# ENVIRONMENT IN THE COURTROOM

UNIVERSITY OF CALGARY
Press

# ENVIRONMENT IN THE COURTROOM

EDITED BY
Allan E. Ingelson

University of Calgary Press
2500 University Drive NW
Calgary, Alberta
Canada T2N 1N4
press.ucalgary.ca



LIBRARY AND ARCHIVES CANADA CATALOGUING IN PUBLICATION

Environment in the courtroom / edited by Allan E. Ingelson.

Includes bibliographical references and index.
Issued in print and electronic formats.
ISBN 978-1-55238-985-0 (softcover).—ISBN 978-1-55238-987-4 (PDF).—
ISBN 978-1-55238-988-1 (EPUB).—ISBN 978-1-55238-989-8 (Kindle).—
ISBN 978-1-55238-986-7 (open access PDF)

1. Environmental law—Canada. I. Ingelson, Allan, 1958-, editor

KE3619.E55 2019 344.7104›6 C2018-905874-9
KF3775.ZA2E55 2019 C2018-905875-7

The University of Calgary Press acknowledges the support of the Government of Alberta through the Alberta Media Fund for our publications. We acknowledge the financial support of the Government of Canada. We acknowledge the financial support of the Canada Council for the Arts for our publishing program.

Alberta Government Canada Canada Council for the Arts Conseil des Arts du Canada

Copyediting by Peter Enman
Cover images: COLOURBOX #1300653 and #5185681
Page design and typesetting by Garet Markvoort, zijn digital
Cover design by Melina Cusano

# Table of Contents

## SECTION 3
## Sentencing and Environmental Offences

## SECTION 5

## Inspections and Enforcement Issues: On-site and in Court

# Preface

During the past seven years, the Canadian Institute of Resources Law and its partners at the University of Ottawa and Dalhousie University, the Canadian Bar Association, and the Ontario Bar Association have organized national annual environmental law symposia titled "Environment in the Courtroom." The symposia, which were sponsored by Environment and Climate Change Canada and the Alberta Law Foundation, were held in Calgary, Ottawa, and Halifax. This book is a collection of the essays presented at the national symposia.

This book is focused on providing an overview of current environmental legal issues in Canada in three key areas: the unique nature of environmental harm, prosecution of environmental offences, and sentencing for environmental offences. The essays in this volume represent an attempt by Canadian environmental law scholars, lawyers in private practice, Crown counsel, corporate counsel, administrative lawyers, lawyers employed by NGOs and industry organizations, environmental consultants, and law students to come to grips with the challenges associated with the litigation of environmental cases in Canada. The majority of the essays represent a Canadian perspective and provide insights on the environmental law experience in a variety of Canadian provinces and territories, leading judicial decisions, and the important procedural and theoretical aspects of environmental litigation in Canada, a nation with a shared common law and civil law heritage. However, consideration of the included contributions on Australia and the United States will reveal that Canada shares similar fundamental environmental challenges with some other jurisdictions. Environmental law is a dynamic and exciting area that is playing an increasingly important role in furthering the sustainable development policies adopted by federal, provincial, and territorial governments in Canada.

The book is divided into five thematic headings that reflect the issues discussed in each of the first five symposia:

- Key environmental concepts and the unique nature of environmental damage;
- Environmental prosecutions;
- Sentencing and environmental offences;
- Evidentiary issues in environmental prosecutions and hearings;
- Site inspections, investigations, and enforcement issues.

The first section of the book is intended to strengthen the knowledge of court practitioners and the judiciary about key environmental concepts from a legal perspective and to create an appreciation and understanding of the unique nature of environmental damage. The emphasis throughout this part, which contains 13 essays, is on the practical nature of environmental damage. While there is an abundance of literature on environmental law, less attention has been paid to the practical problems associated with environmental litigation in Canada, for both judges and court practitioners. Many of the key principles at the heart of modern environmental thinking have been incorporated into legislation with little definition or guidance as to how they should be applied. Similarly, the very concept of environmental damage presents practical challenges in the courtroom insofar as much of the harm may be non-pecuniary in nature and inherently subjective in perception. Indeed, there may be fundamental disagreements even over the question of what is to be incorporated into environmental damage. Concepts dealt with in this part include sustainable development, the precautionary principle, public nuisance, ecosystem management, sustainability, and ecological integrity. The practical environmental problems addressed include engagement with indigenous legal traditions, cumulative effects assessment, and environmental damage assessment.

The second section in the volume considers the major issues that can arise in the course of environmental prosecutions in Canada, beginning with the decision to prosecute and proceeding sequentially through key decision points, ending with available defences. This part consists of ten chapters that deal with a variety of issues in environmental prosecutions, including prosecutorial discretion, private prosecutions, federal and provincial jurisdiction over environmental offences, defenses to environmental offences, due diligence in environmental offences, and the interface between Indigenous legal traditions, and the Anglo-Canadian legal system in the prosecution of regulatory offences.

Section 3 comprises 11 chapters and addresses the major issues that can arise in the course of sentencing for environmental offences, including both the basic considerations that attach to environmental sentencing and more advanced topics. A major issue considered by the authors is creative sentencing. One chapter provides perspectives from the experience of creative sentencing in New South Wales, Australia, enabling a parallel to be drawn with Canada, while another chapter provides perspectives from non-governmental organizations and a third one examines the corporate perspective on creative sentences. Other topics dealt with in the section include director and officer liability, administrative penalties, negotiating sentencing, and the law and economics of environmental harm.

Section 4 focuses on evidentiary issues that can arise in environmental prosecutions and hearings and consists of 14 chapters. Issues considered include proof of causation, the role of expert witnesses, admissibility of evidence, the question of privilege in environmental enforcement, and judicial notice of climate change in environmental litigation.

The fifth section of the book, which focuses on site inspections, investigations, and enforcement issues, consists of seven chapters that consider the frontline role played by government agencies and their "boots on the ground" in the litigation of environmental offences in Canada. There exists in both federal and provincial environmental legislation an array of powers—preventive, remedial, and punitive—that the regulated community can expect to encounter. It is difficult to detect any uniform approach throughout legislation, and as a result, the full range of legal implications arising out of such powers and orders is not always well understood by court practitioners, whether at first instance (e.g. on site) or in the context of a prosecution. Some of the issues that are addressed in this final section include the art of responsive regulation, inspections, compliance, and investigations and legal strategies for collecting evidence.

This volume is intended to be a source of relevant, current, and useful information for a wide-ranging Canadian and international audience and will be of use to both lawyers and non-lawyers. *Environment in the Courtroom* discusses significant issues and challenges in Canadian environmental law today. As we have had legal professionals and scholars from outside Canada make invited presentations and participate in the symposia via webcast, individuals in other nations interested in comparative environmental legal studies will also find this book to be a useful reference on contemporary issues in Canadian environmental law.

It is my pleasure to thank and acknowledge the organizations that have contributed to the success of the symposia, in particular Environment and

Climate Change Canada, the Canadian Bar Association, Ontario Bar Association, Centre for Environmental Law & Global Sustainability, Marine & Environmental Law Institute, University of Calgary, University of Ottawa, and Dalhousie University. In addition, I would like to thank Owen Saunders, Jamie Benidickson, Phillip Saunders, Sarah Powell, Jennifer Fairfax, Alastair Lucas, Martin Olszynski, Laura Scott, Chilenye Nwapi, Ian Holloway, Nancy Money, and Jane Rowe for their special contributions that have made *Environment in the Courtroom* such a success.

—Allan E. Ingelson
Executive Director, Canadian Institute of Resources Law *&*
Associate Professor, Faculty of Law, University of Calgary

## SECTION 1

# Key Environmental Concepts and the Unique Nature of Environmental Damage

1

# Sustainable Development under Canadian Law

PAULE HALLEY AND PIERRE-OLIVIER DESMARCHAIS

Sustainable development represents a new paradigm, casting doubt on the belief that development can be based on sporadic and unlimited economic growth thanks to the planet earth's ability to perpetually provide adequate resources to keep pace with it. That belief has been replaced with uncertainty and concern in the face of deteriorating ecosystems, climate and biodiversity, and other risks associated with irreversible changes. Sustainable development is trying to become established for the long term and to sever its ties with any developmental approach that does not take into account the restricted nature of the planet earth's resources.[1]

The implementation of sustainable development has mobilized most national and international organizations and a great number of participants. The task at hand is colossal and meets with much resistance. For legal experts, sustainable development remains a dynamic concept, the subject of much debate and reflection.[2] Here, we will content ourselves with introducing the origins of sustainable development, outlining significant milestones in its development on the international stage, and examining its implementation in Canadian law through its guiding principles.

## Origins and Definitions of Sustainable Development

The concept of "sustainable development" first appeared on the international stage in 1980, in *World Conservation Strategy* published by the International Union for Conservation of Nature and Natural Resources: "For development to be sustainable it must take account of social and ecological factors, as well as economic ones."[3] It then gained prevalence in 1987 with the publication of the report *Our Common Future* by the World Commission on Environment and Development (the *Brundtland Report*): "Sustainable development is development that meets the needs of the present without compromising the ability of future generations to meet their own needs."[4] The two main principles that inform these definitions are equity and integration, which have established the present-day model of sustainable development and influence the legislation and interpretations surrounding its scope, conditions of application, and implementation.

It was at the second *United Nations Conference on Environment and Development*, held in Rio de Janeiro in 1992, that the international community undertook to establish "a new and equitable global partnership" through the integration of the goal of sustainable development in policy and public decision making. The *Rio Declaration on Environment and Development*[5] clearly defines the concept of sustainable development, most notably its conditions of equity: "the right to development must be fulfilled so as to equitably meet developmental and environmental needs of present and future generations";[6] and integration: "in order to achieve sustainable development, environmental protection shall constitute an integral part of the development process and cannot be considered in isolation from it."[7]

Since then, this change in the approach to development has been reiterated by the international community on numerous occasions[8] and has flourished in the areas of both international environmental law and international trade.[9] For example, the preambles to the *Marrakesh Agreement Establishing the World Trade Organization*[10] and the *North American Free Trade Agreement*[11] recognize that the rules governing international trade must favour the sustainable use of resources and that member states are obligated to promote sustainable development.[12]

The goal of sustainable development in international law is given concrete expression in guiding principles that set out its purpose, means of application and implementation. The *Rio Declaration*, for example, lays down 27 guiding principles, among which it is possible to distinguish those that are inherent to sustainable development from those that are operational principles.[13] Today, these guiding principles represent the foundation for many international conventions. Thus, the principle of public participation is at the heart of the *Aarhus Convention on Access to Information, Public Participation in Decision-making and Access to Justice in Environmental Matters*;[14] the precautionary principle was codified in the 1996 *Protocol to the Convention on the Prevention of Marine Pollution by Dumping of Wastes and Other Matter*,[15] while the prevention principle is the basis for the *United Nations Convention on the Law of the Non-navigational Uses of International Watercourses,*[16] and the procedure for evaluating environmental impact contained in the *Convention on Environmental Impact Assessment in a Transboundary Context.*[17]

International organizations have expressed opinions about these governing principles. In 1995, the United Nations Commission on Sustainable Development gathered together a group of experts with a mandate to identify the international legal principles applicable to sustainable development and to promote their translation into national legal systems.[18] For its part, in 2002, the International Law Association adopted the *New Delhi Declaration of Principles of International Law Relating to Sustainable Development* setting out seven main principles necessary for meeting the goal of sustainable development.[19]

The International Court of Justice (ICJ) also played a significant role in the changes introduced in the area of sustainable development and its guiding principles, notably in the 1997 case of *Gabčíkovo-Nagymaros,*[20] which saw Czechoslovakia and Hungary locked in a litigation battle over the development of the Danube for a joint hydroelectric dam project. Examining the potential environmental impact of such a project, the ICJ stated that "in the field of environmental protection, vigilance and prevention are required on account of the often irreversible character of damage to the environment and of the limitations inherent in the very mechanism of reparation of this type of damage."[21] For the court, sustainable development requires that new norms be taken into consideration when states engage in new activity:

> Such new norms have to be taken into consideration, and such new standards given proper weight, not only when States contemplate new activities but also when continuing with activities begun in the past. This need to reconcile economic development with protection of the environment is aptly expressed in the concept of sustainable development.[22]

In a separate opinion, Justice Weeramantry underlined the significance of sustainable development. He stated that it is a principle of international law in that it is "a part of modern international law by reason not only of its inescapable logical necessity, but also by reason of its wide and general acceptance by the global community."[23] The question of whether sustainable development is a legal concept or a principle has not yet been decided, and the issue continues to be the subject of much debate in legal doctrine.[24]

Sustainable development has also been addressed in decisions of the Supreme Court of Canada. The court consults sources of international and environmental law to find the solutions best suited to common problems, citing, among other sources, the *Brundtland Report*, *Our Common Future*, the *Rio Declaration*, *Agenda 21*, and the *Bergen Ministerial Declaration on Sustainable Development*.[25]

## Sustainable Development in Canadian Law

Since the Rio Summit, Canada has signed numerous international declarations and agreements recognizing the need to ensure sustainable development. The concept has been rapidly integrated into Canadian legislation, both at the federal and provincial levels.[26] In 1995, Parliament introduced a definition of sustainable development in the *Auditor General Act* that echoes the principles of the *Rio Declaration*:

> 21.1 In addition to carrying out the functions referred to in subsection 23(3), the purpose of the Commissioner is to provide sustainable development monitoring and reporting on the progress of category I departments towards sustainable development, which is a continually evolving concept based on the integration of social, economic and environmental concerns, and which may be achieved by, among other things:
>
> a) the integration of the environment and the economy;
> b) protecting the health of Canadians;
> c) protecting ecosystems;
> d) meeting international obligations;
> e) promoting equity;
> f) an integrated approach to planning and making decisions that takes into account the environmental and natural resource costs of different economic options and the economic costs of different environmental and natural resource options;
> g) preventing pollution; and
> h) respect for nature and the needs of future generations.[27]

As a result of this, the legislative definitions closely reflect the wording of the *Brundtland Report* and the *Rio Declaration*. For example, the *Canadian Environmental Protection Act, 1999*,[28] and the *Federal Sustainable Development*

*Act* reiterate: "development that meets the needs of the present without compromising the ability of future generations to meet their own needs."[29]

Beyond its legislative definition, the goal of sustainable development raises the question of whether the concept has been effectively implemented within the Canadian legal system. It is through general principles that express its purpose, conditions of application, and the procedures for its implementation that a framework of norms and legal systems required for its successful completion is being built. The role of the principles of sustainable development is to guide any state intervention, whereby the legislator must translate them into law, the executive branch must include them in its strategies, plans, and policies, and the judiciary must interpret the law when deciding litigation.

When sustainable development principles play a deciding role, they grab the attention of national and international institutions and highlight the legal doctrine regarding important questions relating to their legal nature, scope, hierarchical organization, etc. To facilitate their presentation, we can divide the principles into two categories: inherent and operational. The first category contains those principles that can be described as inherent, essential, or basic to sustainable development (they represent its ultimate purpose) and are necessary for its attainment.[30] The second category comprises operational principles,[31] which clearly identify the procedures for the implementation of sustainable development, such as prevention, precaution, the application of the polluter pays principle, and public participation. Despite this distinction, the interconnectedness of these two categories of principles means that the interpretation of operational principles must respect the principles inherent to sustainable development, which are health, quality of life, equity, and the integration of sustainability.

## The Principles Inherent in the Concept of Sustainable Development

The principles that are inherent in sustainable development include its purpose and the conditions necessary for its successful application. Although they cannot be understood and interpreted in isolation from each other, they are discussed individually here.

### HEALTH AND QUALITY OF LIFE: THE PURPOSE

The *Rio Declaration* clearly defines the purpose of sustainable development: "Human beings are at the centre of concerns for sustainable development. They are entitled to a healthy and productive life in harmony with nature."[32]

It refers to the right of human beings to live in a healthy environment, which was recognized by the international community in 1972 in the *Stockholm Declaration*.[33] The basic link between human rights and environmental rights has been repeated numerous times on the international stage.[34] It resides in the threat to human life and health posed by the destruction of the natural world.[35]

Many countries have, in fact, drafted human environmental rights into their constitutions, expressed in different ways and revolving around the protection of such rights from any substantial modifications.[36] The Canadian Constitution does not recognize environmental rights. Nevertheless, Article 7 of the *Canadian Charter of Rights and Freedoms*[37] could be used as the basis for recourse against the state when its intervention infringes upon an individual's environmental rights and has an impact on his or her health and safety,[38] provided that the alleged impact is not considered speculative or fictitious.[39] By way of analogy, we could point to the fact that the European Court of Human Rights has established a link between the right to privacy in private and family life, guaranteed by the *Convention for the Protection of Human Rights and Fundamental Freedoms*,[40] and serious infringements of environmental law.[41]

In Canada, the federal Parliament and the provinces have introduced environmental rights into their legislation, along with the procedural rights intended to ensure their proper application.[42] In the Yukon, for example, the public "is entitled to a clean and healthy environment" and every resident has the right to take legal action in order to protect the environment.[43] In Quebec, the *Charte québécoise des droits et libertés de la personne* has enshrined the right of every person to live in a clean environment that protects biodiversity.[44]

From this perspective, it should be noted that the Supreme Court of Canada has stated that "environmental protection has become […] a fundamental value in the life of Canadian society" and that "we are individually and collectively responsible" for its protection.[45] In 2004, the court recognized the state's right, in its role as *parens patriae*, to represent the public and enforce respect of "the public's interest in an unspoiled environment" and the "inescapable rights of the public with respect to the environment and certain common natural resources," by taking recourse on its behalf to grant injunctions and award compensation for environmental damage.[46]

Environmental rights are applied by way of the principle of public participation, which is expressed in terms of three procedural rights, including access to information, participation in the decision-making process, and access to justice.[47] The first two components are found in the procedures concerning the adoption of laws and regulations, and in the assessment procedures surrounding the environmental impact of large-scale development projects.[48] Environmental legislation includes a variety of provisions granting the public rights of access to environmental information, to take part in the decision-making process, and to initiate recourse to the justice system.[49] Quebec has strengthened the public's right to participate by passing the "anti-SLAPP" act in order to delegitimize strategic lawsuits against public participation, commonly known as SLAPPs.[50]

### THE PRINCIPLE OF EQUITY: AN ESSENTIAL CONDITION

International and Canadian law both recognize the moral and legal obligation to protect the environment in order to preserve the right to development for present and future generations.[51] It is based upon an awareness of the threat to future generations posed by the exhaustion of natural resources and the destruction of the environment, ecosystems, and climate.[52] On the subject, the Supreme Court of Canada recognizes that "[t]oday we are more conscious of what type of environment we wish to live in, and what quality of life we wish to expose our children to" and that this awareness "perhaps indicates the birth of a feeling of solidarity between generations and an environmental debt towards humanity and the world of tomorrow."[53]

According to the *Stockholm Declaration*, the principle of equity applies to the protection of "the natural resources of the earth, including the air, water, land, flora and fauna and especially representative samples of natural ecosystems, [which] must be safeguarded for the benefit of present and future generations through careful planning or management, as appropriate."[54] The principle of equity, which transcends the implementation of sustainable development, is difficult to apply. Protecting the rights of future generations is one of the most difficult things to do.[55] Who can take action? In 1994, the Philippines Supreme Court examined the question of the interest in acting for future generations and recognized the right of young children, representing the future generation, to take legal action in order to challenge forestry exploration permits "for themselves, for others of their generation and the succeeding generations":

> Needless to say, every generation has a responsibility to the next to preserve that rhythm and harmony for the full enjoyment of a balanced and healthful ecology. Put a little differently, the minors' assertion of

> their right to a sound environment constitutes, at the same time, the performance of their obligation to ensure the protection of that right for the generations to come.[56]

This decision illustrates the link between intergenerational environmental and equity rights, including the natural right to survive and to self-perpetuate, "the advancement of which may even be said to predate all governments and constitutions. As a matter of fact, these basic rights need not even be written into the Constitution for they are assumed to exist from the inception of humankind."[57]

The Court of Appeal for Newfoundland and Labrador, for its part, highlighted the existing link between the procedure for assessing environmental impacts and the rights of future generations:

> If the rights of future generations to the protection of the present integrity of the natural world are to be taken seriously, and not to be regarded as mere empty rhetoric, care must be taken in the interpretation and application of the [environmental assessment] legislation. Environmental laws must be construed against their commitment to future generations and against a recognition that, in addressing environmental issues, we often have imperfect knowledge as to the potential impact of activities on the environment.[58]

## THE PRINCIPLE OF INTEGRATION: ANOTHER ESSENTIAL CONDITION

In order to achieve sustainable development, the *Rio Declaration* states that "environmental protection shall constitute an integral part of the development process and cannot be considered in isolation from it."[59] The principle of integration reflects the interrelationship of the social, economic, and environmental objectives of society.[60] In the *Brundtland Report*, this principle speaks to "the idea of limitations imposed by the state of technology and social organization on the environment's ability to meet present and future needs."[61]

The principle of integration is the subject of much discussion and remains equivocal. It is often represented by an iterative triangle or Venn diagram with the three dimensions, or pillars, of sustainable development overlapping. The crucial issue is finding the necessary balance between the three dimensions, as the principle is silent about whether we should reconcile diverging interests, or rather measure the "sustainability" of development, or ensure the mutual support between the dimensions. In the absence of clear indications, the fear is that the integration exercise will create negotiation gaps between the players with differing interests, without regard to the sustainable nature of the development.

Since the beginning of the 1990s, studies have stressed the distinction between the concepts of sustainable development supporting "weak" sustainability and "strong" sustainability.[62] This dichotomy rests mainly on the economic value we place on natural stock and environmental protection. For legislators, it is the opposition between the anthropocentric concept and the ecocentric concept that feeds debate about the significance of sustainable development.[63] The balance being sought between the diverging dimensions of development directly influences the decisions taken in the name of sustainable development and the interpretation of the rule of law.

So-called "weak" sustainability tends to favour economic development by allowing the substitution of natural stock with goods and wealth generated by human activity, with the justification that this wealth might then be invested in environmental protection. On this approach, environmental protection is not viewed as a condition of sustainable development;[64] it merely represents one pillar of sustainable development and is equal to the social and economic pillars.[65] This substitution between the different stocks contradicts the principle of intergenerational equity and the ability to attain the goal of sustainable development.

The assessment of the sustainability of development refers back to a conceptual framework based on the calculation of natural, economic, and social stock.[66] If the total of the sum of the capitals drops, development is not sustainable and the well-being of future generations will be inferior to that of present generations, which contravenes the principle of equity.[67] It is still not easy to assess the monetary value of natural stock, to set a price on air, the ozone layer, or a wetland.[68]

From the perspective of "strong" sustainability, natural stock is not substituted by goods produced by humans.[69] On this approach, natural stock should remain intact or not diminish to such a level that it does not renew itself. Natural stock is given an intrinsic value, totally independent from the needs of humans; it is the condition of its development.[70] Strong sustainability promotes itself as being the only interpretation of sustainable development that is capable of guaranteeing equity between the generations.[71] From this perspective, the state is invited to become involved in order to restrict any negative impact on the environment and to establish indicators that would allow us to follow the evolution of natural stock.

The assessment of sustainable development leads governments to formulate plans for future action within a strategic framework. The experience of other states is also called upon.[72] The trend is to legislate for the implementation of sustainable development, at the centre of power.[73] From this perspective, government action is neither free nor voluntary but mapped out by legislative deadlines, with the goal of sustainable development, guiding principles, periodical accountability, and compliance assessments being carried out by an independent commissioner. These framework laws are not immune from the trend towards "strong" sustainability, as witnessed by the definition of "sustainability" in the *Federal Sustainable Development Act*: "the capacity of a thing, action, activity or process to be maintained indefinitely."[74]

Ancillary to the principles inherent to sustainable development, operational principles represent the procedures to be implemented in order to attain this goal. They are integrated with one or several dimensions of sustainable development to which they lend a precise form. Thus, environmental integrity is expressed through the principles of prevention and precaution; economic efficiency through internalization of costs and the "polluter pays" principle; and the social dimension through the principle of public participation. The transposition of these principles into Canadian law is effectuated through special regimes, such as assessment procedures to measure the impact on the environment based on the principle of prevention[75] and site cleanup obligations based on the polluter pays principle.[76]

We have set out here the general principles and requirements for the dynamic concept of sustainable development. Although the concept is widely accepted, its prescriptive implications seem today to be more complicated and radical than we could ever have expected back in the early 1970s. The devil is in the details! Thankfully, every day, practitioners and scientists in many disciplines are working to make sustainable development an enduring reality.[77]

## NOTES

1 Donella H Meadows, Dennis L Meadows & Jorgen Randers, *Beyond the Limits* (London: Earthscan, 1972).

2 See, for example, David R Boyd, *Unnatural Law: Rethinking Canadian Environmental Law and Policy* (Vancouver: UBC Press, 2003); Klaus Bosselmann, *The Principle of Sustainability: Transforming Law and Governance* (Burlington: Ashgate,

2008); [Bosselmann, "Principle of Sustainability"]; Bruce Pardy, "In Search of the Holy Grail of Environmental Law: A Rule to Solve the Problem" (2005) 1 McGill Int'l J Sust Dev L & Pol'y 29; Staffan Westerlund, "Theory for Sustainable Development: Towards or Against? " in Hans-Christian Bugge & Christina Voigt, *Sustainable Development in International and National Law*, ch 1.3 (Groningen, the Netherlands: Europa Law Publishing, 2008) at 49–66; Massimiliano Montini, "Revising International Environmental Law through the Paradigm of Ecological Sustainability," in Federico Lenzerini & Ana Filipa Vrdoljak, eds, *International Law for Common Goods: Normative Perspectives on Human Rights, Culture and Nature*, ch 13 (Oxford, UK, and Portland, OR: Hart, 2014) at 271–287 [Montini, "Ecological Sustainability"]; Rakhyun E. Kim & Klaus Bosselmann, "Operationalizing Sustainable Development: Ecological Integrity as a Grundnorm of International Law," (2015) 24:2 Review of European Community and International Environmental Law, Special Issue: Public Participation and Climate Governance, 194–208.

3 International Union for Conservation of Nature and Natural Resources, *World Conservation Strategy: Living Resource Conservation for Sustainable Development* (Gland: IUCN, 1980) para 3.

4 World Commission on Environment and Development, *Our Common Future* (1987) (Montreal: Éditions du Fleuve, 1988) at 51.

5 UNCED, *Rio Declaration on Environment and Development*, Off Doc AG UN, 1992, Doc UN A/CONF151/26 (Vol I).

6 *Ibid*, principle 3.

7 *Ibid*, principle 4.

8 United Nations, *Agenda 21*, UN Doc A/CONF151/26 (Vol. I–III); *Agreement on Biodiversity*, 5 June 1992, 1993 QR Can 24 (effective date: 29 December 1993) [*Biodiversity*]; *United Nations Framework Convention on Climate Change*, 9 May 1992, 31 ILM 851 (effective date: 21 March 1994) [*Climate Change*]; *United Nations Convention to Combat Desertification in those Countries Experiencing Serious Drought and/or Desertification*, 5 June 1992, 1996 QR Can 51 (effective date: 26 December 1996); *Barcelona Convention for Protection against Pollution in the Mediterranean Sea*, 16 February 1976, 1102 UNQR 27 (effective date: 12 February 1978); United Nations, *Johannesburg Declaration on Sustainable Development*, Doc off AG UN, 2002, UN Doc A/CONF199/20, para 8; *Great Lakes–St. Lawrence River Basin Sustainable Water Resources Agreement*, 13 December 2005, the preamble; *Declaration on the Establishment of the Arctic Council*, 19 September 1996, 35 ILM 1382, art 1(a).

9 On this subject, see also Philippe Sands, *Principles of International Environmental Law*, 2d ed (New York: Cambridge University Press, 2003) at 253, 281 and 941 [Sands, "Principles of International Environmental Law"]; Patricia Birnie, Alan Boyle & Catherine Redgwell, *International Law and the Environment*, 3d ed (Oxford: Oxford University Press, 2009) [Birnie et al, "International Law and the Environment"]; Jean-Maurice Arbour et al, *Droit international de l'environnement* (Montréal: Éditions Yvon Blais, 2016), at 106 and following [Arbour et al, "Droit international de l'environnement"] .

10 WTO, *Marrakesh Agreement Establishing the World Trade Organization*, 15 April 1994, 1867 UNTS 154, 33 ILM 1144; WTO, Appellate Body, *United States—Import Prohibition of Certain Shrimp and Shrimp Products* (1998), WTO Doc WT/DS58/AB/R paras 185–186.

11 North American Free Trade Agreement between Canada, the United States of America and Mexico, 1 January 1994, QR Can 1994 No 2, 32 ILM 289 (effective date: 1 January 1994).

12 WTO, Ministerial Decision on Trade and Environment, 15 April 1994.

13 Philippe Sands, "International Law in the Field of Sustainable Development,"

(1994) 65 Brit. Y.B. Int. L. 303–381 at 338 [Sands, "International Law in the Field of Sustainable Development"].

14 *Aarhus Convention*, 25 June 1998, 38 ILM 517 (effective date: 30 October 2001).

15 17 November 1996, QR Can 2006 n° 5 (effective date: 24 March 2006). See also *Cartagena Protocol on Biosafety*, 29 January 2000, 39 ILM 1027 (effective date: 11 September 2003).

16 Res AG 229, Off Doc AG UN, 51st Sess, Appendix n° 1, UN Doc A/51/229 (1997). See also *Helsinki Convention on the Protection and Use of Transboundary Watercourses and International Lakes*, 17 March 1992, 31 ILM 1312.

17 25 February 1991, 1989 UNQR 309.

18 United Nations, *Report of the Expert Group Meeting on Identification of Principles of International Law for Sustainable Development*, 18 April–3 May 1996.

19 International Law Association, *New Delhi Declaration of Principles of International Law Relating to Sustainable Development*, ILA Res 2/2002, 2–6 April 2002, New Delhi [New Delhi Declaration].

20 *Gabčíkovo-Nagymaros Project (Hungary v Slovakia)*, [1997] CIJ rec 7.

21 *Ibid* at para 140.

22 *Ibid* at para 140.

23 *Ibid*, separate opinion by Mr. Justice Weeramantry, Vice-President, at 95.

24 On the debate surrounding the legal status of sustainable development, see Jaye Ellis, "Sustainable Development as a Legal Principle: A Rhetorical Analysis" in Hélène Ruiz Fabri, Rudiger Wolfrum & Jana Gogolin, eds, *Select Proceedings of the European Society of International Law*, vol 2 (London: Hart, 2008) at 641; Vaughan Lowe, "Sustainable Development and Unsustainable Arguments" in Alan Boyle & David Freestone, eds, *International Law and Sustainable Development: Past Achievements and Future Challenges* (Oxford: Oxford University Press, 1999) at 19; Sands, "International Law in the Field of Sustainable Development," *supra* note 13 at 305; Ulrich Beyerlin, "Different Types of Norms in International Environmental Law: Policies, Principles, and Rules" in Daniel Bodansky, Jutta Brunnée & Ellen Hey, eds, *The Oxford Handbook of International Environmental Law* (Oxford: Oxford University Press, 2007) at 425; Arbour et al, "Droit international de l'environnement," *supra* note 9 at 109–110. Barral Virginie, *Le développement durable en droit international: Essai sur les incidences juridiques d'une norme évolutive* (Bruxelles: Éditions Bruylant, 2016) at 23–24 and 233–236.

25 *R v Hydro-Québec*, [1997] 3 SCR 213 at para 41 [*Hydro-Québec*]; *114957 Canada Ltd (Spraytech, Sprinkler Company) v Hudson (Town)*, [2001] 2 SCR 241 at para 31 [*Spraytech*]; *Imperial Oil Ltd v Québec (Ministry of the Environment)*, [2003] 2 SCR 624 at para 24 [*Imperial*]; *St. Lawrence Cement Inc. v Barrette*, [2008] 3 SCR 392 at para 80.

26 See, for example, *Loi sur le ministère de l'environnement et de la faune et modifiant diverses dispositions législatives* (SQ 1994, c 17); *Loi modifiant la Loi sur les forêts et d'autre dispositions législatives* (SQ 1996, c 14); *Loi modifiant la loi sur la protection du territoire agricole et d'autres dispositions législatives afin de favoriser la protection des activités agricoles* (SQ 1996, c 26); *Energy Authority Act* (SQ 1996, c 61); *Sustainable Development Act* (LM 1997, c 61, CPLM c S270) [Manitoba, LDD]; *Sustainable Development Act* (SQ 2006, c. 3) [Québec, LDD]; *Act to affirm the collective nature of water resources and to strengthen their protection* (SQ 2009 c 21), s 3; *Law on Sustainable Forest Management* (SQ 2010 c 32); *Loi modifiant la Loi sur les mines* (SQ 2013, c 32), preamble and s 17. See also Stepan Wood, Georgia Tanner & Benjamin J. Richardson, "What Ever Happened to Canadian Environmental Law?" (2010) 37:4 Ecology Law Quarterly 981–1040 at 1031.

27 *Auditor General Act*, RSC 1985, c A-17, s 21.1.

28 *Canadian Environmental Protection Act, 1999*, SC 1999, c 33, s 3.

29 *Federal Law on Sustainable Development Act*, SC 2008, c 33, s 2 [Canada, FLSDA].

30 Sands, "International Law in the Field of Sustainable Development," *supra* note 13. See also Sands, "Principles of International Environmental Law," *supra* note 9 at 253; Philippe Sands, "Environmental Protection in the Twenty-First Century: Sustainable Development and International Law" in Richard L Revesz, Philippe Sands & Richard B Stewart, eds, *Environmental Law, The Economy and Sustainable Development: The United States, the European Union and the International Community* (New York: Cambridge University Press, 2000) 369; Birnie et al, "International Law and the Environment," *supra* note 9 at 115.

31 Sands, "International Law in the Field of Sustainable Development," *supra* note 13. See also Philippe Sands, "International Law in the Field of Sustainable Development: Emerging Legal Principles" in Winfried Lang, ed, *Sustainable Development and International Law* (Boston: Graham Trotman, 1994) 53 at 57; Rudiger Wolfrum, "International Environmental Law: Purposes, Principles and Means of Ensuring Compliance" in Fred L Morrison & Rudiger Wolfrum, eds, *International, Regional and National Environmental Law* (Boston: Kluwer Law International, 2000) 3 at 8.

32 *Supra* note 5, principle 1.

33 United Nations Conference on the Human Environment, *Stockholm Declaration*, 5–16 June 1972, principle 1 ("Man has the fundamental right to freedom, equality and adequate conditions of life, in an environment of a quality that permits a life of dignity and well-being, and he bears a solemn responsibility to protect and improve the environment for present and future generations").

34 See the *World Charter for Nature*, 1982, 48th Plenary Session, Doc UN A/37/7 (1982), principle 6; OÉA, *Additional Protocol to the American Convention on Human Rights*, A-52, (1988), s 11(1); *African Charter on Human and Peoples' Rights*, 27 June 1981, art 24; *World Conference on Human Rights, Declaration and Programme of Action from the Vienna World Conference on Human Rights*, 25 June 1993, Doc UN A/CONF157/23, art 11.

35 See Human Rights Commission, *Review of Further Developments in Fields with which the Sub-committee has been Concerned—Human Rights and the Environment—Final Report prepared by Mrs. Fatma Zohra Ksentini*, Special Rapporteur, Off Doc ESC UN, 1994, Doc UN E/CN4/Sub2/1994/9 at para 21 and following; Dinah Shelton, "Human Rights and the Environment: What Specific Environmental Rights have been Recognized?" (2006) 35 Denv J Int'l L & Pol'y 129; Klaus Bosselmann, "Human Rights and the Environment: Redefining Fundamental Principles?" in Brendan Gleeson & Nicholas Low, eds, *Governance for the Environment: Global Problems, Ethics and Democracy* (London: Palgrave, 2001) at 118–134; David Hunter, James Salzman & Durwood Zaelke, *International Environmental Law and Policy*, 5th ed (St Paul, MN: Foundation Press, 2015) at 1323.

36 See David R. Boyd, *The Environmental Rights Revolution: A Global Study of Constitutions, Human Rights, and the Environment* (Vancouver: UBC Press, 2012); Marie-France Delhoste, "L'environnement dans les constitutions du monde" (2004) 120 RDP 441; Earth Justice, *Issue Paper, Human Rights and the Environment, Materials for the 60th Session of the United Nations Commissions on Human Rights*, Geneva, 15 March–23 April 2004.

37 *Canadian Charter of Rights and Freedoms*, Part I of the Constitution Act, 1982, being Schedule B of Act 1982 of Canada (UK), 1982, v 11.

38 On the link between art 7 and environmental rights, see Sophie Thériault & David Robitaille, "Les droits

environnementaux dans la Charte des droits et libertés de la personne du Québec: Pistes de réflexion" (2011) 57:2 McGill LJ 211 at 240 and following; Andrew Gage, "Public Health Hazards and Section 7 of the Charter" (2003) 13 J Envtl L & Prac 1.

39 *Opération Dismantle Inc* c *R*, [1985] 1 RCS 441.

40 European Council, *Convention for the Protection of Human Rights and Fundamental Freedoms*, CETS n° 005, art 8.

41 *López Ostra v Espagne* (1994) 303C Cour Eur DH (Sér A) 51 at paras 59–60; See also *Moreno Gómez v Espagne*, n° 4143/02, [2004] CEHR 1; *Deés v Hongrie*, n° 2345/06, [2010] CEHR 1.

42 See in Quebec, *Environment Quality Act*, CQLR c Q-2, ss 19.1–2, ss 118.5.1–3 [Québec, LQE]; *Charter of Human Rights and Freedoms*, CQLR c C-12, s 46.1 [Québec, CDLP]; in the Northwest Territories, *Environmental Rights Act*, LRTN-O 1988 c 83 (Supp), ss 4–6; in the Yukon, *Environment Act*, SY 2002, c 76, ss 6, 8, 14, 19, 21 [Yukon, LE]; in Ontario, *Environmental Bill of Rights*, SO 1993, c 28, ss 3 and following [Ontario, EBR]; and federally, *Auditor General Act*, *supra* note 27, ss 11 and following.

43 *Ibid*, Yukon, LE, ss 6 and 8.

44 *Ibid*, Québec, CDLP, s 46.1. See David Robitaille & Sophie Thériault, "Le droit à un environnement sain: normativité et limites d'un principe phare de la charte québécoise des droits," in *Droits fondamentaux et environnement* (Montréal: Wilson & Lafleur, 2013) at 203–229.

45 *Friends of the Oldman River Society v Canada (Ministry of Transport)*, [1992] 1 SCR 3 at paras 16–17 [*Friends of the Oldman River Society*]; *Hydro-Québec*, *supra* note 25 at para 55; *Spraytech*, *supra* note 25 at para 1; *Imperial*, *supra* note 25, para 19; *Ontario v Canadian Pacific Ltd* [1995] 2 SCR 1028 at para 1075.

46 *British Columbia v Canadian Forest Products Ltd*, [2004] 2 SCR 75 at paras 64 and 76 (The majority rejected the claim which was filed late and based on a method of calculation considered to be "too arbitrary and simplistic").

47 *Aarhus Convention*, *supra* note 14, s 1.

48 See, for example, Québec, LQE, *supra* note 42, ss 31.3.1–7; Ontario, EBR, *supra* note 42, Part II; *Canadian Environmental Assessment Act 2012*, SC 2012, c 19, s 52 and ss 4 (1)(e), 24 and following [Canada, LCEE]; *Environmental Management and Protection Act*, SS 2010, c E-10.22, s 98(4). On this topic, see Jamie Benidickson, *Environmental Law*, 3d ed (Toronto: Irwin Law, 2009) at 132 and following.

49 See cited laws, *supra*, note 42. See also Benjamin J Richardson & Jona Razzaque, "Public Participation in Environmental Decision-making" in Benjamin J Richardson & Stepan Wood, eds, *Environmental Law for Sustainability: A Reader* (Oxford: Hart, 2006) at 165; Jonas Ebbesson, "Public Participation" in Daniel Bodansky, Jutta Brunnée & Ellen Hey, eds, *The Oxford Handbook of International Environmental Law* (Oxford: Oxford University Press, 2007) at 686 and following.

50 *Protection of Public Participation Act*, SBC 2001, c 19 [Repealed by *Miscellaneous Statutes Amendment Act*, 2001, SBC2001, c. 32, s. 28]; *Act to amend the Code of Civil Procedure to prevent misuse of the courts and promote respect for freedom of expression and citizen participation in public debate*, LQ 2009, c 12 (*Code of civil procedure*, CQLR c C-25.01); *Protection of Public Participation Act*, SO 2015, c 23 – Bill 52. For a precedential perspective, see *Daishowa Inc v Friends of the Lubicon*, [1998] OJ 1429 (Ont SCJ); *Fraser v Saanich (District)*, [1999] BCJ 3100 (BCCS) (LN/QL) and *Ugo Lapointe v Pétrolia*, 2011 QCCS 4014.

51 See *International Convention for the Regulation of Whaling*, 2 December 1946, 161 UNTS 72, 10 UST 952, preamble; *Convention for the Protection of World Cultural and Natural Heritage*, 16 November 1972, 1037 UNTS 151 (effective date: 17 December 1975) art 4;

*Climate Change*, *supra* note 8, preamble; *Biodiversity*, *supra* note 8, preamble.

52 Edith Brown Weiss, *Intergenerational Fairness and Rights of Future Generations* (Paris: UNU Press, 1993) at 35; Daniel Barstow Magraw & Lisa D Hawke, "Sustainable Development" in Daniel Bodansky, Jutta Brunnées & Ellen Hey, *The Oxford Handbook of International Environmental Law* (Oxford: Oxford University Press, 2007) at 630.Virginie Barral, "Sustainable Development in International Law: Nature and Operation of an Evolutive Legal Norm" (2012) 23:2 European Journal of International Law at 380–381.

53 *Spraytech*, *supra* note 25 at para 1; *Imperial*, *supra* note 25 at para 19.

54 *Supra* note 33, Principle 2.

55 Sumudu A Atapattu, *Emerging Principles of International Environmental Law* (Ardsley: Transnational, 2006) at 116. In Canada, see Jerry V DeMarco, "Law for Future Generations: The Theory of Intergenerational Equity in Canadian Environmental Law" (2005) 15 J Envtl L & Prac1 at 28 and following. Malgosia Fitzmaurice, *Contemporary Issues in International Environmental Law* (Cheltenham, UK: Edward Elgar Publishing, 2009) at 110–169; Gail E. Henderson, "Rawls and Sustainable Development" (2011) 7:1 RDPDD at 1–31.

56 *Decision in Minors Oposa v Sec of DENR*, 30 July 1993, 33 ILM 173 at 185 (1994) (Philippines Supreme Court).

57 *Ibid* at 187.

58 *Labrador Inuit Association v Newfoundland (Minister of Environment and Labour)*, 1997 CanLII 14612 (NL CA) at paras 11 and 12.

59 *Supra* note 5, principles 12, 13 and 14.

60 New Delhi Declaration, *supra* note 19, principle 7.

61 *Supra* note 4 at 51.

62 David Pearce, Kirk Hamilton & Giles Atkinson, "Measuring Sustainable Development: Progress on Indicators" (1996) 1 Environment & Development Economics 85; Andrew Dobson, "Environment Sustainabilities: An Analysis and a Typology" (1996) 5:3 Environmental Politics 401 at 409–412.

63 Bosselmann, "Principle of Sustainability," *supra* note 2 at 34 ("Clearly, the preservation of the natural stock determines the ability to meet the needs of present and future generations"). See also Montini, "Ecological Sustainability," *supra* note 2 at 278–280.

64 Andrea Ross, "Modern Interpretations of Sustainable Development" (2009) 36 JL & Soc'y 32 at 35.

65 *Ibid.* See also Arbour et al, "Droit international de l'environnement," *supra* note 9 at 111.

66 Statistics Canada, *A Proposed Approach to Sustainable Development Indicators Based on Capital*, paper submitted to joint ECE/EuroStat Work Session on Methodological Issues of Environment Statistics, 2001, online: Statistics Canada <http://www.unece.org/fileadmin/DAM/stats/documents/2001/10/env/wp.9.e.pdf>. See also National Round Table on the Environment and the Economy, *Environmental Indicators and Sustainable Development for Canada*, Ottawa, Library and Archives Canada, 2003.

67 OECD, *Measuring Sustainable Development: Integrated Economic, Environmental and Social Frameworks* (Paris: OECD) at 54.

68 See the concept of ecosystem services in *Millennium Ecosystem Assessment – MEA*, *Ecosystems and Human Well-Being: A Synthesis* (Washington, DC: Island Press, 2005), 137 pages, online: <http://www.millenniumassessment.org/documents/document.356.aspx.pdf>; United Nations Environment Programme (TEEB), *The Economics of Ecosystems and Biodiversity: Ecological and Economics Foundations*, ed by Pushpam Kumar (London and Washington, DC: Earthscan, 2010). About payments for ecosystem services, see Philippe Méral & Denis Pesche, eds, *Les services écosystémiques: repenser les relations nature et société* (Versailles: Éditions

Quae, 2016) at 184–200; Jérôme Dupras & Jean-Pierre Revéret, eds, *Nature et économie: un regard sur les écosystèmes du Québec* (Québec: Presse de l'Université du Québec, 2015). For examples, see Québec, Ministère des Forêts, de la Faune et des Parcs, *Estimer la compensation financière lors d'une perte d'habitat faunique – Résumé de l'outil de calcul du ministère des Forêts, de la Faune et des Parcs*, Direction générale de la valorisation du patrimoine naturel, 2016, 10 pp; *Loi concernant la conservation des milieux humides et hydriques* (LQ 2017, c 14); Sophie Lavallée & Jérôme Dupras, "Regards sur les systèmes de paiements pour services *écosystémiques* en milieu agricole au Québec" (2016) 7:1 Développement durable et territoires, 18 pp; Fisheries and Oceans Canada, *Avoid, mitigate or offset harm to fish and fish habitat, including aquatic species at risk*, online: <http://www.dfo-mpo.gc.ca/pnw-ppe/measures-mesures/offset-harm-dommage-comp-eng.html>; Government of Alberta, Alberta Environment and Parks, *Alberta Wetland Mitigation Directive*, Water Policy Branch, Edmonton, 2017, online: <http://aep.alberta.ca/water/programs-and-services/wetlands/documents/AlbertaWetlandMitigationDirective-Jun2017.pdf>.

69 *Supra* note 62 at 37.

70 Klaus Bosselmann, "Rio+20: Any Closer to Sustainable Development?" (2002) 6 NZ J Envtl L 297 at 301–302 ("[T]he natural sphere is paramount and cannot be compromised. The challenge of SD is, therefore, not to find the right 'balance' or 'compromise' between the natural sphere and the human sphere but to adjust the human sphere to the conditions set by the natural sphere").

71 Herman E Daily, "Economics in a Full World" (2005) 293:3 Scientific American 1; Bosselmann, "Principle of Sustainability," *supra* note 2 at 55.

72 See notably *Environment Act 1986* (N-Z), 1986/127, 36 RS 223 (New Zealand) [enacted on 18 December 1986]; *Act on the coordination of Federal Sustainable Development Policy* (*Loi relative à la coordination de la politique fédérale de développement durable*) (BE), SC 97/21155, F 97/1176 (Belgium) [enacted on 5 May 1997]; *Commissioner for Environmental Sustainability Act 2003* (Vic) (State of Victoria, Australia) [enacted on 13 May 2003]; *Act of June 25, 2004 on the coordination of national sustainable development policy* (LU), 2 July 2004, JO A No 102/1621 (Luxembourg).

73 Canada, LCEE, *supra* note 48; *supra* note 28; Ontario, EBR, *supra* note 42; Manitoba, LDD, *supra* note 25, Scheds A and B (directions and principles); Québec, LDD, *supra* note 26, art 6 (16 principles); Newfoundland, *An Act Respecting the Sustainable Development of Natural Resources in the Province*, SNL 2007, c S-34; Nova Scotia, *Environmental Goals and Sustainable Prosperity Act*, NSS 2007, c 7. See also Paule Halley & Denis Lemieux, "La mise en œuvre de la Loi québécoise sur le développement durable: un premier bilan," *Conférence des juristes de l'État, XVIIIe Conférence: Vert, le droit ?*, Québec, 2009.

74 Canada, FLSDA, *supra* note 29, s 2.

75 *Friends of the Oldman River Society*, *supra* note 45 at 71.

76 *Imperial*, *supra* note 25 at para 24.

77 Jonathan M Harris, *Basic Principles of Sustainable Development*, Working Paper 00-04 (Medford, MA: Global Development and Environment Institute, June 2000).

# 2

# A Precautionary Tale: Trials and Tribulations of the Precautionary Principle

CHRIS TOLLEFSON*

## 1. Introduction

The rise to prominence of the precautionary principle both as a legal concept and a public policy tool has prompted extraordinary attention and debate. Considered by many to be one of the foundational principles of modern environmental law, it increasingly is being incorporated into federal and provincial legislation, and invoked in litigation before domestic courts and tribunals.

This chapter reflects on the challenges and opportunities associated with litigating the precautionary principle as a basis for seeking review of governmental action. In so doing, it builds on and revisits themes and questions originally addressed in a paper authored in 2007.[1] Since that time, a critical mass of domestic jurisprudence on the application and interpretation of the principle has continued to emerge. To date, however, within much of this jurisprudence, the principle continues to be adverted to as a discretionary consideration or background interpretive canon. Nevertheless, there is also growing evidence of a judicial appetite to engage with the principle in a more systematic doctrinal fashion: in the words of one leading jurist, to give it "some specific work to do."[2] Whether and to what extent this aspiration can be realized depends on whether the precautionary principle can be rendered sufficiently coherent and predictable to serve as a basis for judicial decision making.

In Part 2 of this chapter, I offer some introductory thoughts on the principle and the challenges associated with its deployment as an adjudicative tool. Part 3 surveys the various avenues and legal theories through which litigants

* *The author is grateful for the research and editorial contributions of Ethan Krindle and Anthony Ho.*

have sought to invoke the principle in domestic litigation. Part 4 then considers the growing Canadian jurisprudence that has emerged out of these efforts, offering some views on overarching trends and themes. And, finally, in Part 5, I return to the question of how and whether the principle can be given some specific work to do by exploring some recent Australian case law that has directly taken up this challenge.

## 2. The Precautionary Principle: An Overview

The origins and implications of the precautionary principle are the subject of a considerable and growing scholarly literature.[3] Derivative of the maxim "better safe than sorry," at its core the principle seeks to formalize precaution as a regulatory obligation in the face of environmental threats and scientific uncertainty. In the domain of international law, the principle began to emerge in the early 1980s, most notably in the *World Charter for Nature* (1982). Since that time, it has become a central feature of close to one hundred international agreements and has been incorporated into scores of domestic environmental and public health laws worldwide.

There are many differing formulations of the precautionary principle. The most widely cited version of the precautionary principle is found in Principle 15 of the *Rio Declaration on Environment and Development* (1992):

> Where there are threats of serious or irreversible damage, lack of full scientific certainty shall not be used as a reason for postponing cost-effective measures to prevent environmental degradation.[4]

This relatively permissive or "weak" version of the principle is frequently contrasted with a more rigorous version famously approved by environmental activists and scholars at the 1998 Wingspread Conference:

> When an activity raises threats to the environment or human health, precautionary measures should be taken, even if some cause-and-effect relationships are not fully established scientifically.[5]

The chameleon-like nature of the principle has tended to undermine reasoned consideration and debate of its precise meaning and implications. In an effort to provide an operational taxonomy of the principle, Sandin argues that its various formulations can be usefully analyzed along four key dimensions: threat, uncertainty, action, and command.[6] Under Sandin's approach, threat refers to

**Table 2.1 | Four dimensions of the Rio and Wingspread articulations of the precautionary principle**

| | *Rio Declaration* | *Wingspread Conference* |
|---|---|---|
| Threat | Serious or irreversible damage | Threats to environment or human health |
| Uncertainty | Lack of full scientific uncertainty | Cause-and-effect relationships are not fully established scientifically |
| Action | Postpone cost-effective measures to prevent environmental degradation | Precautionary measures |
| Commmand | Shall not | Should |

the nature of the imminent harm to the "state of the world" (particularly its seriousness and (ir)reversibility), while uncertainty connotes "our (lack of) knowledge as [to] whether and how this threat might materialize." Under most formulations of the principle, where both the threat and uncertainty meet defined thresholds, an action obligation is triggered (e.g., to consider "cost effective measures to prevent environmental degradation," "preventative measures" or "regulatory steps"). Finally, the command dimension prescribes the legal status of the action to be taken, which may be framed in either mandatory or permissive language, "shall" or "may."[7] According to Sandin, a key challenge to operationalizing the precautionary principle lies in the imprecision with which the dimensions of "threat," "uncertainty," "action," and "command" are typically framed. Table 2.1 depicts and compares the *Rio Declaration* (1992) version of the principle with the later Wingspread Conference (1998) version using the Sandin framework.

Sandin's work in the realm of risk assessment has parallels in the legal scholarship of Professor Applegate. Applegate argues that a "tamed" understanding of the precautionary principle is beginning to emerge.[8] In particular, he argues that, through this taming, "the constituent elements of the precautionary principle have been altered over time to be less stringent or to narrow the scope of the principle."[9] This emerging, tamed version of the principle has the potential to provide a procedural vehicle for decision making in the face of uncertainty. Traditionally, where the principle has not been considered as part of a decision-making process, regulators have only taken a risk into account when it rises to a relatively high standard of certainty. In contrast, where the principle is part of the regulatory equation, a decision maker is empowered (and, in some instances, obliged) to take it into account. However, this response must be proportional to the risk, and must adapt as knowledge of the risk becomes more certain.

If Applegate and other legal scholars are correct that a tamed version of the precautionary principle can offer decision makers the procedural means to take risk into account in a manner that is consistent with established administrative law principles, a host of important questions about the meaning and implications of the principle arise. These include:

- *When should the principle apply?* In other words, should it apply generically or only when certain threshold requirements relating to environmental damage and scientific uncertainty are met?
- *How should it apply?* Who should bear the burden of proof, should the burden shift at some juncture, what form of evidence should be considered, and what standard(s) of proof should apply?
- *What remedial consequences should flow from its application?* To what extent and how should an adjudicative body prescribe measures necessary to achieve compliance with the principle?

## 3. Enter Precaution: The Emergence of the Principle in Domestic Environmental Litigation

There are two distinct avenues for the precautionary principle to enter domestic litigation: through the domestic application of international law, or through its application as a principle of domestic law.[10] Each of these categories may be further subdivided. International law may be applied directly, as binding in its own right; or it may apply indirectly, as an interpretive aid. Likewise, standalone principles of domestic law may be derived either from common law or statutory sources.

### APPLICATION OF INTERNATIONAL LAW

To date, few courts have accepted that the precautionary principle, as a rule of international law, can be directly applied in domestic litigation. One prominent exception is the Supreme Court of India. In *Vellore Citizens Welfare Forum v. Union of India*, it held that the principle had become a part of customary international law and as such was binding domestic law.[11]

An alternative way for international law to affect domestic litigation is for it to be applied indirectly as an interpretive aid. Generally, courts will be reluctant to apply the precautionary principle in this way if it is inconsistent with applicable domestic law. However, if domestic law is capable of being interpreted in a manner consistent with the principle, it may play a persuasive interpretive role.

The Supreme Court of Canada's decision in *Spraytech*[12] is an illustration of the indirect application of international law. While the status of the principle in international law was not fully argued before the court, the majority reasons cite scholarly opinion to the effect that "a good argument" could be made that it had become "a principle of customary international law."[13] The majority went on to employ the principle as a relevant consideration in upholding the validity of a municipal ban on pesticide use. As such, the decision makes it clear that principles of international law—even those that are not binding on Canada—may be taken into account when interpreting domestic law.

In 2013, the Supreme Court of Canada reinforced the views it expressed in *Spraytech*. In *Castonguay*[14] the court relied on the principle to interpret a provision in the *Ontario Environmental Protection Act*[15] (*EPA*). The provision in question made it an offence to discharge a contaminant into the environment [see s. 15(1) *EPA*]. Abella J., writing for the court, describes the *EPA* as "Ontario's principal environmental protection statute," concluding that "its status as remedial legislation entitles it to generous interpretation."[16]

In support of the conclusion that a broad purposive approach should be given to the interpretation of section 15(1) of the *EPA*, Abella J. specifically relies on the precautionary principle even though the *EPA* makes no specific mention of the principle. In the words of the court:[17]

> As the interveners Canadian Environmental Law Association and Lake Ontario Waterkeeper pointed out in their joint factum, s. 15(1) is also consistent with the precautionary principle. This emerging international law principle recognizes that since there are inherent limits in being able to determine and predict environmental impacts with scientific certainty, environmental policies must anticipate and prevent environmental degradation (O. McIntyre and T. Mosedale, "The Precautionary Principle as a Norm of Customary International Law" (1997), 9 *J. Envtl. L.* 221, at pp. 221–222; *114957 Canada Ltée (Spraytech, Société d'arrosage) v. Hudson (Town)*, 2001 SCC 40, [2001] 2 SCR 241, at paras. 30–32).

## THE COMMON LAW

The precautionary principle may also emerge as a principle of common law within a domestic legal system. This process can occur through the direct or indirect application of international law; or it can occur independently of international law. The jurisdiction that has been the most receptive to the notion that the principle has or is destined soon to achieve common law status is Australia, where some scholars argue that this has already occurred.[18]

One of the earliest and most oft-cited Australian decisions marshalled in support of this claim is *Leatch v. National Parks and Wildlife Service*.[19] This case involved a review of a permit to kill endangered fauna issued to a local government in connection with a road-building project. The relevant legislation did not require the precautionary principle to be applied; as a result, the plaintiffs argued that the principle was binding by virtue of international law. Stein J., of the New South Wales Land and Environment Court, demurred:

> It seems to me unnecessary to enter into this debate. In my opinion the precautionary principle is a statement of common sense and has already been applied by decision-makers in appropriate circumstances prior to the principle being spelt out. It is directed towards the prevention of serious or irreversible harm to the environment in situations of scientific uncertainty. Its premise is that where uncertainty or ignorance exists concerning the nature or scope of environmental harm (whether this follows from policies, decisions or activities), decision makers should be cautious.[20]

As a principle of "common sense" not excluded by the relevant legislation, he held that the precautionary principle should be taken into account when deciding whether the permit to take or kill should be issued.

## STATUTORY ADOPTION

By far the most common way that the principle finds its way before domestic courts and tribunals is through its implicit or explicit adoption in domestic statutes. A growing number of jurisdictions have enacted legislation that explicitly incorporates the precautionary principle either as a substantive decisional criterion or in preambular language. In Canada, the principle is now found, in various iterations, in most federal environmental laws, including the *Species at Risk Act* (SARA), the *Oceans Act*, the *Canadian Environmental Protection Act* (CEPA), the *Canadian Environmental Assessment Act* (CEAA), and the *Pest Control Products Act* (PCPA). It was also included in recently proposed amendments to the *Fisheries Act*.

Currently, the principle appears in the preambles to CEPA, SARA, and the *Oceans Act*, in the purposes section of CEAA (s. 4) and as a mandatory strategic management principle under the *Oceans Act* (s. 30). It is also expressed as a relevant consideration in the exercise of administrative duties vested in the Government of Canada and its agencies under CEPA and CEAA.[21] Moreover, in several instances, as set out below, the principle operates as a substantive decisional criterion:

- When conducting various assessments of potentially toxic substances, federal Ministers shall "apply ... the precautionary principle": section 76.1, CEPA.
- In preparing a recovery strategy, action plan, or management plan the competent minister shall "consider the principle that, if there are threats of serious or irreversible damage to the listed wildlife species, cost effective measures to prevent the reduction or loss of the species should not be postponed for lack of full scientific certainty": section 38, SARA.
- When conducting a re-evaluation or special review of a registered pesticide product, the minister must take the precautionary principle "into account" when deciding whether "a situation ... endangers human health or safety or the environment": see subsections 20(1) and (2), PCPA.

It is also, somewhat more slowly, finding its way into provincial legislation. In this regard, Ontario has led the way, generating a growing case law discussed in Part 4 below. Here the principle has come to be incorporated in many of the Statements of Environmental Values (SEVs) that every provincial government ministry is obliged to develop and apply. For example, the Ontario Ministry of the Environment and Climate Change's SEV commits it to "exercising a precautionary approach in its decision making."[22] Where a ministry's SEV contains language to this effect, public interest litigants have argued that a subsequent failure by ministry officials to comply with the principle, in the issuance of a permit or the exercise of a regulation making power, provides a basis for seeking leave to appeal from a ministry action under the *Environmental Bill of Rights*.[23]

Endangered species legislation in Ontario provides for a more direct way to pursue judicial review invoking the principle. Under the *Endangered Species Act* (ESA), the principle must be considered in the development of species recovery strategy: see subsection 11(3), ESA. This provision is analogous to the requirement under section 38 of SARA.

The principle also appears in provincial environmental statutes in other jurisdictions. To date, however, such references are relatively rare and are typically restricted to preambular language: see section 2 of the Nova Scotia *Environment Act*, and section 2 of the New Brunswick *Clean Air Act*.

## 4. Trials and Tribulations: The Precautionary Principle Case Law Post-*Spraytech*

If the precautionary principle is to find traction and yield real benefits in the adjudicative context, courts and tribunals must find ways to engage with it in the process of legal reasoning. When the principle is viewed as little more than "common sense," at best it provides little decisional guidance and at worst promotes uncertainty and subjectivity. The principle must likewise respect the discretion of elected decision makers to make judgments about the public good. Leaving aside concerns about interpretive uncertainty, courts are unlikely to adopt a principle that is perceived as fettering judicial discretion to balance competing interests.[24] In this Part, therefore, I consider whether and to what extent the emerging Canadian case law interpreting the principle mirrors these various and related concerns about uncertainty, subjectivity, deference, and institutional competence.

To date, as discussed above, the Supreme Court of Canada has directly opined on the precautionary principle in two cases. In *Spraytech*, writing for the majority, L'Heureux-Dubé J. relied upon the principle as an emerging norm of international law to assist in a domestic interpretive task, namely determining the validity of local government bylaws. And, in *Castonguay*, the court has now affirmed this majority judgment in a case involving the interpretation of a provincial environmental protection law where the statute in question made no mention of the principle. But while the Supreme Court of Canada has encouraged tribunals and courts to deploy the principle, at the very least as an interpretive tool, this invitation has not always been accepted.

One tribunal that has tended to resist arguments that it should give the principle work to do is the Environmental Appeal Board of British Columbia (EAB). Shortly after the *Spraytech* decision came down, the EAB was asked to consider the principle in the context of an appeal of a pesticide-permitting decision. At issue in the case was whether the proposed pesticide usage would cause an "unreasonable adverse effect." The statute in question did not mention the principle specifically. The EAB, at first instance, rejected the argument that its inquiry into this issue should be expanded to take account of the precautionary principle as set out in *Spraytech*. On judicial review, however, the BC Supreme Court disagreed, holding that *Spraytech* and in particular the precautionary principle mandated a broader analysis than the board had undertaken[25]

Notwithstanding this admonition, however, the EAB has remained reluctant to accede to arguments that the principle should be "read into" or even deemed relevant to the merits-based review of permitting or approval decisions where the statute is otherwise silent. For example, in *Burgoon v. B.C. (Ministry of Environment)*, the EAB rejected an argument that water licensing decisions should be subjected to scrutiny under the principle, distinguishing *Wier* on the footing that water licensing decisions, unlike pesticide use decisions, do not entail considerations of "reasonableness."[26] Another reason proffered in *Burgoon* for declining the invitation to apply the principle, according to the EAB, is that there are several different versions of the principle and it is unclear, "in the absence of clear statutory direction," which one ought to be applied.[27] It has maintained this approach in later cases: see *Toews v. Minister of Environment*[28] and *Shawnigan*.[29]

Some courts and tribunals elsewhere in Canada have likewise displayed, at least at times, a reluctance to apply the principle or, alternatively, a tendency to "read down" the principle so as to circumscribe its interpretive relevance and weight. In Ontario, several of these cases arise in connection with language contained in ministerial statements of environmental values (SEVs) that invoke the principle. A helpful summary of the tribunal jurisprudence on the subject is provided in *Greenspace Alliance v. Ontario (Ministry of Environment)*.[30] In this case, the applicants argued that the principle required that "if there is any uncertainty, then the decision maker is required to presume that the activity will be as hazardous as it could possibly be."[31] The Environmental Review Tribunal (ERT) held, however, that "to demand absolute proof … is not a realistic expectation of science, or of the Director."[32] In its view, the principle should instead be interpreted to require that proponents provide credible scientific evidence as to whether and to what extent the proposed activity will cause environmental harm. At this juncture, according to the ERT:

> Where there is credible evidence that shows that harm is unlikely, the degree of uncertainty is significantly reduced and it is consistent with the precautionary approach for the Director to approve the activity and include measures to prevent harm or to confirm the predictions. On the other hand, where there is a great deal of scientific uncertainty … the Director must presume there will be harm. In that case,

a reasonable person having regard for the precautionary approach would refuse the permit.[33]

There has also been resistance to attempts to invoke the principle in recent decisions of the Ontario Divisional Court. In *Sierra Club of Canada v. Ontario,* the applicant challenged a permit issued by the Ministry of Natural Resources (MNR) under the *Endangered Species Act* (ESA) that authorized the disturbance of endangered species habitat in connection with a major bridge-building project.[34] The applicant argued that the principle was binding upon the MNR (by virtue of its inclusion in the *ESA* preamble and the MNR's SEV), and that by issuing the permit the MNR was in breach of its duty to comply with the principle. The court rejected both propositions. It held that the principle was "not a statutory or regulatory requirement" and that in any event the MNR had "accounted for and considered" the principle, to the extent that this was mandated in its SEV, in its deliberations prior to issuance of the permit.[35]

Allegations of a failure to comply with the principle also played a central role in another judicial review decided by the Divisional Court: *Hanna v. Ontario (Attorney General)*.[36] This case sought to strike down regulations that prescribed setback requirements for wind energy developments that had been promulgated by the Ministry of Environment. This challenge contended that these setbacks were inadequate and inconsistent with the precautionary principle, which was applicable by virtue of its inclusion in the ministry's SEV. The Divisional Court dismissed the application, holding that the precautionary principle was only one of ten principles set out in the SEV, that there was no "clear evidence" that the setback was inadequate, and that the applicant retained the remedy of challenging site-specific wind turbine approvals on their merits to the ERT.[37]

In contrast, in the Federal Court the precautionary principle is most assuredly being put to work. In jurisprudence dating back to 2009, a much more sanguine perspective on the role and future of the principle emerges. Three of these decisions arise in connection with the interpretation of statutory provisions that specifically mandate consideration of the principle as a decisional criterion; significantly, however, in the fourth and most recent of these decisions the principle is considered and applied in the context of a statutory regime (the *Fisheries Act*) that makes no reference to the principle.

The first two of these cases were rendered in 2009 in litigation brought to compel the federal government to designate critical habitat in recovery strategies prepared under subsection 41(1) of *SARA*. The provision in question makes it mandatory to designate such habitat "to the extent possible" based on best available information.[38] The species at issue in these cases were the Greater Sage-Grouse and the Nooksack Dace; in both instances, the argument was that the federal government had acted unlawfully in failing to designate critical habitat where the facts suggested that it was possible to do so.

As noted earlier, *SARA* incorporates the precautionary principle not only in preambular language but also as a mandatory decisional consideration in the preparation of a recovery strategy, action plan, or management plan: see section 38, *SARA*. In both decisions, the Federal Court interpreted the habitat designation obligation under section 41 of *SARA* as reflecting and embodying the principle, concluding that the government's failure to designate habitat was not only inconsistent with the principle but also unlawful. Indeed, the judgment in the *Nooksack Dace* case goes even further. Noting that the precautionary principle is "an important feature of the [Biodiversity] Convention" that Canada has ratified, it held that *SARA* must be construed "to conform to the values and principles of the Convention [and that] the court must avoid any interpretation that could put Canada in breach of its Convention obligations."[39]

The third decision was rendered in late 2011: *Wier v. Canada (Health)*. The applicant in this case had requested the federal Minister of Health to initiate a "special review" (under subsection 17(1) of *PCPA*) of a registered pesticide, namely a variety of glyphosate-based product regularly sprayed to control forest undergrowth.[40] The minister declined. On judicial review, the applicant contended that there was uncertainty within the scientific community about the effects of the pesticide on amphibians in wetland areas. In light of this uncertainty, she therefore argued subsection 20(2) of *PCPA* (described in Part 3 above) made it mandatory for the minister to take the principle "into account" when deciding whether a special review was justified.

Kelen J.'s ruling in the case sets out in considerable detail the scientific assessment process undertaken on the minister's behalf by the Pest Management Regulatory Agency. This internal assessment revealed some differing views as to the toxicity of the pesticide in issue. Accordingly, Kelen J. concluded that this was a situation in which application of the principle required him to rule in favour of the applicant:

> With opinions within the Regulatory Agency on both sides of the question as to whether the pesticide presents an unacceptable environ-

> mental risk to amphibians in ephemeral wetlands, the precautionary principle would require the Minister initiate a special review into that issue.[41]

Finally, a recent decision of Rennie J. (as he then was) strongly reinforces relevance of the precautionary principle even to where the statute in question does not make explicit reference to the precautionary principle.[42] In *Morton v. Canada (Minister of Fisheries and Oceans)*, at issue was the validity of licences issued under the *Fisheries Act* that allowed for the transfer of "smolts"—"that is, salmon which have undergone a physical change … enabling them to live in sea water."[43] The applicant was concerned that licences had been improperly issued by the Department of Fisheries and Oceans (DFO) to a large fish farm operator (Marine Harvest) that allowed for the transport of smolts diseased with PRV (piscine reovirus).[44] The applicant argued that the issuance of such licences was inconsistent with the overarching obligation of the minister under the *Fisheries Act* to ensure "conservation and protection of fish."[45]

A central scientific issue in the case was the relationship between PRV and a disorder known as HSMI (heart and skeletal muscle inflammation). HSMI is known to cause anorexia and mortality in farmed salmon and is capable of wiping out entire stocks.[46] It would appear that the applicant brought this suit out of concern that there was a potential causal connection between PRV and HSMI, and that licences that allowed for the transport of smolts afflicted with PRV therefore posed a threat to wild and farmed salmon stocks.[47] In determining the validity of these licences, the applicant contended that the Federal Court should employ the precautionary principle notwithstanding that the *Fisheries Act* makes no mention of the principle. The Federal Court agreed.

Marine Harvest and DFO vigorously disputed the existence of a causal link between PRV and HSMI.[48] In the end, the court agreed that prevailing science did not support the conclusion that PRV caused HSMI. In its view, however, while there was a "body of credible science" supporting the theory of a causal relationship, such a link had yet to be proven. In its words,

> although there is a healthy debate between respected scientists on the issue, the evidence suggests that the disease agent (PRV) *may* be harmful to the protection and conservation of fish, and therefore a "lack of full scientific certainty should not be used as a reason for postponing measures to prevent environmental degradation": *Spraytech* at 31. In sum, it is not, on the face of the evidence, open to the respondents

> to assert that the licence conditions permitting a transfer of PRV infected smolts reflect the precautionary principle. The Minister is not, based on the evidence, erring on the side of caution.[49]

After citing *Spraytech* and *Castonguay*, Rennie J. offers the following observations about the principle:[50]

> The precautionary principle recognizes, that as a matter of sound public policy the lack of complete scientific certainty should not be used as a basis for avoiding or postponing measures to protect the environment, as there are inherent limits in being able to predict environmental harm. Moving from the realm of public policy to the law, the precautionary principle is at a minimum, an established aspect of statutory interpretation, and arguably, has crystallized into a norm of customary international law and substantive domestic law: *Spraytech* at paras 30–31.

In justifying reliance on the precautionary principle to interpret the *Fisheries Act* (a statute that does not mention the principle directly), Rennie J. notes that "the precautionary principle has been applied in international agreements to which Canada is a party (such as the *Convention on Biological Diversity*), and domestic legislation (for example the *Oceans Act* or the *Species at Risk Act*)." He also notes the Supreme Court of Canada's reliance on the principle in "interpreting regulations directed to public health and the environment" in the *Spraytech* and *Castonguay* cases.[51] Moreover, he underscores that use of the principle is consistent with the relevant language of the *Fisheries Act*:[52]

> In the language of "… the protection and conservation of fish," the word "protection" does not stand for "management"; rather the word means "preservation": *Canada (Minister of Fisheries and Oceans) v. David Suzuki Foundation*, 2012 FCA at para 114.

## INSIDE THE JUDICIAL MINDSET

From these early cases, some themes are beginning to emerge. For one, there has been little patience for claims that the precautionary principle is a trump card that when played clinches the case.[53] Courts and tribunals have, likewise, been unsympathetic to claims that compliance with the principle requires decision makers to defer approval for potentially harmful activities wherever any scientific uncertainty, no matter how remote or speculative, about the nature or extent of the harm exists.[54] What level of scientific uncertainty is required, and what forms of scientific evidence can and should be relied in this assessment, is unclear. Where, however, there are diverging opinions within the "regulatory community," and especially among a government's own scientific advisors, as to the nature or extent of the harm, it would appear that the test is met.[55] Likewise, adjudicators also seem clearly to want compelling evidence that a proposed action or standard poses a serious risk to human health or the environment before concluding that the principle applies.[56] Moreover, what quantum of risk is necessary, once again, is unclear.

Secondly, it would appear that, at least judicially, there is a growing appetite to consider the principle and give it work to do. This is certainly reflected in the Supreme Court of Canada (*Spraytech* and *Castonguay*) and, as well, in Federal Court jurisprudence (*Greater Sage Grouse*, *Nootsack Dace*, *Wier v. Canada (Health)* and *Morton*). And, of course, we can add to this list *Wier v. BC (EAB)* in the BC Supreme Court involving the same Dr. Wier.[57] It is notable that, in three of these seven cases, courts have chosen to deploy the principle even where the principle itself has not been referenced in the legislation being interpreted.

Finally, however, both in cases where courts and tribunals have demurred from considering the principle and where they have chosen to engage with it, there is a very discernible sense that the "legal contours" of the principle remain uncertain. Can the principle become more than an interpretive "straw in the wind"? Can it offer guidance as a decisional criterion? The Divisional Court in *Sierra Club* is illustrative, dismissing the idea that preambular language referring to the principle does anything more than serve "to introduce the ideas and concerns that inform the legislation that follows."[58] Cases in which references to the principle in preambular and purpose provisions have been interpreted in a more robust light have tended, almost invariably, to be ones where the principle is also incorporated into a substantive decisional criterion within the same statutory regime.[59] Yet, where the precautionary principle is framed as a substantive decisional criterion, what guidance can be relied upon to apply that criterion? In the next part, I discuss possible ways through which the principle can be applied.

## 5. Can the Principle Be Given some "Specific Work To Do"?

Although there has been very little judicial consideration of the precautionary approach or 'precautionary principle' ... the clear thread which emerges from what consideration has been given to the approach is that it does dictate caution, but it does not dictate inaction, and it will not generally dictate one specific course of action to the exclusion of others.

—JUSTICE CHRISTINE WHEELER, COURT OF APPEAL OF WEST AUSTRALIA[60]

I now propose to return to a question posed at this beginning of this chapter: assuming that courts or tribunals are inclined or required to apply the principle, to what extent can it be given specific work to do? As noted earlier, a variety of legal scholars have argued in favour of "taming" the principle, enabling it to provide useful guidance to decision makers, rather than dictating to them.[61] Whether this can occur—in effect, whether the principle can be rendered justiciable—depends heavily on the creativity and initiative of lawyers and courts alike. Ten years ago, in the predecessor to this article, I profiled and critiqued a new decision of the Land and Environment Court of New South Wales which, in my view, represented an important step in this direction: *Telstra Corporation Ltd. v. Hornsby Shire Council*.[62] In the balance of this part, I want to revisit *Telstra* and consider whether it has indeed given the principle something specific to do.

## TELSTRA AND ITS PROGENY

The *Telstra* case arose out of a proposal to construct a mobile telephone base station in a suburb of Sydney, Australia.[63] The Shire Council, in response to community fears about the health effects of radiofrequency electromagnetic energy, refused the development application for the base station despite the fact that the installation complied with a peer-reviewed, applicable national safety standard. The council's decision was appealed to the Land and Environment Court of New South Wales, pursuant to the *Environmental Planning and Assessment Act*, 1979 (EPAA).[64] The EPAA requires the principles of sustainable development, including the precautionary principle, to be taken into account when considering development applications.[65]

Under the *Telstra* approach, determining whether and how to apply the precautionary principle in a particular case occurs in three discrete steps: (1) deciding whether the principle applies; (2) if so, reversing the onus of proof; and (3) identifying the appropriate governmental response.

An important feature of *Telstra* is its recognition of the importance of restricting the application of the principle to situations where it can add analytic value. As such, it holds that before the principle can be applied the applicant must establish two conditions precedent: (1) the existence of a threat of serious or irreversible environmental damage; *and* (2) the existence of scientific uncertainty as to the environmental damage.[66] Whether these preconditions exist are questions of fact.

The first condition precedent requires that impending environmental damage must be *serious or irreversible*. This, according to *Telstra*, can be measured using a variety of factors including:

> (a) the spatial scale of the threat (eg local, regional, statewide, national, international);
> (b) the magnitude of possible impacts, on both natural and human systems;
> (c) the perceived value of the threatened environment;
> (d) the temporal scale of possible impacts, in terms of both the timing and the longevity (or persistence) of the impacts;
> (e) the complexity and connectivity of the possible impacts;
> (f) the manageability of possible impacts, having regard to the availability of means and the acceptability of means;
> (g) the level of public concern, and the rationality of and scientific or other evidentiary basis for the public concern; and
> (h) the reversibility of the possible impacts and, if reversible, the time frame for reversing the impacts, and the difficulty and expense of reversing the impacts.[67]

Under this approach, the seriousness of the threat is primarily a "values" as opposed to a "science" question, to be judged by consultations with a broad range of experts, stakeholders, and right-holders. This does not mean, however, that science is irrelevant at this stage of the inquiry: indeed, Preston C.J. specifically notes "the threat of environmental damage must be adequately sustained by scientific evidence."[68]

The second condition precedent is that there be *a lack of full scientific certainty*. In assessing this question of fact, *Telstra* posits another menu of factors, including:

> (a) the sufficiency of the evidence that there might be serious or irreversible environmental harm caused by the development plan, programme or project;
> (b) the level of uncertainty, including the kind of uncertainty (such as technical, methodological or epistemological uncertainty); and
> (c) the potential to reduce uncertainty having regard to what is possible in principle, economically and within a reasonable time frame.[69]

*Telstra* leaves open the question of what constitutes a requisite level of scientific uncertainty sufficient to trigger application of the principle; in its view, this standard may differ depending upon the nature of the impending environmental damage. In a leading case that has recently applied *Telstra*, a standard of "substantial uncertainty" was adopted.[70]

If these conditions precedent are met, the precautionary principle is then triggered. This means that the burden of proof shifts to the proponent to show that the threat of serious or irreversible environmental damage does not in fact exist or is negligible. If the proponent cannot do so, the government decision maker must assume that serious or irreversible damage will occur.

In this situation, the decision maker must respond in a manner that is consistent with the principle. The response that is required by the precautionary principle will depend on the outcome of a risk assessment. The overarching goal of the response is proportionality. The more significant and likely the threat, the greater the degree of precaution required. Where uncertainty exists, a margin of error should be left so that serious or irreversible harm is less likely to occur. This margin of error may be maintained through step-wise or adaptive management plans.

In the result, the carefully elaborated approach set out in *Telstra* was not put to the test on the facts of the case. Preston C.J. decided that the party seeking to rely upon the principle (in this case, the Shire Council) had failed to lead evidence capable of supporting the conclusion that the proposed cell tower presented a threat of serious or irreversible harm. As a result, the precautionary principle did not apply and it was unnecessary to proceed further with the analysis.

The *Telstra* approach has, however, been applied in a more fulsome fashion in several subsequent cases.[71] Among these, the case that most faithfully applies the framework, *Environment East Gippsland Inc. v. VicForests*,[72] involves a familiar scenario, especially for those of us from the Canadian West Coast. The conflict here arose in a remote region in southern Australia, and was triggered by logging plans in an old growth Crown-owned forest that were said to threaten a variety of endangered species. It is instructive to reprise how Osborn J. for the Supreme Court of Victoria analyzes this complex dispute employing the *Telstra* framework.

In this case, the plaintiff environmental group commenced an action seeking an injunction against proposed logging to be undertaken by the defendant, a state-owned forest company. The defendant had secured timber-harvesting approvals for an area known as Brown Mountain, in the East Gippsland region of the state of Victoria, southeast of Melbourne. Surrounded by conservation reserve areas, Brown Mountain contains areas of old growth forest with high timber values and ecological significance. The area in contention was home to over a dozen threatened or endangered species, including the Long-footed Potoroo, the Powerful Owl, and the Giant Burrowing Frog.[73] Under a legally binding Code of Practice, the defendant was obliged to plan and undertake harvesting in accordance with the precautionary principle.

The case makes fascinating reading for Canadian environmental lawyers more accustomed to the highly constrained manner in which judicial supervision of natural resource decision making occurs in Canada. Osborn J.'s careful reasons for judgment help, in my view, to dispel the notion that the principle can at best play a background or ancillary role in domestic adjudication.

The case arises in the context of what Osborn J. characterizes as a "labyrinthine" maze of legislation and regulation. A central issue to be decided was whether and to what extent the precautionary principle applied to the defendant's tree harvesting plans, and what implications (in terms of injunctive relief) flow. The court heard evidence over the course of sixteen days. Ultimately, for five species—the Powerful Owl and the Spotted Owl, the Spot-tailed Quoll, the Giant Burrowing Frog, and the Large Brown Tree Frog—the principle played a decisive role in the court's conclusion that logging should be enjoined pending further studies aimed at determining what measures were necessary to maintain species viability.

To provide a sense of how Osborn J. assessed the evidence in applying the *Telstra* test, it is worthwhile to reprise his analysis with respect to two of the species at issue: the Giant Burrowing Frog and the Large Brown Tree Frog. For these species, he concluded as follows:

> (a) that the proposed logging presents a *real threat of serious or irreversible damage* to the environment (i.e. these two species) for a variety of reasons including their 'threatened' status and relevant expert evidence;
> (b) that this damage is attended by *a lack of full scientific certainty* including evidence with respect to very significant uncertainties relating to their respective distribution, biology and conservation;
> (c) the defendant has not demonstrated that the threat is *negligible* insofar as it led 'no evidence from an expert with specialist qualifications relating to the biology and conservation of frogs;
> (d) the threat can be addressed through *adaptive management*, including 'management measures, which would significantly better inform a

further judgment as to the relevant conservation values of the Brown Mountain ... [reducing] ... uncertainty with limited cost and within a reasonable timeframe';

(e) the 'measures proposed are *proportionate* to the threat in issue. They are limited operations. Further, they are capable of definition and ... controlling supervision ... In addition there is satisfactory evidence that postponement of timber harvesting pending the completion of such surveys would cause VicForests significant economic damage'. [Emphasis added.][74]

While these excerpts may be not adequately convey the point, I would argue that this judgment grapples impressively with a dispute that is extraordinarily complex both in legal and scientific terms. And, I would argue, far from being a "make-work" project for the precautionary principle, the judgment shows in convincing fashion that the principle—appropriately "tamed"—can indeed be a powerful tool for analyzing and resolving disputes of this kind. Among other reasons, I think that this is attributable to the care with which the Osborn J. applies the *Telstra* framework, particularly in relation to the conditions precedent to the principle and the need to calibrate a judicial response that is proportionate to the risk.[75]

As discussed at the end of Part 2, turning the precautionary principle into a workable framework raises three important questions:

- When should the principle apply?
- How should it apply?
- What remedial consequences should flow from its application?

*Telstra* is a compelling illustration of how these three questions can be addressed in a manner that allows the principle to play a constructive role in a variety of administrative and adjudicative settings. The *Telstra* approach accomplishes this by responding to concerns about overbreadth by Professor Applegate and others: see Part 2 above. To this end, it injects into the principle a proportionality mechanism that calibrates the precautionary measures required to the degree of risk that is present. Moreover, as knowledge of the risk grows more certain through adaptive management and learning, these precautionary measures can be fine-tuned.

Finally, the two conditions precedent under the *Telstra* approach offer another "taming" mechanism that clarifies and constrains what the precautionary principle is supposed to do. By requiring courts to first determine whether the principle applies in the first place, and then providing a framework for application where the principle is found to be applicable, the *Telstra* approach affirmatively answers Stein J.'s question about whether the principle can be given "specific work to do."

## Conclusion

It is now almost a decade since I first began writing on this topic. Back then, in an article I wrote with Jamie Thornback, we emphasized that these were early days in the judicial development of the principle, and expressed the hope that lawyers would "advocate for a nuanced approach to implementing the principle capable of persuading courts that, it adds value to and is consistent with their competence and jurisdiction to supervise administrative action."[76] These remain early days. However—now more than ever—lawyers have the tools and precedents necessary to persuade courts not only of the desirability but the viability of putting the precautionary principle to work.

### NOTES

1 C Tollefson & J Thornback, "Litigating the Precautionary Principle in Domestic Courts" (2008) 19 JELP 33.

2 See the extra-judicial reflections of Stein J of the NSW Court of Appeal in "A Cautious Application of the Precautionary Principle" (2000) 2 Environmental Law Review 1 at 2.

3 See generally David Freestone & Ellen Hey, eds, *The Precautionary Principle and International Law* (The Hague: Kluwer Law International, 1996); Arie Trouwborst, *Evolution and Status of the Precautionary Principle in International Law* (The Hague: Kluwer Law International, 2002); Harold Hohmann, *Precautionary Legal Duties and Principles of Modern International Environmental Law* (London: Graham & Trotman, 1994); Ronnie Harding & Elizabeth Fisher, *Perspectives on the Precautionary Principle* (Sydney: Federation Press, 1999); Simon Marr, *The Precautionary Principle in the Law of the Sea* (The Hague: Kluwer Law International, 2003); Joakim Zander, *The Application of the Precautionary Principle in Practice: Comparative Dimensions* (Cambridge: Cambridge University Press, 2010); Jocelyn Stacey, "Preventive Justice, the Precautionary Principle and the Rule of Law" (2016) in Tamara Tulich et al, *Regulating Preventive Justice* (New York: Routledge, 2016) 23.

4 United Nations Conference on Environment and Development, *Rio Declaration on Environment and Development*, Principle 15.

5 See generally the discussion in Per Sandin, "Dimensions of the Precautionary Principle" (1999) 5 Human and Ecological Risk Assessment 889 at 891.

6 *Ibid.*

7 *Ibid* at 891–895.

8 John S Applegate, "The Taming of the Precautionary Principle" (2002–2003) 27 Wm & Mary Envtl L & Pol'y Rev 13 [Applegate]. In a similar vein, see Elizabeth Fisher, "Is the Precautionary Principle Justiciable?" (2001) 13 JELP 315.

9 Applegate, *ibid* at 15–16.

10 For a comparative review of the precautionary principle case law see B Preston, CJ, "The Role of the Judiciary in Promoting Sustainable Development: The Experience of Asia and the Pacific" (2005) 9:2–3 Asia Pac J Envtl L 109.

11 *Vellore Citizens Welfare Forum v Union of India*, WP 914/1991 (28 August 1996) at para 15. The *Vellore* decision was later affirmed in *MC Mehta v Kamal Nath* (1997), 1 SCC 388.

12 *114957 Canada Ltee (Spraytech) v Hudson (Town of)*, [2001] 2 SCR 241.

13 *Ibid* at para 32.

14 *Castonguay Blasting Ltd v Ontario (Environment)*, 2013 SCC 52 at para 20 [*Castonguay Blasting Ltd*].

15 RSO 1990, c E.19.

16 *Castonguay Blasting Ltd*, *supra* note 14 at para 9.

17 *Ibid* at para 20.

18 Charmian Barton, "The Status of the Precautionary Principle in Australia: Its Emergence in Legislation and as a Common Law Doctrine" (1998) 22 Harv Envtl L Rev 509 at 535.

19 *Leatch v National Parks and Wildlife Service* (1993), 81 LGERA 270.

20 Ibid.

21 See *CEPA*, s 2 and *CEAA*, s 4(2).

22 Other ministries make more equivocal commitments: for example, the Ontario Ministry of Natural Resources does not use the word "precaution" in its SEV; however it does recognize that need for its staff to "exercise caution and special concern for natural values in the face of uncertainty" about "... the way the natural world works and how our actions affect it": see discussion in *Sierra Club Canada v The Queen*, 2011 ONSC 4655 (Ont Sup Ct Gen Div) at para 46.

23 See *Dawber v Ontario (Director, Ministry of the Environment)* (2007), 28 CELR (3d) 281 aff'd (2008), 36 CELR (3d) 191 (Ont Sup Ct Gen Div).

24 In this vein, consider the words of the European Court of Justice: "[T]he precautionary principle has a future only to the extent that, far from opening the door wide to irrationality, it establishes itself as an aspect of the rational management of risks, designed not to achieve a zero risk, which everything suggest does not exist, but to limit the risks to which citizens are exposed to the lowest level reasonably imaginable": see *National Farmers' Union v Secretary Central of the French Government*, ECJ C-241/01 (2 July 2002) at 76.

25 *Wier v BC (EAB)*, [2003] BCJ No 2221 at paras 33–38.

26 *Burgoon v British Columbia (Ministry of Environment)*, [2010] BCEA No 5, 53 CELR (3d) 1 at para 127 [*Burgoon*].

27 *Ibid* at para 132. To a similar effect see *City of Cranbrook v British Columbia (Ministry of Environment)*, [2009] BCEA No 2, 42 CELR (3d) 240 at para 38.

28 *Toews v British Columbia (Director, Environmental Management Act)*, [2015] BCEA No 25.

29 *Shawnigan Residents Assn v British Columbia (Director's Delegate, Environmental Management Act)*, 2015 CarswellBC 802.

30 *Greenspace Alliance of Canada's Capital v Ontario (Ministry of Environment)* (2009), CELR (3d) 216 [*Greenspace Alliance*].

31 *Ibid* at para 135.

32 *Ibid* at para 139.

33 *Ibid* at para 138.

34 *Sierra Club of Canada v Ontario (Natural Resources and Transportation)*, 2011 ONSC 4655 [*Sierra Club*].

35 *Ibid* at paras 53 and 60.

36 *Hanna v Ontario (Attorney General)*, 2011 ONSC 609 [*Hanna*].

37 *Ibid* at paras 28–31.

38 *Alberta Wilderness Assn v Canada (Minister of Environment)*, [2009] FCJ 876 (the *Greater Sage-Grouse* case) and *Environmental Defence Canada v Canada (Minister of Fisheries and Oceans)*, [2009] FCJ 1052 (the *Nooksack Dace* case) [*Environmental Defence*].

39 *Environmental Defence*, ibid at paras 34 and 38.

40 See *Wier v Canada (Health)*, 2011 FC 1322. The applicant in this case was the redoubtable Josette Wier, a non-practising, French-trained medical doctor living in Smithers, BC. Ms Wier, who describes herself as an "environmental researcher," also successfully litigated another precautionary principle case initiated before the BC Environmental Appeal Board in 2003 discussed *infra* in text accompanying note 57.

41 *Ibid* at para 101.

42 Examples where the relevant statute is silent in this regard include *Spraytech, supra* note 12; *Castonguay Blasting Ltd, supra*, note 14; *Wier, supra*, note 40; and *Morton, infra*, note 43.

43 *Morton v Canada (Minister of Fisheries and Oceans)*, 2015 FC 575.

44 *Ibid* at paras 1–3.

45 *Ibid* at para 11.

46 *Ibid* at para 33.

47 *Ibid* at paras 2, 19, 33–35.

48 *Ibid* at paras 37–39.

49 *Ibid* at paras 45–46.

50 *Ibid* at para 43.

51 *Ibid* at para 58.

52 *Ibid* at para 23.

53 See *Hanna, supra* note 36 at para 30, and *Sierra Club, supra* note 34 at para 49.

54 See *Greenspace Alliance, supra* note 30 at paras 135–138.

55 See *Wier v Canada (Health), supra* note 40 at para 101.

56 See, for example, *Hanna, supra* note 36 at para 34, where the Divisional Court uses the term "clear evidence."

57 See *supra* note 24: *Wier v BC (EAB)*, [2003] BCJ No 2221.

58 See *Sierra Club, supra* note 34 at para 54.

59 See, for example, references to the preambular language in *SARA* (in the *Greater Sage-Grouse* and *Nooksack Dace* judgments) and to the preambular language in *PCPA* (in *Wier v Canada*).

60 *Bridgetown/Greenbushes Friends of the Forest Inc v Executive Director of Conservation and Land Management* (1997), 18 WAR 102 per Wheeler J (decided prior to her elevation to the Court of Appeal).

61 See Applegate, *supra* note 8.

62 [2006] NSWLEC 133 [*Telstra*].

63 Telstra, ibid.

64 *Environmental Planning and Assessment Act*, 1979 (NSW). The Land and Environment Court of New South Wales is a specialist superior court of record. Its jurisdiction includes merits review, judicial review, civil enforcement, criminal prosecution, criminal appeals and civil claims in planning, environmental, land, and mining matters. It was created by statute in 1979.

65 *Telstra, supra* note 62 at paras 121–26.

66 *Ibid* at para 128.

67 *Ibid* at para 131.

68 *Ibid* at para 134.

69 *Ibid* at para 141.

70 *Environment East Gippsland Inc v VicForests*, [2010] VSC 335 at para 197 [*EEG Inc*].

71 Some examples include *Environment East Gippsland Inc v VicForests*, [2010] VSC 335; *Rosen & Anor v Macedon Ranges Shire Council*, [2010] VSC 583; *Newcastle & Hunter Valley Speleological Society Inc v Upper Hunter Shire Council and Stoneco Pty Ltd*, [2010] NSWLEC 48; *GHD Pty Ltd v Palerang Council*, [2009] NSWLEC 1342; and *Royal Motor Yacht Club*, [2008] NSWLEC 1126.

72 [2010] VSC 335.

73 *EEG Inc, supra* note 70 at para 316.

74 *Ibid* at para 506.

75 The *Telstra* approach has been applied in various other New Zealand cases, e.g.: *Southern Highlands Coal Action Group v Minister for Planning and Infrastructure*, [2013] NSWLEC 1032; *Newcastle v. Hunter Valley Speleological Society v Upper Hunter Shire*, [2010] NSWLEC 48; *Sustain our Sounds Inc v The New Zealand King Salmon Co Ltd*, [2014] NZSC 40.

76 Tollefson & Thornback, *supra* note 1 at 58.

# 3

# Ecosystem Management: It's Imperative ... Whatever It Is

MICHAEL M. WENIG

## 1. Introduction

Ecosystem management has fundamentally changed the field of environmental protection, from a narrow focus on individual sources of harm to a more holistic focus on entire ecosystems, the multiple human sources of harm within ecosystems, and the complex social context (including political boundaries and economic institutions) in which those sources exist. US legal scholar Oliver Houck described ecosystem management as a "whole new species of thought—half science and half religion—[that] has arisen in research, articles, books, management plans and litigation, a new field of conservation biology" that is "changing the language of the game."[1]

This approach was not a new concept when Professor Houck commented on it in 1998, but it had gained an unprecedented level of acceptance in recent years leading up to his paper. According to another US writer, the ecosystem concept, together with the related concept of "sustainable development," were "sweeping through international, national, state, and local policy and reshaping the appearance of environmental law at all levels."[2] For another author, it is a "true paradigm shift."[3]

In Canada, the call for ecosystem management has existed for at least four decades, but has gained considerable traction in recent years.[4] Canadian legislation is jumping on the ecosystem management bandwagon. At a basic level,

* *Thanks to Mount Royal University Professor Michael S. Quinn for his recommendations on the voluminous ecosystem management literature and for his long-term input and advice on ecosystem thinking.*

several Canadian statutes now define the "environment" in holistic, ecosystem-like terms.[5] Others link the objectives of "environmental" and "ecosystem" protection.[6] Numerous other Canadian statutes now aim generally to protect "ecosystems" instead of or in addition to the "environment."[7] Several statutes provide for ecosystem protection as a target or basis for government's use of specific regulatory tools[8] and for the development of broad-brush "strategies."[9] Two federal statutes provide general endorsement for the "ecosystem approach" for achieving the Acts' objectives.[10]

Canadian environmental managers have also shared the enthusiasm for ecosystem management. For example, Environment Canada has been engaged in several "ecosystem initiatives," including those relating to the Great Lakes, the St. Lawrence River, the Atlantic Coast, and the Georgia Basin.[11] Canada's federal Department of Fisheries and Oceans (DFO) has adopted the "ecosystem approach" as a basis for fisheries management.[12] In addition, Canadian provinces and territories have made numerous gestures toward embracing the ecosystem approach.[13] And at least several Canadian post-secondary schools now have degree programs or faculties focused on ecosystem management.[14]

Although there is widespread support for ecosystem management, there remains considerable ambiguity over what it entails and what it is for. As one author stated: "If there is one thing about ecosystem management upon which people agree, it is that the term means different things to different people."[15] This ambiguity is reflected in the lack of consensus over whether "ecosystem management" is even an appropriate name. While many people refer to ecosystem "management," that term is often criticized as reflecting an overly techno- and homo-centric view of the environment as an object that is subject to human manipulation. Others refer to an ecosystem "approach" or ecosystem "protection," both of which at least purport to reflect a more reverential or respectful view of humans' relation to the environment. Another variation is the term "ecosystem-based," in reference to either "management" or "approach" (or some other descriptor).[16] However, to some commentators, the debate over terminology detracts from the development of general principles or elements of the ecosystem concept.[17] This chapter uses the term "ecosystem management," but solely for practical reasons; it does not purport to take a stand on the debate noted above.

The purpose of this chapter is to provide a broad, general outline of ecosystem management. The chapter first addresses the need or imperative for this approach and then discusses several of the approach's principles or components, noting the areas of uncertainty and challenges.

## 2. The Ecosystem Management Imperative

Advocates for ecosystem management generally agree that it is needed because environmental problems often involve linkages among physical, biological, and social components within and among ecosystems.[18] For example, a watershed ecosystem includes four sets of complex physical linkages: vertical (surface to ground water), horizontal (up- and down-stream), lateral (river channel to riparian zone to flood plain), and temporal (changes in each of the above linkages over time). Those physical watershed components are linked, in turn, to biological and, in most cases, human, communities within watersheds. To make matters more complicated, there are physical, biological, and social linkages among watersheds and among watersheds and other kinds of ecosystems.[19]

These linkages show that environmental problems within a given watershed cannot be solved by focusing on one watershed component without considering how that component is linked to others.[20] For example, regulatory efforts to protect fish in a watershed must focus not only on the harm to fish from pollution discharged from a domestic sewage plant but also on the threats to fish from all other sources of water pollution, as well as sources of damage to riparian vegetation and reductions in stream flows. Moreover, those myriad threats must be evaluated in the context not only of the range of often disjointed laws available to reduce them but also the laws and other social factors that may be encouraging them. Ecosystem management provides a comprehensive analytical framework for assessing and addressing these interconnected physical and social factors. Advocates for ecosystem management also generally agree that it can promote the social values of equity and efficiency, as well as environmental protection, by simultaneously addressing all physical, biological, and social causes of environmental problems. Ecosystem management provides a flexible framework for fairly and efficiently allocating the social costs of environmental protection among all public and private interests.[21]

Advocates generally agree, not only on the imperatives for ecosystem management, but also that the holistic approach is difficult to define and implement because of the same complex physical, biological, and social linkages that necessitate the approach in the first place.[22] Professor Adler observes that the advantages and problems inherent in the ecosystem approach present a paradox: the larger the ecosystem unit and the more comprehensive the harms and social causes addressed, the more holistic the approach. Yet, the larger the scale and scope of the ecosystem approach, the more difficult it will be to implement, in terms of scientifically modelling the complex physical and biological linkages and coordinating among all the interested bureaucrats, politicians, citizens, and commercial interests.[23]

## 3. Ecosystem Type and Scale

"Ecosystem" is defined as an "assemblage of species plus the interacting physical and biological processes upon which the species depend."[24] While this definition is intuitive and makes scientific sense, the concept is problematic in that there are no inherent or objective ecosystem "units." While it is useful to define ecosystem scales or boundaries for management purposes, these line drawings are essentially arbitrary (i.e. non-natural) exercises.[25] They are also problematic because defining one type or scope of "assemblages" masks another or other "assemblages" relating to the same biophysical components. For example, a "watershed" is a type of ecosystem that is commonly defined as the geographic area of land drained by a particular body or segment of flowing water. A "basin" is the largest form of "watershed," encompassing the land mass drained by an entire river system.[26] Watershed ecosystems like the Mackenzie, Columbia, South Saskatchewan, and Mississippi River basins may have numerous components, which can be broken up into multiple smaller watersheds based on each of the numerous tributaries that feed those large river systems.

It may be even more difficult to define the appropriate ecosystem scale using kinds of ecosystems other than watersheds. For example, an alpine meadow in the Canadian Rockies can be viewed as a local ecosystem providing habitat for local insects and rodents. But the meadow may also lie within a range for grizzly bears and migrating eagles. It may also contain wetlands adjacent to a creek which is part of a larger watershed that ultimately drains sub-alpine forests and prairies. Should the meadow be viewed as an isolated system, or as part of an alpine Rocky Mountain ecosystem, part of the watershed to which it belongs, or part of a "grizzly-shed" or "eagle-shed"?

Intuitively, watersheds are an appealing ecosystem "unit" for planning purposes because they can be used to cover an entire land mass without overlap, unlike other categories of ecosystems that may overlap and may not cover an entire land mass, such as bird and mammal migration corridors. However, watersheds are not the only ecosystem categories that can be used to cover an entire land mass.[27]

The wide variation among ecosystems arguably suggests that there is no "one size fits all" unit for ecosystem management. Thus, it is not surprising that, while several Canadian statutes provide for the management of marine, forest, or freshwater ecosystems generally, none specifies an ecosystem unit of concern for management purposes.[28] A lack of consistency in the choice of unit or boundary among different ecosystem management prorams may impede necessary efforts to coordinate or link these programs to achieve regional, national, or international goals.

## 4. Governance

Whatever ecosystem unit is used for management purposes, the unit's geographic boundaries are unlikely to coincide with the geographic boundaries of political jurisdictions. In addition, the complex interactions within ecosystems require interdisciplinary management perspectives that are arguably difficult to promote in agencies whose staff have been trained in specific disciplines and who may have historically been organized along lines that correspond to those disciplines. Both of these factors make it a challenge to design a governance system for ecosystem management.

Another challenge arises from choosing the roles of government staff and non-governmental parties, especially those living or working within the relevant ecosystem boundaries. Ecosystem management proponents generally favour a greater role for local stakeholders—typically, through their participation in watershed councils or other area-based planning organizations—than in more conventional or traditional environmental regulatory and natural resource management regimes.[29] No doubt this view stems, in part, from the notion that the people living and working in a given place are the most affected by place-based management decisions, and that locals may be best able to develop creative, effective solutions to problems occurring in their area.[30] This notion seems even more persuasive in an ecosystem management context where an array of local factors is on the table than in a management regime focused more narrowly on a single issue or natural resource.

Locally based decisions can also help take the political "heat" off a regional or national agency on controversial environmental issues and can lighten the agency's workload. In short, broad and strong local participation seems preferable in ecosystem management in order to provide the necessary expertise and power base to address the myriad harms to ecosystems.

On the other hand, there is concern that local citizen and government decision makers are more likely to be corrupted by powerful corporate interests. In addition, even geographically "local" ecosystems have aspects or components that may be of regional, national, or global importance. These facets include the survival of plant and animal species (and arguably even populations) and the protection of publicly owned lands, waters, and other public resources. These non-local interests suggest that environmental regulators and land managers should not completely abdicate their decision-making roles to local bodies that may not see or at least share the non-local interests.

The challenges to defining an appropriate governance model are reflected not only in the lack of consensus on a *uniform* model but in uncertainties with respect to individual governance models. For example, Alberta has arguably sent mixed messages regarding the roles of its "watershed and planning advisory councils" in provincial watershed planning.[31]

Of course, the question of whether ecosystem management decision making should be made by local bodies need not be viewed in black and white. In reality, there exist a variety of decision-making roles, from establishing overall goals and objectives, performance and environmental quality standards, and plans for achieving those targets, to developing in-place solutions, monitoring, enforcement, and follow-up, among other functions. Strong regional or federal leadership may be appropriate for some of these roles but not for others, and other roles may require close coordination at two or more political levels.

As with the variability in types of ecosystem units, there is arguably a wide variability in socio-political circumstances among ecosystems. This socio-political variability suggests that ecosystem governance models themselves may need to vary. However, there is also arguably a need for consistency in governance models to ensure a high degree of coordination and cooperation among governance institutions and that regional, national, and international interests are met. Consistency may also be needed to promote fairness to, and ensure equivalent levels of rights and responsibilities among, all ecosystem management participants and citizens generally.

## 5. Ecosystem Management Objectives

What is ecosystem management for? What are the ultimate aims or purposes of ecosystem management? To some, ecosystem management is just an analytical framework (holistic, place/system-based) for environmental decision making and a decision-making process (problem identification and goal setting, local decision making, adaptive management, planning, etc.). However, to many of its proponents, ecosystem management also includes an objective of achieving, maintaining, or restoring some level of ecosystem condition that is desired for all ecosystem management applications.[32] Many scientists now favour ecosystem "resilience" as the condition of concern.[33]

Varying expressions of the "optimum" ecosystem condition reflect an evolving scientific understanding of ecosystems, from the concept of an ideal ecosystem condition as a static or "equilibrium" state to the notion that ecosystems are inherently dynamic and evolving.[34] Of course, the moving nature of the target makes it even more challenging to define an "ideal" ecosystem condition.

Canadian legislation runs the gamut of these varying approaches. For example, some statutes require or enable watershed or water management planning but provide little or no detail on the target of such planning effort.[35] By contrast, several Canadian statutes focus on maintaining or restoring ecosystem "integrity."[36] Several others aim for ecosystem "integrity" along with "health" or other co-conditions.[37] Other statutes aim to protect ecosystem "structure and function," "productive capability" or "capacity" and "stability" or "diversity," among other targets.[38] There can be a wide range of target conditions specified in different statutes within a single province.[39]

An ethical issue that underlies the debate about ecosystem management objectives is whether its purpose—and the expression of any desired ecosystem condition—should be driven solely by anthropocentric, utilitarian concerns, or by some non-anthropocentric, non-utilitarian notion of ecosystems in their "natural" or "undisturbed" state.[40] (A related conceptual conflict relates to whether ecosystem management views humans as part of or separate from ecosystems.) There is some common ground between these two ethical poles in the sense that an ecosystem approach is arguably necessary from a purely anthropocentric view, because humans themselves are ultimately better off living in healthy ecosystems.

Some question whether humans are really capable of constructing a non-anthropocentric ethic (and accompanying management framework), given that ethics itself is a human construct and human interests must still be considered in any method for implementing a non-anthropocentric ethic.[41]

This logic is supported by Aldo Leopold's justification for his influential "land ethic," which has been cited as providing the ethical justification for ecosystem management.[42] Under that ethic, the morality of various human actions is judged according to whether they preserve or destroy the "land," a term Leopold defined broadly along ecosystem lines.[43] Although Leopold's "land ethic" is commonly associated with a non-anthropocentric environmental ethic, much of his justification for his "land ethic" is based on humans' physical or biological dependence on healthy ecosystems.[44] One could also argue that humans are psychologically or spiritually dependent on them as well.[45]

## 6. Tools for Ecosystem Management

Regardless of the lack of consensus about the objectives of ecosystem management, there is arguably a consensus that "planning" is the foundational tool for achieving its objectives. However, this consensus belies a debate as to whether plans should include or be based on quantitative thresholds or *limits* to define boundaries for permissible human activities across the entire ecosystem of focus. There are numerous proponents of ecosystem-based limits.[46] Limits provide a "bottom line" or system of accountability, but they can be scientifically or technically difficult to determine, especially at an ecosystem scale. A limits-based approach also requires the development of potentially complex systems for fairly and efficiently deciding the appropriate mix of present and future activities that collectively stay within the limits of choice.

Several Canadian statutes provide for ecosystem-based planning, for example, for public forests or other public lands, based on considerations of desired ecosystem conditions. For example, subsection 11(1) of the *Canada National Parks Act* requires the adoption of park management plans that include a "long-term ecological vision" and "ecological integrity objectives and indicators."[47] Section 68 of Ontario's *Crown Forest Sustainability Act* requires the adoption of a "Forest Management Planning Manual" that must, in turn, require that every "forest management plan" adopt objectives based on considerations of the "abundance and distribution of forest ecosystems" and a recognition that "healthy forest ecosystems are vital" to Ontarians' "well-being."[48]

Several Canadian endangered species statutes provide that species recovery strategies or management plans may be based generally on "ecosystem management principles" or other broad criteria.[49] Similarly, the *Canada National Marine Conservation Areas Act* calls for the development of marine conservation area management plans based in part on "principles of ecosystem management."[50]

While Canadian statutes endorse ecosystem management or ecosystem-based planning, the author is unaware of any Canadian statutes that prescribe ecosystem-based limits, or that require the establishment of such limits, as a starting point or target for ecosystem management plans.

## 7. Adaptive Management

Because of the scientific and technical uncertainties inherent in a holistic, ecosystem perspective, there is general consensus among proponents of ecosystem approaches that they require adaptive management. This approach is essentially a circular process in which problems are identified and hypotheses about cause and effect are made, followed by the adoption and implementation of management tools. The effectiveness of these tools is then studied and assessed, leading to reconsiderations of problems and appropriate solutions and adjustments of previously chosen tools, as necessary.[51]

Adaptive management is inherently sensible, but it is also problematic. Besides requiring the commitment of often scarce funds and personnel, it logically calls for a flexible approach that may conflict with the oft-stated need for certainty in regulatory and planning regimes, certainty that is needed, in turn, for effective business and land use decision making. There is also a risk that adaptive management may be used to avoid making controversial or difficult decisions in the first instance.

## Conclusion

Ecosystem management is not just a passing fad. For all of its uncertainties and challenges, its holistic, ecosystem focus makes sense. And the alternative—narrowly focusing on protecting or maximizing the yield of individual natural resources—is inherently flawed. As one textbook suggests, ecosystem management must be approached with "caution and humility," but it is nevertheless "necessary and urgent."[52] Another author similarly observed that "striving for some aspect of an ecosystem approach, as difficult as it might be, is better than what we are doing now."[53]

The idea that ecosystem management is an approach to "striv[e] for" is particularly important. Like the principles of "equality" and "democracy," ecosystem management may be impossible to achieve in its purest or absolute form, but it is nevertheless worth pursuing. In Yaffee's words, "movement toward the ecosystem management end of the spectrum is good," even if each step does not achieve a perfectly holistic result.[54]

### NOTES

1 Oliver A Houck, "Are Humans Part of Ecosystems?" (1998) 28 Envtl L 1 at 2.

2 JB Ruhl, "An Environmental Rights Amendment: Good Message, Bad Idea" (1997) 11 Nat Res & Envt 46 at 47.

3 Fred Van Dyke, *Conservation Biology: Foundations, Concepts, Applications*, 2d ed (Dordrecht: Springer, 2008) at 351 [Van Dyke].

4 Michael M Wenig, *The Fisheries Act as a Legal Framework for Watershed Management* (LLM Thesis, University of Calgary Faculty of Law, June 1999) at 4–5 [Wenig].

5 For example, several Alberta statutes define the "environment" broadly as the "components of the earth" including in turn "air, land and water," the "layers of the atmosphere," "organic and inorganic matter and living organisms," and the "interacting natural systems that include" these other components. *Alberta Land*

*Stewardship Act*, SA 2009, c A-26.8, s 2(1)(j); *Environmental Protection and Enhancement Act* (*EPEA*), RSA 2000, c E-12, s 1(t). The Yukon's *Environment Act* defines the "environment" in similarly broad terms but also specifically includes in its list of "environment" components "the ecosystem and ecological relationships." RSY 2002, c 76, s 2.

6 For example, the purpose statements of both Nova Scotia's *Environment Act* and Alberta's *Environmental Protection and Enhancement Act* include a recognition that environmental protection is "essential to the integrity of ecosystems." SNS 1994–95, c 1, s 2; *EPEA*, s 2.

7 For example, at the federal level, the *Auditor General Act* provides that the federal Sustainable Development Commissioner's role includes monitoring and reporting on federal departments' progress in achieving "sustainable development," which concept itself includes "protecting ecosystems." RSC 1985, c A-17, s 21.1(c). Similarly, the *Canada National Marine Conservation Areas Act* states that "[m]arine conservation areas [should] be managed and used in a sustainable manner that meets the needs of present and future generations without compromising the structure and function of the ecosystems, including the submerged lands and water column, with which they are associated." SC 2002, c 18, s 4(3). See also, e.g., *Species at Risk Act* (*SARA*), SC 2002, c 29 (preamble "recognizing" that Canadian "ecosystems" are "part of the world's heritage"), and *Saguenay-St Lawrence Marine Park Act*, SC 1997, c 37, s 4 (Act's purposes include to "increase ... the level of protection of the ecosystems of a representative portion of the Saguenay River and the St. Lawrence estuary for conservation purposes"). Examples at the provincial or territorial level include Manitoba's *Provincial Parks Act*, whose purposes include "to conserve ecosystems." CCSM c P20, s 5. Manitoba's *Water Protection Act* states that its purpose is to "provide for the protection and stewardship of Manitoba's water resources and aquatic ecosystems." CCSM c W65, s 2. Similarly, the preamble to British Columbia's *Muskwa-Kechika Management Area Act* states that the purpose of the legislatively created Muskwa-Kechika Management Area is to "maintain in perpetuity the wilderness quality, and the diversity and abundance of wildlife and the ecosystems on which it depends." SBC 1998, c 38. In the Northwest Territories, the *Environmental Rights Act* states that the people of the Northwest Territories have the "right to protect the integrity, biological diversity and productivity of the ecosystems in the Northwest Territories." RSNWT 1988, c 83, Preamble.

8 For example, the *Canadian Environmental Protection Act* (*CEPA*) authorizes the federal cabinet to adopt regulations for "preventing or reducing the growth of aquatic vegetation that is caused by the release of nutrients in waters and that can interfere with the functioning of an ecosystem or degrade or alter, or form part of a process of degrading or altering, an ecosystem to an extent that is detrimental to its use by humans, animals or plants." SC 1999, c 33, s 118(1). Similarly, Manitoba's *Water Rights Act* states that, in reviewing applications for licences issued under that Act, the relevant minister must consider "scientific and other information relating to the groundwater and water body levels, and the in-stream flows, that are necessary to ensure that aquatic ecosystems are protected and maintained." The Act then enables the minister to deny a licence application if the proposed activity would "negatively affect an aquatic ecosystem." CCSM c W80, ss 9.1(1) and (2). British Columbia's *Local Government Act* states that a "community plan" may include "policies" relating to the "preservation, protection, restoration and enhancement of the natural environment, [and] its ecosystems." RSBC 1996, c 323, s 474(1).

9 For example, the federal *Oceans Act* provides for the "development and implementation of a national strategy for the management of [Canada's] estuarine, coastal and marine ecosystems." SC 1996, c 31, s 29. Similarly, Alberta's *Water Act* requires the Minister of Environment and Water to adopt "a strategy for the protection of the aquatic environment" that may include "matters relating to the protection of biological diversity," which the Act defines as the "variability among living organisms and the ecological complexes of which they are a part, and includes diversity within and between species and ecosystems." RSA 2000, c W-3, ss 8(1), (2) and (3)(c).

10 See *Oceans Act*, *ibid* (preamble stating that "[marine] conservation, based on an ecosystem approach, is of fundamental importance"); and *CEPA*, *supra* note 8 (preamble recognizing the "importance of an ecosystem approach" and stating that the Government of Canada will "continue to demonstrate national leadership in establishing ... ecosystem objectives ...") and s 2(1)(c) (stating that the Government of Canada's "duties" include "implement[ing] an ecosystem approach that considers the unique and fundamental characteristics of ecosystems").

11 Government of Canada, "Ecosystem Initiatives" (accessed 12 December 2017), online: <http://www.ec.gc.ca/nature/default.asp?lang=En&n=2C63408C-1>.

12 Department of Fisheries and Oceans, "Principles of Ecosystem-based Fisheries Management" (accessed 12 December 2017), online: <http://www.dfo-mpo.gc.ca/reports-rapports/regs/sff-cpd/ecosys-back-fiche-eng.htm>.

13 For example, Alberta's 2003 *Water for Life Strategy* stated that its "focus" is to adopt a "watershed approach to management." Accordingly, the landmark policy called for the development of "watershed plans" for setting water management objectives and priorities and for the support of watershed planning and advisory councils. Government of Alberta, *Water for Life – Alberta's Strategy for Sustainability* (November 2003, accessed 14 December 2017), online: <http://aep.alberta.ca/water/programs-and-services/water-for-life/strategy/documents/WaterForLife-Strategy-Nov2003.pdf> at 7–8 and 15.

14 These are Lethbridge College (online: <https://lethbridgecollege.ca/programs/ecosystem-management-bachelor-of-applied-science>), University of Northern British Columbia (online: <https://www.unbc.ca/ecosystem-science-management>), and York University (online: <https://futurestudents.yorku.ca/program/ecosystem-management>).

15 Steven L Yaffee, "Three Faces of Ecosystem Management" (1999) 13 Conservation Biology 713 [Yaffee]. See also, e.g., Van Dyke, *supra* note 3 (stating that, of "all modern efforts in conservation, none has proven more elusive in definition ... than 'ecosystem management.'").

16 See Wenig, *supra* note 4 at 3.

17 See, e.g. Yaffee, *supra* note 15 at 723 (noting that the ecosystem management "term itself is not sacrosanct, but the direction it implies is").

18 For a good discussion of the "ecological imperative" for ecosystem management, see Robert W Adler, "Addressing Barriers to Watershed Protection" (1995) 25 Envtl L 973 at 981–991 [Adler].

19 *Ibid* at 981–986.

20 *Ibid* at 982–983.

21 *Ibid* at 995–1000.

22 *Ibid* at 991–994.

23 *Ibid* at 1088–1104.

24 Peter F Brussard et al, "Ecosystem Management: What Is It Really?" (1998) 40 Landscape and Urban Planning 9.

25 Thus, Kennett rightly observed that ecosystems "are not self-defining as focal points for ... management.... [T]hey are human constructs designed to capture ecological processes and relationships that are deemed to be important." Steven

A Kennett, *New Directions for Public Land Law*, CIRL Occasional Paper #4 (Calgary: Canadian Institute of Resources Law, 1998) at 18 [Kennett].

26 Adler, *supra* note 18 at 976.

27 The Government of Canada has divided the country into a hierarchy of 20 distinct, non-overlapping "ecozones." The 15 terrestrial ecozones are broken down, in turn, into 53 "ecoprovinces" and in turn into 194 "ecoregions," based on their physical and social characteristics. See Natural Resources Canada, "Forest Classification" (accessed 12 December 2017), online: <http://www.nrcan.gc.ca/forests/measuring-reporting/classification/13179>.

28 For example, s 4(4) of the *Canada National Marine Conservation Areas Act*, *supra* note 7, requires that each marine conservation area subject to the Act be divided into "zones," at least one of which must "fully protect[t] special features or sensitive elements of ecosystems." But the Act does not specify the ecosystem unit of concern. Similarly, both British Columbia's *Ecological Reserves Act* and Alberta's *Wilderness Areas, Ecological Reserves, Natural Areas and Heritage Rangelands Act* provide for the provinces' adoption of "ecological reserves" that are representative examples of natural ecosystems in each of those provinces. RSBC 1996, c 103, s 2(b); RSA 2000, c W-9, s 4(1)(b).

29 E.g., Van Dyke, *supra* note 3 at 351.

30 See, e.g., Adler, *supra* note 18 at 1091–1092.

31 See Michael M Wenig, *Understanding Local Albertans' Roles in Watershed Planning – Will the Real Blueprint Please Step Forward?*, CIRL Occasional Paper #28 (Calgary: Canadian Institute of Resources Law, 2010).

32 E.g., Van Dyke, *supra* note 3 at 350; Averil Lamont, "Policy Characterization of Ecosystem Management" (2006) 11 Envtl Monitoring & Assessment 5 at 6. For an interesting and enlightening debate on the objectives and ethics of ecosystem management, see Bruce Pardy, "Changing Nature: The Myth of the Inevitability of Ecosystem Management" (2003) 20 Pace Envtl L Rev 675; JB Ruhl, "The Myth of What Is Inevitable under Ecosystem Management: A Response to Pardy" (2004) 21 Pace Envtl L Rev 315; Bruce Pardy, "Ecosystem Management in Question: A Reply to Ruhl" (2005–2006) 23 Pace Envtl L Rev 209; JB Ruhl, "The Pardy-Ruhl Dialogue on Ecosystem Management, Part IV: Narrowing and Sharpening the Questions" (2007) 24 Pace Envtl L Rev 25; and Bruce Pardy, "The Pardy-Ruhl Dialogue on Ecosystem Management Part V: Discretion, Complex-Adaptive Problem Solving and the Rule of Law" (2007) 25 Pace Envtl L Rev 341.

33 See, e.g., Brian Walker & David Salt, *Resilience Thinking: Sustaining Ecosystems and People in a Changing World* (Washington: Island Press, 2006). The authors define "resilience" as the "ability of a system to absorb disturbance and still retain its basic function and structure." *Ibid* at 1.

34 *Ibid* at 8.

35 See *Water Protection Act*, *supra* note 7 (preamble committing the Manitoba government to "watershed planning as an effective means to address risks to water resources and aquatic ecosystems," and stating the government's belief that "residents of watersheds should be consulted when watershed plans are developed"); *Water Act* (Alberta), *supra* note 9, ss 9 and 11 (discussed in Wenig, *supra* note 31 at 3–6).

36 *Canada National Parks Act*, SC 2000, c 32, ss 2(1) and 8(2); *Species at Risk (NWT) Act*, SNWT 2009, c 16, s 1(1); *Provincial Parks and Conservation Reserves Act, 2006*, SO 2006, c 12, ss 2(1), 3(1) and 5(2)–(3).

37 See, e.g., *Environmental Rights Act* (NWT), *supra* note 7 (preamble referencing ecosystem "integrity, biological diversity and productivity"); *Crown Lands Act*, RSNS 1989, c 114, ss 25(1) (forest ecosystem "productivity, diversity

and stability") and 25(2) ("integrity of water-supply watersheds"); *Environment Act*, SNS 1994–95, c 1, ss 2(a) ("integrity") and 104(d) and 105(3)(d) (aquatic ecosystem "health and integrity").

38 See *Canada National Marine Conservation Areas Act*, *supra* note 7, s 4(3) (ecosystem "structure and function"); *Sustainable Development Act*, CCSM c S270, Sched A, s 5(d) (ecosystem "long-term productive capability, quality and capacity"); *Crown Forest Sustainability Act*, 1994, SO 1994, c 25, s 68(5)(b)(i)–(ii) ("natural landscape patterns, forest structure and composition, habitat for animal life and the abundance and distribution of forest ecosystems … healthy forest ecosystems"); and *Forests Act*, RSNS 1989, c 179, s 10 (forest ecosystem "long term diversity and stability").

39 See *Sustainable Forest Development Act*, RSQ, c A-18.1, ss 2(2) and (4) (forest ecosystem "condition and productivity" and "contributions to major ecological cycles") and 4(2) (ecosystem "biodiversity and viability"); *Sustainable Development Act.*, RSQ, c D-8.1.1, s 6(m) (ecosystem "support capacity" and "perenniality"); *Environment Quality Act*, RSQ, c Q-2, s 31.9(b) (ecosystem "balance").

40 For the latter perspective, see, e.g., Yaffee, *supra* note 15 at 715 and 719; and Van Dyke, *supra* note 3 at 351.

41 See Wenig, *supra* note 4 at 18–25.

42 See, e.g., Kennett, *supra* note 25 at 19 (referring to Leopold's "land ethic" as providing the "normative basis of ecosystem management"); and Adler, *supra* note 18 at 1000–1003 (referring to ecosystem management as a means for "harnessing bioregionalism" in order to promote widespread public adoption of Leopold's ethic).

43 Aldo Leopold, *A Sand County Almanac* (New York: Ballantine Books, 1968) at 262.

44 Wenig, *supra* note 4 at 19 and n. 58.

45 This view is reflected in the observation of a BC judge in deliberating on the appropriate sentence in a prosecution for violation of the federal *Fisheries Act*, RSC 1985, c F-14. According to the judge, the "ecological system that was threatened in this case is of such immense value that it is impossible to put a value and figure on it. It must be, above all, protected in this community, because it is, in fact, the basis and the *soul of the community* in so many aspects, and to pollute it would be a loss without and beyond measure." *R v Island Industrial Chrome, Ltd* (1989) 5 FPR 163 at 185 (BC Prov Ct) (emphasis added).

46 See, e.g., Heather Tallis et al, "The Many Faces of Ecosystem-Based Management: Making the Process Work Today in Real Places" (2010) 34 Marine Policy at 340 at 347–48; Pardy (2007), *supra* note 32 at 10; Michael M Wenig, Arlene Kwasniak & Dr Michael S Quinn, "Water Under the Bridge? The Role of IFN Determinations in Alberta's River Management" in H Epp, ed, *Water: Science & Politics*, Proceedings of the Alberta Society of Professional Biologists, Annual Conference and Workshop, 25–28 March 2006, Calgary, Alberta; Michael M Wenig & Dr Michael S Quinn, "Integrating the Alberta Oil and Gas Tenure Regime with Landscape Objectives: One Step Toward Managing Cumulative Effects" in H Epp, ed, *Access Management: Policy to Practice*, Proceedings of the Conference presented by the Alberta Society of Professional Biologists in Calgary, 18–19 March 2003 (Edmonton: ASPB, 2004); and Kennett, *supra* note 25 at 22.

47 *Supra* note 36.

48 *Supra* note 38 at ss 61(1)(1), (5)(i)–(ii).

49 See SARA, *supra* note 7, ss 41(3) and 67; *Species at Risk (NWT) Act*, *supra* note 36, s 61(8), *Endangered Species Act, 2007*, SO 2007, c 6, s 13; and *Endangered Species Act*, SNS 1998, c 11, s 15(5).

50 *Supra* note 7, s 9(1) and (3).

51 See, e.g., Van Dyke, *supra* note 3 at 351, 354–355; Lamont, *supra* note 32 at 7.

52 Van Dyke, *supra* note 3 at 378.

53 Yaffee, *supra* note 15 at 715.

54 *Ibid* at 721.

# 4

# Public Nuisance: Public Wrongs and Civil Rights of Action

ALASTAIR R. LUCAS, Q.C.

## Introduction

Historically, the common law developed doctrine to protect the health and safety of the general public. The Supreme Court of Canada (SCC) has summed up the concept of public nuisance as "any activity which unreasonably interferes with the public's interest in questions of health, safety, morality, comfort or inconvenience."[1] But this doctrine has not meshed smoothly as the modern law has evolved.

There are two principal problems. One is that though the concept of public nuisance was originally part of the domain of criminal law, a related civil right of action emerged. The concepts thus straddled somewhat uncomfortably criminal law and civil law. The second problem involves the question of who has this right. Who has standing to seek judicial remedies for public nuisance?

## The Crime

As common nuisance, it was an offence to endanger the lives, safety, or health of the public. It now appears in this form as subsections 180(1) and (2) of the *Criminal Code*, which states:[2]

> 180.(1) Every one who commits a common nuisance and thereby
>
> (a) endangers the lives, safety or health of the public, or
> (b) causes physical injury to any person,
>
> is guilty of an indictable offence and liable to imprisonment for a term not exceeding two years.

*Definition*

(2) For the purposes of this section, every one commits a common nuisance who does an unlawful act or fails to discharge a legal duty and thereby

(a) endangers the lives, safety, health, property or comfort of the public; or
(b) obstructs the public in the exercise or enjoyment of any right that is common to all the subjects of Her Majesty in Canada.

What is the "public" appears to be a question of fact in particular circumstances. But it cannot be a single person or even a small group[3] of individuals. However, in principle, these individuals might still have a remedy in private nuisance.[4]

## The Common Law Tort

The common law has also recognized a civil right of action to remedy a public nuisance.[5] Initially in the 18th and 19th centuries, this appeared to function as a supplement to the criminal law in order to fully address common issues of the day such as disputes about access and passage on public highways. Thus, any rights flowed from establishment of an unlawful act. However, public nuisance has developed into an independent common law tort.[6] This has been recognized by the Supreme Court of Canada in *Ryan v. Victoria*[7] and acknowledged in *British Columbia v. Canadian Forest Products Ltd.*[8]

Public nuisance involves interference with the use and enjoyment of a group of properties. It differs from private nuisance in its scope. Harm must be sufficiently widespread.[9] There is no bright line test, but the scale of damage in relation to that suffered by others is an important factor.[10]

## Standing for Civil Actions

This brings us to the second fundamental problem associated with public nuisance. In general, actions cannot be initiated by individuals to remedy public nuisances.[11]

## The Attorney General as Plaintiff

The general principle is that actions in public nuisance can be brought only by the Attorney General acting as an officer of the Crown.[12] This means either the federal or the provincial Attorney General (A-G), depending on the circumstances in the context of constitutional jurisdiction or perhaps intergovernmental arrangements. The theory is that the A-G acts as *parens patriae* to vindicate public rights vested in the Crown.[13] Sometimes the A-G has sued at the request of individuals. In other cases, the A-G has acted in a relator capacity, agreeing to a nominal plaintiff role at the request of a private party or parties.[14] In both cases, the decision whether or not to sue is entirely within the A-G's discretion.[15] There is little scope for judicial review. However, there is authority to the effect that the A-G must consider the issue in good faith and if he or she refuses leave, "in a proper case, or improperly or unreasonably delays in giving leave, or if the machinery works too slowly, then an action for injunctive relief by a member of the public may be entertained."[16]

## Private Plaintiffs

A private plaintiff may sue in public nuisance directly, without the A-G's consent, where that individual can establish that he or she suffered "special" or "peculiar" damage.[17] A key difference from private nuisance is that no interest in land must be shown.[18] What constitutes special damage for this purpose has been problematic for over a century and a half.

## Special Damage

The general principle is that special damage is extraordinary—in some way greater than that suffered by the general public. In 1874, Justice Brett in the English Court of Common Pleas expressed this idea in *Benjamin v. Storr* as follows:

> [T]he plaintiff must show] a particular injury to himself beyond that which is suffered by the rest of the public. It is not enough for him to shew that he suffers the same inconvenience in the use of the highway as other people do (if the alleged nuisance be the obstruction of a highway).[19]

This injury, said his Lordship, must be particular and it must also be:

1. direct and not merely consequential,
2. of a substantial character, 'not fleeting and evanescent.'[20]

This definition of special damage has proven resilient in Canada.

It is worth noting that establishing special damage in cases of personal or property damage is relatively straightforward. In fact, in these circumstances the elements necessary for a claim in private nuisance are likely to be present. It is where the loss asserted is to public lands or natural resources and the claim is concerned either with protecting the public or the fundamental ecological values of a natural resource, or with consequential economic loss, that establishing special damage is problematic. Thus in *McKie v. KVP Co.*[21] the owner of a common law right to fish, but not financially harmed resort owners, was held to have suffered special damage as a result of water pollution that killed fish.

For Canadian environmental law, the classic case is a 1970 decision of the Newfoundland Supreme Court Trial Division, *Hickey v. Electric Reduction Company of Canada Ltd.*[22] Hickey and the other plaintiffs fished commercially in Placentia Bay, Newfoundland. Fish life in the bay was largely destroyed as a result of discharges from an electric reduction company's phosphorus plant in Long Harbour. The plaintiffs alleged that this created a public nuisance that resulted in damage to their fishing livelihoods.

The court accepted that serious harm to the fishery had been caused. But Furlong C.J. concluded that the action should fail because, "while the pollution created a nuisance to all persons," it was not, he said, "a nuisance peculiar to the plaintiffs, nor confined to their use of the waters of Placentia Bay. It was a nuisance committed against the public."[23]

His Lordship rejected the argument that the plaintiffs should succeed because they had suffered "special" or "direct" damage. The "right view," he said, is that "a person who suffers peculiar damage has a right of action, but where damage is common to all persons of the same class, then a personal right of action is not maintainable."[24] The result was that all of the fishers had a right to fish in the area, but no remedy if the fish were destroyed as a result of activity acknowledged to create a public nuisance. Only proof of unique adverse effects would suffice, a requirement characterized by Klar as "illogical."[25] The Attorney General could initiate an action. However, unspoken was the reality that many factors may militate against the A-G choosing to pursue this remedy.

A further complication may be a negligence requirement. This may become an issue where the public harm is caused by inadvertent discharge of pollutants rather than operational discharge that can be characterized as intentional.[26]

There is ample authority for *Hickey's* requirement that standing founded upon public nuisance must be different in kind and not merely in degree from that of the remainder of the class. But even in 1970, there were inconsistent cases.[27] In particular, financial loss resulting from obstruction of access was considered to be special damage in several cases.[28]

In *Canfor*, Binnie J. commented on the efficacy of public nuisance in remedying environmental damage. He stated that "class actions will have a role to play," but he quoted Klar's assessment that "[w]hat has made public nuisance a particularly ineffective private law remedy is the special damages requirement."[29] "The reality," according to Binnie J.,

> is that it would be impractical in most of these environmental cases for individual members of the public to show sufficient 'special damages' to mount a tort action having enough financial clout to serve the twin policy objectives of deterrence to wrongdoers and adequate compensation for their victims: *Bazley v. Curry*, [1999] 2 SCR 534.[30]

## Statutory Modification

The special damage requirement has been removed in varying degrees by statute in several Canadian jurisdictions. The most significant is provisions of the *Ontario Bill of Rights*,[31] which gives individuals standing to commence action in certain circumstances. These are: (1) a person has or will contravene an environmental law as defined; (2) the contravention causes or will cause significant harm to an Ontario public resource; and (3) the plaintiff has applied under the Act for an investigation into the matter and has received either no response or an unreasonable response. Remedy is limited to injunction, and courts may consider the potential efficacy of other processes and even government plans. It is apparent that this is a narrow right, but one that may alert and even mobilize relevant government agencies. Environmental rights of action of this general type are also found in Yukon[32] and the Northwest Territories.[33]

## Availability of Damages

Traditionally, public nuisance actions have involved the A-G seeking to enjoin activities that infringe public rights. The injunction was regarded as an appropriate public remedy. This has led to the assumption that injunction, but not damages, is the only available remedy.[34] However, to this narrow view there have been exceptions.[35] Binnie J. in *Canfor* made his "impracticability for individuals" comments quoted above. But he went on to acknowledge that Canadian courts "have not universally adhered to a narrow view of the Crown's available remedies in civil proceedings for nuisance." In addition to cases,[36] he cited reports by the British Columbia and Ontario law reform commissions.[37] His conclusion was that the Crown represented by the A-G could indeed "pursue compensation for environmental damage in a proper case."[38]

Binnie J. then moved to create a broader context for this principle. He noted Canadian judicial reference to the idea of municipalities as trustees of the environment, citing L'Heureux-Dubé J. in *Spraytech v. Town of Hudson*,[39] and at least alluded to the older, deeper common law fiduciary idea of public trust, including US law where monetary compensation has been awarded.[40] These latter US cases were actions in which the government in a *parens patriae* capacity sought damages for harm to the trust in public natural resources.

The conclusion in *Canfor* was that "there is no legal barrier to the Crown suing for compensation as well as injunctive relief in a proper case on account of public nuisance or negligence causing environmental damage to public lands."[41]

But his Lordship then noted that it was also open to the Crown to base the claim on its private law property rights in the forest lands in question. Further, the claim based on a broader public right was not fully argued in the lower courts. Consequently, the SCC majority considered the Crown's claim only as landowner.

## Novel and Important Policy Questions

In *Canfor*, Binnie J. somewhat qualified his conclusion that the Crown could sue for damages in public nuisance and on other tort theories by stating that "there are clearly important and novel policy questions raised by such actions." These include:

1. potential Crown liability for inactivity in relation to environmental threats,
2. whether or not there are enforceable fiduciary duties on the Crown,
3. limits to the Crown's role, function and available remedies, and
4. the potential burden on private interests of this kind of 'indeterminate liability.'[42]

However, the court concluded that it was not a "proper appeal to embark on a consideration of these difficult issues."[43] Indeed, several of the questions are heavy with policy considerations difficult for courts to handle.

But it is question 2 that has caught the attention of environmental lawyers. It raised issues that have been debated since the beginnings of Canadian environmental law: Is the Crown subject to some kind of fiduciary duty to protect and perhaps to preserve public natural resources for the benefit and enjoyment of the public? If so, can this public duty be judicially enforced through actions by citizens? Are relevant US authorities persuasive? This is the essence of a set of legal principles known as the public trust doctrine.

## Public Trust

The public trust doctrine has received much discussion and analysis but little judicial acceptance in Canadian environmental law. It is based on common law public rights of access, including fishing and navigation, with origins in Roman Law.[44] The modern concept, which involves fiduciary obligations on government to preserve public resources for public use, emerged in the United States in the late 19th century.[45] It was popularized in the early 1970s by several judicial decisions[46] and through scholarly writings, particularly the articles of Professor Joseph Sax.[47] Sax described the modern public trust doctrine as follows:

> When a state holds a resource which is available for the free use of the general public, a court will look with considerable scepticism upon any government conduct which is calculated either to reallocate that resource to more restricted uses or to subject public uses to the self interest of private parties.[48]

The concept is thus essentially a presumption. It can be qualified and even overridden by statute. However, it has been adopted explicitly in a number of US federal and state statutes. Since the 1970s, public trust has found its greatest expression in US water resources law.

Public trust has been considered in few Canadian cases. An early attempt to incorporate US doctrine foundered in *Green v. The Queen in Right of Ontario*[49] on difficult facts (the alleged harm occurred adjacent to but outside the Ontario Provincial Park alleged to be subject to a public trust) and apparent confusion between the fiduciary principles of public trust and the criteria for common law private trusts. Subsequently, while there was considerable academic writing,[50] with some scholars arguing the existence of a public trust doctrine in Canadian law,[51] some direct or apparent statutory incorporation, and allowance in Quebec of an analogous class action claim against government for failing to effectively enforce environmental laws,[52] there was no explicit judicial adoption.

Then in 2006, the thread was picked up by the Supreme Court of Canada majority in *Canfor*. The door has opened on potential government and, subject to what may be left of the special damage requirement, even private actions for injunctions and damages for harm to public natural resources. But explicit judicial recognition must await fuller consideration, including assessment of the policy issues outlined by Binnie J. in *Canfor*. An intriguing possibility is connection with the fiduciary concepts in Aboriginal law. There is some indication of this in the US jurisprudence.[53]

## Conclusion

While public nuisance has clearly emerged from its criminal law beginnings to offer a tort with potential for remedying environmental harm, it remains an imperfect instrument, inconsistent and even irrational in its operation. Availability of damages in public nuisance actions received Supreme Court of Canada support in *Canfor*. But the core problem—extreme uncertainty of the special damage requirement—remains.

Binnie J.'s comments in *Canfor* may be a prelude to judicial rethinking of the special damage requirement. But perhaps more promising is the public nuisance concept serving as a springboard for development of other public remedies, particularly public trust and related theories of Crown fiduciary duties to protect and preserve the environment.

### NOTES

1 *Ryan v Victoria (City)*, [1999] 1 SCR 201 at para 32, cited with approval in *British Columbia v Canadian Forest Products Ltd*, 2004 SCC 38, [2004] 2 SCR 74 at para 66 [*Canfor*].

2 *Criminal Code*, RSC 1985, c C-46, s 180(1)(2).

3 Such as the Placentia Bay, Newfoundland, fishers in *Hickey v Electric Reduction Co of Canada* (1970), 21 DLR (3d) 368 (Nfld SC) [*Hickey*]. In *Rex v Lloyd* (1803), 4 Espinasse 200 (*Nisi Prius*), the inhabitants of three chambers of Clifford's Inn, London, were held not a sufficient public to maintain a public nuisance indictment against owners of adjacent tin works.

4 As the court noted in *Rex v Lloyd*, *ibid*.

5 A-G *Can v Ewen* (1895), 3 BCR 468 (SC) [*Ewen*]; *Benjamin v Storr* (1874), LR 9 CP 400 [*Benjamin*]. See John McLaren, "The Common Law Nuisance Actions and the Environmental Battle—Well-Tempered Swords or Broken Reeds?" (1972) 10:3 Osgoode Hall LJ 505 at 511–515.

6 See *Benjamin*, *ibid*.

7 [1999] 1 SCR 201 at para 52.

8 2004 SCC 38 at para 66.

9 *A-G v PYA Quarries Ltd*, [1957] 2 QB 169.

10 Keith Stanton & Christine Willmore, "Tort and Environmental Pluralism" in John Lowry & Rod Edmunds, eds, *Environmental Protection and the Common Law* (Oxford: Hart, 2000) ch 5 at 100.

11 *Stein v Gonzales* (1984), 14 DLR (4th) 263 (BCSC, McLachlin J).

12 *Ibid*; *Ewen*, *supra* note 5; *Canfor*, *supra* note 1 at para 67.

13 *Canfor*, *ibid*, citing Wilfred Estey, "Public Nuisance and Standing to Sue" (1972) 10 Osgoode Hall LJ 563 at 566, 576.

14 *British Columbia (AG) v Haney Speedways Ltd* (1963), 39 DLR (2d) 48 (BCSC).

15 *Ewen*, *supra* note 5.

16 A-G *ex rel McWhirter v Independent Broadcasting Authority*, [1972] 2 WLR 344 (Eng CA).
17 See *Hickey, supra* note 3 at 372.
18 *Hunter v Canary Wharf Ltd*, [1997] AC 655 (HL).
19 *Supra* note 5 at 438.
20 *Ibid* at 439.
21 *McKie v KVP Co*, [1948] 3 DLR 201 (Ont HC), aff'd [1949] 1 DLR 39 (Ont CA), aff'd [1949] SCR 698.
22 *Hickey, supra* note 3.
23 *Ibid* at 370.
24 *Ibid* at 372.
25 Lewis Klar, *Tort Law*, 4th ed (Toronto: Carswell, 2008) at 717.
26 *Ibid* at 720–721.
27 See, Robert Mansell, "Civil Liability for Environmental Damage" in Alastair Lucas, ed, *Canadian Environmental Law*, 2d ed (Toronto: LexisNexis, 2017) ch 18, para 18.15.
28 *Ibid*, para 18.16 n 2.
29 *Canfor, supra* note 1 at para 68; Klar, *supra* note 25 at 647.
30 *Ibid.*
31 *Ontario Environmental Bill of Rights*, SO 1993, c 28, Part VI.
32 *Environment Act*, SY 1991, c 5.
33 *Environmental Rights Act*, SNWT 1990, c 38.
34 *Canfor, supra* note 1 at para 68.
35 Including *The Queen v The Ship Sun Diamond*, [1984] 1 FC 3 (TD) (damages awarded to the federal Crown for oil spill cleanup costs); A-G *Ontario v Fatehi*, [1984] 2 SCR 536. (province entitled to damages for public highway cleanup cost). Both cases were cited by Binnie J in *Canfor, supra* note 1 at paras 69–70.
36 *Canfor, supra* note 1 at paras 69–70.
37 British Columbia Law Reform Commission, "Report on Civil Litigation in the Public Interest" (1980) No 46 at 70–71; Ontario Law Reform Commission, "Report on Damages for Environmental Harm" (1990) at 11–13.
38 *Canfor, supra* note 1 at para 72.
39 *114947 Canada Ltée (Spraytech Société d'arrosage) v Hudson (Town)*, 2001 SCC 40 at para 27.
40 *Canfor, supra* note 1 at paras 79–80.
41 *Ibid* at para 81.
42 *Ibid* at para 87.
43 *Ibid* at para 82.
44 *Ibid* at paras 74–75 and authorities cited.
45 *Ibid* at paras 78–79 and authorities cited, including *Georgia v Tennessee Copper Co*, 206 US 230 (1907), in which Holmes J at 237 spoke of the state having "an *interest independent* of and behind the titles of its citizens in all the earth and air within its domain" (emphasis added), and the leading case, *Illinois Central Railroad Co v Illinois*, 146 US 387 (1892).
46 Including *Gould v Greylock*, 215 NE 2d 114 (1966) (Mass SC) (Massachusetts statute purporting to approve development of a private ski resort in a state park held unlawful).
47 Joseph Sax, "The Public Trust Doctrine in Natural Resources Law: Effective Judicial Intervention" (1970) 68 Mich L Rev 471; Joseph Sax, *Defending the Environment: A Strategy for Citizen Action* (New York: Knopf, 1971).
48 Sax, "The Public Trust Doctrine," *ibid* at 484–485.
49 [1973] 2 OR 396 (HC).
50 See Constance Hunt, "The Public Trust Doctrine in Canada" in John Swaigen, ed, *Environmental Rights in Canada* (Toronto: Butterworths, 1981).
51 Robert Franson, "Legislation to Establish Ecological Reserves for the Protection of Natural Areas" (1972) 10 Osgoode Hall LJ 582, 589.
52 *Girard v 2944-7828 Quebec Inc*, [2003] JQ No 9105.
53 *Sierra Club v Department of Interior*, 376 F Supp 90 (1974) (US Dist Ct).

# 5

# The Incorporation of an Environmental Ethic in the Courtroom

HEATHER McLEOD-KILMURRAY

## Introduction: Ethics in Law

In "a discipline deeply influenced by positivism, any inquiry into the moral underpinnings of a field of law tends to be regarded with no small degree of suspicion."[1] Yet ethics are present in law:

> [L]aw and ethics support each other. Ethical standards are a means of criticizing the law, revealing its unstated value judgments. Uncertainties and conflicts in the law can often be traced to the absence of common ethical ground. A convincing ethical justification helps to make a law or a court's decision respected. Legal regulation, particularly if it allows negotiation between regulator and regulated, may help to shape ethical attitudes. Ethical arguments can be used as ammunition in litigation.[2]

How can judges make use of, and interpret, concepts of environmental ethics in environmental law and policies? Environmental ethics can help courts be aware of the underlying ethics in legislation or common law rules, and in the arguments of the parties.[3] They can help judges to be more explicit about ethics that may influence their analyses and conclusions. This is important because environmental judgments are essential to the evolution of cultural perceptions and priorities in environmental protection.[4] This chapter will briefly outline the field and main strands of environmental ethics, point to several environmental ethics in environmental legislation, and conclude by analyzing some cases in which judges have made use of and interpreted concepts of environmental ethics.

## Environmental Ethics

The field of environmental ethics (EE) is defined as "a relatively new field of philosophical ethics concerned with describing the values carried by the non-human world and prescribing an appropriate ethical response to ensure preservation or restoration of those values."[5] This suggests EE can help in the judicial tasks of both describing the values in a given case and prescribing possible solutions. The field of EE addresses several important concepts and has different branches.[6]

### CRITERIA FOR BEING VALUABLE

This philosophical question arises in environmental and animal rights law, but also in the evolution of human rights. Who is deserving of, and capable of enjoying, rights, and why? Potential criteria for being valuable include sentience, ability to feel pain, or mere existence. Just as the class of those deemed capable of holding rights has expanded in law, from propertied white males to all men, women, and other groups, some environmental ethicists argue that this evolution will progress to include higher primates, all animals, and eventually trees,[7] rocks, and ecosystems.

### ANTHROPOCENTRISM VS. ECOCENTRISM

Anthropocentrism regards nature as a tool for human consumption and need fulfillment; ecocentrism views humans as one element of nature. Strong anthropocentrism takes a utilitarian view, while weak anthropocentrism[8] sees a fuller range of human benefits, such as spiritual, cultural, and other, less economic goods. Some argue that weak anthropocentrism is sufficient to produce legal rules that protect nature, particularly where "humans" is understood to include future generations. Others say that only a shift to ecocentric thinking can lead to environmentally sustainable laws and policies.

### INDIVIDUALISM VS HOLISM

This dichotomy asks: is it the individual or the whole that is the priority? Is it the interrelationships that are essential? For example, human rights are often regarded as individual, yet their protection also benefits the community. An environmental example is the debates around culling individuals for the protection of the herd or of other species coexisting within the particular ecosystem. Where certain collective environmental interests are preferred over individual ones, critics have made accusations of "ecofascism."[9]

## ALTERNATIVE/RADICAL APPROACHES

Deep ecologists[10] argue that a complete overhaul of human–ecological relations is necessary to achieve environmental protection. Our economic, political, legal, and social structures are the causes of the ecological crisis, and each needs to be completely altered in order to truly address the problem; tinkering with existing laws will not suffice. Both ecofeminism[11] and social justice strands of EE will be more familiar to jurists. Ecofeminism mirrors the main strands of feminism, arguing that the same social and economic concepts and structures that undervalue and disempower women have undervalued and disempowered the environment. The struggles against dichotomies, exploitation, and hierarchies that will renew respect for and empower women will also generate a greater understanding of the value and rights of the environment. Similarly, social ecology emphasizes that it is not humans *per se* but our current structures of domination, hierarchies, and discrimination that hurt some humans but also the environment we live in. A more egalitarian, democratic society would be more respectful of nature.

Environmental justice,[12] a related yet distinct movement, began in the 1970s in the United States. It investigates the issues of ecoracism, such as why environmentally harmful facilities are more often located in lower-income or racialized neighbourhoods, and why some disadvantaged groups bear disproportionate environmental burdens without enjoying the related benefits.

## ECOLOGICAL JUSTICE

Bossleman[13] argues that just as justice is a core principle of law, ecological justice should be a core element of environmental law. Ecological justice consists of three elements: (i) intergenerational justice; (ii) intragenerational justice; and (iii) interspecies justice. Intergenerational justice refers to the rights of future generations. Intragenerational justice argues that within the current generation, the environmental harms and goods should be distributed equitably (e.g. a crucial aspect of climate justice). Interspecies justice suggests that anthropocentrism is a kind of speciesism, and another form of discrimination. This is sometimes raised by advocates of a plant-based diet, not only for the non-human animals who are the first victims of meat-eating, but also for present and future generations of human animals who suffer the pollution and climate change harms resulting from these practices. We turn now to investigate the environmental ethics in Canadian environmental statutes.

## Ethics in Canadian Legislation

Mickelson and Rees argue that "environmental law in Canada reflects the current dominant scientific and ethical perspective of industrial cultures everywhere, but there is nothing 'natural' … about that perspective." Freyfogle observes that environmental law has viewed pollution as an isolated problem, and focused on human utility, on effects rather than causes and on isolated spheres such as air, water, or land. Environmental ethics concepts such as no net loss, long-term thinking, precaution, and prevention are relevant to the evolution of legislative and judicial lawmaking. EE can justify treating the environment not as a separate consideration or special "interest" but as an element in all policy and decision making.[14] Environmental legislation requires interpretation, and some statutes contain preambles or purposes with principles and ethics intended to guide their application. Since ethics are part of environmental legislation, they should also be part of environmental adjudication.

In Ontario, the purpose of the *Environmental Assessment Act*[15] is "the betterment of the people of … Ontario by providing for the protection, conservation and wise management … of the environment." This reflects an anthropocentric, instrumentalist perspective. By contrast, the *Environmental Bill of Rights, 1993*[16] provides that "[t]he people of Ontario recognize the inherent value of the natural environment [… and] have a right to a healthful environment," and that they "have as a common goal the protection … of the natural environment for the benefit of present and future generations." This refers to the inherent value of nature, the deontological creation of a right to a healthful environment, and the duties of intergenerational equity. It refers to community benefits and values, not just individual concerns. There is no mention of competing interests such as development. The *Environmental Protection Act*[17] contains no preamble, but its declared purpose "is to provide for the protection and conservation of the natural environment."[18]

In Quebec, section 6 of the *Sustainable Development Act*[19] lists 16 principles of sustainable development. The first is "health and quality of life," a highly anthropocentric principle, while the second is "social equity and solidarity," which means that "development must be undertaken in a spirit of intra- and inter-generational equity and social ethics and solidarity," emphasizing two of the three branches of ecological justice. Even its most ecocentric principles are closely tied to human interests: principle 12 addresses biodiversity preservation because "[b]iological diversity offers incalculable advantages and must be preserved for the benefit of present and future generations." However, it emphasizes "respect for ecosystem support capacity" to "ensure the perenniality of ecosystems," which is more ecocentric.

Federally, the preamble to the *Canadian Environmental Protection Act, 1999* (*CEPA*)[20] includes virtually all leading environmental law principles: sustainable development, pollution prevention, ecosystem approach, the precautionary principle, the polluter pays principle, biological diversity, and "short- and long-term human and ecological benefits." The Act recognizes the intrinsic value of biodiversity and creates enforceable legal duties of precaution, considering the environment for its own sake, and an ecocentric approach.[21] The preamble to the federal *Species at Risk Act*[22] is perhaps the most clearly ecocentric, explicitly providing that "wildlife, in all its forms, has value in and of itself," and that "the Government of Canada is committed to conserving biological diversity." Both individuals (s. 32) and species (s. 6) are protected.

The idea that environmental ethics play a role in environmental law-making has also been embraced by the Canadian judiciary, as the following cases will illustrate.

## Ethics in Canadian Environmental Case Law

### ENVIRONMENTAL JURISDICTION: *HYDRO QUEBEC*[23]

Hydro Quebec, charged with dumping PCBs, argued that *CEPA*[24] was *ultra vires* in regulating toxic substances. The majority held this was a valid exercise of the federal criminal law power, while the dissent disagreed because pollution was merely regulated, not prohibited. First, the division of powers in Canada itself presents a challenge to the holistic or ecosystem perspective, revealing an anthropocentric perspective by putting politics above environmental realities. Secondly, different ethics may explain the divided reasons. La Forest J., for the majority, emphasized that environmental protection is "a public purpose of superordinate importance."[25] This led him to reason that courts "must be mindful that the Constitution must be interpreted in a manner that is fully responsive to emerging realities and to the nature of the subject matter sought to be regulated. Given the pervasive and diffuse nature of the environment, this reality poses particular difficulties in this context."[26] He further held that "stewardship of the environment is a fundamental value of our society and ... Parliament may use its criminal law power to underline that value. The criminal law must be able to keep pace with and protect our emerging values."[27] Notably, the legislation is used both to achieve practical environmental protection and in its educational, norm-creating role of "underlining" values.

Finally, a weak anthropocentric perspective is endorsed in the phrase "[h]umanity's interest in the environment surely extends beyond its own life and health."[28] The provisions of *CEPA* dealing with toxic substances[29] themselves separate environmental protection from concerns for human life and health, indicating an ecocentric approach: "Parliament's clear intention was to allow for federal intervention where the environment itself was at risk, whether or not the substances concerned posed a threat to human health and whether or not the aspect of the environment affected was one on which human life depended."[30] Yet this ecocentrism was the problem because it took the legislation away from the health branch of the criminal law power. This is an example of how EE may conflict with deeply embedded anthropocentrism in dominant legal frameworks.

### INTERPRETING ADMINISTRATIVE RULES: *IMPERIAL OIL*

Justice LeBel applied environmental ethics in *Imperial Oil*.[31] "Although the appeal heard by the Court raises an environmental law issue in the context of an application for judicial review, the question relates to an environmental protection problem in Quebec."[32] The decision starts from a very broad view of environmental concerns and the goals of the Quebec regulation, mentioning "the collective desire to protect [the environment] in the interest of the people" and of "an emerging sense of inter-generational solidarity and acknowledgement of an environmental debt to humanity and to the world of tomorrow."[33] The court applied the polluter pays principle in finding that conflict of interest rules applied differently in the context of enforcing environmental statutory discretion, and were powerful enough to legitimize retroactive liability. Judges can therefore bring environmental ethics and principles to bear in the interpretation of broader rules such as administrative conflicts of interest.

### ENVIRONMENTAL SENTENCING: *VAN WATERS*

Another example of applied EE is in the environmental sentencing in *Van Waters*.[34] The judge quoted at length from the Law Reform Commission paper *Sentencing in Environmental Cases*:[35]

> [I]n environmental cases ... the effect of the principle that the protection of society is paramount is to underline the serious nature of the

> offence.... It supports the use of strong deterrents and punishments even in the absence of serious harm to individuals or the environment. Perhaps its importance lies in supporting an environmental ethic which holds that the "various elements of the community of earth [have] an intrinsic value rather than an instrumental or utilitarian one," and consequently, "decisions have become more significant because of the vastly increased capacity of human beings to influence the nature of their environment, seen most graphically in pollution of the air, water, sea, and land."[36]

The court cites the report specifically referring to judicial ecological consciousness:

> Environmental cases put the courts in the difficult position of having to impose a sentence in the context of uncertainty about the degree of risk inherent in the offence or the amount of damage caused.... In the face of this uncertainty, some courts are willing to impose substantial sentences, while others hold out for proof of substantial risk or harm. The difference ... lies in the ecological consciousness of the judge. Ecological consciousness is an ability to see past the obvious and immediate conflicting interests.... It requires an understanding that everything in the environment is interdependent, and that harm to one aspect of the environment, no matter how insignificant it might seem or how unrelated to human concerns it might appear, has the potential to accumulate and ultimately to diminish the diversity and strength of the ecosystem. Some judges have this consciousness; some do not.[37]

The fact that the court would go to such lengths to include lengthy excerpts such as these shows that it felt that these environmental ethics should guide environmental sentencing.

## COMMON LAW PRINCIPLES

Environmental ethics can also be relevant in applying common law rules. In recent class actions such as *Hollick*,[38] *Hoffman*[39] and *Pearson*,[40] the courts have appeared reluctant to broaden common law causes of action such as nuisance, trespass, and strict liability to tackle the new types of harm in environmental cases. In some cases, there is a preference for competing ethics. In *Hoffman*, where organic canola farmers sought class certification to sue genetically-modified (GM) canola manufacturers for harm, the court held that merely marketing GM canola is not direct enough to constitute a trespass,[41] and nuisance may be difficult to make out because it is possible that the prevalence of GM canola farming has made organic canola farming an "overly sensitive" use of land and the seeds did not come directly from the manufacturers but through the intermediary farmer. The court also held that the case was not appropriate for class certification because each defendant experienced different levels of harm, so individual issues would outweigh common issues. The court seemed to be more influenced by the traditional ethics of common law rules such as individual harm, economic damages, and the bipolar structure of litigation than the collective, ecosystem-based harm that was arguably the true nature of the problem.[42]

By contrast, in *Ciment St. Laurent*,[43] the court interpreted the civilian concept of "troubles de voisinage,"[44] similar to common law private nuisance, in an environmentally protective way. It held that environmental nuisance is a strict liability offence, ensuring that the polluter pays, and held that private law prevails even against regulatory authorization of the undertaking.[45] These contrasting cases show that different environmental perspectives and ethics can affect how common law principles are interpreted and applied. The Supreme Court of Canada itself has said that "there is no reason to neglect the potential of the common law, if developed in a principled and incremental fashion, to assist in the realization of the fundamental value of environmental protection."[46]

## REMEDIES

In *Canadian Forest Products (Canfor)*,[47] the Supreme Court of Canada was asked to assess damages resulting from a forest fire. The court was willing to consider arguments about the "inherent value" of the forest as well as its public interest value, not just its utilitarian timber value. The court held that if it was given "the tools to quantify the 'ecological or environmental' loss,"[48] which could include such things as "use value, passive use or existence value, and inherent value,"[49] it was willing to consider these, yet the parties failed to provide such tools in this case.

## PROCEDURAL RULES

In a procedural context, the court in *Platinex*[50] was asked to halt exploratory mining on claimed Aboriginal land. One part of the test for an injunction is whether the refusal to grant it would cause irreparable harm to the applicant. The court held that

> irreparable harm may be caused to KI [Kitchenuhmaykoosib Inninuwug First Nation] not only because it may lose a valuable tract of land…, but also, and more importantly, because it may lose land that is important from a cultural and spiritual perspective. No award of damages could possibly compensate KI for this loss.… Aboriginal identity, spirituality, laws, traditions, culture, and rights are connected to and arise from this relationship to the land. This is a perspective that is foreign to and often difficult to understand from a non-Aboriginal viewpoint.[51]

These ethical strands influenced the court to grant the interlocutory injunction. The fact that judges are called upon to hear evidence of these varying ethical perspectives shows the utility of environmental ethics in understanding the positions of the parties and in resolving the dispute.

## Conclusion

To what extent can courts incorporate environmental ethics? VanderZwaag suggests that one role of the courts is to develop and enforce principles until other branches begin to do so effectively: "[J]udges may play a backstop role in pushing societies in the direction of sustainable development. Not simply guided by personal philosophical passions or class ideology, judges might explicitly refer to the evolving international principles as a checklist for deciding whether the public trust is infringed."[52] The same can be argued of environmental ethics. Familiarity with these concepts can help judges identify, assess, and express competing interests and perspectives in environmental cases more clearly and fairly, leading to better environmental protection.

### NOTES

1 K Mickelson & W Rees, "The Environment: Ecological and Ethical Dimensions" in EL Hughes, AR Lucas & WA Tilleman, eds, *Environmental Law and Policy*, 2d ed (Toronto: Edmond Montgomery, 1998) 1 at 17.

2 J Alder & D Wilkinson, *Environmental Law and Ethics* (Hampshire, UK: MacMillan Press Ltd, 1999) at 10–11.

3 ET Freyfogle, "The Ethical Strands of Environmental Law" (1994) 4 U Ill L Rev 819.

4 Flournoy argues that the lack of clarity in identifying and justifying the values in environmental laws, both as written and as interpreted, impedes democratic accountability, as it prevents the evolution of environmental laws to reflect social priorities and achieve societal goals. A. Flournoy, "Building an Environmental Ethic from the Ground Up" (2003–2004) 37 UC Davis L Rev 53.

5 A Light & H Rolston III, "Introduction: Ethics and Environmental Ethics" in A Light & H Rolston III, eds, *Environmental Ethics: An Anthology* (Malden, MA: Blackwell, 2003) at 1.

6 Detailed analyses and references for these various branches can be found in the excellent JR DesJardins, *Environmental Ethics: An Introduction to Environmental Philosophy*, 2d ed (Belmont, CA: Wadsworth, 1997).

7 C Stone, "Should Trees Have Standing? Toward Legal Rights for Natural Objects" (1972) 45 S Cal L Rev 450.

8 Bryan G Norton, "Environmental Ethics and Weak Anthropocentrism" in Light & Rolston III, eds, *supra* note 5 at 163; and Eugene Hargrove, "Weak Anthropocentric Intrinsic Value" in Light & Rolston III, eds, *ibid* at 175.

9 E.g., T Regan, *The Case for Animal Rights* (Berkeley: University of California Press, 1983), as referred to in Clare Palmer, "An Overview of Environmental Ethics" in Light & Rolston III, eds, *ibid* at 25.

10 E.g., Arne Naess, "The Shallow and the Deep, Long Range Ecology Movements: A Summary" (1973) 16 Inquiry 95, and *Ecology, Community and Lifestyle*, translated by David Rothenberg (Cambridge: Cambridge University Press, 1989).

11 See references in H McLeod-Kilmurray, "An Ecofeminist Legal Critique of Canadian Environmental Law: The Case Study of Genetically Modified Foods" (2009) 26 Windsor Rev Legal Soc Issues 129.

12 See sources in H McLeod-Kilmurray, "Does Preserving the Environment Advance or Conflict with Social Justice and Human Rights?" in S Rodgers & S McIntyre, *The Supreme Court of Canada and Social Justice: Commitment, Retrenchment or Retreat?* (Markham: LexisNexis Canada, 2010) at 466.

13 K Bosselman, "Ecological Justice and Law" in BJ Richardson & S Wood, *Environmental Law for Sustainability* (Oxford: Hart, 2006) at 146.

14 "We are naïve if we assume that the environment is one choice among others. Instead, it is time that we paid heed to the fact that the environment constitutes the very sustenance of all life. 'The environment' is the inescapable condition of the possibility of the emergence of other sectoral priorities." IL Stefanovic, *Safeguarding Our Common Future: Rethinking Sustainable Development* (Albany: State University of New York Press, 2000) at 42.

15 RSO 1990, c E.18, s 2.

16 SO 1993, c 28.

17 RSO 1990, c E.19.

18 Section 2. For analysis of the policy objectives in legislation from other provinces, see the Introduction in J Benidickson, *Environmental Law*, 3d ed (Toronto: Irwin Law, 2009).

19 RSQ, c D-8.1.1.

20 SC 1999, c 33.

21 See s 2(1).

22 SC 2002, c 29.

23 *R v Hydro-Québec*, [1997] 3 SCR 213 [*Hydro-Québec*].

24 SC 1999, c 33.

25 *Hydro-Québec*, *supra* note 23 at 266.

26 *Ibid* at 267.

27 *Ibid* at 297.

28 *Ibid* at 300.

29 Section 11. See also s 35(1).

30 *Ibid* at 247.

31 *Imperial Oil Ltd. v. Quebec (Minister of the Environment)*, [2003] 2 SCR 624, 2003 SCC 58.

32 *Ibid* at para 18.

33 *Ibid* at para 19, citing *114947 Canada Ltée (Spraytech Société d'arrosage) v Hudson (Town)*, 2001 SCC 40.

34 *R v Van Waters & Rogers Ltd*, 1998 ABPC≈55.

35 John Swaigen & Gail Bunt, *Sentencing in Environmental Cases*, Protection of Life Study Papers (Ottawa: Law Reform Commission of Canada, 1985), online: <http://www.lareau-legal.ca/Sentencing.pdf>.

36 *Supra* note 34 at para 23, citing *ibid* at 9.

37 *Ibid* at para 27.

38 *Hollick v Metropolitan Toronto (Municipality)* (1998), 27 CELR (NS) 48 (Ont Ct Gen Div); rev'd (1999), 28 CELR (NS) 198 (Ont Ct Gen Div), aff'd (2000), 32 CELR (NS) 1 (Ont CA), aff'd (2001), 205 DLR (4th) 19 (SCC).

39 *Hoffman v Monsanto Canada Inc*, 2005 SKQB 225, aff'd 2007 SKCA 47, leave to appeal refused [2007] SCCA No 347 [*Hoffman*].

40 *Pearson v Inco Ltd* (2001), 42 CELR (NS) 273 (Ont Sup Ct J), aff'd (2002), 45 CELR (NS) 317 (Ont Sup Ct J, Div Ct), rev'd (2005), 261 DLR (4th) 629 (Ont CA); costs award (2006), 146 ACWS (3d) 600 (Ont CA); application for leave to appeal dismissed with costs (without reasons) [2006] SCCA No 1.

41 *Hoffman*, *supra* note 39 at para 131.

42 H McLeod-Kilmurray, "*Hoffman v Monsanto*: Courts, Class Actions and Perceptions of the Problem of GM Drift" (2007) 27:3 Bull Science, Techn & Soc 188.

43 *Ciment St. Laurent c Barette*, 2008 SCC 64 [*Barette*].

44 *Civil Code of Quebec*, SQ 1991, c 64, art 976.

45 *Barette*, *supra* note 43 at para 80.

46 *British Columbia v Canadian Forest Products*, 2004 SCC 38.

47 *Ibid*.

48 *Ibid* at para 137.

49 *Ibid* at para 138.

50 *Platinex Inc v Kitchenuhmaykoosib Inninuwug First Nation* (2006), 272 DLR (4th) 727 (Ont Sup Ct J).

51 *Ibid* at paras 79–80, varied (2007), 29 CELR (3d) 116.

52 DL VanderZwaag, "The Concept and Principles of Sustainable Development: 'Rio-formulating' Common Law Doctrines and Environmental Laws" (1993) 13 Windsor YB Access Just 39 at 66.

# 6

# The Intersection of Human Rights Law and Environmental Law

NICKIE NIKOLAOU

Clean water and clean air are believed to be ours by birth; we somehow assume that such important and fundamental rights are protected by law.

—ELIZABETH SWANSON & ELAINE HUGHES[1]

## 1. Introduction

Decision makers, scholars, and litigants are increasingly viewing environmental impacts—for example, air and water pollution—as human rights issues. In Canada, a lawsuit that started in 2010 alleged violations of sections 7 and 15 of the *Canadian Charter of Rights and Freedoms* (the *Charter*) in the context of exposure to toxins in Sarnia's Chemical Valley.[2] Landowners in Alberta have alleged violations of section 7 *Charter* rights in the context of environmental impacts from oil and gas facilities.[3] The European Court of Human Rights has repeatedly recognized that human rights may be infringed by environmental harm caused by industrial activities.[4] Courts in Nigeria have struck down regulations authorizing gas flaring on human rights grounds.[5]

This chapter explores the intersection between human rights law and environmental law by examining why and how human rights are relevant in the context of environmental harm. Part 2 considers how human rights law differs from traditional environmental law and why it is increasingly being referred to by people affected by environmental degradation. Part 3 outlines the different approaches currently in use internationally for using human rights in the environmental context. Part 4 reviews the current state of the law in Canada, and Part 5 concludes by noting the key challenge with applying human rights law in this context.

## 2. Why Human Rights?

The idea of addressing questions of environmental pollution through the lens of human rights is a marked departure from traditional approaches to environmental protection. Sax exposed the differences between the traditional regulatory model of environmental protection and what a rights-based regime would look like.[6] The traditional regulatory model is characterized by broad governmental powers, sweeping administrative discretion, and various procedural rights such as the right to be consulted or to be heard in a decision-making forum. By contrast, as Sax argued, a truly rights-based regime would be one which granted its citizens clear substantive environmental rights that would have to be balanced against other legally recognized interests (property rights, for example). In his view:

> The citizen who comes to an administrative agency comes essentially as a supplicant, requesting that somehow the public interest be interpreted to protect the environmental values from which he[/she] benefits. The citizen who comes to court has quite a different status—he[/she] stands as a claimant of rights to which he/she is entitled.[7]

Thus, one reason to pursue human rights claims in the context of actual or potential environmental harm is their legal force in the decision-making process. Human rights are not on par with other "interests" to be taken into account in public interest calculations (typical of traditional environmental law decision-making approaches). Rather, they may trump in a balancing of interests where the decision would amount to an unjustifiable human rights violation. As noted by Swaigen and Woods:

> Sometimes a right may preclude any balancing of interests; for example, when a fundamental constitutional right prevents the majority from overriding the interest of an individual or minority group, even to serve a public interest or provide some benefit to the community.[8]

Another reason for using human rights law in this context is because of its post-decision application. Where a decision maker has not struck the right balance and has exercised its discretion in a manner that violates fundamental human rights, the decision is reviewable even by a stakeholder that was not involved in the decision-making process at first instance.[9] Further, human rights not only provide a vehicle to influence or challenge a decision but also allow for challenges to environmental laws, regulations, and standards that have the effect of infringing on fundamental human rights.[10]

## 3. Which Human Rights?

The literature reveals three possible approaches to human rights in the environmental context: (i) the creation of procedural environmental rights; (ii) the recognition of a substantive right to environmental quality (e.g. a right to a healthy environment); and (iii) the recognition of infringements on existing human rights through adverse environmental conditions.[11]

### PROCEDURAL ENVIRONMENTAL RIGHTS

Procedural environmental rights include access to environmental information, participation in environmental decision making, and access to justice in environmental matters.[12] Such rights are recognized at the international level and domestically throughout the world.[13] In Canada, federal and provincial law implements procedural environmental rights in various ways, "including environmental assessment statutes, environmental bills of rights, and administrative regulatory schemes that provide members of the public with a right to challenge environmental decisions made by government."[14]

While procedural rights are important, scholars agree that they cannot, in themselves, provide a remedy for impacts from state-sponsored environmental harm. "Substantive" concerns matters of substance (i.e. what the right consists of), and "procedural" refers to the process through which the right can be enforced.[15] Without substantive rights of some kind, procedural rights allow for a balancing of interests (as opposed to rights) only. They may get parties to the table, but they do not place outer limits on which decisions are acceptable. They also do not direct the course of decision making in an obvious way.

### SUBSTANTIVE ENVIRONMENTAL RIGHTS

Two possibilities exist for recognizing substantive human rights in the environmental context: (i) the recognition of a free-standing right to environmental quality; and (ii) the recognition that environmental rights are implicit within already-established human rights.

#### A Free-Standing Environmental Right

A free-standing environmental right has been variously described as a right to a healthy, safe, clean, and/or ecologically-balanced environment.[16] Although there is some overlap, a free-standing environmental right is one that extends beyond other existing rights.[17] The idea is that, by virtue of being human, each person has a right to a basic level of environmental quality.

Scholars note that, internationally, such a right has been recognized expressly or implicitly in a substantial body of global human rights treaties (e.g. the *International Covenant on Economic, Social and Cultural Rights* and the *Convention on the Rights of the Child*), declarations (e.g. the *Stockholm* and *Rio Declarations*), and regional human rights treaties (e.g. the *African (Banjul) Charter on Human and Peoples' Rights*, the *Additional Protocol to the American Convention on Human Rights in the Area of Economic, Social and Cultural Rights*, and the *Aarhus Convention*).[18] Human rights tribunals enforcing international and regional human rights treaties have built a "substantial body of decisions enforcing the right to a healthy environment."[19] Ninety national constitutions recognize that their citizens have a substantive right to live in a healthy environment.[20]

Nonetheless, there is debate as to whether a free-standing environmental right has emerged as a principle of customary international law, binding on all nations even without their consent. Some conclude that it has.[21] Others are more cautious and say that, although not there yet, it may be *emerging* as customary international law.[22]

In Canada, there is no explicit recognition of a free-standing environmental right in the Constitution. Even environmental bills of rights statutes do not set up enforceable substantive rights to a healthy or clean environment.[23] Quebec is the only province that recognizes a right to a healthy environment in its human rights legislation.[24]

Is it possible that a free-standing environmental right exists implicitly within Canada's Constitution or within Canadian common law? The Supreme Court of Canada has acknowledged that "a fundamental and widely shared value is indeed seriously contravened by some environmental pollution, a value which we will refer to as the *right to a safe environment*."[25]

It is unclear what the legal status of such a right is in Canadian law. To the extent that it is a rule of customary international law, it is "arguably part of Canadian common law."[26] At a minimum, though, scholars note that developments internationally could (and according to some, should) be used as interpretive aids in construing existing provisions in Canadian constitutional and statutory law. The Supreme Court of Canada has indeed used international hard and soft (i.e. binding and non-binding) law repeatedly to determine Canadian law, especially in cases involving the *Charter* and environmental protection.[27] The contextual approach to statutory interpretation requires legislation to be read in a broader legal context that includes any relevant values and principles expressed by the international community (binding and non-binding) and reflected in Canadian law or policy.[28]

### Environmental Protections within Existing Human Rights

The third and "most established"[29] approach to environmental human rights involves the recognition that existing human rights may be violated by adverse environmental conditions. The idea is that "damage to the environment can impair and undermine all the human rights spoken of in the *Universal Declaration* and other human rights instruments."[30] Scholars note that environmental degradation can result in violations of various human rights recognized around the world, including the right to life, to health, privacy and family life, adequate standard of living, religion, and culture. Tribunals at the international, regional, and domestic levels have "taken an ecologically literate approach to their respective human rights instruments, in order to protect basic human rights from state-sponsored environmental harm."[31]

The most widely recognized human right of relevance is the right to life, which is variously stated in international conventions, declarations, regional treaties, and national constitutions. As Neil Popovic says:

> The right to life represents the most basic human rights doctrine, the essential and non-derogable prerequisite to the enjoyment of all other rights. Environmental problems that endanger life—directly or indirectly—implicate this core right.[32]

Although there has yet to be a definitive statement by an international legal body in an actual case, tribunals and scholars have fleshed out the environmental dimensions of this right. The United Nations Human Rights Committee, for example, has stated that the right to life, liberty, and security in international law has been interpreted too narrowly and that it does include state obligations to protect people from threats (including environmental ones) to survival or quality of life.[33] Earlier, in *EHP v. Canada*,[34] the committee stated that the storage of radioactive waste near homes raised "serious issues" with respect to state obligations to protect human life. It directed the Canadian applicants to seek a remedy under section 7 of the *Charter*.[35]

Regional human rights tribunals have also held the right to life may be violated in the context of environmental risks or harm. For example, in *Yanomami Indians v. Brazil*,[36] the Inter-American Commission on Human Rights held that Brazil had violated the Yanomami peoples' rights to life, liberty, and personal security when it failed to prevent serious environmental damage caused by natural resources development. Elsewhere, the European Court of Human Rights has exposed the links between the right to life and environmental pollution in several decisions. In one case, a complaint was brought about a chemical factory close to the complainants' homes that released large amounts of toxic substances. In finding that the government had failed to adequately protect the complainants in the circumstances, the court held that a violation of the right to "private and family life" and the "right to life" had occurred.[37]

Similarly, domestic courts have exposed the environmental dimensions of the right to life. Courts in India, Pakistan, Bangladesh, and Nigeria, for example, have repeatedly said the right to life in their constitutions includes the right to live in a safe and pollution-free environment. They have required governments to clean up unsafe pollution causing serious health risks or effects.[38]

## 4. Current State of the Law in Canada

The most fertile ground for human rights claims in the context of environmental harm in Canada is section 7 of the *Charter*,[39] which states:

> Everyone has the right to life, liberty and security of the person and the right not to be deprived thereof except in accordance with the principles of fundamental justice.

Scholars considering whether, based on current case law, section 7 has environmental dimensions have concluded that it undoubtedly does.[40] Although there has yet to be a definitive ruling on the matter, cases that have come before the courts have hinted that a remedy may be available on the right facts. Such facts would have to evidence significant physical or psychological health risks or impacts.[41]

To date, section 7 has been argued in the environmental context in several cases that, by and large, have been dismissed on other grounds. These include: *Coalition of Citizens for a Charter Challenge v. Metropolitan Authority*[42] (alleged violation of section 7 based on the threat to human health posed by the operation of a waste incinerator); *Manicom v. Oxford*[43] (alleged violation of section 7 by a government decision to locate a landfill near the plaintiffs' homes); *Energy Probe v. Canada (Attorney General)*[44] (alleged violation of section 7 in the context of a liability limitation for nuclear power generation); two cases alleging breaches in the context of environmental impacts from oil and gas operations;[45] two cases involving health risks and impacts from fluoridated drinking water;[46] and a lawsuit alleging section 7 infringements in the context of emissions from refinery and chemical facilities.[47]

Case law developed under section 7 strongly suggests that it protects against unreasonable risks or impacts to human health.[48] According to Collins, "state action that results in a clear increase in the risk of death may result in a deprivation of this right."[49] As for "security of the person," courts have said it encompasses a right to bodily integrity and a right to be free from harm and from threats to that integrity, including risks to health.[50] Section 7 also protects against serious interference with the psychological integrity of a person.[51] As Gage notes, "where a person has a credible and real fear of his or her physical well-being and safety, personal security issues are likely to arise."[52]

Even if life, liberty, or the security of the person is impacted, section 7 is not violated unless the infringement is not in accordance with the "principles of fundamental justice." While these principles include the usual procedural guarantees (e.g. right to a fair hearing), the cases reveal substantive elements as well. These include "the sanctity of human life," which, according to Collins, means that government conduct which results in actual or potential loss to human life would be unsustainable no matter what decision-making process was followed. There is also a prohibition against deprivations of life, liberty, or security of the person that would "shock the conscience" of Canadians. Collins suggests some state-sponsored environmental harm may result in health effects so "serious and wide-ranging" as to "shock the conscience."[53]

As Canadian courts interpret section 7 in the environmental context, they will likely be guided by international developments. As noted, both international and regional human rights tribunals as well as numerous domestic courts (including from common law jurisdictions) have held that, in certain circumstances, state-sponsored environmental harm can amount to a violation of the right to life. These developments should be highly persuasive to Canadian courts and tribunals.[54]

## 5. Conclusion

Human rights law and environmental law intersect when human rights are impacted by environmental degradation. Internationally, there has been significant movement towards applying human rights law in the context of state-sponsored environmental harm. In Canada, while the application of human rights law in this context is in its infancy, there are no doctrinal reasons why the *Charter* may not provide a remedy in some circumstances. Still, scholars note that proving causation will be a significant challenge. It will have to be proven that state action caused actual or threatened harm sufficient to make out a deprivation of life, liberty, or security of the person.[55] Given the difficulties in establishing causation generally in the environmental context, this will likely prove to be the greatest hurdle for any human rights claim in this context. It remains to be seen whether the evidence in the ongoing litigation relating to Sarnia's Chemical Valley will be able to overcome this hurdle.

## NOTES

1 Elizabeth Swanson & Elaine Hughes, *The Price of Pollution* (Edmonton: Environmental Law Centre, 1990) at 205.

2 *Ada Lockridge and Ronald Plain v Director (Ministry of the Environment) et al*, Notice of Application to Divisional Court for Judicial Review, 29 October 2010 (Ontario).

3 *Domke v Alberta (Energy Resources Conservation Board)*, 2008 ABCA 232; and *Kelly v Alberta (Energy and Utilities Board)*, 2008 ABCA 52.

4 For example, *Lopez Ostra v Spain*, 20 Eur HR Rep 277 (1994); and *Guerra & Others v Italy*, 26 Eur HR Rep 357 (1998).

5 *Gbemre v Shell Petroleum Development Co Nigeria Ltd et al*, Order of the Federal High Court of Nigeria in the Benin Judicial Division Holden at Court Benin City, 14 November 2005.

6 Joseph P Sax, *Defending the Environment: A Strategy for Citizen Action* (New York: Knopf, 1970).

7 *Ibid* at 58.

8 John Swaigen & Richard E Woods, "A Substantive Right to Environmental Quality" in John Swaigen, ed, *Environmental Rights in Canada* (Toronto: Butterworths, 1981) at 197.

9 In Canada, statutory decision makers must comply with the *Charter* in exercising their discretion: see Nickie Vlavianos, "Alberta's Energy and Utilities Board and the Constitution of Canada" (2005) 43 Alta L Rev 369; Lynda M Collins, "An Ecologically Literate Reading of the *Canadian Charter of Rights and Freedoms*" (2009) 26 Windsor Rev Legal & Soc 7 [Collins]; Andrew Gage, "Public Health Hazards and Section 7 of the *Charter*" (2003) 13 J Env L & Prac 1; and Nickie Vlavianos, "Public Participation and the Disposition of Oil and Gas Rights in Alberta" (2007) 17 J Env L & Prac 205.

10 Although human rights law typically protects against state rather than private action, state action is engaged in the environmental harm context in three ways: (i) where government runs industrial operations that may discharge harmful contaminants; (ii) where government permits or authorizes private conduct that causes environmental harm; and (iii) where government sets statutory or regulatory standards that allow for emissions of harmful levels of environmental pollution: see Collins, Gage and Vlavianos articles, *ibid*. The term "state-sponsored environmental harm" has been used to refer broadly to harm falling within any of these categories: see Collins and Gage articles, *ibid*.

11 Collins, *supra* note 9 at 10.

12 *Ibid*.

13 The most significant statement at the international level is the *Convention on Access to Information, Public Participation in Decision-Making and Access to Justice in Environmental Matters* (the *Aarhus Convention*), 25 June 1998.

14 Collins, *supra* note 9 at 10. According to Boyd, Canadian legislation fails to meet the standards set by the *Aarhus Convention* (to which Canada is not a

party): David R Boyd, *The Environmental Rights Revolution: A Global Study of Constitutions, Human Rights, and the Environment* (Vancouver: UBC Press, 2011) [Boyd].

15 Swanson & Hughes, *supra* note 1 at 206.

16 See Boyd, *supra* note 14; James T McClymonds, "The Human Right to a Healthy Environment: An International Legal Perspective" (1993) 37 NYL Sch L Rev 583; and Diana Shelton, "Human Rights, Environmental Rights, and the Right to Environment" (1991) 28 Stanford J of Int'l L 103.

17 Collins, *supra* note 9 at 10.

18 See: Lynda M Collins, "Are We There Yet? The Right to Environment in International and European Law" (2007) McGill JSDLP 119; and John Lee, "The Underlying Legal Theory to Support a Well-Defined Human Right to a Healthy Environment as a Principle of Customary International Law" (2000) 25 Colum J Envt'l L 238.

19 Boyd, *supra* note 14 at 165.

20 *Ibid* at 91.

21 See Collins, *supra* note 9; Boyd, *supra* note 14; and L Rodriguez-Rivera, "Is the Human Right to Environment Recognized under International Law? It Depends on its Source" (2001) 12 Col J Int'l Envt'l L 1.

22 See McClymonds and Shelton, both *supra* note 16.

23 Five provinces/territories in Canada have enacted environmental bills of rights: Quebec, Ontario, the Yukon, the Northwest Territories, and Nunavut. Despite some mention of a right to a healthy environment in the purposes/preamble sections, they focus on procedural environmental rights: Boyd, *supra* note 14.

24 *Charter of Human Rights and Freedoms*, RSQ c C-12. But the provision's restrictive language (guaranteeing the right "to the extent and according to the standards provided by law") means it is likely of limited effect: Boyd, *supra* note 14.

25 See *Ontario v Canadian Pacific*, [1995] 2 SCR 1031 at para 55 (emphasis in original) and *R v Hydro-Québec*, [1997] 3 SCR 213.

26 Collins, *supra* note 9 at 20.

27 See Boyd, *supra* note 14; and Elizabeth Brandon, "Does International Law Mean Anything in Canadian Courts?" (2001) 11 J Envt'l L & Prac 399.

28 *Baker v Canada (Minister of Citizenship & Immigration*, [1999] 2 SCR 817.

29 Collins, *supra* note 9 at 11.

30 *Case concerning the Gabcikovo-Nagymaros Project (Hungary v. Slovakia)*, [1997] ICJ Rep 92, separate but concurring opinion of Judge Weeramantry.

31 Collins, *supra* note 9 at 17. For summaries of the relevant decisions, see: Collins and Gage, both *supra* note 9; Boyd, *supra* note 14; and Nickie Vlavianos, *Health, Human Rights and Resource Development in Alberta: Current and Emerging Law*, Human Rights Paper #1 (Calgary: Canadian Institute of Resources Law, 2003).

32 Neil Popovic, "In Pursuit of Environmental Human Rights: Commentary on the Draft Declaration of Principles on Human Rights and the Environment" (1996) 27 Colum Human Rts L Rev 487 at 512.

33 General Comment on art 6 of the *International Covenant on Civil and Political Rights* issued by the United Nations Human Rights Committee in *Compilation of General Comments and General Recommendations adopted by Human Rights Treaty Bodies*, UN Doc HRI/GEN/1/Rev 3 (1997).

34 *Communication No 67/1980, EHP v Canada*, 2 Selected Decisions of the Human Rights Committee (1990), 20 (UNDOC CCPR/C/OP/2).

35 *Ibid*. Although a *prima facie* claim was made out, the case was dismissed for failure to exhaust domestic remedies.

36 (1985), Inter-Am Comm HR 7615, *Annual Report of the International American Commission on Human Rights: 1984085*, OEA/Ser L/V/II.62, Doc 10.

37 As protected by the *European Convention for the Protection of Human Rights and Fundamental Freedoms*, 4 November 1950, 213 UNTS 222.

38 See: Collins, *supra* note 9; and Boyd, *supra* note 14.

39 Other provisions may have limited application. For example, s 15 may apply "[i]n the environmental arena, [...] when a particular marginalized group in society receives less environmental protection than comparator groups.": Collins, *supra* note 9 at 43.

40 See: Boyd, *supra* note 14; Collins and Gage, both *supra* note 9; and Vlavianos, *supra* note 31.

41 One case may suggest no role for s 7 in the environmental context: *Kuczerpa v Canada* (1993), 152 NR 207 (Fed CA). But scholars have emphasized the case's peculiar circumstances (a self-represented litigant, the improper pleading of the *Charter* claim, and the tort cause of action in negligence): Gage and Collins, both *supra* note 9.

42 (1993), 108 DLR (4th) 145 (NSCA), leave to appeal to SCC denied [1999] 1 SCR vii.

43 (1985), 52 OR (2d) 137 (Div Ct).

44 (1989), 58 DLR (4th) 513 (Ont CA).

45 *Domke* and *Kelly*, both *supra* note 3.

46 *Locke v Calgary* (1993), 15 Alta LR 70 (Alta QB); and *Millership v British Columbia*, 2003 BCSC 82.

47 *Lockridge*, *supra* note 2. See also Ecojustice, "Chemical Valley Challenge" (accessed 31 January 2012), online: <http://www.ecojustice.ca/cases/chemical-valley-charter-case>.

48 As for risks, there is no doubt that the *Charter* provides *prospective* protection: see *Operation Dismantle v The Queen*, [1985] 1 SCR 441.

49 Collins, *supra* note 9 at 22, citing *Chaoulli v Quebec*, [1995] 1 SCR 791.

50 *R v Morgentaler (No 2)*, [1988] 1 SCR 30.

51 *New Brunswick v G(J)*, [1999] 3 SCR 46.

52 Gage, *supra* note 9. Collins notes that it is "well established that persons exposed to known environmental risks frequently experience substantial psychological effects, including anxiety sometimes rising to the level of a phobia.": *supra* note 9 at 25.

53 Collins, *supra* note 9 at 27–28. See also Gage, *supra* note 9.

54 *Charter* issues in the environmental context may arise not only before the courts but also before administrative tribunals. Barring legislation to the contrary, tribunals empowered to determine questions of law must determine questions of constitutional law: *Nova Scotia (Workers' Compensation Board) v Martin*, [2003] 1 SCR 504.

55 Collins, *supra* note 9.

# 7

# Practical Engagement with Indigenous Legal Traditions on Environmental Issues: Some Questions

HADLEY FRIEDLAND

It is better to know some of the questions than all of the answers.

—JAMES THURBER

## Introduction

In this chapter, I argue that serious and sustained practical engagement with Indigenous legal traditions by legal practitioners is important and possible. It is important in the context of environmental issues because it may enable us to move past some "sticking points" in conflicts over resource development and cumulative impacts on traditional lands. It may help us better understand Indigenous perspectives on the impacts of environmental damage and what adequate consultation and reasonable accommodation entails. On a broader level, it also may contribute to a robust reconciliation between peoples within Canada. While practical engagement with Indigenous legal traditions is possible, there are intellectual hurdles to overcome before addressing the legal, political, or institutional questions that are often raised regarding greater formal recognition of these legal traditions within Canada. In this chapter I suggest some methods legal practitioners might use in approaching the intellectual work of engagement.

## Practical Engagement with Indigenous Legal Traditions

Even if we agree that both recognition of and engagement with Indigenous legal traditions would be relevant to a better understanding of the Indigenous perspective on environmental issues on traditional lands, we are still left with the very real question of *how*? Indigenous legal traditions may be deeply meaningful or have great impact in the lives of people within Indigenous communities,[1] but I have come to accept that outside those communities, they are largely invisible or incomprehensible. This perception is illustrated in Professor John Borrows' book, *Canada's Indigenous Constitution*, where he relates a personal conversation with an unnamed chief justice of a provincial appellate court. The chief justice states bluntly to him: "You say Indigenous law exists; I don't believe it for a minute."[2] However, even people who want to know more about Indigenous legal traditions struggle to understand how to do so. Professor Val Napoleon tells the story of a well-known lawyer for Indigenous groups saying to her: "We all know there is *something* there—but we don't know how to *access* it."[3]

When we discuss more public, explicit, and integrated use of Indigenous legal traditions in Canada generally, there are many legal, practical, and institutional issues to address. But there are also very real intellectual issues. I believe that how well we are able to address the legal, practical, and institutional issues will depend on whether we actually address the intellectual ones, or whether we skip this step and assume we already know certain answers about the substantive content of Indigenous legal traditions. So, the first step toward practical engagement is finding ways to start engaging with Indigenous legal traditions in a substantive way. Really, it is about us: How can we start asking better questions?

In order to start asking better questions, I suggest we need three main things, which I will elaborate on in this chapter. First, we need a logical starting point. Second, we need to make some reasonable working assumptions, and third, we need a way to get beyond generalities and generalizations. Then we can begin to ask targeted and useful questions about the specific issues we are focused on at any given time.

## A LOGICAL STARTING POINT

I will start from a very basic level, for people who may not be Indigenous or even have any prior experience directly interacting with Indigenous communities. I want to suggest a logical starting point for inquiries into Indigenous legal traditions generally, and Indigenous legal principles related to environmental issues specifically, that I do not think requires any prior knowledge whatsoever.

Prior to European contact or "effective control," Indigenous peoples lived here, in this place, in groups, for thousands of years. We know that when groups of human beings live together, they have ways to manage themselves and all their affairs.[4] This task of coordination is "the most common of common denominators in law."[5] Indigenous societies harvested resources and used the land in a variety of ways for millennia. Therefore, as a matter of logic alone, our starting point for any inquiry has to be that, *at some point*, and for a very long time, Indigenous peoples coordinated resource harvesting, management, and land use successfully enough to continue on as societies.

It feels a bit embarrassing to even have to point this out as a logical starting point, but it is important to do so, because the myth of Indigenous people as lawless, and without any regulation of land or methods for resource management, has too often been used as a trope for European theorists and jurists in making claims about property rights, with no basis whatsoever.[6] There have been devastating political and *legal* consequences for Indigenous societies based on illogical assumptions about an absence of law.[7]

Dispensing with illogical starting points doesn't lead us to subscribe to a utopian vision of Indigenous legal traditions generally, or resource management specifically. However, we have no logical reason to think Indigenous laws didn't work well enough for thousands of years.[8] Scholars have begun to describe specific resource management regulation in several Indigenous societies in both the past and present, making some of these processes more accessible to outsiders.[9] We can approach Indigenous legal traditions, not as paragons of perfection but as reasonable legal orders with reasoning people. This logical starting point gives us some clues as to how to frame further inquiries more logically and productively about the *content* of these legal traditions.

## REASONABLE WORKING ASSUMPTIONS

There are some reasonable working assumptions that flow from this logical starting point, and these can help us productively frame our inquiries into Indigenous legal traditions. They are just assumptions, but they may serve to keep from us getting stuck in intellectual traps that stem less from facts and more from the ample negative stereotypes about Indigenous people, or from images of Indigenous people that are really just tropes invented by European theorists.

Reasonable working assumptions can help frame relevant questions about aspects of Indigenous legal traditions, including (a) sources of Indigenous law, (b) practitioners and teachers of Indigenous law, and (c) methods for recording and promulgating Indigenous law.

### One reasonable working assumption is that there must be sources of Indigenous law that are not courts or parliament.

As there were no courts or parliament before European control, and there was law, there logically must be other sources of law. So, a useful question is: What are some of these sources of Indigenous law? Borrows has written about five sources of Indigenous law: (1) Sacred, (2) Natural, (3) Deliberative, (4) Positivistic, and (5) Customary.[10] He also makes the important point that the "proximate source" of most Indigenous law, like laws in the common law legal tradition, is deliberation. This means that interpretation and persuasion are vital aspects of legal reasoning within Indigenous legal traditions too.[11]

**A second reasonable assumption is that there have to be practitioners and teachers of Indigenous law who are not lawyers or law professors.**

As there were no lawyers or law professors before European control, and there was law, there logically must be other practitioners and teachers of law. So, again, it makes sense to ask: Who are some of the practitioners? Who are some of the teachers?

Borrows suggests that Indigenous laws are more broadly dispersed in a more decentralized way than in the court cases and written legislation we are accustomed to.[12] He argues that part of the strength and resiliency of Indigenous laws is that they have been practised and passed down through "Elders, families, clans, and bodies within Indigenous societies."[13]

**A third reasonable assumption is that there have to be methods to record and promulgate laws that are not court cases, statutes, or texts.**

As there were no law texts, statutes, or written records of cases before European control, and there was law, there logically has to be other ways Indigenous laws are recorded and promulgated. Therefore, a useful question is: What are some of the ways Indigenous laws can be recorded and promulgated? Again, Borrows explains that Indigenous laws can be recorded and shared in different forms, and in a more broadly dispersed and decentralized way than the statutes and court cases legal practitioners may be accustomed to, and that Indigenous laws can be recorded and promulgated in various forms, including stories, songs, practices, and customs.[14] Napoleon explains that law "setting out the legal capacities, relationships, and obligations" can be embedded and recorded in narrative, practices, rituals, and conventions."[15] The Canadian Law Commission's *Justice Within* Report stated that some Indigenous people suggest that law can be found in dreams, dances, art, the land, and nature.[16]

It is clear from this brief overview that when legal scholars use these types of reasonable working assumptions to frame their inquiries about Indigenous legal traditions, they are starting to come up with relevant questions and to theorize reasonable answers. This begins to make these intellectual resources more explicit and accessible. If we start from our logical starting point and our reasonable working assumptions, we can start to generate some relevant questions for practically engaging with Indigenous legal traditions regarding environmental issues. Some of these questions might be:

- What are some of the sources of Indigenous laws related to the environment?
- Who are some of the practitioners or the teachers we can turn to for information about Indigenous laws related to the environment?
- What are some of the ways Indigenous laws related to the environment may be recorded and promulgated?

The first question in this set is a fundamental one about a community's legal foundations.[17] The next two questions are primarily questions about what resources are available for exploring issues within a particular Indigenous legal tradition or even a specific community.[18]

Starting our inquiry from this angle allows us greater perspective to understand *why* Indigenous communities might be adopting the positions they are in relation to specific development.[19] As Anishinabek legal scholar Aaron Mills points out, looking seriously at the reasons behind such positions "would be infinitely more productive than not caring about the motivations for the behaviour and focusing solely on its result."[20] One thing that is immediately apparent in asking these questions, and looking at some of the answers being theorized, is that this inquiry can lead us to recognize and reflect on a whole other level of environmental impacts.

If the natural world is one vital source of Indigenous laws,[21] then environmental damage may be viewed as damaging the very foundations of these laws. If observations of the natural world or inscriptions upon a landscape are used as pedagogical resources for recording, remembering, and promulgating Indigenous laws,[22] then changes to the environment may erase some essential resources for passing on these laws. Thus, in addition to other effects, it is possible that the cumulative impacts of environmental damage may also constitute real damage to the basic maintenance of social order within particular Indigenous communities.

## GETTING BEYOND GENERALITIES AND GENERALIZATIONS

Once we have framed our inquiry broadly by grounding it in a logical starting point and adopting some reasonable working assumptions so we are asking relevant questions, we still need a way to get "into" the nitty-gritty details of Indigenous legal traditions. This inquiry can potentially move us beyond increasing our insight into the perspectives behind certain positions to actually increasing our capacity to develop constructive ways forward.

It is crucial to get beyond generalities and generalizations if we are going to practically engage with Indigenous legal traditions. From the outside, looking into a legal tradition, we pay attention to the aspects that directly affect our lives or that bother us. We look for simple answers and we look for "the rules." Before I started law school, I assumed that law was an immovable object and I would be memorizing a bunch of answers. I didn't realize how diverse and complex law actually was. Or that I would never be given a book of answers. The difference between before and after law school for me, as for many others, was the difference between an internal and external view of a legal tradition. I started with an external point of view, where I saw the aspects of the law that came to my attention through my work or the media, as well as particular instances of the law's impact on people I knew. In law school, I moved to an internal point of view, where I understood the language and debates within Canadian law and learned how to argue within its parameters.[23] Most importantly, I went from seeing the law as a static "thing" to memorize to seeing it as a fluid, dynamic conversation, in which I could participate if I knew the terms of the debate and the forms and limits of argumentation.

This personal experience helps me understand why, when practitioners look at Indigenous legal traditions from the outside, they focus on the particular aspects of them that are immediately impacting them, and they expect something simple and they expect rules. But the problem that has arisen is that, over time, this has reduced the way we talk about Indigenous legal traditions to rhetoric or oversimplified, rule-bound accounts. This feeds both negative stereotypes about Indigenous law within broader Canadian society and fundamentalism within Indigenous communities. It doesn't give us any way to understand Indigenous legal traditions as fluid, dynamic conversations, in their rich complexity, and it doesn't give us any way to competently question, clarify, or challenge concepts within them.

When we stay at the level of generalities and generalizations, we often end up stuck in discussions that never seem to go anywhere productive. A good example of this is divergent views on whether or not the earth is a living being[24] or whether or not animals can bear rights and obligations.[25] I have heard people argue, from both sides, that these divergent world views are insurmountable obstacles to bridging the chasm between Indigenous and non-Indigenous

**Table 7.1 | Shifts in Questions***

| *From:* | *To:* |
|---|---|
| What is Aboriginal justice? | What are the legal concepts and categories within this Indigenous legal tradition? |
| What are the cultural values? | What are the legal principles? |
| What are the "culturally appropriate" or "traditional" dispute resolution forms? | What are the legitimate procedures for collective decision making? |
| *Overall Shift:* | |
| What are the rules?<br>What are the answers? | What are the legal principles and legal processes for reasoning through issues? |

* These shifts were first published in Hadley Friedland, "Reflective Frameworks: Methods for Accessing, Understanding and Applying Indigenous Laws" (2013) 11:2 Indigenous Law Journal 1.

approaches to natural resource management and other environmental issues. I don't have any definitive answers, but I do think issues look very different when framed in terms of generalizations about cultural world views and incommensurable absolutes than when issues are instead framed in terms of living legal principles, *some* of which may conflict but some of which may provide legitimate ways for resolving the particular issues at hand.

Table 7.1 sets out just a few examples of the shifts in questions that occur when we reframe our inquiries to engage with Indigenous Legal traditions as *legal traditions*, and on a more specific and substantive level.

Following these shifts, our second set of questions could be:

- What are the legal concepts and categories within this particular Indigenous legal tradition relevant to the specific environmental issue at hand?
- What are the legal principles relevant to the environmental issue?
- What are the legitimate procedures for collective decision making regarding the environmental issue?

Overall, we are asking: What are the legal principles and legal processes for reasoning through this environmental issue within this legal tradition?

This shift in questions moves us from a conversation about how legal practitioners should deal with or respond to isolated cultural practices or commitments they may not understand or agree with, and which may not be easily translatable to a common law right or obligation, to a conversation about reasoning through principles as integral but flexible parts of a comprehensive whole.[26] To return to our example, Borrows argues that the earth as living is a "present day principle of central significance," in an Anishinabek legal tradition.[27] This highlights its importance while making it possible to imagine balancing it with other principles, just as we do constantly in Canadian law. Critically, Borrows also gives examples of legitimate community processes and procedures through which legitimate collective decisions have been debated and reached regarding specific environmental issues within his home community.[28] This inquiry may help us identify and proceed through productive and legitimate avenues, from Indigenous legal perspectives, for consultative processes and possible accommodation measures.

For a particular issue in specific circumstances, we might ask:

- What are the general principles regarding this environmental issue?
- How do we interpret these principles?
- What are the exceptions?
- What other principles can or should be considered on these specific facts?
- How are legitimate decisions about such issues reached?
- How does this law change in new circumstances?

These types of questions could move us from understanding a position to understanding a *legal reasoning process*. It won't be easy, and it shouldn't be. Serious and sustained engagement requires hard intellectual work, pushing beyond generalizations and generalities to treat Indigenous laws as we do other laws.

## Conclusion

Practical engagement with Indigenous legal traditions regarding environmental issues is both important and possible for legal practitioners. I suggest this engagement could start with the intellectual work described in this chapter: asking better questions, grounded in logic, built on reasonable working assumptions, and pushing past generalities and generalizations. Serious and sustained engagement between legal traditions may increase understanding of Indigenous perspectives on environmental damage and expand our understanding of legitimate and effective processes for consultation, accommodation, and, ultimately, reconciliation.

Let me close with one thought on the endeavour of robust reconciliation and why I see it as so important to all of us. Robert Cover once famously described law as "not merely a system of rules to be observed, but a world in which we live"—a "resource in signification."[29] Legal traditions are not only prescriptive. They are descriptive. They ascribe meaning to human events, challenges, and aspirations. They are intellectual resources that we use to frame and interpret information, to reason through and act upon current problems and projects, to work toward our greatest societal aspirations. There are many intractable problems and deep disagreements regarding complex environmental issues that impact us all, as well as the generations after us. We do not have all the answers. One way of looking at the project of greater recognition and engagement with Indigenous legal traditions in Canada is that it is about recovering normative possibilities. It is also about how we will tell the story of our shared future on and with this land.

#### NOTES

1 John Borrows, *Canada's Indigenous Constitution* (Toronto: University of Toronto Press, 2010) at 23 [Borrows].

2 *Ibid* at 46.

3 Personal conversation with Val Napoleon (April 2010).

4 Lon Fuller describes law as "a direction of purposive human effort" consisting in "the enterprise of subjecting human conduct to the governance of rules": Lon Fuller, *The Morality of Law* (New Haven, CT: Yale University Press, 1964) at 130.

5 Jeremy Webber, "The Grammar of Customary Law" (2009) 54 McGill LJ 579 at 583 [Webber].

6 *Ibid* at 591.

7 See, for example: James Tully, *Strange Multiplicity: Constitutionalism in an Age of Diversity* (Cambridge: Cambridge University Press, 1995) at 65; and Michael Asch & Patrick Macklem, "Indigenous Rights and Canadian Sovereignty: An Essay on *R v Sparrow*" (1991) 29:2 Alta L Rev 498 at 507.

8 In Val Napoleon, *Ayook: Gitksan Legal Order, Law, and Legal Theory* (PhD Dissertation, University of Victoria Faculty of Law, 2009) [Napolean], this argument is made persuasively throughout.

9 See, for example, Webber, *supra* note 5 at 591 (detailed regulation of hunting by the James Bay Cree); and Brenda Parlee, Fikret Berkes & Teet'lit Gwich'in, "Health of the Land, Health of the People: A Case Study on Gwich'in Berry Harvesting in Northern Canada" (2005) 2:2 Ecohealth 127.

10 Borrows, *supra* note 1, ch 2 at 23–58.

11 *Ibid* at 35–36.

12 *Ibid* at 139.

13 *Ibid* at 179.

14 *Ibid* at 139.

15 Napoleon, *supra* note 8 at 71.

16 Law Commission of Canada, *Justice Within, Indigenous Legal Traditions*, DVD (Ottawa: Minister of Supply and Services Canada, 2006).

17 Borrows, *supra* note 1 at 23.

18 Possible resources for judges in accessing Indigenous laws, as well as their limitations, are discussed in the American tribal court context in Mathew LM Fletcher, *Rethinking Customary Law in Tribal Court Jurisprudence*, Working Paper 2006-04 (East Lasing,

MI: Indigenous Law and Policy Centre, Michigan State University College of Law, 2006) at 36–38, online: <http://www.law.msu.edu/indigenous/papers/2006-04.pdf>.

19 See a discussion of the benefits of this for Crown and third-party actors in Aaron Mills, "Aki, Anishinaabek, Kaye Tahsh Crown" (2010) 9 Indigenous LJ 107 at 123.

20 *Ibid.*

21 This is a common, even dominant theme in many Indigenous scholars' work. See, for example, CF Black, *The Land is the Source of the Law: A Dialogic Encounter with Indigenous Jurisprudence* (New York: Routledge, 2011), generally; and Tracey Lindberg, *Critical Indigenous Legal Theory* (PhD Dissertation, University of Ottawa, 2007) at 41–51.

22 For some examples of this, see Borrows, *supra* note 1 at 29–30 (his mother's legal reasoning related to observation of butterflies and milkweeds) and at 32–35 (Gitksan legal reasoning "reading" a landmark connected to the *Adaawk* regarding respect of animals).

23 Webber contrasts this with legal scholarship from an external viewpoint, which focuses on "historical and sociological accounts of the very same body of law": Jeremy Webber, "The Past and Foreign Countries" (2006) 10 Legal History 1 at 2.

24 Borrows, *supra* note 1 at 238.

25 Webber, *supra* note 5 at 590.

26 Napoleon, *supra* note 8 at 47–48.

27 Borrows, *supra* note 1 at 243.

28 *Ibid* at 30–32 (fishing stock conservation issue) and 246–248 (alvar prairie development issue).

29 Robert Cover, "Nomos and Narrative" (1983) 97 Harv L Rev 4 at 5.

# 8

# The Legal Concept of Sustainability

NATASHA AFFOLDER*

## 1. Introduction

Over one hundred Canadian federal, provincial, and territorial statutes now recognize the legal concepts of sustainability and sustainable development.[1] But accusations that these concepts are meaningless continue to mount. Ambiguous, vague, amorphous, and inadequate are other frequently voiced charges.[2] Have over one hundred Canadian laws been drafted or rewritten to incorporate a meaningless concept? The purpose of this chapter is to argue that the legal concept of sustainability is meaningful and a significant factor in the current Canadian legal landscape. The compilation of references to "sustainable development" (in Table 8.1) and "sustainability" (in Table 8.2) in Canadian federal, provincial, and territorial statutes, together reveal a widespread legislative intent to integrate sustainability thinking into Canadian law. This transformation might be missed if the sustainability language of only a single statute is viewed in isolation. What these compilations together evidence is the cumulative impact of the rewording, redrafting, and amending of legislation to acknowledge sustainability in Canadian law. The challenges inherent in articulating the precise definition and contours of the concept of sustainability do not rob it of meaning or legal significance.

Operationalizing sustainability is challenging, but it does not require the assertion of a single, precise, limited, and uncontroversial definition. To operationalize means to put something into effect, and it is here, at the operational stage, that sustainability has sputtered and stalled. Sustainability, like justice

* *The author thanks Sascha Paruk and Nicholas Healey for their excellent research assistance, especially the compilation and updating of the tables of legislation that appear in Tables 8.1 and 8.2.*

or democracy or equality or fairness, is a contestable concept.[3] This does not mean that it lacks meaning. Rather, like other contestable concepts, the challenge is to interpret the meaning of sustainability in practice. This is a task that courts have long undertaken with other contestable concepts and which this chapter seeks to advance. Consider, for example, the important contributions of Canadian judges in developing thoughtful and multi-dimensional understandings of equality and fairness. This work has advanced through individual judgments that are alert to both formal and substantive dimensions of equality, to differential treatment, and to the dimensions of accountability and transparency of decision making that shape the concepts of fairness and equality. Similar work can be done with the concept of sustainability.

Of course, sustainability is about more than law. It is about moving society towards ecologically sustainable patterns of production and consumption. But law is an integral part of this shift. This chapter proceeds in six parts. Following this introduction, Part 2 discusses how legal meaning can be gleaned from the concept of sustainability. It draws on both the history of the concept of sustainability and multidisciplinary sources. It also further refines the concept of sustainability by pushing beyond the idea that sustainability is simply about "balancing" competing demands. The core principles or components of the legal concept of sustainability are the subject of Part 3. Part 4 discusses the integration of sustainability in Canadian statutes. Part 5 reinforces the legal significance of the international origins of the concept of sustainability. And Part 6 concludes.

## 2. Finding Meaning in the Concept of Sustainability

Before engaging with the legal concept of sustainability in more depth, some introductory comments on the relationship between sustainability and sustainable development are needed. Sustainable development and sustainability are used interchangeably, although they have distinct meanings. Sustainability focuses on the capacity for humans to live within environmental and social constraints.[4] It incorporates respect for ecological limits in affirming that economic activity must proceed within the limits of ecological systems. Indeed, ecological integrity is at the very core of the concept of sustainability. Sustainability thus predates the late twentieth-century concept of sustainable development.[5] Sustainable development has emerged as the principal expression and application of sustainability. Sustainable development has traditionally been the favoured way of framing concerns about sustainability in Canadian legislation, although a number of recent statutes, particularly in

British Columbia and Ontario, have adopted the language of sustainability instead.[6] "Sustainable" development is economic development that is based on ecological sustainability.

The starting point for this discussion of the legal concept of sustainability is that sustainability is both meaningful and significant.[7] The Ministry for the Environment in New Zealand expressed the primacy of sustainability in this way: "Sustainability is a general concept and should be applied in law in much the same way as other general concepts such as liberty, equality and justice."[8] By approaching sustainability like other fundamental concepts, we can at once appreciate the meaning that sustainability can have, despite the difficulty in categorically defining the concept.[9] Thinking about sustainability in a way similar to how we think about justice is not misguided. Living at the expense of future generations and the natural environment is unsustainable and unjust.[10] The environmental and social justice underpinnings of the concept can thus be mutually reinforcing.

## FRAMING SUSTAINABLE DEVELOPMENT: THE *BRUNDTLAND REPORT* DEFINITION

The definition of sustainable development advanced in the *Brundtland Report*—"development that meets the needs of the present without compromising the ability of future generations to meet their own needs"—now dominates Canadian statutory definitions of sustainable development.[11] The *Brundtland Report* recognizes that human needs must be met within environmental limitations. A weak approach to interpreting sustainable development in the wake of the *Brundtland Report* frames sustainable development as requiring a consideration of environmental effects.

A stronger approach to sustainable development mandates the *integration* of sustainability considerations in the development process. This stronger approach is more consistent with the international legal articulations of sustainable development that have followed the *Brundtland Report*, notably Principle 4 of the *Rio Declaration*, which asserts that "in order to achieve sustainable development, environmental protection shall constitute *an integral part of the development process* and cannot be considered in isolation from it."[12] Such an approach is consistent with the *Brundtland Report* itself, which urges the "merging" of environment and economics in decision making. This means not only that environmental impacts should be taken into account, but that the objective and substance of policies and legal approaches should be modified to give effect to ecological integrity. The *Brundtland Report* definition offers guidance in asserting that, in order for development to be sustainable, "the ability of future generations to meet their own needs" cannot be compromised.

While the *Brundtland Report* serves as the basis for the definition of sustainable development in Canadian statutes, it is also the source of significant misunderstanding about the meaning of sustainable development. A common misperception about sustainable development is that it simply requires the balancing of three equally important "pillars"—economic, environmental, and social.[13] Formulated in such a way, it is easy to sympathize with critics who suggest sustainable development is an unhelpful concept, largely devoid of meaning. No guidance on this balancing appears to be given.

## UNDERSTANDING INTEGRATION: BEYOND BALANCING

Part of the challenge of relying on the *Brundtland Report's* definition of sustainable development as a basis for the concept in Canadian law arises from the fact that the report was written to respond to a particular *international* context. The *Brundtland Report* explicitly addresses the task of reconciling the needs of the global "North" and "South" and contemplates "development" in those terms. The emphasis on development thus emerges from a context of respect for the right of development in developing nations. And the social justice underpinning of the concept is animated by the goals of reducing and eliminating extreme poverty in the world. In some ways, the economic development language of the report has been speciously carried over to the domestic contexts of industrialized countries, trapping sustainable development in an unhelpful tripartite language that downgrades the ecological core of the concept and obscures its social dimensions. As a result, it is easy to get lost in the enormous "idea space" that sustainable development has come to envelop, particularly given the wide scope of the United Nation's Sustainable Development Goals.[14]

Sustainability qualifies development. It requires development to be approached in a manner that is sustainable, meaning *ecologically* sustainable. There is a difference when a statute talks about "water resource management" versus "sustainable water resource management." The intentional introduction of the word "sustainable" *cannot* be presumed to be without meaning. Sustainable modifies the term that follows, and signals that water resource management, for example, is to be based on ecological sustainability. John Dernbach usefully centres the word "development" in sustainable development. He explains that, given the fact that *integrated* decision making is the fundamental action principle in sustainable development, that development is a concept that risks being misunderstood.[15]

Finding meaning in the concept of sustainability (and its application through sustainable development) involves moving beyond the language of balancing, and recognizing instead the ecological and social core of this concept. Sustainable development is development that can happen within the "carrying capacities" of the biosphere. This idea draws from two sources. First, it derives from the ecological concept of "carrying capacity"—which reflects the population that an ecosystem can support. The second source is the economic concept of "maximum sustainable yield," which reflects the upper limit of use of resources that will permit the same level of use in the future.[16] Central to both the ecological and economic concepts here is that natural ecosystems can only sustain a certain amount and type of economic activity.

Sustainability thinking has evolved considerably in the years since the original 1987 *Brundtland Report* was released. Much of this evolution has emerged through international policy developments, and through an ongoing diffusion of ideas between and among national and sub-national governments, international lawmaking venues, and non-state actors. As a result, significant legal content resides in the environmental principles that underlie conceptions of sustainable development. Together these principles infuse the language of sustainability with meaning, and recalibrate the core of the concept to emphasize integration, rather than a simple and unweighted "balancing" of interests.

## 3. Key Components

Sustainability functions as an overarching principle that is intended to reorient economic activity away from "business as usual" and unsustainable approaches to more systematically incorporate social and ecological concerns. It has both procedural and substantive implications. The normative aspect of sustainability is rarely discussed absent reference to certain principles, including the principle of integration, the principle of intergenerational equity, the precautionary principle, the polluter pays principle, the principle of ecological integrity, and the principle of participation. This is not to suggest that sustainability is simply an umbrella term encompassing these other principles. Sustainability has legal meaning on its own. Vaughan Lowe suggests that a useful way to approach the relationship between sustainable development and its constituent parts is to think about sustainability as a meta-principle.[17] Klaus Bosselmann writes:

> [O]ne premier role of the law is to promote fundamental principles, often expressed in constitutions and human rights catalogues, and

> ensure that the legal process is reflective of them. If sustainability is perceived as one of such fundamental principles, the legal process will have to be reflective of it. If, by contrast, the principle of sustainability is perceived as just one of any array of environmental principles, it will compete with these and almost certainly vanish in the politics of governments still fixated on economic growth and international competition.[18]

For lawyers, a key question is the legal status of these principles, many of which derive from international law. A disciplined approach to using these principles acknowledges that their legal status differs. One example is the precautionary principle, which in some legal systems is a principle of law, and in other systems is an approach that guides decision making. In European Union law, the precautionary principle has achieved constitutional recognition in the form of Article 191 of the *Treaty on the Functioning of the European Union*.[19] In Canada, the precautionary principle is reflected in a growing number of statutes.[20] Below, I highlight a number of principles that are especially pertinent to the Canadian context. This is an admittedly cursory and incomplete treatment of the principles shaping discussions of sustainability in Canadian law. Numerous authors have developed much fuller discussions of these principles and their relevance for "court practitioners."[21] Some frequently cited environmental principles relevant to sustainability thus include:

(a) *Precautionary Principle* – The precautionary principle stipulates that "[w]here there are threats of serious or irreversible damage, lack of full scientific certainty should not be used as a reason for postponing measures to prevent environmental degradation."[22] This principle asserts that in cases dealing with environmental harm, it is not necessary to await full proof or certainty of that harm. The principle has been widely accepted in many countries, including Canada.

(b) *Intergenerational Equity* – The theory of intergenerational equity forces today's decision makers to explicitly consider future generations. Central to the theory is the requirement that each generation use and develop its natural and cultural heritage in such a way that it can be passed onto future generations in no poorer condition than it was received.[23] The principle of intergenerational equity is central to the *Brundtland Report* definition of sustainable development: "development that meets the needs of the present without compromising the ability of future generations to meet their own needs."[24] This principle highlights the long-term time frame inherent in sustainability decision making. Intergenerational equity is operationalized in Canadian legislation through, for example, commitments to keep protected areas intact for future generations and requirements to sustain renewable natural resources.[25]

(c) *Conservation of Biological Diversity and Ecological Integrity* – While the principles of conservation of biological diversity and ecological integrity are principles of sustainable development in their own right, the operation of other elements of sustainability, such as the precautionary principle and intergenerational equity, also serve to advance these principles.[26] Biological diversity describes genetic diversity, species diversity, and ecosystem diversity.[27] Ecological integrity is described as "the conservation of the earth's life-support systems."[28] It signals the need to maintain ecosystem health and ecosystem services.

(d) *Environment-Economy Integration* – The concept of integrating environmental considerations into economic planning is pivotal to sustainable development. One commentator goes so far as to suggest that this principle of integrated decision making is what holds the other principles together.[29] The formal application of the principle of integration requires, at the very least, the collection of appropriate environmental information and the performance of appropriate environmental impact assessment.[30] Integration takes seriously the need to "green" the economy and extends far beyond traditional environmental or resource management legislation.

(e) *Internalization of Environmental Costs* – Internalization of environmental costs requires accounting for both the short and long-term external environmental impacts of development.[31] One aspect of the internalization of environmental costs, the polluter pays principle, has been described by the Supreme Court of Canada as "firmly entrenched in environmental law in Canada."[32] However, the principle of internalization of environmental costs extends beyond the polluter pays principle to require pricing that reflects full life cycle costs of producing and disposing of goods, also known as the "user pays" principle.

(f) *Participation* – Participation is particularly critical to implementing sustainability. Sustainability depends, to a considerable degree, on the way that environmental, social, and economic considerations are integrated in decision making. Participatory rights have been articulated as including the opportunity to participate in decision-making processes, access to information, and access to justice.[33]

These principles do not exist in isolation from one another. Indeed, courts have advanced the legal concept of sustainability by recognizing the interaction of these principles. One example of this emerges from the Land and Environment Court in New South Wales. In *Gray v. The Minister for Planning*,[34] Justice Pain interpreted the legal concept of sustainability, through the precautionary principle and the principle of intergenerational equity, as requiring the provision of certain types of information in the environmental impact assessment process. She held that in order to account for intergenerational equity, as the statute required, an "assessment of cumulative impacts of proposed activities on the environment"[35] had to be included.

## 4. Sustainability and Canadian Statutes

This is not the place for a detailed analysis of sustainability in Canadian statutes. But a few observations are in order. First, as Tables 8.1 and 8.2 reveal, the legal concept of sustainability has made significant inroads in Canadian statutes. The legislative landscape is certainly uneven, but it is not barren. While the tables of legislation only reference legislative incorporation of sustainable development and sustainability, the key principles underlying these concepts are, at times, independently asserted in Canadian statutes.[36] Moreover, there are some powerfully developed conceptions of sustainability and what it requires now contained in some of the provincial statutes. The Quebec *Sustainable Development Act* deserves special mention here, as it highlights the "necessary change within society" required to reorient development away from unsustainable economic activity:

> The measures introduced by this Act are intended, more specifically, to bring about the necessary change within society with respect to non-viable development methods by further integrating the pursuit

> of sustainable development into the policies, programs and actions of the Administration, at all levels and in all areas of intervention. They are designed to ensure that government actions in the area of sustainable development are coherent and to enhance the accountability of the Administration in that area, in particular through the controls exercised by the Sustainable Development Commissioner under the Auditor General Act.[37]

Given the significance of "objects and purposes" language such as this, and indeed given the sheer number of statutes now referencing sustainability in some way, it is perhaps surprising that little judicial ink has yet to be spilt elaborating the meaning of sustainable development in Canadian legislation. Adjudicating the significance of legislative references to sustainability is admittedly an unenviable task given the lack of developed definitions in existing statutes and the widespread and often overgeneralized scholarly and policy backdrop to the relevant terminology. This chapter has sought to clarify the meaning of the legal concept of sustainability and, in so doing, to allow the underlying principles to emerge, principles that assist with the task of interpreting this body of legislation.

While judicial consideration of Canadian statutory provisions on sustainability is not extensive, the ecological core of sustainability has been identified and acknowledged by Canadian judges. The importance of ecological integrity as a "fundamental value in Canadian society" has been affirmed by the Supreme Court of Canada in a series of judgments. Justice Binnie, writing for the majority in *British Columbia v. Canadian Forest Products*, summarized this judicial history:

> As the Court observed in *R. v. Hydro-Québec*, [1977] 3 SCR 213, at para. 85, legal measures to protect the environment "related to a public purpose of superordinate importance." In *Friends of the Oldman River Society v. Canada (Minister of Transport)*, [1992] 1 SCR 3, the Court declared at 16 that "[t]he protection of the environment has become one of the major challenges of our time." In *Ontario v. Canadian Pacific Ltd.*, [1995] 2 SCR 1031, "stewardship of the natural environment" was described as a fundamental value (para. 55; italics in original). Still more recently, in *114957 Canada Ltée (Spraytech Société d'arrosage) v. Spraytech (Town)*, [2001] 2 SCR 241, 2001 SCC 40, the Court reiterated at para. 1: "... our common future, that of every Canadian community,

> depends on a healthy environment ..." This Court has recognized that "[e]veryone is aware that individually and collectively, we are responsible for preserving the natural environment .... Environmental protection [has] emerged as a fundamental value in Canadian society."[38]

Significantly, Canadian judges have also used the concept of sustainable development to give legal meaning to other statutory requirements, such as the polluter pays principle. In *Imperial Oil v. Quebec (Minister of the Environment)*, Justice LeBel, writing for a unanimous full bench of the court, situated the polluter pays principle in the context of sustainable development:

> *To encourage sustainable development*, [the polluter pays] principle assigns polluters the responsibility for remedying contamination for which they are responsible and imposes on them the direct and immediate costs of pollution. At the same time, polluters are asked to pay more attention to the need to protect ecosystems in the course of their economic activities.[39]

Importantly, Canadian judges and administrative decision makers have also rejected an approach to sustainable development that frames this concept as simply a balancing of competing pressures. The appellant in *Re Ainsworth Lumber Co.*[40] argued that the principle of sustainable development requires that environmental protection measures be weighed against economic factors. In this case, that would mean an abandonment of the requirement of the best available technology, as there were economic arguments to favour a lower-cost approach. The Alberta Environmental Appeal Board firmly concluded that sustainable development did not support the use of the lowest-cost emissions control alternative by the appellant.[41] In so doing, the board affirmed that the core of sustainable development requires "that resources should be developed in a manner that is sustainable for the use by future generations."[42]

The legal concepts of sustainability and sustainable development have not been introduced in a mere handful of Canadian statutes over the past two decades. They have been inserted into over one hundred pieces of legislation. The cumulative impact of this rewriting of Canadian law to respect the concept of sustainability signals something greater than a requirement that competing interests be balanced. Rather, the density of references in Canadian legislation to sustainability and sustainable development suggests that legally significant expectations are crystallizing around these concepts.

## 5. A Concept of International Relevance

International law is relevant in interpreting Canadian statutory approaches to sustainability for at least two reasons: first, because of the presumption of conformity with international law, a rule of legal interpretation that mandates that Canadian law be read consistently with Canada's international law obligations;[43] and second, through the incorporation of customary international law and the implementation of treaties.[44] The legal concept of sustainability is grounded in the historical development of international law and continues to operate in an international normative context.

More pragmatically, it is also instructive to look to the practice of international courts and tribunals to understand how to operationalize the legal concept of sustainability. I turn now to two such examples, one from the International Court of Justice and one from the Appellate Body of the World Trade Organization.

### THE GABČÍKOVO-NAGYMAROS DAM CASE (HUNGARY/SLOVAKIA)

In the *Gabčíkovo-Nagymaros Dam Case*, the concept of sustainability is evoked by Judge Weeramantry of the International Court of Justice absent a specific treaty provision on sustainability or even arguments on sustainability by counsel. Judge Weeramantry drew upon the legal concept of sustainable development as an element of legal reasoning at the discretion of the court. This use is consistent with the status of sustainability as a fundamental legal principle. Judge Weeramantry explains how sustainability forces us to depart from traditional approaches to decision making:

> Throughout the ages, mankind has, for economic and other reasons, constantly interfered with nature. In the past, this was often done without consideration of the effects upon the environment. Owing to new scientific insights and to a growing awareness of the risks for mankind—for present and future generations—of pursuit of such interventions at an unconsidered and unabated pace, new norms and standards have been developed, set forth in a great number of instruments, during the last two decades. Such new norms have to be taken into consideration, and such new standards given proper weight, not only when States contemplate new activities but also when continuing with activities begun in the past. This need to reconcile economic development with protection of the environment is aptly expressed in the concept of sustainable development.

> For the purposes of the present case, this means that the Parties together should look afresh at the effects on the environment of the operation of the Gabčíkovo power plant.[45]

Judge Weeramantry asserts that sustainable development demands "looking afresh" at environmental impacts that may have been acceptable in the past. This need to force decision-making practices to catch up with the demands of sustainable development and the prioritization of ecological integrity is a theme that is affirmed by the Appellate Body of the WTO in its Shrimp-Turtle I decision.

### SHRIMP-TURTLE I

The wording of the Preamble of the *Marrakesh Agreement Establishing the World Trade Organization* (*WTO Agreement*) provides that WTO members' relations in the field of trade and economic endeavors should be conducted in a way that "[allows] for the optimal use of the world's resources in accordance with the objective of sustainable development, seeking both to protect and preserve the environment and to enhance the means for doing so in a manner consistent with their respective needs and concerns at difference levels of economic development."[46]

In the 1998 Shrimp-Turtle I dispute, the Appellate Body of the WTO was tasked with interpreting the meaning of "exhaustible natural resources" in Article XX(g) of GATT. The provision had been written 50 years earlier. The Appellate Body held that these words "must be read by a treaty interpreter in the light of contemporary concerns of the community of nations about the protection and conservation of the environment."[47] It relied upon the preambular reference to sustainable development in the 1995 *WTO Agreement* quoted above in its decision: "As [the preambular reference to sustainable development] reflects the intentions of negotiators of the WTO Agreement, we believe it must add colour, texture, and shading to our interpretation of the agreements."[48] Such a reading led to the interpretation that the protection of sea turtles fell within the meaning of exhaustible natural resources.

These two examples illustrate that the task of clearly articulating the legal concept of sustainability remains a work in progress. It is a task being taken up by judges and court practitioners around the world.[49] The legal concept of sustainability is an evolving concept but one which, at its core, affirms that economic activity happens within an acceptable framework of social justice and within ecological limits.

## 6. Conclusion: Defining Sustainability by Its Absence

Sustainability is a concept with legal meaning. It recognizes the social and ecological limits on economic activity. It is easy to understand how attempts to apply sustainability, through sustainable development, have obscured the legal meaning and significance of sustainability. Sustainable development has mistakenly been framed as containing only the normative content of mandating balancing, requiring compromise between economic, environmental, and social demands.

This chapter has sought to clarify these concepts and the key principles underlying sustainability. In so doing, examples of how Canadian, foreign, and international courts and tribunals have sought to operationalize these principles have been provided. The task now is to move beyond simply recognizing that sustainability is a meaningful legal concept to demonstrating how it can also be a powerful concept in Canadian law. To do this, the unsustainable practices and trajectories upon which the Canadian economy is proceeding must be identified and addressed.[50] Ultimately, the content of the legal concept of sustainability in Canada will only develop when there is a willingness to identify and name unsustainable development.

**Table 8.1 | References to Sustainable Development in Canadian Legislation**

| *Jurisdiction* | *Name of Legislation* | *Section Number and Heading* | *Language* |
|---|---|---|---|
| Canada (Federal) | *Agreement on Internal Trade Implementation Act*, SC 1996, c 17 | Preamble | "Sustainable development" |
| | | S 2 - definitions | "Sustainable development" |
| | | S 7(2)(f) - Annual and additional reports [by the Auditor General] to the House of Commons | "Sustainable development" |
| | *Auditor General Act*, RSC 1985, c A-17 | S 7.1(1)(e) - Inquiry and report | "Sustainable development" |
| | | S 15.1(1) - Appointment of Commissioner | "Sustainable development" |
| | | S 15.1(2) - Commissioner's duties | "Sustainable development" |
| | | S 21.1 - Purpose | "Sustainable development" |
| | | S 22(1) - Petitions received | "Sustainable development" |
| | | S 23(1)(a) - Duty to monitor | "Sustainable development" |

**Table 8.1 | *continued***

| *Jurisdiction* | *Name of Legislation* | *Section Number and Heading* | *Language* |
|---|---|---|---|
| | | S 23(2)(a)&(c) - Commissioner's report | "Sustainable development" |
| | | S 23(3) - Duty to examine | "Sustainable development" |
| | *Budget Implementation Act*, 2007, SC 2007, c 29 | S 124 - Maximum payment of $30,000,000 [to BC] | "Fair and equitable economic development, in an environmentally sustainable and ecologically integrated manner" |
| | *Canada-Chile Free Trade Agreement Implementation Act*, SC 1997, c 14 | Preamble | "Sustainable development" |
| | *Canada-Colombia Free Trade Agreement Implementation Act*, SC 2010, c 4 | S 7(h) - Purpose | "Sustainable development" |
| | *Canada-Costa Rica Free Trade Agreement Implementation Act*, SC 2001, c 28 | Preamble | "Sustainable development" |
| | *Canada-European Union Comprehensive Economic and Trade Agreement Implementation Act*, SC 2017, c 6 | S 7(i) - Purpose | "Sustainable development" |
| | *Canada-Honduras Economic Growth and Prosperity Act*, SC 2014, c 14 | S 7(h) - Purpose | "Sustainable development" |
| | *Canada-Jordan Economic Growth and Prosperity Act*, SC 2012, c 18 | S 7(f) - Purpose | "Sustainable development" |
| | *Canada-Korea Economic Growth and Prosperity Act*, SC 2014, c 28 | S 7(h) - Purpose | "Sustainable development" |
| | *Canada-Panama Economic Growth and Prosperity Act*, SC 2012, c 26 | S 7(h) - Purpose | "Sustainable development" |
| | *Canada-Peru Free Trade Agreement Implementation Act*, SC 2009, c 16 | S 7(h) - Purpose | "Sustainable development" |
| | *Canada-Ukraine Free Trade Agreement Implementation Act*, SC 2017, c 8 | S 7(g) - Purpose | "Sustainable development" |

**Table 8.1 | *continued***

| *Jurisdiction* | *Name of Legislation* | *Section Number and Heading* | *Language* |
|---|---|---|---|
| | *Canada Foundation for Sustainable Development Technology Act*, SC 2001, c 23 | S 2 - Definitions | "Sustainable development" |
| | | S 11(a)(i)&(c) - Director representation and experience | "Sustainable development" |
| | | S 15(a)(i)&(c) - Member representation and experience | "Sustainable development" |
| | | S 32(1) - Property to be divided [upon winding up of the Foundation] | "Sustainable development" |
| | *Canadian Environmental Assessment Act*, 2012 - SC 2012, c 19, s 52 | S 2 - Definitions | "Sustainable development" |
| | | S 4(1)(h) - Purposes | "Sustainable development" |
| | *Canadian Environmental Protection Act*, 1999, SC 1999, c 33 | Preamble | "Sustainable development" |
| | | S 3 - Definitions | "Sustainable development" |
| | | S 54(2)(d) - Scope of [Minister's] objectives | "Sustainable development" |
| | *Department of Foreign Affairs, Trade and Development Act*, SC 2013, c 33, s 174 | S 10(2)(f) - Powers, duties and functions of Minister | "Sustainable international development" |
| | | S 10(3)(b) - Programs | "Sustainable international development" |
| | | S 14 - Minister for International Development | "Sustainable international development" |
| | *Department of Industry Act*, SC 1995, c 1 | S 5(a) - Objectives | "Sustainable development" |
| | *Department of Natural Resources Act*, SC 1994, c 41 | S 2 - Definitions | "Sustainable development |
| | | S 6(a) - General duties | "Sustainable development" |
| | *European Bank for Reconstruction and Development Agreement Act*, SC 1991, c 12 | S 7 - Annual Report | "Sustainable development" |
| | | Schedule, Ch 1, Art 2(1)(vii) - Functions | "Sustainable development" |
| | *Federal Sustainable Development Act*, SC 2008, c 33 | S 2 - Definitions | "Sustainable development" |
| | | S 3 - Purpose | "Sustainable development" |
| | | S 5 - Basic principles of sustainable development | "Sustainable development" |
| | *First Nations Fiscal Management Act*, SC 2005, c 9 | S 29(f) - Mandate | "Sustainable economic development" |
| | *National Seal Products Day Act*, SC 2017, c 5 | Preamble | "Sustainable development" |
| | *North American Free Trade Agreement Implementation Act*, SC 1993, c 44 | Preamble | "Sustainable development" |

**Table 8.1 | *continued***

| *Jurisdiction* | *Name of Legislation* | *Section Number and Heading* | *Language* |
|---|---|---|---|
| | *Oceans Act*, SC 1996, c 31 | Preamble | "Sustainable development" |
| | | S 30(a) - Principles of [national oceans] strategy | "Sustainable development" |
| | | S 40(2) - encouragement of activities [by the relevant Minister] | "Sustainable development" |
| | *Official Development Assistance Accountability Act*, SC 2008, c 17 | S 2(1) - Purpose | "Sustainable development" |
| | | S 3 - Definitions | "Sustainability" |
| | *Pest Control Products Act*, SC 2002, c 2 | Preamble | "Sustainable pest management" and "sustainable development" |
| | | S 4(2)(a) - Ancillary objectives | "Sustainable development" and "sustainable pest management" |
| | *Standards Council of Canada Act*, RSC, 1985, c S-16 | S 4 - Mandate | "Sustainable development" |
| | *World Trade Organization Agreement Implementation Act*, SC 1994, c 47 | Preamble | "Sustainable development" |
| Alberta | *Alberta Land Stewardship Act*, SA 2009, c A-26.8 | S 1(2)(d) - Purposes of Act | "Sustainable development" |
| | *Climate Change and Emissions Management Act*, SA 2003, c C-16.7 | Preamble | "Environmentally sustainable technologies" and "sustainable development" |
| | *Environmental Protection and Enhancement Act*, RSA 2000, c E-12 | S 2(c) - Purpose of Act | "Sustainable development" |
| | | S 6(1) - Purpose of Co-ordinating Council | "Sustainable development" |
| | | S 40(a) - Purpose of environmental assessment process | "Sustainable development" |
| British Columbia | *Park Act*, RSBC 1996, c 344 | S 5(3.1)(d) - Classification of parks, conservancies and recreation areas | "Development ... in a sustainable manner" |
| Manitoba | *The Capital Region Partnership Act*, SM 2005, c 32, CCSM c C23 | S 2(c) - Purpose | "Sustainable economic development" |
| | *The Climate Change and Emissions Reduction Act*, SM 2008, c 17, CCSM c C135 | Preamble | "Sustainable economic development" |
| | | S 2 - Purpose | "Sustainable economic development" |
| | *The Conservation Agreements Act*, SM 1997, c 59, CCSM c C173 | Preamble | "Sustainable development" |

## Table 8.1 | *continued*

| *Jurisdiction* | *Name of Legislation* | *Section Number and Heading* | *Language* |
|---|---|---|---|
| | *The Conservation Districts Act*, RSM 1987, c C175, CCSM c C175 | S 3(4) - Appointing public representatives [to the Conservation Districts Commission] | "Sustainable development" |
| | *The Contaminated Sites Remediation Act*, SM 1996, c 40, CCSM c C205 | S 1(1) - Purpose | "Sustainable development" |
| | | S 1(2) - Principles of sustainable development | "Sustainable development" |
| | *The East Side Traditional Lands Planning and Special Protected Areas Act*, SM 2009, c 7, CCSM c E3 | S 10(1)(a) - Agreement to develop management plan | "Sustainable development" |
| | *The Energy Act*, SM 1994, c 3, CCSM c E112 | S 2 - Objects and Purposes | "Sustainable development" |
| | | S 3 - Principles of sustainable development | "Sustainable development" |
| | | S 4(f)&(l) - Functions of the department | "Sustainable development" |
| | *The Fisheries Act*, RSM 1987, c F90, CCSM c F90 | S 14.3(1)(f) - Powers of Minister | "Develop ... in a sustainable manner" |
| | *The Mines and Minerals Act*, SM 1991-92, c 9, CCSM c M162 | S 2(1) - Object and purpose of Act | "Sustainable development" |
| | | S 2(2) - Sustainable development | "Sustainable development" |
| | *The Oil and Gas Act*, SM 1993, c 4, CCSM c O34 | S 2(1)(a) - Objects and purposes of act | "Sustainable development" |
| | | S 2(2) - Principles of sustainable development | "Sustainable development" |
| | | S 113(3)(b) - Consideration of application by Minister | "Sustainable development" |
| | | S 149(3)(b) - Consideration of application by Minister | "Sustainable development" |
| | | S 153(4)(b) - Consideration of application by Minister | "Sustainable development" |
| | | S 162(2)(b) - Consideration of application by Minister | "Sustainable development" |
| | *The Peatlands Stewardship Act*, SM 2014, c 27, CCSM c P31 | S 3(1)(b) - Purposes | "Development ... in a sustainable manner" |
| | | S 3(2)(d)&(f) - Principles | "Sustainably managed" and "sustainability" |
| | *The Planning Act*, SM 2005, c 30, CCSM c P80 | S 4(1) - Provincial land use policies | "Sustainable land use and development" |
| | | S 17(1) - Establishment of planning district | "Sustainable land use and development" |
| | | S 42(1) - Requirements of development plan | "Sustainable land use and development" |

**Table 8.1 | *continued***

| *Jurisdiction* | *Name of Legislation* | *Section Number and Heading* | *Language* |
|---|---|---|---|
| | | S 62.2(3)(b)(iii) - Content [of drinking water and wastewater management plans] | "Sustainability" |
| | *The Provincial Parks Act*, SM 1993, c 39, CCSM c P20 | Preamble | "Sustainable development" |
| | *The Sustainable Development Act*, SM 1997, c 61, CCSM c S270 | S 1 - Definitions | "Sustainability" and "sustainable development" |
| | | S 2 - Purpose | "Sustainable development" |
| | | S 4(1)(b) - Manitoba Round Table Established | "Sustainable development" |
| | | S 4(2)(a)&(f) - Duties of Manitoba Round Table | "Sustainable development" and "sustainability" |
| | | S 4(3)(c)(d)&(d.1) - Powers of the Manitoba Round Table | "Sustainable development" |
| | | S 5(b)(c)(i)(iii)(iv)&(v) - Responsibilities of the Department of Conservation and Water Stewardship | "Sustainable development" and "sustainability" |
| | | S 6(1)&(2) - Principles and guidelines for sustainable development enumerated | "Sustainable development" |
| | | S 7(1)(2)&(3) - Sustainable development strategies | "Sustainable development" and "sustainability" |
| | | S 9(1) - Provincial sustainability indicators established | "Sustainability" |
| | | S 10(1)(2)&(4) - Provincial sustainability report required | "Sustainability" |
| | | S 11(1)(a) - Provincial Code shall be established | "Sustainable development" |
| | | S 12(1)(a)&(c) - Financial management guidelines and reporting | "Sustainability" and "sustainable development" |
| | | S 12(2)(a)(i)&(ii) - Procurement guidelines | "Sustainable development" |
| | | S 13 - Crown corporations to adopt [sustainable development] code of practice | "Sustainable development" |
| | | S 14(e) - Crown corporations to adopt [sustainable development] guidelines | "Sustainable development" |

**Table 8.1 | *continued***

| *Jurisdiction* | *Name of Legislation* | *Section Number and Heading* | *Language* |
|---|---|---|---|
| | | S 15(a) - Guidelines for local authorities and others - "sustainability" | "Sustainability" |
| | | S 16(1)(a)&(b) - Review may be required [by Minister] | "Sustainable development" |
| | | S 17(2)(a)&(b) - Purpose of [the Sustainable Development Innovations] Fund | "Sustainability," and "sustainable development" |
| | | Schedule A - Principles of Sustainable Development | "Sustainable development" |
| | | Schedule B - Guidelines for Sustainable Development | "Sustainable development" |
| | *The Waste Reduction and Prevention Act*, SM 1989-90, c 60, CCSM c W40 | S 1(1) - Purpose | "Sustainable development" |
| | | S 1(2) - Principles of sustainable development | "Sustainable development" |
| New Brunswick | *Environmental Trust Fund Act*, RSNB 2011, c 151 | S 3(a)(iii)&(v) - Uses of assets of Fund | "Sustainable development" |
| | *Maritime Economic Cooperation Act*, SNB 2014, c 118 | S 3(1)(d) - Maritime cooperation | "Sustainable development" |
| | *Seafood Processing Act*, SNB 2006, c S-5.3 | S 79(c) - Agreements | "Sustainable development" |
| | | S 80(b) - Policies, guidelines, programs and other measures | "Sustainable development" |
| Newfound-land and Labrador | *Aquaculture Act*, RSNL 1990, c A-13 | S 4(6)(a)(ii) - Aquaculture licence | "Sustainable development" |
| | | S 11.2(a) - Regulations | "Sustainable development" |
| | *Cruiseship Authority Act*, SNL 1998, c C-44 | S 7(l) - Powers of Authority | "Sustainable development" |
| | *Environmental Protection Act*, SNL 2002, c E-14.2 | S 2(kk) - Definitions | "Sustainable development" |
| | | S 5(1)(a)(c)(e)&(f) - Research | "Sustainable development" |
| | *Foresters Act*, SNL 2011, c F-22.1 | S 2(j)(i) - Definitions | "Sustainable forest management" |
| | *Forestry Act*, RSNL 1990, c F-23 | S 2(f)(f.2)(r)(r.1)&(s) - Definitions | "Sustainable forest management" and "sustainable development" |
| | | S 6(2)(3)(4)&(5) - Timber resource analysis | "Sustainable forest management strategy" |
| | | S 7(3)(4)(5)(6)&(7) - Forest Management District | "Sustainable forest management" and "sustainable development" |

**Table 8.1 | *continued***

| *Jurisdiction* | *Name of Legislation* | *Section Number and Heading* | *Language* |
|---|---|---|---|
| | | S 38(o) - Regulations | "Sustainable forest management" |
| | | S 113(1)&(2)(a) - Construction or abandonment to be approved | "Sustainable forest management" and "sustainable forestry practices" |
| Northwest Territories | *Northwest Territories Business Development and Investment Corporation Act*, SNWT 2005, c 3 | S 5(3.1) - Considerations [in the Board of Directors exercising its powers and performing its duties] | "Sustainable development" |
| | | S 40(a) - Regulations | "Sustainable development" |
| Nova Scotia | *Environment Act*, SNS 1994-95, c 1 | S 2(b) - Purpose of Act | "Sustainable development" |
| | | S 3(as)&(aw) - Interpretation | "Sustainability," and "sustainable development" |
| | | S 8(2)(a) - Minister responsible for Act | "Sustainable development" |
| | | S 9(3)(b) - Advisory committees, experts and Round Table | "Sustainability" |
| | | S 27(1)(a)(c)(e)&(f) - Education and research | "Sustainable development" |
| | | S 104(a)&(b) - Lead agency | "Sustainable development" |
| | | S 156(1)&(2)(c) - Lead agency | "Sustainable environmental industries, innovations and technologies" and "sustainable environmental innovations, technologies and services" |
| | *Environmental Goals and Sustainable Prosperity Act*, SNS 2007, c 7 | S 2(g)&(h) - Interpretation | "Sustainability" and "sustainable prosperity" |
| | | S 3(2)(b)(f)&(g) - Foundation and principles of Act | "Environmentally sustainable economic development," "sustainability" and "sustainable prosperity" |
| | | S 4(1)(a)(2)(a)(q)(r)(s)& (3)(b) - Long-term objectives of Province | "Sustainable prosperity," "sustainable practices," "sustainable management," and "sustainable uses of energy" |
| | | S 5(m) - Sectoral agreements | "Sustainable prosperity" |
| | | S 6(1) - Review and annual reports | "Sustainability," and "sustainable prosperity" |
| | | S 7(1)(da)&(f) - Programs and measures | "Sustainable practices," and "sustainable prosperity" |
| | | S 8(2) - Agreements | "Sustainable prosperity |

Table 8.1 | *continued*

| *Jurisdiction* | *Name of Legislation* | *Section Number and Heading* | *Language* |
|---|---|---|---|
| | *Foresters Association Act*, SNS 1999 (2d Sess), c 6 | S 2(k) - Interpretation | "Sustainable development" |
| | *Internal Trade Agreement Implementation Act*, SNS 1995-96, c 8 | S 2 - Purpose of Act | "Sustainable development" |
| | *Maritime Economic Cooperation Act*, SNS 1992, c 7 | S 3(1)(d) - Guiding principles | "Sustainable development" |
| | *Mineral Resources Act*, SNS 1990, c 1 | S 1A - Purpose of Act | "Sustainable development" |
| | *Municipal Government Act*, SNS 1998, c 18 | Schedule B - Statements of Provincial Interest, Introduction | "Sustainable development" |
| Ontario | *Endangered Species Act*, 2007, SO 2007, c 6 | Preamble | "Sustainable social and economic development" |
| | | S 48(h) - Advisory committee | "Sustainable social and economic activities" |
| | *Far North Act*, 2010, SO 2010, c 18 | S 5 - Objectives for Land Use Planning | "Sustainable economic development" |
| | *Planning Act*, RSO 1990, c P.13 | S 1.1(a) - Purposes | "Sustainable economic development" |
| | | S 2(q) - Provincial interest | "Development that is designed to be sustainable" |
| | | S 42(6.2) - Redevelopment, reduction of payment | "Sustainability" |
| Prince Edward Island | *Maritime Economic Cooperation Act*, RSPEI 1988, c M-1.1 | S 3 - Principles [of Maritime Cooperation] | "Sustainable development" |
| Québec | *Act Establishing the Eeyou Istchee James Bay Regional Government*, CQLR c G-1.04 | S 32 - Miscellaneous provisions | "Sustainable development" |
| | *Act Respecting Commercial Aquaculture*, CQLR c A-20.2 | S 2 - Frameworks for Aquaculture Development | "Sustainable development" |
| | *Act Respecting Contracting by Public Bodies*, CQLR c C-65.1 | S 2(4) - Purpose and scope | "Sustainable development" |
| | *Act Respecting La Financière Agricole du Québec*, CQLR c L-0.1 | S 3 - Establishment and mission | "Sustainable development" |

Table 8.1 | *continued*

| *Jurisdiction* | *Name of Legislation* | *Section Number and Heading* | *Language* |
|---|---|---|---|
| | *Act Respecting Land Use Planning and Development*, CQLR c A-19.1 | S 2.24 - Content of metropolitan plan | "Sustainable development" |
| | | S 6(8)&(9) - Contents of the plan | "Sustainable development," "sustainable forest development" and "sustainable land use and development" |
| | | S 79.1 - Planting or felling of trees | "Sustainable development" |
| | | S 84(8) - Contents of the planning program | "Sustainable urban planning" |
| | | S 113(12.1) - Zoning by-laws | "Sustainable development" |
| | *Act Respecting the Autorité Régionale de Transport Métropolitain*, CQLR c A-33.3 | S 5 - Mission | "Sustainable development" |
| | *Act Respecting the Conservation and Development of Wildlife*, CQLR c C-61.1 | Preliminary provision | "Sustainable development" |
| | *Act Respecting the Institut de la Statistique du Québec*, CQLR c I-13.011 | S 3.1 - Establishment, mission and functions | "Sustainable development" |
| | *Act Respecting the Ministère de l'Agriculture, des Pêcheries et de l'Alimentation*, CQLR c M-14 | S 2(1) - The Minister and his functions | "Sustainable development" |
| | | S 23 - Development of the agricultural and food sectors | "Sustainable development" |
| | *Act Respecting the Ministère de l'Enseignement Supérieur, de la Recherche, de la Science et de la Technologie*, CQLR c M-15.1.0.1 | S 2 - Responsibility of the Minister | "Sustainable development" |
| | *Act Respecting the Ministère des Affaires Municipales, des Régions et de l'Occupation du Territoire*, CQLR c M-22.1 | S 21.4.1 - Table Québec-Montréal Métropolitain pour l'Aménagement et le Développement | "Sustainable development" |
| | | S 21.4.3 - Table Québec-Québec Métropolitain pour l'Aménagement et le Développement | "Sustainable development" |
| | | S 21.7 - Regional Development in the Nord-du-Québec Region | "Sustainable development" |

**Table 8.1 | *continued***

| *Jurisdiction* | *Name of Legislation* | *Section Number and Heading* | *Language* |
|---|---|---|---|
| | *Act Respecting the Ministère des Ressources Naturelles et de la Faune*, CQLR c M-25.2 | S 11.1 - Functions and powers of the Minister | "Sustainable development" |
| | | S 11.3 - Functions and powers of the Minister | "Sustainable development" |
| | | S 17.12.12(2) - Natural resources fund | "Sustainable forest development" |
| | | S 17.12.15 - Natural resources fund | "Sustainable forest development" |
| | | S 17.14 - Regional development program | "Sustainable development" |
| | | S 17.24.1 - Management delegation | "Sustainable development" |
| | *Act Respecting the Ministère du Développement Durable, de l'Environnement et des Parcs*, CQLR c M-30.001 | S 10 - Functions and powers | "Sustainable development" |
| | | S 12(2.1) - Functions and powers | "Sustainability" |
| | | S 15.1(2) - Green fund | "Sustainable management of hazardous materials" |
| | | S 15.4(4) - Green fund | "Sustainable development" |
| | | S 15.4.7 - Establishment of the Conseil du Gestion du Fonds Vert | "Sustainable development" |
| | | S 15.4.40(5) - Fund for the protection of the environment and the waters in the domain of the state | "Sustainable development" |
| | | S 15.4.41 - Fund for the protection of the environment and the waters in the domain of the state | "Sustainable development" |
| | *Act Respecting the Ministère du Développement Économique, de l'Innovation et de l'Exportation*, CQLR c M-30.01 | S 2 - Minister's responsibilities | "Sustainable development" |
| | *Act Respecting the Ministère du Tourisme*, CQLR c M-31.2 | S 2 - Minister's responsibilities | "Sustainable development" |
| | *Act Respecting the Preservation of Agricultural Land and Agricultural Activities*, CQLR c P-41.1 | S 1.1 - Interpretation and scope | "Sustainable development" |
| | | S 59.2 - Applications of collective scope [regarding Agricultural Zones] | "Sustainable development" |

**Table 8.1 | *continued***

| *Jurisdiction* | *Name of Legislation* | *Section Number and Heading* | *Language* |
|---|---|---|---|
| | *Act Respecting the Régie de l'Énergie*, CQLR c R-6.01 | S 5 - Establishment | "Sustainable development" |
| | | S 74.1 - Obligations of the electric power carrier and of distributors | "Sustainability" |
| | *Act Respecting the Société du Plan Nord*, CQLR c S-16.011 | S 4 - Mission | "Sustainable development" |
| | *Act Respecting Transition Énergétique Québec*, CQLR c T-11.02 | S 4 - Mission and activities | "Sustainable economic development" |
| | *Act to Affirm the Collective Nature of Water Resources and to Promote Better Governance of Water and Associated Environments*, CQLR c C-6.2 | Preamble | "Sustainable development," and "sustainably use [environments associated with water resources]" |
| | | S 3 - Water, a collective resource | "Sustainable development" |
| | | S 13 - Measures related to governance of water and associated environments | "Sustainable development" |
| | | S 15.2(1)(c) - Regional planning related to wetlands and bodies of water | "Sustainable use" |
| | | S 15.9(6) - Program to promote the restoration and creation of wetlands and bodies of water | "Sustainability" |
| | *Act to Ensure the Occupancy and Vitality of Territories*, CQLR c O-1.3 | Preamble | "Occupancy and vitality ... in a sustainable manner" |
| | | S 3 - Purpose and scope | "Sustainable development" |
| | | S 5 - Strategy | "Sustainable development" |
| | *Act to Modify Mainly the Organization and Governance of Shared Transportation in the Montréal Metropolitan Area*, CQLR c O-7.3 | S 2(2) - Purpose | "Sustainable development" |
| | *Auditor General Act*, CQLR c V-5.01 | S 17 - The Auditor General | "Sustainable development" |
| | | S 26(8) - Audit and reports | "Sustainable development" |
| | | S 43.1 - Annual and special reports | "Sustainable development" |
| | *Charter of Ville de Montréal*, CQLR c C-11.4 | S 86.1 - General provisions | "Sustainable development" |
| | *Cultural Heritage Act*, CQLR c P-9.002 | S 1 - Objects, definitions and scope | "Sustainable development" |

**Table 8.1 | *continued***

| *Jurisdiction* | *Name of Legislation* | *Section Number and Heading* | *Language* |
|---|---|---|---|
| | *Environment Quality Act*, CQLR c Q-2 | Preamble | "Sustainable development" |
| | | S 31 - Protection of the environment | "Sustainable development" |
| | | S 31.76 - Withdrawal of surface water or groundwater | "Sustainable ... management of the resources" |
| | | S 31.101(4)&(1) - Withdrawal of surface or groundwater | "Sustainable use of the waters" and "sustainable management" |
| | | S 46.0.1 - Wetlands and bodies of water | "Sustainable development" |
| | | S 95.10 - Strategic environmental assessment | "Sustainable development" |
| | *James Bay Region Development Act*, CQLR c D-8.0.1 | S 4 - Constitution of the Société [de développement de la Baie James] | "Sustainable development" |
| | *Mining Act*, CQLR c M-13.1 | Preamble | "Sustainable diversification of the regions' economies" |
| | | S 17 - Object and scope | "Sustainable development" |
| | *Sustainable Development Act*, CQLR c D-8.1.1 | S 1 - Preliminary provisions | "Sustainable development" |
| | | S 2 - Preliminary provisions | "Sustainable development" |
| | | S 5 - Sustainable development principles and strategy | "Sustainable development" |
| | | S 6 - Sustainable development principles and strategy | "Sustainable development," and "sustainability" |
| | | S 7 - Sustainable development principles and strategy | "Sustainable development" |
| | | S 9 - Sustainable development principles and strategy | "Sustainable development" |
| | | S 10 - Sustainable development principles and strategy | "Sustainable development" |
| | | S 11 - Sustainable development principles and strategy | "Sustainable development" |
| | | S 12 - Sustainable development principles and strategy | "Sustainable development" |
| | | S 13 - Sustainable development principles and strategy | "Sustainable development" |

Table 8.1 | *continued*

| *Jurisdiction* | *Name of Legislation* | *Section Number and Heading* | *Language* |
|---|---|---|---|
| | | S 14 - Sustainable development principles and strategy | "Sustainable development" |
| | | S 15 - Sustainable development principles and strategy | "Sustainable development" |
| | | S 17 - Sustainable development principles and strategy | "Sustainable development" |
| | *Sustainable Forest Development Act*, CQLR c A-18.1 | Preamble | "Sustainable development" and "sustainable forest development" |
| | | S 1(1) - Object, scope and other provisions | "Sustainable forest development" |
| | | S 5 - Object, scope and other provisions | "Sustainable forest development" |
| | | S 6 - Provisions specific to Native communities | "Sustainable forest development" |
| | | S 7 - Provisions specific to Native communities | "Sustainable forest development" |
| | | S 8 - Provisions specific to Native communities | "Sustainable forest development" |
| | | S 9 - Consultation policy | "Sustainable forest development" |
| | | S 11 - Sustainable forest development strategy | "Sustainable forest development" |
| | | S 12 - Sustainable forest development strategy | "Sustainable development" and "sustainable forest development" |
| | | S 16 - Development units | "Sustainable forest development" |
| | | S 20 - Teaching and research forests | "Sustainable forest development" |
| | | S 38 - Forest development standards | "Sustainable forest development" |
| | | S 45 - Chief forester | "Sustainable development" |
| | | S 46(3)(5)(7)&(9) - Chief forester | "Sustainable forest development" |
| | | S 46.1 - Chief forester | "Sustainable forest development" |
| | | S 48(1) - Chief forester | "Sustainable forest development" and "sustainability" |
| | | S 52 - Responsibilities of the Minister | "Sustainable development" and "sustainable forest development" |

Table 8.1 | *continued*

| *Jurisdiction* | *Name of Legislation* | *Section Number and Heading* | *Language* |
|---|---|---|---|
| | | S 54 - Integrated forest development plans | "Sustainable forest development" |
| | | S 55 - Integrated forest development plans | "Sustainable forest development" |
| | | S 86.3 - Forestry permits | "Sustainable development" |
| | | S 88 - Timber supply guarantees | "Sustainable development" |
| | | S 119 - Timber marketing | "Sustainable development" |
| | | S 128 - Plans and programs | "Sustainable development" |
| | | S 149 - Objects | "Sustainable forest development" |
| | | S 224(2)&(3) - Reporting | "Sustainable forest development" |
| Saskatchewan | *The Agri-Food Innovation Act*, SS 1995, c A-15.3 | S 4(2)(c) - Objects and purposes | "Sustainable agricultural development" |
| | *The Fisheries Act (Saskatchewan), 1994*, SS 1994, c F-16.1 | S 9(k) - Powers of Minister | "Conserve, develop, maintain, enhance, manage and utilize ... in a sustainable manner" |
| | *The Forest Resources Management Act*, SS 1996, c F-19.1 | S 3 - Purpose | "Sustainable use of forest land |
| | | S 6(1)(j) - Powers of minister | "Utilize ... in a sustainable manner" |
| | | S 7(1)(k) - Power to enter into agreements | "Conserving, developing, enhancing, maintaining, managing, protecting and utilizing ... in a sustainable manner" |
| | | S 12(1) - Provincial forests | "Managed in a sustainable manner" |
| | | S 45(1.1) - Plans re term supply licence | "Sustainability" |
| | *The Litter Control Act*, RSS 1978, c L-22 | S 2.1(d)(iii) - Powers of Minister | "Sustainable development" |
| | *Natural Resources Act*, SS 1993, c N-3.1 | S 4(1)(h) - Powers of the Minister | "Conserve, develop, manage and utilize ... in a sustainable manner" |
| | *Planning and Development Act*, 2007, SS 2007, c P-13.2 | S 3(c) - Purposes of the Act | "Development of ... sustainable communities" |
| | | S 32(2)(a) - Contents of [an official community] plan | "Sustainable ... land use and development" |
| | | S 97(1)(a)(ii)(c) - Agreement for establishment of planning district | "Sustainability" |
| | | S 111(3)(e) - Northern planning commission | "Sustainability" |

**Table 8.1 | *continued***

| *Jurisdiction* | *Name of Legislation* | *Section Number and Heading* | *Language* |
|---|---|---|---|
| Yukon | *Economic Development Act*, RSY 2002, c 60 | Preamble | "Sustainable economy," "sustainable development goals" and "sustainable economic development" |
| | | S 1 - Interpretation | "Sustainable development" |
| | | S 2(c) - Goals of the Government | "Sustainable development" |
| | | S 3(2)(e) - Work of the Department | "Sustainable development" |
| | | S 7(1)(e) - Yukon Council on the Economy and the Environment | "Sustainable development" |
| | *Environment Act*, RSY 2002, c 76 | S 2 - Definitions | "Sustainable development" |
| | | S 5(1)(c) - Objectives | "Sustainable development" |
| | | S 39(1)(a)&(c) - Responsibilities of the members of the executive council | "Sustainable development" |
| | | S 41(1)&(2)(d) - Powers and duties of the Council | "Sustainable development" |
| | | S 44(b) - Purpose of the Yukon conservation strategy | "Sustainable development" |
| | | S 52(1)(c) - Inter-jurisdictional and circumpolar cooperation | "Sustainable development" |
| | | S 54(b) - Partnership with the Government of Canada | "Sustainable development" |
| | | S 57(a) - Incentives and assistance | "Sustainable development" |
| | | S 82(a) - Purpose of development approval process | "Sustainable development" |
| | | S 141(b) - Regulations concerning Part 3 | "Sustainable development" |
| | *Oil and Gas Act*, RSY 2002, c 162 | S 2(b) - Objectives of the Act | "Sustainable development" |
| | *Parks and Land Certainty Act*, RSY 2002, c 165 | Preamble (i) | "Sustainable economic development" and "sustainable development" |
| | *Yukon Development Corporation Act*, RSY 2002, c 236 | S 5(c) - Objects | "Sustainable development" |

**Table 8.2 | References to other Sustainability Language in Canadian Legislation**

| *Jurisdiction* | *Name of Legislation* | *Section Number and Heading* | *Language* |
|---|---|---|---|
| Canada (Federal) | *Canada Marine Act*, SC 1998, c 10 | S 25(a)(iii) - No appropriation | "Sustainability" |
| | *Canada National Marine Conservation Areas Act*, SC 2002, c 18 | Preamble | "Ecologically sustainable" |
| | | S 4(3) - Management and use | "Managed and used in a sustainable manner" |
| | | S 4(4) - Zones | "Ecologically sustainable" |
| | *Canada Transportation Act*, SC 1996, c 10 | S 5 - Declaration [on National Transportation Policy] | "Sustainable environment" |
| | *Farm Income Protection Act*, SC 1991, c 22 | S 4(2)(e) - Statement of principles | "Sustainability" |
| | | S 5(2)(e) - Environmental requirements to be provided for in agreements | "Sustainability" |
| | *Fisheries Act*, RSC 1985, c F-14 | S 6.1 - Purpose | "Sustainability" |
| | *International Boundary Waters Treaty Act*, RSC 1985, c I-17 | S 37(1)(f) - Orders of Court | "Sustainable water resource management" |
| | *International River Improvements Act*, RSC 1985, c I-20 | S 45(1)(g) - Orders of Court | "Sustainable water resource management" |
| | *Migratory Birds Convention Act*, 1994, SC 1994, c 22 | Schedule | "Sustainable uses [in migratory bird population management]" |
| | *Official Development Assistance Accountability Act*, SC 2008, c 17 | S 3 - Definitions | "Sustainability" |
| | *Parks Canada Agency Act*, SC 1998, c 31 | Preamble (h) | "Ecologically sustainable" |
| | *Pest Control Products Act*, SC 2002, c 2 | Preamble | "Sustainable pest management" and "sustainable development" |
| | | S 4(2)(a) - Ancillary objectives | "Sustainable development" and "sustainable pest management" |
| | *Rouge National Urban Park Act*, SC 2015, c 10 | Preamble | "Sustainable farming practices" |
| | | S 9(2)(b) - Area management approach | "Sustainable farming practices" |
| Alberta | *Agricultural Service Board Act*, RSA 2000, c A-10 | S 2(d) - Agricultural service board duties | "Sustainable agriculture" |
| | *Climate Change and Emissions Management Act*, SA 2003, c C-16.7 | Preamble | "Environmentally sustainable technologies" and "sustainable development" |

**Table 8.2 | *continued***

| *Jurisdiction* | *Name of Legislation* | *Section Number and Heading* | *Language* |
|---|---|---|---|
| | *Forests Act*, RSA 2000, c F-22 | S 16(1) - Forest management agreements | "Sustainable forest management" |
| | *Renewable Electricity Act*, SA 2016, c R-16.5 | S 1(l)(v) - Definitions | "Sustainable biomass [as a form of renewable energy resource]" |
| British Columbia | *Nisga'a Final Agreement Act*, RSBC 1999, c 2 | Ch 8, s 39 - General [on Nass steelhead] | "Sustainable harvest [of Nass steelhead]" |
| | | Ch 9, s 99(b) - Objects of [Lisims Fisheries Conservation] Trust | "Sustainable management of fisheries" |
| | *Range Act*, SBC 2004, c 71 | S 53(4) - Earned increase in animal unit months or quantity of hay | "Sustainable [increase in animal unit months or quantity of hay on Crown range]" |
| | *Tla'amin Final Agreement Act*, SBC 2013, c 2 | Schedule, Ch 7, s 22(a) - Groundwater | "Sustainability" |
| | *Water Protection Act*, RSBC 1996, c 484 | S 2 - Purpose | "Sustainable use of British Columbia's water resources" |
| | *Water Sustainability Act*, SBC 2014, c 15 | S 1(1) - Definitions | "Water sustainability plan" |
| | | S 17(3)(a)(i) - Sensitive streams mitigation | "Sustainability" |
| | | S 128(2)(a) - Regulations respecting sensitive streams | "Sustainability" |
| Manitoba | *The CentrePort Canada Act*, SM 2008, c 45, CCSM c C44 | S 3(a)(iv) - Mandate of the Corporation | "Environmentally sustainable" |
| | *The Labour-Sponsored Venture Capital Corporations Act*, SM 1997, c 39, CCSM c L12 | S 6(1)(b) - Investment policies and criteria | "Sustainability" |
| | *The Manitoba Agricultural Services Corporation Act*, SM 2005, c 28, CCSM c A25 | S 1 - Definitions | "Sustainability" |
| | | S 9(a) - Purposes | "Sustainability" |
| | *The Peatlands Stewardship Act*, SM 2014, c 27, CCSM c P31 | S 3(2)(d)&(f) - Principles | "Sustainably managed" and "sustainability" |
| | *The Planning Act*, SM 2005, c 30, CCSM c P80 | S 62.2(3)(b)(iii) - Content [of drinking water and wastewater management plans] | "Sustainability" |
| | *The Sustainable Development Act*, SM 1997, c 61, CCSM c S270 | S 1 - Definitions | "Sustainability" and "sustainable development" |
| | | S 4(2)(a)&(f) - Duties of Manitoba Round Table | "Sustainable development" and "sustainability" |

Table 8.2 | *continued*

| *Jurisdiction* | *Name of Legislation* | *Section Number and Heading* | *Language* |
|---|---|---|---|
| | | S 5(b)(c)(i)(iii)(iv)&(v) - Responsibilities of the Department of Conservation and Water Stewardship | "Sustainable development" and "sustainability" |
| | | S 7(1)(2)&(3) - Sustainable development strategies | "Sustainable development" and "sustainability" |
| | | S 9(1) - Provincial sustainability indicators established | "Sustainability" |
| | | S 10(1)(2)&(4) - Provincial sustainability report required | "Sustainability" |
| | | S 12(1)(a)&(c) - Financial management guidelines and reporting | "Sustainability" and "sustainable development" |
| | | S 15(a) - Guidelines for local authorities and others - "sustainability" | Sustainability" |
| | | S 17(2)(a)&(b) - Purpose of [the Sustainable Development Innovations] Fund | "Sustainability" and "sustainable development" |
| | *The Water Protection Act*, SM 2005, c 26, CCSM c W65 | S 25(e) - Responsibilities of the Water Council | "Sustainability" |
| | *The Water Resources Conservation Act*, SM 2000, c 11, CCSM c W72 | Preamble | "Sustainable water resource management practices" |
| New Brunswick | *Community Planning Act*, SNB 2017, c 19 | S 2(a) - Purposes of Act | "Development of environmentally, economically, socially and culturally sustainable communities" |
| | | S 13(2)(b) - Establishing statement of provincial interest | "Development of environmentally, socially and culturally sustainable communities" |
| | *Electricity Act*, SNB 2013, c 7 | S 100(2) - Integrated Resource Plan | "Sustainability" |
| Newfoundland and Labrador | *Foresters Act*, SNL 2011, c F-22.1 | S 2(j)(i) - Definitions | "Sustainable forest management" |
| | *Forestry Act*, RSNL 1990, c F-23 | S 2(f)(f.2)(r)(r.1)&(s) - Definitions | "Sustainable forest management" and "sustainable development" |
| | | S 6(2)(3)(4)&(5) - Timber resource analysis | "Sustainable forest management strategy" |

Table 8.2 | *continued*

| *Jurisdiction* | *Name of Legislation* | *Section Number and Heading* | *Language* |
|---|---|---|---|
| | | S 7(3)(4)(5)(6)&(7) - Forest Management District | "Sustainable forest management" and "sustainable development" |
| | | S 38(o) - Regulations | "Sustainable forest management" |
| | | S 113(1)&(2)(a) - Construction or abandonment to be approved | "Sustainable forest management," and "sustainable forestry practices" |
| Northwest Territories | *Community Planning and Development Act*, SNWT 2011, c 22 | S 3(1) - Purpose [of community plans] | "Sustainability" |
| Nova Scotia | *Community Easements Act*, SNS 2012, c 2 | S 4(2)(f) - Nature and purpose of community easement | "Sustainable and responsible use of lands" |
| | *Endangered Species Act*, SNS 1998, c 11 | S 2(1)(b)&(g) - Purpose | "Use ... in a sustainable manner" and "sustainable management practices" |
| | *Environment Act*, SNS 1994-95, c 1 | S 3 (as)&(aw) - Interpretation | "Sustainability" and "sustainable development" |
| | | S 9(3)(b) - Advisory committees, experts and Round Table | "Sustainability" |
| | | S 156(1)&(2)(c) - Lead agency | "Sustainable environmental industries, innovations and technologies" and "sustainable environmental innovations, technologies and services" |
| | *Environmental Goals and Sustainable Prosperity Act*, SNS 2007, c 7 | S 2(g)&(h) - Interpretation | "Sustainability" and "sustainable prosperity" |
| | | S 3(2)(b)(f)&(g) - Foundation and principles of Act | "Environmentally sustainable economic development," "sustainability" and "sustainable prosperity" |
| | | S 4(1)(a)(2)(a)(q)(r)(s)& (3)(b) - Long-term objectives of Province | "Sustainable prosperity," "sustainable practices," "sustainable management" and "sustainable uses of energy" |
| | | S 5(m) - Sectoral agreements | "Sustainable prosperity" |
| | | S 6(1) - Review and annual reports | "Sustainability" and "sustainable prosperity" |
| | | S 7(1)(da)&(f) - Programs and measures | "Sustainable practices" and "sustainable prosperity" |
| | | S 8(2) - Agreements | "Sustainable prosperity" |

**Table 8.2 | *continued***

| *Jurisdiction* | *Name of Legislation* | *Section Number and Heading* | *Language* |
|---|---|---|---|
| | *Fish Harvesters Registration and Certification Board Act*, SNS 2012, c 5 | S 2(d) - Purpose of Act | "Sustainability" |
| | *Forests Act*, RSNS 1989, c 179 | S 7 - Principles of forest management programs | "Sustainable forest management" |
| | | S 19(2) - Buyer of forest products | "Sustainable basis" |
| | | S 40(j) - Regulations | "Sustainable forest practices" |
| | *Fur Industry Act*, SNS 2010, c 4 | S 4(f)&(g) - Powers of Minister | "Sustainability" |
| | *Petroleum Resources Removal Permit Act*, SNS 1999, c 7 | S 2 - Purpose of Act | "Sustainable use of petroleum resources" |
| | *Public Service Act*, RSNS 1989, c 378 | S 38(b) - Powers of Minister | "Sustainability" |
| | *Tourism Nova Scotia Act*, SNS 2015, c 10 | S 14 - Objects of Corporation | "Sustainable tourism" |
| | *Water Resources Protection Act*, SNS 2000, c 10 | Preamble | "Sustainability" |
| Nunavut | *Wildlife Act*, SNu 2003, c 26 | S 1(2)(i) - Values | "Use in a sustainable manner" |
| Ontario | *City of Toronto Act, 2006*, SO 2006, c 11, sched A | Preamble | "Sustainable city" |
| | *Climate Change Mitigation and Low-Carbon Economy Act*, SO 2016, c 7 | Preamble | "Live, work and travel in sustainable ways ..." |
| | *Crown Forest Sustainability Act, 1994*, SO 1994, c 25 | S 1 - Purposes | "Sustainability" |
| | | S 2(1)(2)&(3) - Sustainability | "Sustainability" |
| | | S 9(2) - Criteria for approval [of a forest management plan] | "Sustainability" |
| | | S 26(1) - Sustainable forest licenses | "Sustainability" |
| | | S 27(3)(a) - Agreements | "Sustainability" |
| | | S 42(2) - Exception [to conduct of forest operations] | "Sustainability" |
| | | S 55(1) - Damage by forest operations | "Sustainability" |
| | | S 68(3)(b)(c)&(d) - Forest management planning manual | "Sustainability" |

Table 8.2 | *continued*

| *Jurisdiction* | *Name of Legislation* | *Section Number and Heading* | *Language* |
|---|---|---|---|
| | *Electricity Act*, 1998, SO 1998, c 15, sched A | S 1(a)&(g) - Purposes | "Sustainability" |
| | *Environmental Bill of Rights*, 1993, SO 1993, c 28 | S 2(1)(b) - Purposes of Act | "Sustainability" |
| | *Great Lakes Protection Act*, 2015, SO 2015, c 24 | S 1(2) - Purposes | "Environmentally sustainable economic opportunities, innovation and environmentally sustainable use of natural resources" |
| | *Greenbelt Act*, 2005, SO 2005, c 1 | S 5(k) - Objectives | "Sustainable resource use" |
| | *Housing Services Act*, 2011, SO 2011, c 6, sched 1 | S 4(1)(l) - Provincial interest | "Sustainability" |
| | *Lake Simcoe Protection Act*, 2008, SO 2008, c 23 | Preamble | "Environmentally sustainable land and water uses" |
| | | S 4(b)(h)&(i) - Objectives of [the Lake Simcoe Protection] Plan | "Environmentally sustainable recreational activities" and "environmentally sustainable land and water uses" |
| | *Metrolinx Act*, 2006, SO 2006, c 16 | S 5(1)(a)(iii) - Objects | "Sustainable environment" |
| | *Nutrient Management Act*, 2002, SO 2002, c 4 | S 1 - Purpose | "Sustainable future for agricultural operations and rural development" |
| | *Ontario Forest Tenure Modernization Act*, 2011, SO 2011, c 10 | S 5 - Objects of [an Ontario local forest management] corporation | "Sustainability" |
| | *Ontario Water Resources Act*, RSO 1990, c O.40 | S 0.1 - Purpose | "Sustainable use [of Ontario's waters]" |
| | | S 75(1.5) - Regulations, charges | "Sustainable use [of Ontario's waters]" |
| | *Planning Act*, RSO 1990, c P.13 | S 2(q) - Provincial interest | "Development that is designed to be sustainable" |
| | | S 42(6.2) - Redevelopment, reduction of payment | "Sustainability" |
| | *Provincial Parks and Conservation Reserves Act*, 2006, SO 2006, c 12 | S 1 - Purpose | "Ecologically sustainable recreation" |
| | | S 2(1) - Objectives: provincial parks | "Ecologically sustainable outdoor recreation" |
| | | S 2(2) - Objectives: conservation reserves | "Ecologically sustainable land uses" |
| | *Water Opportunities Act*, 2010, SO 2010, c 19, sched 1 | S 1(1)(c) - Purposes | "Conserve and sustain water resources for present and future generations" |
| | | S 25(1) - Water sustainability plan | "Sustainability" |

**Table 8.2 | *continued***

| *Jurisdiction* | *Name of Legislation* | *Section Number and Heading* | *Language* |
|---|---|---|---|
| Prince Edward Island | *Institute of Man and Resources Act*, RSPEI 1988, c I-3 | S 3(a)&(d) - Objects and purposes | "Ecologically sustainable" and "environmentally sustainable" |
| | *Trails Act*, RSPEI 1988, c T-4.1 | S 7(a) - Principles of management | "Sustainable use of the trail as a public resource" |
| Québec | *Act Respecting Land Use Planning and Development*, CQLR c A-19.1 | S 84(8) - Contents of the planning program | "Sustainable urban planning" |
| | *Act Respecting the Ministère du Développement Durable, de l'Environnement et des Parcs*, CQLR c M-30.001 | S 12(2.1) - Functions and powers | "Sustainability" |
| | | S 15.1(2) - Green fund | "Sustainable management of hazardous materials" |
| | *Act Respecting the Régie de l'Énergie*, CQLR c R-6.01 | S 74.1 - Obligations of the electric power carrier and of distributors | "Sustainability" |
| | *Act to Affirm the Collective Nature of Water Resources and to Promote Better Governance of Water and Associated Environments*, CQLR c C-6.2 | Preamble | "Sustainable development" and "sustainably use [environments associated with water resources]" |
| | | S 15.2(1)(c) - Regional planning related to wetlands and bodies of water | "Sustainable use" |
| | | S 15.9(6) - Program to promote the restoration and creation of wetlands and bodies of water | "Sustainability" |
| | *Act to Ensure the Occupancy and Vitality of Territories*, CQLR c O-1.3 | Preamble | "Occupancy and vitality ... in a sustainable manner" |
| | *Environment Quality Act*, CQLR c Q-2 | S 31.76 - Withdrawal of surface water or groundwater | "Sustainable ... management of the resources" |
| | | S 31.101(4)&(1) - Withdrawal of surface or groundwater | "Sustainable use of the waters," and "sustainable management" |
| | *Mining Act*, CQLR c M-13.1 | Preamble | "Sustainable diversification of the regions' economies" |
| | *Natural Heritage Conservation Act*, CQLR c C-61.01 | S 1 - Objects, definitions and scope | "Sustainable use [of natural heritage and the ecosystem it comprises]" |
| | *Sustainable Development Act*, CQLR c D-8.1.1 | S 6 - Sustainable development principles and strategy | "Sustainable development" and "sustainability" |
| | *Sustainable Forest Development Act*, CQLR c A-18.1 | S 48(1) - Chief forester | "Sustainable forest development" and "sustainability" |

**Table 8.2 | *continued***

| *Jurisdiction* | *Name of Legislation* | *Section Number and Heading* | *Language* |
|---|---|---|---|
| Saskatchewan | *The Forest Resources Management Act*, SS 1996, c F-19.1 | S 3 - Purpose | "Sustainable use of forest land |
| | | S 6(1)(j) - Powers of minister | "Utilize ... in a sustainable manner" |
| | | S 12(1) - Provincial forests | "Managed in a sustainable manner" |
| | | S 45(1.1) - Plans re term supply licence | "Sustainability" |
| | *The Forestry Professions Act*, SS 2006, c F-19.2 | S 2(m) - Interpretation | "Sustainability" |
| | *The Innovation Saskatchewan Act*, SS 2009, c I-9.02 | S 4(a) - Purpose of agency [Innovation Saskatchewan] | "Long-term sustainable growth of Saskatchewan's economy" |
| | *The Irrigation Act*, SS 1996, c I-14.1 | S 12(c) - Objects and purposes [of an irrigation district] | "Sustainable irrigation" |
| | | S 43(d) - Objects and purposes of the Irrigation Crop Diversification Corporation | "Sustainable irrigation" |
| | *Planning and Development Act*, 2007, SS 2007, c P-13.2 | S 3(c) - Purposes of the Act | "Development of ... sustainable communities" |
| | | S 32(2)(a) - Contents of [an official community] plan | "Sustainable ... land use and development" |
| | | S 97(1)(a)(ii) (c) - Agreement for establishment of planning district | "Sustainability" |
| | | S 111(3)(e) - Northern planning commission | "Sustainability" |
| Yukon | *Economic Development Act*, RSY 2002, c 60 | Preamble | "Sustainable economy," "sustainable development goals" and "sustainable economic development" |
| | *Forest Resources Act*, SY 2008, c 15 | S 2 - Purpose | "Sustainable use ... for the benefit of current and future generations" |
| | | S 20(4) - Restrictions on harvesting licences | "Harvested sustainably" |
| | | S 27(4)(c) - Cutting permits | "Sustainability" |
| | *Quartz Mining Act*, SY 2003, c 14 | S 130 - Purpose of Part [land use and reclamation] | "Development and viability of a sustainable, competitive and healthy quartz mining industry" |

**Table 8.2 | *continued***

| *Jurisdiction* | *Name of Legislation* | *Section Number and Heading* | *Language* |
|---|---|---|---|
| | *Wilderness Tourism Licensing Act*, RSY 2002, c 228 | Preamble | "Sustain continuing public access and wilderness tourism sector use" |
| | | S 1 - Objective | "Sustain the wilderness quality of Yukon lands and waters" |
| | | S 14(1)(c) - Regulations | "Sustainability" |

## NOTES

1 See, at the end of this chapter, Table 8.1 and Table 8.2 – References to Sustainability and Sustainable Development in Canadian Legislation.

2 John C. Dernbach and Federico Cheever respond to three of the most pernicious challenges to sustainable development—that it is "too boring," "too vague," and "too late." John C. Dernbach and Federico Cheever, "Sustainable Development and Its Discontents" (2015) 4:2 Transnational Environmental Law 247.

3 Michael Jacobs, "Sustainable Development as a Contested Concept" in Andrew Dobson, ed, *Fairness and Futurity* (Oxford: Oxford University Press, 2004) 21 at 25 [Jacobs].

4 John Robinson, "Squaring the Circle? Some Thoughts on the Idea of Sustainable Development" (2004) 48 Ecological Economics 369 at 370.

5 Klaus Bosselmann, "Sustainability and the Courts: A Journey Yet to Begin?" (2010) 3:1 Journal of Court Innovation 337 at 338 [Bosselmann, "Courts"].

6 See Table 8.1 (tracking statutory use of "sustainable development") and Table 8.2 (listing the use of other "sustainability" language in statutes) to this chapter.

7 Klaus Bosselmann, *Principles of Sustainability: Transforming Law and Governance* (Abingdon, UK: Ashgate, 2008) at 9 [Bosselmann, "Principles"].

8 New Zealand, Ministry for the Environment, *Resource Management Law Reform: Sustainability, Intrinsic Values and the Needs of Future Generations*, Working Paper 24 (Wellington: Ministry for the Environment, 1989) at 9.

9 Bosselmann, "Principles," *supra* note 7 at 9.

10 *Ibid* at 10.

11 World Commission on Environment and Development, *Our Common Future* (Oxford: Oxford University Press, 1987) [*Brundtland Report*].

12 For a discussion of the principle of integration as articulated in other international instruments, see Alan Boyle & David Freestone, "Introduction" in Alan Boyle & David Freestone, eds, *International Law and Sustainable Development* (Oxford: Oxford University Press, 1999) 1 at 10.

13 Bosselmann, "Principles," *supra* note 7 at 23.

14 See United Nations, Sustainable Development Goals, online: <https://sustainabledevelopment.un.org/?menu=1300>.

15 Dernbach suggests that in countries like the United States there is a failure to grapple with the idea of the law of development, as such law is dismissed as only relevant to "developing countries." John C. Dernbach, "Creating the Law of Environmentally Sustainable Economic Development" (2011) 28:3 Pace Environmental Law Review 614.

16 Jacobs, *supra* note 3 at 31–32.

17 Vaughan Lowe, "Sustainable Development and Unsustainable Arguments" in Boyle & Freestone, *supra* note 12, 19 at 31.

18 Bosselmann, "Courts," *supra* note 5 at 346.

19 This is now reflected in art 191(2) of the Lisbon Treaty.

20 See Chris Tollefson & Jamie Thornback, "Litigating the Precautionary Principle in Domestic Courts" (2008) 19:1 J Envtl L & Prac 33.

21 See, e.g., Brian J. Preston, "The Role of the Judiciary in Promoting Sustainable Development: The Experience of Asia and the Pacific" (2005–06) 9:2–3 Asia Pacific Journal of Environmental Law 109; Eloise Scotford, *Environmental Principles and the Evolution of Environmental Law* (Oxford: Hart, 2017).

22 *114957 Canada Ltée (Spraytech Société d'arrosage) v Spraytech (Town)*, 2001 SCC 40, [2001] 2 SCR 241 at para 31, citing *Bergen Ministerial Declaration on Sustainable Development*, GA Res 44/228, UN GAOR, 1990, UN Doc A/CONF 151/PC/10.

23 See Edith Brown-Weiss, *In Fairness to Future Generations* (Dobbs Ferry, NY: Transnational Publishers, 1989).

24 *Brundtland Report*, *supra* note 11 at 43.

25 See Jerry DeMarco, "Law for Future Generations: A Theory of Intergenerational Equity in Canadian Environmental Law" (2005) 15 J Envtl L & Prac 1 at 27.

26 Hon Justice Brian J Preston, "Judicial Implementation of the Principles of Ecologically Sustainable Development in Australia and Asia" (Paper delivered at the Law Society of New South Wales Regional Presidents Meeting, Sydney, 21 July 2006) [Preston] (on file with author).

27 The components of biological diversity are discussed in John Moffet & Francois Bregha, "The Role of Law in the Promotion of Sustainable Development" (1996) 6 J Envtl L & Prac 1 at 5.

28 *Ibid* at 4.

29 John Dernbach, "Achieving Sustainable Development: The Centrality and Multiple Facets of Integrated Decision-Making" (2003) 10 Ind J Global Legal Stud 247 at 248.

30 Philippe Sands, "International Law in the Field of Sustainable Development: Emerging Legal Principles" in Winfried Lang, ed, *Sustainable Development and International Law* (London: Graham & Trotman, 1995) 53 at 61.

31 Preston, *supra* note 26 at 30.

32 *Imperial Oil Ltd v Quebec (Minister of the Environment)*, 2003 SCC 58 at para 23, [2003] 2 SCR 624 [*Imperial Oil*].

33 These three pillars of participation have emerged from the *Aarhus Convention*, signed in 1998. *Convention on Access to Information, Public Participation in Decision-making and Access to Justice in Environmental Matters*, 25 June 1998, 2161 UNTS 450, 38 ILM 517 [*Aarhus Convention*].

34 *Gray v The Minister for Planning*, [2006] NSWLEC 720.

35 *Ibid* at para 122.

36 See, e.g., the incorporation of the precautionary principle in the *Canadian National Marine Conservation Areas Act*, SC 2002, c 18, s 9(3); in the *Canadian Environmental Protection Act, 1999*, SC 1999, c 33, ss 2(1), 6(1); in the *Canadian Environmental Assessment Act*, SC 1992, c 37, s 4(2); in the *Oceans Act*, SC 1996, c 31, s 30; and in the *Federal Sustainable Development Act*, SC 2008, c 33, ss 2, 9(1).

37 *Sustainable Development Act*, RSQ c D-9.1.1, s 1.

38 *British Columbia v Canadian Forest Products Ltd*, 2004 SCC 38 at para 7, [2004] 2 SCR 74 [*Canfor*].

39 *Imperial Oil*, *supra* note 32 at para 24 (emphasis added).

40 *Re Ainsworth Lumber Co*, [2000] AEABD No 33.

41 *Ibid.*

42 *Ibid.*

43 *R v Hape*, 2007 SCC 26 at para 53.

44 For a fuller discussion of the reception of international environmental

law in Canada, see Natasha Affolder, "Domesticating the Exotic Species: International Biodiversity Law in Canada" (2006) 51 McGill LJ 217.

45 *Case Concerning the Gabčíkovo-Nagymaros Project (Hungary v Slovakia)*, [1997] ICJ Rep 7 at para 140.

46 *Marrakesh Agreement Establishing the World Trade Organization*, 15 April 1994, 1867 UNTS 154, 33 ILM 1144, at preamble [WTO *Agreement*].

47 WTO, Appellate Body, *United States—Import Prohibition of Certain Shrimp and Shrimp Products*, WTO Doc WT/DS58/AB/R (1998) at para 129, online: WTO <https://www.wto.org/english/tratop_e/dispu_e/58abr.pdf>.

48 *Ibid* at para 153.

49 In 2002, senior judges and chief justices from around the world signed the *Johannesburg Principles on the Role of Law and Sustainable Development*, affirming principles that should guide the judiciary. *Johannesburg Principles on the Role of Law and Sustainable Development* (Statement adopted at the Global Judges Symposium on Sustainable Development and the Role of Law, Johannesburg, South Africa, 18–20 August 2002) (2003) 15 J Envtl L 107.

50 On the problem of "Unsustainability" in Canada, see C. Scott Findlay, Jamie Benidickson, Hugh Benevides & Karen Kraft Sloan, "Sustainability Lost: Comments on 'Planning for a Sustainable Future: A Federal Sustainable Development Strategy for Canada'" (2010) 22:1 JELP 77 at 80.

# 9

# How Legal Design May Constrain the Power of Law to Implement Environmental Norms: The Case of Ecological Integrity in Canada's National Parks

SHAUN FLUKER

## Introduction

The struggle between advocates of "parks for people" and "parks for preservation" defines the modern history of Canada's national parks.[1] Historians and other scholars generally agree that Parliament designated Canada's early national parks to fulfill the public policy objective of nation building and to generate economic returns. At the forefront of any identifiable parks purpose was the satisfaction of recreational, economic, or spiritual interests of Canadians.[2] Since the late 1960s preservationists have battled this "parks for people" ideology governing Canada's national parks, applying pressure on Parliament to assert the preservation of nature *for its own sake* as the primary purpose in the parks. This pressure, in conjunction with various government studies conducted during the 1980s and 1990s, led to the enactment of new federal national parks legislation in 2001 that categorically mandates the maintenance or restoration of ecological integrity as the first priority in the national parks. This legislative priority for ecological preservation in national parks decision making has curiously not produced any discernible change from the "parks for people" ideology. Indeed, recent evidence suggests economic and recreational interests are actually becoming more rather than less influential in management decisions for certain parks.[3]

The objective of this chapter is twofold. First, the chapter sets out doctrinal analysis of applicable case law to support the view that the 2001 ecological integrity amendments to national parks legislation have had little impact on the "parks for people" ideology governing national parks. In a series of decisions interpreting this legislation, the Federal Court has repeatedly emphasized that maintaining ecological integrity is simply one of many factors for parks decision makers to consider in their mandate. Second, the chapter offers a critical reading of these Federal Court decisions to support the hypothesis that there is a problem of legal design here that constrains the power of law to implement the ecological integrity preservation norm.

## The Norm of Ecological Integrity

Ecological integrity has a long association with North American environmental discourse dating back to Aldo Leopold's 1949 Land Ethic: "A thing is right when it tends to preserve the integrity, stability and beauty of the biotic community. It is wrong when it tends otherwise."[4] With these words, Aldo Leopold gave ecological integrity popular recognition as a norm to guide human activity in relation to the rest of the biotic community. The last decades of the 20th century saw extensive growth in the literature describing the meaning of ecological integrity and how to measure for it. Most commentators associate ecological integrity with an ecological state free of any human disturbance. On this view, human activity necessarily impairs ecological integrity, and thus paradigm ecological integrity is found in ecosystems protected from human disturbance. These commentators tend to advocate for the preservation of core protected areas wherein humans have little or no presence.[5]

### ECOLOGICAL INTEGRITY AS A PRIORITY IN LEGISLATION AND POLICY

Ecological integrity was first expressed in Canadian national parks policy in 1979, and several years later Parliament amended the *National Parks Act* to state the maintenance of ecological integrity is the first priority in national park zoning and visitor use management.[6] While this statutory provision was subsequently cited in several judicial decisions, it was not the focus of litigation and its meaning was never thoroughly considered.[7] While not having much legal significance, this enactment did symbolize a strengthening of the ecological integrity mandate in national parks decision making.

In 1998, the Minister of Canadian Heritage appointed a panel of scientists to assess the ecological integrity of the national parks. In 2000 the panel provided the minister with its conclusion that the ecological integrity of most national parks was in peril. The panel set out various recommendations on actions to enhance the ecological integrity of the parks.[8] One such recommendation was for legislative amendments to ensure the maintenance or restoration of ecological integrity as the *overriding* priority in national parks management.[9] The consensus among panel members was that a stronger legal mandate was necessary to provide authority for Parks Canada to say "no" to excessive human activity in the parks, because the panel had concluded from its field visits that human activity was largely responsible for the ecological decline in the parks.[10]

Parliament responded in February 2001 by legislating an expanded ecological integrity mandate in the *Canada National Parks Act* with the following additions to sections 2 and 8 in the legislation:

> Section 2(1) – Definitions
> "ecological integrity" means, with respect to a park, a condition that is determined to be characteristic of its natural region and likely to persist, including abiotic components and the composition and abundance of native species and biological communities, rates of change and supporting processes;
>
> Section 8(2) – Ecological Integrity
> Maintenance or restoration of ecological integrity, through the protection of natural resources and natural processes, shall be the first priority of the Minister when considering all aspects of the management of parks.[11]

These ecological integrity provisions were enacted by Parliament alongside the existing subsection 4(1), which dedicates the parks to the use and enjoyment of Canadians:

> Section 4(1) – Parks dedicated to public
> The national parks of Canada are hereby dedicated to the people of Canada for their benefit, education and enjoyment, subject to this Act and the regulations, and the parks shall be maintained and made use of so as to leave them unimpaired for the enjoyment of future generations.[12]

The categorical priority in subsection 8(2) afforded to the maintenance or restoration of ecological integrity in the national parks, combined with the emphasis on natural conditions and native species in the legislated definition, makes a convincing case that these legislative provisions require national parks to be managed as places where the preservation of nature for its own sake is the first priority, with human interest of secondary concern. In its literal terms, subsection 8(2) requires that national parks be managed as core preservation areas with little human presence or influence.

## The Application of Ecological Integrity in Law

The Federal Court of Canada has directly considered subsection 8(2) in two cases, and has referred to the section in several others. All judicial consideration has resulted from an application for judicial review of a Parks Canada decision concerning parks management. The first consideration of subsection 8(2) was provided by Justice Gibson of the Federal Court Trial Division in a 2001 judicial review of the Parks Canada decision to approve the construction of a road in Wood Buffalo National Park.[13] In 2003, Justice Gibson's interpretation of subsection 8(2) was upheld by Justice Evans in the Federal Court of Appeal.[14] These two decisions remain the leading authority on the meaning and scope of the subsection 8(2) ecological integrity mandate for Parks Canada.

Wood Buffalo National Park straddles the northeast corner of Alberta and southern edge of the Northwest Territories, covering approximately 45,000 kilometres.[15] Parliament established the park in 1922 to protect the declining population of wood buffalo.[16] In 1983 the park received international recognition as a United Nations World Heritage Site as habitat for threatened wood buffalo and whooping crane species, as well as being recognized for protecting one of the world's largest inland freshwater deltas.[17]

In 1998 the municipality of Fort Smith, located on the northern boundary of the park in the Northwest Territories, submitted an application to Parks Canada seeking approval to construct and operate a road crossing the park from east to west along the Peace River. Parks Canada commissioned an environmental assessment, which concluded that a new road would have some environmental impact on the park, but taking into account mitigation measures this impact was not likely to be significant. In May 2001 Parks Canada (as the Minister's delegate) approved construction of the road.

The Canadian Parks and Wilderness Society (CPAWS) viewed these facts as the ideal case to test the new ecological integrity provisions that had recently been enacted by Parliament in the *Canada National Parks Act*.[18] CPAWS has a long history in national parks issues dating back to the early 1960s, and was an active contributor to the policy work that led to the 2001 ecological integrity legislative amendments. Parks Canada acknowledged on the record that the road did not serve a park purpose. The environmental assessment provided evidence that construction of the road and its subsequent use would disturb the ecology in a national park known internationally for protecting endangered species. Parks Canada had failed to even mention ecological integrity in its May 2001 written approval of the road construction. CPAWS applied to the Federal Court in June 2001 seeking judicial review of the road approval on the basis that these facts made for a clear violation of the new ecological integrity rule in the *Canada National Parks Act*.

Justice Gibson ruled that Parks Canada had the statutory authority to approve the road, and he was not swayed by the evidence on environmental impacts or the fact that Parks Canada failed to mention ecological integrity in its decision.[19] In dismissing the CPAWS application, Justice Gibson referenced the new statutory provisions as non-substantial changes to the legislation and provided a remarkable interpretation of the subsection 8(2) ecological mandate and its relationship to subsection 4(1):

> Further, I agree with counsel for the respondents that the record, when read in its totality, is consistent with the Minister and her delegates according first priority to ecological integrity in arriving at the decision under review. That the decision is clearly not consistent with treating ecological integrity as the Minister's *sole* priority is clear. However, that is not the test. I reiterate: subsection 4(1) of the new *Act* requires a delicate balancing of conflicting interests which include the benefit and enjoyment of those living in, and in close proximity to, Wood Buffalo National Park. This is particularly so when that Park is as remote from services and facilities as is in fact the case and as is likely to remain the case for some time. In the circumstances, while Wood Buffalo National Park, like other National Parks, is dedicated to the people of Canada as a whole, it is not unreasonable to give special consideration to the limited number of people of Canada who are by far most directly affected by management or development decisions affecting the Park. I am satisfied that it was reasonably open to the Minister and her delegates to conclude that the interests of those people overrode the first priority given to ecological integrity where

> impairment of such integrity can be minimized to a degree that the Minister concludes is consistent with the maintenance of the Park for the enjoyment of future generations.
>
> … Subsection 8(2) of the *Act* does not require that ecological integrity be the "determinative factor" in a decision such as that under review. Rather, it simply requires that ecological integrity be the Minister's "first" priority and, as indicated immediately above, I am satisfied on the totality of the evidence before the Court that it was her first priority in reaching the decision here under review. I acknowledge that the record before me does not disclose that the Minister and her delegates used the phrase "ecological integrity" in their decision making process, or, in fact, in the decision that is under review itself. That reality does not lead inexorably to a conclusion that ecological integrity was not considered or was not given a first priority. I am satisfied on the record that it is clear that ecological integrity was taken into account by the Minister and her delegates. I am further satisfied that it was, as well, given first priority notwithstanding that it was not found to be the determinative factor in all of the circumstances.[20]

Justice Gibson provides an interpretation of subsection 8(2) that differs significantly from the literal wording of the provision. Not only does he employ utilitarian logic to read down the ecological integrity priority as just another factor for Parks Canada to weigh in carrying out its subsection 4(1) mandate to balance use with preservation, he concludes that a parks decision can promote the interests of people over the maintenance of ecological integrity and still comply with subsection 8(2).

CPAWS arguably fared worse at the Federal Court of Appeal. Justice Evans confirmed that the court owed significant deference to Parks Canada in the exercise of its statutory authority to manage the national parks, and accordingly he ruled that the court would not revisit how Parks Canada weighed ecological integrity and other factors in its management decisions.[21] Moreover, in dismissing the CPAWS appeal, Justice Evans placed the onus on CPAWS to establish what components of restoring or maintaining ecological integrity were missing in the Parks Canada approval or, alternatively, to submit evidence on how the road construction would impair the park's ecological integrity.[22] Justice Evans not only read down subsection 8(2), he placed a new evidentiary burden on CPAWS as the applicant seeking to challenge Parks Canada under subsection 8(2).

These two decisions in the case of the Wood Buffalo National Park road approval provide Parks Canada with the legal authority to consider the maintenance or restoration of ecological integrity as just another factor in parks decision making; moreover, ecological integrity is a factor that can be overridden by human commercial or economic interests.[23] The doctrinal analysis here demonstrates that judicial interpretation of subsection 8(2) has significantly undermined the normative influence of the ecological integrity rule on parks management. Another effect of these decisions has been to intimidate public interest environmental groups away from using the law to challenge Parks Canada decision making in the national parks.

The Mikisew Cree First Nation also applied to the Federal Court for judicial review of the Parks Canada road approval in Wood Buffalo National Park, filing their application in June 2001, just one week after the CPAWS application was filed with the court. The Mikisew application asserted the decision by Parks Canada was an unlawful infringement of Aboriginal rights under section 35 of the *Constitution Act*.[24]

Madam Justice Hansen ruled the road approval infringed upon Mikisew section 35 rights to hunt and carry on their traditional lifestyle in Wood Buffalo National Park, and as such she set aside the Parks Canada decision.[25] The reasoning provided by Justice Hansen to support her ruling offers an interesting contrast to that of Justice Gibson and Justice Evans in the CPAWS application.

Justice Hansen found the infringement on Mikisew Aboriginal rights partially on the evidence of adverse environmental impacts from the proposed road, including habitat fragmentation, adverse impacts to wildlife that rely on undisturbed wilderness for sustainable populations, and loss of vegetation.[26] Justice Hansen concluded:

> Subsistence hunting and trapping by traditional users of the Park's resources has been in decline for many years. Opening up this remote wilderness to vehicle traffic could potentially exacerbate the challenges facing First Nations struggling to maintain their culture. For example, if the moose population is adversely affected by increased poaching or predation pressures caused by the road, Mikisew will be forced to change their hunting strategies. This may simply be one more incentive to abandon a traditional lifestyle and turn to other modes of living. Further, Mikisew argues that keeping the land around the reserve in its natural condition and maintaining their hunting and trapping traditions is important to their ability to pass their skills on to the next generation of Mikisew.[27]

The decision was ultimately heard at the Supreme Court of Canada, and it is noteworthy for present purposes that a unanimous Supreme Court agreed with Justice Hansen that the Mikisew Aboriginal rights were infringed by the adverse environmental impacts of the proposed road.[28]

Also noteworthy in the Mikisew application is the fact that Parks Canada led evidence on environmental impacts to oppose the Mikisew application. It is hard to miss the irony of Parks Canada asserting that hunting is incompatible with maintaining the ecological integrity of Wood Buffalo National Park, while at the same time asserting the road will have no adverse impact on ecological integrity in the CPAWS application. Justice Hansen has little difficulty in rejecting this argument by giving significant weight to the evidence on the proposed road's environmental impacts and emphasizing that Aboriginal hunting is intertwined with the ecology of the park.[29]

The ecological integrity of Wood Buffalo National Park is given priority in Justice Hansen's reasoning that is nowhere to be found in the court's reasons for dismissing the CPAWS application. The remoteness and wild nature of Wood Buffalo National Park informs her analysis on the lawfulness of the proposed road and its impact on both the Mikisew Cree First Nation and the ecology of the park.

## A Problem of Institutional Design

The foregoing analysis provides for a couple of observations. The first observation is that judicial interpretation of the ecological integrity rule in subsection 8(2) of the *Canada National Parks Act* has significantly read down the priority for ecological integrity in parks management. The Federal Court has effectively ruled that ecological integrity is simply one of many factors for Parks Canada to consider in exercising its legal power to manage the national parks, despite how poorly this reading fits with the literal terms of subsection 8(2).

The second observation is the distinction in legal reasoning evident in a comparison between the CPAWS decisions and the Mikisew decision concerning the impacts of the road on the ecology of Wood Buffalo National Park. Ironically, the Mikisew decision gives ecological integrity the priority called for in the *Canada National Parks Act*, notwithstanding that the parks legislation is not at issue in the Mikisew application.

The most compelling explanation for these observations might rest in the statutory nature of the ecological integrity rule in the *Canada National Parks Act*. Many legal scholars have noted a strong correlation between utilitarian ethics and statutory rules.[30] The general argument is that an application of statutory rules is predisposed towards the balancing of competing interests and polycentric considerations. The categorical or deontological nature of certain environmental norms, such as the norm of preserving ecological integrity, is perhaps too rigid to be operationalized as a statutory rule. The reason might simply be that a categorical assertion of authority in legislation is inextricably linked to the policy debates underlying its enactment, and thus a statutory rule is especially vulnerable to being read down to accommodate competing interests. Or perhaps worse, the rule may be completely flipped on its head when necessary to satisfy these competing interests. I have previously suggested this is exactly what Justice Gibson does in the CPAWS decision: The human–wilderness dualism underlying the meaning of ecological integrity whereby park wilderness is idealized over human interests in the literal wording of subsection 8(2) is untenable to Justice Gibson, who simply flips the dualism in his application of subsection 8(2) to assert human interests over park wilderness.[31] There are exceptional cases where a deontological statutory rule on environmental preservation prevails against competing interests and the court expressly refuses to engage in utilitarian reasoning, but these really are exceptions.[32]

The statutory nature of the ecological integrity rule also seems to dictate that legal reasoning will be predominantly concerned with principles of statutory interpretation and judicial review. These principles inject a formalism into legal argument and legal reasoning that negates the creativity and imagination in legal thought required to develop and implement complex and difficult norms. Legal reasoning in the CPAWS decisions concerning ecological integrity, and presumably the arguments of the parties before the court, focuses on dissecting the wording of subsection 8(2) and adjudicating the lines of authority between the judiciary, legislature, and the executive. The court never seriously engages with the norm of ecological integrity preservation and what it means for national park management. The contrast between how the CPAWS decisions and the Mikisew decision assess the impact of the proposed road on the ecological integrity of Wood Buffalo National Park demonstrates how constraining this formalism can be.

## NOTES

1 See generally Claire Campbell, *A Century of Parks Canada* (Calgary: University of Calgary Press, 2011).

2 The literature on Canada's national parks is vast. The most recent publication is Campbell, *ibid*. See also WL Lothian,

*A History of Canada's National Parks* (Ottawa: Minister of Indian Affairs and Northern Development, 1976); Sid Marty, *A Grand and Fabulous Notion: The First Century of Canada's Parks* (Toronto: NC Press, 1984); Leslie Bella, *Parks for Profit* (Montreal: Harvest House, 1987); Rick Searle, *Phantom Parks: The Struggle to Save Canada's National Parks* (Toronto: Key Porter Books, 2000); Alan MacEachern, *Natural Selections: National Parks in Atlantic Canada, 1935–1970* (Montreal: McGill-Queen's University Press, 2001); Paul Kopas, *Taking the Air: Ideas and Change in Canada's National Parks* (Vancouver: UBC Press, 2007); IS MacLaren, *Culturing Wilderness in Jasper National Park: Studies in Two Centuries of Human History in the Upper Athabasca River Watershed* (Edmonton: University of Alberta Press, 2007).

3 Jeff Gailus, "All Sizzle, No Stake" (23 December 2011) Alternatives Journal, online: <http://www.alternativesjournal.ca/articles/all-sizzle-no-stake>. See also Jeff Gailus, *The Grizzly Manifesto* (Victoria: Rocky Mountain Books, 2010).

4 Aldo Leopold, *A Sand County Almanac and Sketches Here and There* (New York: Oxford University Press, 1949) at 224–225.

5 I canvass the literature in detail in Shaun Fluker, "Ecological Integrity in Canada's National Parks: The False Promise of Law" (2010) 29 Windsor Rev Legal Soc Issues 89 at 90–99.

6 *National Parks Act*, RSC 1985, c N-14, s 5(1.2).

7 See, e.g., *Sunshine Village Corp v Canada (Minister of Environment and Minister of Canadian Heritage)* (1996), 44 Admin LR (2d) 201, 202 NR 132.

8 Panel on the Ecological Integrity of Canada's National Parks, *"Unimpaired for Future Generations"? Conserving Ecological Integrity with Canada's National Parks*, vol 1 (Ottawa: Parks Canada Agency, 2000); Panel on the Ecological Integrity of Canada's National Parks, *"Unimpaired for Future Generations"? Conserving Ecological Integrity with Canada's National Parks*, vol 2 (Ottawa: Parks Canada Agency, 2000) [Ecological Integrity Panel Report].

9 Ecological Integrity Panel Report, *ibid* at Appendix C.

10 Ecological Integrity Panel Report, *ibid* at 1–11 to 1–17.

11 *Canada National Parks Act*, SC 2000, c 32, ss 2(1), 8(2).

12 *Ibid*, s 4(1).

13 *Canadian Parks and Wilderness Society v Canada (Minister of Canadian Heritage)*, 2001 FCT 1123 [*CPAWS Trial Division*].

14 *Canadian Parks and Wilderness Society v Canada (Minister of Canadian Heritage)*, 2003 FCA 197 [*CPAWS Court of Appeal*].

15 Wood Buffalo National Park, online: Parks Canada <http://www.pc.gc.ca/eng/pn-np/nt/woodbuffalo/natcul.aspx> [Parks Canada].

16 Janet Foster, *Working for Wildlife: The Beginnings of Preservation in Canada* (Toronto: University of Toronto Press, 1978) at 104–116.

17 Parks Canada, *supra* note 15.

18 Taken from interview notes on file with the author.

19 *CPAWS Trial Division*, *supra* note 13 at para 47.

20 *Ibid* at paras 52–53 (emphasis in original).

21 *CPAWS Court of Appeal*, *supra* note 14 at paras 68–99.

22 *Ibid* at paras 89, 101–105.

23 This conclusion is reinforced by the second case involving the consideration of s 8(2), wherein the Federal Court dismissed an application by the Mountain Parks Watershed Association for judicial review of a Parks Canada water permit renewal issued to Chateau Lake Louise. *Mountain Parks Watershed Assn v Canada (Minister of Canadian Heritage)*, 2004 FC 1222.

24 *Constitution Act, 1982*, being Schedule B to the *Canada Act, 1982* (UK), 1982, c 11.

25 *Mikisew Cree First Nation v Canada (Minister of Canadian Heritage)*, 2001 FCT 1426 [*Mikisew Trial Division*].

26 *Ibid* at paras 87–98. This evidence came from both the environmental

assessment report and cross-examination of the Wood Buffalo National Park Superintendent, who admitted that the road construction would adversely impact wildlife habitat in the park.

27 *Ibid* at para 98.

28 *Mikisew Cree First Nation v Canada (Minister of Canadian Heritage)*, [2005] 3 SCR 388, 2005 SCC 69 at para 44.

29 *Mikisew Trial Division*, *supra* note 25 at paras 67–74, 87–98.

30 See, e.g., Sean Coyle & Karen Morrow, *The Philosophical Foundations of Environmental Law* (Portland: Hart, 2004).

31 Fluker, *supra* note 5 at 121–122.

32 The paradigm example of deontological over utilitarian reasoning in the application of statutory environmental law is perhaps the 1978 decision of the United States Supreme Court in *Tennessee Valley Authority v Hill*, 437 US 153 (1978).

# 10

# Applying International Law to Canadian Environmental Law

CHARLES-EMMANUEL CÔTÉ

## Introduction

In order to understand how international law can be applied to Canadian environmental law,[1] we must first clarify certain basic concepts. By "international law," we are referring to international public law, which is the law applicable to the international community made up of sovereign states and international intergovernmental organizations (IOs). This means the legal system out of which Canada's obligations arise in its relationship with other sovereign states and IOs.

Canada's international obligations basically originate from two main sources. On the one hand, they arise from customary international practices, or customary international law, which consists of general domestic practices accepted as law. The teaching methods for this customary practice are empirical and hard to pinpoint, as is unavoidable for Canada, which has established neither a specific procedure nor implicit consent for this. Generally speaking, it is international jurisdictions that ascertain the existence of any customary international rules. Otherwise, the existence of a customary rule is ascertained by way of scattered measures (national standards, national jurisdictions, non-binding IO resolutions, legal doctrine, etc.).

On the other hand, Canada's international obligations flow from treaties entered into with other sovereign states or IOs. Treaties are voluntary agreements between sovereign states or IOs intended to have legal effect, regardless of their designation (agreement, convention, exchange of notes, understanding, protocol, treaty, etc.). For Canada to be bound by a treaty, it must have specifically consented to it. According to well-established governmental practice and based on the principles of the *Constitution of the United Kingdom*, which are referred to in the preamble of the *Constitution Act, 1867*,[2] it is the federal government that has a monopoly over the correct procedures for entering into treaties, without any intervention on the part of the federal Parliament or the provinces.

Canada is bound by numerous customary or conventional international obligations concerning environmental protection. These international obligations can be applied as sources of positive law or as interpretive sources for Canadian environmental law.

## International Law as a Source of Positive Law for Canadian Environmental Law

Canada's international obligations can be a source of positive law in Canadian environmental law. This means that they can give rise to rights and obligations that may then be relied upon as the foundation of a claim when pleading before a Canadian judge. This first application of international law respects specific rules depending on the customary or conventional nature of the obligation in question.

### CUSTOMARY INTERNATIONAL LAW AS A SOURCE OF POSITIVE LAW

In the judicial ruling *R. v. Hape*[3] rendered in 2007, the Supreme Court of Canada ended the uncertainty surrounding the status of customary international practice in Canadian law. It is now clear that this is automatically accepted into *common law*, without the requirement for any special procedure or action on the part of the federal or provincial government, provided that it is not incompatible with the Constitution, federal legislation, or provincial legislation.[4] Only "prohibitive rules" in customary international law are automatically accepted: if a rule does not prohibit a course of conduct in Canada but rather the jurisdiction to act in a given manner, it is not automatically accepted and then requires the adoption of an Act on the part of the legislator having jurisdiction.

In order to decide whether a Canadian customary international obligation is part of the current law in effect in Canada, the Canadian judge must complete the following steps:

(a) ascertain the existence of the prohibitive customary rule in international law based on a precedent established in an international jurisdiction, or else establish such a rule himself;

(b) ascertain that the acceptance of the customary rule in Canadian law is not contrary to a constitutional or legislative provision that is incompatible with the customary rule.

If these steps are completed successfully, the customary rule will then form part of the current law in effect in Canada and the judge may proceed to apply it.

The automatic acceptance of customary international law in Canadian law raises the question of the evidentiary rules that apply. Under *common law*, the practice of Canadian courts stipulates that a judge must always have knowledge of customary international law, which means that it does not require evidentiary proof, unlike the law of a foreign state.[5] Under Quebec Civil Law, a Quebec judge must also have knowledge of customary international law, but it must only be argued before the judge—without evidentiary proof—even if it is included in the current law in effect in Quebec.[6] This special rule concerning evidentiary proof implies that a judge is not required to apply customary international law himself, if the parties to the claim do not request it.[7]

A Canadian judge thus becomes a compliance officer for customary international law in Canadian environmental law, watching over Canada's compliance to its international obligations. He can also contribute by verifying the existence of a customary rule concerning environmental protection, not only for the purposes of the case he must decide but also to advance international law for the benefit of environmental protection around the world. The challenges in his role are that these actions result in the establishment of the existence of a customary rule and its contents.

## THE TREATY AS A SOURCE OF POSITIVE LAW

Contrary to international custom, treaties entered into by Canada cannot apply to Canadian law without the legislator's intervention. Only an Act can transform Canada's international obligations into a source of positive law under Canadian law.[8] In its famous *Decision on the Conventions of the International Labour Organization*, in 1937, the Judicial Committee of the Privy Council decided that the legislative authority required to implement a treaty under Canadian law is an ancillary power to the normal division of legislative jurisdictions.[9] There is no general authority for the implementation of treaties in Canada: the federal or provincial legislator has the authority according to the matter targeted by the treaty. In spite of an old controversy concerning the denial of a general federal jurisdiction for the implementation of treaties, the 1937 ruling still constitutes the leading decision on this issue.[10]

The concept of the implementation of a treaty by Canada reverts to the performance of its conventional international obligations. The legal status of a treaty under Canadian law depends on the legislative procedure applied in its implementation.

### Treaty Applicable under Canadian Law

A treaty that is applicable under Canadian law is one whose very text forms part of the law in effect in Canada. The text of the treaty becomes a source of positive law that can be invoked before the Canadian judge as the basis for a claim. This first hypothesis is not the most common one in Canadian legislation. It assumes that the law governing the implementation of the treaty shows the "clear and unequivocal" intention by the legislator to incorporate the text of the treaty, or a portion thereof, into Canadian law. The incorporation of the treaty into Canadian law is a legal concept: it does not mean that the text of the treaty should be attached to the implementation legislation! If the implementation legislation does actually incorporate the treaty, it then becomes directly applicable under Canadian law. It then follows that it occupies the same rank as its incorporation legislation in the Canadian normative hierarchy.

#### INCORPORATION ACT WITH ANNEXATION OF THE TREATY TEXT

The competent legislator may want to incorporate a treaty and attach its text to the Incorporation Act. The determining legal criterion is always a clear and unequivocal indication of the intention to incorporate the text of the treaty into Canadian law. The annexation of the text alone is not enough. An example in federal legislation of an incorporation act with annexation of the text of a treaty is the *Foreign Missions and International Organizations Act*, which states that:

> Articles 1, 22 to 24 and 27 to 40 of the Vienna Convention on Diplomatic Relations ... have the force of law in Canada in respect of all foreign states, regardless of whether those states are parties to those Conventions.[11]

The integral text of the *Vienna Convention on Diplomatic Relations*[12] is reproduced in Appendix II of the Act. The incorporated provisions thus form an integral part of the law in effect in Canada and are directly applicable under Canadian law.

### INCORPORATION ACT WITHOUT ANNEXATION OF THE TREATY TEXT

On the other hand, even if the treaty text is not annexed to the Act, this does not necessarily mean that the legislator did not express a clear and unequivocal intention to incorporate the treaty into Canadian law. The legislator might well express his intention to render the text directly applicable under Canadian law without annexing it to the Incorporation Act. An example in federal legislation of an incorporation act without annexation of the text of a treaty is found in the *Canadian International Trade Tribunal Procurement Inquiry Regulations*, which states that:

> If the Tribunal conducts an inquiry into a complaint, it shall determine whether the procurement was conducted in accordance with the requirements set out in whichever of NAFTA, the Agreement on Government Procurement, the CCFTA, the CPFTA, the CCOFTA, the CPAFTA, the CHFTA, the CKFTA, CETA, the CFTA or CUFTA applies.[13]

This regulatory provision simply refers back to Chapter 10 of the North American Free Trade Agreement between the government of Canada, the government of Mexico, and the government of the United States of America (NAFTA),[14] which deals with procurement carried out by federal government entities or federal government business enterprises. The NAFTA text is not reproduced, but this does not prevent the text of its Chapter 10 from being incorporated into Canadian law and being invoked before a judge during an inquiry into a federal government contract.

As the incorporated treaties are part of the law in effect in Canada, a judge automatically has knowledge of their texts. Under *common law*, tribunals have knowledge of all treaties entered into by Canada, whether or not they have been incorporated into Canadian law. This rule contributes to the general evidentiary rule which requires that a *common law* judge have knowledge of all actions by the government carried out through the exercise of Crown prerogatives.[15] Under Quebec civil law, the decision to annex or not annex the text of the treaty to the Incorporation Act has an effect on the applicable evidentiary rules. Unlike customary international law, a treaty whose text is not reproduced in the Incorporation Act must be submitted so that the judge automatically has knowledge of it.[16] However, the judge cannot ask for evidence, unlike with the law of a foreign state. As for the treaty whose text is annexed to the Act, the

Quebec judge automatically has knowledge of it without the requirement for it to be claimed by a party.

Incorporation under Canadian law allows for the most extensive use of treaties as a source of positive law. These are considered to be part of the law in effect in Canada and are directly applicable, allowing for their texts to be invoked before a Canadian judge as the basis for a claim.

#### Treaty Inapplicable under Canadian Law

A treaty that is inapplicable under Canadian law is one whose text does not form part of the law in effect in Canada. This would include any treaty that was correctly entered into by Canada in the international legal system, but whose provisions have not been incorporated into Canadian law by way of an Act. It does not matter what Canada did to implement the treaty, in the performance of its conventional international obligations, if no clear and unequivocal intention to incorporate the treaty exists in federal or provincial legislation.

### IMPLEMENTATION ACT WITHOUT ANNEXATION OF THE TEXT OF A TREATY

The most common hypothesis is that of a treaty that is the subject of an implementation Act on the part of the competent legislator, who has no intention to incorporate the treaty under Canadian law. The purpose of the implementing Act is to change Canadian law in such a way as to ensure the performance by Canada of its conventional international obligations. This could be either a new Act adopted specially for the implementation of a treaty, or else changes made to an already existing Act. The provisions of the treaty itself remain inapplicable in Canadian law: only the legislative provisions for implementation are part of the law in effect in Canada. The text of the treaty itself cannot under any circumstances be invoked before the judge as the basis for a claim.

An example of an Act adopted specifically for the purpose of implementing a treaty is the *World Trade Organization Agreement Implementation Act*, which states that "The purpose of this Act is to implement the Agreement" and "The Agreement is hereby approved."[17] The Act then sets forth over two hundred articles that aim to change the federal legislation in a surgical and timely manner, in order to fulfill Canada's international obligations. In the matter of *Pfizer Inc. v. Canada (1st inst.),*[18] a private individual attempted to use this Act to directly invoke the implemented treaty in order to challenge the compatibility of the federal law respecting patents with Canada's international obligations.

The Federal Court rejected this use of the implemented treaty, with approval from the Federal Court of Appeal, in the following terms:

> Parliament, in my view, manifestly indicated its intention as to how it was implementing the WTO Agreement and its annexed TRIPS Agreement or any part thereof. Parliament gave legal effect to its WTO obligations by carefully examining the nature of those obligations, assessing the state of the existing federal statutory and regulatory law and *then deciding the specific and precise legislative changes which were required* to implement the WTO Agreement.[19]

A similar act was adopted in Quebec in order to implement several international trade agreements. The *Act respecting the Implementation of International Trade Agreements*[20] states that its purpose "is to implement the following agreements," and it then goes on to list four agreements, including the *North American Agreement on Environmental Cooperation.*[21] The Quebec Court of Appeal also rejected a similar attempt to invoke the text of one of the agreements implemented by the Act in the matter of *UL Canada v. Québec (AG).*[22]

### IMPLEMENTATION ACT WITH ANNEXATION OF THE TEXT OF THE TREATY

Whatever the implementation method used by the legislator, the only criterion that counts when deciding whether the treaty is incorporated and forms part of the law in effect in Canada is that of the legislator's clear and unequivocal intention. Even the annexation of the text of the treaty in an implementation Act is insufficient to conclude that this intention exists![23] A rare example of this hypothesis is to be found in the *Canada-United States Free Trade Agreement Implementation Act*, which stipulates firstly that "The purpose of this Act is to implement the Agreement" and that "The Agreement is hereby approved." It then proceeds to make more than one hundred changes to the federal legislation.[24] The integral text of the *Canada-United States Free Trade Agreement*[25] is then annexed to the Act.

The same evidentiary rules apply to the treaty that is inapplicable in Canadian law. A *common law* judge has knowledge of all of the treaties entered into by the Canadian government. A Quebec civil law judge also has knowledge of these treaties, except that the treaties whose texts are not reproduced in an Act must then be placed before the judge so that he definitely has knowledge of them.

## International Law as a Source Of Interpretation for Canadian Environmental Law

Quite apart from the question of the applicability of a treaty under Canadian law as a source of positive law, a treaty may also be used as a source for the interpretation of Canadian law. It is no doubt a very useful tool to allow a Canadian judge to use international law in Canadian environmental law, independently of the question of the incorporation of the treaty and the changes made to Canadian law by the legislator to implement Canada's international obligations.

### THE PRINCIPLE OF CONSISTENT INTERPRETATION

In the 2007 *Hape* ruling, the Supreme Court of Canada referred to the existence of the principle of consistent interpretation in Canadian law:

> It is a well-established principle of statutory interpretation that *legislation will be presumed to conform to international law*. The presumption of conformity is based on the rule of judicial policy that, *as a matter of law, courts will strive* to avoid constructions of domestic law pursuant to which the state would be in violation of its international obligations, unless the wording of the statute clearly compels that result.[26]

This established principle, which was inherited from British constitutional law, means that the Canadian judge must choose the interpretation of Canadian law that most closely conforms to Canada's international obligations. This only applies to treaties entered into by Canada and international customary law, but it applies whether the nature of the treaty is applicable or not applicable or whether the custom has been accepted into Canadian law.[27] The principle of consistent interpretation allows the judge to complete the implementation of Canada's international obligations, while interpreting Canadian law; it does not, however, allow for changes in the case of obvious incompatibility.

The matter of *114957 Canada Ltd. (Spraytech, Sprinkler Company) v. Hudson (Town)*[28] presents an interesting case of application of the principle of consistent interpretation in environmental law. In order to reconcile her interpretation of the prescribed authority attributed to Quebec municipalities with empowering legislation, Justice L'Heureux-Dubé referred to the precautionary principle, which would from that day forward be included in customary international law.[29] In doing so, not only did the Supreme Court of Canada use international environmental law to interpret Canadian law, but its ruling in and of itself constitutes a contribution to the development of customary international law.

## THE INTERPRETATION OF IMPLEMENTATION LEGISLATION AS IT APPLIES TO A TREATY

The wording of the principle of consistent interpretation in the *Hape* decision does not include any reference to the condition of the existence of ambiguity in the provision of the Canadian law to be interpreted.[30] However, the lack of such a doubt blocked the application of the principle in earlier decisions of the Supreme Court of Canada, and certain lower courts continue to apply this condition.

The scope of any possible condition of preliminary ambiguity was, however, severely limited by the Supreme Court of Canada in 1992 in the matter of *National Corn Growers v. T.C.I.*[31] Whenever the court has to interpret the implementation Act with respect to a treaty in accordance with the treaty, a Canadian judge does not first have to identify ambiguity in the Act: even clear legislative provisions must be interpreted in accordance with the implemented treaty, except in the case of obvious incompatibility.

When a Canadian judge applies an implementation Act with respect to an international environmental agreement, he must be able to make reference to the agreement in question to ensure that his interpretation of the Act is in accordance with Canada's international obligations. For example, a judge who applies the *Wild Animal and Plant Protection and Regulation of International and Interprovincial Trade Act*[32] can make reference to the *Convention on International Trade in Endangered Species.*[33] The close relationship between a treaty and its implementation Act allows the judge to be proactive in the application of international law and to improve Canada's performance of its international obligations.

### NOTES

1 The expression "Canadian environmental law" refers to both federal environmental law and provincial environmental law.

2 (UK), 30 & 31 Vict, c 3, reprinted in RSC 1985, App II, No 5.

3 [2007] 2 SCR 292 [*Hape*].

4 *Ibid* at 39, *per* LeBel J.

5 Gibran van Ert, *Using International Law in Canadian Courts*, 2d ed (Toronto: Irwin Law, 2008) at 45 [van Ert]; Ronald St. John Macdonald, "The Relationship between International Law and Domestic Law in Canada" in Ronald St. John Macdonald, Gerald L Morris & Douglas M Johnston, eds, *Canadian Perspectives*

*on International Law and Organization* (Toronto: University of Toronto Press, 1974) 88 at 113.

6 *Québec Civil Code*, SQ 1991, c 64, art 2807, para 2 [QCC].

7 Léo Ducharme, "Le nouveau droit de la preuve en matières civiles selon le code civil du Québec" in Barreau du Québec et Chambre des notaires du Québec, ed, *La réforme du Code civil*, v 3 (Québec : Presses de l'Université Laval, 1993), 443 at 445.

8 *Canada (AG) v Ontario (AG)*, [1937] AC 326 at 347–348 (PC). (*Decision on the Conventions of the International Labour Organization*).

9 *Ibid* at 351.

10 In the matter of the controversy surrounding the *Decision on the Conventions of the International Labour Organization* and its outdated aspects, see Charles-Emmanuel Côté, "Applying international law to Canadian law" ("La réception du droit international en droit canadien") (2010) 52 SCLR (2d) 483 at 513–521.

11 SC 1991, c 41, s 3(1).

12 18 April 1961, Can TS 1966 No 29.

13 SOR/93-602, art 11.

14 17 December 1992, Can TS 1994 No 2.

15 van Ert, *supra* note 5 at 56. See *Pan-American World Airways Inc v Department of Trade*, [1976] 1 Lloyd's Rep 257 at 261 (Eng CA).

16 QCC, *supra* note 6, art 2807, para 2; Québec, Ministère de la Justice, *Commentaires du Ministre de la Justice : le Code civil du Québec*, v 2 (Québec : Publications du Québec, 1993) at 1757.

17 SC 1994, c 47, arts 3 and 8. See *Marrakesh Agreement Establishing the World Trade Organization*, 15 April 1994, 1867 UNTS 3.

18 [1999] 4 CF 441, aff'd 1999 CanLII 8952 (CAF) [*Pfizer Inc*].

19 *Ibid* at para 45 (CF) (emphasis added).

20 RSQ, c M-35.2.

21 *Ibid*, art 2; *North American Agreement on Environmental Cooperation*, 14 September 1993, Canada–United States–Mexico, 32 ILM 1499.

22 [2003] QLR 2729 (CA Qué) at para 80, aff'd [2005] 1 RCS 143. See also *Entreprise de rebuts Sanipan v Québec (AG)*, [1995] QLR 821 at 846.

23 See *Pfizer Inc*, *supra* note 18 at para 43 (CF).

24 SC 1988, c 65, arts 3, 8, 23–148.

25 2 January 1988, TR Can 1989 No 3.

26 *Hape*, *supra* note 3 at para 53 (main reasons) [emphasis added].

27 See *Daniels v White*, [1968] SCR 517; *Arrow River & Tributaries Slide & Boom Co v Pigeon Timber Co*, [1932] SCR 495.

28 [2001] 2 RSC 241.

29 *Ibid* at paras 30–32 (main reasons).

30 See Côté, *supra* note 10 at 541–544.

31 [1990] 2 SCR 1324 at 1371 (Gonthier J, main reasons).

32 SC 1992, c 52, art 4.

33 2 July 1974, TR Can 1975 No 32.

# 11

# The Role of International Environmental Law in Canadian Courts

PHILLIP M. SAUNDERS, Q.C.

## Introduction

International law has been a major force in the development of environmental law in the last half-century, as global solutions are sought for common problems, and treaty regimes are used to promote domestic implementation of international standards. Canada has been an active participant in this process and has implemented numerous agreements in legislation, but the direct application of international environmental law in Canadian courts has at times been hesitant and confusing. This chapter provides a brief overview of the use of this body of law in the courts and an assessment of the prospects and challenges facing its application in the future.

## Public International Law in Canadian Courts

The principles governing the application of international law in Canadian courts are the subject of a separate chapter in this volume, and accordingly will not be addressed in detail here.[1] However, it is necessary to note some of the general principles prior to the discussion of international environmental law in particular.

First, in most cases, Canada's obligations under international conventions "must be implemented by statute in order to alter domestic law."[2] Second, the existence of an international agreement, validly concluded by the federal government, does not confer legislative authority over the subject matter of the agreement on the federal legislature.[3] Third, "prohibitive" rules of customary international law are "adopted" into Canadian law without the necessity of any act of the legislature or executive (subject to the legislature's power to expressly reject or derogate from such rules).[4] Fourth, for treaties that have been brought into Canadian law through implementation in a statute, the treaty obligations may become part of domestic law. The treaty text may constitute a "direct source of rights and obligations" if incorporated in the statute, or may be applied via a statute that "reflects the treaty's substance."[5]

Fifth, where a treaty has been implemented by legislation (which requires that the legislative intent be "manifest"),[6] the "underlying" convention may be used to interpret the implementing statute, both to determine whether there is any ambiguity between treaty and statute and to resolve ambiguity where it is found.[7] Furthermore, the international rules of treaty interpretation, as reflected both in the *Vienna Convention on the Law of Treaties*[8] and in customary law, should be applied in the interpretation of the treaty.[9] Finally, treaties that have been concluded and ratified by Canada, but which remain unimplemented in domestic law, still have an impact through their application in the interpretation of legislation. The "presumption of conformity" requires courts to interpret federal statutes (where possible and in absence of an express contrary intent) to be in compliance with Canada's international obligations.[10]

It is important to note that the presumption of conformity has taken on a dual aspect that can lead to confusion, particularly in the environmental context. In *Ordon Estate v. Grail* in 1998, the Supreme Court of Canada (SCC) expressed the rule as follows:

> Although international law is not binding upon Parliament or the provincial legislatures, a court must presume that legislation is intended to comply with Canada's obligations under international instruments and as a member of the international community. In choosing among possible interpretations of a statute, the court should avoid interpretations that would put Canada in breach of such obligations.[11]

This test held the statutory provision up against "obligations" binding on Canada in international law. In both *Hape* and *Baker*, by contrast, the court at once accepted this more limited purpose and confirmed another, less precise element rooted in the court's general "contextual" approach to statutory interpretation: "[T]he values reflected in international human rights law may help inform the contextual approach to statutory interpretation and judicial review."[12] These cases leave open how far a court might go in using the "values and principles" of international law[13] as part of the "contextual approach" to statutory interpretation, and whether this cuts the exercise loose from the firmer moorings of a definable international *legal* "obligation" against which a statute might be measured.

## International Environmental Law: Application In Canada

Despite the general applicability of the principles summarized above, there are certain unique characteristics of international *environmental* law, and the manner in which it has been incorporated in Canada. First, whereas much of the jurisprudence on international law has dealt with the application of *unimplemented* obligations or customary law, in the environmental context, Canada has been quite active in statutory implementation. Second, environmental agreements often require complex programs of action, which are only capable of implementation through legislation (as opposed to court decisions that interpret existing law). Third, the obligations set out in these agreements are primarily owed to other states,[14] and generally do not create rights that allow challenges by individuals in domestic courts (as in the human rights setting). Finally, this is a field in which there exists a great variety of international documents, often non-binding in a formal legal sense, but nonetheless influential as so-called "soft law," or as evidence of policy directions at the international level.

### STATUTORY IMPLEMENTATION

There has been an extensive practice in Canada of implementing environmental conventions (in whole or in part) in statutes—even a short list of examples of such instruments[15] makes it clear that this is a significant source of substantive law:

- Part VII, Division 3 of the *Canadian Environmental Protection Act 1999* (*CEPA 1999*)[16] implementing the Convention on the Prevention of Marine Pollution by Dumping of Wastes and Other Matter, 1972.[17]
- The Ozone-depleting Substances and Halocarbon Alternatives Regulations 2016,[18] made under *CEPA 1999*, implementing the Montreal Protocol on Substances that Deplete the Ozone Layer, 1987 (as amended).[19]
- Vessel Pollution and Dangerous Chemicals Regulations,[20] made under the *Canada Shipping Act 2001*,[21] implementing the provisions of Annex I of the International Convention for the Prevention of Pollution from Ships, 1973 as amended by the Protocol of 1978 relating to the International Convention for the Prevention of Pollution from Ships.[22]

- The *Migratory Birds Convention Act* (MBCA), 1994,[23] implementing the Convention for the Protection of Migratory Birds in Canada and the United States, 1916.[24]
- The *Coastal Fisheries Protection Act*[25] and regulations,[26] which provide, inter alia, for the application of obligations arising under the Convention on Future Multilateral Cooperation in the Northwest Atlantic Fisheries, 1978[27] and other agreements.
- The *Species at Risk Act* (SARA),[28] implementing (in part) Canada's obligations under the *Convention on Biological Diversity, 1992*.[29]

The *means* of implementation, and the sources that must therefore be consulted, are quite varied. For example, in SARA the direct mention of the *Biodiversity Convention* is limited to preambular statements "recognizing" that Canada has ratified it and that protection for species at risk "will, in part, meet Canada's commitments under that Convention."[30] By contrast, the detailed scheme in Annex I of *MARPOL 73/78* is incorporated, along with other obligations into the *Pollution Prevention Regulations*, and the *Migratory Birds Convention* is annexed as a Schedule to the MBCA. Moreover, legislation can provide for incorporation of the underlying international agreement as it may be amended over time,[31] requiring reference to the international sources to determine their current status. Nor is the incorporation process limited to the actual agreement itself—a number of instruments require reference to decisions that may be made by international bodies empowered by the relevant convention,[32] or conservation schemes established by an international organization.[33] If a treaty is determined to be implementing a convention, then the interpretive rules in *Pushpanathan*[34] clearly apply, and any interpretation must conform to the treaty obligation. Perhaps less clearly stated is the approach to be taken to interpretation of such sources as conservation regulations, which do not have the status of a treaty and are not subject to any defined set of interpretation rules at international law.

### JUDICIAL APPLICATION OF INTERNATIONAL ENVIRONMENTAL "LAW"

When we move beyond the application of treaties implemented in legislation, the interpretive waters become somewhat murkier, and Canadian courts dealing with environmental law have been willing to look beyond well-defined conventional obligations. In the following sections some examples are considered that may make it possible to draw out a few general lessons.

### From *Crown Zellerbach* to *Spraytech*

In a series of five cases beginning with *R. v. Crown Zellerbach Canada Ltd.*[35] in 1988, and ending with *114957 Canada Ltée (Spraytech, Société d'arrosage) v. Hudson (Town)*[36] in 2001, the Supreme Court of Canada turned to the international level, with varying degrees of precision, in its consideration of domestic environmental law. While some have referred to developments in this period as "progressive" and ground breaking,[37] other observers have been more skeptical about the inherent limitations of the court's approach.[38]

In *Crown Zellerbach*, the court considered the constitutionality of the *Ocean Dumping Control Act*,[39] as it applied to internal waters within a province. The Act was passed in implementation of the *London Convention*, but this was not explicitly stated in the legislation, and the application to internal waters went beyond the convention's provisions. In finding that the relevant section was valid federal legislation under the "national concern" branch of the "peace order and good government" power, the majority looked to the provisions of the convention, but primarily as evidence that ocean dumping constituted a "distinct and separate form of water pollution," so as to qualify as a "a single, indivisible matter."[40]

In *Friends of the Oldman River Society v. Canada (Minister of Transport)* in 1992,[41] the court considered, inter alia, the statutory validity and mandatory status of the Environmental Assessment and Review Process Guidelines Order.[42] In support of the integration of environmental and economic concerns, La Forest J. turned to a report of the Canadian Council of Resource and Environment Ministers, which referred to the Report of the World Commission on Environment and Development (WCED) (the *Brundtland Report*).[43] Beyond this once-removed acknowledgement of a non-binding international document, and a brief mention of the work of international organizations, the decision took no further notice of the international level, and never mentioned international law in explicit terms.

In 1995, the SCC returned in passing to international matters in *Ontario v. Canadian Pacific Ltd.*[44] In considering whether a statutory prohibition on "impairment of the quality of the natural environment for any use that can be made of it," was unconstitutionally vague, the court noted that an international panel of experts had recommended a definition of "use of natural resources"; this was just one piece of extrinsic evidence in support of the argument that "use" was capable of legal definition.[45] Again, no binding international *law* was applied, or even considered.

In *R. v. Hydro-Québec*[46] in 1997, La Forest J., in considering whether jurisdiction for environmental protection (through regulation of PCBs) could be based on the criminal law power, turned to a number of sources of evidence, including views expressed by the WCED.[47] Further, he looked to a series of international scientific reports for confirmation that PCBs constituted a "significant danger to the environment or to human life or health," as required by the statute.[48] No actual international obligations binding upon Canada were identified, but Justice La Forest, writing for the majority, was still able to conclude as follows:

> I am confident that Canada can fulfil its international obligations, in so far as the toxic substances sought to be prohibited from entering into the environment under the Act are concerned, by use of the criminal law power.[49]

The final case of interest is *Spraytech*, which has perhaps had the most lasting impact. At the conclusion of her analysis of the statutory authority for the impugned municipal pesticide bylaw, L'Heureux-Dubé J., for the majority, observed that a reading of the statute to permit the town to regulate pesticide use would be "consistent with principles of international law and policy," and that the "interpretation of By-law 270 contained in these reasons respects international law's 'precautionary principle,'" as "defined" in the non-binding 1990 *Bergen Ministerial Declaration on Sustainable Development*.[50] The decision listed a number of sources, mostly academic commentators, in support of the controversial contention that the "precautionary principle" had by 2001 attained the status of binding customary international law, but did not offer any firm conclusion to that effect. Rather, the decision offered merely the observation that in "the context of the precautionary principle's tenets, the Town's concerns about pesticides fit well under their rubric of preventive action."[51]

These cases give rise to three general observations. First, despite the enthusiasm with which they were viewed by some at the time, there is not much by way of adoption of international law in the decisions. Only one, *Spraytech*, even purports to apply international law, and then in a clearly secondary manner, after the substantive decision has been reached. Second, the cases did generally accept the idea that environmental protection was a "fundamental value of Canadian society,"[52] and this broad finding was rooted in part in the "values and principles" of international law and "policy." Third, and perhaps most important, it seems clear that these cases turned to international sources as part of the contextual approach to interpretation, and not in seeking conformity with actual *obligations*. Even in *Spraytech*, the precautionary principle is only invoked to show that the court's interpretation was "consistent with principles of international law and policy," and as part of the "legal context."[53] A similar use of the precautionary principle is seen in *Castonguay Blasting Ltd. v. Ontario (Environment)*,[54] in which the SCC noted that the legislative provision at issue was "also consistent with" the precautionary principle, which was described only as an "emerging international law principle,"[55] and this was ten years after *Spraytech*.

### Post-*Spraytech*

In recent years, Canadian courts have returned to the application of international environmental law in the domestic context, and similar issues have arisen.

First, the line between a presumption of conformity with a binding obligation and a "contextual" analysis of international sources remains somewhat blurred. For example, in *Environmental Defence Canada v. Canada (Minister of Fisheries and Oceans)*,[56] a judicial review application dealing with a minister's decisions under SARA, Campbell J. turned to Canada's obligations under the *Biodiversity Convention* for guidance. He found that section 38 of SARA requires the minister, in preparing recovery strategies or action plans for species at risk, to consider Canada's "commitment" to "the principle that, if there are threats of serious or irreversible damage to the listed wildlife species, cost-effective measures to prevent the reduction or loss of the species should not be postponed for a lack of full scientific certainty." In determining that this was a "mandatory interpretive principle" to be applied by the minister, Campbell J. took account of the fact that Canada had ratified the convention and was therefore "committed to apply its principles."[57]

What is unclear is whether the relevant provisions of the convention (which are not identified) are being applied: (a) as a binding obligation, subject to interpretation under treaty law; (b) to enforce a rebuttable presumption of conformity with some unimplemented part of the convention; or (c) as part of the general context of interpretation. The answer may indeed be "all of the above," given the court's explicit approval of the formulation put forward by the applicant:[58]

> The *Convention* is a binding treaty, and SARA was enacted in part to implement Canada's treaty commitments. Furthermore, the *Convention* is part of the "entire context" to be considered in interpreting the

SARA. Therefore, not only must the SARA be construed to conform to the values and principles of the *Convention*, but the Court must avoid any interpretation that could put Canada in breach of its *Convention* obligations.

Second, it is still the case that the application of international law often occurs in a secondary manner, to buttress a decision already supported on other grounds. In *Environmental Defence*, for example, section 38 contained a version of the precautionary principle as a required ministerial consideration, and the wording of section 41 was similarly mandatory. Likewise, in *Adam v. Canada (Minister of the Environment)* (another *SARA* case), the court noted that section 38 was "enacted in part to satisfy Canada's obligations" under the convention, but ultimately relied on the clear words of the statute in any event.[59]

## Conclusions: Prospects and Remaining Challenges

This review of the experience with international environmental law as applied in Canadian courts suggests a few general conclusions to date, and potential challenges for the future.

First, it seems clear that the most important substantive impacts will continue to be through direct implementation of international obligations in Canadian legislation, because of the nature of environmental agreements and their emphasis on positive programs of action. As shown in the litigation under *SARA*, one important impact of the reference to international principles in interpreting such legislation is likely to be the limitations imposed on the exercise of discretion in environmental decision making.[60]

Second, as courts continue to address the interaction between international environmental law and its domestic implementation, some attention must be paid to the practical evidentiary problems in an area as fluid as environmental law. Although Canadian courts are presumed to be aware of international law, there has certainly been a practice of accepting expert evidence on its current state (especially with regard to customary law),[61] and this may be relevant in more complex situations in the environmental field as well.

Finally, where there is no implementing statute, or only partial implementation of a convention, clarity is needed as to the distinction between the rebuttable presumption of conformity with a binding obligation, and reference to international "policy" in a contextual approach to interpretation. There is, as noted above, a vast array of international documents of variable provenance and expressing extensive commitments, but that states explicitly chose to make non-binding. Further, some "obligations" within binding agreements are themselves aspirational and effectively non-binding. The use of such instruments in a loosely structured contextual interpretation may obscure the real status of international law, and create binding commitments where none were intended. To date, it seems that this has been avoided by the secondary or supportive role assigned to this aspect of interpretation, but the issue still requires attention.

### NOTES

1 See chapter 10 in this volume. For the most comprehensive study of this issue, see generally Gibran van Ert, *Using International Law in Canadian Courts* 2d ed (Toronto: Irwin Law, 2008). See also Hugh Kindred, Phillip Saunders, Robert Currie et al, *International Law: Chiefly as Interpreted and Applied in Canada* 8th ed (Toronto: Emond Montgomery, 2014) at ch 3 [Kindred et al].

2 Gibran van Ert, "Using Treaties in Canadian Courts" (2000) 38 Can YB Int'l Law 3 at 16 ["Using Treaties"]. This rule, which would not be relevant to self-executing treaties, was stated by Lord Atkin in *Attorney General for Canada v Attorney General for Ontario (Labour Conventions Case)*, [1937] AC 326 at 347 (PC) [*Labour Conventions Case*]. An exception to this requirement for legislative action is found in treaties that can be "given effect by administrative action," as described by Kindred et al, *supra* note 1 at 174: "If existing law grants a minister of the government regulation-making authority of sufficient scope to include the provisions of the treaty, they may be given internal force of law by executive act, such as an Order in Council of the appropriate government(s)." For an endorsement of this view, see *Turp v. Canada (Foreign Affairs)*, 2017 FC 84 at para 63.

3 *Labour Conventions Case*, *supra* note 2. There is no independent head of jurisdiction for "treaty implementation" in the *Constitution Act*, 1867 (UK), 30 & 31 Vict, c 3, reprinted in RSC 1985, App II, No 5, except for "Empire" treaties under s 132. On the controversy over this decision see van Ert, "Using Treaties," *ibid* at 67–78.

4 *R v Hape*, [2007] 2 SCR 292 at para 39 [*Hape*].

5 Kindred et al, *supra* note 1 at 180.

6 *Macdonald et al v Vapor Canada Ltd*, [1977] 2 SCR 134 at 171.

7 *National Corn Growers Assn v Canada (Import Tribunal)*, [1990] 2 SCR 1324 at 1371–1372 [*Corn Growers*]. This case confirmed that resort could be had to the international source of law for interpretive purposes without any precondition of ambiguity: see the discussion at Gibran van Ert, "The Reception of International Law in Canada – Three Ways We Might Go Wrong," *Paper No. 2, Canada in International Law at 150 and Beyond* (Waterloo, ON: Centre for International Law and Governance, 2018) at 3–6.

8 27 January 1980, Can TS 1980 No 37.

9 See, e.g., *Pushpanathan v Canada (Minister of Citizenship and Immigration)*, [1998] 1 SCR 982 at paras 51–52 [*Pushpanathan*]. This may lead, where appropriate, to use of the *travaux préparatoires* and other sources relevant to the purposes of the treaty.

10 *Hape*, *supra* note 4 at para 53. See also *Baker v Canada (Minister of Citizenship and Immigration)*, [1999] 2 SCR 817 at paras 70–71 [*Baker*]. The legislature may, of course, still choose to act expressly in contravention of the international obligation.

11 [1998] 3 SCR 437 at para 137.

12 *Baker*, *supra* note 10 at paras 69–70.

13 See *Hape*, *supra* note 4 at para 53: "[T]he legislature is presumed to comply with the values and principles of customary and conventional international law. Those values and principles form part of the context in which statutes are enacted, and courts will therefore prefer a construction that reflects them."

14 See, e.g., the observation of Barnes J with regard to the *Kyoto Protocol to the United Nations Framework Convention on Climate Change*, 2303 UNTS 148, to the effect that the agreement has its own "its own formal system of accountability." *Friends of the Earth v Canada*, 2008 FC 1183 at note 3, aff'd 2009 FCA 297.

15 Provinces, within their jurisdiction, may also legislate for the implementation of international agreements, but given the space available this review is limited to examples of federal legislation.

16 SC 1999, c 33 [*CEPA 1999*], as amended; *Disposal at Sea Regulations*, SOR/2001-275, as amended (last amended 24 September 2009).

17 Can TS 1979/36 [*London Convention*] and *1996 Protocol*, 7 November 1996, Can TS 2006/5. The regulations go further than the convention, in that they apply to internal waters, beyond the scope of the convention's application.

18 SOR/2016-137 [*ODSHAR*].

19 Can TS [*Montreal Protocol*]. The *Montreal Protocol* is a protocol to the 1985 *Vienna Convention for the Protection of the Ozone Layer*, Can TS 1988/23.

20 SOR/2012-69 [Pollution Prevention Regulations].

21 SC 2001, c 26 [*CSA*]. As set out in s 29(1), Sched 1 of the *CSA* lists various conventions which the Minister of Transport "has determined should be brought into force, in whole or in part, in Canada by regulation."

22 1340 UNTS 61 [*MARPOL 73/78*].

23 SC 1994, c 22, as amended [*MBCA*]. See also *Migratory Birds Regulations*, CRC, c1035.

24 UKTS 1917, No 17 [*Migratory Birds Convention*].

25 RSC 1985, c C-33, as amended.

26 *Coastal Fisheries Protection Regulations*, CRC, c 413, as amended [*CFP Regulations*].

27 Can TS 1979, No 11, as amended [*NAFO Convention*].

28 SC 2002, c 29 [*SARA*].

29 Can TS. 1993, No 24 [*Biodiversity Convention*].

30 *SARA*, Preamble.

31 See, e.g., s 1 of the *ODSHAR*, which makes reference to the *Montreal Protocol* "in its most recent version," and a similar provision in s 2 of the *MBCA*, referring to the convention "as amended from time to time."

32 See, e.g., the references to "Decisions" of the parties to the *Montreal Protocol* at ss 1 and 29(1) of the *ODSHAR*.

33 See. e.g., the application of "NAFO measures," "as amended from time to time," in the *CFP Regulations*, s 2, and throughout the regulations.

34 *Pushpanathan*, *supra* note 9.

35 [1988] 1 SCR 401 [*Crown Zellerbach*].

36 [2001] 2 SCR 241 [*Spraytech*].

37 Jerry V DeMarco & Michelle Campbell, "The Supreme Court of Canada's Progressive Use of International Environmental Law and Policy in Interpreting Domestic Legislation" (2004) 13:3 RECIEL 320 at 330, referring to the "enlightened approach" of the court.

38 See, e.g., Jutta Brunnée, "International Environmental Law in Canadian Courts" (1998) 7:1 RECIEL 47 at 50 and 53.

39 SC 1974-75-76, c 55, repealed and replaced by Part VII, Division 3 of *CEPA 1999*.

40 *Crown Zellerbach*, *supra* note 35 at 436–438. The court also considered international scientific reports for the same purpose.

41 [1992] 1 SCR 3 [*Oldman River*].

42 SOR/84-467 (repealed with the coming into force of the *Canadian Environmental Assessment Act*, SC 1992, c 37, which was then repealed by SC 2012, c 19, s 66).

43 *Oldman River, supra* note 41 at 37.
44 [1995] 2 SCR 1031 [*Canadian Pacific*].
45 *Ibid* at para 69.
46 [1997] 3 SCR 213 [*Hydro-Québec*].
47 *Ibid* at para 126.
48 *Ibid* at para 157.
49 *Ibid* at para 127.
50 *Spraytech, supra* note 36 at paras 30–31.
51 *Ibid* at para 32. The precautionary principle is addressed by another chapter in this collection, and the question of its actual status (i.e. as a binding norm) in international law in 2001 will not be addressed further here.
52 See, e.g., *Canadian Pacific, supra* note 44 at para 55 and *Oldman River, supra* note 41 at 16–17.
53 *Spraytech, supra* note 36 at para 30.
54 [2013] 3 SCR 323.
55 *Ibid* at para 20.
56 2009 FC 878, [2009] FCJ No 1052 [*Environmental Defence*].
57 *Ibid* at paras 34–35. Campbell J also found at para 40, that s 41 of SARA, requiring the minister to meet certain criteria in identification of critical habitat, was a mandatory provision. In this he applied the reasoning in *Alberta Wilderness Association v Canada (Minister of the Environment)*, 2009 FC 710 at para 25. The approach in *Environmental Defence* has been adopted and applied in a case dealing with judicial review of ministerial actions to protect killer whales under SARA: *David Suzuki Foundation v Canada (Minister of Fisheries and Oceans)*, 2010 FC 1233 at paras 103–104, aff'd in part 2012 FCA 40.
58 *Environmental Defence, supra* note 56 at para 38.
59 2011 FC 962 at para 71 [*Adam*]. See also *Imperial Oil Ltd v Quebec (Minister of the Environment)*, [2003] 2 SCR 624 at para 23, where the "polluter pays" principle is applied because of its presence in the legislation, although it is also noted that the principle is "recognized" at the international level.
60 In this context, note also that governments are not only *limited* in their actions but may also be *empowered* to take action, due to the possibility of treaty implementation through executive action, as discussed *supra* note 2.
61 See, e.g., *Bouzari v Islamic Republic of Iran* (2004), 243 DLR (4th) 406 (Ont CA), where expert evidence of customary law and Canada's international obligations had been presented at trial.

# 12

## Article removed at author's request

*This page left blank.*

*This page left blank.*

*This page left blank.*

*This page left blank.*

*This page left blank.*

*This page left blank.*

*This page left blank.*

*This page left blank.*

*This page left blank.*

# SECTION 2

# Environmental Prosecutions

# 13

# The Exercise of Prosecutorial Discretion: Challenges to Environmental Prosecutions

ALEX IKEJIANI

## Introduction

The position of a Crown counsel is unique in that the goal of the Crown is not entirely predicated on seeking a conviction. Instead, the goal of the Crown is to assist the trier of fact in ensuring that all of the credible evidence is put before the court. This chapter will examine some of the factors that shape and guide Crown counsel in exercising their discretion to prosecute environmental cases. Environmental cases carry some inherent challenges that will influence and shape a Crown counsel's discretion in various elements of the decision-making process, such as determining plea resolution, whether to proceed to trial or discontinue a prosecution, private prosecutions, entering a stay of proceedings, and appeals.

## Crown Discretion: A Brief History

The Crown counsel has a duty to ensure the proper administration of justice and in doing so must take into account the fairness of the accused, victims of crime, and the public interest. The public confidence in the administration of justice is strengthened where the system encourages Crown counsel to be strong and effective advocates.[1] The role of a Crown counsel has been described as a symbol of fairness within a complex system of law and order. The Supreme Court of Canada in *R. v. Boucher*[2] provided the following comments concerning the role of a Crown counsel:

> It cannot be overemphasized that the purpose of a criminal prosecution is not to obtain a conviction; it is to lay before a jury what the

> Crown considers to be credible evidence relevant to what is alleged to be a crime. Counsel have a duty to see that all available legal proof of the facts is presented; it should be done firmly and pressed to its legitimate strength, but it must also be done fairly. *The role of prosecutor excludes any notion of winning or losing; his function is a matter of public duty than which in civil life there can be none charged with greater responsibility*. It is to be efficiently performed with an ingrained sense of the dignity, the seriousness, and the justness of judicial proceedings.[3] [Emphasis added.]

The Attorney General has the responsibility to carry out prosecutions independent of pressure from interest groups and free from political influence. This unique and powerful position is fundamental in enabling the balance of power within the criminal-regulatory justice system. Prosecutorial discretion has been described as the discretion exercised by the Attorney General in matters within his or her authority in relation to the prosecution of criminal offences.[4] The Attorney General is the chief law officer of the Crown and a member of the Cabinet within the government. This unique relationship was discussed in *Kreiger*[5] by the Supreme Court of Canada, whereby the court referred to prosecutorial discretion as follows:

> Significantly, what is common to the various elements of prosecutorial discretion is that they involve the ultimate decisions as to whether a prosecution should be brought, continued or ceased, and what the prosecution ought to be for. Put differently, prosecutorial discretion refers to decisions regarding the nature and extent of the prosecution and the Attorney General's participation in it. Decisions that do not go to the nature and extent of the prosecution, i.e., the decisions that govern a Crown prosecutor's tactics or conduct before the court, do not fall within the scope of prosecutorial discretion. Rather, such decisions are governed by the inherent jurisdiction of the court to control its own processes once the Attorney General has elected to enter into that forum.[6]

## Decision to Prosecute

The Crown counsel must consider two factors in determining whether to prosecute a case. The first question to ask is—*Is there is a reasonable prospect of conviction based on evidence that is likely to be available at trial?*; and secondly: *Would a prosecution best serve the public interest?*[7] The courts will afford a

Crown counsel with a high degree of deference, but the scope of the deference is not unlimited. In determining whether there is enough evidence to support a proceeding, the courts have specified a test that encompasses both subjective and objective elements. In *Proulx v. Quebec (Attorney General)*,[8] the Supreme Court of Canada determined that there must be an actual reasonable belief on the part of the prosecutor—it must be reasonable in the circumstances—that there is enough evidence to support a prosecution. As this determination is one of law, not fact, the judge is tasked with the responsibility to make that determination.

With that said, in Canadian legal jurisprudence, the scope of prosecutorial discretion and what constitutes Crown misconduct continues to receive considerable judicial attention in the context of malicious prosecutorial actions against Crown counsels. In these cases,[9] the courts continue to afford a high level of deference to the decisions made by the Crown.

## THE SUFFICIENCY OF EVIDENCE

There are a number of factors a Crown may consider in determining the sufficiency of the evidence. The list of factors is not exhaustive and will be based on the circumstances of the case. Environmental prosecutions present a unique set of challenges to a Crown counsel in determining the sufficiency of the evidence. This unique class of prosecutions are considered to be regulatory prosecutions rather than true criminal law offences. This is an important distinction because it places environmental offences within the category of strict liability offences. This was discussed in great detail by the Supreme Court of Canada in *R. v. Sault Ste. Marie*,[10] which held that strict liability offences do not require *mens rea* but only an *actus reus* to prove the elements of the offence. In addition, it was reasoned that the defence of due diligence was available to the defendant.

### Credible Witnesses and the Expert

As part of a Crown counsel's exercise of reviewing the evidence, the Crown must assess the credibility of a variety of potential witnesses. In doing so, counsel must take into account such matters as the availability, competence, and the credibility of various witnesses. This becomes a more difficult exercise when applied to an expert witness. The expert witness plays a crucial role in explaining the scientific elements of an offence in most environmental prosecutions.[11] Unlike other witnesses, an expert witness is viewed as having *special knowledge* in his or her respective discipline. This knowledge may assist the trier of fact in understanding the case before the accused. Once a witness is qualified under a *voir dire* as an expert, the expert witness may provide opinion evidence. A court may rely on the expert evidence in reaching its decision.

The high degree of deference that a court may grant an expert witness will have an impact on the discretion exercised by Crown counsel. The challenge for the Crown is not limited to the assessment of the credibility of the expert witness; in addition, the Crown is required to present the special knowledge of an expert in an attempt to aid and assist the trier fact. This raises questions such as: Who is the right expert? What is the experience of the expert? Is the data quantifiable? Is there a shortage of experts? Is the debate of the experts one of data or methodology?—all of which must be given great scrutiny by the Crown in relation to the overall reasonable expectation of conviction.

### Admissibility of Evidence (Section 8 of the *Charter*)

It can be argued that the admissibility of evidence is one of the most important factors affecting the discretion of a Crown counsel. This includes all aspects of the Crown's case and, in particular, the evidence gathered as a result of an inspection and search. In most environmental legislation there are distinct powers that enable designated authorities to conduct inspections to ensure compliance with legislation or regulations. In this context, a Crown counsel must dedicate extra scrutiny to the examination of the evidence, as it relates to the use of the inspection authority by agents of the state.

A number of key cases involving section 8 of the *Canadian Charter of Rights and Freedoms* have caused Crown counsel to revisit the law associated with the authority to conduct an inspection and investigate regulatory offences.[12] In the regulatory world, the courts have acknowledged that inspection powers are necessary in order to ensure compliance with the legislation in question. The facts of a particular case will determine what test a court will apply in a given factual circumstance. In *R. v. Jarvis*,[13] the question for the court to determine was at what point a government-appointed investigator crosses the threshold—often referred to as the "*Rubicon*"—that results in the suspension of an inspection and the application of the *Charter*. In *Jarvis*,[14] the Supreme Court of Canada, in deciding the breadth of an inspection power, reasoned that an inspection will violate section 8 of the *Charter* if the predominant purpose of the site visit is to gather evidence for the purpose of a prosecution. This was articulated by Iacobucci and Major JJ. for the court:

> In our view, where *the predominant purpose of a particular inquiry is the determination of penal liability*, CCRA officials must relinquish

> the authority to use the inspection and requirement powers under ss. 231.1(1) and 231.2(1). In essence, officials "cross the Rubicon" when the inquiry in question engages the adversarial relationship between the taxpayer and the state. There is no clear formula that can answer whether or not this is the case. Rather, to determine whether the predominant purpose of the inquiry in question is the determination of penal liability, one must look to all factors that bear upon the nature of that inquiry.[15] [Emphasis added.]

In *R. v. Nolet*,[16] the Supreme Court of Canada considered the authority of an inspection in the context of a routine highway stop under the authority of provincial legislation. In that case, the court distinguished the *Jarvis* decision and created a new test in determining when the Rubicon has been crossed and when section 8 will be triggered. Although the court recognized the "*Jarvis* test" as the appropriate test for the particular facts of that case, it did—however—distinguish those facts from *Nolet*. Binnie J., for the majority of the court, reasoned that in cases where the intent of the search is penal, the question for the court to determine is whether the search was reasonable in the *totality of the circumstances*.[17] The distinguishing factor between the two cases suggests that a Crown counsel must determine whether the facts and the legislation support a situation where there is a "crossing of the Rubicon" from a civil dispute into an adversarial relationship with penal liability (*Jarvis*)—whereas, in *Nolet*, the courts determined the inspection had a penal consequence and there was no option to solve the matter through civil means. In essence, there was no Rubicon to cross in the case of *Nolet*. Binnie J. provided a summary:

> The present case is wholly different. We are not "crossing the Rubicon" from a civil dispute into penal remedies. Here the context was always penal. The *Charter* applies to provincial offences as well as to criminal offences. The shifting focus argument was appropriate in *Jarvis*, but I do not think it helps in the solution of this appeal. The issue here is whether the police search of the duffle bag did "in the totality of the circumstances" invade the reasonable privacy interest of the appellants. I would hold that it did not.[18]

The *Nolet* decision was followed in *R. v. Mission Western*,[19] which dealt with an inspection of a construction site under the authority of the *Fisheries Act*.[20] In *Mission*, the British Columbia Court of Appeal held that a court must review the actions of the officers and determine if those actions were reasonable in the totality of the circumstances. Bennett J. held:

> Like the inspection in *Nolet*, the DFO employees' actions always took place, broadly speaking, in a "penal" or "adversarial" context, in the sense that s. 49(1) of the *Fisheries Act* grants powers of entrance and inspection "for the purpose of ensuring compliance with this Act and the regulations". Ultimately, the proper question for consideration, as Binnie J. held in *Nolet*, is whether the officers' regulatory inspection powers were exercised reasonably in the totality of the circumstances.[21]

The case law surrounding section 8 of the *Charter* and the use of inspection powers by environmental agents will continue to challenge Crown counsel. In that respect, the test developed in *Jarvis* is still considered valid law in Canada. The challenge of a Crown counsel is to understand which test should be used based on the facts and the legislation in question. In addition, the Crown must assess the facts in order to determine if any evidence-gathering was carried out in contravention of section 8. These factors will have a critical impact on the discretion exercised by the Crown as it pertains to the approval of charges. The existence of a *Charter* violation may lead to an exclusion of evidence that may be essential to sustain a conviction—all of which weighs on the Crown counsel to make a sound decision based on an accurate interpretation of the law and fact.

### Possible Defences

A zealous consideration of potential defences should be part of a Crown counsel's routine assessment of a case. Although in theory, a Crown counsel must consider all the evidence available at the time it is presented by an investigator, this may not be possible in certain environmental cases. One example is the submission of a defence counsel's expert report. The Crown is not entitled to the expert report of an accused until the close of the Crown's case.[22] In such cases, a Crown counsel must consider a number of defences that are open to an accused, None of which are required to be disclosed to the Crown before trial. There is a range of defences available that will impact a Crown counsel's discretion:

### Due Diligence

- In *R. v. Gemtec Ltd. and Robert Lutes*, the New Brunswick Court of Appeal convicted an engineering consulting company of violating federal environmental laws based on a failure to incorporate environmental compliance into their advice. As a result, Crown counsel must anticipate due diligence defences of all parties involved: landowners, operators, subcontractors, and consultants;[23]

- In *R. v. Syncrude Canada Ltd.*, the Alberta Provincial Court described the due diligence test: "To meet the onus, Syncrude is not required to show that it took all possible or imaginable steps to avoid liability. It was not required to achieve a standard of perfection or show superhuman efforts. It is the existence of a "proper system" and "reasonable steps to ensure the effective operation of the system" that must be proved. The conduct of the accused is assessed against that of a reasonable person in similar circumstances; [Emphasis added.]"[24]
- Despite the fact that an employee of the defendant poured several thousand litres of a liquid substance into a storm drain on the defendant's property in contravention of provincial legislation, the Ontario Court of Justice, in *Ministry of the Environment v. Control Chem Canada Ltd.*, dismissed all charges and reasoned that the "scope of the Defendant's efforts to avoid and remediate any out of doors spills or discharge was broad, thorough, detailed, well documented, understood by employees and subject to frequent internal and external compliance review."[25]

#### Act of God

- In *R. v. British Columbia Hydro and Power Authority*,[26] Lamperson J. stated that a one in one thousand year event is to be treated as an act of God. However, he held that one in one hundred year events are "routinely planned for" and cannot be treated as such. The Ontario Provincial Court in *R. v. Weyerhaeuser* took a different position and considered a one in one hundred year rainfall to be an act of God—despite evidence of a lack of maintenance and care of the collapsed road crossing.[27] Such inconsistencies provide little to no guidance to Crown counsel in circumstances where a large unexpected event is alleged to have contributed to the offence.

#### Science vs. Law (Adequate Science)

- In *R v. Weyerhaeuser*, the Ontario Court of Justice reasoned that the science discrepancy between experts from the defence and the Crown was not enough to enter a conviction.[28] Crown counsel must consider the complexity and adequacy of the expert evidence. In doing so, a

Crown must determine if an expert's evidence will offer a convincing opinion that a court will understand and relate to the elements of the offence in question.

### Officially Induced Error

- The Supreme Court of Canada considered the defence of officially induced error in *La Souveraine, Compagnie d'assurance générale v. Autorité des marchés financiers.*[29] In doing so, Abella J. endorsed the six criteria for this defence as elaborated by Lamer CJ in *R. v. Jorgensen.*[30]

1. that an error of law or of mixed law and fact was made;
2. that the person who committed the act considered the legal consequences of his or her actions;
3. that the advice obtained came from an appropriate official;
4. that the advice was reasonable;
5. that the advice was erroneous; and
6. that the person relied on the advice in committing the act.

## PUBLIC INTEREST

If there is enough evidence to support the institution or continuation of a prosecution, Crown counsel must consider whether, in light of the evidence, the public interest requires a prosecution. The meaning of the public interest was considered by Sir Hartley Shawcross, QC, former Attorney General of England:

> It has never been the rule in this country—I hope it never will be—that suspected criminal offences must be subject to prosecution. Indeed, the very first regulations under which the Director of Public Prosecutions worked provided that he should … prosecute, amongst other cases: "wherever it appears that the offence or the circumstances of its commission is or are of such a character that a prosecution in respect thereof is required in the public interest." That is still the dominant consideration.[31]

In the exercise of the discretion by the Crown counsel, a number of different factors may guide a Crown in deciding whether to institute proceedings. In theory, the more serious the offence, the more likely the public interest will weigh on that discretion. With that said, it does not suggest that lesser offences should employ a lesser threshold. Consultation with the investigative agency can help a Crown counsel in such cases, but ultimately such decisions reside with the prosecution.

### Seriousness or Triviality of the Alleged Offence (*de minimis non curat lex*)

In most circumstances, Crown counsel is required to consider the public interest, even in cases where an alleged offence is not serious. With that said, Crown counsel may be presented with an occurrence that may appear to be a trivial violation of the Act. The difficulty with the concept of *de minimis* is that case law has suggested that *de minimis* does not apply to public welfare offences or strict liability. Platana J, in *R. v. Williams Operating*,[32] stated as follows:

> The trial judge used the maxim of *de minimis non curat lex* to determine that the quantities of the substances deposited were so insignificant as not to constitute an offence. I accept the Appellant's argument that based on the principles in *R. v. Sault Ste. Marie*, *R. v. Goodman* and *R. v. Croft*, *de minimis* does not apply to public welfare offences or strict liability offences.[33]

In essence, it could be argued that one drop of oil in a large water body with fish could potentially trigger a regulatory prosecution.[34] The question to consider is whether the public interest is satisfied in such cases—in other words, should limited resources be assigned to trivial matters? This determination becomes a difficult exercise in the balance between the public interest and application of *de minimis* to environmental prosecutions.[35] This can only be answered on a case-by-case basis with a delicate consideration of the facts.

### Significant Mitigating or Aggravating Circumstances

The behaviour of an accused will likely affect the way a Crown counsel will exercise their discretion during a prosecution.[36] For example, if an accused remediates a site soon after the commission of the offence, this may be seen as a mitigating factor in determining whether to pursue charges or in a sentencing hearing. In contrast, an accused that knowingly breaches environmental laws—and does so as a cost of doing business—would likely be viewed as aggravating.

This issue was discussed in *R. v. Ivy Fisheries*,[37] where a court ordered a fine in the amount of $650,909 for fishing tuna contrary to *Fisheries Act* licence conditions. Of that fine, $625,909 was ordered to be paid under section 79 of the *Fisheries Act*, which deals with an additional fine. The court reasoned that the additional fine was required to offset proceeds from the sale that was made as a result of the licence breach.

## SENTENCING CONSIDERATIONS

The goal of an environmental prosecution is not necessarily to seek punishment of an accused. For example, in some cases, Crown counsel should be guided by the principle of seeking a remediation plan that would put the environment in a position as if the offence had not been committed. In addition, Crown counsel must understand what type of sentence is appropriate and proportional to the offence committed. In other words, does the offence match the fine? Some environmental legislation may have abundant case law that will aid a Crown counsel in such circumstances, but this may not always be the case. The latter consideration will place the Crown in a position of trying to decide if the case is worth prosecuting based on the prospect of a low fine amount. For example, in cases where a Crown counsel is tasked with deciding whether to prosecute a particular case—where the allegation against the accused is one drop of oil in a large body of water—what factors should a Crown consider in the assessment of the public interest?

Such decisions can be said to be based on the public interest. However, it is understood in these cases that Crown counsel may be motivated to make a decision that will undoubtedly be influenced by the prospect of a low fine amount. I don't intend to suggest that a fine amount is the only factor to consider in such cases. However, it certainly is a factor that a Crown counsel will be unable to overlook, depending on the circumstances. Some other factors a Crown counsel may take into account are as follows:

- Do the facts support a low fine that is not worth pursuing?
- Will the court order technical details for a restorative action? (e.g. under s. 79.2 of the *Fisheries Act*)
- What are the estimated costs of the prosecution? Will the cost of the prosecution surpass the fine and remediation estimates?
- Remediation: Will the court order remediation in addition to a separate fine?[38]
- Will the case provide a bad precedent (bad facts can create bad law)?

### Alternatives to Prosecution

In some cases, Crown counsel may consider it to be in the public interest to pursue a prosecution. However, this may not be the most appropriate course of action in every circumstance. If that is the case, Crown counsel may consider alternatives to prosecution. The availability of alternatives to prosecution will depend on the facts of each case and the legislation in question.

This may include, for example, the use of corrective measures[39] under the *Fisheries Act*, aimed at stopping an actual deposit of a deleterious substance from entering waters frequented by fish; or an occurrence that results in serious harm to fish that are part of a commercial, recreational, or Aboriginal fishery; or to fish that support such a fishery. The above-noted authority can only be issued by a designated fishery officer or an inspector under the *Fisheries Act*. In such cases, a Crown counsel could decide that such an order may suffice and a prosecution under the general prohibition[40] would be unwarranted.

In addition, subsection 717(1) of the *Criminal Code*[41] provides in certain circumstances the option to consider the use of the alternative measure. The measures may be considered by Crown counsel if certain conditions are satisfied. Similarly, alternative measures may be considered if it is part of the legislation under which charges have been laid. For example, section 296 of the *Canadian Environmental Protection Act*[42] provides the option for alternative measures to a Crown counsel only if the alternative measure is not inconsistent with the purposes of the Act and the conditions set out under the section have been satisfied.

## Conclusion

This chapter has attempted to examine the role of a Crown counsel and the exercise of discretion. In particular, the chapter focuses on the challenges to environmental prosecutions. It is clear that Crown counsel face many challenges in deciding how to exercise their unique form of discretion. It can be argued that environmental cases carry some inherent challenges that may affect the discretion to prosecute or continuance of a case. Although such challenges may exist, there is a body of case law that can aid the Crown in determining the proper exercise of discretion.

### NOTES

1 *R v Cook* (1997), 114 CCC (3d) 481 (SCC) at 489.
2 [1955] SCR 16 (Rand J).
3 *Ibid* at 23–24.
4 *Krieger v Law Society of Alberta*, 2002 SCC 65.
5 *Ibid* at paras 23–32.
6 *Ibid* at para 47.
7 Public Prosecution Service of Canada, *The Federal Prosecution Service Desk Book*, c 2.3, online: <http://www.ppsc-sppc.gc.ca/eng/pub/fpsd-sfpg/fps-sfp/tpd/p2/ch03.html#section_2>.
8 [2001] 3 SCR 9.
9 *Nelles v Ontario* (1989), 60 DLR (4th) 609 (SCC); *Proulx v Quebec (Attorney*

*General)*, 2001 SCC 66. There are four necessary elements that must be proved for success in an action for malicious prosecution: A. the proceedings must have been initiated by the defendant; B. the proceedings must have terminated in favour of the plaintiff; C. the plaintiff must show that the proceedings were instituted without reasonable cause, and D. the defendant was actuated by malice. *Nelles*, *ibid* at 615.

10 [1978] 2 SCR 1978.

11 *Fisheries Act*, RSC 1985, c F-14, ss 35–36(3) [*Fisheries Act*]. Both sections of the *Fisheries Act* require expert opinion evidence to prove certain elements of the offence. The exception to this general rule is offences under s 36(3) where the deleterious substance in question that was deposited, and its quantity or concentration, is authorized by regulations. In such instances the requirement of leading expert evidence is lifted. This was the subject of debate in *Williams Operating*, *infra* note 27; the court deemed expert evidence unnecessary if by way of regulation substances are deemed to be deleterious.

12 The *Constitution Act, 1982*, Sched B to the *Canada Act 1982* (UK), 1982, c 11.

13 [2002] 3 SCR 757.

14 *Ibid.*

15 *Ibid* at para 88.

16 [2010] 1 SCR 851.

17 *Ibid* at para 86.

18 *Ibid* at para 86.

19 2012 BCCA 167. (Important to note: this case was a decision on leave to appeal to the BCCA. The BCCA denied the appeal.)

20 *Fisheries Act*, *supra* note 11.

21 *Ibid* at para 40.

22 *Criminal Code*, RSC 1985, c C-46, s. 657.3(c): in addition to complying with paragraph (a), an accused, or his or her counsel, who intends to call a person as an expert witness shall, not later than the close of the case for the prosecution, provide to the other party or parties the material referred to in paragraph (b).

23 *R v Gemtec Ltd* (2007), 321 NBR (2d) 200 (CA).

24 *R v Syncrude Canada Ltd*, 2010 ABPC 229.

25 *Ministry of the Environment v Control Chem Canada Ltd* (15 March 2016), ON Prov Ct No. Burlington 139537-01.

26 [1997] BCJ No 1744

27 *R v. Williams Operating* (2008), CanLII 48148 (ON SC) [*Williams Operating*].

28 *R v. Weyerhaeuser* (2007), ON COJ [Unreported].

29 [2013] SCJ No 63.

30 [1995] 4 SCR 55.

31 UK, House of Commons Debates, vol 483, col 681 (29 January 1951).

32 (2008), CanLII 48148 (ON SC).

33 *Ibid* at para 86.

34 The release of oil could be considered a deleterious substance which is prohibited under s 36(3) of the *Fisheries Act*.

35 Various cases have ruled that *de minimis* does not apply to strict liability offences—*Williams Operating*, *supra* note 27; *R v Croft* (2003), NSCA 109, 218 NSR (2d) 184; *R v Goodman*, [2005] BCJ No 542 (Prov Ct – Crim Div).

36 Other factors to consider: the accused's alleged degree of responsibility for the offence, previous convictions, other records of non-compliance.

37 (2006), 245 NSR (2d) 381 (Prov Ct).

38 The *Fisheries Act* supports separate fine amounts under ss 40, 79, and 78 and restoration under s 79.2.

39 *Fisheries Act*, *supra* note 11 at s 38(7.1).

40 *Fisheries Act*, *ibid* at s 36(3), general prohibition against the release of a deleterious substance.

41 RSC 1985, c C-46.

42 *Canadian Environmental Protection Act, 1999*, SC 1999, c 33.

# 14

# Regulatory Negligence in Environmental Law

LYNDA COLLINS AND JASMINE VAN SCHOUWEN

## Introduction

Canada enjoys a strong regulatory regime of statutory environmental law, ranging from municipal bylaws to nation-wide pollution provisions enacted by the federal government. Statutory environmental law covers the full universe of environmental issues, including waste management, toxic substances, natural resources, and air, land, and water pollution. In addition, Canadians benefit from the efforts of thousands of specialized public servants who work in the various environmental and natural resource ministries across the country, including prosecutors. Despite these laudable efforts, Canada's environmental performance ranks quite poorly in comparison to other developed nations, and available data indicates a disturbing persistence of hazardous contaminants in environmental media and human bodies.[1] One of the reasons for the dissonance between the stated goals of Canadian environmental legislation and the reality of widespread contamination is the non-enforcement of environmental laws in Canada.

This chapter will consider the civil liability of governments for environmental non-enforcement, with a focus on negligence. It should be noted at the outset that absent a showing of malice or impropriety, specific decisions as to whether or not to prosecute a particular polluter for a particular incident will likely remain immune from tort liability given the high degree of deference accorded to prosecutorial decision making.[2] However, plaintiffs in environmental non-enforcement cases frequently base their tort claims on the cumulative impact of a pattern of both acts and omissions resulting in harm. In these cases, the claim amounts to an assertion that, while government had discretion as to choice of regulatory tool, it had a duty to act with due care in its regulation of polluting enterprises.[3]

## Why Sue Government?

Suits against government defendants make up a significant area within the law and practice of toxic torts. Because government enjoys the unique ability to regulate the characteristics of both products and contaminant emissions, it has significant exposure to toxic tort liability. In the environmental arena, for example, government is the only actor that can substantially influence the ambient air or water quality in a region. Any individual emitter is simply one contributor to the overall problem. Thus, if a plaintiff's illness results from the accumulation of emissions in a given air- or watershed, it is unsurprising that recourse would be sought from the regulator. Similarly, where government has approved a particular toxic pharmaceutical or food product, plaintiffs will frequently join the regulator as a co-defendant along with the product's manufacturer. In addition to its regulatory liability, governments also carry out large-scale infrastructure projects and other activities (e.g. energy production) that may result in losses to private individuals, and, therefore, attract liability in tort.[4]

Although a variety of civil causes of action are theoretically maintainable against environmental regulators (including novel theories in breach of public trust and s. 24 damages for environmental *Charter* violations, for example), by far the most common tort claim against government is that of negligence. The tort of negligence includes the elements of duty of care, breach of the relevant standard of care, factual causation, proximate causation (i.e. the absence of remoteness), and actual loss. The elements of causation, remoteness, and actual loss are generally unchanged in government negligence actions as opposed to suits involving private parties only. Although the governmental standard of care analysis is somewhat unique, the single most distinctive characteristic of the government negligence action is the duty analysis.

Duty of care involves a two-stage inquiry, which asks first whether there is a *prima facie* duty owed by the defendant to the plaintiff, and second whether such duty should be negated or limited due to policy considerations. Step one includes the criteria of foreseeability of harm and proximity, and it is this latter factor that has most often defeated negligence actions against government defendants. Courts have frequently held that there is inadequate proximity between the regulator and the plaintiff because there is no difference between the plaintiff and the general public in relation to whom the entity in question regulates. This of course was the result in *Cooper v. Hobart*,[5] and has likewise defeated a number of prominent toxic tort claims against government. In claims involving West Nile virus, Severe Acute Respiratory Syndrome (SARS), and regulation of drugs and medical devices, courts have refused to hold that the regulator's general statutory duty crystallized into a private law duty to the particular plaintiff at issue.

In *Eliopoulos v. Ontario*,[6] for example, the Court of Appeal held that Ontario had no private law duty of care to Mr. Eliopoulos, who died from West Nile Virus from a mosquito bite.[7] The plaintiffs argued that since the province had developed a plan to prevent the spread of the virus, and Mr. Eliopoulos still became ill, this was an operational failure and liability should lie. Ruling that this was a new duty of care, the court was prepared to assume foreseeability, but held that there was no proximity, since the statutory powers of the Ontario government[8] were to be exercised in the "general public interest," not for the benefit of any particular individual.[9] In terms of broader policy implications (the second branch of *Anns/Cooper*), "to impose a private law duty of care … would create an unreasonable and undesirable burden on Ontario that would interfere with sound decision-making in the realm of public health. Public health priorities should be based on the general public interest."[10] Similar results and rationales were given in the SARS cases[11] and in several drug or medical device regulation cases.[12]

One significant difference between the duty of care analysis involving private defendants and that involving regulators is that the latter often begins with a consideration of the statutory scheme under which the entity operates in order to determine whether the statute creates a private duty of care distinguishable from the government's duty to the public as a whole.[13] The analysis of this factor aims to determine whether there is something in the statute that distinguishes the relationship between this plaintiff and the regulator from the relationship that exists between the regulator and all those affected by the regulator's actions.[14] The analysis of the wording of the statutory scheme is, however, intended to be a single factor among many in establishing proximity; it is not a necessary source of proximity, and is unlikely to be a sufficient source of proximity alone, although "it may play a positive role in establishing proximity, provided the resulting duty would not conflict with the statutory scheme."[15]

This being said, some courts have focused on the regulator's enabling statute as the sole potential source of proximity and have concluded that "there is no sufficient proximity in the circumstance of a regulatory failure to enforce a statute or regulation of public rather than private interest."[16] Despite acknowledging the statute as one factor among many, these courts tended to focus almost exclusively on the text of the enabling statute, often ending their analysis after concluding that the statutory scheme does not give rise to a private duty of care.[17] Claims for regulatory non-enforcement were struck on this basis in environmental class actions in *Pearson v. Inco* (contamination from nickel refinery) and *MacQueen v Sidbec Inc.*[18] (Sydney Tar Ponds).

Jurisprudence from the Supreme Court of Canada, however, counsels that factors to be considered in evaluating proximity go beyond the relevant statute(s) and include "expectations, representations, reliance, and the property or other interests involved."[19] A recent line of cases clarifies the role of government representations in establishing proximity; although these cases are not specifically environmental in character, they clarify the general principles to be applied in assessing proximity in government negligence suits.

In *Sauer v. Canada*, cattle farmers suffered loss as a result of the emergence of "mad cow disease" in Canadian herds. The plaintiffs alleged that the federal government was negligent in continuing to permit the addition of ruminant remains in cattle feed. The court made a finding of proximity, noting in particular Canada's "many public representations" that it regulates cattle feed to protect "commercial farmers among others."[20] In *Taylor v. Canada*,[21] Justice Cullity certified a class action involving plaintiffs injured by temporomandibular implants (TMJ implants). Justice Cullity held that on the facts alleged, there was sufficient proximity between the parties to meet the duty of care requirement, relying in part on the 2007 decision in *Sauer*. In 2008, the Ontario Court of Appeal dismissed appeals in *Drady v. Canada (Minister of Health)*[22] involving TMJ implants, and *Attis v. Canada (Minister of Health)*,[23] involving breast implants. The court declined to find proximity in these cases, distinguishing them from *Sauer* on the basis that there was an absence of the kinds of government representations alleged by the cattle farmers in *Sauer*. The Supreme Court of Canada denied leave to appeal in both cases. In the 2009 decision in *Knight v. Imperial Tobacco Canada Ltd.*,[24] the BC Court of Appeal found that there was a sufficient allegation of proximity against the federal government in a suit based on negligent misrepresentation and negligent development of tobacco strains for mild and light cigarettes.

In 2010, on a motion to decertify in *Taylor*, Justice Cullity found that he could not distinguish the pleadings before him from those in *Attis* and *Drady* and struck the plaintiffs' statement of claim with leave to amend. Justice Cullity later upheld Taylor's fresh statement of claim, which included allegations that Health Canada had made various representations that the regulatory scheme governing medical devices was intended to protect individual consumers like the plaintiffs. Finally, the Supreme Court of Canada ruled in the *Knight v. Imperial Tobacco* appeal that Canada did not owe a *prima facie* duty of care to consumers of low-tar cigarettes. The statute did not impose a private law duty, there were no specific interactions between Canada and the class members, and Canada's statements to the general public regarding the characteristics of light cigarettes did not suffice.[25]

In an attempt to reconcile the disparate holdings in regulatory negligence jurisprudence, the Ontario Court of Appeal accepted a special case in *Taylor* posing the question as to what allegations are necessary to establish a viable argument for proximity in a regulatory negligence action. In reasons released in July 2012, the court explained that in regulatory negligence actions, "the proximity inquiry will focus initially on the applicable legislative scheme and secondly on the interactions, if any, between the regulator or governmental authority and the putative plaintiff."[26] If the applicable legislation imposes or forecloses a private law duty of care,[27] this is the end of the inquiry. If the legislation leaves the question of tort liability open, then the court proceeds to examine the interaction between the parties.[28] The court noted that cases in which a finding of proximity has been made involve a relationship with the plaintiff that is "distinct from and more direct than the relationship between the regulator and that part of the public affected by the regulator's work."[29] Secondly, the proposed private law duty must not be inconsistent with the regulator's public duties.[30] The court held that the existence of particular representations to the plaintiff may give rise to proximity, and this factor will not be satisfied by general public representations concerning the regulator's public duties.[31]

However, the Court of Appeal clarified that specific representations to the plaintiff are not *necessary* for a finding of proximity, and the court will look at the totality of the interactions between the plaintiff and defendant, including the defendant's public representations.[32] Noting Chief Justice McLachlin's admonition in *Imperial Tobacco* that "where the asserted basis for proximity is grounded in specific conduct and interactions, ruling a claim out at the proximity stage may be difficult,"[33] the court upheld the plaintiffs' statement of claim in *Taylor*. It held that the proximity requirement could be met by the combined effect of allegations that (i) Health Canada erroneously represented that the certain implants had met regulatory requirements, (ii) Health Canada was informed of defects in the implants and resulting harm to patients, (iii) Health Canada took no adequate steps in response to this information, (iv) Health Canada represented throughout that it monitored and ensured the safety of medical devices, and (v) the plaintiffs relied on these representations.[34] Health Canada's misrepresentation as to regulatory compliance, and its failure to correct this misrepresentation, were clearly salient. The defendants did not seek leave to appeal the Ontario Court of Appeal's decision to the Supreme Court of Canada, and the *Taylor* action is accordingly ongoing.

The Ontario Court of Appeal's decision in *Taylor* notes that proximity has been found where the regulator was aware of a specific threat against a relatively small and well-defined group and where the defendant has a statutory obligation to monitor and protect.[35] This suggests that proximity in environmental cases is most likely to be found where plaintiffs are harmed by a specific polluting facility that posed foreseeable risks of harm to its neighbours. This is particularly true where the plaintiff has solicited advice or assurances from the regulators and has relied on the information provided. Although prosecutorial discretion itself is generally non-reviewable, a pattern of non-prosecution coupled with an absence of alternative effective measures to curb pollution may give rise to liability. The Supreme Court of Canada's decision in *Fullowka*[36] suggests that when regulatory officials have visited a particular site and are aware of specific hazards, proximity is more likely to be recognized. Thus, when a particular facility has a pattern of environmental non-compliance that has impacts on a discrete geographic area, a finding of proximity appears likely. Where an environmental regulator has not only failed to enforce relevant standards in statute and/or regulation but has also affirmatively facilitated the harmful conduct by issuing specific pollution permits, the argument for proximity is even stronger.

This possibility has been confirmed by the Ontario Superior Court of Justice's recent decision in *Swaita v Her Majesty the Queen in Right of Ontario (Environment)*.[37] In this case, the Ontario Ministry of the Environment became involved in the cleanup of an oil spill affecting the plaintiff's property. The ministry decided where the excavation of contaminants should stop and erred in failing to ensure that the contaminants were contained; as a result, the plaintiff's property became contaminated, and the plaintiff sustained damages. The court dismissed the defendant's motion to strike the plaintiff's claim, concluding that:

> Once the defendant embarks on a course of action (whether obliged to do so under a legislative scheme, or has chosen to do so under discretionary powers) the defendant is obliged to carry out that course of conduct without negligence. There is then a sufficient proximity for the basis of a private law duty of care.[38]

However, the Alberta Court of Appeal has recently indicated that it may not be willing to recognize a duty of care, even in such circumstances: In *Ernst v Alberta (Energy Resources Conservation Board)*,[39] the Alberta Energy Resources Conservation Board, tasked with overseeing hydraulic fracturing (fracking) in Alberta, allegedly failed to conduct proper investigations into fracking-related contamination in Rosebud, Alberta, after the plaintiff raised concerns about methane contamination of her well water.[40] When the board intervened to conduct an investigation into the contamination, it allegedly did not follow a sampling protocol, used unsterilized equipment when taking samples, committed sampling errors, lost, destroyed, or otherwise disposed of data, failed to test water wells for various substances that could be indicative of industry contamination, and failed to test or investigate specifically identified gas wells that potentially caused water contamination.[41] In its decision granting the board a motion to strike the claim, the Court of Appeal of Alberta concluded:

> Forcing the Board to consider the extent to which it must balance the interests of specific individuals while attempting to regulate in the overall public interest would be unworkable in fact and bad policy in law. Recognizing any such private duty would distract the Board from its general duty to protect the public, as well as its duty to deal fairly with participants in the regulated industry. Any such individualized duty of care would plainly involve indeterminate liability, and would undermine the Board's ability to effectively address the general public obligations placed on it under its controlling legislative scheme.[42]

Should the plaintiff survive the proximity hurdle, proving the foreseeability of physical harm is generally unproblematic, and the inquiry therefore proceeds to stage two of the *Anns/Childs* analysis. This step of the duty test addresses "residual policy considerations," or those that are unrelated to the relationship between the parties.[43] One such factor is the character of the government decision at issue; if it is one of "policy," then no liability will attach. If the decision is found to be "operational" in nature, then the duty may be sustained.[44] In *Brown v. British Columbia (Minister of Transport and Highways)*, the court held that policy decisions "involve social, political and economic factors, [and ...] the authority attempts to strike a balance between efficiency and thrift, in the context of planning and predetermining the boundaries of its undertakings and of their actual performance. True policy decisions will usually be dictated by financial, economic, social and political factors or constraints."[45] By contrast, operational decisions are "concerned with the practical implementation of the formulated policies" and "will usually be made on the basis of administrative direction, expert or professional opinion, technical standards or general standards of reasonableness."[46] Although the policy–operational dichotomy has been strongly criticized as a touchstone for liability, the test has persisted in Canadian negligence law. In order to establish tort liability for environmental non-enforcement, plaintiffs will be required to show that the regulator had a policy of pursuing environmental protection and/or enforcing the relevant standards and that the failure to do so was an operational one, rather than a decision of policy. This has proven problematic for plaintiffs in previous cases.

In *Pearson v. Inco*,[47] for example, the plaintiff class alleged that as a result of the Ministry of Environment's (MOE's) negligent regulation of an Inco metals refinery over a period of decades, they had been exposed to unsafe levels of air emissions and their properties had become contaminated. On a motion to strike, the court found that the plaintiffs could not succeed in their claim against the Crown because they failed to allege that the MOE was negligent in the implementation of any "policy, practice or procedure" regarding Inco.[48] Prior to the certification hearing, the plaintiffs amended their claim to allege (*inter alia*) that during the course of its operations, the ministry had made hundreds of investigations of the refinery and issued more than 70 Certificates of Approval affirmatively permitting Inco's activities.[49] Indeed, the MOE conceded that it had issued approvals, performed hundreds of investigations, received complaints from members of the public, closely monitored Inco's emissions, and "encouraged Inco to abate both its air emissions and water emissions, either by voluntary or regulatory means such as control orders."[50]

Although the court allowed claims based on the negligent implementation of affirmative policies of inspection, approvals, etc., it struck the cause of action based on the MOE's failure to enforce the *Environmental Protection Act*.[51] Indeed, the court treated this claim as a challenge to prosecutorial discretion and found that unless malice was alleged the claim must fail.[52] This decision predates *Fullowka*, however, and might have been decided differently had that authority been available at the time.

## Conclusion

Although negligence actions against regulators fail more often than they succeed, liability for environmental non-enforcement remains a live issue. Particularly in cases where regulators are both failing to protect environmental quality and affirmatively authorizing harmful pollution, plaintiffs could plausibly succeed in clearing the hurdle of duty of care. Assuming there is further evidence linking unreasonable conduct with a resulting harm on a balance of probabilities, liability would ensue. For now, liability for environmental non-enforcement remains an emerging area in Canadian tort law.

### NOTES

1 See generally Office of the Auditor General, *The 2004 Report of the Commissioner of the Environment and Sustainable Development* (Ottawa: Minister of Public Works and Government Services, 2004); Jana Neuman et al, *Toxic Nation: A Report on Pollution in Canadians* (Toronto: Environmental Defence, November 2005); OECD, *OECD Environmental Performance Reviews: Canada* (Paris: OECD Publications, 2017), online: <http://www.oecd.org/environment/oecd-environmental-performance-reviews-canada-2017-9789264279612-en.htm>.

2 See, e.g., *Pearson v Inco* (2002), 115 ACWS (3d) 564 [*Pearson (2002)*] [affirmed on appeal to the Divisional Court in *Pearson v Inco Ltd* (2004), 128 ACWS (3d) 875, overturned by the Ontario Court of Appeal on other grounds in *Pearson v Inco Ltd* (2005) 143 ACWS (3d) 973]; *Werring v British Columbia*, [1997] BCJ No 2952 (QL), and more recently *Ernst v Alberta* 2014 ABCA 285 (Energy Resources Conservation Board) [*Ernst*] (affirmed in *Ernst v Alberta Energy Regulator*, 2017 SCC 1), and *MacQueen v Sidbec Inc*, 2006 NSSC 208 [*MacQueen*].

3 See, e.g., *Procureur général du Québec v Girard*, [2003] JQ no 9105 at paras 414, 417–419, varied on appeal in *Girard v 2944-7828 Québec inc*, [2004] JQ No 13624.

4 See, e.g., *Sydney Steel Corporation v MacQueen*, 2013 NSCA 5 at paras 6–7.

5 *Cooper v Hobart*, 2001 SCC 79, [2001] 3 SCR 537.

6 *Eliopoulos v Ontario* (2006), 82 OR (3d) 321 (CA) [*Eliopoulos*], leave to appeal refused [2006] SCCA No 514.

7 *Ibid* at para 12: "There is plainly no category of cases that supports the respondents' assertion that Ontario owes a private law duty to protect all persons within its boundaries from contracting a disease."

8 Under the *Health Protection and Promotion Act*, RSO 1990, c H.7.

9 *Eliopoulos*, *supra* note 6 at paras 17, 20.

10 *Ibid* at para 33.

11 See, e.g., *Williams v Canada (Attorney General)*, 2009 ONCA 378, 310 DLR (4th) 710, leave to appeal refused [2009] SCCA No 298; *Abarquez v Ontario* (2005), 257 DLR (4th) 745 (Ont Sup Ct), varied on appeal 2009 ONCA 374, 310 DLR (4th) 726; *Jamal Estate v Scarborough Hospital – Grace Division*, [2005] OTC 726 (Ont Sup Ct), varied on appeal 2009 ONCA 376, 95 OR (3d) 760.

12 *Klein v American Medical Systems Inc* (2006), 84 OR (3d) 217 (Div Ct); *Attis v Canada (Minister of Health)*, 2008 ONCA 660, 93 OR (3d) 35, leave to appeal refused [2008] SCCA No 491 (government regulation of breast implants—chilling effect on public health mandate and spectre of indeterminate liability if government seen as guarantor of public health).

13 *R v Imperial Tobacco Canada Ltd*, [2011] 3 SCR 45, 2011 SCC 42 at paras 43–45; *Klein v American Medical Systems Inc* (2006), 84 OR (3d) 217; 278 DLR (4th) 722 at paras 23–25.

14 *Taylor v Canada (Health)*, 2009 ONCA 487, 309 DLR (4th) 400 at para 104.

15 Peter W Hogg, QC, Patrick J Monahan and Wade K Wright, *Liability of the Crown*, 4th ed (Toronto: Carswell, 2011) at 231.

16 *MacQueen*, *supra* note 2 at para 48.

17 *Klein v American Medical Systems Inc* (2006), 84 OR (3d) 217, 278 DLR (4th) 722 (Div Ct).
18 *Pearson (2002)* and *MacQueen*, both *supra* note 2.
19 *Cooper v Hobart, supra* note 5 at para 34.
20 *Sauer v Canada (Attorney General) et al*, 2007 ONCA 454 at para 62.
21 *Taylor v Canada (Attorney General)*, 2011 ONCA 181.
22 (2008), 300 DLR (4th) 443 (Ont CA).
23 (2008), 93 OR (3d) 35 (CA).
24 (2009), 313 DLR (4th) 695 (BCCA).
25 *R v Imperial Tobacco Canada Ltd*, 2011 SCC 42 at paras 49–50 [*Tobacco (2011)*].
26 *Taylor v Canada (Attorney General)*, 2012 ONCA 479 at para 75 [*Taylor (2012)*].
27 *Ibid* at para 77.
28 *Ibid* at para 79.
29 *Ibid* at para 80.
30 *Ibid* at para 88.
31 *Ibid* at para 95.
32 *Ibid* at para 96.
33 *Tobacco (2011), supra* note 25 at para 47, cited in *Taylor (2012), supra* note 26 at para 103.
34 *Taylor (2012), ibid* at para 109.
35 See *Doe v. Metropolitan Toronto (Municipality) Commissioners of Police* (1990), 74 OR (2d) 225 (Div. Ct.) and *Fullowka, infra* note 36.
36 *Fullowka v Pinkerton's of Canada Ltd*, 2010 SCC 5, [2010] 1 SCR 132 at paras 37–55.
37 2016 ONSC 5785 (CanLII).
38 *Ibid* at para 15.
39 *Ernst, supra* note 2 at para 17.
40 Amended Statement of Claim, *Ernst v EnCana Corporation, Energy Resources and Conservation Board and Her Majesty the Queen in Right of Alberta*, court file 0702-00120, online: <http://www.ernstversusencana.ca/wp-content/uploads/2010/10/ Statement-of-Claim.pdf> at para 132.
41 *Ibid* at para 162.
42 *Ernst, supra* note 2 at para 18.
43 *Cooper v Hobart, supra* note 5 at para 37; see also *Childs v Desormeaux*, 2006 SCC 18, [2006] 1 SCR 643 at para 12.
44 See generally LM Collins, "Tort, Democracy and Environmental Governance: Crown Liability for Environmental Non-Enforcement" (2007) Tort L Rev 107.
45 *Brown v British Columbia (Minister of Transport and Highways)*, [1994] 1 SCR 420 at para 38.
46 *Ibid.*
47 See *Pearson (2002), supra* note 2.
48 *Pearson v Inco*, [2001] OJ No 4990 at para 22 [*Pearson (2001)*]. As in *Cooper v Hobart, supra* note 5, Nordheimer J found that there was insufficient proximity to establish a duty of care (*ibid* at paras 30–31) but also held that the negligent claim was an impermissible attack on the MOE's failure to adopt a particular policy with respect to *Pearson (2001), ibid* at 24. The finding on proximity was apparently not fatal to plaintiffs' claims; in the subsequent certification motion Nordheimer J permitted the plaintiffs to proceed with amended negligence claims alleging negligence in the implementation of policy. See *Pearson (2002), supra* note 2 at paras 85–86, 109.
49 *Pearson (2002), supra* note 2 at para 27.
50 *Ibid* at paras 62–65.
51 The court also allowed a claim for negligent misrepresentation based on communications from the MOE to residents allegedly suggesting that residents were not being exposed to a health threat from the refinery's emissions. However, it found that such a claim could not be adjudicated as a class proceeding. See *ibid* at paras 66, 103.C.(iv), 109–112.
52 *Ibid* at para 86. Note, however, that the court ultimately dismissed the motion for certification on the grounds that the plaintiffs failed to satisfy the requirements under s 5(1) of the CPA.

# 15

# Strategic Decisions in Environmental Prosecutions

PAUL McCULLOCH AND DANIELLE MEULEMAN

## The Nature of Environmental Offences

Most environmental offences are regulatory in nature. The general purpose of regulatory legislation, as explained by Justice Cory in the Supreme Court's 1991 decision in *R. v. Wholesale Travel Group Inc.*, is to protect public and societal interests:

> The objective of regulatory legislation is to protect the public or broad segments of the public (such as employees, consumers and motorists, to name but a few) from the potentially adverse effects of otherwise lawful activity. Regulatory legislation involves a shift of emphasis from the protection of individual interests and the deterrence and punishment of acts involving moral fault to the protection of public and societal interests. While criminal offences are usually designed to condemn and punish past, inherently wrongful conduct, regulatory measures are generally directed to the prevention of future harm through the enforcement of minimum standards of conduct and care.[1]

Regulatory offences are typically strict liability regimes in which the prosecutor is not required to prove a mental element. Rather, the prosecutor must simply prove, beyond a reasonable doubt, that the violator carried out all the elements of the offence (the *actus reus*). The onus then shifts to the defendant, who may choose to raise a defence, the most common being due diligence, in which the defendant must disprove the presumption of negligence by establishing, on a balance of probabilities, that it exercised all due care to foresee and prevent the commission of the offence.[2] This reverse onus plays an important role in some of the most important strategic considerations: what to investigate, who to charge, and what to charge them with, which jurisdiction to hold the trial, when to enter into a plea arrangement, will the evidence be admissible, what can't be argued, and, perhaps the most important question, why are charges warranted. Both the prosecutor and defence counsel must consider these questions throughout the prosecution process, including the investigation stage.

## What To Investigate?

Before laying a charge, there must be sufficient evidence to demonstrate that there are reasonable and probable grounds to believe that an offence has been committed.[3] This threshold is usually reached when an investigator or inspector has amassed enough information to form the necessary belief. Therefore, the first strategic decisions involve the collection of evidence.

Enforcement agencies become aware of potential offences through a variety of means: random and targeted inspections to confirm compliance with environmental laws, complaints received from the public, information received from other regulatory agencies, self-reporting mechanisms, and whistleblowers. The regulated community and the enforcement agency alike should be aware of and prepared to respond to each of these situations.

During an inspection process the regulated community is generally subject to warrantless inspections and is required to provide a range of information upon request. Inspection powers are typically expansive and allow the regulator to enter any property to obtain information, samples, and documents, and take photos or video recordings.[4] If the subject of the inspection refuses entry, it may be charged with obstruction.[5] It is also an offence to provide false or misleading information.[6]

However, at a certain point, an enforcement agency may overstep its bounds and instead of conducting an inspection for the purpose of determining whether a person is complying with regulatory requirements, begin collecting evidence for the purpose of laying charges. The distinction between an inspection on the one hand and an investigation on the other may be a fine line, but it is an important one. If the "predominant purpose" behind the use of these powers was to obtain evidence for the purpose of laying a charge, the prosecutor may not be able use this evidence (or evidence that flowed directly from this information), as the use of "super powers" in the course of an investigation may be found to breach a person's privacy interests.[7]

A key decision that must be made is to determine what information is available as evidence of an offence, and what information is off limits because it is inculpatory and was obtained through the use of "super powers" after the investigation was commenced.

## What Charge?

If a decision is made to launch an investigation, the investigator will assess the range of possible offences and proceed to gather evidence. There are many different types of environmental offences. Common offences include:

- failure to comply with administrative orders;
- failure to obtain licence/approval/permit;
- failure to comply with conditions in licence/approval/permit;
- failure to keep records;
- depositing waste without an approval or in area not approved for disposal;
- discharges that exceed approved limits.

Typically, some of the more serious offences include:

- discharging contaminants that cause adverse effect or impair the environment;
- failure to report discharges/spills/upsets/accidents;
- obstruction;
- submitting false and misleading information;
- offences involving toxic/hazardous substances;
- habitat destruction.

A single complaint, incident, or inspection can lead to a mix of different types of offences, and can involve a single offence over a period of time or discrete offences on the same day. Therefore, once an investigator determines that he or she has reasonable and probable grounds, the next important step is to decide what charge(s) to proceed with. Some of the considerations that go into this determination are the seriousness of the offences, the number of offences, the complexity of the evidence needed to prove each charge, and what statutory regime to proceed under. As well, some statutes have prescribed minimum penalties for certain offences, and the investigator may consider (and the defendant may want to try to influence) whether to charge with a more serious or with a lesser offence.[8]

## Who To Charge?

Another strategic decision involves considering who should be charged or whether the right person was charged. In some situations, it is fairly simple as there is only one perpetrator. However, the simple situation may be the rare one. More often, there are many complicated facts that involve a number of possible parties, such as subcontracting or landlord-tenant arrangements. Some transactions may involve multiple steps, with each step being carried out by a different person, for example when hazardous waste is generated by one person, a second person is contracted to transport the waste, often to a transfer and processing centre operated by a third person, where it may be picked up by a fourth person and taken to its final disposal destination owned another separate person. If it turns out that the waste was not managed properly, or is spilled, or disposed of inappropriately because it wasn't classified properly, it can be very difficult to determine which party(ies) was/were ultimately responsible.

As well, as with criminal law, regulatory offences do not limit liability to persons who actually commit offences, but normally extend it to parties to an offence—those who aid, abet, counsel, or procure another person to commit an offence. This extension of liability can be based in the procedural statute governing the legislation;[9] however, many environmental offences specifically provide for multiple ways in which an offence can be committed. A second issue, which arose in the seminal *Sault Ste. Marie* decision, is the explanation of the scope of the terms "cause" and "permit." The City of Sault Ste. Marie was charged with depositing waste into a water body that impaired the quality of the water even though the municipality had hired a contractor to manage the city's waste. The offence in question provided that "every municipality or person that discharges or deposits or causes or permits the discharge or deposit of any material into water … that may impair the quality of the water … is guilty of an offence." Justice Dickson (as he then was) noted that this style of legislation is not duplicitous as it "is aimed at one class of offender only, those who pollute."[10]

In addition to these general provisions that expand liability from the "active" offender to include "passive" offenders, many environmental statutes also impose a separate duty on corporate directors and officers to take all reasonable to ensure that a corporation complies with its environmental responsibilities.[11]

Additional considerations arise where the offender is a corporation. Most environmental statutes provide that the acts of an employee are considered to be the acts of an employer.[12] Therefore, if an employee contravenes a statute in the course of his or her duties, it is possible to charge one or both of the employee(s) involved and the corporate employer. Another consideration is whether to proceed with a prosecution when a corporation has become insolvent or has even been dissolved.[13] As corporations can be revived, it may still be worthwhile pursuing. Furthermore, if the prosecution results in a conviction, the sentence may act as a useful deterrent to others.

So, an investigator and prosecutor must determine (and defence counsel may wish to challenge) who is liable for an offence, who may be a party to an offence, and if anyone had a statutory duty to prevent the commission of the offence. Based on these considerations, the decision will be made as to who should be charged.

## Trial Jurisdiction

One important consideration that is unique to Ontario is to decide which justice should preside over the case—a justice of the peace or a provincial court judge. Justices of the peace hear most matters under Ontario's *Provincial Offences Act* (POA). Generally, POA matters include highway traffic act contraventions, municipal bylaw infractions, and other less serious offences. However, environmental offences, including ones with serious consequences to both the environment and potentially the defendant, will also be heard by a justice of the peace, many of whom are not legally trained prior to being appointed to the bench.

Many statutes permit the prosecutor to elect, as a right, to have a matter heard by a provincial court judge instead of a justice of the peace.[14] The defendant may also request, but does not have a right, to have the matter heard by a judge. However, due to the differing caseloads, it may take much longer to schedule a trial before a judge as opposed to a justice of the peace. Therefore, in most cases, the prosecutor will not exercise the right to elect a judge. It is generally only when there are complex and/or legal arguments anticipated, such as a new type of *Charter* claim or complicated statutory interpretation issues, that such an election or request will be made.

## When to Make a Plea Offer

Many of the strategic decisions outlined above come to the fore during resolution discussions. The prosecutor is required to disclose all evidence in its possession and is not concerned with "winning" or ensuring that a defendant is convicted, but instead is responsible for ensuring that the evidence is presented in a manner that is fair and truthful.[15] However, the prosecutor is not necessarily required to reveal exactly how the case will be run. The Ontario Court of Appeal has recognized that "trials are dynamic and as events unfold, prosecution and defence may find that they have to respond quickly to changes in strategy."[16] Defence counsel have virtually unlimited latitude, subject to the rules of professional conduct, to decide whether to disclose in advance any evidence in its position or the defences that will be argued in advance. On the one hand, providing such information to the prosecutor may result in a better resolution for the defendant, such as a lower fine. On the other hand, doing so may often enable the prosecutor to prepare better for the trial.

The *Canadian Environmental Protection Act, 1999* (CEPA) sets out the fundamental purposes for sentencing offences under that Act, and arguably the principles in this section are applicable to most environmental offences:

> **287.** The fundamental purpose of sentencing for offences under this Act is to contribute, in light of the significant and many threats to the environment and to human health and to the importance of a healthy environment to the well-being of Canadians, to respect for the law protecting the environment and human health through the imposition of just sanctions that have as their objectives:
>
> (a) to deter the offender and any other person from committing offences under this Act;
> (b) to denounce unlawful conduct that damages or creates a risk of damage to the environment or harms or creates a risk of harm to human health; and
> (c) to reinforce the "polluter pays" principle by ensuring that offenders are held responsible for effective clean-up and environmental restoration.[17]

In addition to these principles, case law and various environment statutes set out a number of factors that should be considered when determining an appropriate sentence: damage to the environment, the nature and extent of the damage, whether the defendant is a repeat offender, the moral blameworthiness of the defendant, and whether the offence resulted in a monetary benefit, among others.[18] Another factor is the current status of compliance. If the charge relates to an ongoing offence (e.g. an order to clean up a site, a requirement to submit records to the ministry) or if the defendant has ongoing compliance issues (e.g. a waste transfer site that continually fails to store liquid industrial waste in designated areas, exceeds its capacity, etc.) then continued non-compliance is certainly an aggravating factor. In these cases, a prosecutor may refuse to agree to a lower plea arrangement until compliance is achieved, or look to have the defendant agree to a court order to come into compliance.[19] Another consideration may be restitution: Is there an innocent victim who has paid for the consequences of a defendant's actions (e.g. a municipality who has paid for the cleanup from an illegal dumping)? Finally, as many environmental offences provide for the possibility of imprisonment, the prosecutor will need to assess whether jail time is warranted or a probation order appropriate.

Plea resolution discussions can also be used to achieve other objectives. A prosecutor will often use the negotiation process to canvass any admissions that can be made by a defendant to narrow the issues in contention at a trial. An agreed statement of fact may be used to shorten the trial where, for example, the only issue being contested is due diligence. Even when the facts of the *actus reus* are being contested, facts such as the existence of the corporation, the ownership of property, and the admissibility of certain documents can often be agreed to.

## Will the Evidence Be Admissible?

Environmental prosecutions are no different than any other trial, and inevitably involve a myriad of tactical decisions regarding the presentation of evidence by both the prosecutor and the defence. Two topics that are perhaps more common to environmental prosecutions are the admissibility of statements made by agents of the defendant and the introduction of lab results.

Environmental regulation is full of self-reporting requirements that have generally been upheld as constitutional in a regulatory context.[20] One question that often arises is: What do you do when the sole evidence that forms the basis of an offence was supplied to the enforcement agency by the defendant, either directly or through an agent? Many licences require companies to test emissions or effluent on a regular basis, and the reports must be submitted to the regulator periodically. The results are generally reported by submitting a letter or, more recently, uploading the data into a database through a Web-enabled portal. These reports may contain lab results demonstrating that the company exceeded an emission limit, which constitutes an offence.

So how should the prosecutor go about proving this offence? One avenue would be to call all the witnesses involved in obtaining the sample, delivering it to the lab, and conducting the testing. In this scenario, the prosecutor would have to call a large number of witnesses: the employee who took the sample, any employee who handled it and transported it to the lab, or perhaps an employee of the courier company, the person who received it at the lab, all the technicians who processed the samples for testing, and the analyst who signs the final test result. This evidence would likely take days of trial time. Alternatively, the prosecutor could call one witness: the inspector who received the letter and attached lab results from the company and perhaps followed up with the environmental manager at the facility and discussed the results afterward. The second avenue is permitted under the evidentiary rule allowing admissions made by an agent of the defendant to be entered into evidence through a third party (the inspector).[21] This is potentially a much more efficient use of court time and avoids the prosecutor needing to call employees from the defendant company. Defence counsel should of course consider whether to challenge through a *voir dire*, the use of the hearsay exception in this manner, considering, for example: Was the report made to the enforcement agency by an agent or employee authorized to make the admissions? Can it be demonstrated that the sampling and testing procedures are unreliable?

As described above, proving the reliability of test results can involve a significant amount of evidence detailing the entire chain of events from the time the sample was taken, in what type of container, how it was handled and transported, what control methods were employed (multiple samples, travel blanks, background samples), the test method used, the quality control and assurance processes employed by the lab, and the qualifications and background of the lab technicians. Some statutes create an evidentiary rule dispensing with the need for any of this evidence where the lab or personnel meet certain qualifications, permitting the prosecutor to simply enter the test result as evidence. However, it is left open to the defendant to provide evidence to the contrary. Furthermore, most test results have standard margins of error. A prosecution should rarely proceed where the exceedance of a limit is within the margin of error.

## What Can't Be Argued?

Once the prosecutor has proven the *actus reus* of the offence, it is then open to the defendant to escape liability by demonstrating a valid defence. Many of these defences are described in chapter 20 of this volume by Ronda M. Vanderhoek and chapter 21 by Jean Piette. This chapter will focus on one defence that is not available—collateral attacks.

Environmental prosecutions may involve failure to comply with requirements set out in different types of administrative instruments that can take many forms: licences, permits, approvals, orders, directives. The governing statute often provides a right to the instrument holder to appeal or seek a review of the instrument if it is believed that the terms and conditions are unfair. It is important that persons avail themselves of these appeal rights. If they don't, and are later found to be in non-compliance with a condition, it is likely that a defendant will not be permitted to attack the basis of the instrument as unreasonable or even assert that the enforcement agency was without jurisdiction to impose the condition. The prosecutor will argue that the defence is a collateral attack on the instrument, relying on the decision in *R. v. Consolidated Maybrun Mines Ltd.*[22] In that case, the Supreme Court of Canada sets out five factors to consider as to whether a collateral attack should be permitted, but the most important was the right of the person to appeal and the nature of the appellate body. In Ontario, licences and orders can be appealed to the Environmental Review Tribunal, a quasi-judicial adjudicative body with specific expertise in environmental issues.[23] This was a key factor the Supreme Court of Canada took into account in determining that under the Ontario *Environmental Protection Act* (EPA), it was the intention of the legislature that the tribunal should determine the appropriateness and reasonableness of approvals and licences, not the court in a penal proceeding. A defendant should not sit on their objections and wait to see if a prosecution is pursued.

Therefore, the key strategic decision is really whether to appeal the approval or order in the first place, and if so, within the statutory time limit if one is prescribed. If the defendant doesn't do so, and later fails to comply with a requirement, it may not have any decision left to make at prosecution stage (other than what the size of the penalty should be).

## To Charge or Not to Charge?

Some enforcement agencies will seek the advice of the prosecutor prior to laying a charge, but in many cases the decision is left to the individual inspector/investigator. In either case, the prosecutor must ultimately determine whether to proceed with a prosecution. In Ontario, the Ministry of the Attorney General has a specific charge screening policy used to guide this decision for all regulatory offences. The two main factors are whether there is a reasonable prospect of conviction (lower standard than beyond a reasonable doubt) and whether there are any public interest factors that weigh against proceeding.

The decision to lay a charge is a key moment in any enforcement action. Once the charge is laid, it sets in process the quasi-criminal process and all the procedural rights that it entails. At times, the process can be complex and drawn out, requiring both the prosecutor and defence counsel to make strategic decisions in furthering the case.

## NOTES

1 *R v Wholesale Travel Group Inc*, [1991] SCJ No 79 at para 129.
2 *R v Sault Ste Marie (City)*, [1978] SCJ No 59, [1978] 2 SCR 1299 [*Sault Ste Marie*].
3 See *Provincial Offences Act*, RSO 1990, c P.33, as amended [*POA*], s 23.
4 See *Environmental Protection Act*, RSO 1990, c E.19, as amended [*EPA*], s 156.
5 *Ibid* at s 184(1).
6 *Ibid* at s 184(2).
7 The leading case on the use of information gathered using a regulator's "super powers" is the Supreme Court of Canada case *R v Jarvis*, [2002] SCJ No 76, [2002] 3 SCR 757; see also *R v Nolet*, 2010 SCC 24, [2010] 1 SCR 851; *R v Larsen*, 2012 CarswellBC 1101, 2012 BCCA 167.
8 See *EPA*, s 187, which sets out statutory minimums for certain offences. Individuals are subject to $5,000/day minimum fines for first offences, $10,000/day for second offence and $20,000/day for any subsequent offence and/or imprisonment for up to five years less one day; corporate minimum fines start at $25,000/day and go up to $100,000/day.
9 See *POA*, *supra* note 3 at ss 77 and 78.
10 *Sault Ste Marie*, *supra* note 2 at 1309, SCR version.
11 See *EPA*, *supra* note 4 at s 194.
12 See *EPA*, *supra* note 4 at s 192.
13 For a recent example of issues that may arise for both environmental prosecution units and provincial regulators responsible for environmental oversight, see *Orphan Well Assn. v Grant Thornton Ltd.*, 2017 ABCA 124 (leave to appeal to the Supreme Court of Canada granted on 9 November 2017) regarding implications for environmental cost and/or damage claims in insolvency proceedings under the federal *Bankruptcy and Insolvency Act*, RSC 1985 c B-3 [*BIA*], in particular with respect to constitutional paramountcy of *BIA* provisions over provincial environmental legislation.
14 See *EPA*, *supra* note 4 at s 185.
15 *R v Boucher*, [1954] SCJ No 54.
16 *R v Horan*, [2008] OJ No 3167 (CA) at para 26.
17 *Canadian Environmental Protection Act, 1999*, SC 1999, c 33, s 287 [*CEPA*].
18 See *CEPA*, *ibid* at s 287.1 and *EPA*, *supra* note 4 at s 188.1. See also *R v Bata Industries Ltd*, [1992] OJ No 667.
19 See s 190 of the *EPA*, *supra* note 4.
20 *R v Fitzpatrick*, [1995] 4 SCR 154.
21 The original case recognizing this exception to the hearsay rule is *R v Strand Electric Ltd*, [1968] OJ No 1291 (CA); also see *R v Syncrude Canada Ltd*, [2010] AJ No 421 (Prov Ct) for a thorough review of the development of this exception.
22 [1998] 1 SCR 706,, 158 DLR (4th) 193.
23 There are similar tribunals in Alberta and British Columbia—the Alberta Environmental Appeals Board and the British Columbia Environmental Appeal Board, in addition to others in other provinces and other tribunals that deal with a range of environmental issues such as forestry, oil and gas, energy projects, and planning decisions.

# 16

# Federal vs. Provincial Crowning

SUSAN McRORY *

## Background to the Discussion

This is not an academic paper or a statement of policy. I was a prosecutor for Alberta Justice for over 30 years, the last 20 exclusively in the business of running or overseeing every environmental prosecution done by the province. As a result, the issue of provincial and/or federal jurisdiction over environmental files was a very personal one for me. Every file that crossed my desk had to be evaluated to see which level of government had jurisdiction and what I had to do about it.

There were two major considerations for me: one, primarily legal; the other, primarily practical. First, by law, any release to the environment that might affect fish-bearing waters or federally protected wildlife could create a situation where both Crown offices would be involved. In cases where both jurisdictions had a vested interest, there was always a delicate balancing act involving statutory and common law powers, interests, and resources—which is where the practical considerations became important.

On the practical side, there are never enough Crowns to go around. When I began in 1993, I was the only environmental prosecutor for the Alberta Crown. Even now there are only two lawyers to cover the entire province. In the federal regulatory unit, there are just three prosecutors who specialize in environmental offences. In Alberta, we can't afford not to play well together. And, with so few players to choose from, personal relationships become of vital importance. I hired the two lawyers who are doing the work for the province today, and I worked very closely with the federal Crown for many years. On files where the defendants

* *The author is grateful for the editorial contributions of Timothy McRory.*

were often one or more multinational corporations, with well-funded defence teams, we had no choice but to cooperate if we wanted our files to go forward with any hope of presenting a solid case.

## Who Is to Act for the Crown?

### THE LAW

As this chapter is not intended to be a comprehensive review of legislation or the case law regarding Crown jurisdiction, I can tell you three things for sure.

First, when you are dealing with provincial environmental charges, even in combination with *Criminal Code* charges, the provincial legislation adopts the *Code* provisions *mutatis mutandis* and the province of Alberta prosecutes. Section 2 provides as follows:

> "Attorney General" … with respect to proceedings to which this Act applies, means the Attorney General or Solicitor General of the province in which those proceedings are taken.

Second, for charges under federal environmental legislation, if the information is laid by the Government of Canada AND the federal Crown appears, then the Attorney General of Canada takes exclusive jurisdiction. But the kicker is that if the Attorney General of Canada chooses not appear on federal charges, then counsel is the provincial Attorney General (See *Stevenson v. Queen*,[1] upholding the decision of the New Brunswick Court of Appeal in *R. v. Sacobie*.[2]

Third, for all private prosecutions under any legislation, the provincial Crown has a right of first refusal. Only if the province doesn't step in does the federal government have the power to do so in accordance with section 579.1(1) of the *Criminal Code*, as follows:

> The Attorney General of Canada or counsel instructed by him or her for that purpose may intervene in proceedings in the following circumstances:
>
> (a) the proceedings are in respect of a contravention of, a conspiracy or attempt to contravene or counseling the contravention of an Act of Parliament or a regulation made under that Act, other than this Act or a regulation made under this Act;
> (b) the proceedings have not been instituted by an Attorney General;

(c) judgment has not been rendered; and
(d) the Attorney General of the province in which the proceedings are taken has not intervened.

In fact, the first really serious environmental prosecutions in Alberta began as private prosecutions under federal legislation but were then taken over by the province.

Summing up: The province prosecutes all charges under provincial legislation, but it may handle charges under federal legislation, or private prosecutions. The federal Crown may or may not prosecute charges under federal legislation, and may take over private prosecutions of certain federal laws if where the province declines.

#### But ...

Simple and logical as the above may sound, section 579.01 of the *Code* adds a note of confusion to the process by positing a fourth scenario. It allows a private prosecutor to *present* the case while the relevant Attorney General (as determined in the three steps listed above), appears only as a *party*, albeit one with the rights of a party opposed in interest, as follows:

> If the Attorney General intervenes in proceedings and does not stay them under section 579, he or she may, without conducting the proceedings, call witnesses, examine and cross-examine witnesses, present evidence and make submissions.

See, for a brief comment, *Canadian Broadcasting Corporation et al. v. Morrison,*[3] where the Court of Appeal noted in passing that the Attorney General has an obligation to "supervise" all prosecutions and, in the circumstances anticipated by s. 579.01, may do as laid out in the legislation. As nearly as I can tell, the mechanics of how that task might be accomplished have not been the subject of any judicial direction in Canada.

This brings us to the question of who *should* be the Crown. Here, we leave the realm of the theoretical and approach the realm of the practical in the following areas:

### THE POLICY

In 1990, Canada and Alberta produced a policy document under the title "Federal/Provincial Cooperation in the Prosecution of Offences in Alberta." With respect to pollution cases at that time, the direction was as follows:

> In certain types of particularly sensitive cases, such as those involving the pollution of the environment and the transportation of dangerous goods, both the Attorney General of Alberta and the Attorney General of Canada will be instructing their own counsel to assume conduct of concurrent resulting prosecutions.

Theoretically, this allows for two separate sets of charges and two parallel prosecutions. And, presumably, that could lead to two separate trials, two different decisions, etc., etc. It seldom, if ever, has come to that particular duplication of effort.

## THE PRACTICE

First, as I mentioned, there are very few environmental Crowns available to cover an entire province. It makes little sense to duplicate effort. Second, it creates some very real difficulties in both communications and provision of disclosure with the investigators who originate it and the defence counsel who receive it. Third, it could take up valuable court time for no apparent good reason. Fourth, and perhaps most persuasive given the Crown's duty of fairness, it could lead to inconsistent verdicts.

I found that the best way to divide responsibility for files where there is overlapping jurisdiction was through very informal discussions. (In my case, at any rate, these usually took place over a nice lunch.) The questions we discussed over the salad revolved around capacity, interest, and in some rare cases, conflict.

### Capacity

Holidays, maternity and paternity leave, secondments, and teaching assignments mean that we are not always operating at full strength. And even if we have all hands on deck, a mega-trial sucks up all of our time and energy. In my day, when the federal Crown was short staffed, we helped them out. Sometimes that meant taking over the whole file; sometimes it was just a question of a division of labour on joint prosecutions. Sometimes it meant sharing resources. When the province had the ability to hire expert witnesses, they did. At a time when the federal Crown had a full time paralegal and I didn't, I was allowed to "borrow" her services.

### Interest

Every lawyer has different strengths, and it makes sense to play to them. On *Syncrude,* Alex Bernard handled the legal research on constitutional challenges because he likes that sort of thing. We had another lawyer in our office with a talent for research and an interest in obscure legislation, so she enjoyed working on dangerous goods and PCB files, in which there is a lot of overlap between the federal and provincial legislation. She got involved in the federal files because she wanted to.

#### A Conflict

As to a conflict, there were a few files where the accused was another provincial department. In those cases, we needed the federal Crown to assume conduct of the provincial proceedings. We "paid it back" by assuming conduct of some of their files. (In one particularly ugly file, we agreed that we owed the feds at least two files in return!)

So does this mean that provincial/federal relations were all happiness and light in Alberta? Sometimes yes, and sometimes no, but there was always a way to make things work. And it is much easier to find one by sitting down and talking it out then by spouting policy at each other over emails.

### RUNNING JOINT PROSECUTIONS

Sometimes the files are just too big or too important to be handled by one branch of government, *R. v. Syncrude* being the prime example. When cases like that came along, we had to find a way to work together. I would like to pass on to you what we learned to do to handle the challenge.

#### Be proactive, be proactive, be proactive

You must assume that another mega-trial is just down the road. First of all, there really is always one lurking just over the horizon and, second, the more you prepare for these files, the better you can handle the details of the smaller ones.

#### Be prepared to give quick advice about differing search and seizure powers under all relevant legislation

The early hours of an investigator's file are often critical, and evidence needs to be collected appropriately and legally from the beginning. So Crowns are often consulted in the early days with respect to evidence gathering, and this is an area where you need to be proactive in preparing your responses. Case in point: one of the counsel in my office got a call from an investigator asking what his powers of search and seizure were on a particular file. The lawyer in question was meticulous and thoughtful, and she spent almost half an hour summarizing the various options. At the end, the investigator blew up: "Lady, I'm in a metal boat on the North Saskatchewan River and it's 20 below! Just tell me what to do!"

One of our major roles is to clarify what powers of search and seizure are allowed under what Acts, and the differences from one Act to another can be vast. For legislation where the resource is Crown-owned, as in the *Water Act* or the *Public Lands Act* (what I like to call "owner's legislation"), the investigators have wide-ranging powers. There are also broad powers under the provincial environmental legislation (section 198, *Environmental Protection and Enhancement Act*), but those powers are pretty much limited to the *early* days of the investigation. It is vital for the investigators to be aware of the exact differences. But other relevant legislation can have much more restrictive clauses.

Finally, there is the question of how evidence gathered under one Act can be used in a prosecution under other legislation. The differences in powers can lead to very different approaches in execution.

And, of course, where legislative regimes overlap, the potential problems multiply. A proactive approach to the difficult questions will allow you to be ready to go when you need to be.

### Agree on who is responsible for disclosure up front

Disclosure is the Achilles' heel in every mega-file. Managing the vast amount of information and proving that it was delivered to defence counsel is a huge undertaking. There is a Major Case Management System for investigations that has been proven to work. Unfortunately, not every investigating agency uses it. And sometimes those agencies that do use it are required to work with agencies that do not. Protocols and a division of responsibility on disclosure *have* to be worked out in advance.

### Have a common file review process

There are two basic, and mutually exclusive, ways in which an investigation file results in charges. If the involved Crown agencies are not using the same one, disaster can ensue. The more traditional model is that the police or other investigating agency lays the charges before the file ever reaches the Crown. Only when a trial date has been set is it sent to a Crown for review and trial prep. (This was my understanding of how the *Wabumun* file was handled.) That might work for small files, but for the "mega-file" (which describes many environmental files) the poor Crown is stuck reading thousands of pages of materials under the threat of the 18-month timeline set by *Jordan* (more on that later).

The other is the "pre-charge approval" system, which we used in Specialized Prosecutions where the file was almost "trial ready" at the point when charges were approved. That meant the Crown would read every page of the thousands of pages in a major file more than once, produce a status report detailing the strengths and weaknesses in the case and summarize the evidence in support of a recommendation to proceed. It is a lot of work! Within the Specialized Prosecutions Branch, we had the luxury and the privilege of having the time to do that kind of intensive review. The file review took a long time, but setting a matter down for trial didn't. (If I may, I would like to say a word of thanks to Alberta Justice for giving me the time and freedom to handle these files—mostly!—in the way I thought they needed to be done. I realize now how very lucky I was.)

Early consultation on which system is to be used on joint files is crucial to the smooth running of a prosecution file. Otherwise, the differing time constraints of opposing systems can create unbearable friction between offices. On the *Syncrude* file, planning and discussion allowed the federal and provincial Crown to receive the file on the same day. Then we worked together to have the file "trial ready" (or almost) on the day that we jointly recommended that charges proceed. And, by the way, disclosure was then ready to go out, too.

### Work towards the shortest limitation period

Under the provincial legislation, you have two years from the offence date (or its discovery) to lay charges—period, no exceptions. Federal legislation usually contains an option to proceed by way of indictment, which means no statutory time limit. If the feds choose to proceed summarily, of course, they may face similar constraints. (Note: The *Jordan* "clock" starts ticking when the charges are laid.)

So the time crunch is a constant for provincial investigators and Crown. We must get charges out the door in less than two years, regardless of the seriousness of the offence or the size of the investigation. Adding to the pressure on the provincial side is the practice of allowing the accused an opportunity to provide additional information prior to a final decision to proceed. If they choose to provide it, it must be reviewed (however lengthy) and may trigger the necessity of follow-up investigations. But the 24-month deadline does not change in any way to allow for the additional time.

Our federal colleagues don't face the same time constraints, but it really helps when they understand what we on the provincial side might face. On one particularly memorable file (for me), the federal investigators and Crown weren't in any particular hurry, but on my side I was told that a failure to get the matter to trial quickly might be "career-ending." Frankly, I wasn't terribly concerned, but it was nice when my federal colleagues made a point of speeding up their work to allow me to avoid finding out if the threat was real.

### *Jordan* and the right to a speedy trial

The 2016 decision of the Supreme Court of Canada in *R. v. Jordan*[4] has put new pressure on both the federal and provincial Crown to get their act in order. In *Jordan*, the court held that there is a presumption that the accused's right to a trial within a reasonable time (s. 11(b) of the Charter) is violated if more than 18 months elapse between first appearance and trial. Delay attributable to the defence doesn't count towards the 18-month limit, but assuming that isn't a factor, then the onus shifts to the Crown to prove that the delay was reasonable. The importance of the charge isn't a consideration; basically it's only the complexity of the trial that counts. I am not aware of any decisions that have given *Jordan* rights to corporate accused but can certainly see it is a possibility. Crown working in the area had best be aware of the arguments that might be made about just that issue. Any defence lawyer worth his salt certainly will be!

### Don't get *Kienapple*'d

It's very hard when so much work and resources go into a file when at the end of the day, one set of charges may be stayed by reason of the rule in *Kienapple* against duplicitous charges. We knew that might happen heading into *Syncrude*. So before we ever got to the courthouse steps, we had our strategy already laid out in the event of a successful defence application. The investigators and Crown on both sides agreed that the federal charge was the better one on which to proceed based on the option for dual procedure, potential custodial sentences, and greater fines based on a per-bird calculation.

### Beware of *Criminal Code* Section 725(2)

Although the federal Crown cannot directly withdraw provincial charges, and *vice versa*, there is a provision in the *Code* that, *de facto,* allows precisely that thing to happen. In sentencing, unless the court decrees otherwise, the Crown and the accused can agree to read in facts supporting other offences with the result that "no further proceedings may be taken with respect to any offence described in those charges or disclosed by those facts."

In theory, that means I could craft a statement of facts that includes evidence which would have been used in support of a federal offence, thus precluding federal charges down the road. Talk about a quick way to end good federal-provincial relations!

### Solve the problem on a personal level, not in head office

Now this is just me. My experience is that there is an immediacy and incentive to solve problems, when you are the poor bastard who will be standing before the court in the near future, that no head office manager could appreciate. Enough said.

### The only folks allowed to make decisions on a file are the folks who have read the damn file

Another personal "rule." The typical accused on an environmental file is a very different creature than the traditional criminal. They are multi-million, if not billion, dollar corporations who in other circumstances are good corporate citizens. They commit offences not because they want to but because they assign such a low priority to environmental protection. The strategies and approaches to charging, negotiations, and sentencing that work for a bank robber don't work here. Unless the traditional criminal prosecutions boss has read the file and knows the relevant law, his or her suggestions aren't very helpful or welcome and may even interfere with proper and due process. Therefore, improper instructions are to be resisted at all costs.

### The health of the file should be the overriding consideration, not turf protection

When conflict arises as to whose file it is, it's easy to get your back up. Little things like determining who is lead counsel can cause friction. Even though I did not always remember it right away during difficult moments, it helped to be reminded that at all times "the file must come first." Being frustrated with the federal investigator or Crown is a luxury that I don't have if it interferes with the progress of the file. Leave your ego at the door if you want to do your job well.

### Invest in each other

There will be bad days and conflict with any joint enterprise, and it's worse when there is a ton of publicity on a file, so it is important to invest in the relationship with the other office well in advance. It may be as simple as going for lunch and keeping each other up to date on files of mutual interest. It might extend to helping out on research or even sending each other to conferences. Federal/provincial relations were at an all-time high when we sent the federal Crown to one of our conferences in California. (Note: funding was provided by the Western States Project, a federation of American environmental prosecuting agencies that makes it possible for our lawyers to attend their conferences.)

### Establish the business rules BEFORE the big file

In the early days of the *Syncrude* investigation, the Crown and investigators from both sides agreed in advance that regardless of which charges went ahead, we would help each other. We divided up the work on the file, and we agreed to follow the Alberta Specialized Prosecutions' process for recommending charges.

### Cross-appoint agents

This is new to me, and it is based on reading the case law in preparing for this chapter. Where there have been challenges as to who the Crown ought to be, they are solved easily by having written appointments identifying each other as agent for the other guy. You might even consider filing them with the court, the way defence counsel do.

### Invest in the investigative services

This is not just about federal versus provincial investigators; it's about cross training for all government investigating agencies. In reality, some of these files are so big that no one agency could handle them. Examples in my career where cooperation between investigators was vital included the Hub Oil explosion in Calgary, the derailment of a CN train at Lake Wabumun or Syncrude, or every big pipeline rupture. On a major file, investigators from multiple agencies will be involved, and the time to make introductions is not at the scene.

Since 2006 we have hosted an annual one-week conference for investigators from agencies across government, provincial and federal alike, using instructors from the RCMP, the city police forces, Fish and Wildlife, or whoever else had the expertise. We also have fought to have Major Case Management adopted as the system for managing all investigations, so that when there is a joint venture the investigators will know how to communicate and work with each other.

### Never proceed on the expectation that there will be a guilty plea

This one is hard. The stats say that something like 80 to 90 percent of criminal trials are resolved by way of a guilty plea, and if you were looking at the world from a time management perspective, it would make sense to defer the effort in preparation until such time as a trial was inevitable.

But we are not in the time management business. Files only proceed if the Crown determines that there is a reasonable expectation of conviction and that the prosecution is in the public interest. The strengths and weaknesses of the Crown's case are revealed through an intensive review of the file. Recommending the appropriate sentence requires an in-depth understanding of the file. And let's be practical: the defence counsel who handle big environmental files are some of the best in the business. They can smell the lack of preparation from a mile off. Seldom are they afraid to take a matter to trial and will certainly do so if there is even a sniff of a possibility that it is in their client's best interests. If you are not ready for them, rest assured they will be ready for you.

## Conclusion

I enjoyed tremendously my chance to work on environmental and regulatory files. They certainly present unique challenges! They are big, complex, hard-fought, and cover areas of law that are unfamiliar to most courts. Just the jurisdictional questions alone between the two senior levels of government require special handling, and as to the actual investigations and taking the matters to trial, well, anyone to wants to prosecute these cases had better like hard work. When I look back at what I have written, I realize that most of my recommendations come down to "work hard and play nice with the other people on your team."

Perhaps it did not require 4,000 words to say it, but I hope that my suggestions are useful to anyone who has the courage and the desire to get a mega-trial into a courtroom. I wish you the best of luck. May you enjoy yourself as much as I always do!

### NOTES

1 1983 CanLII 3141 (SCC).
2 (1979), 51 CCC (2d) 430).
3 2017 MBCA 36 at para 24.
4 [2016] 1 SCR 631.

# 17

# Who Should Prosecute: Intragovernmental Aspects

MARTIN Z.P. OLSZYNSKI*

**Scenario 1 ("Mexican fish oil"):** On a late afternoon, the flight crew of a Transport Canada Dash 8 surveillance aircraft is conducting a routine aerial patrol above and along the shipping lanes off the west coast of Vancouver Island. The crew detects and observes an oily slick on the surface of the ocean. Proceeding to make several passes over one of the ships in the area—the M/T *Champion*—the crew further observes and records a hose connected to one of the manifolds on the port side of the ship dangling above the surface of the ocean and discharging a brownish-coloured oily substance, leaving a slick approximately 35 miles in length.[1]

**Scenario 2 ("Mudfest"):** A conservation officer observes an off-road race involving large trucks. Two hours later, he observes sediment entering into a nearby river, which turns the river from transparent to opaque. The silt is entering the river from a storm sewer connected to a ditch. Upon entering the property, the conservation officer videotapes one of the trucks from the race being washed with a fire hose. It is apparent that the sediment being washed off was running down off the property into the ditch, into the storm sewer, and into the river. The river is a fish migratory route, a spawning habitat, and fishing grounds.[2]

## Introduction

The purpose of this chapter is to provide some insight into the federal environmental regime, and the prosecution of federal environmental offences in

* *The views and opinions expressed herein are those of the author alone.*

particular. After setting out in general terms some of the federal environmental offences that judges and practitioners are most likely to encounter, the chapter describes the roles of the various actors, including departmental officials, prosecutors, and legal services lawyers, in carrying a prosecution forward, as well as some of the considerations that influence whether and which charges are ultimately laid. While these generally fall into one of two groups—the sufficiency of the evidence and the public interest in prosecuting an offence—their content is influenced by the different perspectives brought by each of the relevant actors.

## Common Federal Environmental Offences

While there is now in Canada a relatively robust jurisprudence with respect to regulatory offences generally[3] and environmental offences specifically,[4] it is useful to remember that, unlike some other jurisdictions that have established specialized environmental courts,[5] in Canada most (if not all) environmental offences are tried in generalist provincial courts where they form only a fraction of the judiciary's caseload.[6] In addition to informing the discussion that follows, therefore, this part is intended to serve as a bit of a primer on the federal environmental regime.

While there are over 30 different federal laws that may be considered environmental in character,[7] most federal environmental prosecutions are for offences under one of the following four statutes: the *Fisheries Act*,[8] the *Canadian Environmental Protection Act, 1999* (*CEPA, 1999*),[9] the *Migratory Birds Convention Act, 1994* (*MBCA, 1994*)[10] and the *Canada Shipping Act, 2001*.[11] The first three of these are described in some detail below.

### THE *FISHERIES ACT*: HABITAT PROTECTION AND POLLUTION PREVENTION

Since the introduction in 1976 of the habitat protection provisions, the *Fisheries Act* has been widely considered one of Canada's most important environmental laws. The most relevant provisions for our purposes here are subsections 35(1) and 36(3). Currently, subsection 35(1) prohibits the carrying on of any work, undertaking, or activity that results in the harmful alteration, disruption, or destruction (HADD) of fish habitat, which the Act defines as spawning grounds and other areas (nursery, rearing, food supply, and migration) on which fish depend.[12] In *R. v. Posselt*, the court held that "the offence is established if the Crown proves beyond a reasonable doubt that the accused interfered with the fish habitat in a way that has impaired the value or the usefulness of the habitat for one or more of the purposes described in the definition of 'fish habitat.'"[13]

As for subsection 36(3), it prohibits the deposit of "deleterious substances," a defined term pursuant to section 34, in waters frequented by fish or in any place where that substance, or some resulting deleterious substance, may enter such waters. In contrast to some other regimes—including the prohibition against HADD—the jurisprudence is clear that the focus is on the substance being deposited, and whether or not it is deleterious to fish, not on the receiving environment: "What is being defined is the substance that is added to the water, rather than the water after the addition of the substance."[14]

Contravention of subsections 35(1) or 36(3) is an offence pursuant to subsections 40(1) and (2), respectively. Importantly, neither prohibition is absolute. Works, undertakings, and activities resulting in HADDs can be authorized by the minister or by regulations pursuant to paragraphs 35(2)(a)–(c). The deposit of deleterious substances can also be authorized, but at present only through regulations promulgated pursuant to subsection 36(5). The *Metal Mining Effluent Regulations* (*MMER*)[15]—the primary federal regulation aimed at mining effluent and tailings disposal—are one example of such regulations.[16]

## *CEPA, 1999*: HAZARDOUS SUBSTANCES AND DISPOSAL AT SEA

*CEPA, 1999* is often referred to as Canada's "flagship environmental legislation," the primary purpose of which is "to contribute to sustainable development through pollution prevention."[17] With 12 distinct parts and over 340 sections, this multifaceted legislation covers such matters as pollution reporting (Part 3), pollution prevention (Part 4), controlling toxic substances (including animate products of biotechnology—Parts 5 and 6), and controlling pollution and managing waste, which includes marine and air pollution (Part 7). The focus here is on Part 5 and Part 7.

While a comprehensive explanation of Part 5 is well beyond the scope of this chapter,[18] the basic objective of the regime is to assess, characterize, and manage (as necessary) the approximately 23,000 substances already in use in Canada as well as new ones (whether manufactured or imported into Canada). Where, following assessment, a substance is determined to be "toxic,"[19] it is placed on the *Toxic Substances List*[20] and may then be subject to regulations by the Governor in Council (GiC) dealing with a wide range of issues including its manufacture, processing, sale, import, export, and release. There are now over 25 such regulations (roughly half of all regulations under *CEPA, 1999*), regulating such chemicals as PCBs, ozone depleting substances, benzene, and mercury.

With respect to marine pollution, these provisions are essentially the same as those considered in the constitutionally significant *R. v. Crown Zellerbach*,[21] and they implement some of Canada's commitments pursuant to the *Convention on the Prevention of Marine Pollution by Dumping Wastes and Other Matter, 1972*, and the related *1996 Protocol*. Division 3 sets out the regime for disposals at sea. Paragraph 125(1)(a) prohibits disposal of a substance at sea, other than those substances incidental to or derived from the normal operations of a ship, unless it is done in accordance with a Canadian permit.

Offences under *CEPA, 1999* are set out in sections 272 to 274, each of which sets out a different fine regime (different minimums and maximums). Contravention of paragraph 125(1)(a) (disposal at sea) is an offence pursuant to both paragraphs 272(1)(a) (for persons and corporations) and 272.4(1) (for ships). Contravention of regulations, which as noted above play a primary role in the toxic substances regime, is an offence pursuant to various sections depending on the specific regulatory provisions in question. Paragraph 272(1)(h) makes it an offence to contravene any provision of regulations "designated by regulations made under section 286.1." According to the *Regulatory Impact Analysis Statement* (*RIAS*) that accompanied these regulations, their objective is to secure the imposition of the new—and higher—fine scheme[22] for offences involving "harm or risk of harm to the environment, or obstruction of authority."[23] Applying these criteria, Environment Canada (EC) identified over 80 provisions from 25 different *CEPA, 1999* regulations, the vast majority of which regulate toxic substances.[24] Contravention of other regulatory provisions is an offence *per* section 272.1 and does not attract the higher fine regime.

### *THE MIGRATORY BIRDS CONVENTION ACT, 1994*: PROTECTING MIGRATORY BIRDS

The *MBCA, 1994* implements Canada's international obligations under the *Migratory Birds Convention*.[25] As noted by the Court in *R. v. Carriere*,[26] the preamble to the original 1916 *Convention* recognized that migratory birds "are of great value as a source of food or in destroying insects which are injurious to forests and forage plants on the public domain."[27] In amendments to the *Convention* in 1995, the parties reiterated their commitment to

> the long-term conservation of shared species of migratory birds for their nutritional, social, cultural, spiritual, ecological, economic, and

> aesthetic values through a more comprehensive international framework that involves working together to cooperatively manage their populations, regulate their take, protect the lands and waters on which they depend, and share research and survey information.[28]

Common offences under the *MBCA, 1994* include illegal hunting activities[29] as well as contraventions of sections 5 and 5.1. Section 5 prohibits the unlawful possession of migratory birds or nests, including for commercial transactions. Subsections 5.1(1) and (2) are similar to subsection 36(3) of the *Fisheries Act*, in that they prohibit any person or vessel from depositing or permitting the deposit of a substance harmful to migratory birds in waters or areas frequented by migratory birds, or in a place where the substance may enter such waters or a place. The subsection 5.1(1) offence was most recently explained in the relatively high-profile prosecution of a Canadian oil sands company following the death of approximately 1,500 birds after these landed on one of its tailings ponds in the spring of 2008.[30]

Finally, because the *MBCA, 1994* applies not only to persons but also *vessels*, paragraph 5(3)(a) explicitly exempts deposits authorized by the *Canada Shipping Act, 2001*.

## The Players

### ENFORCEMENT PERSONNEL

Except in the case of a private prosecution, enforcement personnel (variously designated) are usually the first to learn about a potential offence, either in the course of an inspection or as a result of a reporting requirement.[31] Under the *Fisheries Act*, for example, enforcement personnel are designated by the minister as "fishery officers" or "fishery guardians" (per section 5), or as "fishery inspectors" pursuant to section 38. Fisheries officers and guardians have the authority to enforce all *Fisheries Act* provisions,[32] while fishery inspectors are limited to matters relating to habitat protection and pollution prevention:

> **38**(3) An inspector may, for a purpose related to verifying compliance with this Act, enter any place or premises, including a vehicle or vessel—other than a private dwelling-place … in which the inspector believes on reasonable grounds that
>
> (a) there is anything that is detrimental to fish habitat; or

(b) there has been carried on, is being carried on or is likely to be carried on any work, undertaking or activity resulting or likely to result in
    (i) the alteration or disruption of fish habitat, or
    (ii) the deposit of a substance in water frequented by fish.[33]

Generally speaking, enforcement personnel are guided by compliance and enforcement policies that are often publicly available. With respect to the *Fisheries Act*, fishery officers and guardians are guided by the 2001 *Compliance and Enforcement Policy for the Habitat Protection and Pollution Prevention Provisions of the Fisheries Act* (*Fisheries Act Enforcement Policy*),[34] a joint effort by the Department of Fisheries and Oceans (DFO) and EC to promote consistency in their compliance and enforcement activities, bearing in mind the bifurcation since 1978 of responsibility for the environmental provisions of the Act, with section 35 remaining with DFO and subsection 36(3) administered by EC.[35]

Compliance and enforcement policies usually set out a range of potential enforcement activities (e.g. inspections, investigations, the issuance of warnings, and prosecution), and then set out the criteria to be considered in response to alleged violations. For example, the above noted *Fisheries Act Enforcement Policy* lists the following criteria:

- Nature of the alleged violation;[36]
- Effectiveness in achieving the desired result with the alleged violator;[37]
- Consistently in enforcement;[38]

According to that same policy, prosecution will always be pursued where evidence establishes that:

- there is evidence that the alleged violation was deliberate;
- the alleged violator knowingly provided false or misleading information to enforcement personnel;
- the alleged violator obstructed enforcement personnel in the carrying out of their duties or interfered with anything seized under the Act;
- the alleged violator concealed or attempted to conceal or destroy information or evidence after the alleged offence occurred; or
- the alleged violator failed to take all reasonable measures to comply with a direction or an order issued pursuant to the Act.

While federal enforcement personnel may in some jurisdictions (e.g. Ontario) lay charges for alleged offences without first consulting with the Attorney General of Canada (AGC), the ultimate decision on whether to *proceed* with prosecution of the charges rests with the AGC as represented by the Public Prosecution Service of Canada (PPSC) (discussed in the next section).

A final note, and a relatively recent development that is relevant to the discussion here, is the nearly ubiquitous adoption of "risk-based" approaches to compliance and enforcement in the regulatory world, including in the environmental context. As a practical matter, while a prosecutor makes the ultimate determination about whether or not to proceed with a prosecution, alleged violations must first be detected. Risk-based regulation in this context has been described as:

> a targeting of inspection and enforcement resources that is based on *an assessment of the risks that a regulated person or firm poses to the regulator's objectives.* The key components of the approach are evaluations of the risk of non-compliance and calculations regarding the impact that the non-compliance will have on the regulatory body's ability to achieve its objectives. Risk-based regulation thus offers an evidence-based means of targeting the use of resources. It differs from "pyramidic" approaches by emphasizing analysis and targeting rather than a process of responsive escalation.[39]

While the *Fisheries Act Enforcement Policy* discussed above has some risk-based characteristics, especially some of the factors pertaining to the nature of the alleged violation,[40] the second and third criteria, as well as the list of facts that favour the initiation of a prosecution, are more reflective of the pyramidic approach: "A range of enforcement sanctions extending from persuasion, at its base, through warning and civil penalties up to criminal penalties."[41]

A clearer example of risk-based regulation can be found in the *Compliance and Enforcement Policy* for CEPA, *1999*.[42] This enforcement policy states that "the schedule of inspections will be determined by *the risk that the substance or activity presents* to the environment or to human health, and by the compliance record of the individual, company or government agency."[43]

### THE PUBLIC PROSECUTION SERVICE OF CANADA (PPSC)

Formerly known as the Federal Prosecution Service, a branch within the Department of Justice, the PPSC is now an independent organization that reports to Parliament through the AGC. By a fairly wide margin, Crown prosecutors have the most decision-making authority with respect to whether a prosecution will proceed to court. In some jurisdictions (e.g. British Columbia), their approval is necessary before charges are laid. Even in those jurisdictions where pre-approval is not required, however, prosecutors retain the discretion to stay a prosecution if the circumstances do not satisfy the following criteria (relevant to both pre-approval and stays), which are also publicly available in what is referred to as the FPS *Deskbook*:

1. Is the evidence sufficient to justify the institution or continuation of proceedings?
   a. A bare *prima facie* case is not enough; the evidence must demonstrate that there is a *reasonable prospect of conviction.*

2. If it is, does the public interest require a prosecution to be pursued?
   a. The factors here will vary from case to case, but generally the more serious the offence, the more likely it is that a prosecution is in the public interest.[44]

With respect to the second criterion, the FPS *Deskbook* makes clear—and current practice bears this out—that prosecutors ought to consult with the relevant investigative agencies:

> This may be particularly important in the case of prosecutions under statutes such as the … the *Fisheries Act* … or the *Income Tax Act*, where the offence provisions serve important regulatory goals. Consideration of what the public interest requires will of necessity require consideration of how the regulatory purpose of the statute might best be achieved. If, for example, the relevant regulatory authority has a mechanism for dealing with the alleged offender such as a compliance program, Crown counsel should consider whether an alternative such as this might better serve the public interest than prosecution.[45]

## DEPARTMENTAL LEGAL SERVICES

Finally, most federal departments and agencies have their own legal services unit (LSU), often staffed by counsel from the Department of Justice. The role of legal services counsel in the prosecution context varies with the circumstances. In the past, counsel have acted as agents for the Crown in prosecutions involving their client department. In most instances, however, counsel play a supporting role, first assisting enforcement personnel in assessing an alleged violation and then, if charges are laid, assisting the Crown prosecutor in understanding the relevant provisions (as necessary) and the client department's objectives in the prosecution. This is especially the case on appeal, where the primary concern may not be directly related to the specific violation at issue but rather an important question of law, such as the correct interpretation of a key provision or complex regulatory scheme.

## Application

### WHICH SHOE FITS BEST?

As noted above, among the primary considerations for determining whether to proceed with a prosecution is whether the evidence demonstrates a reasonable prospect of conviction.[46] As the two scenarios set out at the outset of this chapter make clear, however, occasionally multiple violations may be at play.

With respect to the Mexican fish oil scenario, and bearing in mind the discussion in Part 2, potential offences include contravention of *CEPA, 1999* (para. 125(1)(a)—unlawful disposal at sea) and the *MBCA, 1994* (subs. 5.1(1)—deposit of a substance harmful to migratory birds), both of which are administered by EC. With respect to the second scenario, Mudfest, both the subsection 35(1) prohibition against HADD (administered by the DFO) and the subsection 36(3) prohibition against the deposit of a deleterious substance (administered by EC) are on their face applicable.

In such instances, prosecutors may properly be influenced by strategic considerations. With respect to the Mudfest scenario, for example, an experienced prosecutor would know that in order to secure a conviction for a HADD, the evidence must demonstrate—beyond a reasonable doubt—that some identifiable habitat was actually harmfully altered, disrupted, or destroyed. Though by no means impossible, such site-specific harm is often difficult to prove and generally requires expert evidence.[47] In order to secure conviction for contravening subsection 36(3), on the other hand, the evidence must simply show that the substance being deposited is deleterious to fish when deposited into any water. The choice may further be simplified where judges in previous cases have taken judicial notice of some element of the offence, for example, that a particular substance is a deleterious substance, as they have in the case of silt.[48]

### DEPARTMENTAL POLICIES AND PRIORITIES

In the regulatory context—and the environmental context in particular—determining whether a prosecution is in the public interest is very much an exercise in cost-benefit analysis (CBA). Simply put, the gathering of evidence and its presentation in court, which includes the preparation of witnesses, can be costly endeavours. A department or agency may not feel justified in incurring such costs where the violation is not considered a significant risk (under a risk-based approach)—even where the available evidence suggests a reasonable prospect of conviction. In the Mexican fish oil scenario, for example, it is worth recalling that the occurrence was first observed by a Transport Canada (TC) flight crew. TC also has a mandate with respect to ship pollution under the *Canada Shipping Act, 2001*. Nevertheless, charges were laid under *CEPA, 1999*. One possible explanation is that TC did not consider a prosecution under its legislation to be necessary or useful in achieving its mandate in this context. While such views are theoretically not binding on a prosecutor, proceeding with a prosecution is difficult if the necessary evidence supporting a charge is not collected at the time.

That being said, most federal departments with an environmental protection mandate have entered into information-sharing arrangements with other departments, such as the National Aerial Surveillance Program (NASP) operated by TC that detected the Mexican fish oil incident. The NASP crew in that case informed EC of the incident, which then conducted its own follow-up and determined that the accused likely violated the disposal at sea provisions of *CEPA, 1999*. As another example, the *Deposit Out of the Normal Course of Events Notification Regulations*[49] under the *Fisheries Act* designate both provincial and federal officials for the purposes of spill notification, a system that ensures the dissemination of knowledge about pollution events to both federal and provincial officials. Such arrangements increase the chances that at least one agency will consider a prosecution to be in the public interest.

#### NOTES

1 This scenario is based on the facts in a recent prosecution from British Columbia—*R v Champion Shipping A/S*, Court File No 157673-1 (2013).

2 This scenario is based on the facts in *R v Jackson* (2002), 48 CELR (NS) 259 (Ont Sup Ct).

3 *R v City of Sault Ste-Marie*, [1978] 2 SCR 1299, being the foundational authority establishing that regulatory offences, also referred to as public welfare offences, are not "true crimes" and generally fall within the "strict liability" category of offences.

4 Indeed, whole volumes are now written on the subject, most notably Stanley Berger, *The Prosecution and Defense of Environmental Offences* (Toronto: Canada Law Book, 2012).

5 On the merits of such courts, see Brian J Preston (Chief Justice), "Benefits of Judicial Specialization in Environmental Law: The Land and Environment Court of New South Wales as a Case Study" (2011–12) 29 Pace Envtl L Rev 396.

6 Having searched various court websites (e.g. Ontario, British Columbia), I found that no specific statistics on the number

of environmental offences prosecuted annually were available. According to Statistics Canada, however, in 2011 there were 2,277,258 violations, of which 2,121,131 were under the *Criminal Code*. Of the remaining federal violations, the vast majority were drug offences (113,144). This leaves 21,344 for *all* other federal statutes, or slightly less than 1%. See online: <http://www.statcan.gc.ca/tables-tableaux/sum-som/index-eng.htm>.

7 Environment Canada (EC) alone "administers nearly two dozen acts either in whole or in part. It also assists with the administration of many others." EC, online: <http://www.ec.gc.ca/default.asp?lang=En&n=48d356c1-1>.

8 RSC 1985, c F-14.

9 SC 1999, c 33 [*CEPA, 1999*].

10 SC 1994, c 22 [*MBCA, 1994*].

11 SC 2001, c 26.

12 The *Fisheries Act* was amended in 2012 (see SC 2012, c 19, s 142) to prohibit works, undertakings, and activities that result in "serious harm" to fish that are part of, or support, a commercial, recreational or Aboriginal fishery. The Act also now defines "serious harm" as the death of fish and the permanent alteration, or destruction, of their habitat. However, the current government has recently introduced legislation to restore the previous prohibition against HADD, such that the case law referred to in this chapter should once again be relevant. For a discussion of the current proposed amendments, see Martin Olszynski, "In Search of #BetterRules: An Overview of Federal Environmental Bills C-68 and C-69" (15 February 2018), online: <http://ablawg.ca/wp-content/uploads/2018/02/Blog_MO_Bill68_Bill69.pdf>.

13 *R v Posselt*, [1999] BCJ No 1141 (SC) at para 23.

14 *R v Kingston* (2004), 240 DLR (4th) 734 (Ont CA) at para 64, citing with approval the decision of Seaton JA in *R v MacMillan Bloedel* (1979), 47 CCC (2d) 118 (BCCA).

15 SOR/2002-222 [*MMER*].

16 See *R v Williams Operating Corporation*, 2008 CanLII 48148 (Ont SC) for a relatively recent interpretation of the *MMER* scheme.

17 *CEPA, 1999*, *supra* note 9, "Declaration."

18 See ch 13 in Jamie Benidickson, *Environmental Law*, 3d ed (Toronto: Irwin Law, 2009), for a general overview of the toxic substances regime; and Meinhard Doelle, *Canadian Environmental Protection Act and Commentary*, 2008 ed (Markham: LexisNexis Canada, 2008) for a detailed understanding.

19 *CEPA, 1999*, s 64: "… a substance is toxic if it is entering or may enter the environment in a quantity or concentration or under conditions that (a) have or may have an immediate or long-term harmful effect on the environment or its biological diversity; (b) constitute or may constitute a danger to the environment on which life depends; or (c) constitute or may constitute a danger in Canada to human life or health."

20 Being Schedule 1 to *CEPA, 1999*, *supra* note 9.

21 [1988] 1 SCR 401.

22 This newer and higher fine scheme was introduced into *CEPA, 1999* and eight other federal environmental statutes administered by EC—including the *MBCA, 1994*—through the 2009 federal *Environmental Enforcement Act*, SC 2009, c 14 [*EEA*]. For more information about the *EEA*, see online: <http://www.ec.gc.ca/alef-ewe/default.asp?lang=En&n=A72F150D-1>.

23 *Regulations Designating Regulatory Provisions for Purposes of Enforcement (Canadian Environmental Protection Act, 1999)* (SOR/2012-134). The *RIAS* is available online: <http://gazette.gc.ca/rp-pr/p2/2012/2012-07-04/html/sor-dors134-eng.html>.

24 Examples include the *PCB Regulations*, the *2-Butoxyethanol Regulations*, the *Ozone-depleting Substances Regulations, 1998*, the *Benzene in Gasoline Regulations*, the *Pulp and Paper*

*Mill Effluent Chlorinated Dioxins and Furans Regulations*, and the *Chlor-Alkali Mercury Release Regulations*.

25 See Sched II of the *MBCA, 1994*, *supra* note 10.

26 *R v Carriere* (2005), 272 Sask R 13 [*Carriere*].

27 *Supra* note 25.

28 Ibid.

29 See, e.g., *Carriere*, *supra* note 26.

30 *R v Syncrude Canada Ltd*, 2010 ABPC 229 at paras 87–94.

31 Most environmental statutes contain provisions that require the regulated community to report spills, deposits, or releases and to take remedial measures related thereto. See, e.g., subss 38(5)–(6) of the *Fisheries Act*, paras 95(1)(a)–(c) of the *CEPA, 1999*, and ss 13 and 15 of Ontario's *Environmental Protection Act*, RSO 1990, c E.19.

32 See *Fisheries Act*, *supra* note 8, ss 49–54, for the full suite of fishery officer and guardian powers.

33 For enforcement officer and inspector powers under *CEPA, 1999*, the relevant provisions are ss 217–241. For the *MBCA, 1994*, see ss 6–9.

34 EC, online: <http://www.ec.gc.ca/alef-ewe/default.asp?lang=en&n=D6B74D58-1> [*Fisheries Act Enforcement Policy*].

35 For the *CEPA, 1999* enforcement policy, see online: <https://www.ec.gc.ca/lcpe-cepa/default.asp?lang=En&n=5082BFBE-1>.

36 The factors to be considered here include "the seriousness of the damage or potential damage to fish habitat, the fishery resource, or the risks associated with the human use of fish; the intent of the alleged violator; whether it is a repeated occurrence; and whether there were attempts by the alleged violator to conceal information or otherwise circumvent the objectives and requirements of the habitat protection and pollution prevention provisions": *Fisheries Act Enforcement Policy*, *supra* note 34.

37 The factors to be considered include "the alleged violator's history of compliance with the habitat protection and/or pollution prevention provisions; the alleged violator's willingness to co-operate with enforcement personnel; evidence and extent of corrective action already taken; and the existence of enforcement actions by other federal or provincial/territorial authorities": *ibid*.

38 The *Fisheries Act Enforcement Policy* states: "Enforcement personnel aim to achieve consistency in their responses to alleged violations. Accordingly, they will consider how similar situations in Canada are being or have been handled when deciding what enforcement action to take."

39 Robert Baldwin & Julia Black, "Really Responsive Regulation" (2008) 71:1 Mod L Rev 59 at 17 [emphasis added].

40 See *supra* note 36.

41 Baldwin & Black, *supra* note 39.

42 *Supra* note 35.

43 *Ibid* [emphasis added].

44 These criteria, as well as other useful information about the PPSC's role in the Canadian legal system, are publicly available online: <http://www.ppsc-sppc.gc.ca/eng/pub/fpsd-sfpg/index.html> [*FPS Deskbook*].

45 *Ibid*.

46 *Ibid*.

47 For a recent case, see *R v Northwest Territories Power Corp*, 2011 NWTTC 3 at para 89: "The difficulty of proving an ascertainable and quantifiable harm is present in most environmental cases."

48 *R v Jourdain*, [1999] BCJ 1186: "It is now trite law that silt and sand can be a deleterious substance to fish habitat."

49 SOR/2011-91.

# 18

# Science and Advocacy

HEATHER McLEOD-KILMURRAY

What does an environmental advocate need to know about science? What does she need to help judges to understand about science? Analysis of the interrelationship between science and law has been extensive and is still evolving.[1] The focus of this chapter is on a much narrower aspect of this debate, namely the role of science in advocacy in environmental prosecutions.

The first obvious but important point is that the majority of lawyers and the judges they appear before are not scientists themselves. It is therefore crucial for them to know when, what kind, and how much science is necessary, whether to prove the environmental offence or to substantiate the defence of due diligence. It is important to be clear on the different goals of, and standards of proof in, law and in science. Finally, in environmental cases, the issue of scientific uncertainty is relevant and must be dealt with by advocates.

## Purposes and Standards in Science and Environmental Prosecutions

Deciding when, what kind, and how much science is necessary in a legal case depends on the purpose of the litigation in question. What is the purpose of science and what is its role in law? It is sometimes argued that both science and law seek "the truth," but the US Supreme Court in *Daubert* noted some of the differences in these quests:

> Scientific conclusions are subject to perpetual revision. Law, on the other hand, must resolve disputes finally and quickly. The scientific project is advanced by broad and wide-ranging consideration of a multitude of hypotheses, for those that are incorrect will eventually be shown to be so, and that in itself is an advance. Conjectures that

are probably wrong are of little use, however, in the project of reaching a quick, final, and binding legal judgment—often of great consequence—about a particular set of events in the past.[2]

While the purposes of science and law may be seen to vary from each other, the purposes of law also vary across legal fields. In tort law, the primary purpose is corrective justice between the parties, and therefore the balance of probability is the test. In administrative law, the purpose is to determine whether executive actions were fair, efficient, and legitimate, and therefore the standard is usually reasonableness.[3] In criminal cases, the goals are different again, and they are even more specific in environmental prosecutions. What is required to be proved in these cases?

Some harms to the environment might be caught by the *Criminal Code*[4] itself,[5] in which case the full criminal law standard of proof beyond a reasonable doubt would apply to proof of both the crime and any defences to it. The penalty for *Code* offences is often incarceration. Further, a significant social stigma is attached to being charged with a crime, even if the ultimate verdict is not guilty. The courts, therefore, tend to be heavily influenced by the need to avoid wrongful convictions.

Yet the majority of environmental harms are caught by specific environmental legislation that creates prohibitions or offences punishable primarily by fines (though very rarely incarceration is ordered, particularly for repeat offences or failure to comply with court orders). Benidickson provides several examples of such provisions, including section 30 of the *Ontario Water Resources Act*[6] and subsection 36(3) of the federal *Fisheries Act*,[7] noting that "[o]ffences in the environmental context are generally described as *regulatory* or *public welfare offences*" that "may be further subdivided into three classifications—*mens rea*, strict liability, and absolute liability offences," and that environmental offences … fall overwhelmingly within the strict liability category."[8]

The goals of these three types of offences differ in important ways. Full *mens rea* means the full criminal code burden of proof, with the rationale that severe penalties such as incarceration require higher standards of proof and greater intention on the part of the defendant. Absolute liability offences represent a drastically different social decision—that the prevention and penalization of particular kinds of conduct are more important than fairness to the accused.

Strict liability offences, which most environmental offences are, provide a kind of middle ground. They require the prosecutor to prove the *actus reus* to the criminal standard of beyond a reasonable doubt, but then the burden shifts to the defendant to prove that he or she showed due diligence, to be proved on the civil standard of a balance of probabilities.

This is because, as stated in *Wholesale Travel*,[9] "[t]he objective of regulatory legislation is to protect the public ... from the potentially adverse effects of otherwise lawful activity.... The concept of fault in regulatory offences is based upon a reasonable care standard and, as such, does not imply moral blameworthiness in the same manner as criminal fault." That case also stated that "[w]hile criminal offences are usually designed to condemn and punish past, inherently wrongful conduct, regulatory measures are generally directed to the prevention of future harm through the enforcement of minimum standards of conduct and care."[10]

This underlines several important aspects of strict liability offences. They are intended to "protect the public ... from ... *potentially* adverse risks," which suggests that there is greater emphasis on risk prevention in these cases than in criminal law, as well as a focus on prevention of future harm, rather than punishment of past wrong, a very different goal from *Criminal Code* offences and therefore requiring a different standard of proof. This is important in selecting the types of science to be used, the approach to interpreting it in court, and the degree of certainty required.

## Uncertainty, Standards of Proof, and Fields of Science

Environmental cases often involve not only science but scientific uncertainty. Just as with standards of proof, there are various kinds of uncertainty, with differing causes. There are, for example, "preventable scientific uncertainties"[11] that result from a lack of research, but there are also uncertainties even in cases where the highest degree of scientific investigation has been undertaken, because the current state of science simply cannot answer with certainty the question of whether this particular contaminant caused this particular environmental or health effect. There is also an important difference between awareness of uncertainty, where we can predict and articulate with some degree of accuracy at least the level of potential risk, and situations where "we don't know that we don't know" and therefore proceed as if we have certainty when in fact we do not.

Scientific uncertainty is more likely to arise in prosecutions for violations of qualitative, rather than quantitative, standards. Consider, for example, subsection 36(3) of the *Fisheries Act*, which has been the subject of many environmental prosecutions, as we will see below:

> **36**(3) … no person shall deposit or permit the deposit of a deleterious substance of any type in water frequented by fish or in any place under any conditions where the deleterious substance or any other deleterious substance that results from the deposit of the deleterious substance may enter any such water.

"Deleterious substance" is defined in section 34 of the Act as "any substance that, if added to any water, would degrade or alter or form part of a process of degradation or alteration of the quality of that water so that it is rendered or is likely to be rendered deleterious to fish or fish habitat or to the use by man of fish that frequent that water." Whether a substance is deleterious is a qualitative question. These kinds of offence provisions are more subject to interpretation than quantitative standards, which are based on numerical and measurable limits on substances or emissions. However, the kinds of cases that do raise scientific uncertainty may involve significant environmental or health risks, and it is therefore essential to have an effective approach to deal with scientific uncertainty fairly and effectively.

Various tools have been proposed to deal with the different kinds and degrees of scientific uncertainty at the interface between law and science. Charles Weiss has developed a "subjective scale of scientific uncertainty," which is "a tool to help increase the precision and rationality of discourse in controversies in which generalists untrained in natural science must judge the merits of opposing arguments in dispute among scientific experts" to clarify the risk probabilities.[12] He states that this is similar to the quantitative scale of scientific uncertainty used by the Intergovernmental Panel on Climate Change to provide clarity on the numerical probability of their conclusions about the science of climate change being accurate.[13] However, Weiss's scale is subjective in that it is intended to allow scientific experts to express their subjective degree of uncertainty about their opinion. He states that this table may help to avoid the problem that "issues of scientific uncertainty become inextricably intertwined with differences in policy and philosophy."[14]

Weiss tries to help lawyers and scientists to talk to one another by lining up scientific uncertainty with legal standards of proof. For example, Weiss equates "beyond a reasonable doubt" with the scientific level of certainty of "rigorously proven; Critical experiment(s) give(s) a clear an unambiguous result, excluding alternative explanations," and gives the example of "AIDS is caused by HIV." The lower civil standard of a balance of probability is similar to the scientific approach of "more likely than not. If I have to choose, this seems more likely to be true than untrue," and the corresponding example is "there has been liquid water on the surface of Mars at some time within the past 100 million years."[15]

Effective environmental advocacy in prosecutions will ensure that the uncertainty in expert testimony is addressed and clarified. In regulatory offences, it could be argued that since the goals are somewhat different from those involved in "true" crimes and the goal is to protect the environment and human health and prevent risk of harm, the precautionary approach should apply, and uncertainty should be resolved in favour of penalizing risk creation and preventing risk.

In addition to uncertainty, another issue in relation to science and advocacy arises from the many different branches of science that can be involved in environmental prosecutions. Jurists require awareness of the different approaches in these branches of science, and of the advantages and disadvantages of relying on them in environmental cases. For example, scientific evidence in environmental situations can include scientific fields as varied as medicine, epidemiology, public health, environmental health, hydrogeology, geology, environmental engineering, environmental chemical engineering, toxicology, hematology, and oncology, among many others.

It is also important to understand that some of these fields of science have different goals, time frames, and standards than others, just as the various branches of law do. For example, epidemiologists can wait generations to reach a result, and tend to prefer Type I over Type II errors.[16] They wait until they reach almost complete certainty before providing opinions. By contrast, clinical doctors have to treat a patient now, based on the evidence they have, however limited it may be. They proceed on what is more like a balance of probabilities because they have a short time frame and a need for an immediate decision to solve a current problem. As a result, this field of medicine is much closer to the role and realities of litigators and judges.[17] This understanding may also inform the types of scientific evidence advocates may wish to put before the court in a given environmental case.

## Expert Evidence, Novel Science, and Admissibility

Advocates must choose the appropriate type of scientific evidence and meet the appropriate standard of proof, but they also have to pass the admissibility threshold. This has been the subject of much debate in the United States since the 1993 US Supreme Court decision in *Daubert*, a toxic tort case about an allegedly defective drug, which dealt with "novel science" and established a greater "gatekeeping" role for judges. The court set out the "standard for determining the admissibility of novel scientific evidence at trial,"[18] developing a four-part test that more strongly emphasized peer review and "general acceptance" by the scientific community than the prior test. The court emphasized that the methodology, not the results, are the focus. It is interesting that the court admitted that "there are no certainties in science" and required that "the known or potential rate of error ... and the existence and maintenance of standards controlling the technique's operation" be clarified. In *Daubert*, the court recognized the risks in this stricter approach to admissibility:

> We recognize that, in practice, a gatekeeping role for the judge, no matter how flexible, inevitably on occasion will prevent the jury from learning of authentic insights and innovations. That, nevertheless, is the balance that is struck by Rules of Evidence designed not for the exhaustive search for cosmic understanding but for the particularized resolution of legal disputes.[19]

Canadian courts tend to be more generous with admissibility. The Supreme Court of Canada, in the criminal case of *R. v. Mohan*,[20] provided the four Canadian criteria for admissibility of expert evidence:

(a) relevance;
(b) necessity in assisting the trier of fact;
(c) the absence of any exclusionary rule; and
(d) a properly qualified expert.[21]

Relevant means logically relevant and also entails an assessment of whether "its probative value is overborne by its prejudicial effect, if it involves an inordinate amount of time which is not commensurate with its value or if it is misleading in the sense that its effect on the trier of fact, particularly a jury, is out of proportion to its reliability" which they call the "reliability versus effect factor."[22] Another element of relevance is to ask whether "the jury is likely to be overwhelmed by the 'mystic infallibility' of the evidence" because of its complexity and the status of the experts.[23] The court added that "a novel scientific theory or technique is subjected to special scrutiny to determine whether it meets a basic threshold of reliability and whether it is essential in the sense that the trier of fact will be unable to come to a satisfactory conclusion without [it]."[24]

In a medical device liability case, the court also addressed weight, stating that "the underlying message of *J.-L. J.*, echoed in *The Goudge Report*, is that in assigning weight to individual pieces of scientific evidence, the court must pay attention to its purpose and underlying methodology and be guided by the methods and principles generally accepted and applied in the relevant scientific communities."

It is noteworthy that the leading cases in Canada on the issue of admissibility—*Mohan, Trochym*, and *J.-L.J.*—are criminal cases. In *Trochym*, the court emphasized "the need to carefully scrutinize evidence presented against an accused for reliability and prejudicial effect, and to ensure the basic fairness of the criminal process"[25] to avoid wrongful convictions, "particularly ... where, as here, an accused person's liberty is at stake."[26] Canadian courts tend to be fairly generous with admissibility, but advocates must still turn their minds to this potential barrier for scientific evidence. It is also once again important to emphasize that in the context of environmental regulatory offences, there is an even greater argument for generous approaches to admissibility.

## Examples

A brief review of some examples of environmental prosecutions will provide some illustration of how science arises, and the types of science presented, in environmental prosecutions.

Several cases have dealt with subsection 36(3) of the *Fisheries Act* and the issue of deleterious substances. In *R. v. Williams*,[27] the Ministry of Fisheries and Oceans prosecuted the defendant mining company for discharging deleterious substances, including arsenic, cyanide, and copper, into Moose Lake. This resulted from an overflow of "3,000 gallons of mine and storm water" from a sedimentation pond into the lake, due to a plugged intake screen in a pump in the sedimentation pond. The issue was whether "deleterious" under the Act refers to the nature of the substance itself or its effect on the receiving waters. This issue has been repeatedly litigated, and in *R. v. Kingston*[28] and *R. v. MacMillan Bloedel (Alberni) Ltd.*[29] both the Ontario and BC Courts of Appeal held that "[w]hat is being defined is the substance that is added to the water, rather than the water after the addition of the substance."[30] The court in *Williams* agreed.[31]

*R. v. Kingston*, in fact, was a leading example of a case started as a private prosecution, and was begun when Janet Fletcher launched a private suit against the City (the Ontario Ministry of the Environment (MOE) then began its own prosecution). It involved the escape of leachate from a municipal landfill.

Scientifically, Ms. Fletcher had had samples taken for her on four occasions, and the MOE later obtained its own samples. All of these samples and the results of their testing served to provide the evidence on which the City was convicted, and the municipality provided no adequate evidence of due diligence. The trial lasted for 25 days and again involved significant scientific evidence on the tests of deleteriousness and acute lethality, among other things. The trial judge stated that this was a difficult case, indicating that "many witnesses were necessary to establish the legality of a chain of evidence for the samples, the analysis, the charts and exhibits—two hundred and twenty-seven exhibits in all."[32]

While the core issue in all of these cases ultimately turned on the statutory interpretation of subsection 36(3), the science played a significant role. Indeed, on appeal in *Kingston*, one of the issues raised was whether the trial judge had ignored relevant evidence. The Court of Appeal upheld the decision, stating that "[a]lthough the trial judge's reasons are not exhaustive, his reasons nevertheless demonstrate a full understanding of the complex issues of scientific evidence that were before him. I therefore conclude that the record does not disclose a lack of appreciation of relevant evidence."[33]

Another high-profile prosecution was *R. v. Syncrude Canada Ltd.*, in which the defendant corporation was charged with "failing to store a hazardous substance in a manner that ensured that it did not come into contact with any animals, contrary to section 155 of Alberta's *Environmental Protection and Enhancement Act*, and with depositing a substance harmful to migratory birds in an area frequented by migratory birds, contrary to subsection 5.1(1) of Canada's *Migratory Birds Convention Act*."[34] Over one thousand birds died when they became trapped in bitumen in the tailings pond. The evidence involved several experts, including an "expert in conservation behaviour and specialized research dealing with avian deterrence," who explained to the court the qualities of a "minimum reasonable deterrent system" for birds. Much of the scientific information presented was to substantiate the due diligence defence. The court had to assess the scientific issues of the working of tailings ponds and the composition of the substances within them, the technology of bird deterrent systems, and the flight patterns and migratory habits of birds, among other things. These were presented by expert witnesses as well as experienced employees of the defendants. The diversity and complexity of the science was remarkable.

Finally, another successful private prosecution was *Podolsky v. Cadillac Fairview Corp.*, about offences resulting in fatalities, once again to birds, but in this case from hitting office buildings, under the Ontario *Environmental Protection Act* (EPA) and the federal *Species at Risk Act*.[35] The private prosecutor, which was the environmental advocacy group Ecojustice and not a private individual, was able to prove the offences, but the due diligence defence was accepted. Scientific evidence was presented, including expert evidence related to ornithology, "the physics of light and radiation," and growing social awareness of "bird strikes." Once again, much of the evidence related to the due diligence analysis, yet expert opinion about the physics of light was instrumental in having the court accept the prosecution's novel argument that discharging a contaminant in section 14 of the *EPA* could include emitting light radiation.[36]

## Conclusion

Science is an essential element of environmental prosecutions. Advocates and judges need to understand what kinds of scientific evidence are necessary, as well as the purposes, methodologies, and standards in each of those fields of science, and they need to apply them appropriately to the applicable legal standards of proof. They also need to be aware of scientific uncertainties of various kinds, and to become familiar with tools such as the Weiss scale of uncertainty, to ensure that advocates and scientists can talk to each other, if not in the same language, at least in a way that enables them to understand each other.

### NOTES

1 Sidney N Lederman, "Judges as Gatekeepers: The Admissibility of Scientific Evidence Based on Novel Theories" in Joost Blom & Hélène Dumont, eds, *Science, Truth and Justice* (Canadian Institute for the Administration of Justice, Themis, 2000) 218–242; Justice Ian Binnie, "Science in the Courtroom: The Mouse that Roared" (2007) 56 UNBLJ 307; Susan Haack, "Of Truth, in Science and in Law" (2008) 73:3 Brook L Rev 985–1008; John M Eisenberg, "What Does Evidence Mean? Can the Law and Medicine be Reconciled?" (2001) 26:2 J Health Pol 369–381 [Eisenberg]; Michelle M Mello & Troyen A Brennan, "Demystifying the Law/Science Disconnect" (2001) 26:2 J Health Pol 429–438.

2 *Daubert v Merrell Dow Pharmaceuticals, Inc*, 509 United States Reports 579 (US SC, 1993) at 596–597 [*Daubert*].

3 H McLeod-Kilmurray "Placing and Displacing Science: Science and the Gates of Judicial Power in Environmental Cases" (2009) 6 U Ott Law & Tech J 25.

4 RSC 1985, c C-46.

5 For example, criminal negligence, common nuisance, dangerous (explosive) and offensive volatile substances—see "Bringing a Private Prosecution" (East Coast Environmental Law Summary, Vol III, Summer 2009) at 1, online: <https://www.ecelaw.ca/images/PDFs/EnviroLaw_SS_2009_Bringing_a_Private_Prosecution.pdf>.

6 RSO 1990, c O.40.

7 RSC 1985, c F-14.

8 Jamie Benidickson *Environmental Law*, 3d ed (Toronto: Irwin, 2009) at 159–160.

9 *R v Wholesale Travel*, [1991] 3 SCR 154 at 219 (as cited in Benidickson, *ibid*).

10 *Ibid* at paras 25–26.

11 W Wagner, "Choosing Ignorance in the Manufacture of Toxic Products" (1997) 82 Cornell L Rev 733 at 780–782.

12 Charles Weiss, "Expressing Scientific Uncertainty" (2003) 2 Law, Probability and Risk 25 at 25.

13 The IPCC 2001 report provides: "The following words have been used throughout the text of the Synthesis Report ...: *virtually certain* (greater than 99% chance that a result is true); *very likely* (90–99% chance); *likely* (66–90% chance); *medium likelihood* (33–66% chance); *unlikely* (10–33% chance); *very unlikely* (1–10% chance); and *exceptionally unlikely* (less than 1% chance). An explicit uncertainty range (±) is a *likely* range." *Climate Change 2001 Synthesis Report: Summary for Policymakers* (Box SPM-1), online: <http://www.ipcc.ch/pdf/climate-changes-2001/synthesis-spm/synthesis-spm-en.pdf>.

14 Weiss, *supra* note 12 at 26.

15 *Ibid*, table 2.

16 Type I errors are. e.g., saying that a substance is safe, when it is later revealed to be dangerous. Type II errors assert that a substance is dangerous when in fact it was safe. See US, *Reference Manual on Scientific Evidence*, 3d ed (Federal Judicial Centre, National Research Council: 2011) at 176.

17 See Eisenberg, *supra* note 1, as summarized in Mello & Brennan, *supra* note 1 at 430.

18 *Ibid.*

19 *Daubert*, *supra* note 2 at 596–597.

20 [1994] 2 SCR 9. The case was about when "expert evidence is admissible to show that character traits of an accused person do not fit the psychological profile of the putative perpetrator of the offences charged" (para 1).

21 *Ibid* at para 17.

22 *Ibid* at para 18.

23 *Ibid* at para 19.

24 *Ibid* at para 28.

25 *R v Trochym*, 2007 SCC 6, [2007] 1 SCR 239 at para 1.

26 *Ibid* at para 33.

27 2007 ONCJ 163.

28 (2004), 70 OR (3d) 577 (ONCA) [*Kingston*].

29 (1979), 47 CCC (2d) 118 (BCCA).

30 *R v McMillan Bloedel (Alberni) Ltd*, 1979 BCCA 693 at para 10.

31 *R v Williams Operating Corp*, 2008 ONSC 5646 at paras 85 and 87.

32 *Kingston*, *supra* note 28 at para 93.

33 *Ibid* at para 95.

34 *R v Syncrude Canada Ltd*, 2010 ABPC 229 at para 1.

35 *Podolsky v Cadillac Fairview Corp*, 2013 ONCJ 65 at para 3: "causing or permitting the discharge of a contaminant, namely radiation (light), from reflective glass, including windows, that caused or was likely to cause an adverse effect, namely death or injury to birds, contrary to subs. 14(1) of the *Environmental Protection Act*, RSO 1990, c E.19" and "killing, harming, or taking individuals of a wildlife species, namely Canada Warblers or Olive-sided flycatchers, that are listed as a 'threatened' species, by having or using highly reflective glass, including windows, contrary to the *Species at Risk Act*, s 32(1)."

36 *Ibid* at paras 15–18, 68–71.

# 19

# Private Prosecutions Revisited: The Continuing Importance of Private Prosecutions in Protecting the Environment

JOHN SWAIGEN, ALBERT KOEHL, AND CHARLES HATT

While under Canadian law the private prosecutor is granted considerable power to pursue his case, in practice it is a power that is very rarely exercised. The frequency of the use of the power is not in our view an accurate measure of its value.[1]

Society as a whole is the beneficiary where formal, positive citizen interaction with the justice system results in some additional control over official discretion.[2]

—LAW REFORM COMMISSION OF CANADA, 1986

In the late 1960s and early 1970s, when Canadians awakened to the reality of a growing environmental crisis, lawyers, environmental groups, and concerned citizens urgently searched for effective legal remedies. Civil actions and judicial review were largely unavailable because of the absence of substantive environmental rights, the discretion granted by statute to government, the threat of adverse costs awards, *locus standi* requirements, and other barriers to environmental justice. One of the first tools citizens turned to was the private prosecution. Forty years later, the urgency of the need to protect the environment persists, and private prosecution is sometimes still the most effective legal tool available to individuals and Environmental Non-Governmental Organizations (ENGOs) to combat violations of environmental laws. The continuing relevance and importance of environmental private prosecutions is demonstrated by the recent success of private prosecutions in the *Syncrude* and *Cadillac Fairview* cases described below.

## Requests for Investigation (Prior to Private Prosecution)

In the best of all worlds, private prosecutions would not be necessary. If a citizen brought concerns about violations of the law to police or a regulatory agency, they would be investigated and, if those concerns were supported by the evidence, the law would be enforced by trained and objective Crown Attorneys or lawyers employed by regulatory agencies to enforce the law. However, this ideal world does not exist. In the real world, law enforcement agencies are often understaffed, under-resourced, untrained, and reluctant to prosecute or employ other enforcement tools such as orders—particularly where the alleged offender is another government body or even their own department.

In view of the obvious challenges, few people contemplating a private prosecution of a regulatory offence will launch into such a case without first seriously considering or exhausting other options. The first option is always to report an infraction to the relevant government agency, such as the abatement or investigations branch of the Ministry of Environment. Where this is unsuccessful, a more formal request for investigation (pursuant to relatively new citizen engagement tools) can be made. Unfortunately, since the history of such requests is quite discouraging,[3] the person involved will want to carefully consider likely delays—and the impact on the evidence or limitation periods—to reach a realistic expectation of government involvement.

Various federal laws also provide *request for investigation* rights. For example, section 17 of the *Canadian Environmental Protection Act* provides for formal requests for investigation by a citizen along with relevant timelines that are to be followed. A similar process exists under section 93 of the *Species at Risk Act*. Under subsection 22(1) of the *Auditor General Act*, individuals may file *petitions* with a federal government ministry. The petition can include a formal request that a particular violation be investigated.[4] In practice, such requests more often lead to frustration instead of action on alleged violations.

As a matter of public policy, a government monopoly on law enforcement is not necessary. Private prosecutions are essential to promoting the societal goals of access to justice, government transparency, and government accountability. Nowhere is this more true than in environmental protection regimes. As noted by the Law Reform Commission of Canada in 1986:

> Certain kinds of offences may be more likely to inspire a citizen or a group to launch a private prosecution. Offences relating to environmental quality and consumer protection ... are those that most readily spring to mind.... Large groups of people are committed to the

enforcement of the values contained in this type of legislation. It is this type of quasi-crime or regulatory offence that seems most likely to be given a lower priority in the public prosecutor's or Crown attorney's scale of importance.[5]

## The Role of the Private Prosecutor at Common Law and under Canadian Statutes

Historically, a citizen in Britain had a generally unrestricted common law right to prosecute any statutory offence. This ability to prosecute offences has been referred to as a "basic" right and continues to this day.[6] Under its *Criminal Code*, Canada has adopted the criminal law of England except as altered or varied by the *Code* or any other federal statute. As the *Code* and other federal statutes have not prohibited private prosecutions (except in a few situations where a statute provides, for example, that prosecution requires the consent of the Attorney General or a minister of an enforcement agency), the Canadian citizen has the same right to prosecute criminal and other federal offences as he or she had at common law, at least for summary conviction offences.[7]

The same is true of provincial offences, whether prosecuted under the summary conviction procedures in the *Criminal Code* or under provincial statutes. For example, in Ontario prosecutions for violations of provincial statutes and municipal bylaws are conducted under the *Provincial Offences Act* (POA), rather than under the summary conviction provisions of the *Criminal Code*. The POA explicitly provides for private prosecutions for any proceedings commenced by an Information.[8]

## The Role of the Attorney General in Private Prosecutions

Although well established, the right to prosecute privately is not entirely unfettered. The Attorneys General of the provinces have the right to intervene in a private prosecution. They may withdraw or stay charges or proceed with the charges. If the Attorney General withdraws or stays a charge, he or she may substitute his or her own Information and proceed or simply prevent the prosecution from proceeding. One of the few restraints placed on this discretion is that once an Information is before a justice, the Attorney General cannot *withdraw* charges until after the justice has decided whether to issue process.[9] However, this restriction does not prevent the Attorney General from *staying* charges at any time after the Information has been laid.[10] It has been held that the constitutional duty of the Crown to consult First Nations before making decisions affecting their rights does not include a duty on the part of the

Attorney General to consult a First Nations informant before staying his or her prosecution.[11]

## The Role of the Courts in Supervising Private Prosecutions

While the Attorney General has almost limitless power to stay or take over a private prosecution, the courts have much more limited powers that are largely restricted to preventing abuse of process. Basically, the courts have the same power to control the integrity of their process in private prosecutions as they do in relation to public prosecutions. As one Ontario court stated, "proceeding with a private prosecution under the *POA* is a statutorily granted right which the courts should be loath to tamper with lightly."[12]

## Recommendations for Reform of Private Prosecution

Where the British or the Canadian system of penal law has been examined, private prosecutions have either been considered so uncontroversial as to merit little or no mention (for example, the Martin Committee Report)[13] or the commentators have recommended that private prosecutions be retained.[14] When Ontario passed its *POA* in 1979, the legislature provided for the right of any person to commence a private prosecution by laying an Information, on the basis that the obligation of a private prosecutor to satisfy a justice of the peace that there are reasonable and probable grounds for believing the offence has been committed and to swear that belief provides an adequate safeguard to prevent abuse of the prosecution process.[15]

The key reasons for retaining private prosecutions (apart from the fact that there are very few of them) is that they provide access to justice (recognized as a "*Charter* value") and that they enhance government accountability. One commentator went so far as to suggest that it was not only the privilege but the duty of the private citizen to preserve the King's Peace and bring offenders to justice.[16]

A related reason for supporting private prosecutions is that they help the state to enforce its laws when it has insufficient resources for vigorous enforcement. Although seldom recognized today, the need for such assistance was once considered so important that statutes were passed that encouraged private prosecutions by providing that fines levied by the courts be shared with the prosecutor. At least one of these provisions has survived for centuries and remains in our statute books to this day.[17] The view that government officials no longer need private assistance in carrying out their enforcement duties is undermined by the fact of cutbacks to government enforcement staff and department budgets, as recorded in recent Hansard debates and the media.[18]

## Advantages of Private Prosecution as a Tool for Citizens: Costs and Standing Issues

As indicated earlier, prosecutions have a number of advantages over civil actions and applications for judicial review as a method of enforcing environmental laws. Most importantly, there is no "standing" barrier, since the prosecutor need suffer no harm or loss from the offence in order to have the right to prosecute. Secondly, although the prosecutor cannot recover costs from the defendant if successful, no costs may be awarded against the prosecutor who fails to secure a conviction, except in the most exceptional circumstances.[19] Moreover, this immunity from costs largely also applies to an appeal of an acquittal.

## Disadvantages of Private Prosecutions: The Difficulty of Securing Evidence (and Disclosure)

Success in a prosecution, whether by a public or a private prosecutor, is challenging because the prosecutor must meet the criminal onus of proving the offence beyond a reasonable doubt rather than the civil burden of proof on the balance of probabilities. One reason there will never be an "open floodgate" problem with private prosecutions is the difficulty of securing sufficient evidence to meet this onus or to rebut a due diligence defence. Although it is not necessary for the prosecutor to prove a lack of due diligence to the criminal standard, it can be difficult for any prosecutor to obtain even enough evidence of lack of due diligence to rebut the evidence of reasonable care adduced by a defendant. It is particularly difficult for a private prosecutor to obtain evidence of lack of due diligence. Although the prosecutor has no legal onus to prove lack of due diligence, as a practical matter it is difficult to succeed without at least some such evidence. As Dickson C.J.C. pointed out in *Sault Ste. Marie*, it is fair to put the onus on the defendant to establish due diligence because the defendant will usually have whatever information exists about the steps taken to prevent the offence.[20] Despite the onus on the defendant, prudence usually dictates that a public enforcement body or a private prosecutor have at least some evidence of lack of due diligence, rather than relying solely on the defendant's onus.

The most serious practical problems facing the private prosecutor, especially with respect to environmental statutes, relate to obtaining the evidence necessary to prove the charge.[21] The government enforcement agency has inspectors and investigators. The inspectors have authority to enter business premises to carry out inspections, while the legislation often contains a requirement that a regulated business cooperate with the inspector. The private prosecutor has no such tool available. Once the focus of an inspection turns to investigation and the collection of evidence for possible prosecution, a search warrant may be needed.[22] The *Criminal Code* and provincial offences legislation do not appear to prevent a justice issuing a search warrant to a private individual, but the authors are not aware of a private prosecutor ever successfully applying for a search warrant—and the request for a warrant by a private party is very likely to be met with significant skepticism. Freedom of information statutes provide for access to certain government information on request, but they are subject to broad exceptions and involve lengthy delays that may exceed prescribed time limits for the laying of charges.

Government officials may choose to voluntarily share evidence with a private prosecutor without the need for a formal request under freedom of information laws, but as noted by S.H. Berner in a study on private prosecutions,[23] "the government may, in effect, be indifferent, in the sense that it would neither assist the private prosecutor nor actively hinder him in his efforts; or the government may be quite antipathetic and prepared to bar the private prosecutor's way entirely if it can."

In addition, a private prosecutor may persuade a justice to issue a subpoena to government officials to attend court and bring with them the relevant evidence. This is a gamble, however, as the government official has no duty to speak to or to produce the documents to the prosecutor until called to the witness stand. Moreover, a subpoena can be issued only after process has been issued, and the prosecutor must obtain sufficient evidence to be able to swear that he or she has reasonable grounds for laying charges (and in the case of prosecutions for federal offences, to satisfy a *pre-enquete* justice) *before* the court issues process.

In addition, since disclosure obligations almost certainly apply equally to a private prosecutor as they do to a public prosecutor, a private prosecutor must both anticipate this obligation in terms of gathering documentary and other evidence and also be diligent in terms of its disclosure.

## Practices of Difference Jurisdictions on Whether to Allow Private Prosecutions to Proceed

Whether you will be allowed to pursue a prosecution depends on where you live. British Columbia and Alberta have traditionally stayed private prosecutions. Alberta had a "blanket policy that the Attorney General takes conduct of all criminal prosecutions in Alberta (other than those conducted by the federal Attorney General) and that such prosecutions are based on an investigation conducted by the appropriate government agency."[24] However, in recent years, the Alberta Crown has at least once laid its own charges and pursued the case to trial. After a private prosecutor laid charges against Syncrude under Alberta's *Environmental Protection and Enhancement Act* for the April 2008 deaths of 1,600 ducks that landed on a Syncrude tailings pond, Alberta substituted its own charges and proceeded to trial on those charges. The company was found guilty in June 2010 and fined $800,000 as well as agreeing to donate over $2,200,000 to various environmental projects.

The federal government has also stayed environmental private prosecutions. For example, in 2004, the Attorney General of Canada stayed private prosecutions against the Province of Newfoundland and Labrador for allowing the destruction of fish habitat contrary to the federal *Fisheries Act*. However, the federal government does not have a policy of staying all prosecutions. The Department of Justice Federal Prosecution Service Deskbook, which guides the exercise of prosecutorial discretion by federal prosecutors, has a chapter on private prosecutions that "endorses the important role that members of the public play in enforcement of the law." The federal government's policy on whether to intervene in private prosecutions requires Crown counsel to consider, *inter alia*:

- The need to strike an appropriate balance between the right of the private citizen to conduct a prosecution as a safeguard in the justice system and the responsibility of the Attorney General for the proper administration of justice;
- The seriousness of the offence;
- Whether there is a reasonable prospect of conviction;
- Whether the public interest would not be served by continuing the proceedings;
- Whether the decision to prosecute was made for improper motives; and
- Whether it is in the interests of the proper administration of justice for the prosecution to remain in private hands.[25]

On at least two occasions the federal government has laid its own charges following initiation of a private prosecution. In the *Syncrude* case above, in addition to the charges laid by the Alberta government under the provincial environmental statute, the federal government laid charges of harming the ducks contrary to the *Migratory Birds Convention Act*. In British Columbia, the private prosecution of Alexandra Morton against a salmon farm company for killing wild salmon was stayed, but the federal Public Prosecutions Service then laid four of its own charges on the same facts (the case is ongoing).[26]

In contrast, Ontario allows private prosecutions to proceed or takes them over but may proceed to trial rather than staying or withdrawing them. Ontario has obtained convictions on cases in which it intervened, such as the *Snow* case referred to below. In 2001, the Attorney General of Ontario took over a private prosecution against the Ontario Ministry of the Environment for violations of the *Ontario Water Resources Act* alleging continuous discharges of heavy metals into the Moira River from the former Deloro mine site. The trial became the longest environmental trial in Canadian history. At its end, the court ruled that the ministry had committed the *actus reus* of the offence but acquitted on the basis that the ministry had exercised due diligence.[27]

Whether it is healthy for the integrity of the administration of justice to have some provinces in which meritorious private prosecutions are allowed to proceed while other provinces have a blanket policy of staying all or most private prosecutions is a matter that deserves serious consideration.

## Crown Consent, Notice to Crown, and the *Pre-Enquete*

In a number of jurisdictions around the world, the prior consent of the Crown is required for a private prosecution. This requirement has generally not been adopted in Canada given the continuing acceptance of the importance of such prosecutions. There are, however, particular provisions of acts such as the *Criminal Code* that specifically require the Attorney General's consent. Various federal and provincial laws in Canada require some form of notice of the private prosecution to the Crown. Where federal criminal procedure applies, then the notice also serves to allow the federal Crown to participate in the *pre-enquete* hearing.

The *pre-enquete* is an additional screening measure to prevent improper private prosecutions under the *Criminal Code* and other federal regulatory statutes such as the *Fisheries Act* or the *Species at Risk Act*. A justice who receives an Information laid by a private prosecutor and determines that it complies with the requirements for a valid Information must select a date upon which a hearing (the *pre-enquete*) will be conducted to determine whether to issue a summons or warrant to the person accused in the Information. The justice is required to hear and consider "the allegations of the informant and the evidence of the witnesses." Section 507.1 (*Referral when private prosecution*) of the *Criminal Code* requires that the Attorney General receive a copy of the Information, notice of the hearing, and an opportunity to attend and participate in the hearing by calling or cross-examining witnesses. In doing so, the Attorney General is not considered to have intervened in the case—and the private prosecutor can therefore retain carriage of the case.

The purpose of the *pre-enquete* is also to prevent frivolous or vexatious prosecutions from reaching the courts.[28] In *R. v. Vasarhelyi*, the Ontario Court of Appeal emphasized the gatekeeping function of the *pre-enquete*, holding that it "serves as an important control over invocation of the criminal process to further the fevered imaginings of a private informant."[29]

The accused need not be notified and has no right to participate in the *pre-enquete*, which is usually conducted *ex parte* and *in camera*.

The current regime for private prosecutions, including the procedure for the *pre-enquete*, came into force on July 23, 2002. However, the taking of evidence at a *pre-enquete* is governed by provisions for evidence at preliminary inquiries that were added by amendment in 2004.[30] Unlike a pre-hearing on an Information laid by a law enforcement officer, where evidence must only be presented if required by the presiding justice, paragraph 507.1(3)(a) of the *Criminal Code* requires a private informant to provide evidence of witnesses at the *pre-enquete*.[31] This evidence must show or tend to show the commission of the offence.[32] By contrast, evidence that amounts to an "amalgam of unshakeable beliefs, unbridled speculation and patent animus," and which leaves "untouched many, if not most essential elements of the offences alleged in the Information" will not meet the standard in section 507.1.[33]

Under subsection 579(1) of the *Criminal Code*, the Attorney General may, at any point after proceedings are commenced and prior to the conclusion of the case, intervene to stay the charges or take over carriage of the prosecution. Under section 579.01, the Attorney General is allowed to call evidence in the trial itself and to cross-examine witnesses without actually intervening in the case.

### PROVINCIAL CHARGES

The Ontario POA does not require that the Crown be notified of a private prosecution. However, since the *Crown Attorneys Act* gives the Crown the right to oversee private prosecutions and to intervene,[34] there are obvious advantages to notifying the Crown early to avoid an intervention at a later stage in the trial. The same is true of comparable British Columbia legislation, namely the *Offence Act* and the *Crown Counsel Act*.

Under Ontario's POA, the requirements that an informant swear an Information based on reasonable and probable grounds, together with the ability of a justice of the peace to refuse to issue process and the power of the Attorney

General to intervene, have been considered sufficient safeguards against abusive private prosecutions.

## The Power to Appeal

The private prosecutor has a common law right to bring a prosecution. However, there is no common law right carried over from British law for any prosecutor, public or private, to appeal an acquittal. Accordingly, the private prosecutor, like the public prosecutor, can appeal an acquittal only where given this power by statute. Appeals from *Criminal Code* summary trial acquittals can be taken by a private prosecutor because subsection 748(b) of the *Criminal Code* provides for this. There is no similar statutory power to appeal in relation to indictable proceedings, so no such power exists. In practice, this is of little consequence, since environmental prosecutions will almost always proceed by way of summary conviction.

Under Ontario's POA, the "prosecutor," defined as the person who lays the Information or his or her agent, has the same right to appeal an acquittal as the Attorney General.[35]

## Costs

As noted earlier, unlike in civil litigation, a private or public prosecutor need not fear an adverse costs award if the case results in an acquittal. By the same token, the private prosecutor will not benefit monetarily if a conviction results. If a fine is imposed in the case of a successful private prosecution, then the fine will simply be paid into government coffers. One notable exception is the *Fisheries Act*, which stipulates that the private prosecutor will receive half of any penalty imposed.[36] This "fine-splitting" provision enables a private prosecutor to recover some of the significant costs that may have been incurred in mounting a case.[37] In this way, private prosecutions may actually be encouraged.[38]

In both provincial offences and criminal cases the underlying philosophy is that costs are neither sought nor paid by the Crown because, unlike the situation in civil proceedings, the Crown is bringing its cases in the public interest. This applies to private prosecutions as well. The fact that costs are not awarded to a winning party might also be seen as a deterrent to private prosecutions given the significant expense involved. This is particularly true in regulatory, public welfare law cases—and more so where the prosecution is brought merely as a "test case."[39]

At the trial stage, while there is no statutory right to costs on acquittal under the POA,[40] a defendant may have a *Charter*-based right to costs if the prosecutor demonstrated "a marked and unacceptable departure from the standards customarily expected of the Crown" during the trial.[41] This standard is a high one and is rarely met.

Beyond this *Charter* right, section 809 of the *Criminal Code* allows for the making of a costs award in summary conviction matters, but these costs are restricted to nominal amounts set out in the Schedule (s. 840) to the Act for such things as the attendance of a witness ($4).

A costs award[42] at the appeal stage is only slightly more likely but still rare—whether in the case of a public or private prosecutor. The case law reveals only the rarest of cases where costs are actually awarded, and the standard used is the same as that for a *Charter*-based right to costs upon acquittal—namely, "a marked and unacceptable departure" from the proper standard of conduct.[43]

In *R. v. Goodfellow* (2009), costs were awarded on appeal because at trial the prosecutor demonstrated a "basic misunderstanding of the law," did not provide disclosure of essential witness statements, and failed to correct the presiding justice of the peace when it was objectively clear his "lack of patience and … biting sarcasm" created an unfair trial process.[44]

The biggest hurdle for a private prosecutor will simply be the cost of mounting a prosecution. The cost of sampling, analysis, and experts—if they have to be paid in full—will present a significant impediment. In addition, time and resources that have to be dedicated to meeting disclosure obligations are equally, if not more, onerous.

A prosecutor (whether private or public) may also face a civil suit for malicious prosecution. The burden on a plaintiff for proving this tort, however, is so high that the prospect of such a suit need never worry a prosecutor proceeding in good faith.

## Examples of Successful or Influential Private Prosecutions

Private prosecutions are usually brought as a last resort, after repeated requests to government officials to enforce the law have been rebuffed. One environmental private prosecutor has noted that typically she launched a private prosecution only after government bodies had been trying unsuccessfully to negotiate compliance for a prolonged period of time but remained unwilling to turn to prosecution.[45] As one of the authors of this chapter has noted elsewhere, prosecution often succeeds in quickly getting offenders to spend money on corrective actions where prolonged efforts to persuade or to negotiate compliance have had no results.[46] This is true of both government and private prosecutions.

Private environmental prosecutions have historically been very successful in setting positive legal precedents, influencing government policy, publicizing serious environmental concerns, and spurring industries (and government offenders) to greater action to prevent the continuation of breaches of statutory duties. They continue to be effective in achieving those goals even today.

Private prosecutions have been successful in achieving some of these goals even when unsuccessful in court. For example, private charges against a noisy bedspring factory in Toronto in 1976 were quashed because of a drafting error in the Information. The charges, however, led to the Ministry of Environment issuing a control order. Ultimately, the company was prompted by the charges and the control order to move to a more isolated location. In addition, the publicity generated by the prosecution resulted in the ministry announcing that it was reversing its policy of not prosecuting noise violations under the *Environmental Protection Act* (EPA). The ministry had drafted a regulation but later abandoned this approach in favour of drafting a model municipal noise control bylaw to be enforced by municipalities. During both these periods, which together lasted several years, the ministry refused to enforce section 14 of the *EPA*, which made it an offence to emit noise likely to interfere with the enjoyment of property.[47]

Other cases with successful or influential results include:

### *Podolsky v. Cadillac Fairview Corporation Ltd.* (2013) (Ont CJ)[48]

The City of Toronto lies in the path of an important migratory bird flyway. On their migratory journeys, birds will be drawn into cities by bright lights or to replenish their stores of energy. Daytime images of the sky or trees reflected in windows routinely delude birds into fatal collisions. A Toronto-based non-profit group routinely collects birds that have been killed or injured in window strikes—and for over a decade had unsuccessfully tried to get building owners and managers to take action.[49] It is estimated that upwards of one million birds die in Toronto each year in such collisions despite the existence of known solutions involving the application of visual markers on the windows of a building's lower floors.

In a February 2013 judgment, Ontario Judge Melvyn Green found that the prosecutor had proved beyond a reasonable doubt that Cadillac Fairview killed or injured hundreds of birds, including several birds of "threatened" species, as a result of window collisions at its Toronto office complex. In coming to this conclusion, Judge Green interpreted section 14 of Ontario's *Environmental Protection Act* and section 32 of the federal *Species at Risk Act* to cover the unintentional killing or injuring of birds from window strikes.

The company was ultimately acquitted of the charges, having satisfied the judge that it acted reasonably in pursuing innovative measures to prevent the window strikes. The ruling, however, will now require all building owners and managers (as well as corporate directors and officers) to implement remedial measures where birds are being killed or injured in window strikes.

#### *Schultz v. Menkes Developments et al.* (2012) (Ont CJ)

This case preceded the Cadillac Fairview case noted above and was based on a similar fact scenario. The justice of the peace dismissed charges against the accused companies for the death or injury of hundreds of migratory birds in window strikes at the defendants' office complex. The court concluded that reflected light could not have been contemplated as a pollutant under the *EPA*. In the subsequent Cadillac Fairview decision, Judge Green noted that the legal analysis of the justice of the peace in coming to his decision was "unencumbered by any reference to the governing jurisprudence." The acquittal was overturned on appeal. In light of the fact that prior to the commencement of the trial the entire complex had been retrofitted with window films to deter strikes, making it the first commercial structure of its kind, the prosecutor withdrew the charges rather than seek an order for a new trial.[50]

#### *R. v. Syncrude Canada Ltd.* (2010) (Alta Prov Ct)[51]

In January 2009, after both the federal and Alberta governments ignored requests to prosecute Syncrude for the killing of more than 1,600 ducks that landed on the company's tar sands tailings pond, Ecojustice laid a charge against Syncrude under the *Migratory Birds Convention Act* (*MBCA*). Before the *pre-enquete*, the federal and provincial Crown committed to laying charges under Alberta's *Environmental Protection and Enhancement Act* and the *MBCA* in exchange for withdrawal of the privately laid charge. The government prosecutions resulted in convictions and $800,000 in fines plus additional penalties amounting to $3 million, among the highest amounts ever levied for an environmental offence.

#### *Lukasik v. City of Hamilton* (1999) (Ont CJ – Prov Div)[52]

In 1999, Sierra Legal Defence Fund (now Ecojustice) brought a private prosecution against the City of Hamilton, Ontario, for violating the *Fisheries Act* by discharging toxic leachate into Red Hill Creek. The Ontario Ministry of the Environment brought separate charges for the same matter under the Ontario *Water Resources Act*. Hamilton pleaded guilty to both charges and was fined $480,000. The fine was subject to the *Fisheries Act* fine-splitting provision. $150,000 of this money was then used to establish Environment Hamilton, an ENGO.[53]

### *Fletcher v. Kingston (City)* (1998) (Ont CJ - Prov Div)[54]

In 1999, a private prosecutor represented by lawyers from Sierra Legal Defence Fund obtained a conviction against the City of Kingston under the *Fisheries Act* and a fine of $120,000, one of the highest fines ever levied against a municipality for environmental offences, for discharges of toxic effluent from a former waste dump into the Cataraqui River. As soon as the charges were laid, the City installed pumps and a collection system to prevent the leachate from polluting the river. The case was, however, appealed and the conviction on the private Information charges was overturned.

### *R. v. Suncor Inc.* (1982), *R. v. Suncor Inc.* (1983); *R. v. Suncor Inc.* (1985)[55]

In 1982, five Informations were laid by the Chief of the Fort McKay Indian Band under the *Fisheries Act* for discharges of effluent from the accused's upstream oil sands operation along the Athabasca River. Subsequently, the Alberta Attorney General's office laid additional charges under the *Fisheries Act* and the provincial *Clean Water Act* and assumed carriage of the prosecutions. The multitude of charges proceeded via separate trials. In the first trial, Suncor was acquitted of all but one charge (failure to notify), but the subsequent trials resulted in convictions and fines totalling $38,000. The actions were Alberta's first environmental prosecutions and, at an estimated cost of several million dollars, they provided the impetus for significant reforms to the province's environmental enforcement regime.[56]

### *R. v. Snow* (1981) (Ont Prov Ct)[57]

In 1981, a private prosecution for violation of the *Environmental Assessment Act* (EAA) was taken over by the Attorney General. An Ontario cabinet minister and deputy minister pleaded guilty to violating the EAA and were given substantial fines. They had approved the construction of a road without preparation of the environmental assessment required by the EAA. The court stated that it was imposing a substantial penalty because of the need to ensure respect for the law.

### *R. v. Cherokee Disposals and Construction Ltd.* (1973) (Ont Prov Ct – Crim Div); *R. v. Sault Ste. Marie* (1978) (SCC)[58]

Informations in both cases were laid by Mark Caswell, a landowner along watercourses polluted by a waste disposal company under contract to the City of Sault Ste. Marie. The Crown eventually took carriage of both prosecutions and, in the latter case, pursued the matter to the Supreme Court of Canada. The result was the landmark decision establishing strict liability offences in Canadian law.

### *R. ex rel. Tyson v. Hale* (1976) (Ont Prov Ct – Crim Div)[59]

In 1976, the Canadian Environmental Law Association (CELA) conducted the first successful prosecution for the violation of waste disposal standards under the *Environmental Protection Act*. The prosecution was launched after two years of unsuccessful efforts to persuade the ministry to enforce these standards.

### *R. ex rel. Strathy v. Konvey Construction Company Ltd.* (1975) (Ont Prov Ct – Crim Div)[60]

In 1975, a construction company was convicted of injuring a maple tree during construction activities at an elementary school under the little-used *Trees Act* of Ontario. The conviction resulted in front-page coverage in both the *Toronto Star* and *Globe and Mail*, as well as worldwide in *Reader's Digest*, giving widespread publicity to the plight of urban trees. The informant, Shirley Strathy, was later given an award by the Ontario Association of Landscape Architects for her action.

### *R. ex rel. Johnston v. Lieberman* (1974) (Ont Prov Ct – Crim Div)[61]

After Ontario's *Environmental Protection Act* was passed in 1971, the first prosecutions for violating the Act were taken not by the Ministry of the Environment but by the CELA. The cases included a prosecution of a homeowner, Ms. Lieberman, who was convicted of operating an excessively noisy air conditioner, as well as a prosecution of the Adventure Charcoal company for operating a source of air pollution without the required permit.

### *R. ex rel. Mackinnon v. International Nickel Company of Canada* (1974) (Ont Prov Ct – Crim Div)[62]

In the 1970s, the International Nickel Company of Canada Ltd. (INCO) had a reputation as one of Canada's worst polluters. The first prosecution of INCO for air pollution was brought in July 1973, not by the Ministry of the Environment but by a group of students, the Sudbury Environmental Law Association. INCO was charged with two counts of emitting black smoke contrary to the "smoke density" regulation under the *EPA* and one count of failing to notify the ministry of the smoke emission. INCO was convicted of one count of emitting black smoke and acquitted on the second black smoke account and the charge of failing to notify the ministry.

## In Whose Name Is a Private Prosecution Brought—The Informant or the Crown?

The previous section makes clear the lack of consistency in the citation of case names. In the past, it mattered little whether a prosecution proceeded in the name of the Crown or in the prosecutor's name. There was some disagreement about this among commentators, but perhaps the only thing that turned on this was whether the court's decision was reported as "*R. v. Defendant*," "*X v. Defendant*," "*R. on the relation of (ex rel) X v. Defendant*," or "*R. on the Information of X v. Defendant*," where "X" is the informant/private prosecutor. After the passage of the *Canadian Charter of Rights and Freedoms*, however, whether a private prosecution proceeds in the name of the Crown or the informant's name may have implications for matters such as whether disclosure is required or whether the prosecutor or persons assisting the prosecutor who obtain evidence are conducting a search or seizure that is subject to the requirements of section 8 of the *Charter*.

This is now a potential issue because the *Charter* applies only to governmental action; that is, action by government officials and their agents. For example, if a prosecutor is not considered the Crown or an agent for the Crown, theoretically, he or she may not be subject to disclosure duties required by the *Charter*. The simplest solution to this dilemma may be to recognize that while an Information is sworn in the prosecutor's own name, process issues in the name of the Crown, and therefore *Charter* requirements for disclosure and reasonable search and seizure apply, just as they apply to the Crown.

We have been unable to find case law that discusses whether private prosecutors have a duty of disclosure. However, there is little reason to doubt that the disclosure obligation of the Crown also applies to private prosecutors, as a decision to the contrary would result in manifest and unacceptable unfairness to the defendant. In the *Cadillac Fairview* case noted above, Ecojustice gave extensive disclosure, a matter upon which the trial judge commented favourably.

## Conclusions

Private prosecutions remain an important legal tool available to individuals and community groups that might otherwise become frustrated with the lack of action by public officials for an ongoing or serious environmental violation. The challenges in launching a private prosecution, including evidentiary issues, disclosure obligations, the *pre-enquete*, and the risk of a government intervention to stay charges mean that private prosecutions will continue to be used sparingly. Nonetheless, the history of success and influence of private prosecutions over the last decades means that this tool ought to continue to be both protected and respected.

### NOTES

1 Law Reform Commission of Canada, *Private Prosecutions*, Working Paper 52 (Ottawa: Law Reform Commission of Canada, 1986) at 27, online: Law Reform Commission of Canada <http://caledoniavictimsproject.files.wordpress.com/2010/04/1986-law-reform-commission-working-paper-privateprosecution.pdf>. The commission noted that these powers are greater in summary conviction matters. The commission also recommended that the anomalies restricting the rights of a private prosecutor for indictable offences be removed.

2 *Ibid* at 28. The commission goes on in the same paragraph to say:

> … the form of retribution which is exacted by the citizen's resort of legal processes is clearly preferable to other unregulated forms of citizen self-help. Further, the burgeoning case-loads which our public prosecutors routinely shoulder are, in some small measure at least, assisted by a system which provides an alternative avenue of redress for those individuals who feel that their cases are not being properly attended to within the public prosecution system. Finally, it is our belief that this form of citizen/victim participation enhances basis democratic values while at the same time … promotes the general image of an effective system of administering justice within the Canadian state.

3 Section 74 of Ontario's *Environmental Bill of Rights, 1993*, SO 1993, c 28, for example, allows two citizens to sign a formal request for investigation to prescribed ministries under prescribed Acts, including the *Environmental Protection Act*, *Ontario Water Resources Act*, and other environmental statutes. The Environmental Commissioner of Ontario (ECO) reports that in the first decade of this provision, about 36% of requests for investigation were investigated (Source: ECO, PowerPoint presentation, 17 June 2008, David McRobert, Legal Counsel, at ENGO EBR workshop). However, even where such requests lead to an "investigation," this is often little more than a bureaucratic exercise not involving investigators but rather a decision based on political considerations aimed at forgoing non-compliance charges. Investigations very rarely lead to charges.

4 Such petitions are forwarded to the relevant ministries and timelines and responses reviewed by the Commissioner for Sustainable Development and the Environment (CESD)—an office created under the Act. (The CESD, however, has

no authority to force a minister to act—and there is little redress where legislated timelines by government actors are ignored.)

5 Law Reform Commission of Canada, *supra* note 1 at 3.

6 Richard Jackson, *The Machinery of Justice in England*, 5th ed (Cambridge: Cambridge University Press, 1967) at 129–301.

7 Section 504 of the *Criminal Code* provides that "anyone" who has reasonable grounds to believe that another person has committed an indictable offence may lay an Information before a justice of the peace. "Anyone" clearly includes a private prosecutor. *Criminal Code*, RSC 1985, c C-46, s 504.

8 *Provincial Offences Act*, RSO 1990, c P.33, s 23 [*POA*]; s 3 of Alberta's *Provincial Offences Procedure Act*, RSA 2000, P-34 [*POPA*], provides that the provisions of the *Criminal Code* dealing with summary conviction offences apply to all matters to which the *POPA* applies; therefore, it does not prevent private prosecutions for violations of Alberta statutes and municipal bylaws.

9 *Dowson v The Queen*, [1983] 2 SCR 144. See also *Buchbinder v The Queen*, [1983] 2 SCR 159.

10 *R v McHale*, 2010 ONCA 361.

11 *Labrador Metis Nation v Canada (Attorney General)*, 2005 FC 939. The case, incidentally, was an environmental prosecution—a charge against the Province of Newfoundland and Labrador for alleged destruction of fish habitat contrary to s 35 of the *Fisheries Act*. Upheld, 2006 FCA 393.

12 *Sanford v Ontario Realty Corp* (2003), 2 CELR (3) 288 (ONSC).

13 G Arthur Martin, Chair, ed, *Report of the Attorney General's Advisory Committee on Charge Screening, Disclosure, and Resolution Discussions* (Toronto: Queen's Printer for Ontario, 1993) [Martin Committee Report]; Criminal Justice Review Committee, *Report of the Criminal Justice Review Committee* (Toronto: Queen's Printer for Ontario, 1999); Law Commission of Ontario, *Modernization of the Provincial Offences Act: Final Report* (Toronto: Law Commission of Ontario, August 2011), online: <http://www.lco-cdo.org>.

14 *Supra* note 1; Justice (Society) Criminal Justice Committee, *The Prosecution Process in England and Wales* (London, UK: Justice Educational and Research Trust, 1970); Peter Burns, "Private Prosecutions in Canada: The Law and a Proposal for Change" (1975) 21 McGill LJ 269 [Burns]; Law Reform Commission of Canada, *supra* note 2.

15 JD Drinkwalter & JD Ewart, *Ontario Provincial Offences Procedure* (Toronto: Carswell, 1980) at 79. Drinkwalter and Ewart note at 48 that while private prosecution may continue under Part III of the *POA*, which deals with prosecutions commenced by the traditional Information, private prosecutions are not available under Part I, which provides for the more streamlined approach of issuing "tickets" because of the default consequences and because the Act ensures ministerial accountability for issuing offence notices or a Part I summons.

16 See BM Dickens, "Control of Prosecutions in the United Kingdom (1973) Int'l & Comp LQ 1, 2, cited in Burns, *supra* note 14.

17 The *Fishery (General) Regulation*, SOR/93-53, s 62, issued pursuant to the *Fisheries Act*, RSC 1985, c F-14, provide that one half of any fine resulting from a private prosecution is paid to the private informant.

18 See, for example, Paul McLeod, "Ottawa axes fisheries staff, offices," *The Chronicle Herald* (27 June 2012), online: <http://thechronicleherald.ca/canada/111543-ottawa-axes-fisheries-staff-offices>; Fisheries and Oceans Canada, "Quarterly Financial Report for the quarter ended June 30, 2012," online: <http://www.dfo-mpo.gc.ca/qfr-rft/2012-13/Q1-eng.htm>; Mark Hume, "Austerity Measures threaten to

sink salmon biologist jobs" *The Globe and Mail* (26 October 2012), online: <http://www.theglobeandmail.com/news/british-columbia/austerity-measures-threaten-to-sink-salmon-biologist-jobs/article4677593/>; Rob Ferguson, "Ministry of Natural Resources job cuts, office closures coming, province says" *The Toronto Star* (28 June 2012), online: <http://www.thestar.com/news/canada/2012/06/28/ministry_of_natural_resources_job_cuts_office_closures_coming_province_says.html>.

19 In one of Ontario's earliest private prosecutions, the court convicted the defendant of operating a charcoal plant without the required approval under the *Environmental Protection Act*. But the judge, feeling that the prosecution was unnecessary since he considered the Ministry of the Environment to have matters well in hand, awarded costs against the successful prosecutor. The costs award was overturned on appeal. See *R v Adventure Charcoal Enterprises Ltd* (1972), 9 CCC (2d) 81; see also "Charcoal plant fined $500 in first private prosecution under Ontario *Environmental Protection Act*," Canadian Environmental Law News (April 1972) at 1.

20 *R v Sault Ste Marie*, [1978] 2 SCR 1299 at 1325, per Dickson CJC, "In a normal case, the accused alone will have knowledge of what he has done to avoid the breach and it is not improper to expect him to come forward with the evidence of due diligence."

21 See, for example, SH Berner, *Private Prosecution & Environmental Control Legislation: A Study Commissioned by the Department of the Environment* (Vancouver: Faculty of Law, University of British Columbia, September 1972) at 22–26 [Berner].

22 An inspection becomes an investigation, necessitating a warrant, where the predominant purpose of an inquiry is the determination of a person's penal liability: see *R v Jarvis*, 2002 SCC 73; *R v Ling*, 2002 SCC 74.

23 Berner, *supra* note 21 at 23.

24 Shaun Fluker, "Remembering Martha Kostuch: The Private Prosecution and the Oldman River Dam" (29 September 2008), online: <http://ablawg.ca/2008/09/29/remembering-martha-kostuch-the-private-prosecution-and-the-oldman-river-dam/>.

25 Public Prosecution Service of Canada, "The Federal Prosecution Service Deskbook—Chapter 26 Private Prosecutions," online: <http://www.ppsc-sppc.gc.ca/eng/fps-sfp/fpd/ch26.html>.

26 Mark Hume, "Ottawa takes over prosecution of salmon farm" *The Globe and Mail* (21 April 2010), online: <http://www.theglobeandmail.com/news/british-columbia/ottawa-takes-over-prosecution-of-salmon-farm/article1541338/>.

27 *R v Ontario (Ministry of the Environment)* (27 June 2001) (Ont CJ), per Dorval J.

28 *McHale v Ontario (Attorney General)*, 2010 ONCA 361 at para 65, per Watt JA.

29 *Vasarhelyi*, *infra* note 30 at para 39.

30 Subsections 540(7)–(9) of the *Criminal Code* govern what evidence must be adduced at a *pre-enquete*. These provisions have been in force since 1955. One must connect a series of related provisions to reach this result: subs 507.1(8) incorporates by reference subss 507(2)–(8), which includes para 507(3)(b). This section requires "evidence to be taken in accordance with s 540 in so far as that section is capable of being applied." Subsections 540(7)–(9) therefore set the standard for *what* the justice may receive as evidence at a *pre-enquete*. For a full discussion, see *R v Vasarhelyi*, 2011 ONCA 397 at paras 39–48 [*Vasarhelyi*], per Watt JA.

31 *Ibid.*

32 *Ibid* at para 56.

33 *Ibid* at para 63.

34 RSO 1990, c C.49, s 11(1).

35 *POA*, *supra* note 8, ss 1 and 116(1).

36 *Fishery (General) Regulation*, *supra* note 17, states in s 62(1) that:

Where an information is laid by a person in circumstances other than those referred to in section 60 [federal prosecutor] or 61 [provincial prosecutor] relating to an offence under the Act, the payment of the proceeds of any penalty imposed arising from a conviction for the offence shall be made

(a) one half to the person; and
(b) one half to the Minister or, where all of the expenses incurred in the prosecution of the offence are paid by a provincial government, to that provincial government.

37 The "fine-splitting" provision in the *Fisheries Act* was challenged by the defendants in a private prosecution for the escape of landfill leachate involving the City of Kingston on the basis that it violated the common law relating to maintenance and champerty. The case was ultimately decided on other grounds. *Fletcher v Kingston (City)* (2004), 70 OR (3d) 577 (Ont CA), varying in part *Fletcher v Kingston (City)* (7 June 2012) (Ont SCJ); overturning convictions of the private informant *Fletcher v Kingston (City)* (1998), 28 CELR (NS) 229 (Ont CJ – Prov Div).

38 In his foreword to Linda Duncan, *Enforcing Environmental Law: A Guide to Private Prosecution* (Edmonton: Environmental Law Centre, 1990), John Swaigen notes that:

Perhaps it is because of the potential of private prosecutions to reveal so dramatically government ineptitude, that governments are so hostile towards private prosecutions, and attempt to establish a monopoly over prosecution of environmental statutes. This was not always the case. There was a time when government welcomed the assistance of the private prosecutor. During the eighteen hundreds, government agencies and the courts explicitly recognized the need for such assistance from the public and encouraged private prosecutions by providing that half of any fine imposed by the court was payable to the person laying the charge. Ontario's Municipal Act contained such a provision until the 1960s.

39 *R v Garcia* (2005), 194 CCC (3d) 361 (Ont CA).

40 *R v Roberts*, [2001] OJ No 4645 (CJ).

41 *Ontario v 974649 Ontario Inc*, [2001] SCJ No 79, 159 CCC (3d) 321 [*Dunedin Construction*].

42 Subsection 129(1) of Ontario's *POA* reads: "Where an appeal is heard and determined … the court may make any order with respect to costs that it considers just and reasonable."

43 *R v Hallstone Products Ltd* (1999), 140 CCC (3d) 145 (Ont SCJ). Furthermore, there is no jurisdiction at the Ontario Court of Appeal to award costs on a leave application: *R v Laundry* (1996), 93 OAC 100 (Ont CA); *R v Rankin*, 2007 ONCA 426. There is a "reluctance" to order costs on prerogative writ matters, as well as their appeals: *R v 1353837 Ont Inc* (2005), 74 OR (3d) 401 (Ont CA); *R v Felderhoff* (2004), 180 CCC (3d) 498 (Ont CA).

44 2009 ONCJ 543 at paras 24–34, per Bishop J.

45 Marilyn Kansky, "Private Prosecutions from the Public's Perspective" in Linda Duncan, ed, *Environmental Enforcement: Proceedings of the National Conference on the Enforcement of Environmental Law* (Edmonton: Environmental Law Centre, 1985).

46 *Ibid.*

47 In February of 1973, the ministry stated that it expected to announce noise regulations "in the near future." See "Noise regulations expected soon," Canadian Environmental Law News (April 1974) at 47. These regulations still had not been released, and the ministry still continued to refuse to prosecute noise violations under s 14 of the *EPA*, when a private prosecutor obtained such a conviction in February 1974. (See "Noisy neighbour's air conditioner," *infra* note 61). In early

1976, CELA initiated a private prosecution against a noisy bedspring factory after negotiating unsuccessfully for about two years. See "CELA action leads to second Ontario Noise Control Order," CELA Newsletter (April 1976). These charges led to the ministry issuing its second control order in relation to noise. As stated in the article, at the time CELA's charges were laid the *EPA* had been in effect for four years with no noise prosecutions by the ministry and only one control order being issued against noise polluters in early 1976.

48 2013 ONCJ 65, online: <http://canlii.org/en/on/oncj/doc/2013/2013oncj65/2013oncj65.html>. For a brief analysis of the case, see Dianne Saxe, "Canada: It Is Now An Environmental Offence To Kill Birds With Buildings," *Mondaq* (4 March 2013), online: <http://www.mondaq.com/canada/x/224868/Environmental+Law/It+Is+Now+An+Environmental+Offence+To+Kill+Birds+With+Buildings>.

49 Fatal Light Awareness Program (FLAP), online: <http://www.flap.org/>.

50 CBC Metro Morning, audio interview with new building owner (13 February 2013), online: <http://www.cbc.ca/metromorning/episodes/2013/02/13/bird-safe-buildings/>.

51 *R v Syncrude Canada Ltd*, 2010 ABPC 229, Tjosvold J; CBC News, "Syncrude to pay $3M penalty for duck deaths" (22 October 2010), online: <http://www.cbc.ca/news/canada/edmonton/story/2010/10/22/edmonton-syncrude-dead-ducks-sentencing.html>.

52 Environmental Bureau of Investigation, "Hamilton Environmentalist Succeeds in Private Prosecution – City of Hamilton fined $450,000 for toxic waste dump" (18 September 2000), online: <http://ebi.probeinternational.org/prosecutions/city-of-hamilton/news-releases/september-18-2000/>; Also, see "Hamilton bleeding PCBs," Sierra Legal Defence Fund Newsletter (December 1999) at 4; "City of Hamilton fined a record $450,000 for toxic dumping," Sierra Legal Defence Fund Newsletter (October 2000) at 1.

53 Environment Hamilton, online: <http://environmenthamilton.org/view/page/about>.

54 At trial, defendant was convicted on one ministry charge, acquitted on one ministry charge, and convicted on all privately laid charges, *Fletcher v Kingston (City)* (1998), 28 CELR (NS) 229 (Ont CJ – Prov Div); appeal to Ont SC allowed in part (new trial ordered on both ministry charges, new trial ordered for all privately laid charges) (7 June 2012) (Ont SCJ), McWilliam J; leave to appeal to Ont CA granted for ministry charges; appeal allowed in part (original conviction and acquittal for ministry charges restored) 70 OR (3d) 577 (CA); leave to appeal to SCC denied [2004] SCCA No 347. Also see "Prosecutions prompt quick clean-ups," Sierra Legal Defence Fund Newsletter (December 1999) at 5.

55 *R v Suncor Inc* (1983), 3 FPR 264 (Alta Prov Ct); *R v Suncor Inc*, [1983] AWLD 881, 3 FPR 270 (Prov Ct); *R v Suncor Inc* (1985), 4 FPR 409 (Alta Prov Ct).

56 For a detailed summary of the *R v Suncor Inc* cases, see Kernaghan Webb, "Taking Matters Into Their Own Hands: The role of Citizens in Canadian Pollution Control Enforcement" (1991) 36 McGill LJ 770 at 809–814, online: <http://lawjournal.mcgill.ca/documents/36/3/03.pdf>.

57 *R v Snow* (1981), 11 CELR 13 (Ont Prov Ct).

58 *R v Cherokee Disposals and Construction Ltd*, [1973] 3 OR 599 (Prov Ct), Greco J; *R v Sault Ste Marie*, [1978] 2 SCR 1299. See also Jamie Benidickson, *Water Supply and Sewage Infrastructure in Ontario, 1880–1990s: Legal and Institutional Aspects of Public Health and Environmental History*, Issue Paper for the Walkerton Inquiry (Toronto: 2002) at 109–112, online: <https://ospace.scholarsportal.info/bitstream/1873/7663/1/10294043.pdf>; Also, see "Private prosecutions can succeed," Canadian Environmental Law News (December 1973) at 158–161.

59 *R ex rel Tyson v Hale* (30 November 1976) (Ont Prov Ct – Crim Div), Baxter J; Also, see "CELA wins first case under EPA garbage regulations," CELA Newsletter (December 1976). The ministry relied on this conviction several years later in support of its own application for an injunction to prevent the continued operation of this waste disposal site.

60 *R ex rel Strathy v Konvey Construction Company Ltd* (February 27, 1975) (Ont Prov Ct – Crim Div), Newall J; Also, see "CELA obtains conviction for damage to maple tree," Canadian Environmental Law News (April–May 1975) at 36; "CELA plaintiff honoured," Canadian Environmental Law News (June 1975) at 105.

61 *R ex rel Johnston v Lieberman* (28 February 1984) (Ont Prov Ct – Crim Div), Pearce J; See "Noisy neighbour's air conditioner leads to first noise conviction under Ontario *Environmental Protection Act*," Canadian Environmental Law News (April 1974) at 47 ["Noisy neighbour's air conditioner"].

62 *R ex rel Mackinnon v International Nickel Company of Canada* (4 May 1974, sentencing 11 June 1974) (Ont Prov Ct – Crim Div) Michel J; Also, see "Private citizens succeed in first air pollution charge in northern Ontario as INCO fined for polluting Sudbury Air," Canadian Environmental Law News (June 1974) at 75; Brian Chang, "The Canadian Environmental Law Association: Selected highlights from the first decades of CELA's work" (2010) at 27–28, online: <http://www.cela.ca/sites/cela.ca/files/789CELA40years.pdf>.

# 20

# Due Diligence in Environmental Offences

RONDA M. VANDERHOEK

Today we see an ever-increasing societal focus on the environment. That focus ranges from consumer considerations such as which liquid detergent is least detrimental to the water table, to whether it is all right to pour used paint thinner down the household drain. It is clear the public is increasingly mindful of the impact our actions have on the shared environment. Likewise, businesses are making ever greater efforts to ensure that they too are seen as respecting the environment in the production of products and the provision of services. As such, lawyers have never been more focused on participating in ongoing legal training directed at helping clients to avoid regulatory prosecutions. All those involved in pursuits that bring them within a regulatory environment are heeding the call to ensure that they are demonstrably diligent in their actions in the unenviable event of prosecution.

When a prosecution does arise, the most common defence advanced is due diligence. But what exactly is due diligence and how is it being used in the courts? This chapter serves as primer on the defence of due diligence from the perspective of a presenter familiar with the defence as it arises in federal regulatory prosecutions, such as those under the *Fisheries Act*. While the chapter will focus on cases arising in the Atlantic Provinces, the principles have general application throughout the country for conducting a prosecution.

The defence, generally speaking, arises in the prosecution of regulatory offences. Depending on the area in which a court is situated, it may not be unusual for a provincial court judge to have infrequent experience with the defence. As a result, the case law is replete with examples of lower court decisions overturned on appeal as a result of the failure to properly apply the defence of due diligence. But whether common or not, it is necessary to be well prepared to consider the defence when it does arise in a trial.

## Strict Liability

Before exploring the defence, it is necessary to first consider the nature of the offences in which it may arise—the regulatory offence. Regulatory offences are, more often than not, strict liability offences. Strict liability offences are a fairly new creature, established in the seminal case *R. v. Sault Ste. Marie.*[1] *Sault Ste. Marie* involved charges under the *Ontario Water Resources Commission Act*[2] against a city contractor charged with discharging pollutants into a watercourse. *Sault Ste. Marie* provided an opportunity for the Supreme Court of Canada to establish a middle ground between full *mens rea* offences and absolute liability offences. As a result, the Crown was required to prove the *actus reus* beyond reasonable doubt, but the accused could avoid conviction by establishing, on a balance of probabilities, that he had taken all reasonable steps to avoid the commission of the offence. The court addressed it as such:

> Offences in which there is no necessity for the prosecution to prove the existence of *mens rea*; the doing of the prohibited act *prima facie* imports the offence, leaving it open to the accused to avoid liability by proving that he took all reasonable care. This involves consideration of what a reasonable man would have done in the circumstances. The defence will be available if the accused reasonably believed in a mistaken set of facts which, if true, would render the act or omission innocent, or if he took all reasonable steps to avoid the particular event. These offences may properly be called offences of strict liability.[3]

Aspects of the defence have been evolving since 1978, and case law has been answering such questions as, who is the "reasonable man" and what exactly are "reasonable steps." A survey of some representative case law will serve to assist in considering these and other questions, as well as provide direction as to what facts might support a finding of due diligence.

## Onus Is on the Defendant to Establish Due Diligence

A frequent source of trouble in the regulatory trial is a failure to appreciate that the burden of proof to establish the defence rests firmly with the defendant. There is no obligation on the Crown to establish that a defendant was *not* diligent. That said, it is not uncommon for defence counsel to attempt to shift the burden or try to create new burdens for the Crown. Likewise, some counsel will ignore the burden altogether and simply try to persuade the court, based solely on closing submissions, that the defendant was diligent. Other arguments include a simple suggestion that the legislation placed too high an onus on the defendant to avoid the commission of the offence or I "had no real choice."[4] But the law is clear, the defence must *prove* due diligence.

Equally important, the defendant must establish due diligence on a *balance of probabilities* as it relates to the external elements of the specific offence charged. It is a positive onus, and the defendant will be convicted if he does not meet it.[5]

In *R. v. Keough*,[6] the Newfoundland and Labrador Supreme Court addressed both the onus and the standard of proof in overturning an acquittal. The case took an interesting twist when the trial judge tried to apply the test in *R. v. S. (W.D.)*,[7] to the due diligence defence:[8]

> [32] The trial judge achieved the wrong result by mistakenly applying the W.D. test to the defence evidence about due diligence. His approach to the evidence effectively relieved Mr. Keough of his onus of proving on a balance of probabilities that he had exercised due diligence to avoid committing the offences....
>
> [38] The trial judge was right when he said that applying the W.D. "... becomes a little bit complicated when you get into regulatory offence[s]...." Breaking the trial into two phases, with shifting and differing onuses of proof, is what complicates the procedure. The W.D. test did not fit into this case at all. It might only have applied in the first phase but the Crown and defence agreement on the essential facts turned that part of the trial into a perfunctory exercise. If the trial judge had ignored the W.D. test and assessed the evidence about due diligence on a balance of probabilities it would have been patently obvious to him that Mr. Keough had not met his burden of proof. Then the trial judge would have reached a different verdict.

To meet the onus, a defendant is not required to prove that he took all possible or imaginable steps to avoid commission of the offence. Nor is he held to a standard of perfection requiring superhuman effort. But he must prove that he has in place a "proper system" and took "reasonable steps to ensure the effective operation of the system." He will then be assessed against the standard of the reasonable person in similar circumstances.[9]

Since every case is factually different, the court will ask what a reasonable person in the particular circumstances (occupation of the defendant, i.e., fisher, farmer, business owner, consultant, etc.) would have done to avoid the commission of the offence. A useful list of considerations was set out in *R. v. Commander Business Furniture Inc.*:[10]

1) the nature and gravity of the adverse effect;
2) the foreseeability of the effect, including abnormal sensitivities;
3) the alternative solutions available;
4) legislative or regulatory compliance;
5) industry standards;
6) the character of the neighbourhood;
7) what efforts have been made to address the problem;
8) over what period of time, and promptness of response;
9) matters beyond the control of the accused, including technological limitations;
10) skill levels expected of the accused;
11) complexities involved;
12) preventative systems;
13) economic considerations;
14) actions of officials.

A court is entitled to consider the defendant's character and experience, and it is appropriate to distinguish between the onus placed on an ordinary person and that of the licensed fisherman.[11] In the fishing context, courts have interpreted the due diligence defence in the context of "what a reasonable fisherman would do to take all reasonable steps to avoid the particular breach."[12] To take it a step further, the reasonable man standard will also include a fisher in the specific fishery at issue.[13] For example, in *R. v. Gould*,[14] a conviction was entered for possession of undersized lobsters. Gould, an experienced lobster fisher, could not rely on the defence of due diligence where he had measured the lobsters using a gauge that had not been certified as accurate by visual comparison with the gauges used by the Department of Fisheries.

Likewise, in considering the second prong of due diligence, "if the accused reasonably believed in a mistaken set of facts which, if true, would render the act or omission innocent,"[15] the court will consider whether the defendant could reasonably believe certain facts. In *R. v. Harris*,[16] such proved to be the case when the trial judge accepted the defence of due diligence when, had the crew followed Captain Harris's instructions, no offence would have been committed. In that case the crew had previously followed the captain's instructions for well over a year and it was reasonable to believe they would continue to do so.

However, reasonable actions must relate to the offence charged and not some broader notion of acting reasonably, in which case the defence will fail.[17] In *R. v. Boyd*,[18] a crab fisher negligently set traps very near the line between the open and closed fishing areas on May 2, 2009, and as a result the traps migrated into the closed area. The next day his traps were located fishing in the closed area, whereupon he acted admirably in contacting the Department of Fisheries and Oceans (DFO). On charges related to fishing in the closed area on May 2, the trial judge found that the respondent's positive and forthright activities the next day established due diligence. In overturning the acquittal, the appeal court said:

> [35] As noted in *R. v. Alexander, supra*, the due diligence defence must "relate to the external elements of the specific offence that is charged." In this instance, the Trial Judge, when considering the charge relating to May 2, 2009, properly found that the Respondent was not diligent. The inquiry should have ended at that point. To extend the examination of the Respondent's actions beyond the date of the offence, was as described by the Court in *R. v. Kurtzman, supra*, improperly considering "some broader notion of acting reasonably."

While we know a determination of what constitutes due diligence will require consideration of such things as the standards of a particular industry, what information was available to the defendant, policies of the regulator,[19] etc., in some cases the legislation that regulates the activity will itself serve as a guide. A recent example of the latter arose in the Nova Scotia Supreme Court decision *R. v. Arbuckle*.[20] The respondents had been charged with being in possession of undersized herring contrary to subsection 41(1) of the *Atlantic Fishery Regulations*. At trial, the Crown led evidence from fishery officers that the catch contained short herring. More specifically, the officers testified that they had sampled the catch in accordance with the sampling method set out in subsection 44(3) of the *Atlantic Fishery Regulations*, determining that there were significantly more than the permissible 10 percent short herring in that catch. The defence called no evidence of due diligence at all, instead focusing the attack on whether the samples taken by the fishery officers were random.

The trial judge interpreted subsection 44(3) as an element of the offence and concluded the Crown had not established, beyond a reasonable doubt, that the samples taken by the officers were taken in compliance with subsection 44(3) of the *Atlantic Fishery Regulations*; the samples were not random. Without considering due diligence, the trial judge determined the Crown did not prove beyond a reasonable doubt that the provisions of subsection 44(2) of the Regulations *do not apply* and acquitted. It is useful at this stage to review the section of the *Atlantic Fishery Regulations*:

> 44. (1) Subject to subsections (2) and (4), no person shall fish for, buy, sell or have in his possession any herring that is less than 26.5 cm in length.
>
> (2) Subsection (1) does not apply with respect to herring that are less than 26.5 cm in length where
>
> (*a*) the catching of the herring was incidental to the catching of longer herring; and
> (*b*) the number of herring less than 26.5 cm in length retained during any one fishing trip does not exceed 10% of the number of longer herring that were caught and retained during that fishing trip.
>
> (3) For the purposes of subsection (2), the percentage shall be determined on the basis of four or more samples taken from the catch, with each sample containing 50 or more herring.

The Crown appealed, asking the court to clarify whether subsection 44(3) was really just a codification of the due diligence defence. In overturning the acquittal and entering a conviction, the appeal court confirmed that proof that the provisions of subsections 44(2) and (3) *did not* apply is not an essential element of the offence under subsection 44(1). Rather, subsections 44(2) and (3) constitute a statutory due diligence defence. Since the defence called no evidence of due diligence, a conviction was entered.

The case serves to remind prosecutors that a careful analysis of the legislation may serve to demonstrate that the legislator has set out the standard for defendants to meet in certain cases. So, with respect to herring fishing, a fisher will be diligent if he employs the sampling method outlined in subsection 44(3) to ensure that the catch does not exceed 10 percent short herring, and if it does he must employ proper measures to bring his fishing into line with the regulations.[21]

## Planning for the Due Diligence Defence

Not all cases will contain a statutory example of what will constitute diligence. Instead, prosecutors will frequently rely on investigators to gather evidence related to diligence at the same time they investigate an offence. And while the Crown need not establish a lack of diligence at trial, it has to be prepared to assess and, where necessary, challenge the defence evidence. This will require the Crown to gain familiarity with the standards in the specific regulatory environment and break new ground in prosecuting those who may have avoided responsibility in the past.

For a long time, it proved singularly difficult to successfully prosecute consultants for environmental offences arising in their work. That was the case until *R. v. Gemtec Ltd. and Robert Lutes*[22] turned due diligence in the environmental context on its head, when for the first time an engineering consultant company was convicted of providing advice to a client that resulted in the client violating federal environmental law. This case demonstrated that consultants who fail to incorporate environmental compliance into their advice to clients can and may be held accountable for their role in any resultant environmental offence. Consultants are now well advised to ensure they are duly diligent in both the advice provided a client and the subsequent implementation of that advice.

This case involved the convictions that arose from the appellants' involvement in recommendations and implementation of plans to close the former City of Moncton landfill site. In particular, they were convicted of charges of depositing or permitting the deposit of landfill leachate into the Petitcodiac River. The facts: the City of Moncton retained Gemtec to conduct a study for the closure of the landfill and to implement the closure plan that it had recommended. The purpose of the plan was to provide an environmentally acceptable closure plan, compatible with long-term land use objectives for the property. The company provided a plan and designated Robert Lutes, its president, as the project leader. The closure plan recommended an option that would see harmful leachate continue to flow into the river environment. Concerns about the leachate were raised; however, the City adopted the plan and Gemtec was advised to proceed. Under the direction of the appellants, part of the work involved the installation of a 400-metre-long pipe to collect leachate, flowing from various seeps, and drain it directly into the adjacent Jonathan Creek.

The trial judge had little difficulty in concluding that the defendants had failed to meet the onus of establishing due diligence:

> [57] In my view, the due diligence raised by the defendants has not been made out. Evidence at trial established that the defendants either, at best, did not know, or at worst, were "wilfully blind" as to the requirements of s. 36(3) of the Fisheries Act. Further, the defendants were forewarned, via the correspondence of Dr. Louis Lapierre that the closure option they were recommending may not comply with Fisheries Act requirements. No evidence has been presented that they did consult Environment Canada, or the Department of Fisheries and Oceans as to whether the closure plan complied with federal regulatory requirements.
>
> [58] Between 1995 and 2001, the defendants neither recommended nor implemented any reasonable measures to prevent toxic leachate from being deposited into the Petitcodiac River system. In fact, during that time, the defendants recommended and oversaw the installation of the Jonathan Creek pipe which collected and deposited leachate directly into Jonathan Creek. This involved the installation of approximately 400 meters of perimeter drain in 1998. The drain collected leachate from various points on the site and piped it directly into Jonathan Creek....
>
> [60] In my view the evidence presented does not support the conclusion that the defendants either recommended or implemented any measures to avoid the "prohibited act", i.e., the deposit of leachate into the Petitcodiac River system. There were no provisions for proper leachate management or collection in order to minimize leachate deposits as the defendants' approach was predicated on allowing leachate to flow directly into the river system and relying on its dilution capacity to mitigate any environmental harm. [Emphasis added.]

The appellants had argued their actions should be judged diligent in light of obligations imposed on them by the province. The appeal court found the trial judge had correctly rejected these arguments.

In my view, the trial judge properly directed and instructed herself on the defence of due diligence when she stated:

> … my duty in this matter is not to evaluate the defendants' action in respect to the environmental and financial requirements imposed by the Department of Environment of the Province of New Brunswick, but to determine whether the evidence supports the conclusion, on a balance of probabilities, that the defendants took reasonable steps to avoid committing the statutorily-barred activity described in section 36(3) of the Fisheries Act.[23]

Ultimately, a nuanced understanding of the industry coupled with a firm understanding of the law relating to due diligence led to this successful prosecution.

## Conclusion

This chapter has sought to clarify the defence of due diligence available in regulatory prosecutions. In doing so, some examples of how Atlantic Canadian courts have applied the defence have been provided as well as some interesting examples of the defence gone awry. Ultimately, where individuals and businesses enter regulated environments with a sound plan to avoid the commission of offences, coupled with reasonable action in that regard, the defence of due diligence may be available. When available, the defence of due diligence will require a factual foundation, established by the defence on the balance of probabilities. Where the Crown is well informed as to industry standards and, where appropriate, challenges the reasonableness of actions taken, courts should have no difficulty assessing the defence and finding it applicable in the appropriate circumstances.

### NOTES

1 [1978] SCR 1299 [*Sault Ste Marie*].

2 RSO 1970, c 332.

3 *Sault Ste Marie*, *supra* note 1 at 1326.

4 *R v Zellstoff Celgar Limited Partnership*, 2012 BCPC 38.

5 See *R v Henneberry*, 2009 NSCA 112 at para 31; *R v Gemtec Ltd and Robert Lutes* (2007), 321 NBR (2d) 200 (CA) [*Gemtec*]; *R v Petten* (1995), 129 Nfld & PEIR 37 (Nfld TD) at para 53; *R v Keough* (2006), 260 Nfld & PEIR 278 (Nfld SC) at para 8.

6 *Keough*, *ibid*.

7 [1994] 3 SCR 521.

8 This is the test, in three parts, as stated by Cory, J:

> First, if you believe the evidence of the accused, obviously you must acquit;

Secondly, if you do not believe the testimony of the accused but you are left in reasonable doubt by it, you must acquit; and

Thirdly, even if you are not left in doubt by the evidence of the accused, you must ask yourself whether, on the basis of the evidence which you do accept, you are convinced beyond a reasonable doubt by that evidence of the guilt of the accused.

9 *Levis (City) v Tetreault*, [2006] 1 SCR 420 at para 15; *R v Edmonton (City)*, 2006 ABPC 56 at para 703; *R v JD Irving Ltd*, [2008] NBJ No 371 at paras 42–43.

10 (1992), CELR (NS) 185 (Ont CJ) at 212.

11 *R v Jarvis* (1993), 120 NSR (2d) 354 (SC).

12 *R v Symmonds* (RP), 138 Nfld & PEIR 109 (Nfld PC) at para 31.

13 Also see *R v McIntyre*, [1999] NBR (2d) (Supp) No 15 at para 15 and *R v Bell*, [1992] BCJ No 2829 (SC) at 2, 4.

14 (1995), 136 Nfld & PEIR 58 (Nfld TD).

15 *Sault Ste Marie*, *supra* note 1.

16 (1997), 165 NSR (2d) 73 (CA).

17 *R v Alexander*, [1997] NJ No 19 (Nfld CA) at paras 17–18.

18 2010 NSSC 417.

19 In *Keough*, *supra* note 5 at para 22: "Generally, fishermen are required to contact DFO and request permission to recover the gear. Sometimes fishermen are required to carry observers on board when they go for the gear and normally only one trip is allowed for this purpose."

20 2013 NSSC 2.

21 Also see *R v Neary*, 2010 NSSC 466, which dealt with a similar issue in the context of mackerel.

22 (2007), 321 NBR (2d) 200 (CA).

23 *Gemtec*, *supra* note 5 at para 36.

# 21

# Certain Defences in Criminal Law of the Environment

JEAN PIETTE

## Introduction

This chapter presents certain defences used in criminal law of the environmental other than the due diligence defence set forth in *R. v. Sault Ste. Marie,*[1] which has since been codified in various ways in many provincial and federal environmental protection Acts. Most of these defences are known in penal or criminal law. They have been adapted to environmental law and have been subject to various interpretations and applications by different courts across Canada. Defences of particular interest from this standpoint, which have selected for this chapter, are the abuse of process, officially induced error of law, the defence of impossibility, the defence of necessity, and the defence of *de minimis non curat lex.*

We will therefore describe these defences and show how the courts have dealt with them considering the nature and particular purpose of environmental law. Our remarks are not intended to be exhaustive, as there are other defences that address procedural or constitutional issues or deal with the interpretation of statutory law, which creates duties, obligations, and prohibitions specific to environmental law.

## Abuse of Process

The defence of abuse of process is well known in criminal law. It enables the accused to have the proceedings stayed or the charge dismissed if it can demonstrate that the authorities have treated it in an unfair or abusive manner, thus compromising the integrity of the judicial process. The conditions for using this defence in criminal law were established by the Supreme Court of Canada in *R. v. Jewitt.*[2] In *Re Abitibi Paper Co. Ltd. and the Queen,*[3] the Court of Appeal for Ontario established the circumstances and rules under which a justice may find an abuse of process in the context of environmental law. This defence is applicable only "in the most exceptional circumstances," where the behaviour of the Crown may be described as "vexatious, unfair and oppressive," to use the words of Justice Jessup.[4] It should be noted that, like most defences, abuse of process must be proved by a preponderance of evidence submitted by the accused after the Crown has presented the evidence proving that the accused is guilty of the charge against it.

In *Abitibi Paper*,[5] the Court of Appeal reversed the trial judgment and ordered a stay of proceedings because the charges regarding violations of the Ontario *Environmental Protection Act*[6] and the *Ontario Water Resources Act*[7] had been filed before the deadline set by the Ministry of the Environment for the accused to complete work in order to stop polluting the Abitibi River.

In another interesting case, *Attorney General of Quebec v. Balmet Canada Inc.*,[8] a motion to stay the proceedings was granted. The defence argued that there had been an abuse of process by the Attorney General of Quebec and that the proceedings against the defendant were oppressive and vexatious. In this case, the department had waited almost two years after the initial inspection had revealed a fault before instituting proceedings. On this point, the court wished to mention that even if it did not approve of the department's behaviour, the defendant could expect to be prosecuted because the requirement had not been fulfilled. The court also reiterated the principle that a stay of proceedings may be ordered only in the clearest cases. Justice Mayrand nevertheless granted the motion because the Crown sought to punish the defendant for an offence committed on March 3, 1988, while the Department of the Environment had granted the defendant a written extension until March 25, 1988 to comply with a condition of its certificate of authorization. Justice Mayrand wrote the following regarding this matter:

> [Translation] It is inconceivable and disgusting to think that the Department may institute legal proceedings to impose penalties in regard of a situation that it implicitly allows. Because written permission was provided on February 8, 1988 for the situation to continue until March 25, 1988, the defendant could not expect to be prosecuted for this violation on March 3, 1988.

In an occupational health and safety case, *R. v. Toddglen Construction Ltd.*,[9] the court also issued a stay of proceedings based on the evidence that the Ministry of Labour's inspector had agreed not to prosecute the accused if a company representative testified that a subcontractor was responsible for having performed a dangerous excavation.

A similar situation arose in *R. v. Loblaw Properties Inc.*,[10] where a Ministry of Labour inspector had promised that no charges would be laid against the accused if one of its representatives provided an incriminating statement. A stay of proceedings was also ordered in *R. v. Northwood Pulp Timber Limited*,[11] where the accused had implemented a process water treatment pilot project within a period specified by the Ministry of the Environment, but failed to reduce the illegal discharges.

In cases of environmental law, "vexatious, unfair and oppressive" behaviour has often been associated with the conduct of Ministry of the Environment officials and their interaction with the Crown prosecutor responsible for instituting criminal proceedings.

To mount a successful defence of abuse of process in environmental law, the accused must show that clear promises not to institute proceedings were made and even constituted a contractual agreement between the parties. This defence was therefore rejected in *R. v. Laidlaw Waste Systems Limited*[12] because the department's commitments had more to do with an impression of a commitment than a formal commitment.

The defence of abuse of process was also rejected in *R. v. Placages Techno-Spec*,[13] where the defendant argued that the sampling method used by the Department of the Environment prevented it from mounting a full and complete defence because it did not allow the defendant to provide a sample. This defence was also rejected in *R. v. Syncrude Canada Limited*,[14] where the accused argued that it had complied with the provisions of the permit obtained under the Province of Alberta's environmental legislation. It was the same in *R. v. Canada (Northwest Territories Commissioner)*,[15] where the argument of compliance with a permit to refute a charge of non-compliance with the law was rejected because the permit included the following clause: "Compliance with the terms and conditions of this permit does not exempt the holder from having to comply with the requirements of other federal and territorial legislation."[16]

## Officially Induced Error of Law

There is a fundamental rule in our society that ignorance of law is no excuse. The courts have always been reluctant to accept an error of law as a defence or excuse in criminal matters. However, given the number of regulations in modern life, the courts now recognize an exception to this rule when an officially induced error of law is involved. An error of this nature can therefore have an exculpatory effect under appropriate conditions.[17]

Case law has set out certain conditions that have to be met in order for this defence to be used to excuse the commission of the offence by the accused. In *R. v. Jorgensen*,[18] Justice Lamer stated and updated the conditions for this defence, which may be established by an accused only after the Crown has proved all the elements of the offence.[19] These conditions, which must be established by the defendant by a preponderance of evidence, are as follows:

(1) There must have been an error of law or an error of mixed law and fact;
(2) The accused must have questioned the legality of his or her actions;
(3) The accused must have consulted with or received advice from a person in authority who is competent in the matter, that is to say, a reasonable person normally responsible for enforcing a law or providing advice on the law in question, and to whom questions were asked, or from whom advice was obtained regarding the particular situation in question;
(4) The advice obtained must be reasonable in the circumstances;
(5) The advice obtained must have been erroneous (the accused is not required to demonstrate this because the Crown will have already established what the correct law is);
(6) The accused performed an act or engaged in conduct based on this advice.

If the court allows this defence, it will generally grant a stay of proceedings because this defence functions as an excuse rather than a full defence.[20] However, a court will sometimes grant an acquittal based on this defence.[21]

Although Justice Lamer stated the conditions for officially induced error of law in 1995, that defence had already been recognized for several years. The following cases are prime examples: *MacDougall*,[22] *Cancoil*,[23] and *Gravel Chevrolet Oldsmobile*.[24]

This defence has often been used in criminal law of the environment. In *Québec (P.G.) v. Allard*,[25] the defendants had dug a boat trench at Lac-Kénogami. They had obtained a permit from the municipality but had not obtained a certificate of authorization from the Department of the Environment. The defendants believed that they had all the necessary permits. Given all the circumstances, including a dispute between the municipality and the department, which the accused could not be blamed for not being aware of, their error was deemed inadvertent; that is to say, it was an honest mistake made in good faith. The defence was therefore allowed.

As a general rule, the absence of legal proceedings, silence on the part of the Crown[26] or the authorities' tolerance may be the source of the error recognized by this defence.[27] An accused who invokes this defence must have inquired about the rules of law governing a particular activity and obtained advice in this regard. The advice issued by the competent authority will be deemed reasonable unless it appears unreasonable on its face.[28] However, this defence was still allowed where the defendants claimed that although their activities were illegal, they had continued for several years with the tacit approval of the authority responsible for enforcing the law, the Department of Fisheries and Oceans.[29]

In *Balmet*,[30] which we have already discussed in the context of the defence of abuse of process, the court stated that the situation was similar to cases in which a defence may be allowed based on officially induced error of law. In this case, the defendant knew that it had violated the terms of the licence issued to it by the department, but it had been misled by a letter from the department, which tolerated this situation until a specified date.

The Superior Court of Quebec also ruled on this defence in a case of environmental law that went to trial in 1992.[31] In this case, the defendant was acquitted on a defence of officially induced error of law. The company claimed that it had been working under the supervision and responsibility of the Quebec Department of Transport and that a department supervisor responsible for enforcing the contract specifications and applicable regulations had approved the release of materials in an unauthorized location, an offence for which it was being now charged.

The case involved an offence under the Quebec *Environment Quality Act*, and the official who had "approved" the release of materials in an unauthorized location was a Quebec Department of Transport official. However, in *Jorgensen*, Justice Lamer wrote that to be eligible, the error had to be induced "in general" by an official responsible for enforcing the law in question.[32] In practice, the courts seem to show flexibility in this regard and allow this defence when, from the accused's point of view, the officer is seen as a duly authorized representative of the public authority even if he or she is not an official responsible for enforcing the law that has been violated. The same situation arose in *Dow Chemical Canada Inc.*[33] and *MacPherson*.[34]

When a court recognizes this defence, it seeks to understand the accused's perception of the Crown (or "authorities"). Thus, in *Forest v. Pointe-Fortune*

*(Municipality)*,[35] a private citizen misled by the mayor of a small town on the need for a permit was granted a stay of proceedings based on this defence. In *R. v. Vostis*,[36] the accused was less fortunate, undoubtedly because he was an experienced businessman who had relied on a receptionist's statements. However, in *Maitland Valley Conservation Authority v. Cranbrook Swine Inc.*,[37] the court accepted the defendants' good faith because they had verified the applicable laws and the Ontario *Building Code Act, 1992*[38] indicated that the approval obtained included a reference to compliance with other applicable laws.

In another case,[39] the accused was charged with making false statements. He relied on the defence of officially induced error because the alleged statements were made in the presence of a wildlife officer who was fully aware of all relevant facts, since he had witnessed them. The defence was accepted for one of the charges.

Sometimes the distinction between the defence of officially induced error and the due diligence defence seems rather tenuous. Thus, in *MacPherson*,[40] cited as an example of officially induced error, the defence appears to be more like a defence of due diligence. In this case, the defendant, Mr. Macpherson, had a pond, which according to the inspectors, did not meet current standards. They then asked him to suspend his operations and make some changes. The defendant made the changes based on his understanding of the instructions, but the inspectors said that they were not satisfied and initiated proceedings. Mr. Macpherson was acquitted because he had made considerable efforts to comply with the inspectors' requirements and believed that he had made the required changes.

When the defence of officially induced error of law is dismissed, it is because the applicable criteria have not been met.[41] It is obvious that honest and reasonable error ceases immediately when an accused receives a letter or notice indicating that a situation or behaviour is contrary to the law.[42]

## Defence of Impossibility

"No one is obliged to do the impossible." This truism also applies to environmental law. To successfully establish a defence of absolute impossibility, the accused must be in a situation in which he was unable to act because of a fortuitous event or *force majeure*. Obviously, the impossible situation must not have been created by the defendant. Instead, he must have done everything reasonably possible to avoid committing an offence. The cause must be external, beyond the control of the accused, unpredictable, and unavoidable.[43]

In the recent case of *Directeur des poursuites criminelles et pénales v. Lapointe*,[44] the defendant was accused of having allowed a contaminant (sewage from a mobile home park) to be released into a stream. The defendant claimed that he had made every effort to find a solution to the pollution problem but that it was impossible for him to correct the situation without the municipality's help. The court considered the defence in light of Paule Halley's work[45] on criminal law of the environment and found that this defence was not admissible in the circumstances of this case. The court wrote the following:

> 44 [Translation] With respect to the defence of impossibility, it is clear that relative impossibility was involved because the situation did not involve an unpredictable event over which the defendant had no control. The evidence showed that he was aware of the pollution situation long before he became the owner of polluting facilities. He was also aware of the high costs that these repairs could entail because the former owner had not been able to afford them and the municipality of Notre-Dame-du-Portage had refused to become involved.

In *Québec (P.G.) v. Récupère-Sol Inc.*,[46] the defendant operated a contaminated soil and water treatment centre and was accused of failing to comply with the conditions of the certificate of authorization granted by the Minister of the Environment, as a result of having received and stored pieces of concrete larger than it was authorized to receive. The defendant pleaded that it was impossible to dispose of the concrete in question because the only company capable of receiving these types of pieces of concrete in Canada was no longer in business. However, the evidence showed that the defendant accepted the concrete after the company had gone out of business, which was common knowledge. The court wrote, "[Translation] Therefore, it knows or should know that it will not be able to dispose of it. No one may invoke their own turpitude as a defence."[47] The defendant did not meet the following essential criterion for establishing a defence of impossibility: "Finally, the accused must not have placed himself in an unavoidable infringement situation." [48]

In PG *du Québec v Beaulieu*,[49] the court ruled in favour of the defendant accused of having discharged wastewater into a ditch, and ordered a stay of proceedings. The accused lived in an area without a sewer system and his lot was too small to accommodate a septic field. Also, installing a septic tank was not practical. The case was declared very exceptional and the defence was described as very unusual. The court stated that the impossible situation in which defendant found himself was "acceptable and reasonable." Because potential solutions were extremely costly and unreasonable, the court ordered a stay of proceedings based on "society's sense of fair play and decency." This economic argument is more consistent with the relative impossibility of complying with the law and is rarely admitted in a criminal court.

A few years later, the same defendant was prosecuted again for the same offences.[50] The defendant entered a plea of abuse of process, which was rejected this time. The court stated that the doctrine of abuse of process applied only when the facts and the dispute were the same as in the previous case. In this case, the evidence revealed that the circumstances had changed since the first trial: the accused was no longer unable to comply with the law because he could purchase a lot for $500 in order to comply with the standards.

In *R. v. Grégoire*,[51] the accused faced three counts for having discharged manure into a river and having contaminated drinking water. The accused was convicted on two of the three counts, since the court was not satisfied beyond reasonable doubt of his guilt on the first count. The justice wrote:

> [Translation] On February 4, 1980, the defendant cited various events relating to the atmosphere and the temperature, which he described as uncontrollable. These events made it reasonable to assume that on that date it was impossible for him to act differently and that the discharge observed by the inspectors was an overflow from the basin caused by an accumulation of natural rainwater. When the wind picked up, it caused the basin to overflow.

The court therefore accepted a defence of impossibility with respect to the first charge. It considered that the explanations provided by the accused had weakened the prosecution's position, and the court was not satisfied beyond reasonable doubt of the guilt of the accused for the event that occurred February 4, 1980.

The judgment provided few details on the nature and intensity of the weather conditions cited in support of the defence. However, we must remember that the defence of impossibility requires a fortuitous event or *force majeure* to have occurred. However, abnormal weather conditions are predictable and cannot be described as fortuitous events or *force majeure*.

## Defence of Necessity

In order to mount a successful defence of necessity against a criminal charge, some essential elements are required. First, the accused must establish that he was in an urgent situation and that in the circumstances it was extremely difficult for him to comply with the law. Second, the offence must have been committed in order to avoid a greater evil. The defendant chose the lesser of two evils. However, it cannot be a real choice made by the accused since the illegal act was committed in circumstances where it was deemed morally involuntary.

A defendant who wants to use this defence must demonstrate that it was necessary in the circumstances to break the law in order to prevent an event with more serious consequences and that it was better and reasonable to act in this manner. Where an accused reasonably believes that a great evil will occur, committing an offence may be justified if committing the offence prevents a greater evil and if he is in such an urgent situation that no other way to avoid the evil appears reasonably possible.[52]

*Perka v. R.*[53] established three conditions for the operation of this defence:

(1) The moral involuntariness of the act committed by the accused;
(2) The existence of an urgent situation; and
(3) The harm inflicted is less than the harm the accused sought to avoid.

The defence of necessity has been used in some cases involving criminal law of the environment. However, the courts rarely accept this defence. Thus, in a case in which liquid manure was spread in contravention of section 20 of the *Environment Quality Act*[54] and the *Regulation respecting the prevention of water pollution in livestock operations*,[55] the justice rejected the defence of necessity and found the defendant guilty.[56] As an excuse or rationale for its act, the accused pleaded that it had to spread the manure out of necessity. It submitted that it was in an urgent situation and if it had not spread the manure when the earth was not very frozen or covered with snow, the pit that it used to store its cattle manure would have overflowed before spring, which would have caused greater harm. However, the court came to the following conclusion:

> [Translation] [...] that he did not seek other solutions and his choice to spread the manure during the prohibited period was an economic choice rather one motivated by a sincere desire to comply with environmental protection regulations. The situation was not urgent and there was no imminent danger because it was December and he expected the harm to occur at the end of winter. The accused had the means to find a legal solution. For example, he could have hired a septic service company to remove the manure. Obviously, it would have cost some money and the accused would have lost some manure, but that would have been a potential solution.

However, this defence has been accepted in circumstances where the accused had chosen to protect the life and health of a person rather than comply with the provisions of the *Fisheries Act*,[57] which ensures the protection of fish. The same thing occurred in *R. v. Milaster*[58] and *R. v. Western Forest Industries Limited.*[59] The protection of human life, health, and safety prevails over protection of the environment, which reflects the hierarchy of social values.

In *R. v. Saint-Cajetan d'Armagh*,[60] the municipality had dredged a river without first conducting an environmental impact assessment and obtaining a certificate of authorization. The court found that the public authority had failed to act with due diligence but that the defendant had to intervene to prevent a disaster similar to that which had already occurred, that is, frequent flooding. In this case, the court permitted an offence under the *Environment Quality Act* in respect of an activity conducted in the public interest to prevent the catastrophic effects of flooding that would have harmed taxpayers and their property. The court chose to protect the community rather than the environment, even if the protection of life did not seem to be involved. It should be noted, however, that the offence in this case was a violation of an administrative nature, that is, failure to obtain a certificate of authorization to perform work, and that the certificate of authorization would probably have been issued if it had been demonstrated that the work was necessary and if measures had been taken to minimize the environmental impact of the work.

## The Defence of *De Minimis Non Curat Lex*

This defence is used when the facts constituting the offence appear so ridiculous that it seems unlikely that the legislation was meant to address these types of situations. The defence then claims that minor contraventions of the law should not give rise to criminal penalties.

This maxim has existed for very long time, but its relevance in environmental law was formally established in *Ontario v. Canadian Pacific Ltd.*,[61] where the Supreme Court of Canada was asked to consider paragraph 13(1)(a) of the Ontario *Environmental Protection Act*,[62] which contains a general prohibition against releasing contaminants into the environment. This provision is somewhat similar to the ban adopted by the Quebec legislature as a residuary clause at the end of the second paragraph of section 20 of the *Environment Quality Act.*[63] The prohibition of the Ontario legislation forbids the discharge of any contaminant that can cause "impairment or serious risk of impairment of the quality of the natural environment for any use that can be made of it."[64] This is obviously a very broad and vague provision. However, this is one way of legislating to protect the environment. The other is to prohibit the discharge of a particular contaminant based on a very specific quantity or concentration, generally determined by regulations[65] or by enacting highly targeted legislative prohibitions. The defence of *de minimis non curat lex* applies only to prohibitions phrased in general terms.

In its judgment, the court considered that the general prohibition of the Ontario Act was not vague in the constitutional sense but sought to determine the area of risk created by the prohibition and wrote the following in this regard:

> Because the legislature is presumed not to have intended to attach penal consequences to trivial or minimal violations of a provision, the absurdity principle allows for the narrowing of the scope of the provision. In this regard, the principle of absurdity is very closely related to adage of *de minimis non curat lex* (the law does not concern itself with trifles).[66]

This defence, now officially recognized by the Supreme Court of Canada, has not had significant success in the courts. In Quebec, it was accepted in *P.G. du Québec v. Naud*,[67] where the court dismissed the charge of having maintained a dump within 500 feet of a road maintained by the Minister of Highways because the "dump" consisted simply of an automobile body, a small pile of scrap metal and a pile of wood. The court ruled that the law could not deal with such an insignificant matter. This defence was also allowed in the case of a soil remediation activity that was considered a "negligible"[68] activity, but it was rejected in the three other cases in Quebec.[69]

## Conclusion

This overview of various defences in criminal law of the environment shows that the courts always seek to maintain balance and equity between the need to protect society's environmental interests and the behaviour of individuals and companies that are subject to the requirements and ever-increasing expectations of environmental legislation.

Environmental law reflects the increasing importance of environmental protection in the hierarchy of social values and the coexistence of this concern with the rights and freedoms recognized in a society governed by the rule of law.

## NOTES

1 [1978] 2 SCR 1299.
2 [1985] 2 SCR 128.
3 (1979), 24 OR (2d) 742, 47 CCC (2d) 487 (CA).
4 *Ibid* at 496.
5 *Supra* note 3.
6 RSO 1990, c E.19.
7 RSO 1990, c O.40.
8 *Procureur général du Québec v Balmet Canada Inc*, CQ (Crim Div), Nos 755-27-000012-908, 755-27-000013-906, and 755-27-000014-904, 12 March 1992, Yvan Mayrand J [*Balmet*]; reported in No 88 of Y Duplessis, J Hétu & L Vézina, *Jurisprudence inédite du droit de l'environnement: 1980–1992* (Cowansville: Éditions Yvon Blais Inc, 1994).
9 1994 CLB 15993 (Ont Sup Ct, Prov Div).
10 [2002] OJ No 4324 (CJ).
11 (1992), 9 CELR (NS) 289 (BC Prov Ct).
12 [1995] OJ No 4279 (Prov Ct).
13 JE 92 1270 (Montreal Mun Ct).
14 2010 ABPC 229.
15 (1993), 12 CELR (NS) 25 (NWT Terr Ct), upheld on appeal 15 CELR NS [85].
16 *Ibid* at 103 (author's translation).
17 See Jean Piette & Isabelle Fournier, "Le développement des moyens de défense en droit pénal de l'environnement" in Service de la formation continue du Barreau du Québec, *Développements récents en droit de l'environnement* (Cowansville: Yvon Blais, 1994) 291 at 297; Paule Halley, *Le droit pénal de l'environnement* (Cowansville: Éditions Yvon Blais, 2001) at 253 ff [Halley]; *Québec (Attorney General) v MJ Robinson Trucking Ltd*, CQ Hull, No 550-27-005452-906, 4 December 1991, JE 92-1221 (SC); *R v Macpherson* (1983), 3 FPR 329 at 331 (BC Prov Ct) [*Macpherson*].
18 [1995] 4 SCR 55 at 77–84 [*Jorgensen*].
19 *Ibid* at 81.
20 *Ibid.*
21 For example, in PG *du Québec v Allard*, JE 2001-401 (CA) [*Allard*].
22 It was without a doubt *R v MacDougall*, [1981] 2 SCR 605 [*MacDougall*] that officially recognized the existence of this defence.
23 *R v Cancoil Thermal Corp* (1986), 27 CCC (3d) 295 (Ont CA) [*Cancoil*].
24 JE 91-1697 (CA).
25 JE 98-2179 (CQ), Micheline Paradis J; appeal judgment, *supra* note 21.
26 *Halton Conservation Authority v Cristiano* (1992), 10 CELR (NS) 154 at 160 (Ont CJ, Prov Div).
27 G Côté-Harper & A Manganas, *Droit pénal canadien*, 3d ed (Cowansville: Éditions Yvon Blais, 1984) at 532.
28 *Jorgensen*, *supra* note 18 at 80.
29 *R v Johnson & Wilson* (1988), 2 WCB (2d) 194 (NB Prov Ct).
30 *Balmet*, *supra* note 8 at 14.
31 *Québec (Attorney General) v MJ Robinson Trucking Ltd*, *supra* note 17.
32 *Jorgensen*, *supra* note 18 at 79.
33 (1987), 1 CELR (NS) 169 at 172–174 (Ont Prov Ct, Crim Div).
34 *Macpherson*, *supra* note 17.
35 (2004), JQ No 7390 (SC).
36 (2006), 21 CELR (3d) 218 (Ont CJ), aff'd 35 CELR (3d) 109 (CJ).
37 (2004), OJ No 5724 (CA).
38 SO 1992, c 23.
39 *David v PG du Québec*, JE 93-127 (CS).
40 *Macpherson*, *supra* note 17.
41 *Marcheland v R*, [1991] Recueil de jurisprudence du Québec 799 (CS); *Lalonde v Savard*, JE 88-354 (CA); *Séguin v R*, JE 88-584 (CS); *R v Gruber* (1982), WCB 65 (CTY).
42 *Allard*, *supra* notes 21 and 25; *Québec (Procureur général) v Entreprises A Stabile & Fils*, JE 94-1096 (CQ) at 22.
43 See Piette & Fournier, *supra* note 17 at 300–302; Halley, *supra* note 17 at 213 and ff; *Strasser v Roberge*, [1979] 2 SCR 953, studied the defence of impossibility but did not consider it. In this case, the defendant was charged with having participated in an unlawful strike. The road leading to the mine was blocked, but the mine could be reached by another road and 40% of the other employees ultimately went to work.

44 2012 QCCQ 6464, Julie Dionne J.
45 Halley, *supra* note 17.
46 [2003] JQ No 418, Jean-Yves Tremblay J (CQ).
47 *Ibid* at para 128.
48 *Ibid* at para 127, citing *L'environnement au Québec* des publications CCH.
49 *PG du Québec v Beaulieu*, CSP Rivière-du-Loup, No 250-27-000321-863, 21 October 1987, Marc-André Drouin J; reproduced in No 36 of Duplessis, Hétu & Vézina, *supra* note 8.
50 *PG du Québec v Beaulieu*, JE 91-1487 (CQ).
51 *R v Grégoire*, CP Saint-Hyacinthe (Crim Juris) No 27-001200-81, 11 December 1981, Denis Robert J; reproduced in Duplessis, Hétu & Vézina, *supra* note 8.
52 See in particular *Morgentaler v R*, [1976] 1 SCR 616.
53 [1984] 2 SCR 232.
54 RSQ, c Q-2.
55 RRQ 1981, c Q-2, r 18.
56 *PG du Québec v Ferme du Clan Gagnon Inc*, Alma PC (Crim Div), 29 February 1988, Claude Gagnon J; reproduced in No 33 of Duplessis, Hétu & Vézina, *supra* note 8.
57 RSC 1985, c. F-14.
58 (1982), 3 FPR 403 (BC Prov Ct).
59 (1978), 9 CELR 57, 2 FPR 269 (BC Prov Ct).
60 *R v Corporation municipale de la paroisse de Saint-Cajetan d'Armagh*, QC Montmagny (Crim Div), 16 February 1990, Yvon Sirois J; reproduced in No 52 of Duplessis, Hétu & Vézina, *supra* note 8.
61 [1995] 2 SCR 1031.
62 *Supra* note 6.
63 *Supra* note 54.
64 *Supra* note 6, s 1 (definition of the term "adverse effect").
65 As the Ontario legislature did in subs 6(1) of the *Environmental Protection Act*, *supra* note 6, and as the Quebec legislature did in the first para of s 20 of the *Environment Quality Act*.
66 *Ontario v Canadian Pacific Ltd*, *supra* note 61, at 1081.
67 *PG du Québec v Naud*, CSP Mégantic, No 358-75, 4 February 1976, Gérald Boisvert J; reproduced in Y Duplessis, J Hétu & J Piette, *La protection juridique de l'environnement au Québec* (Montréal: Éditions Thémis, 1982) at 595.
68 *Québec (Procureur général) v Ultramar Canada Inc*, JE 98-745 (CQ).
69 *Québec (Procureur général) v 139452 Canada Inc*, JE 96-550 (CQ); *Québec (Procureur général) v Dyfotech Inc*, [1999] RJQ 2496 (CQ); *Granicor Inc v Québec (Procureur général)*, JE 97-1631 (CS); the following article by Paule Halley is worthwhile reading: "La règle de *minimis non curat lex* en droit de l'environnement" in Service de la formation continue du Barreau du Québec, *Développements récents en droit de l'environnement*, vol 214 (Cowansville: Yvon Blais, 2004) 253 (CAIJ). See also *Québec (Procureur général) v 3766063 Canada Inc*, 2007 QCCQ 866, Richard Laflamme J at para 71.

# 22

# Aboriginal Law in the Context of Regulatory Prosecutions

CHERYL SHARVIT

The history of the interface of Europeans and the common law with aboriginal peoples is a long one. As might be expected of such a long history, the principles by which the interface has been governed have not always been consistently applied. *Yet running through this history, from its earliest beginnings to the present time is a golden thread—the recognition by the common law of the ancestral laws and customs of the aboriginal peoples who occupied the land prior to European settlement....*

Most recently in *Mabo*, the Australian High Court, after a masterful review of Commonwealth and American jurisprudence on the subject, concluded that the Crown must be deemed to have taken the territories of Australia subject to existing aboriginal rights in the land, even in the absence of acknowledgment of those rights. As Brennan J. put it at p. 58: "an inhabited territory which became a settled colony *was no more a legal desert than it was 'desert uninhabited'* ...." Once the "fictions" of *terra nullius* are stripped away, "[t]he nature and incidents of native title must be ascertained as a matter of fact by reference to [the] laws and customs" of the indigenous people....

This much is clear: the Crown, upon discovering and occupying a "new" territory, recognized the law and custom of the aboriginal societies it found and the rights in the lands they traditionally occupied that these supported....

... It follows that the Crown in Canada must be taken as having accepted existing native laws and customs and the interests in the land

> and waters they gave rise to, even though they found no counterpart in the law of England. In so far as an aboriginal people under internal law or custom had used the land and its waters in the past, so it must be regarded as having the continuing right to use them, absent extinguishment or treaty.[1]

*R. v. Van der Peet*, the case quoted above that set out the test for proving an Aboriginal right, was, like most of the cases in which the law regarding Aboriginal title, Aboriginal rights, and treaty rights has been developed in Canada, a regulatory prosecution. The defendant, Dorothy Van der Peet, was charged with a *Fisheries Act* offence, as were the defendants in several of the other leading cases on Aboriginal rights.[2] Other cases in which the principles and tests applicable to section 35 of the *Constitution Act, 1982* have been established have stemmed from hunting charges and charges laid for logging without permits.[3] Indigenous individuals, practising their rights under their own laws as they have always done, found themselves being charged with offences under federal or provincial legislation. They raised their Aboriginal and treaty rights as defences to the charges. Few of the Aboriginal rights, Aboriginal title, and treaty rights cases have been brought as civil actions commenced by the Indigenous rights holders.[4]

This chapter does not discuss the tests for proof of rights protected under subsection 35(1) and the analysis and tests developed and applied by the courts for determining whether a right protected by subsection 35(1) has been unjustifiably infringed.[5] The chapter will address two interrelated issues: Are regulatory prosecutions the appropriate forum for working out these issues, and what is the role of Indigenous peoples' laws and legal systems, which, as noted by then Justice McLachlin in the above-quoted excerpts from *Van der Peet*, pre-existed and survived the Crown's assertion of sovereignty over what is now Canada? The chapter concludes with a consideration of the role of negotiations and the courts in bridging the gap between Indigenous and settler legal systems.

## Indigenous Laws and Legal Systems Exist and Are Constitutionally Protected

While Justice McLachlin was dissenting in *Van der Peet*, since its first decision on section 35 of the *Constitution Act, 1982* in *R. v. Sparrow*, the Supreme Court of Canada has consistently identified, as a key principle of Aboriginal law, the requirement to incorporate the Aboriginal perspective,[6] including

Indigenous legal systems.[7] In *Van der Peet*, the majority judgment adopted Professor Slattery's characterization of Aboriginal rights as intersocietal law, and held that reconciliation requires that equal weight be placed on the common law and the Aboriginal perspective, which includes Indigenous peoples' laws.[8] Similarly, in *Delgamuukw v British Columbia*, the court confirmed that Aboriginal title is sourced in part from pre-existing Indigenous legal systems.[9] The court held in particular that Indigenous laws regarding land tenure and land use are relevant in establishing occupation of lands for the purpose of proving Aboriginal title.[10]

These principles flow from the law that governed the British Crown in colonial times. The principle of continuity provided that pre-existing rights under local law continued after the Crown asserted sovereignty over lands occupied by Indigenous peoples.[11] As noted by the Supreme Court of Canada in *Mitchell v. M.N.R.*,[12] Aboriginal laws survived the assertion of sovereignty and were absorbed into the common law as rights. Those rights now receive constitutional protection under section 35 of the *Constitution Act, 1982*. In *Campbell v. British Columbia*, Justice Williamson of the British Columbia Supreme Court held that section 35 protects the right of Indigenous peoples holding Aboriginal title "to make decisions as to the use of the land and therefore the right to have a political structure for making those decisions."[13] The Supreme Court of Canada confirmed in *Tsilhqot'in Nation v. British Columbia*[14] that Aboriginal title includes the right to make land use decisions. Where there are treaties, the Indigenous signatories arguably did not surrender their jurisdiction over natural resources.[15]

Chief Justice Finch, formerly of British Columbia's Court of Appeal, has urged judges, the legal profession, and society to learn about Indigenous laws and legal systems, and to make space for the operation of Indigenous legal orders.[16] In his words, "the current legal system must reconcile itself to co-existence with pre-existing Indigenous legal orders."[17] Professor Jeannette Armstrong refers to the recognition of Indigenous legal traditions and to collaboration between the Crown and Indigenous governments as a shift towards "bio-justice."[18]

Indigenous laws include land tenure systems and rules governing the use of land and resources. These Indigenous laws need to be recognized and integrated into resource management in Canada. One result would be fewer prosecutions of Indigenous individuals taking part in traditional resource use practices. What might be labelled and prosecuted as an "offence" when considered from the perspective of a Canadian or provincial law might, when considered from the Indigenous perspective, be an exercise of an Aboriginal right, in compliance with the Indigenous legal system. The Indigenous legal system is likely to have its own rules for taking care of the lands and resources. Two examples illustrate how the failure to make space for the operation of Indigenous laws and systems has led to charges, prosecutions of Indigenous people, and protracted litigation.

### *R. V. MORRIS*

In *R. v. Morris*,[19] the accused were charged under British Columbia's *Wildlife Act*. The accused were members of the Tsartlip Band of the Saanich Nation, who are signatories to a treaty entered into with the Crown in 1852. The treaty provided that the Saanich Nation would be "at liberty to hunt over the unoccupied lands; and to carry on our fisheries as formerly." The accused hunted at night with aid of illumination, which was prohibited by the *Wildlife Act* on the basis that such practices are unsafe. The accused hunters were trapped by a decoy operation and charged with offences. Under their Indigenous legal system, hunting at night with the aid of illumination is permitted, and the evidence was that the Indigenous laws governing this practice were effective: the Tsartlip people have engaged in this practice since time immemorial, and there is not one known accident resulting from it.[20]

Three levels of court convicted, and upheld the convictions of, the accused.[21] The Supreme Court of Canada overturned the convictions, ten years after the defendants were arrested and seven years after they were convicted. There are likely many Indigenous individuals who have been charged with similar offences, and who have not been able to pursue their defences all the way to the Supreme Court of Canada. The defendants in *Morris* might have remained convicted of an offence or pled guilty despite having engaged in the exercise of a treaty or Aboriginal right in accordance with their own peoples' laws. The lower courts accepted the assumption underlying the province's law: that hunting at night with an illuminative device is inherently unsafe.[22] A majority of the Supreme Court of Canada, however, did not accept this assumption, because the evidence established that night hunting with illumination is safe when done in accordance with Tsartlip laws and practices.

The court concluded that both parties to the treaty shared a common intention that the treaty right to hunt would not include a right to hunt in an unsafe manner;[23] however, the accused did not engage in an unsafe practice, and the court concluded that they were engaged in the exercise of their treaty right to hunt. The court, therefore, found the ban on hunting at night with an illuminating device to be an infringement of the treaty right, and because of the division of powers in the *Constitution Act, 1867* and section 88 of the *Indian Act*, the provision was therefore inapplicable and the court set aside the convictions.[24] Had the province been willing to learn about and make space for the operation of Tsartlip law, there would have been no need for the Indigenous defendants to be charged and prosecuted.[25]

### *BRITISH COLUMBIA V. OKANAGAN INDIAN BAND*

In 1999, the Okanagan Nation issued a permit to one of its member Bands, the Okanagan Indian Band (OKIB), to log trees in an area in close proximity to the OKIB reserve. The community was in desperate need for housing for its members, and the logs were to be used to build a home for an elder who suffered from health risks because he lived in a house with a leaky roof, no central heating, no plumbing, and no toilet facilities.[26] The Band was in a deficit position and could not get any funding for housing for this elder or anyone else on the reserve in need of housing.[27]

The OKIB carried out the selective harvest of logs under the permit issued by the Okanagan Nation,[28] and the OKIB was charged with cutting, damaging, or destroying "Crown timber" without authorization under the provincial forestry legislation. The OKIB were unsuccessful in obtaining access to timber under that legislation.[29]

The dispute between the First Nation and British Columbia laws ran much deeper than the conflict between the Okanagan Nation's issuance of a permit to cut timber and the province's prohibition of cutting timber without its authorization. There was a long-standing dispute between the Okanagan and the province about the management of the forests and watersheds.[30] For many generations, the Okanagan people managed the watersheds under their laws. Their laws give them the responsibility to take care of the land; when the people were created, "a covenant was made that we, as humans, were required to do things in a certain way and in return we would be looked after."[31]

One of the practices the Okanagan engaged in under their own laws and systems for managing the use of natural resources was the practice of controlled burns.[32] Based on Okanagan ecological knowledge, controlled burns were used to take care of the forest ecosystem. If a natural burn cycle did not burn an area periodically, overgrowth would prevent understory plants from growing, including berries and medicines used by the Okanagan and plants relied on by animals and birds. The Okanagan have knowledge about the time of year, and how to read wind cycles and air pressure cycles so that the burns could be carried out safely. The Okanagan have not been able to carry out these burns because they are illegal under British Columbia's laws. In addition, also under British Columbia's laws, vast areas of the Okanagan peoples' forests have been clearcut. The Okanagan believe that the clearcutting and replacement of their forests with less diverse tree farms, combined with the prohibition on Okanagan management practices, contributed to the Mountain Pine Beetle epidemic that has in recent years devastated much of their forests and led to an accelerated rate of clearcutting of the forests in order to salvage the economic value of the trees before the beetles reduce their commercial value.[33]

## Are Regulatory Prosecutions the Appropriate Context for Developing Aboriginal Law?

In *Sparrow*, the first decision of the Supreme Court of Canada regarding section 35 rights, the court noted that "the trial for a violation of a penal prohibition may not be the most appropriate setting in which to determine the existence of an aboriginal right."[34] Similarly, 16 years later, in his minority concurring reasons in *Marshall; Bernard*,[35] Justice LeBel opined that prosecutions for regulatory offences are not an ideal forum for the development of Aboriginal law.

In *Marshall; Bernard*, the accused raised Aboriginal title as a defence to regulatory prosecutions for harvesting timber without authorization. Justice LeBel noted that in *Delgamuukw*, the court held that physical occupation is only one source of Aboriginal title; the other source is Indigenous peoples' laws:

> 139 The aboriginal perspective on the occupation of their land can also be gleaned in part, but not exclusively, from pre-sovereignty systems of aboriginal law. The relevant laws consisted of elements of the practices, customs and traditions of aboriginal peoples and might include a land tenure system or laws governing land use.
>
> 140 … anyone considering the degree of occupation sufficient to establish title must be mindful that aboriginal title is ultimately premised upon the notion that the specific land or territory at issue was of central significance to the aboriginal group's culture. Occupation should therefore be proved by evidence not of regular and intensive

> use of the land but of the traditions and culture of the group that connect it with the land. Thus, intensity of use is related not only to common law notions of possession but also to the aboriginal perspective.

While Justice LeBel concurred with the majority judgment, holding that the Aboriginal title claim had not been made out, he cautioned that the decision ought not to be considered a final pronouncement on Aboriginal title in the area at issue, partly because the nature of the proceedings led to an inadequate record being before the court. Part of what was missing was the Indigenous legal perspective:

> 141 The record in the courts below lacks the evidentiary foundation necessary to make legal findings on the issue of aboriginal title in respect of the cutting sites in Nova Scotia and New Brunswick and, as a result, the respondents in these cases have failed to sufficiently establish their title claim. In the circumstances, I do not wish to suggest that this decision represents a final determination of the issue of aboriginal title rights in Nova Scotia or New Brunswick. *A final determination should be made only where there is an adequate evidentiary foundation that fully examines the relevant legal and historical record. The evidentiary problems may reflect the particular way in which these constitutional issues were brought before the courts.* [Emphasis added.]
>
> IV. Summary Conviction Proceedings
>
> 142 Although many of the aboriginal rights cases that have made their way to this Court began by way of summary conviction proceedings, *it is clear to me that we should re-think the appropriateness of litigating aboriginal treaty, rights and title issues in the context of criminal trials. The issues that are determined in the context of these cases have little to do with the criminality of the accused's conduct*; rather, the claims would properly be the subject of civil actions for declarations. Procedural and evidentiary difficulties inherent in adjudicating aboriginal claims arise not only out of the rules of evidence, the interpretation of evidence and the impact of the relevant evidentiary burdens, but also out of the scope of appellate review of the trial judge's findings of fact.... In addition, special difficulties come up when dealing with broad title

and treaty rights claims that involve geographic areas extending beyond the specific sites relating to the criminal charges.[36] [Emphasis added.]

143 There is little doubt that the legal issues to be determined in the context of aboriginal rights claims are much larger than the criminal charge itself and that the criminal process is inadequate and inappropriate for dealing with such claims.

The court noted again in *Lax Kw'alaams Indian Band v Canada (Attorney General)* (21 years after *Sparrow*) that regulatory prosecutions are not well suited for litigating Aboriginal and treaty rights issues.[37] In *Marshall; Bernard*, Justice LeBel suggested that prosecutions be put on hold while title and rights issues are litigated in the civil courts:

144 The question of aboriginal title and access to resources in New Brunswick and Nova Scotia is a complex issue that is of great importance to all the residents and communities of the provinces. The determination of these issues deserves careful consideration, and all interested parties should have the opportunity to participate in any litigation or negotiations. Accordingly, when issues of aboriginal title or other aboriginal rights claims arise in the context of summary conviction proceedings, it may be most beneficial to all concerned to seek a temporary stay of the charges so that the aboriginal claim can be properly litigated in the civil courts. Once the aboriginal rights claim to the area in question is settled, the Crown could decide whether or not to proceed with the criminal charges.

While summary conviction proceedings may not be the appropriate forum for determinations of Aboriginal title and rights and treaty rights, or for receving evidence of Indigenous laws and legal systems, civil proceedings have thus far not proved to be a great alternative. In the meantime, prosecutions continue, and Indigenous people engaged in practices that have been central to their cultures for countless generations are charged and treated as criminals.

## Civil Actions: Risks and Difficulties

While full evidence can be expected to be put before the court in a civil lawsuit, and the Indigenous Nation's laws can be put before the court, civil lawsuits addressing Aboriginal title and rights are expensive and take many years to litigate, and, thus far, most civil cases brought by Indigenous peoples in Canada to prove their title and rights have been decided at least in part on pleadings or other technical issues raised by the Crown.

## TECHNICALITIES AND PLEADINGS ISSUES

In *Calder v Attorney-General of British Columbia*,[38] three judges of the Supreme Court of Canada held that Aboriginal title had been extinguished, three held that the Nisga'a continued to hold unextinguished Aboriginal title, and the seventh and deciding judge dismissed the case on a technicality because the Nisga'a did not obtain a fiat from the province to proceed with the case.

Initially, the *Delgamuukw* litigation was brought by individual Gitksan and Wet'suwet'en Houses; on appeal, the claims were amalgamated into two collective claims, one by each nation. The Supreme Court of Canada concluded that the respondents suffered prejudice because the Gitsksan and Wet'suwet'en did not amend their pleadings, and it therefore ordered a new trial rather than applying the tests it set out for proof of Aboriginal title to the facts.[39]

At trial, the *Tsilhqot'in* case was decided on a pleadings issue. The trial judge concluded that the wording of the declaration in the Tsilhqot'in statement of claim advanced an "all-or-nothing" claim. Because the trial judge found that the evidence established Aboriginal title to only part of the area claimed, he held that he could not issue any declaration of Aboriginal title.[40] The Supreme Court of Canada disagreed and granted the declaration of Aboriginal title, concluding that: (1) in cases such as this, legal principles may be unclear at the outset; (2) evidence as to how the land was used may be uncertain at the outset and historic practices will be clarified through the course of trial; and (3) "cases such as this require an approach that results in decisions based on the best evidence that emerges, not what a lawyer may have envisaged when drafting the original calim."[41]

In the *Lax Kw'alaams*[42] case, the statement of claim was focused on a right to a commercial fishery. Partway through the trial, the Lax Kw'alaams sought, as alternative relief, declarations of lesser rights, including a right to fish for subsistence purposes. The Supreme Court of Canada held that the defendants "must be left in no doubt about precisely what is claimed" and that the trial judge did not err in refusing to grant a declaration of "lesser" rights.[43] While the evidence established that the Lax Kw'alaams people "largely sustained themselves" by fishing, which ought to give rise to an Aboriginal right to do so, a member of Lax Kw'alaams facing a fishing charge would have to prove an Aboriginal right to raise it as a defence unless the prosecutor admitted the existence of the Aboriginal right.

## COSTS

Around the same time that the defendants in the *Bernard* and *Marshall* cases were logging without provincial authorization on the east coast, in British Columbia, the Okanagan, Neskonlith, Adams Lake, and Splats'in (Spallumcheen) Bands engaged in logging under permits issued by their respective Nations (the Okanagan Nation Alliance and the Secwepemc or Shuswap Nation Tribal Council), rather than under permits issued by the province. The province issued stop work orders under its forestry legislation, seized the logs, obtained injunctions against the Okanagan and Secwepemc, and brought proceedings to enforce the stop work orders. The Okanagan and Secwepemc raised Aboriginal title and rights in defence, and on the province's motion, the summary proceedings were converted into civil trial proceedings; the courts were of the view that discovery and cross-examinations were required in order to properly determine the scope of Okanagan and Secwepemc Aboriginal title.[44]

A civil trial involving claims of Aboriginal title and rights can be prohibitively expensive, as it involves a factual inquiry spanning many years and many witnesses, including experts and oral history witnesses.[45] The Okanagan and Secwepemc could not afford an Aboriginal title trial and so they sought, and were granted, an order requiring the Crown to pay their costs in advance of the trial and in any event of the cause.[46] The Supreme Court of Canada set out a new test for advance or interim costs orders in public interest litigation as follows: (1) the party seeking costs genuinely cannot afford to pay for the litigation, and no other realistic option exists for bringing the issues to trial; (2) the claim to be adjudicated is *prima facie* meritorious; and (3) the issues raised transcend the individual interests of the particular litigant, are of public importance, and have not been resolved in previous cases.[47]

Because of the third requirement, advance cost orders are not available for most Indigenous peoples with unresolved Aboriginal title and rights claims, either as a defence to a regulatory prosecution or in a civil lawsuit. Unless the Indigenous peoples can show that their case is a test case raising an unresolved legal issue, the case will not qualify.[48]

The Tsilhqot'in Nation was already partway through its Aboriginal title and rights trial when the British Columbia Court of Appeal granted the advance costs award to the Okanagan and Secwepemc. The Tsilqhot'in were then granted an advance costs order as well, based on the test set out in the *Okanagan* case.[49] The Crown was then able to rely in part on the *Tsilhqot'in* case to deny to the Okanagan and Secwepmec the ability to prove their Aboriginal title in their cases under their cost order. The Secwepemc case was stayed pending the outcome of the Okanagan case.[50] In 2007, after the Supreme Court of Canada affirmed that the Mi'kmaq and Maliseet have an Aboriginal right to harvest timber for domestic purposes,[51] the province admitted that the Okanagan have this same right. Though the Okanagan and Secwepemc never pled this kind of right, the province successfully applied to defer the Aboriginal title issues in the Okanagan case, to be heard only if necessary after a decision on whether the province could justify the infringement of the admitted right, and after the outcome of the *Tsilhqot'in* litigation.[52] The Okanagan have thus far been deprived the ability to defend themselves on the basis of their title and laws.

## Where To From Here?

The courts have repeatedly called upon the parties to negotiate reconciliation.[53] The closing paragraph of Chief Justice Lamer's decision in *Delgamuukw* was as follows:

> 186 Finally, this litigation has been both long and expensive, not only in economic but in human terms as well. By ordering a new trial, I do not necessarily encourage the parties to proceed to litigation and to settle their dispute through the courts. As was said in *Sparrow*, at p. 1105, s. 35(1) "provides a solid constitutional base upon which subsequent negotiations can take place".... Moreover, the Crown is under a moral, if not a legal, duty to enter into and conduct those negotiations in good faith. Ultimately, it is through negotiated settlements, with good faith and give and take on all sides, reinforced by the judgments of this Court, that we will achieve what I stated in *Van der Peet, supra*, at para. 31, to be a basic purpose of s. 35(1)—"the reconciliation of the pre-existence of aboriginal societies with the sovereignty of the Crown". Let us face it, we are all here to stay.

In *R. v. Marshall*, the court noted that accommodation of treaty rights would be best achieved through consultation and negotiation of an agreement for Mi'kmaq participation in resources.[54] In *Haida*, the court once again called on the parties to engage in negotiations to resolve the outstanding issues between Indigenous peoples and the Crown:

> 20 Where treaties remain to be concluded, *the honour of the Crown requires negotiations leading to a just settlement of Aboriginal claims*: *R. v. Sparrow*, [1990] 1 SCR 1075, at pp. 1105–6. Treaties serve to reconcile pre-existing Aboriginal sovereignty with assumed Crown sovereignty, and to define Aboriginal rights guaranteed by s. 35 of the *Constitution*

> *Act, 1982*. Section 35 represents a promise of rights recognition, and "[i]t is always assumed that the Crown intends to fulfil its promises" (*Badger*, *supra*, at para. 41). *This promise is realized and sovereignty claims reconciled through the process of honourable negotiation.* It is a corollary of s. 35 that the Crown act honourably in defining the rights it guarantees and in reconciling them with other rights and interests. This, in turn, implies a duty to consult and, if appropriate, accommodate. [Emphasis added.]
>
> . . .
>
> 25 Put simply, Canada's Aboriginal peoples were here when Europeans came, and were never conquered. Many bands reconciled their claims with the sovereignty of the Crown through negotiated treaties. Others, notably in British Columbia, have yet to do so. The potential rights embedded in these claims are protected by s. 35 of the *Constitution Act, 1982*. The honour of the Crown requires that these rights be determined, recognized and respected. This, in turn, requires the Crown, acting honourably, to participate in processes of negotiation. While this process continues, the honour of the Crown may require it to consult and, where indicated, accommodate Aboriginal interests.

Justice Vickers, the trial judge in *Tsilhqot'in*, expected the parties to negotiate, and attempted to facilitate those negotiations by making findings about Tsilhqot'in Aboriginal title even though he (in error) concluded that he could not grant a declaration:[55]

> [1136] Over the years, British Columbia has either denied the existence of Aboriginal title and rights or established policy that Aboriginal title and rights could only be addressed or considered at treaty negotiations. At all material times, British Columbia has refused to acknowledge title and rights during the process of consultation. Consequently, the pleas of the Tsilhqot'in people have been ignored....
>
> [1375] I have come to see the Court's role as one step in the process of reconciliation. For that reason, I have taken the opportunity to decide issues that did not need to be decided. For example, I have been unable to make a declaration of Tsilhqot'in Aboriginal title. However, I have expressed an opinion that the parties are free to use in the negotiations that must follow.

> [1376] What is clear to me is that the impoverished view of Aboriginal title advanced by Canada and British Columbia, characterized by the plaintiff as a "postage stamp" approach to title, cannot be allowed to pervade and inhibit genuine negotiations.

Crown positions often fail to comply with the jurisprudence, making a negotiated resolution difficult to achieve. For example, for many years, British Columbia sought to advance its position, supported by various legal arguments, that Aboriginal title had been extinguished throughout the province. These arguments were put to rest by the Supreme Court of Canada in *Delgamuukw*, where the court held that Aboriginal title had not been extinguished and continued to exist in British Columbia.[56]

In response to the *Delgamuukw* decision, rather than acknowledge that Aboriginal title continues to exist and engage in negotiations based on recognition, the province took the position that everything the court said about Aboriginal title was *obiter*, and that as no Indigenous people had actually proven Aboriginal title and received a court declaration, nothing on the ground had changed. It would not recognize Aboriginal title and would not negotiate based on recognition, or even consult with Indigenous people before impacting their interests, unless an Indigenous Nation proved its Aboriginal title and rights in court. This eventually led to the *Haida* case, in which the Supreme Court of Canada rejected the Crown's position that until Aboriginal title is proven, the Crown has no legal obligations.[57]

The province then attempted to confine Aboriginal title to individual small sites, such as villages, fishing rocks, hunting blinds, and buffalo jumps—a theory rejected as "impoverished" at trial in the *Tsilhqot'in* case[58] but successful on appeal to the BC Court of Appeal.[59] This approach to Aboriginal title ignores Indigenous peoples' laws and perspectives despite *Delgamuukw's* requirement to give weight to those laws. It is also an approach that implicitly adopts stereotypes about Indigenous peoples that the Supreme Court of Canada rejected almost 30 years earlier.[60]

The trial judge noted that the Crown's positional and "impoverished" approach to Aboriginal title had stood in the way of negotiations. In response, the Crown appealed, continuing to advance this impoverished approach. *Tsilhqot'in* proceeded to the Supreme Court of Canada, which rejected the Crown's argument and held that a culturally sensitive approach that accounts for the Indigenous perspective—including Indigenous laws—is required.[61] The court granted the Tsilhqot'in a declaration of Aboriginal title to 1,700 square kilometres of land. The court noted that governments are under a legal duty to negotiate in good faith the resolution of land claims,[62] and encouraged governments and proponents not only to negotiate but, more specifically, to seek Indigenous peoples' consent, "whether before or after a declaration of Aboriginal title."[63]

In British Columbia, where most Indigenous nations have never entered into treaty with the Crown, the British Columbia Treaty Commission (BCTC) Process, a tripartite process, was commenced in 1993. Government mandates and policies for treaty negotiations have not changed since, despite developments in the law. Sixty First Nation groups have entered the BCTC process, representing 110 of British Columbia's 203 First Nations; only three final agreements have been ratified in the 25-year history of this process.[64]

Recent developments provide some hope that negotiations could lead to Canadian governments making space for the operation of Indigenous legal systems in the regulation and management of land and resource use.

## The United Nations Declaration on the Rights of Indigenous Peoples

The *United Nations Declaration on the Rights of Indigenous Peoples* (UNDRIP) was adopted by the United Nations in 2007. It sets out rights that "constitute the minimum standards for the survival, dignity and well-being of the Indigenous peoples of the world."[65]

UNDRIP's Articles include the following:

- Article 18: Indigenous peoples have the right to participate in decision-making in matters affecting their rights, and to maintain their decision-making institutions;

- Article 26: Indigenous peoples have the right to their lands, territories and resources, and to own, use develop and control such lands and resources. States must recognize and protect these lands, territories and resources with due respect for the Indigenous customs, traditions and land tenure systems; and

- Article 32: Indigenous peoples have the right to determine priorities and strategies for the development and use of their lands and resources. States shall consult Indigenous peoples in order to obtain their free and informed consent prior to the approval of any project affecting their lands, territories or resources.

Canada was one of four countries to vote against UNDRIP. In 2010, Canada announced its support of UNDRIP as an "aspirational document" that is not legally binding, does not reflect customary international law, and does not change Canadian law. As discussed further below, in 2015, the Truth and Reconciliation Commission released its Final Report, which called on Canadian governments to fully adopt and implement UNDRIP as the framework for reconciliation (Call to Action 43). In 2016, Canada announced that it now fully supports UNDRIP without qualification. In 2015, Alberta announced that it would adopt UNDRIP. In 2017, British Columbia announced that it will adopt UNDRIP.

## The Truth and Reconciliation Commission Calls to Action

The Truth and Reconciliation Commission of Canada (TRC) was established in 2008, and was mandated to:

- reveal to Canadians the complex truth about the history and the ongoing legacy of the church-run residential schools, in a manner that fully documents the individual and collective harms perpetrated against Aboriginal peoples, and honours the resilience and courage of former students, their families, and communities; and
- guide and inspire a process of truth and healing, leading toward reconciliation within Aboriginal families, and between Aboriginal peoples and non-Aboriginal communities, churches, governments, and Canadians generally. The process was to work to renew relationships on a basis of inclusion, mutual understanding, and respect.[66]

The commission released its final report in 2015, including a number of Calls to Action. Of particular relevance to this paper are the following:

> 45. We call upon the Government of Canada, on behalf of all Canadians, to jointly develop with Aboriginal peoples a Royal Proclamation of Reconciliation to be issued by the Crown. The proclamation would build on the Royal Proclamation of 1763 and the Treaty of Niagara of 1764, and reaffirm the nation-to-nation relationship between

Aboriginal peoples and the Crown. The proclamation would include, but not be limited to, the following commitments:

i. Repudiate concepts used to justify European sovereignty over Indigenous lands and peoples such as the Doctrine of Discovery and *terra nullius*.
ii. Adopt and implement the *United Nations Declaration on the Rights of Indigenous Peoples* as the framework for reconciliation.
iii. Renew or establish Treaty relationships based on principles of mutual recognition, mutual respect, and shared responsibility for maintaining those relationships into the future.
iv. Reconcile Aboriginal and Crown constitutional and legal orders to ensure that Aboriginal peoples are full partners in Confederation, including the recognition and integration of Indigenous laws and legal traditions in negotiation and implementation processes involving Treaties, land claims, and other constructive agreements....

50. In keeping with the *United Nations Declaration on the Rights of Indigenous Peoples*, we call upon the federal government, in collaboration with Aboriginal organizations, to fund the establishment of Indigenous law institutes for the development, use, and understanding of Indigenous laws and access to justice in accordance with the unique cultures of Aboriginal peoples in Canada.

## The Government of Canada's "Ten Principles"

In 2017, the Government of Canada announced its commitment to achieve reconciliation through a renewed relationship "based on recognition of rights, respect, co-operation, and partnership as the foundation for transformative change." In particular, Canada "recognizes that Indigenous self-government and laws are critical to Canada's future ..."[67]

The Government of Canada set out ten principles respecting its relationship with Indigenous peoples. The first principle reads as follows: "The Government of Canada recognizes that all relations with Indigenous peoples need to be based on the recognition and implementation of their right to self-determination, including the inherent right of self government." Canada further recognizes that this country's "constitutional and legal order recognizes the reality that Indigenous peoples' ancestors owned and governed the lands," and calls on all governments "to shift their relationships and arrangements with Indigenous peoples so that they are based on recognition and respect for the right to self-determination, including the inherent right of self-government," including "changes in the operating practices and processes of the federal government."

The fourth Principle is that Canada "recognizes that Indigenous self-government is part of Canada's evolving sytem of cooperative federalism and distinct orders of government." Under this principle, Canada recognizes self-government as a right protected by section 35, and states that "Recognition of the inherent jurisdiction and legal orders of Indigenous nations is therefore the starting point of discussions aimed at interactions between federal, provincial, territorial and Indigenous jurisdictions and laws." Canada acknolwedges the need to ensure "space for the operation of Indigenous jurisdictions and laws."

## Judicial Oversight of Rights Implementation and Negotiations

Given recent developments, there is some hope that reconciliation negotiations that make space for the operation of Indigenous laws and legal systems in the regulation and management of Canada's lands and resources will be fruitful. Respect for Indigenous laws and legal orders should in turn end the criminalization and prosecution of Indigenous resource users.

In *Delgamuukw*, the court noted that reconciliation would be best achieved through good faith negotiations "reinforced by judgments of this Court."[68] The courts might also play a role in overseeing reconciliation negotiations as needed in this era of UNDRIP adoption, and cooperation should issues remain unresolvable without further judicial guidance. One role the courts play in advancing reconciliation through negotiation is in settling legal issues whose resolution is necessary to remove barriers to negotiated agreements. An example is the *Tsilhqot'in* decision, which resolved the dispute between the Crown and Indigenous peoples regarding whether Aboriginal title is confined to small sites. Courts have also supervised government/Indigenous relations as an outcome of litigation.

As in Canada, much of the early treaty rights case law in the United States involved defences to prosecutions.[69] In 1968, several tribes brought a civil action against the State of Oregon for failure to protect Indigenous peoples' right to fish under treaty.[70] Judge Belloni held that the treaty fishing right guaranteed to the tribes a fair share of the fish harvest, and that Oregon was required to protect the treaty fishing right. Judge Belloni retained jurisdiction to grant further or amended relief, and supervised allocation decisions for 12 years.[71] Eventually, this decision led to a negotiated salmon management plan under which the fishery became co-managed by Oregon and the tribes.[72]

In *United States v. State of Washington*, a case commonly referred to as the "Boldt" decision,[73] the federal government and Western Washington Tribes commenced a lawsuit alleging that Washington State was not honouring the Tribes' treaty fishing rights. Judge Boldt held that the Tribes were entitled to half of the total salmon catch and should be responsible for regulating the Indian fishery off-reservation, with the state having the power over Indian off-reservation fishing only for the purpose of conservation.[74] Judge Boldt held that Washington's regulations were invalid because they favoured non-tribal fisheries. Washington argued that it was imposing restrictions for the sake of conservation and to stop overharvesting by the tribes, but Judge Boldt found an absence of "any credible evidence showing any instance, remote or recent, when a definitively identified member of any plaintiff tribe exercised his off-reservation treaty rights by any conduct or means detrimental to the perpetuation of any species of anadromous fish."[75] The decision led to controversy and confrontation, and Judge Boldt retained jurisdiction in order to assist the parties in resolving problems and disputes arising from his decision, and to ensure that Washington complied.[76]

In Canada, courts have retained jurisdiction in duty to consult cases, giving the parties leave to apply to the court for further directions;[77] giving the Indigenous party leave to bring the matter back before the court if they are of the view that consultation and accommodation are inadequate, including liberty to reapply to quash the decision or approval in question;[78] and ordering mediation, allowing the Indigenous party to seek further directions from the court if mediation fails.[79]

## Conclusion

As noted above, most prosecutions of Indigenous resource harvesters would be unnecessary if space were made for the operation of Indigenous legal systems in the regulation and management of resource use. While prosecutions of Indigenous resource harvesters are brought on the basis that there is a need to conserve the resource, the real threats to the resource are usually the result of the operation of federal and provincial laws,[80] and prosecutions often result from a failure to recognize and respect that the Indigenous harvester is exercising an Aboriginal right and operating under an Indigenous legal system that ensures safety and protects resources for future generations.

We are at a crossroads in Canada with the recent Report of the Truth and Reconciliation Commission and government responses that pledge adoption of UNDRIP, recognition of Aboriginal title and rights, respect for Indigenous legal systems, and an inclusive cooperative federalism. Negotiations in accordance with these principles should lead to collaborative resource management and make prosecutions of Indigenous harvesters a rare occurrence. What seems certain is that prosecuting Indigenous resource harvesters carrying on practices passed down through the generations does not advance reconciliation.

## NOTES

1 *R v Van der Peet*, [1996] 2 SCR 507 [*Van der Peet*] at paras 263, 265, 268, and 269 (emphasis added).

2 See, for example, *R v Sparrow*, [1990] 1 SCR 1075 [*Sparrow*]; *R v Gladstone*, [1996] 2 SCR 723 [*Gladstone*]; *R v Adams*, [1996] 3 SCR 101; and *R v Côté*, [1996] 3 SCR 139.

3 See, for example, *R v Sioui*, [1990] 1 SCR 1025; *R v Badger*, [1996] 1 SCR 771 [*Badger*]; *R v Sundown*, [1999] 1 SCR 393; *R v Marshall*; *R v Bernard*, 2005 SCC 43 [*Bernard*]; and *R v Morris*, 2006 SCC 59 [*Morris*].

4 The most notable cases that have been commenced by Indigenous peoples as civil actions involve Aboriginal title claims: *Calder v Attorney-General of British Columbia*, [1973] SCR 313 [*Calder*]; *Delgamuukw v British Columbia*, [1997] 3 SCR 1010 [*Delgamuukw*]; and *Tsilhqot'in Nation v. British Columbia*, 2014 SCC 44 [*Tsilhqot'in*]. The Lax Kw'alaams pled both Aboriginal title and fishing rights, but the Aboriginal title issues were severed: *Lax Kw'alaams Indian Band v Canada (Attorney General)*, 2006 BCSC 1463. The case was decided on the basis of the Aboriginal rights claims, and the Aboriginal title claim remains outstanding: *Lax Kw'alaams Indian Band v Canada (Attorney General)*, 2011 SCC 56 [*Lax Kw'alaams*].

5 The leading cases on treaty rights include: *Morris*, *supra* note 3; *R v Marshall*, [1999] 3 SCR 456; *Badger*, *supra* note 3; and *Grassy Narrows First Nation v Ontario (Natural Resources)*, 2014 SCC 48. The cases setting out the tests and analysis under s 35 in the context of Aboriginal rights include: *Sparrow*, *supra* note 2; *Van der Peet*, *supra* note 1; *R v Sappier*, 2006 SCC 54 [*Sappier*]; and *Gladstone*, *supra* note 2. The leading decisions on Aboriginal title are *Delgamuukw*, *supra* note 4; *Bernard*, *supra* note 3; and *Tsilhqot'in*, *supra* note 4. While this is not an exhaustive list of Supreme Court of Canada jurisprudence on these issues, it is worth noting that almost all of these cases began as regulatory prosecutions.

6 *Sparrow*, *supra* note 2 at para 69.

7 *Delgamuukw*, *supra* note 4 at para 147.

8 *Van der Peet*, *supra* note 1 at paras 42 and 49–50.

9 *Delgamuukw*, *supra* note 4 at paras 114, 145, and 147.

10 *Delgamuukw*, *ibid* at para 148.

11 K McNeil, *Common Law Aboriginal Title* (Oxford: Clarendon Press, 1989) at 171–179; M Walters, "British Imperial Constitutional Law and Aboriginal Rights: A Comment on *Delgamuukw v British Columbia*" (1992) 17 Queen's LJ 350 at 407–409; RL Barsh, "Indigenous Rights

and the *Lex Loci* in British Imperial Law" in Kerry Wilkins, ed, *Advancing Aboriginal Claims: Visions/Strategies/ Directions* (Saskatoon: Purich Publishing, 2004) at 91.

12 *Mitchell v MNR*, 2001 SCC 33 at para 10.

13 *Campbell v British Columbia*, 2000 BCSC 1123 at para 137. This case also held that ss 91 and 92 of the *Constitution Act, 1867*, are only exhaustive as between the provinces and the federal government.

14 *Tsilhqot'in*, *supra* note 4.

15 See KL Ladner, "Up the Cree: Fishing for a New Constitutional Order" (2005) 38 Canadian Journal of Political Science 923–953, esp at 924 and 943–944; KL Ladner, "Treaty Federalism: An Indigenous Vision of Canadian Federalisms" in F Rocher & M Smith, eds, *New Trends in Canadian Federalism*, 2d ed (Peterborough: Broadview Press, 2003).

16 Chief Justice Lance SG Finch, "The Duty to Learn: Taking Account of Indigenous Legal Orders in Practice," prepared for the Continuing Legal Education Society of British Columbia, November 2012.

17 Finch, *ibid* at para 44.

18 J Armstrong, "The Salishan Inter-Areal Framework," prepared for the Continuing Legal Education Society of British Columbia, November 2012. Dr Armstrong notes that this approach would be consistent with Article 8J of the United Nations Convention on Biodiversity and with the United Nations Declaration on the Rights of Indigenous Peoples.

19 *Morris*, *supra* note 3.

20 *Morris*, *ibid* at paras 5, 11, 26; 2002 BCSC 780 at paras 29, 31.

21 [1999] BCJ No 3199 (BCPC) (QL); 2002 BCSC 780; and 2004 BCCA 121.

22 *Morris*, *supra* note 3 at para 11.

23 *Morris*, *ibid* at para 56.

24 *Morris*, *ibid* at para 60.

25 Courts have also held that Indigenous individuals accused of an offence were not exercising an Aboriginal right when they have failed to follow the relevant Indigenous laws. An example of the courts recognizing Indigenous laws in this context is the decision of the Provincial Court of British Columbia in *R v Bruce William Wilson Jr*, 2003 BCPC 56. In that case, the evidence was that the individual was not following Gitxsan law, and he was therefore not exercising an Aboriginal right. The accused shot and killed a grizzly bear and two cubs. His defence was that he was exercising an Aboriginal right to kill the bears because they were dangerous and a threat to the local community. The evidence at trial demonstrated that his actions were contrary to Gitxsan law, which requires that grizzly bears be treated with respect. The Gitxsan way to deal with a problem bear is to put out an alert to the community and notify the local Fish and Wildlife office in the hope that they can trap and move the bear. Only if this is not successful will the chief and elders call on a hunter to remove the problem bear, and only an experienced hunter will be called upon for this job. The accused also did not use all of the bear, and this, too, was against Gitxsan laws. The judge held that the exercise of the Aboriginal right would be subject to Gitxsan law (see paras 18 and 27).

26 Affidavit of Chief Dan Wilson, filed 30 November 1999 in *British Columbia (Minister of Forests) v Okanagan Indian Band*, SCBC Vernon Registry, No 23911 [*Okanagan* No 23911].

27 *Ibid.*

28 Affidavit of Chief Dan Wilson, filed 28 October 1999 in *Okanagan* No 23911, *supra* note 26.

29 Affidavit of Dan Wilson #7, filed 5 August 2010 in *Okanagan* No 23911, *ibid.*

30 The province continued to authorize clearcuts in the watersheds at issue while the litigation was ongoing, leading to further litigation in which Tolko, a logging company given cutting rights by province, and the Okanagan Indian Band, each sought injunctions against the other: *Tolko Industries Ltd v Okanagan Indian Band*, 2010 BCSC 24.

31 Affidavit #1 of Jeannette Armstrong, filed 15 May 2007 in *Okanagan* No 23911, *supra* note 26 at para 18.

32 *Ibid* at para 29.

33 *Ibid* at para 30; Affidavit of Fabian Alexis, filed 15 May 2007 in *Okanagan* No 23911, *supra* note 26.

34 *Sparrow, supra* note 2 at para 30.

35 *Bernard, supra* note 3.

36 This problem arose in the Okanagan litigation discussed above, wherein the province attempted to confine the litigation to the cutblock where the logging took place and the stop work order was issued, rather than the watershed area within which the cutblock was located and over which the Okanagan asserted Aboriginal title in defence. The Case Management Judge rejected an application by the province to confine the evidence that the Okanagan could put before the court to evidence of use and occupation of the cutblock, after the proceedings were converted into a civil action: *HMTQ v Chief Jules et al*, 2005 BCSC 1312 at paras 30–52.

37 *Lax Kw'alaams, supra* note 4 at para 11.

38 *Calder, supra* note 4.

39 *Delgamuukw, supra* note 4 at paras 76–77.

40 *Tsilhqot'in Nation v British Columbia*, 2007 BCSC 1700 at paras 120–129 [*Tsilhqot'in* Trial Decision].

41 *Tsilhqot'in, supra* note 4 at paras 21–23.

42 *Lax Kw'alaams*, supra note 4.

43 *Ibid* at para 45.

44 *British Columbia (Minister of Forests) v Okanagan Indian Band*, 2000 BCSC 1135 [*Okanagan 2000*]; *British Columbia (Minister of Forests) v Jules*, 2001 BCCA 647.

45 See, for example, *Tsilhqot'in Nation v British Columbia*, 2006 BCCA 2. The trial in Tsilhqot'in lasted 339 days, over a five-year period.

46 *Okanagan 2000*, supra note 44; *British Columbia (Minister of Forests) v Okanagan Indian Band*, 2001 BCCA 647; *British Columbia (Minister of Forests) v Okanagan Indian Band*, 2003 SCC 71 [*Okanagan 2003*].

47 *Okanagan 2003, ibid.*

48 *Hagwilget Indian Band v Canada (Minister of Indian Affairs and Northern Development)*, 2008 FC 574. While granting an advance costs award, the court suggested at para 19 that if the legal issues were not unique, had been resolved in another case, or were likely to be resolved in another case "at an early date," it would not have made the order.

49 *Xeni Gwet'in First Nations v British Columbia*, 2002 BCCA 434.

50 *HMTQ v Chief Ronnie Jules et al*, 2005 BCSC 1312; *HMTQ v Chief Ronnie Jules et al*, Oral Reasons issued 5 April 2006.

51 *Sappier, supra* note 5; *R. v. Gray*, 2006 SCC 54.

52 *British Columbia (Minister of Forests) v Okanagan Indian Band*, 2008 BCCA 107.

53 See *Van der Peet, supra* note 1 at para 313.

54 *R v Marshall*, [1999] 3 SCR 533 at para 22. See also *Lax Kw'alaams, supra* note 4 at para 11.

55 *Tsilhqot'in* Trial Decision, *supra* note 40 (emphasis added). See also paras 506, 961, and 1349.

56 *Delgamuukw, supra* note 4 at para 172–186.

57 *Haida Nation v British Columbia*, 2004 SCC 73 at paras 8–10, 28–31 [*Haida*].

58 *Tsilhqot'in* Trial Decision, *supra* note 40 at para 1376.

59 *Tsilhqot'in Nation v British Columbia*, 2012 BCCA 285 (*Tsilhqot'in* BCCA) at para 221.

60 *Simon v The Queen*, [1985] 2 SCR 387 at para 21. In that case, the court below had held that as savages, the Indigenous signatories to the treaty in issue lacked the capacity to enter into a treaty. Limiting Aboriginal title to small pieces of land fails to recognize that Indigenous peoples existed as organized societies prior to contact and the Crown's assertion of sovereignty, fails to recognize that the Indigenous sovereignty pre-existed Crown sovereignty (*Haida* at para 20), and fails to incorporate and give weight to the Indigenous perspective.

61 *Tsilhqot'in, supra* note 4 at para 41.

62 *Ibid* at para 18.

63 *Ibid* at para 97.

64 See online: <www.bctreaty.ca>.

65 Article 43.

66 *Honouring the Truth, Reconciling for the Future: Summary of the Final Report of the Truth and Reconciliation Commission of Canada* (2015) at 23.

67 Principles respecting the Government of Canada's relationship with Indigenous peoples, online: <http://www.justice.gc.ca/eng/csj-sjc/principles-principes.html>.

68 *Delgamuukw*, supra note 4 at para 186.

69 See Michael C Blumm & Jane G Steadman, "Indian Treaty Fishing Rights and Habitat Protection: The Martinez Decision Supplies a Resounding Judicial Reaffirmation" (2009) 49 Nat Resources J 653 at 665 and fn 61.

70 *Sohappy v Smith*, 302 FSupp 899 (D Or 1969) (commonly referred to as the "Belloni" decision).

71 Blumm & Steadman, *supra* note 69 at 666 and fn 68.

72 See M Blumm & B Swift, "The Indian Treaty Piscary Profit and Habitat Protection in the Pacific Northwest: A Property Rights Approach" (1998) 69 U Colo L Rev 407 at 460–462; and M Wood, "The Tribal Property Right to Wildlife Capital (Part I): Applying Principles of Sovereignty to Protect Imperiled Wildlife Populations, (2000) 37 Idaho L Rev 1 at 16–17.

73 *United States v State of Washington*, 384 FSupp 312 (WD Wash 1974) [Boldt], aff'd 520 F2d 676 (9th Cir 1975), cer denied 423 US 1086 (1976).

74 Such regulations had to be "reasonable and necessary to the perpetuation of a particular run or species of fish." Boldt, *ibid* at 342.

75 Boldt, *ibid* at 338, fn 26.

76 Boldt, *ibid* at 347. The Boldt decision resulted in further litigation, including a clarification that the treaty right guaranteed no more than was necessary to provide a moderate living, up to 50% of the catch. See, e.g., *Washington v Fishing Vessel Ass'n*, 443 US 658 (1979) at 686–687.

77 *Haida Nation v British Columbia (Minister of Forests)*, 2002 BCCA 147 at paras 58–62; *Homalco Indian Band v British Columbia (Minister of Agriculture, Food and Fisheries)*, 2005 BCSC 283 at para 127 [*Homalco*]; *Heiltsuk Tribal Council v British Columbia (Minister of Sustainable Resource Management)*, 2003 BCSC 1422 at para 129.

78 *Homalco, ibid*; *Gitxsan and other First Nations v British Columbia (Minister of Forests)*, 2002 BCSC 1701; *Gitanyow First Nation v British Columbia (Minister of Forests)*, 2004 BCSC 1734.

79 *Hupacasath First Nation v British Columbia (Minister of Forests)*, 2005 BCSC 1712; *Ke-Kin-Is-Uqs v British Columbia (Minister of Forests)*, 2008 BCSC 1505. The Crown was ordered to pay for the costs of the mediator. Smith J provided the parties with direction as to what would be discussed at the mediation, including, for example, ways of including Hupacasath in discussions regarding environmental, wildlife, and watershed protection on the lands in issue, and accommodation from resources on Crown lands for the impact of the decision in issue on the Hupacasath.

80 See *Tsilhqot'in* BCCA, *supra* note 59 at paras 290–343, where the British Columbia Court of Appeal upheld the trial judge's conclusions that British Columbia's forestry legislation unjustifiably infringes Tsilhqot'in rights to hunt and trap, by directly impacting wildlife, reducing species diversity and populations, and destroying their habitat, including through the removal of coarse woody debris, soil compaction, changes to hydrology, and the resulting slower regeneration of the forests.

## SECTION 3

# Sentencing and Environmental Offences

# 23

# Environmental Sentencing: Making the Best of a Blunt Instrument

BARRY STUART

You can't save the land apart from the people and to save either you must save both.

—WENDELL BERRY

Several times I have been abjectly frustrated and saddened by the failure of our legal system to effectively respond to environmental issues. Today I am optimistic—cautiously optimistic—about, if not what the law is doing, certainly about what the law can do to:

(1) Be an effective part of maintaining the difficult but essential balance between economic development and environmental protection,
(2) Enable citizens to directly participate in our shared fiduciary duty to protect the interests of current and future generations.

We need a good measure of optimism to inspire collaborative efforts in developing the reforms urgently required for the sentencing process to play an effective part in balancing environmental, economic, and social objectives. One needs to begin this work by believing there is an important contribution for sentencing to make. I believe that with some key changes there is. My optimism is fired by:

PROGRESS – We have come a long way from *United Keno Hill*.[1] Yes, we have a way to go for the law to realize its full potential to contribute. Yes, it is important to recognize significant opposition may stand in the way of the reforms needed, but it is equally important to bear in mind how much has changed.

Most reforms needed are within our reach, and some have been reached in other jurisdictions.

ENVIRONMENTAL OFFENCES TREATED AS SERIOUS CRIMES – Courts have begun to treat environmental offences as serious crimes. Environmental offences range from careless littering to premeditated actions that can cause greater harm than any other offence before the court. While the spectrum of penalties must line up to fit the huge spectrum of environmental offences, all must be recognized as criminal behaviour, not merely as bad personal habits or bad business practices.

PUBLIC TRUST – The principles of a public trust are beginning to permeate all actions to protect the environment. When we agree to allow individuals and corporations to undertake for profit activities that place at risk the health of our environment, they take on a public trust to protect the crucial environmental interests of current and future generations. This public trust imposes a fiduciary duty to ensure all their actions are driven by the highest standard of due diligence to prevent harm. Corporations are expected to recognize that public trust responsibilities trump concerns about profit at every step of their activities. These responsibilities must be driven throughout the corporation from top to bottom, from directors to field staff.

The fiduciary responsibilities of public trust fall upon all citizens. All parts of the sentencing process are beginning to reinforce these aspects of the public trust.

COLLABORATIVE PARTNERSHIPS – The complexity of the environmental challenges has fostered an appreciation that, to meet these challenges, hands and minds need to connect across many outdated separations based on laws, on debunked assumptions, and on inane fights over jurisdictional responsibilities. Nor can the public persist in their 9-1-1 mentality of calling in experts to resolve problems. To be successful in the face of these complex challenges everyone needs to be actively involved. The era of abandoning our individual and shared responsibilities to experts has passed. Civic responsibility has never more been more important. Recent successful collaborative initiatives mark the way forward and demonstrate how processes can be designed to foster sharing both responsibility and power among many different interests whose respective histories have been dominated by either fighting with or ignoring each other.

LEVEL PLAYING FIELD – All informed interests are much more aware that a level playing field, transparency, and mutual respect serve everyone's best interests. This recognition is not solely derived from witnessing a burning bush and finding a new religion. In many quarters, genuine soul searching has participated in changing perspectives. It matters less what motivated new perspectives than the fact that changes are occurring to move problem solving into more constructive modes.

While the power of local and global NGOs has not matched the growth of concentrated corporate power, the power and highly developed sophistication of NGOs has immensely increased their influence. Global communication networks enable information and reputations to travel the planet. This has removed the ability for two very different corporate faces, one on home grounds and one in foreign lands. What corporations do away from home follows them home to their governments and shareholders. All these changes have generated a growing awareness that a level playing field is not just good for the environment but good for business.

CHANGES TO THE SENTENCING PROCESS – Developing more punitive criminal sanctions will not have as much impact on outcomes as getting the process right. Process is product. The outcome is determined more by the process used than by anything else. The process used determines which people [and corporations] participate, how they participate, their ongoing relationships, their ability to work together in developing and applying innovative measures, the breadth of what is addressed, and their commitment to outcomes. Process determines whether the enormous energy in conflict is engaged constructively or destructively.

Sentencing is not an event; it is a part of a much larger process that begins before the case finds its way to court and continues long after the imposition of a sentence. What happens before and after court is as important as what happens in court. All stages of the process need to be supported and effective to achieve the core objectives of sentencing and to contribute to the larger regulatory processes governing economic, social, and environmental issues.

There are more corporations than ever before carrying out activities that pose greater risks than ever before to the environment. In relative terms, there are fewer resources invested in monitoring, investigating, and prosecuting environmental activities than ever before. This is a recipe for disaster. There is unlikely to be less corporate activity and less risk to the environment in the future. It is even more unlikely that in the future, governments will increase investment in the resources needed to properly monitor activities and ensure compliance with environmental laws. Consequently, to create a reasonable prospect for high levels of deterrence and compliance, several changes are necessary.

## Suggested Changes

### 1. HIGH EXPECTATION OF APPREHENSION

What will successfully, specifically, and generally deter environmental offences? The harshness of a possible sentence does not top the list of successful deterrents in most studies. These studies repeatedly point to the likelihood of apprehension and the condemnation within one's personal community as more effective deterrent measures.

Creating a high expectation of apprehension currently requires a much greater investment in qualified enforcement officials in the field, armed with the powers and resources to successfully detect, investigate, and prosecute.

Certainly, the outcome of a prosecution is integral to deterrence. A fierce bark and a feckless bite can undermine the effectiveness of creating a high expectation of apprehension. The current arsenal of penalties is almost capable of producing a scary bark, but the lack of resources to prosecute and the relatively light nips on offenders undermine the current capacity of the legal system to effectively deter environmental crime.

### 2. CONDEMNATION FROM PROFESSIONAL AND PERSONAL NETWORKS

This is my hands-down favourite deterrent. The power of family friends, colleagues, and the business community to influence conduct has enormous potential to affect behaviour, for fair or foul. I place enormous hope in the current press by corporations in many different fields to raise the bar on what constitutes good corporate practice. Yup, there are exceptions, but most exceptions remain in the dark ages, dominated by the attitude that no matter what or how business may operate, business is good for the country and community. Currently, corporations, corporate associations, and corporate leaders are proactively raising their standards of practice by developing and pressing for best practices throughout many different business communities. In exemplary ways, some corporations are voluntarily conducting their activities above the minimum requirements imposed by law.

Self-regulation alone is not enough, but without self-regulation, without peer pressure, without immediate community connections, primary reliance on government interventions will never be enough, no matter how much more public funding we dump into failed criminal justice systems. We cannot punish our way to the level of environmental stewardship needed to serve this and future generations. Self-regulation is not a wistful dream but a practical response that serves the best interests of corporations as well as the public. Corporations know more than anyone else when other corporations are violating best practices and offending environmental laws. Their ability to press for best practices and compliant behaviour within their industry is an invaluable and integral part of deterring crimes and securing compliance. Their special privilege to use corporate structures and engage in activities that impose grave risks on people and environments comes with special obligations not just to take care in what they do but also to share in proactively ensuring others take care. The "state" cannot be everywhere all the time. We cannot afford to field enough government officials to effectively detect and prevent environmental offences. All citizens and all corporations have a fiduciary responsibility to establish personal standards of care and to diligently engage in preventing environmental offences.

There are many reasons why self-regulation serves the best interests of corporations:

- Getting rid of the bad apples in the barrel of any industry serves the best interests of all other apples in the barrel;
- Developing the certainty of a level playing field by ensuring universal compliance is a boon to all corporations;
- Attracting and keeping the very best employees is easier when the employees are proud to be a part of a corporation reputed for its responsible and ethical practices;
- Such reputations make it much easier to secure public and political support for their activities.

[Personal note: While I have boundless respect for the work of John Swaigen, I have yet to respond to his admonishment of my implicit belief expressed in *Keno Hill* that corporations have moral standards and do care for more than just bottom line goals. He warned me of the dangers of attributing anthropomorphic capacities to corporations. In my defense, I call on my experience in working with and against corporations that introduced me to corporate leaders who bare-knuckled their way to change corporate behaviour and to corporations that voluntarily raised the bar of good corporate citizenship. These and other experiences founded my belief in the corporate community's capacity to recognize their moral responsibility to lift their game to the level public trust requires. Never will corporate self-regulation alone suffice, no matter how responsible they become. We have accorded corporations more power than ordinary citizens and permitted them to carry out activities that risk lives and critical environments. Too much is at stake to make assumptions at either end of the trust spectrum – to trust all or distrust all. Trusting all is impractical, distrusting is unaffordable. Self-regulation is indispensable to finding an appropriate balance between private and public involvement. Citizens, corporations, and governments need to be actively involved to punish the bad, terminate the ugly, and reward good corporate behaviour.]

### 3. PROCESS IS PRODUCT

When our processes create safe places for difficult exchanges and for developing personal relationships, what seem like miracles become ordinary outcomes. When processes involve direct participation from all levels of community and corporate members in ways that reveal common ground, build mutual respect and trust, the parties will develop the good relationships necessary to negotiate and carry out agreements in good faith. Then there will be winners and winners. Then the risks of anyone being a loser are dramatically reduced. Believing this is possible makes it possible; not believing it is possible makes it impossible.

### 4. PRIVATE PROSECUTIONS

Long before we delegated so much responsibility to police and government agencies, all citizens shared the responsibility to "keep the King's peace." Private prosecutions hearken back to the time when citizens were encouraged to help the King keep peace in the land. *Fisheries Act* regulations encourage citizens to prosecute by awarding half of any fine imposed by the court to the private prosecutor. Half of maximum fines of $500,000 for every day an offence is committed, could be much more than chump change for motivating individuals, NGOs, and community-based organizations to invest the time and energy to monitor and address environmental crimes. If a private prosecution is negotiated out of the criminal court, the private prosecutor must be a full party to any negotiation with government and the alleged offender.

Often without explanation, governments counter this legislative encouragement of citizen engagement by exercising their power to intervene and then terminate the prosecution. In light of the significant lack of funding to support enough prosecutors and enforcement officers to monitor and secure the level of compliance necessary to protect the environment, citizens are desperately needed to help keep the Queen's peace in environmental crimes.

In addition to removing unreasonable restrictions on private prosecutions, many other initiatives are necessary to invite and encourage citizens to become actively engaged in all aspects of decisions affecting our shared environment. Simple legislation such as the *Michigan Environmental Protection Act* invests citizens with the ability to question any decision that fails to manifest reasonable care in actions that impact the environment.

Specific changes needed include:

- Removing exclusive discretion of government to intervene in a private prosecution unless the court approves;
- Requiring courts to provide reasons if a government intervention is approved;
- Subjecting all fines secured in a private prosecution to first pay the private prosecutor's costs, with the remaining fine shared equally among the private prosecutor, enforcement agency involved and any victim whose damages (determined by the court) have not been adequately covered by any other court order or by any other source;
- Creating by legislation an ability for private citizens to initiate private prosecutions of all environmental offences.

### 5. INDEPENDENCE OF PROSECUTORS

Most environmental crimes involve, directly or indirectly, government interests and often investments. In the ongoing debate over whether prosecutors should be vested with the same level of independence as judges, some crimes, including environmental offences, readily tip the scales to warrant carving out unfettered independence for prosecutors to act independently and be seen to do so. *In all prosecutions involving a perceived government conflict of interest, prosecutors should be given clear independence to prosecute.*

### 6. RESPECTING AND INCLUDING VICTIMS

Rendering transparent all phases of the process, particularly plea-bargaining, respects the interests of victims and the public. Victims need to have a voice. Affected communities need to have a voice. Respecting their interests by including their voice significantly assists the court in *getting it right*. Without the victim being directly engaged, the court is left with primarily erroneous assumptions of what best respects the interests of victims. Victims can have very different interests. Only their direct and supported involvement reveals their primary and unique interests. Victim impact statements are unable to respond to changes in the process. Most important, without victim participation offenders rarely appreciate the full nature of harm caused by their actions. In many respects, a victim's perspective enhances the ability of the outcome to achieve many of the core sentencing objectives. A victim should never be pressured to participate in any way, but the opportunity should be open at any time and supported.

### 7. ASSESSING DAMAGES

Leaving assessment of who is a victim and the full measure of their damages exclusively to civil courts assumes civil actions will follow. This imposes both delay and process costs upon victims of environmental offences. The criminal court should, at the very least, take stock of who has been harmed and the extent of the harm. Failing to do so leaves offenders to make their own assessment, which may be woefully minimal and thereby prevent the offender from coming to terms with the full magnitude of their responsibilities. Just as important, failing to measure the harm disrespects the interests of the victim in being fully heard and understood.

Courts should be empowered to order an assessment of who has been harmed and the extent of their harm. The offender should be responsible for the cost of the study and the court responsible to set reasonable guidelines for the scope of the study. There is not any overriding good reason to justify an offender having the fortuitous benefit of his harm being difficult to track. The extent of harm in environmental cases is as important in sentencing as assessing harm in cases of assault causing bodily harm. Guidelines will be needed to avoid extensive hearings in criminal courts.

Compensation has been an integral and effective part of many traditional processes set up to deal with harmful behaviour. However, there is a fundamental difference between how compensation is used traditionally and how it is used in criminal courts. In Papua New Guinea, compensation is called *sorri money*. Traditional compensation payments are carried out through ceremonies designed to mend broken relationships. Compensation is an important part of the ceremony, but more important are the public offering and acceptance of an apology to mark new peaceful beginnings of relationships among the families and communities of the victim and offender.

Many losses cannot be compensated by money. In many cases, money cannot repair relationships and create new beginnings. Traditional ceremonies increase the remedial capacity of compensation. We have learned and have much more to learn from traditional practices about the importance of ceremonies in improving the outcomes in our sentencing processes. Our court ceremonies, dominated by strategies to win, with minimal focus on rebuilding lives, connections, and relationships, undermine prospects for new beginnings.

### 8. TIMELY REVIEWS OF COURT ORDERS

Timely reviews to adjust court orders to changes reward progress by reducing stringent conditions or punishing breaches by taking corrective actions that are essential to secure the full and beneficial use of probation and court orders. Reviews can be expensive. Whenever possible, the offender should pay part or all the costs to review and supervise court orders. Reviews can reduce reliance on jail terms, redress conditions that cause crime, and address many other important sentencing objectives. Paying for the costs of reviews motivates an offender to diligently obey the order to achieve an early termination of the order.

### 9. TRIAGE

A triage is needed at the front door and throughout the sentencing process to determine what at all times is the best process to handle the issues raised in sentencing. All cases are very unique, and in different ways, at different stages in the sentencing process, significant changes will happen. The process must remain flexible enough to engage the appropriate process that fits the changing circumstances. For instance, an accused may, for a variety of reasons, deny responsibility at the outset. At any time, for a host of different reasons, an initial denial may be replaced by a full acceptance of responsibility reinforced by genuine contrition. Changes of this magnitude warrant a triage at all stages to consider the best next steps in the process.

Hospitals depend on front door triage to refer patients to the appropriate response. Public funds are squandered if, without triage, a surgeon handles every case. In the court process, we squander public funds every day by sending all sentencing cases to a formal court hearing presided over by a judge. There are many different, less expensive and more effective options to consider in matching environmental offences to an appropriate process.

**Possible options:**

- Formal court process

- Restorative justice process within formal justice process
- Restorative justice process within community
- Combined community restorative justice and court process.

Within these options, the parties, with the help of facilitators or process managers, have designed many creative processes. In each process, a judge may be engaged in many different ways. The judge may retain control, may play a very minor role, or may simply be called upon if a judicial remedy is an integral part of a consensus proposal or be engaged to determine any outstanding issue that fails to be resolved by consensus.

### 10. RESTORATIVE JUSTICE

These processes are ideally suited for environmental offences, particularly for more serious offences, if:

(1) The offender accepts full responsibility and agrees to participate;
(2) The case returns to court if the offender fails to earnestly participate or agreement is not reached;
(3) Outcomes in more serious cases are included in a binding court order;
(4) Triage used to assess appropriateness of restorative justice is not left solely to the prosecutor but includes the enforcement official, defence counsel, the offender, a community justice representative and victims;
(5) All participants in a triage/assessment are informed and understand the restorative process;
(6) A qualified restorative justice practitioner is available to manage the process.

Too often a restorative process is rejected or not considered because the advantages of a restorative process are not fully appreciated by the parties. The advantages are too many to address here. A sample of some key advantages illustrates how these processes are better suited to realize key environmental sentencing objectives.

FLEXIBILITY – Sentencing for environmental offences can raise complex issues, involve ongoing relationships among the victims, government agencies and the offender, and require several years to implement, review, and adjust the sentence plan. Restorative processes, particularly peacemaking circles, can be adapted to fit the particular circumstances of each case. Court involvement can be retained in many different ways, and all court remedies, including jail terms, can be added to the extensive range of remedies restorative processes can muster.

PROBLEM SOLVING – Restorative processes shift the focus from legal issues to social, economic, and environmental issues, from past behaviour to future behaviour and from symptoms to underlying causes. Courts generally do not, but restorative processes usually do, develop a collaborative process to understand why the offence happened, how to prevent further offences, what can be done to prevent further offences, and what is needed to successfully implement outcomes. Almost always, the outcome embraces issues far beyond the narrow confines of legally defined issues. Restorative processes through collaborative dialogues generate innovative outcomes rarely anticipated by participants.

As important as it is to gather all affected interests to collaboratively develop sentencing plans that effectively repair harm, it is more important, before activities placing environments at risk begin, to gather together all affected interests to collaboratively develop ways to prevent the same or new harm.

CHANGING PERSPECTIVES – Nothing, in my experience, has been more effective in enhancing an offender's appreciation of the harm they have caused than directly facing victims and personally responding. These difficult exchanges forge new understanding and genuine contrition. I have never witnessed in court a genuine transformation of an offender that moves offenders beyond accepting responsibility to earnestly seek ways to demonstrate contrition and change behaviour. Such experiences are common in restorative processes. If changing the behaviour of offenders and addressing in a respectful manner the harm to victims is important, direct interaction in a restorative process readily surpasses the ability of courts to achieve these goals. As important, study after study reveals higher victim satisfaction with restorative processes than with formal court experiences.

PROCESSING ADVANTAGES – Restorative processes usually take less time to begin, and to reach outcomes. They are less expensive to run. Because all participants contribute to the outcome, all feel a pride of ownership in what was achieved. Shared ownership in turn generates a shared commitment to make it work. The parties, having directly participated, have an intimate understanding of the underlying spirit and purpose of the agreement and thereby can readily make adjustments to respond to changes in circumstances and reward progress.

INCLUSIVENESS – Including all affected interests in a process that respects all voices improves mutual understanding, trust, and respect for differences. Generating functional as opposed to dysfunctional relationships, characteristic at the beginning of most environmental sentencing processes, is often the most important outcome of these processes. Improved relationships are essential to working through the ongoing issues among the parties during the life of any project posing a risk to the environment. Improved relationships are invaluable in preventing recidivism.

### 11. SPECIAL ENVIRONMENTAL COURT

Judges, prosecutors, clerks, and probation officers, knowledgeable and skilled in all matters relating to environmental crimes, could contribute on many fronts to improving how environmental cases are handled.

UNIQUE KNOWLEDGE – Environmental trials and sentencing often require very specialized knowledge to appreciate the complex circumstances surrounding the factual basis of the crime and raise unique evidentiary and substantive legal issues. Processing these cases through specialized hands will reduce time and legal errors and build coherent jurisprudence on substantive, evidentiary, and sentencing laws. It took the courts a decade of education to abandon old attitudes and practices in dealing with impaired driving, spousal assaults, and in respecting the needs of victims. Professionals whose work regularly involves environmental offences can develop better insights and more effective responses to the unique challenges of environmental offences.

TIME – Environmental matters, particularly complex cases in both trials and sentencing, can take a long time to process. A court dedicated to these matters can reduce the case processing time and reduce the detrimental effect of bouncing environmental matters from date to date in a busy general purpose court. Sentencing environmental offenders confronts a complex and often conflicting set of objectives. The essential contributions the sentencing process makes, directly and indirectly, to protecting environmental health and to ensuring businesses posing grave risks operate within the safety boundaries defined by law, calls for time, special knowledge, and careful attention to crafting sentences that are effective and constructive.

INNOVATIVE OUTCOMES – The need to fit the process to the fuss is particularly compelling in environmental cases. An environmental court can begin to explore, experiment, and develop innovative alternative processes for handling different cases in ways that achieve the most effective outcomes in each case.

At the very least, if there is not a specialized court, then judges, prosecutors, probation officers, and process managers should be trained and assigned to handle most environmental cases in each jurisdiction. Judges have begun to demonstrate in their sentencing practices recognition of the serious nature of environmental offences. But studies reveal judges remain reluctant to call on severe sentences to rebuke serious environmental offences. A special court or specially trained judges might rectify this reluctance.

Prosecution is a blunt instrument. Prosecutions are essential to generate credibility in any compliance regime and to draw clear lines of significant consequences around initiatives to negotiate settlements or rely upon alternative measures. A full range of appropriate remedies and investing time and care in designing a sentence to fit the special needs of each case can significantly sharpen the effectiveness of prosecutions.

## 12. SENTENCING TOOLS

Achieving unique environmental sentencing objectives calls for a different perception of offences, a different use of traditional sentencing tools, and some new tools. The ability of any penalty to deter criminal activity is related to the kind of criminal activity sought to be deterred. For environmental offences, my three most effective deterrent penalties are stop and control orders, full restitution, and activity bans.

STOP AND CONTROL ORDERS – The mere mention of resorting to these options in a sentencing hearing changes the perspective of offenders from *let's get this over with … just tell me the fine amount so I can get on with my business …* to *… now you have my attention … can you do that!?*

These are the trump cards that immediately grab the attention of the worst environmental criminals. No other legal response to environmental offenders has the same power to:

- Deter environmental crimes;

- Turn on a dime offending behaviour to remedial actions;
- Bring offenders or potential offenders to the table to explore non-offending alternatives.

**Recommendations:**

- Stop and control orders should be applicable to all environmental offences. Guidelines need to be developed to govern their use to prevent misuse of such a powerful remedy. Stop orders are particularly last resort and emergency responses;
- Inputs from victims, relevant agencies, and the offender should be heard to tailor their use to fit the nature of the offence and to minimize unnecessary economic harm to the offender and to others dependent on the offender's operation;
- Offenders should be required to pay the costs of monitoring control or stop orders and of working out the conditions to remove these orders;
- The court should retain a supervisory responsibility, but having set down guidelines only participate upon the request of any party. The negotiations of conditions governing orders should be left to be worked out against court guidelines with the assistance of a skilled process manager appointed by the court, paid for by the offender, and reporting only to the judge.

ACTIVITY BANS – The environmental penalty regime must include significant personal consequences. Money is just money. For many environmental offenders, losing money is just part of doing business and holds little personal stigma or lasting personal consequence. The probable sentence must on many fronts make the risk of offending much more than just a bad business decision.

Licence bans have proved their value in deterring offences [drive drunk, lose your privilege to drive; dangerous use of a firearm, lose your privilege to use a firearm] and in promoting responsible behaviour in many different professions [violate a professional code of conduct, lose your privilege to practise your profession].

The use of a ban is simple and serves as a powerful deterrent. A corporation breaching the public trust implicit in the approval to carry out activities that place the public or environment at risk should face the prospect of a ban from operating in fragile environments, or from carrying on similar activities anywhere.

Executives of corporations are trained as professionals, vested with the responsibilities of a professional, call themselves professionals and use the significant advantages of a corporate structure to carry out their profession. If they breach their professional and fiduciary responsibilities by committing environmental offences, they should be liable to a ban from working in a corporation or in their profession—abuse the privilege, lose the privilege.

An employee, manager, or director whose actions or failure to act relates to the commission of the offence should be liable to similar bans.

Responsible corporations working hard to earn the trust of the public and governments will support bans that remove the bad apples from the barrel.

### 13. REWARDING GOOD BEHAVIOUR

An environmental sentencing process with the appropriate resources, tools, and skilled personnel can make a vital contribution to our generation's fiduciary responsibilities to steward the environment for future generations. To effectively carry out these responsibilities, processes to ensure that bad behaviour is held accountable and punished are essential. As essential, if not more so, are processes that celebrate and reward good behaviour. Providing a regime of incentives rewarding good behaviour by governments, peer business community organizations, and local affected communities has the following advantages over punishing bad behaviour:

- Is more flexible and responsive to changing management priorities;
- Is easier and less expensive to employ [prosecution can be inordinately expensive];
- Responds in a more timely manner;
- While many violations cannot be prosecuted for many different reasons, most exemplary practices can be rewarded;
- Can be applied to individuals and groups and be geographically specific;
- Adds value directly to any activity;
- Does not require legislative changes;
- Can be used by local, regional, and national organizations.

Courts cannot hand out future "get out of jail free" cards as rewards for good corporate citizens, but they can recognize a history of sterling corporate citizenship as a prominent mitigating circumstance in sentencing. Incentives can be particularly effective in engaging public responsibility to keep the Queen's peace by encouraging efforts to detect and report offending behaviour.

## Conclusion

There is no conclusion, in the sense of a final outcome, to developing appropriate responses to the ever-evolving nature of environmental risks. A collaborative effort among all affected interests is necessary to build the essential contribution courts can make to governing private and public activities placing the environment at risk. Resolutions through courts and appropriate processes have a difficult task in developing outcomes among many complex and often conflicting societal interests. This task will always require advancing the economy and caring for our environment in ways that advance the interests of current and future generations of *all our relations*, animate and inanimate.

### NOTES

1 *R. v. United Keno Hill Mines* (1980), 10 CELR 43 (Y Terr Ct).

# 24

# Holding Directors and Officers Liable for Environmental Problems: Sentencing and Regulatory Orders

DIANNE SAXE AND MEREDITH JAMES

For our legal system to effectively respond to environmental issues, law and sentencing can and must:

(1) Be an effective part of maintaining the difficult, but essential, balance between economic development and environmental protection; and
(2) Enable citizens to directly participate in our shared fiduciary duty to protect the interests of current and future generations.

So, what does all this mean with respect to the directors and officers (D&O) who may come before the courts on environmental matters? Charges against D&O have become far more common in recent years and are now routine in Ontario, usually against the directors and officers of small corporations.

D&O may be convicted of an environmental offence as any other offender can, that is, as a conventional principal or party to the offence. But D&O may also end up before the court with much less moral justification, because of broadly written and broadly interpreted environmental statutes, coupled with aggressive use of prosecutorial discretion and flexible or non-existent limitation periods. The challenge in sentencing such individuals is to integrate the complexity of the regulatory structure and the real difficulties of compliance into the usual sentencing matrix, and in earning social trust for the whole process consistent with fairness and the rule of law.

In part 1, this chapter discusses the application of the sentencing principles developed by Chief Justice Stuart in *R. v. United Keno Hill Mines Ltd.*[1] to officers and directors.

In part 2, the chapter discusses the Ontario case of *Baker v. Director, Ministry of Environment*[2] in which a completely innocent former director of a parent company was retroactively held personally liable for a multi-million dollar cleanup related to historic contamination of a site owned by a subsidiary.

## Part 1 – Sentencing Directors and Officers

### ENVIRONMENTAL SENTENCING PRINCIPLES

As Chief Justice Stuart says in his chapter, "We have come a long way from *United Keno Hill*." The following fundamental considerations he laid down in that decision, however, are still the foundation for environmental sentencing for both corporations and their directors and officers:[3]

a. *The nature of the environment affected* – The more sensitive, special, or unique the endangered environment, the greater the penalty should be;
b. *The extent of the damage afflicted* – The more severe the damage, the higher the penalty. In many environmental offences, environmental damage is not a necessary element of the offence. For such offences, absence of damage is not a mitigating factor, but the occurrence of damage is an aggravating factor;[4]
c. *The deliberateness of the offence* – The intent to commit an offence is not a necessary element of most environmental offences but is a significant aggravating factor. Ignoring warning and attempts at concealment are also serious aggravating factors;[5]
d. *The attitude of the accused* – In *R. v. Bata Industries Ltd.*, Justice Ormston of the Ontario Court of Justice (Provincial Division) found that the attitude of the accused could be measured in part by three factors:[6]

    (1) The speed and efficiency of corporate action to rectify the problem;
    (2) Voluntary reporting;
    (3) The personal appearance of corporate executives in court outlining the company's genuine regret and future plans for compliance.

e. *The size, wealth, nature of operations and power of the corporation* – In order to ensure that fines are "felt" and are not treated as mere licence fees, the larger and wealthier the offender, the larger must be the fine;

f. *The extent of attempts to comply* – Any efforts made by the corporation to prevent the offence are mitigating factors, even if they were not adequate to show due diligence;
g. *Remorse* – Speedy and effective action to remedy the problem and to prevent its recurrence are important mitigating factors, although cleaning up spills is no more than the company's legal duty. Similarly, reporting a spill or discharge, while an independent legal duty, has some weight in mitigation. Personal appearance of senior corporate executives in court, compensation paid to those who suffered losses as a result of the offence, and similar means of making public amends are also important indications of remorse. In *Bata*, Justice Ormstrom noted, "The issue of remorse is more significant in sentencing the individual than the corporation";[7]
h. *Profits realized by the offence* – If the defendant has profited through the commission of an offence, whether by benefiting from cheap waste disposal or by avoiding necessary repairs and equipment, no fine will be a deterrent if it is cheaper to pay the fine than to comply. The amount of the fine that would otherwise be imposed should be increased by the amount of the financial benefit.;[8]
i. *Criminal record or other evidence of character* – Repetitions of offences require a higher penalty, even if the current offence is not a "subsequent conviction" in the legal meaning of the phrase.

Over the past 40 years there has been an enormous range in the directors and officers who end up before the courts on environmental matters. How do these principles apply to different types of D&O?

### THE CROOKS

Environmental sentencing principles have not done enough to punish the relatively few crooks who run amok through the rules and the environment for their own profit, sometimes causing immense harm. We do not punish such offenders enough, and we tend not to prevent them from doing it again. Wildlife offences, for example, are a $17 billion a year business, reputedly organized crimes' fourth top money maker, after narcotics, gambling, and people smuggling. Yet they still attract embarrassingly light sentences.[9]

Similarly, consider the infamous Jim Sinclair.[10] He foolishly bought the grossly contaminated Bakelite site after Union Carbide and similar companies were done with it. Sinclair was found guilty of 14 counts in five separate Informations of offences contrary to the *Ontario Water Resources Act*[11] arising out of his attempts to redevelop the property. His two companies, both "one-man operations," were convicted of an additional 23 counts. Completely disregarding both environmental laws and specific orders from the Ministry of Environment (MOE), he bulldozed a drain through a contaminated wetland, releasing PCB-contaminated sediment into the Bay of Quinte, thus contaminating an entire watershed with persistent toxic chemicals.

At trial, the justice of the peace found that Sinclair's aim was to "complete as much work on the property that he could as quickly as possible and hope that he could create such a mess that the Ministries involved would have no opportunity to stop him and would have no choice but to agree to let him do what he wanted with the property."[12] His attitude was described as "obnoxious, despicable, arrogant, deplorable, insulting, demeaning, confrontational, totally incorrigible and completely uncooperative."[13]

At trial, Sinclair was personally fined $71,000 and sentenced to four months in jail; the two corporations were fined a total of $588,000.[14] On appeal, the corporate sentences were reduced by $140,000,[15] but the personal sentence against Sinclair was upheld. As Rommel G. Masse J. of the Ontario Court of Justice wrote:[16]

> [T]he moral culpability of Mr. Sinclair is quite significant. He knew that the site was contaminated with PCBs. He intentionally dug up trenches to drain the wetlands and marshes knowing that by so doing, PCB contaminated sediments would be transported into the Bay of Quinte. His motivation for doing so was to increase profits or to decrease costs. He ignored warnings of the Ministry. He totally disregarded lawful Orders of the Provincial Officers, the Director and even the Court. He devastated the wetlands on the property without regard to the effect of doing so on the environment. There was actual damage to the Bay of Quinte and that damage, in view of the toxicity of PCBs, was significant. He denied the toxicity of PCBs, even though such is well known. His actions were deliberate, flagrant and calculated and continued over a lengthy period of time. He showed no remorse. His attitude towards Ministry personnel was deplorable and extremely insulting. He was totally un-cooperative. His actions were taken with callous disregard for the environment or for the law.

This case attracts the following question: Why was this penalty so light? Other crimes attract much longer jail sentences, with much less harm to the public interest than Sinclair had caused.

## THE WELL INTENTIONED

Mr. Sinclair is, fortunately, fairly unusual. Much more common are offenders who act like those in *United Keno Hill*: well meaning, but not effective enough. For the most part, they are not "bad guys"; they are simply men and women doing their best with too many demands and limited resources, and who are deeply remorseful when things go wrong.

The *United Keno Hill* principles work well for the well-intentioned but ineffective D&O, whether running small family businesses, or waste disposal sites, or sophisticated factories with multiples sites and hundreds or thousands of staff. If they have not done as much as they should, and environmental harm results, it is fair to hold them to account for the consequences. But we have to avoid 20/20 hindsight.

These people now have statutory duties to take reasonable care to have their companies comply with a dizzying array of environmental laws, as well as health and safety laws and many others. These duties appear in provisions such as section 280.1 of the *Canadian Environmental Protection Act, 1999*:[17]

> 280.1 (1) Every director and officer of a corporation shall take all reasonable care to ensure that the corporation complies with
>
> (a) this Act and the regulations, other than Division 3 of Part 7[18] and regulations made under that Division; and
> (b) orders and directions of, and prohibitions and requirements imposed by, the Minister, enforcement officers and review officers, other than those issued or imposed in connection with obligations or prohibitions under that Division or regulations made under that Division.
>
> ...
>
> Liability of directors and officers—Division 3 of Part 7
> (3) If a corporation commits an offence arising out of a contravention of Division 3 of Part 7, a regulation made under that Division or an order or direction of, or prohibition or requirement imposed by, the Minister, an enforcement officer or a review officer in connection with an obligation or prohibition under that Division or a regulation made under that Division, every director and officer of the corporation who directed or influenced the corporation's policies or activities in respect of conduct that is the subject matter of the offence is a party to and guilty of the offence, and is liable to the penalty provided by

> this Act for an individual in respect of the offence committed by the corporation, whether or not the corporation has been prosecuted or convicted.

Once a bad thing happens, it is obvious that it can and will happen. But until then, this particular bad thing is just one of thousands or tens of thousands that can go wrong, not all of which can be prevented. A reasonable process of identifying and addressing hazards ought to offer a defence; but since it has not been accepted as a defence to liability,[19] it must be an important factor in sentencing.

Many environmental offences happen with very little blameworthiness. For example, a highly motivated officer is called to one of the many manufacturing sites he is responsible for, late on a busy workday during a storm. He discovers that a sump pump in the basement has failed and the building has flooded. Contaminated wastewater is escaping the building, but he thinks it is contained on site. It is only hours later that he is told the liquid has escaped off site, and is flowing towards a nearby creek. The drains that should control the liquid on site turn out to have frozen in the severe weather. He works feverishly to get the flooding under control and calls repeatedly for a vacuum truck. Suppliers keep promising to get back to him, but they are very busy with the storm, and do not actually show up until the next morning. Most of his own company's staff has gone home and he is left with a very small team to address the problem. By the time he calls the Spill Action Centre (SAC) Hotline, the spill is several hours old. He is charged with failing to report the discharge. He probably could have called SAC more quickly. But despite failing to do so, his moral culpability is of an entirely different, and much lower, calibre than Mr. Sinclair's.

This officer may choose to plead guilty without attempting a due diligence defence because he cannot afford to fight. Mounting a complete defence to an environmental prosecution is incredibly expensive. In addition to legal fees, it usually requires technical evidence prepared by experts. If his company will not pay the fees, he cannot offer an effective defence.

### THE WELL INTENTIONED BUT CONFUSED

The *United Keno Hill* principles must be applied with special care when the regulated community cannot reasonably determine what the applicable environmental law is, and how to comply with it. Unfortunately, we spend a lot of time on cases like this.

In applying factors (c) and (f), deliberateness of the offence and extent of attempts to comply, judges should pay more attention to the vagueness and inscrutability of many environmental requirements, and the often imperfect conduct of regulators and other government bodies. These issues will have to be part of sentencing, because the Supreme Court of Canada (SCC) has blocked them from being part of a due diligence defence.

For example, in *Castonguay Blasting Ltd. v. Ontario (Environment)*,[20] the defendant reported the discharge of flyrock exactly as required by the province's own contract, and to the satisfaction of the province's supervising contract administrator. The MOE never approached the blasting industry and asked to be notified of the discharged flyrock; they simply began the "conversation" with a summons. This is a poor approach to regulation.

In many another cases, the MOE has issued permits with conditions that they know cannot be met, such as requiring a composting facility to have "100% negative pressure," when the pressure will inevitably fluctuate when there is a gust of wind. In another case, the MOE claimed that a hauler of "solid waste" broke the law whenever it rained, because there was some liquid in the load. The fact that the waste was on its way to be dumped in a landfill where it would also rain was irrelevant to the MOE.

Many environmental regulations and approvals are vague, leaving large grey areas wherein reasonable people may differ. We have long recommended that regulated entities write to regulators explaining their understanding, and requesting a response if the regulators disagree. The SCC has now rejected this practical approach, while offering nothing in its stead.

In *La Souveraine, Compagnie d'assurance générale v. Autorité des marchés financiers*,[21] the SCC made compliance with ambiguous regulations tougher than ever, by ruling that honest efforts to understand the law (however confusing) are not enough.

Sovereign General (SG) was an Alberta insurance company registered with the Quebec Autorité des marchés financiers (AMF) to sell insurance products. It was convicted of 56 counts of offering such products through an unregistered broker, each count with a minimum fine of $10,000.

Before the charges were laid, SG had given AMF a written explanation of why SG believed the broker did not require registration. The AMF did not respond, leading SG to believe that its explanation had been accepted. Then the 56 charges arrived, bearing a minimum $560,000 fine. The AMF punished SG much more severely than the offending broker, a Quebec resident. The SCC upheld all the convictions, despite some sympathy for SG's mistake.

The court rejected SG's argument that it should recognize reasonable mistake of law in the vast mosaic of regulatory offences. "More specifically, [SG] asks that this defence be made available in cases in which reasonable ignorance of or honest confusion about the applicable law is closely tied to improper conduct on the part of a regulatory body."[22] It concluded on this point:[23]

> This Court has held many a time that the fact that a defendant has exercised due diligence to find out and verify the nature of the applicable law is not a defence.
>
> . . .
>
> It should nonetheless be noted that if the rule that *ignorantia juris non excusat*—ignorance of the law excuses no one—were absolute, this could seriously hinder the application of another cardinal rule of our criminal justice system: there can be no punishment without fault. The overlap between these rules is all the more significant given the current simultaneous proliferation of regulatory measures and penal statutes. Indeed, several authors have pointed out that it is now impossible for citizens to have comprehensive knowledge of every law. . . .
>
> . . . [C]onflicts . . . inevitably result from the constantly expanding presence of regulatory measures. Such measures play an essential role in the implementation of public policy. The rule that ignorance of the law is not a valid defence supports the state's duty in this regard. For this reason alone, it needs to be enforced.
>
> At the same time, the rise in the number of statutes coupled with their growing complexity increases the risk that a citizen will be punished in circumstances in which ignorance of the law might nevertheless be understandable. . . .
>
> . . .
>
> The regulator at issue in the instant case, the AMF, is not required by law to reply to those to whom the law applies or to inform them about their rights and obligations. As a result, it was not reasonable in this case for the appellant to view the AMF's silence as a confirmation of its interpretation of that law. This being said, the AMF's attitude is of some concern. Nevertheless, although its attitude does not reflect the greater transparency a regulator is normally expected to show, and as unfortunate as that might be, that attitude cannot be equated with improper conduct or bad faith on its part.

> Furthermore, even if the AMF's conduct were so vexatious as to justify accepting a new exception to the rule with respect to ignorance of the law, which I cannot find to be the case here, I am of the opinion that the steps taken by the appellant to avoid breaking the law do not meet the requirements for the due diligence defence. The appellant relied solely on the legal advice of professionals acting for a third party, Flanders, in Manitoba. A reasonable person would at least have sought an independent opinion from a member of the Barreau du Québec, preferably one who specializes in insurance law. Thus, the appellant in this case has not shown that it took all reasonable steps to avoid breaking the law.

The SCC has left open the possibility that, in future cases, a mistaken understanding of a complex regulatory system could be a defence. In the meantime, however, this issue can only be addressed in sentencing.

In SG's case, the judges were also concerned about AMF's heavy-handedness, in laying 56 charges, each with a minimum $10,000 fine, when one would surely have been sufficient, and a fairer response to SG's honest efforts to understand the law. Three of the judges would have collapsed the 56 counts into a single charge; the others decided not to intervene because the issue had not been fully argued in the courts below. The combination of high minimum fines and a vindictive prosecutor can impose a startling and unjustified burden. However, judges can use their sentencing discretion to avoid saddling companies like AMF with unreasonably high fines.

## Part 2 – Regulatory Orders: Punishing the Innocent D&O

Environmental orders are not supposed to be punitive. Their aim is to ensure protection of the environment. However, orders that impose huge cleanup costs on the innocent certainly feel like punishment to those affected, and they are so instinctively unfair that they can seriously erode the social contract. This is especially so in the many cases where an innocent party has no realistic prospect of compensation, precisely because the original polluter is dead or insolvent.

One example is the case of *Baker v. Director (Minister of the Environment)*.[24] Beginning in the 1960s, chlorinated solvents and chromium were used at a manufacturing site in Cambridge, Ontario, leading to soil and groundwater contamination on and near the property. There was also an overlapping source of trichloroethylene (TCE) nearby.

In 1985, Northstar Aerospace Inc. (Canada) [Northstar Canada] bought the site, without knowledge of the contamination. There was no proof of chlorinated solvent contamination during Northstar Canada's ownership of the site.

In 2004, Northstar Canada discovered the historic contamination, which posed risks to human health and the environment. The company began an extensive voluntary remediation. Unfortunately, the company experienced significant financial difficulties after 2008, and the Cambridge site was vacant by 2009. By August 2012, the company was bankrupt, and its parent company (Northstar Inc.) was insolvent, in CCAA protection, and without assets. All the directors resigned.

The MOE took over the remediation. It tried to claim priority over both companies' secured creditors, but lost in the Court of Appeal.[25] It then looked to the former directors and officers of both companies, perhaps in the hope of seizing a $1.75M directors' charge set up under the CCAA.

In November 2012, the MOE issued a cleanup order to 13 former directors and officers (former D&O group) of both Northstar Canada and its parent company. Our client, Mr. Baker, had only sat on the board of the parent company, and had joined that board only after all manufacturing at the Cambridge site had stopped. It was absolutely clear that no contamination occurred on his watch. In fact, the only thing that happened "on his watch" was that the subsidiary spent a great deal of borrowed money doing a very effective remediation, until the day of its bankruptcy.

The order against Mr. Baker appeared to be, in all respects, illegal.

The MOE claimed authority for the order under section 18 of the *Environmental Protection Act*, which allows preventative orders to be issued to "a person who owns or owned or who has or had management or control of an undertaking or property."[26] The MOE claimed that this authorized them to issue cleanup orders to anyone who *ever* owned, managed, or controlled an "undertaking or property," directly or indirectly, regardless of fault or when the contamination occurred.

The MOE claim stood on two main pillars.

First, shortly before the case was heard, the Ontario Court of Appeal ruled in *Kawartha Lakes (City) v. Ontario (Environment)*[27] that section 18 orders can require innocent owners to clean up contamination caused by others. In that case, the innocent owner was even forbidden to show who was at fault, as it was "irrelevant" to the order against the City. The City had a statutory right to add the cost of the cleanup to the taxes of the responsible home.

Second, in earlier cases, the Environmental Review Tribunal (ERT) had upheld some section 18 orders against directors who *were* at fault because they were the directing minds of private companies and had not been duly diligent when the environmental risk occurred. The ERT created a rebuttable presumption that such directors personally manage and control a corporation's assets. However legally suspect that presumption may be, the results did look a bit like the "polluter pays" principle.

The Northstar former D&O group appealed the order to the ERT. Their request for a stay of the cleanup order pending their appeal was refused. They were required to pay monthly compliance costs of approximately $100,000, in addition to the legal and expert costs required for the appeal. Further, even if they were successful in proving that they did not have "control" of the property or undertaking, and the order was therefore issued without jurisdiction, there is no mechanism under the EPA through which they could recoup these costs. In other words, they could reasonably expect to spend $5 million in unrecoverable compliance costs during the appeal, none of which they could get back, even if they won.

Mr. Baker and others reasonably expected that the courts would eventually strike down the illegal order against them. But given the financial squeeze deliberately created by the EPA and the ERT, there was little point in turning to the courts.

Ultimately, Mr. Baker and others chose to settle the matter before it proceeded to a hearing before the ERT, at a cost of $4.75 million plus the $800,000 already spent to comply pending appeal. The financial impact of this regulatory order is far greater than any environmental fine imposed on an individual, yet it was imposed without any consideration of any of the factors generally applied in environmental sentencing.

The "justification" for such an unfair result is alleged to be the importance of environmental protection, as described by the Ontario Court of Appeal in *Kawartha Lakes*:[28]

> In this case, all agree that the appellant is innocent of any fault for the spill. I agree with the Tribunal and the Divisional Court that evidence that others were at fault for the spill is irrelevant to whether the order against the appellant should be revoked. That order is a no fault order. *It is not premised on a finding of fault on the part of the appellant but on the need to serve the environmental protection objective of the legislation.* [Emphasis added.]

> The tribunal had to determine whether revoking the Director's order would serve that objective. Deciding whether others are at fault for the spill is of no assistance in answering that question. Evidence of the fault of others says nothing about how the environment would be protected and the legislative objective served if the Director's order were revoked. Indeed, by inviting the Tribunal into a fault finding exercise, permitting the evidence might even impede answering the question in the timely way required by that legislative objective.

Imposing cleanup costs on the innocent is akin to an offence of absolute liability – the orderee may be "morally innocent in every sense" and yet subject to huge financial losses. As the SCC famously articulated in *R. v. Sault Ste. Marie*, some claim that absolute liability is justified because it is "efficient" and perhaps will ensure "a high standard of care and attention on the part of those who follow certain pursuits." In fact, though, imposing absolute liability on the innocent is corrosive to our sense of justice, and unlikely to improve behaviour:[29]

> Arguments of greater force are advanced against absolute liability. The most telling is that it violates fundamental principles of penal liability. It also rests upon assumptions which have not been, and cannot be, empirically established. There is no evidence that a higher standard of care results from absolute liability. If a person is already taking every reasonable precautionary measure, is he likely to take additional measures, knowing that however much care he takes, it will not serve as a defence in the event of breach? If he has exercised care and skill, will conviction have a deterrent effect upon him or others? Will the injustice of conviction lead to cynicism and disrespect for the law, on his part and on the part of others? These are among the questions asked. The argument that no stigma attaches does not withstand analysis, for the accused will have suffered loss of time, legal costs, exposure to the processes of the criminal law at trial and, however one may downplay it, the opprobrium of conviction. It is not sufficient to say that the public interest is engaged and, therefore, liability may be imposed without fault.

Chief Justice Stuart is right: we do need vigorous enforcement of environmental laws, and sentences that compel attention. But put yourself in the shoes of a D&O defendant. Could and should that person reasonably have known what was expected of them before the bad thing happened? How much blame does that individual really deserve? Are the regulators or others partly at fault? Environmental protection is essential, but so is fairness and the rule of law. Somehow, we need them all.

## NOTES

1 1980 CarswellYukon 9, 1 YR 299, 10 CELR 43 (Terr Ct) [*United Keno Hill*].

2 See *Baker v Director, Ministry of the Environment* (2013) ERT Case Nos: 12-158 to 12-169 (Ontario Environmental Review Tribunal) [*Baker*].

3 *United Keno Hill*, *supra* note 1 at 48–52; followed in *R. v. Big First Nation*, 2017 SKPC 16; *R v Bata Industries Ltd*, 1992 CarswellOnt 211, 7 CELR (NS) 245, 9 OR (3d) 329, (sub nom *R v Bata Industries Ltd (No 2)*) 70 CCC (3d) 394 [*Bata*].

4 *R v Shamrock Chemicals Ltd* (1989), 7 WCB (2d) 417 (Ont Prov Ct), var'd 9 WCB (2d) 18 (Dist Ct).

5 *R v Canadian Industries Ltd* (1977), 8 CELR 121 (YT Mag Ct); *R v Panarctic Oils Ltd*, 12 CELR 78, [1983] NWTR 143, 43 AR 199, 3 FPR 429 (Terr Ct) [additional reasons to (1982), 12 CELR 29, [1983] NWTR 47, 44 AR 385, 3 FPR 420 (Terr Ct)] at 87–88 [CELR].

6 *Bata*, *supra* note 3 at para 193.

7 *Ibid* at para 235.

8 See, e.g., *Environmental Protection Act*, RSO 1990, c O.40, s 188 [*EPA*].

9 *R v Deslisle*, [2003] BCJ No 662 (CA).

10 *R v Sinclair*, 2009 CarswellOnt 4894, 45 CELR (3d) 222 [*Sinclair*].

11 RSO 1990, c O.40 [*OWRA*].

12 *Sinclair*, *supra* note 10 at para 20.

13 *Ibid* at para 110.

14 *Ibid* at para 4.

15 *Ibid* at para 127.

16 *Ibid* at para 134.

17 Which is based on s 194 of the *EPA*, *supra* note 8.

18 Disposal at sea.

19 *R v Imperial Oil*, 2000 BCCA 553.

20 2013 SCC 52; followed by the Federal Court in *Morton v Canada (Minister of Fisheries and Oceans)*, 2015 FC 575, and *Canadian National Railway Company v Ontario (Environment and Climate Change)*, 2017 CarswellOnt 15472.

21 2013 SCC 63 [*La Souveraigne*].

22 *Ibid* at para 67.

23 *Ibid* at paras 68, 73–75, 78–79.

24 *Baker*, *supra* note 2.

25 *Re Northstar Aerospace Inc*, 2013 ONCA 600.

26 *Environmental Protection Act*, RSO 1990, c E.19, s 18.

27 2013 ONCA 310 [*Kawartha Lakes*].

28 *Ibid* at paras 19–20.

29 *R v Sault Ste Marie*, [1978] 2 SCR 1299 at 1311.

# 25

# The Enforcement of Environmental Law through the Use of Administrative Penalties

JEAN PIETTE*

On October 4, 2011, Bill 89, the *Act to amend the Environment Quality Act in order to reinforce compliance* came into force in Quebec.[1] It established new measures to enhance the repressive nature of the *Environment Quality Act*[2] in order to ensure compliance. These measures include: (1) overhauling criminal provisions to increase penalties that can be imposed by a court, to hold a greater number of individuals accountable and to give a criminal court enhanced power with regard to the environment; (2) enhancing the grounds on which the minister may amend, suspend, or revoke or refuse to issue or renew an authorization certificate; (3) creating a new set of administrative monetary penalties; (4) increasing the government's ability to take civil action to ensure compliance with the *Environment Quality Act*; (5) increasing the power of the minister and his officials to order, inspect, and investigate.

It is difficult to know why all of these measures were justified, except for the need to update certain provisions. It is not known if there was really a high level of delinquency with regard to the requirements of the *Environment Quality Act* or if the problem stemmed from the courts not imposing sufficiently severe penalties on offenders or if the *Ministère du Développement durable, de l'Environnement et des Parcs* (the "MDDEP") was not putting forward enough cases for criminal prosecution. The department's annual reports do

* *The author would like to thank Ms. Miriam Desmarais, whose research and contributions were greatly appreciated by the author.*

not indicate any reasons why this host of new measures was necessary. All that is known is that the data published by the MDDEP in 2011 revealed that Quebec courts imposed $894,400 in fines to 49 offenders who had committed 92 violations of the *Environment Quality Act*. When Bill 89 was introduced in the National Assembly, the minister in charge did not provide many specifics to justify the introduction of the bill except to say that it was being done to "improve the efficiency of the department's response" or because of the delays in imposing fines through the criminal justice system.[3] Among the reasons that were invoked, there was also the perception that the fines were inadequate and the fact that the violation notices were not an effective enough vehicle to secure full environmental compliance.

The fact remains that there seems to be a movement towards modernizing the government's means of intervention and improving its efficiency in order to ensure environmental compliance and crack down on environmental offences. Bill 89 is part of this trend.

## The Nature of Monetary Administrative Penalties

When Bill 89 was introduced for clause-by-clause study, the Minister of Sustainable Development, Environment and Parks made a point of emphasizing that he would amend the bill by replacing the expression "*pénalités administratives*" in the French text with the words "*sanctions administratives pécuniaires*" ("monetary administrative penalties").[4] He felt that this change in terminology would lessen the punitive aspect of the provision. Nevertheless, it is doubtful that this change in terminology will really have any such effect.

The French word "*pénalité*" is defined as follows in the *Nouveau Petit Robert*:

> 1. [Translation] Anything criminal in nature; the application of a sentence; 2. A sentence; financial penalty implemented by the State.[5]

As for the French word "*sanction*," it is defined as follows in the *Nouveau Petit Robert*:

> 1. [Translation] A penalty or reward set forth to ensure compliance with a law; a penalty or reward tied to a prohibition or order, based on merit or demerit; 2. A penalty established by law to suppress an infraction; a repressive measure tied to an unexecuted order or a broken

prohibition; an action through which a country or an international organization suppresses violations of a right.[6]

There is not a lot of difference between a "*pénalité*" and a "*sanction*." Both essentially refer to a penalty aimed at suppressing violations of a law.

When we examine the monetary administrative penalty regime introduced in the *Environment Quality Act*, we find that the National Assembly codified it into 17 sections.[7] All conditions are specified, including the fact that it applies to practically all violations of the Act and regulations.[8] The National Assembly thought it appropriate to establish the regime's parameters itself, without resorting to delegated legislation, as opposed to the federal Parliament and the legislatures of almost every province, which all resort to regulatory power to establish the conditions of the regime and determine the sections of the Acts and regulations to which it applies.[9] The Quebec National Assembly only delegated to the government the power to set by regulation monetary penalties applicable to violations of various regulations that have already been or will be adopted.[10]

Therefore, for this regime, the National Assembly proceeded in the same way it had when it established the regime of criminal penalties that apply to violations of the *Environment Quality Act*, which is codified in 19 sections.

To set the monetary administrative penalty regime apart from the criminal sanction regime, the National Assembly refers to non-compliance with the Act and regulations as "failures to comply."[11] Despite this terminological particularism, the focus must be on the real substance of the new legal system created by the National Assembly and on the way the rights of litigants are handled by said regime, to determine its compliance with rights protected by the Charters of Rights and Freedoms, which we will discuss below.

Before addressing this issue, we should define what this monetary administrative penalty regime involves. In all respects, this regime is one in which a government official designated by the minister imposes a monetary penalty, the amount of which may not exceed $2,000 in the case of an individual and $10,000 in the case of a body corporate, for failing or neglecting to comply with a provision of the *Environment Quality Act* or a regulation adopted under it. However, this official may not impose a prison sentence. Such a sentence may only be imposed through criminal sanction.[12] Below, we will examine the mechanisms by which monetary administrative penalties are imposed and how they can be challenged, as well as the impact of this regime on the rights of litigants.

## The Scope of the Quebec Regime

For environmental issues, Quebec adopted a monetary administrative penalty regime that is different from the types of plans found in enabling statutes enacted in Canada's various provinces and territories and at the federal level. In fact, when we examine the enabling statutes of other Canadian provinces, we immediately notice that, to date, only the provinces of Ontario, Alberta, and New Brunswick have monetary administrative penalty regimes that are operational and in full force. We set out to know to what extent these regimes were effectively applied. Data on the enforcement of these regimes can be found on the websites of the various provinces' departments of the environment. They seem to play some sort of backup role[13] except in Ontario, where the amounts collected are significant[14] because the regime was designed to discipline a well-targeted clientele that is identified in the regulations[15] and is subject to the province's industrial depollution program.

The Quebec regime is particularly characterized by its universal scope. Here again, contrary to what the other provinces and federal government did, Quebec, in fact, created a comprehensive and universal monetary administrative penalty regime in addition to the criminal penalty regime, which is also universal because it applies to all violations of the *Environment Quality Act*.

Elsewhere in Canada, the regime of administrative penalties is usually targeted, complementary in nature, and applicable to particular violations determined by regulation,[16] in order to encourage compliance. These regimes also include an agreement, settlement, or transaction mechanism that aims to bring an offender into compliance with the Act and regulations. This demonstrates a real desire for such a regime to increase compliance, in that this mechanism offers a greater guarantee of results. Instead of suffering a financial penalty or acting to obtain a reduction of such a penalty,[17] the offender can make written commitments or enter into an agreement with the person who imposed the penalty or expressed an intention to do so.[18] Ontario regulations even state that a non-compliant company can have its monetary administrative penalty reduced if it implements an environmental management system[19] or if it implements preventive measures or environmental depollution measures.[20] Officials may also enter into a transaction with anyone who violates the law on order to bring him/her into compliance.[21] Quebec's monetary administrative penalty regime does not provide such mechanisms, despite the fact that they would have been an irrefutable indication of the rapid environmental compliance objective sought out by the regime.

What is surprising about the Quebec regime is that emphasis is placed strictly on imposing financial penalties by administrative means for any violation of the *Environment Quality Act*, without offenders having access to mechanisms for making commitments or entering into compliance agreements.

By acting this way, the Quebec National Assembly took a risk that might undermine the regime itself, which, despite the apparent intention expressed in section 115.13, appears in reality to be designed to impose, by administrative means, monetary penalties on any person who violates the law and regulations, without that person having any of the guarantees that normally apply when a penalty is imposed on someone who does not comply with a law, such as the presumption of innocence, the notion of reasonable doubt, protection from self-incrimination, and the right not to be convicted twice for the same violation. This is, in fact, a regime of financial penalties that are more modest than the criminal penalties found in sections 115.29 to 115.32. We note that the Quebec National Assembly chose to use four separate sections to create four categories of monetary administrative penalties, ranked according to the environmental impact of each violation, which, in a way, closely mirrors the four categories of criminal penalties created in sections 115.29 to 115.32, which are ranked the same way. If this regime proves, legally, to be a mini–criminal law system, it will be subject to all the legal guarantees protected by the federal and Quebec Charters of Rights and Freedoms.[22]

In an article published in 2010, Mr. Robert Daigneault questioned the true nature of the monetary administrative penalty regime in light of the decisions of Canadian courts that were asked to rule on the legality of certain monetary administrative penalty regimes established by laws adopted by Parliament and provincial legislative assemblies.[23] This questioning seems relevant here, given the characteristics of Quebec's monetary administrative penalty regime.

The monetary administrative penalties analyzed by the courts to date are essentially regimes that govern economic and financial activities such as the regulation of foreign investments in Canada, securities regulation, tax regulations, customs regulations, regulations for removing timber in the public forests, etc. These regimes aim to discipline people who have willingly performed a given economic activity.[24] The key decision in this area is *R. v. Wigglesworth*,[25] which dealt with the application of section 11(d) of the *Canadian Charter of Rights and Freedoms*[26] to a federal law that allowed for disciplinary sanctions to be imposed on Royal Canadian Mounted Police officers. In this case, Wilson J. had established the distinction between sanctions for criminal infractions to which the *Canadian Charter of Rights and Freedoms* applies, and sanctions imposed by other punitive regimes involving administrative authorities and quasi-judicial organizations:

> [Translation] In my view, if a particular matter is of a public nature, intended to promote public order and welfare within a public sphere of activity, then that matter is the kind which falls within s. 11. It falls within the section because of its very nature. This is to be distinguished from private, internal or disciplinary matters which are regulatory, protective or corrective and are primarily intended to maintain discipline, professional integrity and professional standards or to regulate conduct within a limited private sphere of activity.[27]

However, the *Environment Quality Act* is a law of general application which aims to protect the environment and maintain public order and welfare through a system of prohibitions and obligations that apply to all citizens, companies, and municipalities in Quebec, including all departments, public organizations, and government corporations.[28] This law reflects society's growing concerns about protecting the environment, as Justice Charles Gonthier of the Supreme Court of Canada acknowledged in the landmark *Ontario v. Canadian Pacific Ltd.* decision.[29] This law establishes public order rules aimed at preserving the environment. Sections 20, 21, and 22, for example, apply to any disposal of contaminants carried out by a person in Quebec, whether the contaminant is regulated or not. If it is not regulated, the disposal will be prohibited based on its impact on the environment, which affects both the environmental factors and resources as well as human quality of life factors.[30] As for the notion of a "contaminant," it is also very broad. As such, according to section 1(5), a "contaminant" is:

> a solid, liquid or gaseous matter, a microorganism, a sound, a vibration, rays, heat, an odour, a radiation or a combination of any of them likely to alter the quality of the environment in any way.

The law, therefore, targets all phenomena that are likely to modify the quality of the environment. It applies to both private and public property.[31] As for section 22, it governs all activities likely to emit contaminants into the environment. The *Environment Quality Act* is certainly not a law that governs "private, internal or disciplinary matters," nor is it intended to "regulate conduct within a limited private sphere of activity," to quote Wilson J. in the *Wigglesworth* decision. The monetary administrative penalty regime can, therefore, be applied to any citizen or company who releases a contaminant into the environment or who conducts activities that are likely to affect the environment.

When determining whether or not section 11 of the *Canadian Charter of Rights and Freedoms* applies, the Supreme Court of Canada indicated, in the *Wigglesworth* and *Martineau* decisions,[32] that it was necessary to verify if the existing sanction regime is a criminal procedure in and of itself or if this sanction will have actual criminal consequences. And, in the *Martineau* case, Fish J. listed three (3) criteria that would help determine if we have a criminal procedure before us:

> [Translation] To determine the nature of the proceeding, the case law must be reviewed in light of the following criteria: (1) the objectives of the law and its relevant provisions; (2) the purpose of the sanction; (3) the process leading to imposition of the sanction.[33]

The objectives of the *Environment Quality Act* are to protect the environment and the public's lives, health, and quality of life. These objectives are quite broad and reach the whole of society. This is not legislation that regulates a specific economic activity. However, some sections of the *Environment Quality Act* do regulate certain specific activities such as, for example, division IV.2 of chapter I on depollution attestations, which apply to certain very precise categories of industrial activities. Nevertheless, it must be noted that the monetary administrative penalty regime does not apply only to the field of activities conducted by depollution permit or attestation holders but applies to all citizens, companies, and municipalities who might release a contaminant into the environment (sections 20 and 21) or who engage in an activity that is likely to modify the quality of the environment (section 22).

In the first paragraph of the second clause of section 115.13, the National Assembly indicates that administrative monetary penalties seek to achieve certain objectives, such as urging rapid compliance and deterring repeat violations. However, we notice the words "such as" (in the legislation), which indicates that these sanctions have other objectives, probably the one that, of course, is associated with the very definition of a "penalty"—penalizing a person or entity that violates a law. In addition, a review of the regime reveals characteristics that are hardly compatible with the regime's stated objective, namely to urge "rapid" compliance and deter repeat violations.

In the legislation,[34] the National Assembly introduced a two-year limitation period starting from the violation date. However, the Act also provides for a virtually unlimited limitation period where the violation deals with misrepresentations, in the case of a violation of section 20, or in the case of a hazardous materials, since in these three types of violation the two-year period, which is absolutely identical to the limitation period of a criminal sanction with regard the same three types of violations,[35] is calculated from the start date of the inspection or investigation that led to the discovery of the violation.[36] These long limitation periods are hardly compatible with objectives such as deterrence or urging "rapid" compliance (as the legislation says). A short limitation period is the only one that will really urge an offender into "rapid" compliance or deter him from reoffending. The deterrent effect of a monetary administrative penalty imposed, for example, a year and a half after a violation is not any different than a criminal penalty imposed after a comparable period following a violation. Similarly, a penalty imposed after such time is hardly compatible with the objective of urging "rapid" compliance.

In the *Martineau* decision,[37] the Supreme Court of Canada sought to determine if the monetary administrative penalty imposed pursuant to the *Customs Act*[38] produced a "true criminal consequence." Speaking for the court, Fish J. looked at various factors that are likely to determine if there is a true criminal consequence and, among them, he mentioned that there was no such consequence in the case of a penalty imposed on goods illegally imported to Canada pursuant to the *Customs Act* because, in this case, it was an *in rem* penalty, meaning "on the thing," and not a penalty imposed on a person guilty of an offence.

However, Fish J. also took an interest in the stigma associated with a criminal conviction compared to a monetary administrative penalty imposed pursuant to the *Customs Act*, which stigmatizes no one. The distinction that Fish J. makes in the case of the *Customs Act* cannot be applied in the case of the *Environment Quality Act*, because the National Assembly provided identical public notice requirements for administrative monetary penalties and criminal penalties.[39] In both cases, monetary administrative penalties and criminal penalties will be posted in a public register that will be available on the website of the Ministère du Développement durable, de l'Environnement et des Parcs.[40] The monetary administrative penalty will also be posted as soon as it is imposed, just like a criminal penalty.

As for the indicator that might be represented by the destination of the administrative penalty or criminal penalty,[41] the legislation calls for both to be paid into the Green Fund established under the *Act respecting the Ministère du Développement durable, de l'Environnement et des Parcs.*[42]

This equal treatment of monetary administrative penalties and criminal penalties indicates that the National Assembly placed equal or comparable emphasis on both types of penalty, especially since the minister is required to publish a host of information related to the offender's identity, the significance of the penalty, and the events that led to the penalties being imposed. People penalized administratively will, therefore, be just as known to the general public as criminally penalized offenders and will have the same stigma on their reputation. Although the procedure for collecting monetary administrative penalties is a civil procedure, we can ask ourselves whether this is basically a procedure that produces actual criminal consequences.

## General Application Framework for Administrative Penalties and Criminal Remedies

When Bill 89 was adopted, the National Assembly broke new ground in creating, within the law, an obligation for the minister to develop and make public a general application framework for administrative and criminal penalties, by specifying five elements that must be found therein. Section 115.13 sets out this obligation and the elements that must be found within this general framework. Thus, the general framework must specify:

(1) the purpose of the penalties, "such as":
  (a) urging "rapid" compliance; and
  (b) deterring repeat violations;
(2) the categories of functions held by the persons designated to impose penalties;
(3) the criteria that must guide the appointed officials, such as the type of failure, its repetitive nature, the seriousness of the effects or potential effects and the remedial measures taken by the person at fault;
(4) the circumstances in which a criminal proceeding will be deemed to have priority; and
(5) the other procedures, such as the requirement to give advance notification of a notice of non-compliance.

This list of elements that must appear in the general application framework reveals the purpose of the monetary administrative penalties, namely:

- urging rapid compliance;
- deterring the repeat violation of the Act and regulations.

A general application framework entitled "Cadre général d'application des sanctions administratives pécuniaires" (General application framework for monetary administrative penalties) was published on the department's website on February 1, 2012, the date on which the monetary administrative penalty regime came into effect.[43] It is accompanied by an administrative directive issued on January 16, 2012, titled "Directive sur le traitement des manquements àa la législation environnementale" (Directive on processing violations of environmental legislation), which describes the administrative function of the *Environment Quality Act*'s enforcement measures.[44]

The adoption of a general application framework addresses a request made by several stakeholders over the years. Ontario and British Columbia have theirs.[45] The federal government has its own.[46] The purpose of this general application framework is to inform the litigant of the circumstances surrounding the administration's choice to proceed with a monetary administrative penalty, a criminal prosecution, or simply a notice of non-compliance, as we will see later on. The review of these documents reveals that the monetary administrative penalty will be applied mainly for violations that have "minor" consequences, particularly in cases of recurring violations or an affront to the department's authority.

## Codification of the Notion of Non-Compliance Notices

Another innovation of Bill 89 involves codifying what was previously known as a "notice of infraction," which was nothing but a warning from a government official that identified an alleged infraction by the person to whom the notice of infraction was served. Obviously, this notice of infraction was not legally binding. It was, in a way, a warning from the government that officials had found certain irregularities during an inspection. The notice of infraction was not legally binding but could be used during forced intervention administrative measures like an order or the revocation of a certificate of authorization during judicial proceedings such as criminal prosecution or an injunction application.

The codification of the notice of infraction, which now bears the name "notice of non-compliance," is an initiative that is found in no other provincial or federal law. The purpose of this procedure is to give the person to whom the notice of non-compliance is served a notice "urging that the necessary measures be taken immediately to remedy the failure."[47] The legislation mentions that this notice must indicate that the violation could lead to a monetary administrative penalty or criminal proceedings. It is not known, however, who will issue these notices of non-compliance. The legislation merely states that such a notice can be served once a "violation" of the Act or a regulation has been identified. However, at this stage, no decision has been made yet as to the imposition of an administrative or criminal penalty. The litigant does not yet know if he or she will be penalized or not. But serving this notice of non-compliance is nonetheless a mandatory precondition for imposing an monetary administrative penalty.[48]

In this respect, this notice reminds us of a formal notice sent before starting legal proceedings.

One can, however, question the adequacy of this type of notice in the context of a monetary administrative penalty. If the government deems that the violation should be subject to a criminal penalty, a notice of infraction will be sent to the subject and he or she will be entitled to all protections provided for in similar matters by the *Canadian Charter of Rights and Freedoms* and the *Charter of Human Rights and Freedoms*.

In some provinces,[49] an administrative penalty is preceded by a prior notice that clearly states the penalty the government intends to impose, which allows the person who receives it to make representations pursuant to the rules of natural justice that apply when the government makes an individual decision that is likely to affect a person's rights. In Quebec, this rule is codified in section 2 of the *Administrative Justice Act*.[50] In fact, for this notice to meet the criteria applicable in similar cases, the notice must generally be detailed enough that the subject can know what he or she is being accused of and present his or her case. To uphold such standards, the notice would have to list, rather clearly, not only the violation of which the subject is accused but also the monetary administrative penalty he or she faces. Moreover, section 4 of the *Administrative Justice Act*[51] requires that the government take appropriate measures to ensure that the citizen is given the opportunity to provide any information useful for the making of any decision which affects him/her.

However, the legislation sets no mechanism or period within which the person named in such a notice can respond or provide explanations. It is not known whether the person who issues the notice will invite the person named therein to respond. In any event, it is highly likely that the subject will be able to further exercise his or her rights when a monetary administrative penalty is reviewed, as we will see below.

## The Initial Decision: Imposing a Monetary Administrative Penalty

The monetary administrative penalty devised by the Quebec National Assembly is not imposed by the minister but by "persons designated by the Minister."[52] The monetary administrative penalty takes the shape of a complaint that states the claimed amount, the reasons for the claim, the time from which it bears interest, the right to challenge the complaint through a review, and information related to the way in which the monetary administrative penalty is to be collected, including the issuance of a recovery certificate set forth in section 115.53 and the consequences of this penalty with respect to the risk of having a certificate of authorization denied or revoked and the risk of criminal penalties that the government reserves the right to take.[53] A monetary administrative penalty may deal with several "failures" and may involve failures having occurred on several different dates, because a failure that continues over several days constitutes as many separate "failures."[54] The cumulative effect of several distinct failures and of failures that continue for several days can lead to claims of tens or hundreds of thousands of dollars, especially in the case of a body corporate.

The amount due bears interest starting from the 31st day following the notice of claim, at the rate set forth in the first clause of section 28 of the *Tax Administration Act*,[55] except that the interest can be suspended if the review decision is rendered more than 30 days after the receipt of the application,[56] and the Administrative Tribunal of Quebec can adjudicate on this question in an action disputing the administrative monetary function.[57] The person who imposes the penalty has significant discretion because it is up to him or her to determine the most "appropriate" penalty[58] when several sanctions could be applied in the case. However, he or she does not have any discretion with regard to the amount of the penalty because the amounts for each violation are set forth in sections 115.23 through 115.26 and will be different for a physical person than for a body corporate. The decision maker's discretion will include whether to impose a monetary administrative penalty, which section of the Act to associate the violation with, and how many days to penalize.

The official who imposes the monetary administrative penalty is not bound by any particular procedural rules except those related to the formalism of the content of his or her decision as explained above. He or she is not required to give notice. He or she must adhere to the directive on processing violations of environmental legislation and the general application framework.[59] He or she is not required to produce or attach to his or her decision any exhibits, photographs or other reports.

Imposing a monetary administrative penalty according to such a procedure is akin, in some respects, both to the accusation and the judgment being rendered against an individual, body corporate, or municipality that is alleged to have committed an infraction, except that the person making the accusation is acting as both the prosecutor and the judge because he or she has the power not only to assess the accuracy of the facts in a notice of non-compliance but also to impose the penalty. He or she is, in a way, both judge and jury. As for the person being penalized, he or she obviously has no right to reasonable doubt. He or she is, for all intents and purposes, presumed to have committed the violation of which he or she is being accused. The person imposing the penalty is not required to provide any evidence. Compared to the criminal system, it is as if the prosecutor demonstrated the *actus reus* of the violation committed.

Starting from the time the penalty is imposed, the burden of proof is reversed,[60] and it will fall upon the defendant to demonstrate that the penalty is not appropriate or justified. There is, therefore, from this point on, a reversal of the burden of proof. The person being penalized must, by a preponderance of evidence, seek to have the penalty reviewed or challenge it, under the procedure and conditions defined by the legislation.

## The Second Step: Reviewing the Penalty

Upon receipt of a monetary administrative penalty, the person or municipality involved can ask for a review of the decision within 30 days of the notice of claim.[61] The review is performed by a person designated by the minister, who must not come under the same administrative authority as the initial decision maker.[62] It is unknown how many people will be designated to review monetary administrative penalties, but the minister announced, in a press release dated February 1, 2012, the creation of a "monetary administrative penalty review office."[63] We do not know anything about these people's training or skills, but we do know that they will be managed by a chief reviewer who has been appointed by the minister.

The legislation provides that the applicant in a review must have the opportunity to submit observations and produce documents to "complete the record."[64] Nowhere is it indicated that the applicant is entitled, at this stage, to have access to his or her record even though one can assume that such access is implicit if the applicant wants the opportunity to "complete the record." How can he or she complete something when he or she is unaware of its content? At this point, the applicant cannot keep quiet. He or she does not have the right to silence or else he or she will be bound by the presumption of guilt created by the penalty imposed by the initial decision maker. In light of the file that he or she will have surely reviewed,[65] the applicant will be entitled to submit arguments and produce evidence to support his or her arguments, if necessary. Section 115.19 states that the person conducting the review decides "on the basis of the record," which means that the applicant is not entitled to a proper hearing that includes the right to produce witnesses and the right to cross-examine the initial decision maker, the inspector, or other witnesses from the department. Nevertheless, the legislation gives the reviewer the opportunity to "proceed in some other manner," at his or her full discretion.[66] This could possibly allow for hearings and the presentation of a more elaborate defence.

Among the "observations" that the litigant can make, he or she will be free to invoke the means of defence and exculpation described below in part 8.

As for the reviewer, he or she has the power to confirm, quash, or vary the original decision.[67] The word "vary" may cause confusion, since the initial decision maker has no discretion with regard to the fine that he or she can impose for each "failure." The amounts of the monetary administrative penalties[68] set forth by the legislation are set amounts that depend on the nature of the "failure" identified. We believe that the power to "vary" the initial decision maker's decision may include the number of days for which a failure will be penalized, or maybe the classification of this "failure" among the four categories set forth in sections 115.23 to 115.26. The legislation expressly requires that a review request be dealt with promptly,[69] which is, in any case, already provided for in similar terms in section 4(1) of the *Administrative Justice Act*. The same goes for the requirement that the reviewed decision be drafted in clear and concise terms and that the right to challenge it before the Administrative Tribunal of Quebec and the period allowed for such a challenge be mentioned.[70] The legislation states that a review decision must be rendered within 30 days after receipt of the application or within the time prescribed for the applicant to submit observations or documents, otherwise the interest is suspended until the decision is rendered.[71]

It is not known what will be the value of such a review, conducted by one government official, of an initial decision made by another official in the same department, even though the reviewing is "not from the same administrative authority." Usually, the trier of fact responsible for reviewing an administrative or quasi-judicial decision must have a certain "distance," a certain detachment or independence from the initial decision maker. This is required to guarantee the credibility of the process and ensure the applicant that he or she is addressing an impartial body. Credibility is, indeed, an essential ingredient in the success of a process of this nature.

## The Third Step: Recourse before the Administrative Tribunal of Quebec

If the applicant is dissatisfied with the decision rendered at the review stage because he or she was unable to successfully convince the "reviewer" of his or her due diligence or any other motive that warrants the monetary administrative penalty being quashed or varied, he or she can bring it before the Administrative Tribunal of Quebec (the "TAQ").[72] This challenge will take place before a tribunal that is completely separate and independent from the MDDEP and the two government officials who rendered the first and second rulings regarding the monetary administrative penalty imposed on the applicant.

For several years, the TAQ has been the tribunal that acts as the appeal (or "challenge") body for administrative decisions rendered pursuant to the *Environment Quality Act*.[73] It is before this tribunal that the applicant can expect to have a truly impartial hearing. The applicant can, indeed, present evidence and have witnesses heard.[74] He or she can invoke the exculpatory means described in part 8 below. He or she must submit a preponderance of proof for each defence chosen. Looking at the TAQ's jurisprudence with respect to the appeals rendered under the *Environment Quality Act*, we note that its rulings have almost always upheld the MDDEP's decisions. Ours is not to analyze the reasons for such rulings in the MDDEP's favour, but it is clear that the litigants had a better chance before the Court of Quebec and the Superior Court.[75]

Within 30 days after receipt of the application to contest, the file for the challenged decision is sent to the TAQ and the applicant.[76] This is somewhat equivalent to the prosecutor disclosing evidence in a criminal case. During an appeal before the TAQ, the tribunal will rule on the merit of the means of challenge invoked by the applicant. It may also be called upon to determine whether the MDDEP's decision is reasonable. In fact, the TAQ holds a sort of *de novo* trial. It can substitute its discretion for that of the two preceding decision makers and even determine whether or not the penalty is appropriate. Since this involves a challenge to a ruling, the second clause of section 15 of the *Administrative Justice Act* allows the TAQ to confirm, vary, or quash the decision and "if appropriate, make the decision which, in its opinion, should have been taken initially."

With regard to the exculpatory means raised by the applicant, the TAQ's role will be similar to that of a criminal court asked to rule on a defence made in regard to a charge involving a criminal infraction. The difference is that, before the TAQ, the applicant is not presumed innocent and has no right to reasonable doubt. However, before the TAQ, MDDEP inspectors and the applicant can be cross-examined, because the rules of procedure are those that apply in civil cases.

## The Means of Defence and Exculpation

The National Assembly did not provide for specific means of defence or exculpation that could be invoked by a person who receives a monetary administrative penalty, unlike the regime in force in Ontario, which has, in section 181(6) of the *Environmental Protection Act*,[77] excluded certain means of defence that could otherwise have been raised by a regulated company, even though it remediated this in the regulations by allowing a company targeted by a penalty to obtain a reduction of the amount if it could demonstrate certain elements of diligence.[78] Since the Quebec legislation does not make any provision to rule out one or several means of defence, one may outline those that could likely be invoked to challenge a monetary administrative penalty. It would indeed go against the elementary rules of justice if a person could be penalized while the violation he or she is accused of can be explained by facts and circumstances that can exonerate him or her. The list of exculpatory means described below is not exhaustive. These means they can be raised both at the review stage and the challenge stage before the TAQ, even though the applicant will have more elaborate procedural means before the TAQ (particularly the production of witnesses, examination, and cross-examination).

### 1. DUE DILIGENCE

The notion of "due diligence" is part of the means of defence that a person can invoke against any accusation of "strict liability," as stated by the Supreme Court of Canada in *R. v. Sault Ste. Marie*.[79] This means of defence applies, among others, to regulatory infractions like environmental infractions. Due diligence has also been recognized as a legitimate means of defence against monetary administrative sanctions.[80] In the context of a monetary administrative sanction, the applicant must demonstrate that he or she took all necessary measures to obey the law and avoid the violation of which he/she is accused.

## 2. MISINTERPRETATION OF FACTS OR LAW

The applicant should be entitled to bring up any error of law in the interpretation of an Act or a regulation, or any error related to the assessment of facts alleged in the violation of which the applicant is accused. The applicant may also find arguments in the enforcement of the *General application framework for monetary administrative penalties (section 115.13 of the Environment Quality Act)*, which was established by the minister pursuant to section 115.13. This is one "official" normative document with unclear legal status adopted by the minister pursuant to the *Environment Quality Act*, which does not have the binding nature of a regulatory text but provides a framework for exercising discretionary powers conferred by law, particularly the powers set forth in sections 115.16 and 115.19.

## 3. ERRORS IN PROCEDURAL LEGALITY

The applicant should be able to obtain redress if there was a breach of the rules of procedural fairness prescribed in section 2 of the *Administrative Justice Act*, including failure to send a prior notice of non-compliance, failure to provide an opportunity to submit observations at the review stage and failure to comply with any of the procedural requirements prescribed in sections 115.14 to 115.22, 115.48, and 115.49 of the *Environment Quality Act*.

## 4. REASONABLE ERROR OF FACT

The notion of a "reasonable error of fact" is a means of defence related to due diligence, which was also recognized in *R. v. Sault Ste-Marie*,[81] and which allows an individual to be exonerated of a charge by invoking an error involving a material fact of the violation of which the person being penalized is accused.[82] This error must be reasonable, meaning that it refers to the behaviour of a reasonable person placed in similar circumstances. As in criminal proceedings, an error of law should not constitute an acceptable means of exculpation except if it is caused by a government official as indicated below.

## 5. DEFENCE OF MISTAKE CAUSED BY THE AUTHORITIES

If a government official has, through his or her writing, words, or behaviour, suggested to an applicant that something was allowed, the applicant may invoke a defence of mistake caused by the authorities.[83] To be admissible, the means of defence must always be reasonable, based on the rule of reasonable behaviour by a person placed in similar circumstances. This means of defence may not be used to justify an applicant's bad faith or negligence. In criminal proceedings, this means of defence may lead to a stay of proceedings[84] or an acquittal.[85] In the case of a monetary administrative penalty, this means of exculpation should be grounds to quash the decision.

### 6. DEFENCE OF NECESSITY

This means of defence applies when a person performs an act in an emergency context because this act seems to be one that will have the fewest consequences on the environment or on the protection of life and property. It must be an act that was not really voluntary because the applicant really did not have any other choices.

### 7. DEFENCE OF IMPOSSIBILITY

This means of defence refers tothea physical impossibility to act due to a fortuitous event or *force majeure* that was out of the applicant's control. Such events create a situation in which the applicant is no longer able to act in compliance with the law.

### 8. *DE MINIMIS NON CURAT LEX*

To be able to invoke this means of defence, the penalty must be trivial or a case of little importance that does not warrant a penalty. This means of defence applies, for instance, when the legislation establishes a legal requirement in general terms, which allows for a certain degree of assessment of the facts with respect to the terms of the law. This means of defence was recognized more notably in *Ontario v. Canadian Pacific Ltd.*[86]

## Classification of Administrative Monetary Penalties

The legislation divides all possible "violations" of the *Environment Quality Act* into four distinct categories, which group the violations together based on their seriousness or their environmental consequences as determined by the legislation. Thus, the model is the same for the monetary administrative penalty regime as for the criminal penalty regime. In addition, we note that the four categories of violations each replicate approximately the same violations referred to as "offences" for the purposes of the criminal penalty regime found in sections 115.29 to 115.32 and "failures" for the purposes of the monetary administrative penalty regime. Table 25.1 lists the monetary administrative penalties set forth by the legislation:

**Table 25.1 | Classification of monetary administrative penalties set forth by the *Environment Quality Act***

| *E.Q.A. Section* | *Natural Person* | *Body Corporate* |
|---|---|---|
| 115.23 | $250 | $1,000 |
| 115.24 | $500 | $2,500 |
| 115.25 | $1,000 | $5,000 |
| 115.26 | $2,000 | $10,000 |

The legislation provides that a monetary administrative penalty imposed pursuant to this regime would be of a fixed amount. Whoever has the power to impose it has no discretion over the amount that can be claimed from the person who committed the violation. He or she can neither increase nor decrease it due to the circumstances of the case.[87] The penalty will be smaller if the violator is a natural person. As such, the most minor violations are punished with fines of $250 for a natural person and $1,000 for a body corporate. The most significant violations are punished with fines of $2,000 for a natural person and $10,000 for a body corporate.

These monetary administrative penalties are about the same as those provided for in other provincial environmental laws. Thus, in Alberta and New Brunswick, the monetary administrative penalty may not exceed $5,000.[88] However, the *Environment Protection Act* in Ontario states that such a penalty can be, in the most serious cases, up to $100,000.[89] A violation that goes unaddressed for some time may be considered a separate violation for each day it continues, which could multiply the total amount of the penalty.[90]

## Enforcement of Monetary Administrative Penalties

The monetary administrative penalty in the *Environment Quality Act*, technically, takes the shape of a notice of claim from the person who imposed the penalty.[91] The amount due bears interest starting on the 31st day following the notice of claim at the rate set forth in the first clause of section 28 of the *Tax Administration Act*.[92] The interest may be suspended if a review decision is not rendered within thirty (30) days of the application or within the time prescribed for the applicant to submit observations or documents.[93] In addition, the TAQ may, when it renders its decision on the challenge of a monetary administrative penalty, rule on the interest incurred during the length of the recourse.[94]

The government has many ways of ensuring that a monetary administrative penalty is paid. For example, section 115.50 states that the directors and officers of a legal person are solidarily liable, with the legal person, for the payment of the monetary administrative penalty. They can exonerate themselves of this responsibility by establishing that they have exercised due care and diligence to prevent the failure that led to the claim. Here we are dealing with a sort of defence of due diligence in civil proceedings. This is referred to as "exercising due care and diligence." Exercising due care and diligence should relate not to the non-payment of the penalty but to the prevention of the violation that led to the penalty.

To ensure payment of the penalty, the government also has a legal hypothec on the payer's movable and immovable property.[95] The legislation also provides that the debtor and the minister may enter into a payment agreement with regard to the amount owing, and also that such an agreement or the payment owing, does not constitute an acknowledgement of the facts giving rise to the penalty.[96]

If the amount owing is not paid in its entirety or the payment agreement is not adhered to, the minister may issue a recovery certificate upon the expiry of any of the following periods:

(i) the time for applying for a review of the decision;
(ii) the period for contesting the decision before the TAQ; or
(iii) thirty (30) days following the TAQ's final decision.[97]

The minister may even issue a recovery certificate before the expiry of these periods if he or she deems that the debtor is attempting to evade payment.[98] Once a recovery certificate has been issued, any refund owed to the debtor by the Minister of Revenue may be withheld.[99] This process was designed to facilitate the collection of monetary administrative penalties as well as any other amounts owing to the minister under the *Environment Quality Act* and its regulations.[100]

In addition, the minister may file his recovery certificate at the office of the competent court, together with a copy of the final decision stating the amount of the debt, which makes the certificate enforceable as if it were a final judgment of that court.[101] The debtor is also required to pay a recovery charge in the cases, under the conditions and in the amount determined by ministerial order.[102] Finally, the minister may delegate to another department or body its powers relating to the recovery of an amount owing.[103]

## Multiple Administrative Monetary Penalties and Criminal Penalties

One of the most controversial aspects of Bill 89 involves multiple monetary administrative penalties and criminal penalties. This means that the MDDEP may, when there is a violation of the *Environment Quality Act*, claim from the offender a monetary administrative penalty followed by a criminal penalty for the same violation. The legislation thus provides that a person could, therefore, be penalized twice for the same violation, albeit in different forms. However, section 115.14 states that no monetary administrative penalty may be imposed if a statement of offence was served for failure to comply with the same provision of the *Environment Quality Act* on the same day, based on the same facts.

The concept of penalizing the same person twice for the same violation goes against the rules that usually apply when sentencing an individual. This important rule was recognized by the Supreme Court of Canada in the *Kienapple* case.[104] It is a rule that is now entrenched in the Constitution and protected in subsection 11(h) of the *Canadian Charter of Rights and Freedoms*[105] and section 37.1 of the *Charter of Human Rights and Freedoms*.[106]

The appropriateness of allowing a double penalty for a violation of the *Environment Quality Act* seems quite debatable. Indeed, one might wonder why the government would bring criminal proceedings against people it has already chosen to penalize administratively. After all, a penalty is a penalty. Furthermore, this type of legislation is not common in the environmental laws of other provinces and at the federal level. In fact, double penalties for the same violation are prohibited under section 41 of the *Marine Transportation Security Act*,[107] section 233 of the *Canada Shipping Act, 2001*,[108] section 237(3) of the *Environmental Protection Enhancement Act* of Alberta,[109] section 115(8) of the *Environmental Management Act* of British Columbia,[110] section 31(8) of the *Clean Air Act* of New Brunswick,[111] and section 13(1) of the *Environmental Violations Administrative Monetary Penalties Act*.[112] Only Ontario allows for criminal proceedings to be taken even when a person has already been subjected to an administrative penalty.[113]

It must be said that deterrence is also a relevant consideration for determining a criminal sentence,[114] and that a return to compliance may be achieved through the implicit threats of the notice of non-compliance process. Finally, aside from the dual conviction aspect, which seems debatable to us, the management of evidence produced during review or before the TAQ is an issue that will also need to be addressed.

## Conclusion

The monetary administrative penalties regime, which was adopted to facilitate the enforcement of the *Environment Quality Act*, has raised serious concerns, particularly with regard to respect for human rights and freedoms. This regime, undoubtedly, allows violators to be penalized more quickly and generates more money for the Green Fund. In this sense, it is a sort of accelerated eco-justice. But does this form of eco-justice comply with the standards of our rules of justice?

By implementing a universal regime, that is, a monetary administrative penalty regime that applies to all of the provisions of the *Environment Quality Act* parallel to the criminal penalties that apply to the same provisions, the National Assembly has, in the same law, enacted two regimes that aim to impose penalties on anyone who violates the *Environment Quality Act* and its regulations, even though the monetary administrative penalty regime seems primarily aimed at certain specific objectives. Although it does not impose prison sentences, the monetary administrative penalty regime is likely to have a significant impact on persons who could then be penalized without enjoying all the rights that normally apply when the government seeks to punish someone who violated the law.

### NOTES

1 Bill 89, *Act to amend the Environment Quality Act in order to reinforce compliance*, 2d Sess, 39th Leg, Quebec, 2011 (assented to 5 October 2011), SQ 2011, c 20 [Bill 89]. Bill n° 102, *An Act to Amend the Environment Quality Act to Modernize the Environmental Authorization Scheme and to Amend Other Legislative Provisions, in Particular to Reform the Governance of the Green Fund*, was passed in 2017 and will come into force on March 23, 2018. The bill will substantially change Quebec's environmental authorization scheme. It also introduces changes to penalties and sanctions. An overview of the amendments is available online: <http://blg.com/en/News-And-Publications/Publication_4884>. There appear to be major incoming changes relating to the issues raised in this chapter.

2 RSQ 1978, c Q-2 [*EQA*].

3 Quebec, National Assembly, Committee on Transport and the Environment, "Bill 89: An Act to amend the Environment Quality Act in order to reinforce compliance" (2011) 42:8 Journal des débats de la Commission des transports et de l'environnement.

4 Quebec, National Assembly, Committee on Transport and the Environment, "Bill 89: An Act to amend the Environment Quality Act in order to reinforce compliance" (Wednesday, 4 May 2011, 3:17 pm) 42:6 Journal des débats de la Commission des transports et de l'environnement.

5 Josette Rey-Debove & Alain Rey, Directors, *Le Nouveau Petit Robert* (Paris: Dictionnaires Le Robert, 1996) at 1624.

6 *Ibid* at 2031.

7 *EQA*, *supra* note 2, ss 115.13–115.28 and 118.5.1.

8 *Ibid*, ss 115.23–115.27.

9 *Environmental Management Act*, SBC 2003, c 53, ss 115 & 119 [*EMA*, BC]; *Environment Protection Act*, RSO 1990, c E.19, ss 14, 93 & 182.1 [*EPA*, Ont]; *Clean Air Act*, SNB 1997, c C-5.2, s 31 [*CAA*, NB]; *Environmental Protection and Enhancement Act*, RSA 2000, c E-12, ss 2 & 237 [*EPEA*, Alb]; *Environmental Management and Protection Act*, RSS 2010, c E-10.22, s 88 [*EMPA*, Sask]; *Marine Transportation Security Act*, SC 1994, c 40, ss 32–41 & 51 [*MTSA*]; *Canada Shipping Act*, SC 2001, c 26, ss 228–232.2 and 244 [*CSA*]; *Canada Environmental Protection Act*, SC 1999, c 33, ss 280, 280.1 and 330 [*CEPA*]; *Environmental Violations Administrative Monetary Penalties Act*, SC 2009, c 14, ss 126 and 5 [*EVAMPA*].

10 *EQA*, *supra* note 2, s 115.27; Bill 89, *supra* note 1, s 61.

11 This term appears for the first time in s 115.13 of the *EQA*. It is systematically used to designate violations of the law subject to an administrative monetary penalty.

12 *EQA*, *supra* note 2, ss 115.31–115.32 and 115.34–115.35.

13 Government of Alberta, "Annual and Quarterly Reports" (Environment and Parks Alberta, accessed 2 February 2018), online: <http://aep.alberta.ca/about-us/compliance-assurance-program/environmental-protection-commission-reports/annual-and-quarterly-reports.aspx>; Government of New Brunswick, "Environment and Local Government – New Brunswick's *Clean Air Act* – Public Register Information" (accessed 2 February 2018), online: <http://www2.gnb.ca/content/gnb/en/departments/elg/environment/content/air_quality/clean_air/public_register_information.html>.

14 Government of Ontario, "Environmental Penalty Annual Report" (accessed 2 February 2018), online: <https://www.ontario.ca/data/environmental-penalty-annual-report>.

15 *Environmental Penalties*, O Reg 222/07, Table 1: This table identifies 115 industrial establishments subject to Ontario's monetary administrative penalty regime.

16 *Ibid*, Tables 2 and 3.

17 *Ibid*, ss 6–18.

18 *Ibid*, s 18; *EPA*, Ont, *supra* note 9, ss 182.1(9)–(10); *EMA*, BC, *supra* note 9, ss 115(4)–(7).

19 *Environmental Penalties*, *supra* note 15, s 17.

20 *Ibid*, s 16.

21 *CSA*, *supra* note 9, s 229(1)(a).

22 *Canadian Charter of Rights and Freedoms*, part I of the *Constitution Act, 1982* attached as Appendix B of the *Canada Act, 1982* (UK), 1982, c 11 and *Charter of Human Rights and Freedoms*, RSQ, c C-12.

23 Robert Daigneault, "Réforme des sanctions environnementales au Québec : droit pénal dérivé ou une dérive du droit pénal ?" in *Service de la formation continue du Barreau du Québec, Développements récents en droit de l'environnement 2010* (Cowansville: Yvon Blais, 2010) vol 329, EYB-2010DEV731 (REJB). See also Marie-Claude Bellemare & Jan-Martin Leblanc, "La Loi sur la qualité de l'environnement et les sanctions administratives pécuniaires: Où en sommes nous" in *Droit de l'environnement*, vol 18 (Cowansville : Yvon Blais, 2013) 1–72.

24 This is also a characteristic that was invoked by the Supreme Court of Canada to allow the admissibility as evidence, for the prosecution, of reports provided by fishermen to the Department of Fisheries and Oceans: *R v Fitzpatrick*, [1995] 4 SCR 154.

25 [1987] 2 SCR 541 [*Wigglesworth*]. See also: *Cartaway Resources Corp (Re)*, [2004] 1 SCR 672; *Lavallée v Alberta (Securities Commission)*, 2009 ABQB 17; and *United States Steel Corporation v AG Canada*, 2011 FCA 176.

26 *Supra* note 22.

27 Wigglesworth, *supra* note 25 at 560.

28 *EQA*, *supra* note 2, s 126.

29 *Ontario v Canadian Pacific Ltd*, [1995] 2 SCR 1028. See also *114957 Canada Ltd. (Spraytech, Société d'arrosage) v. Hudson (City of)*, [2001] 2 SCR 241.
30 *EQA*, *supra* note 2, s 20, c 2 in fine.
31 Yvon Duplessis, Jean C Hétu & Jean Piette, *La protection juridique de l'environnement au Québec* (Montreal: Thémis, 1982) at 49–50.
32 *Martineau v MRN*, [2004] 3 SCR 737.
33 *Ibid* at para 24.
34 *EQA*, *supra* note 2, s 115.21, c 2.
35 *Ibid*, s 115.46
36 *Ibid*, s. 115.21.
37 *Supra* note 32 at para 63.
38 RSC 1970, c C-40, s 124.
39 *EQA*, *supra* note 2, ss 118.5.1–118.5.2.
40 *Ibid*, s 118.5.3.
41 *Wigglesworth*, *supra* note 25 at 561.
42 RSQ 1999, c M-30.001, ss 15.4 (5.1) and (6).
43 Ministère du développement durable, de l'environnement et des parcs du Québec, Centre de contrôle environnemental, *Cadre général d'application des sanctions administratives pécuniaires* (s 115.13 of the Environmental Quality Act) (2012, accessed 2 February 2018), online: <http://www.mddelcc.gouv.qc.ca/lqe/renforcement/cadre-application-SAP.pdf).
44 Ministère du développement durable, de l'environnement et des parcs du Québec, Centre de contrôle environnemental, *Directive sur le traitement des manquement à la législation environnementale* (2012, accessed 2 February 2018), online: <http://www.mddelcc.gouv.qc.ca/publications/2012/env20120309.htm>.
45 Government of Ontario, "Guideline for Implementing Environmental Penalties (Ontario Regulations 222/07 and 223/07)" (2007, accessed 2 February 2018), online: <https://www.ontario.ca/page/guideline-implementing-environmental-penalties-ontario-regulations-22207-and-22307>; Government of British Columbia, Ministry of Attorney General, Administrative of justice, "Administrative Monetary Penalties: A Framework for Earlier and More Effective Regulatory Compliance – A Discussion Paper" (accessed 2 February 2018), online: <https://www2.gov.bc.ca/assets/gov/law-crime-and-justice/about-bc-justice-system/mediation/research-publications/admin-monetary-penalties.pdf >.
46 Environment Canada, "Administrative Monetary Penalty System – Consultation Document" (accessed 2 February 2018), online: <http://www.ec.gc.ca/alef-ewe/default.asp?lang=En&n=465314E0-1>; Environment Canada, "Canadian Environmental Protection Act: compliance and enforcement policy" (accessed 2 February 2018), online: <https://www.canada.ca/en/environment-climate-change/services/canadian-environmental-protection-act-registry/publications/compliance-enforcement-policy.html>; Government of Canada, "Compliance and Enforcement Policy for the Habitat Protection and Pollution Prevention Provisions of the Fisheries Act" (accessed 2 February 2018), online: <https://www.canada.ca/en/environment-climate-change/services/environmental-enforcement/publications/compliance-enforcement-policy-fisheries-act.html>.
47 *EQA*, *supra* note 2, s 115.15.
48 *Ibid*, s 115.13, c 2(5).
49 *Environment Penalties*, *supra* note 15, s 5; *EMPA*, Sask, *supra* note 9, s 88(2); *CAA*, NB, *supra* note 9, s 31(3).
50 *Administrative Justice Act*, RSQ 1996, c J-3, s 2 [*AJA*].
51 *Ibid*, s 4.
52 *EQA*, *supra* note 2, s 115.16.
53 *Ibid*, s 115.48.
54 *Ibid*, s 115.22.
55 RSQ 2001, c A-6.002. [*TAA*].
56 *EQA*, *supra* note 2, s 115.20, c 2.
57 *Ibid*, s 115.49, c 2.
58 *Supra* note 43 at 4.
59 *Ibid*.
60 In *R v Wholesale Travel Group Inc*, [1991] 3 SCR 154, the Supreme Court of Canada ruled that reversing the burden of proof in a case involving a strict liability offence violates s 11(d) of the *Canadian Charter of Rights and Freedoms* because it goes

against the presumption of innocence, which is constitutionally protected, but the court deemed that infringing upon the presumption of innocence is justified in the context of a free and democratic society as set forth in s 1 of the *Charter*.

61 EQA, *supra* note 2, s 115.17.

62 *Ibid*, s 115.18.

63 Cabinet du ministre du Développement durable, de l'Environnement et des Parcs du Québec, Press Release, "Application de la Loi sur la qualité de l'environnement – Mise en place du bureau de réexamen des sanctions administratives pécuniaires" (1 February 2012, accessed 2 February 2018), online: <http://www.mddep.gouv.qc.ca/Infuseur/communique.asp?no=2035>.

64 EQA, *supra* note 2, s 115.19; AJA, *supra* note 50, s 4(2).

65 In criminal matters, the disclosure of evidence to the defendant is mandatory: see *R v Stinchcombe*, [1991] 3 SCR 326.

66 EQA, *supra* note 2, s 115.19.

67 *Ibid*.

68 An amount of $250, $500, $1,000, or $2,000 for a natural person and $1,000, $2,500, $5,000, or $10,000 for a body corporate or municipality based on the classification of the "failure" of which the litigant is accused. EQA, *supra* note 2, ss 115.23–115.26.

69 EQA, *supra* note 2, s 115.20, c 1.

70 AJA, *supra* note 50, ss 4(3) and 8.

71 EQA, *supra* note 2, s 115.20, c 2.

72 *Ibid*, s 115.49.

73 *Ibid*, s 96.

74 AJA, *supra* note 50, ss 128–142.

75 See also: *9007-5193 Québec inc v Québec (Ministre de l'Environnement)*, 2006 QCCS 4527, J Carol Cohen (Request for suspension of upheld enforcement (CA, 2006-11-17), 500-09-017036-062. Appeal denied (CA, 2007-05-10)); *Ferme René Gagnon, senc v Tribunal administratif du Québec*, 2006 QCCS 968, J Michel Richard; *Girard v Tribunal administratif du Québec, Section du territoire et de l'environnement*, JE 2001-1282, J Michael Sheehan (CQ); *Les atocas de l'érables inc v AG*, 2012 QCCS 912, 9047-4784; *Québec inc v Béchard*, 2007 QCCS 710, J Luc Lefebvre (out-of-court settlement); *AG v Aliments Breton inc*, 2008 QCCQ 4715, J Sylvie Marcotte; AG v Produits JCV inc, JE 95-1943, J Denis R Lanctôt (CQ); *AG v Ultramar Canada inc*, JE 98-745, J Jean-Yves Tremblay (CQ).

76 V, *supra* note 50, s 114, c 1.

77 EPA, Ont, *supra* note 9.

78 *Environmental Penalties*, *supra* note 15, ss 16–18. See also EVAMPA, *supra* note 9, s 11.

79 *R v Sault Ste-Marie*, [1978] 2 SCR 1299 [*Sault Ste-Marie*].

80 See also: *Pillar Oilfield Projects Ltd v R*, [1993] TCJ No 764; *Whistler Mountain Ski Corp v British Columbia (Liquor Control & Licensing Branch)*, 2002 BCCA 426; *504174 NB Ltd v New Brunswick (Minister of Public Safety)*, 2005 NBCA 18; *Consolidated Canadian Contractors Inc v Canada*, [1999] 1 FC 209; *Installations électriques Aubert inc v Corp des maîtres électriciens du Québec* (1985) DTE 85T-671 (CA) at 5.

81 *Sault Ste-Marie*, *supra* note 79 at 1326.

82 *R v Chapin*, [1979] 2 SCR 121.

83 Paule Halley, *Le droit pénal de l'environnement: l'interdiction de polluer* (Cowansville, Yvon Blais, 2001) at 242–260.

84 *Lévis (City of) v Tétreault; Lévis (City of) v 2629-4470 Québec Inc*, [2006] 1 SCR 420.

85 *AG of Quebec v Allard*, JE 2001-401.

86 *Supra* note 29.

87 Contrary to Ontario and Alberta, where regulations allow for modulation of the penalty due to the facts and circumstances surrounding the violation. See: *Environmental Penalties*, *supra* note 15, ss 7–18; *Administrative Penalty Regulation*, Alta Reg 23/2003, s 3.

88 *Administrative Penalty Regulation*, *ibid*, s 3(3); CAA, NB, *supra* note 9, s 31(5).

89 EPA, Ont, *supra* note 9, s 182.1(5).

90 EQA, *supra* note 2, s 115.22.

91 *Ibid*, s 115.48.

92 TAA, *supra* note 55.

93 EQA, *supra* note 2, s 115.20, c 2.

94 *Ibid*, s 115.49, c 2.

95 *Ibid*, s 115.51.
96 *Ibid*, s 115.52.
97 *Ibid*, s 115.53.
98 *Ibid*, s 115.53, c 2.
99 *Ibid*, s 115.54.
100 For example, *ibid*, ss 115.01 and 115.1 and the *Règlement sur la redevance exigible pour l'utilisation de l'eau*, RRQ 1981, c Q-2, r 42.1.
101 *EQA*, *supra* note 2, s 115.55.
102 *Ibid*, s 115.56.
103 *Ibid*, s 115.57.
104 *Kienapple v R*, [1975] 1 SCR 729.
105 *Supra* note 22.
106 *Ibid*.
107 *MTSA*, *supra* note 9.
108 *CSA*, *supra* note 9.
109 *EPEA*, Alb, *supra* note 9.
110 *EMA*, BC, *supra* note 9.
111 *CAA*, NB, *supra* note 9.
112 *EVAMPA*, *supra* note 9, s 126.
113 *EPA*, Ont, *supra* note 9, s 182.1(11).
114 *R v Kenaston Drilling (Arctic) Ltd* (1973), 12 CCC (2d) 383 (NWTSC); *AG v Laidlaw Environmental Services (Mercier)*, JE 98-117 (SC) at 13; *R v United Keno Hill Mines Ltd* (1980) 10 CELR 43 (Y Terr Ct).

# 26

# Creative Sentencing in Environmental Prosecutions, the Canadian Experience: An Overview

JOHN D. CLIFFE, Q.C.*

## Background

For obvious reasons the most important hearing in a criminal prosecution is sentencing. The same is true in an environmental prosecution.

Coming clearly from the Supreme Court of Canada is the signal to the trial courts that sentencing offenders for violations of environmental statutes must be taken seriously.[1]

The Supreme Court of Canada has described the prevention of pollution of our lakes, rivers, and streams as a matter of "great public concern."[2] It has also stated that protection of the environment has "emerged as a fundamental value in Canadian society."[3] In *Reference Re Section 94(2)*, the majority of the Supreme Court of Canada, in its analysis of the constitutionality of a provision of the British Columbia *Motor Vehicle Act*, stated that "[i]ndeed, the public interest as regards 'air and water pollution offences' requires that the guilty be dealt with firmly."[4]

In *R. v. Vac Daniels Ltd.*, the Nova Scotia Court of Appeal, hearing sentence appeals by a corporate offender and its president upon their convictions under the provincial *Environmental Protection Act*, acknowledged the seriousness of violating such legislation, and stated: "Violations of rules for the

* *Given that my paper is an overview, I will base my comments upon my experience with creative sentencing in cases heard in the courts of British Columbia, Yukon, the Northwest Territories, and Nunavut. I will also reference some federal environmental legislation.*

protection of the environment strike at the interests of all individuals and call for strongly deterrent penalties."[5]

In *R. v. Terroco Industries Ltd.*, the Alberta Court of Appeal considered a sentence appeal by a corporate offender in relation to a release of chlorine gas from a truck hauling liquid chemicals and stated that "sentencing principles for environmental offences require 'a special approach.'"[6]

Accordingly, both Crown counsel and defence counsel should be familiar with the sentence or penalty provisions in the applicable environmental legislation, and especially the so-called "creative sentence" sections contained therein as well as other "creative" options. I pause to note that not all environmental legislation has creative sentence options.

Counsel should also be familiar with the relevant principles of and factors relating to sentencing set out in the common law and the applicable legislation.[7]

The courts have stated many times that deterrence is the paramount principle of sentencing in prosecutions of environmental offences. In *Terroco*, the Alberta Court of Appeal stated that "[a] key component of sentences imposed for breaches of environmental protection statutes should be specific and general deterrence."[8]

In addition counsel should be aware of different approaches to sentencing depending upon where the offence occurred and the nature of the environment impacted or potentially impacted by the offence. The courts in northern Canada have adopted such an approach.[9]

In *R. v. City of Iqaluit*, the court sentenced a municipal government for release of untreated sewage into arctic marine waters, and stated:

> Experience has shown that damage to an arctic environment is easier to prevent, than it is to repair. All of these circumstances suggest that the commission of an environmental offence in the arctic region should attract severe penalties, penalties commensurate not only with the elevated risk of environmental damage, but with the high costs associated with rehabilitation of the affected areas.
>
> In Nunavut, corporate citizens who knowingly engage in activities that have the potential to cause damage to an arctic environment are "stewards" of the lands and waters upon which they operate. They have a duty when undertaking such a venture to exercise a high standard of care. This duty is owed to the many Inuit and non-Inuit residents who stand to be directly affected by the damage or destruction of wildlife or marine habitat.[10]

Other principles and factors relevant to sentencing environmental offenders include but are not limited to the maximum penalty provided for in the applicable legislation, the purpose of the legislation, criminality of conduct, culpability, resulting damage to the environment, the potential for damage to the environment, cleanup and remediation of the affected environment, timing of reporting to government authorities, cooperation with government investigators, acceptance of responsibility, genuineness of remorse, the standard of care required in the instant case, extent of attempts to comply with the applicable legislation, prior record of conviction and compliance, profit or benefit realized by the offence, financial worth of the offender and, in the case of a corporation, its size, and parity.[11]

## "Creative Sentencing" Defined

Creative sentencing, in the context of environmental prosecutions, refers to a sentence or that part of a sentence imposed upon an offender that does not include a fine or imprisonment. In this regard, the following is relevant.

Since the late 1980s, sentence provisions in environmental legislation have been amended to include an array of so called "creative sentence" options. Common to most legislative creative sentence schemes is the option for the court, in addition to any other punishment imposed, to make orders of prohibition, direction or requirement, upon having regard to the nature of the offence and the circumstances surrounding its commission.

In addition, the *Criminal Code* has been amended to permit the making of probation orders in the case of offending corporation.[12] Pursuant to subsection 34(2) of the *Interpretation Act*, the provisions of the *Criminal Code* in relation to probation orders are applicable to federal environmental legislation unless otherwise stated in that legislation.

Further, Crown counsel and defence counsel are thinking more creatively with respect to what should be an appropriate sentence disposition in any given case.

Finally, the imposition of a creative sentence is not something new. However, it was not often done prior to the aforementioned legislative changes.

## Before the Current Creative Sentence Provisions

Generally, prior to the enactment of the creative sentence provisions now found in many federal environmental protection statutes, penalties were traditional ones, namely fines and imprisonment.[13] A sentence of imprisonment was rarely resorted to, and as a result fines tended to be the most common disposition.

With respect to federal legislation, probation for corporate offenders was not available given the wording of the *Criminal Code* at the time.[14]

As stated above, creative sentencing provisions were few and of limited application, an example of which was subsection 41(2) of the *Fisheries Act* (formerly subsection 33(7)), now repealed and replaced by section 79.2, which gave a court discretion to make an order to refrain or take action in addition to any other penalty imposed by it.[15] The provision stated in part:

> ... the court may ... order that person to refrain from committing the activity that constitutes the offence or to cease to carry on any activity specified in the order the carrying on of which, in the opinion of the court, will or is likely to result in the commission of a further offence *or take such action specified in the order as, in the opinion of the court, will or is likely to prevent the commission of a further offence.* [Emphasis added.]

There are not many examples of this provision being used. In *R. v. Canadian Marine Drilling*, Bourassa T.C.J. described the section as being "virtually unused" but a "potentially far-reaching and effective sentencing tool."[16] Bourassa T.C.J. interpreted the scope of the section and stated:

> ... through this section, a convicting court may intervene in the internal and external operations of a corporation. In fact, it may be able to pierce the corporate veil in significant way if, "in the opinion of the court, [its actions] will or [are] likely to prevent the commission of any further offence".
>
> In proper circumstances, this section may perhaps be used for orders such as restitution, compensation, affirmative action, clean-up or even an order to a defendant to restock a body of water with fish, all, of course, provided that the order prevents or will likely prevent further offence by the defendant. It would appear to me that such an order making a defendant liable financially for damage wrought as a result of its activities could have a significant and positive effect as a deterrent.[17]

I note that the court's above words in *Canadian Marine Drilling* foreshadowed the use of the creative sentence provisions now contained in many federal and provincial environmental protections statutes that became law in the late 1980s, early 1990s, and thereafter.

Having perhaps a cynical view of the effect of a fine, and a desire that sentences in environmental prosecutions be more meaningful, some Crown counsel and defence counsel in British Columbia began to convince the courts to use this provision creatively, although some say in a "tortured" fashion, to make orders, for example: to construct road ditching and a settlement pond, to hydro-seed, remove log jams, and to rip rap;[18] construct a compliant wood treatment dip tank at a sawmill;[19] pay monies for an environmental enhancement program to restore fish populations, implement a fish tagging program, and improve fish habitat;[20] make improvements to a fuel tank farm;[21] remove 200 metres of track and do environment enhancement work;[22] pay monies to Fisheries and Oceans Canada for use in the management and operation of a salmon enhancement hatchery operated by members of a First Nation;[23] and pay monies to a non-profit organization operating a salmon hatchery.[24]

Subsection 41(2) (formerly subsection 33(8)) of the *Fisheries Act* was applied by the courts elsewhere in Canada.[25] Notwithstanding some use by the courts of this provision, most sentences for convictions under the fish habitat protection and pollution prevention part of the *Fisheries Act* remained fines imposed upon corporate offenders.

## The Scope of Creative Sentencing

With respect to sentencing under federal environmental legislation, the scope of creative sentencing is broad, often permitting sentences that embrace a number of penalties, including court orders,[26] additional fines to compensate for accrued monetary benefits resulting from the offence,[27] cancellation of permits and licences and prohibition of application for same,[28] and forfeiture of seized property.[29]

I will focus on court orders that are effective creative sentence options for a number of reasons.

Firstly, specific provisions like those cited above provide numerous options for ordered prohibition, direction, and requirement. For example, the sentencing court may order prohibition of any activity that could continue or repeat the offence; direct the offender to take action to remedy or avoid environmental harm resulting from the offence; direct the offender to conduct environmental monitoring; direct publication of the circumstances of the offence; direct payment of money to the government or any person as compensation for costs of remediation and preventive action incurred by the government; direct payment of compensation; require the offender to surrender permits or authorizations; prohibit the offender from applying for such permits or authorizations; direct community service be performed; direct payment of money to the government for promoting environmental protection and conservation; direct the offender to pay money for scholarships for students enrolled in environmental studies; and direct the offender to post a bond to ensure compliance with orders made.

Secondly, such provisions usually contain a "basket order" requiring the offender to comply with "any other conditions that the court considers appropriate" to ensure the good conduct of the offender, and to deter the offender from committing further offences.[30] Accordingly, counsel and the court are not unduly restricted in their consideration as to what should be an appropriate order or orders.

Thirdly, unless provided otherwise in the legislation, such orders do not have a financial limit.[31] Accordingly, the offender's expenditure upon compliance with the order could exceed the maximum legislated fine.[32]

Fourthly, such orders can be varied by the court, and accordingly there is flexibility. In this regard, it is common, but not universal, that the enabling legislation has provisions for either or both the Crown and the offender to make application to the court to vary the order made because of a change in circumstances.[33] Variation may include changes in the order, relieving the person bound by the order of further compliance with it, or extending or decreasing the term of the order.

In *R. v. City of Dawson*, an application jointly by the Crown and the offender pursuant to section 79.5 of the *Fisheries Act* to vary an order made under section 79.2 of the *Fisheries Act* requiring construction of a sewage treatment plant was granted and the term of the order extended in view of significantly higher capital costs, an increase in the projected annual operating and maintenance costs of the proposed plant, and a change in the financial circumstances of the City.[34]

Fifthly, such orders are enforceable. In this regard, it is common, but not always universal, that the enabling legislation has created an offence for non-compliance with a creative sentence order made under the legislation.[35] In the absence of such a provision, resort can be made to section 126 of the *Criminal Code*, which creates an offence for disobeying a lawful order made by a court other than an order to pay money.

Finally, as stated above, the probation provisions of the *Criminal Code* are applicable to proceedings under federal environmental legislation unless otherwise stated in the applicable statute. As a result, if the governing environmental legislation does not contain creative sentencing provisions such as the above-mentioned court orders, counsel and the courts may consider the use of a probation order to facilitate a creative sentence.[36]

Like creative sentence court orders, probation orders are subject to being varied by the court upon application by the Crown or the offender.[37] Probation orders are enforceable by way of prosecution for breach of the order pursuant to section 733.1 of the *Criminal Code*.

Some examples of court orders made under creative sentence provisions include:

- orders made pursuant to section 664.1 of the *Canada Shipping Act* (the predecessor to section 193 of the *Canada Shipping Act, 2001*) to pay monies to Environment Canada to research and study the conservation and protection of marine birds and habitat;[38]
- orders made pursuant to section 291 of the *Canadian Environmental Protection Act, 1999* to pay monies to Environment Canada to be spent on research into the effects of marine pollutants on birds to be conducted at the university level;[39]
- orders made pursuant to section 79.2 of the *Fisheries Act* to construct and operate a sewage treatment plant whose effluent meets the requirements of section 36(3) of the *Fisheries Act*;[40]
- construct and operate an effluent treatment plant, file with the court an irrevocable letter of guarantee in the sum of $500,000 to ensure such construction, pay monies for environmental improvement purposes, and fund a scholarship in resources technology and environmental science;[41]
- pay monies to Fisheries and Oceans Canada to promote the conservation and protection of fish and fish habitat;[42]
- pay monies to Fisheries and Oceans Canada to fund a river restoration project and a classroom fish incubation facility at a local school;[43]
- pay monies to Fisheries and Oceans Canada to be spent at the direction of their community adviser for a storm drain marking program and to enhance riparian vegetation along a local creek;[44]
- remove a boulder pile from an intertidal zone, plant salt marsh vegetation, and pay monies to Fisheries and Oceans Canada for use in fish and fish habitat conservation and protection projects;[45]
- pay monies to Fisheries and Oceans Canada for the purposes of conservation, protection, and enhancement of fish and fish habitat;[46]

- re-vegetate an impacted stream bank, conduct an assessment of a pollution control centre alarm system, and pay monies to Fisheries and Oceans Canada for the purposes of conservation, protection, and enhancement of fish and fish habitat in a local watershed;[47]
- remove crushed rock from the foreshore under the supervision of a qualified person and pay monies to Fisheries and Oceans Canada for the purposes of conservation and protection of fish and fish habitat at a local lake;[48]
- orders made pursuant to section 16 of the *Migratory Birds Convention Act, 1994* to pay monies to Environment Canada to acquire oiled bird rehabilitation equipment, to develop and present training on oiled bird rehabilitation, and fund research concerning oiled birds;[49]
- pay monies to Environment Canada for the conservation and protection of migratory birds;[50]
- orders made pursuant to subsection 22(6) of the *Wild Animal and Plant Protection and Regulation of International and Interprovincial Trade Act* to pay monies to TRAFFIC of the World Wildlife Fund (WWF) Canada for the operation of its wildlife trade monitoring network;[51]
- pay monies to further plant and animal DNA research;[52] and
- pay monies to Environment Canada for public education purposes and to a local aquarium for compensation for expenditures to care for the animals seized.[53]

## Related Creative Options

Two options that may be considered as "distant relatives" to creative sentencing are worth comment.

Firstly, although uncommon, are works or actions completed by the offender after being charged but before sentence is imposed that would have been the equivalent of conditions of a creative sentence court order. The intention here is that at the sentence hearing, defence counsel makes submissions to the court to the effect that such works or actions are really part of sentence and therefore penalty, usually a fine, should be mitigated. This option is relevant in the case of a prosecution under an environmental statute that does not contain creative sentence provisions.[54]

Secondly, an alternative measures/diversion agreement can be entered into by consent of the parties or pursuant to legislative provision. With respect to the latter, the *Canadian Environmental Protection Act*[55] and the *Species at Risk Act*[56] provide for alternative measures agreements. It should be noted that section 717 of the *Criminal Code* also provides for such measures.

An alternative measures/diversion agreement is just that; namely, it is an agreement between the Crown and the offender to deal with the offence other than by way of prosecution, or in other words "out of court."

Whether entered into between the Crown and the offender by consent or pursuant to the aforementioned legislation, such agreements generally are in writing and include an acknowledgement of responsibility for the offence by the offender and various conditions, including remediation of the impacted environment, changes to operating procedures, and a donation to an environmental community group. In addition, there is usually a condition contained therein that if the offender does not comply with the agreement the prosecution can be reinstated, in the case of an offender entering into such an agreement while charged, or commenced, in the case of an offender who has yet to be charged. It should be noted that such agreements are rare.

## Some Practice Tips

Many of the environmental prosecutions I have handled have ultimately resolved themselves by way of a guilty plea. In many of those cases counsel have made a joint sentence submission in support of a creative sentence based upon an agreed statement of facts.

Whether a creative sentence is the subject of a joint submission or its imposition is contested, counsel must ensure that their respective positions are based on the circumstances of the case and grounded in the principles and factors stated above so that the court can be guided to a reasonable sentence disposition.

With respect to creative sentencing, and in particular court orders, I recommend the following:

(1) Counsel should thoroughly research the available creative sentence options;
(2) For the Crown, consult the investigators local to the offence and the government technical experts as to what would be an appropriate disposition;
(3) For the defence, consult your client and its experts in the same regard. Don't be shy. Contact the Crown's investigators and experts;
(4) Always keep in mind the circumstances of the offence;

(5) If possible, draft and file an agreed statement of facts;
(6) Proportionality and parity cannot be forgotten;
(7) Consider the ability of the offender to comply with the creative sentence. Can they afford it? Can they comply with it?;
(8) Draft a workable, enforceable, and reasonable court order. Sometimes simple is best!;
(9) Last, but most important, ensure that both counsel are communicating with each other and, if possible, have come to agreement with respect to the form and content of the proposed court order.

## NOTES

1 *R v City of Sault Ste Marie* (1978), 40 CCC (2d) 353 at 374; *Reference Re Section 94(2) of the Motor Vehicle Act* (1986), 23 CCC (3d) 289 at 314; *R v Wholesale Travel Group Inc.* (1991), 67 CCC (3d) 193 at 260; *Ontario v Canadian Pacific Ltd*, [1995] 2 SCR 1031 at para 55; *Attorney General of Canada v Hydro Quebec* (1997), 118 CCC (3d) 97 at 163–164; and *114957 Canada Ltée (Spray Tech, Société d'arrosage) v Town of Hudson et al*, (2001) 2 SCR 241 at 248–249.

2 *City of Sault Ste Marie, supra* note 1 at 374.

3 *Canadian Pacific, supra* note 1 at para 55.

4 *Reference Re Section 94(2), supra* note 1 at para 314.

5 *R v Vac Daniels Ltd* (1997), 23 CELR (NS) 127 at 129.

6 *R v Terroco Industries Ltd*, (2005) 196 CCC (3d) 293 at para 34 [*Terroco*].

7 *R v United Keno Mines Ltd*, (1980) 10 CELR 43 (Y Terr Ct); *R v Cotton Felts Ltd* (1982), 2 CCC (3d) 287; *R v Shamrock Chemicals Ltd and Samuel John Shirley*, unreported decision, Ontario Provincial Offences Court, St Thomas, Ontario, 13 February 1989; *Terroco, supra* note 6; and *R v Northwest Territories Power Corp*, 2011 NWTTC 03. See also the sentencing considerations/factors listed in ss 718, 718.1, 718.2(b), and 718.21 of the *Criminal Code*, RSC 1985, c C-46, and, for example, s 50.91, *Antarctic Environmental Protection Act*, SC 2003, c 20; ss 287 and 287.1, *Canadian Environmental Protection Act, 1999*, SC 1999, c. 33; ss 13(4.1), *Migratory Birds Convention Act*, 1994, SC 1994, c 22; and s 102, *Species at Risk Act*, SC 2002, c 29.

8 *Supra* note 6 at para 53.

9 *R v Kenaston Drilling (Arctic) Ltd*, (1973), 12 CCC (2d) 383 at 386 (NWTSC); *United Keno Hill Mines, supra* note 7 at 47–48; *R v Esso Resources Canada Ltd*, (1983) NWTR 59 at 64; and *R v City of Iqaluit*, unreported decision, File No. 08-01-693, Nunavut Court of Justice, 8 August 2002, at paras 8–10.

10 *City of Iqaluit, supra* note 9 at paras 9–10.

11 *United Keno Hill Mines, supra* note 7 at 47–52; *Shamrock Chemicals, supra* note 7 at 3–9; *Terroco, supra* note 6 at paras 35–65; and *Northwest Territories Power Corporation, supra* note 7 at paras 14–47, 92, 105, and 107.

12 See *Criminal Code*, RSC 1985, c C-46, s 732.1(3.1).

13 It should be noted that some provincial/territorial *offence* legislation did provide for collateral orders, including probation, to be made upon sentencing; *Shamrock Chemicals, supra* note 7 at 13–14.

14 *Her Majesty the Queen v Echo Bay Mines Ltd*, Memorandum of Judgment, Appeal #545, Court of Appeal of the Northwest Territories, 11 March 1985; *R v Mainland Sawmills Ltd*, unreported decision, File

# 11016C, Vancouver Registry, Provincial Court of British Columbia, 7 September 1990. Although I have been advised that there were some exceptions by consent of the parties in cases decided in the Territorial Court of Yukon.

15 This provision was applicable to the deleterious substance and destruction of fish habitat prohibitions contained in the *Fisheries Act*, RSC 1985, c F-14.

16 *R v Canadian Marine Drilling Ltd*, [1984] NWTR 48 at para 55.

17 *Ibid.*

18 *R v Jackson Bros Logging Co Ltd*, unreported decision, No CC810445, Vancouver Registry, County Court of Vancouver, 6 September 1983.

19 *R v CIP Inc*, unreported decision, File No 12680, Campbell River Registry, Provincial Court of British Columbia, 16 December 1986.

20 *R v MacMillan Bloedel Ltd*, unreported decision, File No 1777, Masset Registry, Provincial Court of British Columbia, 31 May 1989.

21 *R v Shell Canada Products Ltd*, unreported decision, File No 23343, Richmond Registry Provincial Court of British Columbia, 27 June 1989.

22 *R v British Columbia Railway Company and BC Rail*, unreported decision, File No 6339, Squamish Registry, Provincial Court of British Columbia, 25 January 1990.

23 *R v Rivers Inlet Resort Ltd*, entered order, File No 49576T2, Vancouver Registry, Provincial Court of British Columbia, 29 May 1992.

24 *R v District of Surrey*, unreported decision, File No 52955, Surrey Registry, Provincial Court of British Columbia, 13 January 1992.

25 *R v Robinsons' Trucking Ltd*, (1985), 14 CELR 90 (NWTTC) (The offender was ordered to equip all of its tanker trucks with spill response equipment, designate a corporate officer as an on-scene commander for future oil spills, and designate and train an environmental response team.); *R v Enheat Inc*, unreported decision, Amherst, Provincial Court of Nova Scotia, 13 November 1985 (The offender was ordered to submit to the Department of the Environment a management strategy for dealing with spent chemicals and works to be done with respect to its process chemicals and contaminated rinse waters, and to develop procedures with respect to monitoring and reporting for liquid effluents.)

26 See, e.g., *Antarctic Environmental Protection Act*, SC 2003, c 20, s 66; *Canada Shipping Act*, SC 2001, c 26, s 193; *Canadian Environmental Protection Act*, SC 1999, c 33, s 291; *Fisheries Act*, RSC 1985, c F-14, s 79.2; *Migratory Birds Convention Act*, SC 1994, c 22, s 16; *Species at Risk Act*, SC 2002 c 29, s 105; *Transportation of Dangerous Goods Act*, SC 1992, c 34, s 34; and *Wild Animal and Plant Protection and Regulation of International and Interprovincial Trade Act*, SC 1992, c 52, s 22(6).

27 See, e.g., *Antarctic Environmental Protection Act*, SC 2003, c 20, s 50.7; *Canadian Environmental Protection Act*, SC 1999, c 33, s 274.1; *Fisheries Act*, RSC 1985, c F-14, s 79; *Migratory Birds Convention Act*, SC 1994, c 22, s 13(5); and *Species at Risk Act*, SC 2002, c 29, s 97(6).

28 See, e.g.: *Antarctic Environmental Protection Act*, *ibid*, s 66(5); *Canadian Environmental Protection Act*, SC 1999, c 33, s 291(5); *Fisheries Act*, RSC 1985, c F-14, s 79.1; and *Migratory Birds Convention Act*, SC 1994, c 22, s 18.22.

29 See, e.g., *Arctic Waters Pollution Prevention Act*, RSC 1985, c A-12, s 24; *Antarctic Environmental Protection Act*, SC 2003, c 20, ss 41–42; *Canadian Environmental Protection Act*, SC 1999, c 33, ss 230–231; *Fisheries Act*, RSC 1985, c F-14, s 72; *Migratory Birds Convention Act*, SC 1994, c 22, s 14; and *Species at Risk Act*, SC 2002 c 29, s 103.

30 See, e.g., *Antarctic Environmental Protection Act*, SC 2003, c 20, s 66(1)(n); *Canada Shipping Act*, SC 2001, c 26, s 193(e); *Canadian Environmental Protection Act*, SC 1999, c 33, s 291(1)(q);

*Fisheries Act* RSC 1985, c F-14, s 79.2(i); *Migratory Birds Convention Act*, SC 1994, c 22, s 16(1)(h); *Species at Risk Act*, SC 2002 c 29, s 105(k); and *Wild Animal and Plant Protection and Regulation of International and Interprovincial Trade Act*, SC 1992, c 52, s 22(6)(h).

31 See, e.g., *Transportation of Dangerous Goods Act*, SC 1992, c 34, s 34(3), which limits expenditure to $1 million for a single offence in relation to orders made under s 34.

32 *Robinsons' Trucking, supra* note 25 at 93; and *Northwest Territories Power Corp, supra* note 7 at paras 10, 101 and 102.

33 See, e.g., *Antarctic Environmental Protection Act*, SC 2003, c 20, ss 67–68; *Canadian Environmental Protection Act*, SC 1999, c 33, ss 293–294; *Fisheries Act*, RSC 1985, c F-14, s 79.5; and *Migratory Birds Convention Act*, SC 1994, c 22, ss 16(4)–(6). There is no such provision in the *Species at Risk Act, Transportation of Dangerous Goods Act*, or the *Wild Animal and Plant Protection and Regulation of International and Interprovincial Trade Act*.

34 *R v City of Dawson* (2004), 10 CELR (3d) 197 (Y Terr Ct). Further applications to the court pursuant to the *Fisheries Act*, RSC 1985, c F-14, s 79.5 to vary this order were made and granted before compliance with the order was met.

35 See, e.g., *Antarctic Environmental Protection Act*, SC 2003, c 20, s 50(1)(c); *Canadian Environmental Protection Act*, SC 1999, c 33, s 272(1)(j); *Fisheries Act*, RSC 1985, c F-14, s 79.6; *Migratory Birds Convention Act*, SC 1994, c 22, s 13(1)(c); and *Transportation of Dangerous Goods Act*, SC 1992, c 34, s 34(4).

36 See also *Criminal Code*, RSC 1985, c C-46, s 732.1(3)(h) and (3.1)(g), which give the court discretion respectively in the cases of human offenders and organization to prescribe "other reasonable conditions" the court considers desirable.

37 See *Criminal Code*, RSC 1985, c C-46, s 732.2(3).

38 *R v Motor Vessel "Cape Benat,"* unreported decision, File No 131190, Vancouver Registry, Provincial Court of British Columbia, 21 October 2003; and *R v Motor Vessel "Andre,"* unreported decision, File No 47249-1, North Vancouver Registry, Provincial Court of British Columbia, 21 November 2007.

39 *R v Champion Shipping A/S et al*, unreported decision, File No 157673-1, Victoria Registry, Provincial Court of British Columbia, 25 January 2013.

40 *R v City of Dawson* (2003), 50 CELR (NS) 99 (Y Terr Ct).

41 *R v Corner Brook Pulp and Paper Ltd*, entered order, Corner Brook, Provincial Court of Newfoundland, 14 May 1996.

42 *Northwest Territories Power Corp, supra* note 7.

43 *R v City of Dawson et al*, unreported decision, File Nos TC 95-11049 & TC 95-11050, Whitehorse Registry, Territorial Court of Yukon, 19 January 1996.

44 *R v Town of Gibsons*, unreported decision, File No 11797, Sechelt Registry, Provincial Court of British Columbia, 26 November 2001.

45 *R v Vito Ialungo and Vito's Service Ltd*, unreported decision, File No 12961C2, Sechelt Registry, Provincial Court of British Columbia, 17 March 2003.

46 *R v Cameron Logging Ltd*, unreported decision, File No 13040-1, Powell River Registry, Provincial Court of British Columbia, 3 March 2004.

47 *R v District of Kitimat*, unreported decision, File Nos 23306-1 and 23318-1, Terrace Registry, Provincial Court of British Columbia, 7 September 2004.

48 *R v John Seibold, Dennis Levasseur and Imperial Concrete Floors Ltd*, unreported decision, File No 11720, Sechelt Registry, Provincial Court of British Columbia, 23 October 2000.

49 *R v West Coast Reduction Ltd*, unreported decision, File No C35883-01, Vancouver Registry, Provincial Court of British Columbia, 1 October 1998.

50 *R v Neptune Bulk Terminals (Canada) Ltd*, unreported decision, File No 36550, North Vancouver Registry, Provincial Court of British Columbia, 26 March 2001.

51 *R v Yuk Ming Ho*, unreported decision, File No 51252, Richmond Registry, Provincial Court of British Columbia, 11 October 2007.

52 *R v Sun 2006 Import & Export Ltd et al*, unreported decision, File No 202133-1, Vancouver Registry, Provincial Court of British Columbia, 6 December 2010.

53 *R v Kenneth Grant Howard*, unreported decision, File No 144890-1, Surrey Registry, Provincial Court of British Columbia, 25 October 2005.

54 There is some precedent for this option being the matter of *R v Boart Longyear*, unreported decision, Territorial Court of the Northwest Territories, Hay River Registry, a prosecution under the *Northwest Territories Water Act*, SC 1992, c 39, a statute without creative sentence provisions.

55 SC 1999, c 33, ss 295–309.

56 SC 2002, c 29, ss 108–119.

# 27

# Creative Sentencing: The Experience "Down-Under"

SHARON MASCHER

## Introduction

In Australia, the question of how best to sentence an offender convicted of an environmental crime remains a challenge. Commenting on criminal sentencing more generally, Judge Goldring of the New South Wales (NSW) District Court wrote that "sentencing is the most difficult task that faces any judicial officer in the criminal justice process."[1] Reflecting on this comment in the context of sentencing of environmental offences, Justice Pepper of the New South Wales Land and Environment Court remarked, "Indeed, the time I have spent on the bench [...] has done little to convince me otherwise."[2]

The traditional sanction for environmental crimes in Australia is by way of fine. Yet this approach to environmental sentencing continues to be "variously criticised for imposing mainly fines, for imposing fines too light to deter, for imposing penalties not tailored to the offender or the offence and for not reflecting the moral repugnance of the crime."[3] As in other jurisdictions, these criticisms have been met by many Australian legislatures by both increasing maximum monetary penalties and expanding the range of sentencing tools available to the courts.

This chapter looks at the availability of, and practice around, creative sentencing orders relating to environmental offences in Australia, drawing particularly on the sentencing practice in NSW.

## The Prosecution of Environmental Offences

As in Canada, not all alleged environmental offences are prosecuted, with regulators often reserving prosecution for the most serious of breaches.[4]

This approach is reflected in the NSW Environmental Protection Authority (EPA) Prosecution Guidelines, which state that even when there is sufficient evidence, "(a) ... the laying of charges is discretionary, and (b) the dominant factor in the exercise of that discretion is the public interest."[5] The Guidelines also recognize that prosecution may not always be the appropriate response. In keeping with this, the *Protection of the Environment Operations Act 1997* (the *POEO Act*) provides a variety of non-prosecution options.[6] Prosecution, therefore, is used "as part of the EPA's overall strategy for achieving its objectives [...] as a strategic response where it is in the public interest to do so."[7]

## The Sentencing of Environmental Offences

### SENTENCING PURPOSES

When an environmental offence is prosecuted, there are seven overlapping purposes the court must consider in determining an appropriate sentence: punishment; deterrence; community protection; rehabilitation of the offender; making the offender accountable; denunciation; and recognizing the harm inflicted on the victim and the wider community.[8] While all are relevant, in environmental sentencing the utilitarian purpose of achieving deterrence is of particular importance. This is made explicit in the NSW EPA Prosecution Guidelines, which state that "[i]n criminalising breaches of environmental laws a primary, though not the sole, aim of Parliament is deterrence."[9]

### SENTENCING CONSIDERATIONS

However, courts are required to consider a range of factors in coming to a sentencing decision, to ensure that the sentence reflects both the objective seriousness of the offence and the subjective circumstances of the defendant.[10]

In NSW, section 241(1) of the *POEO Act* requires the court to consider the following five factors when imposing a penalty:

- the extent of environmental harm caused or likely to be caused;
- the practical measures taken to prevent, control, abate, or mitigate the harm;
- the reasonable foreseeability of the harm by the person who committed the offence;
- the extent to which the person who committed the offence had control over the causes that resulted in the offence;
- whether in committing the offence, the person was complying with orders from an employer or supervisor.

The court may also take into consideration any other matters it considers relevant,[11] including:[12]

- evenhandedness;
- the principle of totality;
- the principle of proportionality;
- early entry of a plea of guilty;
- lack of prior convictions;
- genuine contrition;
- cooperation with the investigation;
- remedial measures undertaken;
- whether a repeat offence in likely;
- any agreement voluntarily undertaken between the defendant and the regulator for environmental benefit.

## CUSTODIAL SENTENCES AND FINES

Operating as both "the upper limit on the sentencing judge's discretion"[13] and an expression of the legislative view on the "seriousness of criminal conduct,"[14] the maximum penalties available for an offence play a significant role in determining the objective severity of the offence in the sentencing process.[15] In Australia, the maximum penalties for environmental offences have been increased significantly in recent years. In the *POEO Act*, Tier 1 offences (intentional offences) committed wilfully now carry maximum penalties of $5 million for corporations and $1 million and/or seven years' imprisonment for individuals, while Tier 1 offences committed negligently carry a maximum penalty of $2 million for corporations and $500,000 and/or four years' imprisonment for individuals.[16] Strict liability offences carry maximum penalties of $1 million for corporations and $250,000 for individuals, with further daily maximum penalties of $120,000 and $60,000 respectively.[17] And an indivdual who is convicted of polluting water or land or unlawfully transporting or disposing of waste ("the waste offences) who within five years of that conviction commits a separate subsequent waste offence faces the maximum individual strict liability fine and up to two years' imprisonment.[18]

In Australia, the availability of the increasingly higher maximum penalties for environmental offences is explained on the basis of a desire to achieve greater deterrence. So, for example, when the maximum penalties in the *POEO Act* were increased in 2005, the second reading speech introducing the amendment Act emphasized the need to maintain the "original deterrent value" of the penalties.[19] As Lloyd J. of the NSW Land and Environment Court stated in *Director-General of the Department of Environment and Climate Change v. Taylor*:[20]

> … persons will not be deterred from committing environmental offences by nominal fines. There is a need to uphold the integrity of the planning system of protecting and preserving endangered ecological communities. There is a need to send a strong warning to others who might be minded to breach the law that such actions will be visited upon with significant consequences.

In *Bentley v. BGP Properties*,[21] the NSW Land and Environment Court also emphasized that the penalty not only needs to be designed to deter the offender but "must also serve the purpose of general or public deterrence"[22] to others who might otherwise be tempted to commit similar crimes. This is a factor of particular relevance in the context of environmental offences.[23]

However, the courts have also recognized that the concept of proportionality, together with other subjective sentencing considerations, may operate to constrain the purposes of achieving deterrence through sentencing.[24] Justice Bignold captured this sentiment in *Director-General of the Department of Land and Water Conservation v. Robson*, stating: "I am mindful of […] the need for general deterrence and of the need to apply sentencing policy not unfairly (or out of proportion to the gravity of the offence in penalising the Defendant) but in furtherance of the public educative role of the criminal law."[25]

Other sentencing considerations such as evenhandedness, which requires the court to have regard to the general sentencing patterns in judicially relevant cases, may also have the effect of reducing penalties in a way that correspondingly impacts the message of deterrence.[26]

While perhaps the ultimate deterrent, custodial sentences for environmental crimes are rare in Australia and generally reserved for the most egregious of cases.[27] The much more common sentencing option in Australia is the imposition of a fine.[28] While trends suggest that the fines imposed for environmental crimes in Australia are increasing,[29] in NSW[30] and throughout Australia more generally,[31] the fines imposed are often only a fraction of the maximum fine available.

Regardless of the level of fine imposed, monetary penalties are not always the best means to achieve deterrence or, where warranted, retribution.[32] In particular, there is concern that some defendants, and particularly corporate defendants, have the financial ability to absorb fines as a "cost of business"[33]—with the result that a fine is unlikely to serve as a deterrent to either the individual corporate offender or to corporations more generally.[34] This is particularly so where a corporate offender stands to profit from the commission of an offence, a particular concern in Australia in relation to native vegetation clearing offences and the "waste offences" referred to above.[35] At the other end of the spectrum, the court is also unlikely to impose significant fines on individuals who do not have the capacity to pay,[36] in which case the nominal fine again offers no real deterrent.

In Australia, therefore, the rationale for providing courts with alternative, creative sentencing options is largely referenced in answer to the question—how can the sentencing of environmental crimes "provide a more socially acceptable outcome?"[37] Creative sentencing options allow the courts to "deal with situations where a fine/custodial sentence is considered either an inappropriate or an insufficient sentence."[38]

## CREATIVE SENTENCING OPTIONS

While many Australian legislatures have now introduced a range of creative sentencing options into their environmental legislation, creative sentencing orders are used most commonly in the Australian states of Victoria and NSW.[39] In the case of NSW, this is perhaps partially explained by the fact that the specialist Land and Environment Court has jurisidiction to sentence environmental offenders under the POEO *Act* and other state environmental legislation.

Under the POEO *Act*, the court may order an offender to do one or more of the following:

- take specified actions to publicize the offence, its environmental and other consequences, and any other orders made against the defendant to either a specified class of persons (including for example shareholders) or generally;[40]
- carry out a specified project for the restoration or enhancement of the environment in a public place or for the public benefit,[41] and if the EPA is a party to the proceedings, provide financial assurances to the EPA, of a form and amount specified by the court, for that court-ordered program;[42]
- carry out any social or community activity for the benefit of the community or persons that are adversely affected by the offence (a "restorative justice activity") that the offender has agreed to carry out;43

- undertake specified environmental audits of activities carried on by the offender;[44]
- pay a specified amount into the New South Wales Environmental Trust or to a specified organization, for the purposes of a specified project for the restoration or enhancement of the environment or for general environmental purposes;[45]
- attend specified training or courses or design specified courses for employees or contractors;[46]
- take steps to prevent, restore, and abate any harm to the environment caused by the commission of the offence, to repair any resulting environmental damage, and to prevent the continuance or reccurrence of the offence;[47]
- compensate a public authority or any other person for expenses incurred or damages suffered as the result of the offence;[48]
- pay costs and expenses associated with the investigation of the offence;[49] and
- repay the monetary benefit derived from the offence.[50]

Any such order may be made in addition to, or in lieu of, any monetary penalty or custodial sentence that might otherwise be imposed, and one or more orders may be made against the offender.[51] Importantly, the amount of any such additional penalty is not subject to any maximum amount of penalty provided elsewhere by or under the Act.[52] As an alternative to imprisonment of an individual, a community service order is also available to the court in appropriate situations.[53]

## NSW EPA GUIDELINES FOR SEEKING ENVIRONMENTAL COURT ORDERS

The NSW EPA Guidelines for Seeking Environmental Court Orders[54] divide these sentencing options into two groups: orders aimed at restoring or preventing the recurrence of the offence; and orders aimed at punishing or deterring offenders.

### Orders Aimed at Restoring or Preventing the Recurrence of the Offence

The Guidelines place cleanup orders, compensation orders, investigation costs orders, monetary benefit penalty orders, and environmental orders (meaning orders to restore or prevent harm to the environment) in the first group. The collective purpose of these kinds of orders is "to attempt to return the environment, and those committing/affected by the offence, to the same position it/they were in prior to the offence and also ensure that the offender takes steps to guard against future contraventions."[55]

In accordance with the Guidelines, orders for cleanup or compensation will ordinarily be sought, unless the EPA determines that the defendant does not have sufficient funds. In keeping with the principle that an offender should not profit from committing an offence, monetary benefit orders together with investigation costs orders will generally also be sought. Environmental audit orders, on the other hand, are sought when the offender's operations "lack essential environment protection systems" or "there are serious ongoing failures in those systems."[56] Again, the Guidelines make it clear that this type of order is not intended to punish but rather to ensure that the offender takes steps to undertake its activities in a manner that is environmentally acceptable.

### Orders Aimed at Punishing or Deterring Offenders

Together with fines and custodial sentences, publication orders and environmental service orders are classified as orders aimed at punishing or deterring offenders.

The NSW Land and Environment Court has recognized that publication of both the prosecution and the punishment of environmental offenders improves the effectiveness of general deterrence by bringing broader attention to the consequences of such conduct.[57] However, publication orders are largely used as a response to the criticism that fines alone may be an inadequate deterrent for large corporations. As such, according to the Guidelines, this type of order is mainly reserved for "corporate offenders as it is likely to be of the most deterrent value to them."[58] In determining whether a publication order is appropriate, the EPA is also directed to consider the defendant's culpability and environmental record as well as the threatened or actual environmental harms caused by the incident. After the fact, cooperation or contribution, however, are not relevant factors to consider in determining whether a publication order is appropriate. It is ordinarily the case that the order will specify that the notice be published, at a minimum, in a newspaper circulating state-wide and, in the case of public companies, in the executive summary of the company's annual report.[59]

An environmental service order allows the court to order that a specified project be carried out for the restoration or enhancement of the environment in a public place or for the public benefit. While the result is to deliver a benefit to the public, the Guidelines make clear that such an order is made for the purposes of punishment or deterrence. As such, a publication order will always be sought in conjunction with an environmental service order so that it is understood the project is being carried out because of the commission of the offence, rather than, for example, because the offender "simply being a good citizen."[60] Such an order will only be sought from the court when an appropriate project can be found in the vicinity of the offence, and then only if the offender has the ability, means, and willingness to carry out the project. Only projects with easily measured outcomes will be considered suitable.[61]

## CREATIVE SENTENCING IN PRACTICE IN NSW

The recent sentencing decision in *Environment Protection Authority v Clarence Colliery Pty Ltd; Office of Environment and Heritage v Clarence Colliery*[62] provides a good example of the use of creative sentencing in NSW. The sentencing decision relates to an incident that resulted in coal fines slurry flowing from the defendant's coal mines into an unnamed watercourse and eventually into the Blue Mountains National Park and the Wollangambe River. With approximately 10.3 kilometres of the river affected by the slurry, Clarence Colliery was charged with, and pleaded guilty to, two environmental offences. The first offence, under section 166(1)(a) of the *POEO Act*, was negligently causing a substance to leak, spill, or otherwise escape in a manner that harms or is likely to harm the environment. The second, under section 156A(1)(b) of the *National Parks and Wildlife Act 1974 (NSW)*, related to damaging land reserved under that Act. After considering the relevant sentencing principles, and taking into account the objective and subjective circumstances, Robson J. imposed a total fine for both offences of $1,050,000.[63] As agreed by the prosecutor and Clarence Colliery, the court held that this monetary penalty be paid to the Environmental Trust established under the *Environmental Trust Act 1995* (NSW) pursuant to sections 250(1)(e) of the *POEO Act* and 205(1)(d) of the *National Parks and Wildlife Act* in order to fund the following five specific projects for restoration or enhancement of the environment:

1. "stabilisation of walking tracks in the Newnes Plateau and Wollangambe/Mt Wilson area";
2. "enhancing the survival of the endangered Blue Mountains Water Skink";
3. enhancement of "Farmers Creek Master Plan";
4. Office of Environment and Heritage "water quality and improvement"; and

5. Office of Environment and Heritage "Weed control in Wollangambe Catch."

Significantly, Robson J. was provided with documentation, including detailed descriptions in relation to each of the proposed projects, and was satisfied that each of the projects was designed to meet the principal objective of "reducing the impacts on the water quality of the Wollangambe Catchment in Blue Mountains and Wollemi National Parks by targeted erosion control, weed control and rehabilitation of areas disturbed by illegal use, and improving sanitation facilities at a popular camp area."[64] These projects, in turn, were considered by Robson J. "to be appropriate in the circumstances where Clarence Colliery's commission of the offences has caused harm to the areas generally the subject of the proposed projects."[65]

In addition, Robson J. made two important publication orders. First, all future public references by the defendant, Clarence Colliery, to the payments specified in the order to carry out the specified restoration or enhancement projects were to be accompanied by the following passage:[66]

> Clarence Colliery Pty Ltd's contribution to the funding of the "[insert name of project]" is part of a penalty imposed on it by the Land and Environment Court of NSW after it was convicted of an offence against the *Protection of the Environment Operations Act 1997* (NSW).

Second, Clarence Colliery was ordered to place a notice detailing the offence and penalty in three newspapers (the *Australian Financial Review*, the *Sydney Morning Herald*, and the *Lithgow Mercury*). The order specified the wording of the notice, the minimum size of the notice, and where (how far from the first page) the notice must appear in each newspaper.[67]

Finally, Robson J. also ordered that Clarence Colliery pay investigation costs totalling $106,010 as well as legal costs.[68] As the defendant had already itself undertaken a large-scale cleanup, it also bore these costs, although they did not form part of the order.

## Next Steps in Creative Sentencing for Environmental Offences Taking a Restorative Justice Approach

As noted above, the NSW *POEO Act* allows the court to order an offender "to carry out social or community activity for the benefit of the community or persons that are adversely affected by the offence (a 'restorative justice activity') that the offender has agreed to carry out."[69] This provision, inserted by amendment in 2015,[70] is "sufficiently broad" to allow the court to order restorative justice processes, such as conferences,[71] and restorative justice outcomes in the context of environmental sentencing.[72]

As the Chief Justice Brian Preston of the NSW Land and Environment Court has written, "[r]estorative justice has the potential to be transformative for the offender, the victims, the community, the environment and the justice system."[73] This transformation is possible because "the community, victims[74] and the offender participate together actively in resolving matters arising from the offender's crime, remedying harm caused to the environment and other victims and preventing re-offending, thereby protecting the environment in the future."[75] However, this transformation is not without its challenges. As members of the NSW Land and Environment Court have noted, the main challenge in implementing restorative justice in the sentencing of environmental offences is "responding to the tension between traditional sentencing options and restorative justice outcomes, the latter of which seeks to resolve harm collectively rather than focus on punishment and retribution."[76] While not necessarily making the sentencing purposes identified at the outset unachievable, "[r]estorative justice may alter the usual weighting of these principles."[77] Ultimately, however, the use of restorative processes may allow a more holistic approach to environmental crime, with the potential to transform relationships and behaviours and provide a means to empower and give a voice to the broader community and the environment as victims of environmental crime.[78] In this way, the restorative justice approach now available in NSW should offer something that environmental sentencing, even creative sentencing, to date has not.

## NOTES

1 The Hon Judge J Goldring, NSW Land and Environment Court, "Facts and Statistics in the Sentencing Process" (2009) 32 Austl Bar Rev 281 at 282 and 286.

2 The Hon Justice R Pepper, NSW Land and Environment Court, "Recent Developments in Sentencing of Environmental Offences" (Paper delivered at the Australasian Conference of Planning and Environment Courts and Tribunals, Perth, 28 August–2 September 2012) at 1 [Pepper].

3 *Ibid.*

4 S Bricknell, *Environmental Crime in Australia*, Research and Public Policy Series 109 (Canberra: Australian Institute of Criminology, 2010) at xii; Pepper, *ibid* at 8.

5 NSW Environment Protection Authority, *EPA Prosecution Guidelines* (Sydney, NSW: Dept of Environment and

Conservation, 2013) at 3 [EPA Prosecution Guidelines]. The *EPA Prosecution Guidelines* list several factors that may be considered alone or in conjunction to determine whether the public interest requires prosecution

6 *Protection of the Environment Operations Act* [*POEO Act*], Act 156 of 1997, online: <http://www8.austlii.edu.au/cgi-bin/viewdb/au/legis/nsw/consol_act/poteoa1997455/>. Jurisdictions throughout Australia commonly use administrative tools such as enforceable undertakings, penalty notices, or civil penalty regimes as an alternative to criminal prosecution. For a discussion of guidelines relating to the use of enforceable undertakings in NSW, see NSW Environment Protection Authority, *Guidelines on Enforceable Undertakings* (Sydney, NSW: Dept of Environment and Conservation, 2017), online: <http://www.epa.nsw.gov.au/licensing-and-regulation/legislation-and-compliance/policies-and-guidelines>.

7 EPA Prosecution Guidelines, supra note 5 at para 2.2.7.

8 *Crimes (Sentencing Procedure) Act*, 1999 (NSW), s 3A. The High Court of Australia has stated: "The purposes of criminal punishment are various: protection of society, deterrence of the offender and of others who might be tempted to offend, retribution and reform. The purposes overlap and none of them can be considered in isolation from the others when determining what is an appropriate sentence in a particular case. They are guideposts to the appropriate sentence but sometimes they point in different directions." (*Veen v R (No 2)*, [1988] HCA 14. 164 CLR 465 at 476.) For a full discussion of these sentencing purposes in the context of environmental crime, see Hon Chief Justice B Preston, NSW Land and Environment Court, "Principles Sentencing for Environmental Offences" (Paper presented at the 4th International IUCN Academy of Environmental Law Colloquium, *Compliance and Enforcement: Toward More Effective Implementation of Environmental Law*, Pace University School of Law, 16–20 October 2006) at 1–12 [Preston].

9 EPA Prosecution Guidelines, *supra* note 5 at 2.2.5. See also Preston, *ibid* at 40.

10 *Veen v R (No 1)* (1979), 143 CLR 458 at 490; *Veen v R (No 2)* (1988), 164 CLR 465 at 472; *R v Scott*, [2005] NSWCAA 152 at para 15. For a full discussion of these sentencing considerations, see: Preston, *supra* note 8 at 12–29.

11 *POEO Act*, s 241(2). To increase predictability, consistency, accessibility, and transparency in sentencing for environmental offences, sentencing statistics for criminal matters dealt with by the NSW Land and Environment Court are accessible in graphical form on the Judicial Information Research System, online: <https://www.judcom.nsw.gov.au/judicial-information-research-system-jirs/>. For a discussion of this database, see Hon Chief Justice B Preston and H Donnelly, "The Establishment of an Environmental Crime Sentencing Database in New South Wales" (2008) 32 Criminal Law Journal 214.

12 New South Wales Environmental Defender's Office, "Court Imposed Fines and their Enforcement" (Submission to the NSW Sentencing Council, 8 June 2006), referencing G Bates, *Environmental Law in Australia* (Australia: Butterworths, 2002) at 226–227.

13 Pepper, *supra* note 2 at 3.

14 Preston, supra note 8 at 33. See also *Chief Executive of the Office of Environment and Heritage v Grant Wesley Turnbull*, [2017] NSWLEC 141 at para 24; *Bankstown City Council v Hanna*, [2014] NSWLEC 152 at para 58.

15 Pepper, *supra* note 2 at 3.

16 *POEO Act*, s 119.

17 See, e.g., *POEO Act*, s 123.

18 *POEO Act*, s 144AB. This amendment was introduced by the *Protection of the Environment Operations (Illegal Waste Disposal) Act*, 2013. See P Crofts, "Communicating the Culpability of

Illegal Dumping: Banstown v Hanna (2014)" (2015) 2 AELJ 57 [Crofts] for a discussion of facts resulting in this amendment.

19 Mr Bob Debus, Attorney General, Minister for the Environment, HANSARD, 2nd Reading Speech, 28 November 2005.

20 [2007] NSWLEC 530 at para 32.

21 [2006] NSWLEC 34 (6 February 2006) at para 139.

22 *Bentley, ibid.*

23 *Bentley, ibid.* See, e.g., *Chief Executive of the Office of Environment and Heritage v Cory Ian Turnbull*, [2017] NSWLEC 140 at paras 231–232 for a discussion of specific and general deterrence in the context of a recent decision.

24 R Bartel, "Sentencing for Environmental Offences: An Australian Exploration (Presented at the Sentencing Conference, National Judicial College of Australia, ANU College of Law, February 2008) at 4; and Preston, *supra* note 8.

25 *Director-General of the Department of Land and Water Conservation v MW Robson*, [1998] NSWLEC 174 at para 20.

26 See G Bates, *Environmental Law in Australia*, 7th ed (Australia: LexisNexis Butterworths, 2010) at para 16.83 for a discussion of the application of evenhandedness in the context of environmental sentencing.

27 See, e.g., *Wood v Ivanyi*, [2016] SAERDC 3; *Environment Protection Authority v Hanna*, [2013] NSWLEC 41; *Environmental Protection Authority v Janna*, [2013] NSWLEC 41; *Environmental Protection Authority v Gardner*, [1997] NSWLEC 169; *R v Moore*, [2003] 1 Qld Reports 205; and *R v Dempsey*, [2002] QCA 4.

28 C Abbot, "The Regulatory Enforcement of Pollution Control Laws: The Australian Experience" (2005) 17 J Envtl L 161 at 170.

29 Pepper, *supra* note 2 at 2. See also D Cole, "Creative Sentencing – Using the Sentencing Provisions of the South Australian Environment Protection Act to Greater Community Benefit" (2008) 25 EPLJ 94 at 95 [Cole]. It is difficult to identify a statistical trend because individual penalties are heavily dependent on the objective and subjective considerations that inform the sentencing decision. The NSW Land and Environment Court has created a sentencing database in an attempt to provide judges, legislatures, and members of the public easier access to more nuanced information relating to environmental sentencing: Hon Chief Justice B Preston, NSW Land and Environment Court, "A Judge's Perspective on Using Sentencing Databases" (Presented at the Judicial Reasoning: Art or Science Conference, Australian National University, Canberra, 7–8 February 2009).

30 Crofts, *supra* note 18 at 74, referencing to M Hain and C Cocklin, "The Effectiveness of the Courts in Achieving the Goals of Environmental Protection Legislation" (2001) 18:3 Environment and Planning and Law Journal 319–338; and P Crofts and J Prior, *Environment Protection Authority Responses to Illegal Dumping in NSW: An Analysis of Clean-Up Notices and Prosecutions*, Report submitted to the NSW EPA (University of Technology, Sydney, 2014).

31 Bricknell, *supra* note 4 at xii. Bricknell suggests that these low fines may be explained, in part, by the role of magistrates' courts in environmental sentencing as, unlike the specialist environment courts of NSW and South Australia, magistrates' courts see environmental crimes only intermittently and lack judicial training in dealing with environmental matters.

32 Bricknell, *ibid.*

33 Pepper, *supra* note 2 at 4–5. See also Cole, *supra* note 29 at 96.

34 Pepper, *ibid* at 6; Cole, *ibid*; and Australian Law Reform Commission, *Compliance with the Trade Practices Act 1974*, ALRC Report No 68 (Sydney: Commonwealth of Australia, 1994) at para 10.3. See also NSW EPA, "Guidelines for Seeking Environmental Court

Orders" [NSW EPA "Guidelines"], online: <http://www.epa.nsw.gov.au/licensing-and-regulation/legislation-and-compliance/policies-and-guidelines/guidelines-seeking-enviro-court-orders>. The Guidelines state: "It is certainly arguable that even the maximum fine available for a Tier 2 offence provides no real deterrent to a major corporation."

35 The media release announcing the increased penalties and creative sentencing options for waste offences states: "The current penalties do not outweigh the profits from illegal activity, and as long as that remains, unscrupulous waste operators will continue to exploit the system." Environment Minister Robyn Parker, Media Release, "NSW Government to Crack Down on Illegal Dumping (29 May 2013), online: <http://www.environment.nsw.gov.au/resources/MinMedia/MinMedia13052901.pdf>.

36 NSW EPA "Guidelines," *supra* note 34.

37 Cole, *supra* note 29 at 96.

38 NSW EPA "Guidelines," *supra* note 34.

39 Pepper, *supra* note 2 at 6–7.

40 *POEO Act*, s 250(1)(a)–(b). See, e.g., *Bankstown City Council v Hanna*, [2014] NSWLEC 152; *Environment Protection Authority v Queanbeyan City Council (No 3)*, [2012] NSWLEC 220.

41 *POEO Act*, s 250(1)(c). See, e.g., *Environmental Protection Authority v Yolarno Pty Ltd*, [2004] NSWLEC 264 at para 25.

42 *POEO Act*, s 250(1)(h).

43 *POEO Act*, s 250(1A).

44 *POEO Act*, s 250(1)(d). See, e.g., *Environmental Protection Authority v Ramsay Food Processing Ltd (No 2)*, [2010] NSWLEC 150.

45 *POEO Act*, s 250(1)(e). See, e.g., *Environmental Protection Authority v Caltex Refineries (NSW) Pty Ltd*, [2006] NSWLEC 335.

46 *POEO Act*, s 250(1)(f)–(g).

47 *POEO Act*, s 245. See, e.g., *Environmental Protection Authority v Warringah Golf Club (No 2)*, [2003] NSWLEC 140.

48 *POEO Act*, ss 246 and 247. See, e.g., *Environmental Protection Authority v Obaid*, [2005] NSWLEC 171.

49 *POEO Act*, s 248(1). See, e.g., *Environmental Protection Authority v Centennial Newstan Pty Ltd*, [2010] NSWLEC 211.

50 *POEO Act*, s 249(1).

51 *POEO Act*, s 244(1).

52 *POEO Act*, s 244(2).

53 *Crimes (Sentencing Procedure) Act* (NSW), Act 92 of 1999 at ss 8(1) and 86. The legislation prescribes 500 hours as the maximum number of community service hours: s 8(2). See, e.g., *Environmental Protection Authority v Coggins*, [2003] NSWLEC 111.

54 NSW EPA "Guidelines," *supra* note 34.

55 *Ibid.*

56 *Ibid.*

57 See *Environment Protection Authority v Waste Recycling and Processing Corporation*, [2006] NSWLEC 419 at para 242; *Environmental Protection Authority v Dyno Nobel Asia Pacific Pty Ltd*, [2017] NSWLEC 64 at para 163.

58 *Ibid.*

59 *Ibid.*

60 *Ibid.* See also Preston, *supra* note 8 at 38.

61 *Ibid.*

62 [2017] NSWLEC 82.

63 Robson J found the appropriate monetary penalties to be $1,200,000.00 for the *POEO Act* offence and $550,000 for the *National Parks and Wildlife Act* offence. These amounts were then reduced by 25% for the utilitarian value of the early pleas of guilty. The application of the totality principle resulted in the combined fines being adjusted by a further 20%, resulting in a total fine of $1,050,000 (at paras 135–136).

64 *Supra* note 62 at para 139.

65 *Ibid.*

66 *Ibid* at para 145.

67 *Ibid* at para 145 and Annexure A.

68 *Ibid* at para 145.

69 *POEO Act*, s 250(1A). The proviso that offenders must agree to carry out a restorative justice activity is in keeping with

need for offenders to accept responsibility for their criminal behaviour and for their participation not to be coerced in a restorative justice process. See United Nations Office on Drugs and Crime (UNODC), *Handbook on Restorative Justice Programs* (United Nations, New York, 2006) at 11; Hon Justice B Preston, "The Use of Restorative Justice for Environmental Crime" (2011) 35 Criminal Law Journal 136, online: SSRN <https://ssrn.com/abstract=1831822> at 13 [Preston].

70 *Protection of the Environment Legislation Amendment Act*, 2014 No 65. This Act also amended the *Contaminated Land Management Act 1997* (NSW) and the *Radiation Control Act 1990* (NSW) to include restorative justice activities. Several years prior to this amendment, restorative justice processes were used by Hon B Preston CJ of the NSW Land and Environment Court in *Garrett v Williams*, [2007] NSWLEC 96, 151 LGERA 92.

71 Hon Justice N Pain, Hon Justice R Pepper, M McCreath & J Zorzetto, "Restorative Justice for Environmental Crime: An Antipodean Experience" (International Union for Conservation of Nature Academy of Environmental Law Colloquium 2016, Oslo Norway 22 June 2016) at 9.

72 For a discussion of the use of restorative justice for environmental crimes, see Preston, *supra* note 69. Restorative justice outcomes are also used in the Australian State of Victoria (with the main restorative justice provision, found in s 67AC(2)(c) of the *Environment Protection Act 1970* (Vic), inserted into the Act in 2000) and New Zealand (*Sentencing Act 2002* (NZ)). For a recent discussion of the restorative justice practices in these jurisdictions, see Pain et al, *ibid* at 12–16.

73 Preston, *supra* note 69 at 25.

74 For a detailed discussion of the possible victims of an environmental crime, including specific individuals, classes of persons, members of the community, future generations, and the environment other than humans, see Preston, *supra* note 69 at 8–12. See also Pain et al, *supra* note 71 at 6–8.

75 Preston, *supra* note 69 at 25.

76 Pain et al, *supra* note 71 at 16.

77 Pain et al, *ibid.*

78 Preston, *supra* note 69 at 23–25.

# 28

# Creative Environmental Sentences: The Corporate Perspective

ALLAN E. INGELSON

In a 2012 commentary, "Getting Creative with the Law," Dianne Saxe and Jackie Campbell consider the advantages of creative sentences, including the potential for corporate monies spent on projects to improve the environment and, through corporate involvement and sponsorship, to increase the prospect of environmental compliance in the future. The authors report that, in some cases, corporate offenders can make more valuable contributions to the environment than strictly monetary ones and the participation of corporations in "restoring the natural environment can help rehabilitate offenders, motivate them to care about issues, and set a good example to others."[1] Saxe and Campbell note that three decades ago the Province of Ontario was the leader in creative sentencing, but now federal, British Columbia, and Alberta prosecutors have assumed a national leadership role in creative environmental sentencing.[2]

Rapid and significant development of oil sands projects in recent years has prompted numerous federal and provincial environmental offences in which the courts in Alberta have approved a variety of creative sentences. Why are some corporations open to participating in joint submissions with the Crown for creative sentences? We will examine this question. In light of availability of information on recent creative sentences approved in the province during the last five years, we will examine the orders under which corporations are funding research and education, habitat preservation, water quality monitoring and protection, prohibitions on specified activities, and publication projects.

## The Emergence of Creative Sentences in Canada

What are the objectives of creative environmental sentences in Canada? In the 1980 *Keno Hill*[3] judgment, Chief Justice Barry Stuart laid the foundation for creative sentencing in Canada. The Chief Justice discussed "special considerations" when the court sentenced a major national mining corporation after it discharged waste above the amount allowed under its water licence, contrary to the *Northern Inland Waters Act*.[4] The court considered the following factors in determining the appropriate sentence: the "nature of the environment affected; the extent of injury (the degree of damage inflicted)";[5] the size, wealth, and power of the corporation;[6] the "criminality of the conduct"; "the extent of corporate attempts to comply; remorse; profits realized by the offence; the criminal record of the corporation."[7] Subsequently, the Environmental Damages Fund was created by the Canadian Government to direct monies paid for fines under statutes such as the *Migratory Birds Convention Act* (*MBCA*),[8] the *Fisheries Act*,[9] and the Canadian *Environmental Protection Act*[10] to fund environmental improvement projects rather than depositing such monies into the government's Consolidated Revenue Fund.[11]

Eighteen years after the *Keno Hill* decision, in another case arising from the unlawful release of a substance harmful to the environment, the Provincial Court of Alberta, in *R. v. Van Waters & Rogers Ltd*,[12] considered the following factors when determining the appropriate sentence:

1. Public protection, even in the absence of serious harm;
2. Denunciation of offenders;
3. Deterrence not rehabilitation;
4. Sole potential harm or risk arising from the offence is not a mitigating factor, but actual harm is an aggravating factor;
5. The absence of intent is not a mitigating factor, but willfulness or recklessness is an aggravating factor;
6. Profit or benefit from the environmental offence may be difficult to quantify, but should be considered when appropriate;
7. Imposing the maximum statutory penalty may be appropriate where there is intent, significant discharge, and a prior record;
8. The size and financial resources of the corporation should be considered;
9. Offender remorse needs to be determined (remorse of the offender to be evaluated by considering the corporation's actions, not words);
10. Compliance only after the fact should not be treated as too much of a mitigating factor;
11. Lax government enforcement is not a mitigating factor;

12. Previous convictions must be considered;
13. The availability of easy steps that could have been taken by the corporation to avoid pollution, or carrying on a hazardous activity knowing that pollution will be difficult to control, are both aggravating factors.[13]

In regard to the ninth factor, the conclusion that corporate remorse is to be evaluated based on the actions of the corporation, not words, can be one of the factors that encourages corporations in some cases to participate in the creative sentencing process.

In his 2004 analysis of creative sentencing, Gordon Scott Campbell discussed the role that "non-fine measures" such as beneficial environmental projects, public denunciation, and voluntary compliance measures can play in encouraging environmental compliance.[14] In 2009, Professor Elaine Hughes and Dr. Larry Reynolds examined the "options available" for creative sentences under federal and provincial legislation, including:

- the confiscation of profits from the commission of an environmental offence;
- ordering compensation for property losses;
- payment into trust funds to facilitate environmental restoration or research;
- prevention orders such as "mandatory employee training";
- "compliance with 'voluntary' codes such as ISO 14001 management systems";
- community service orders;
- publication and information orders; and
- probation.[15]

Hughes and Reynolds noted that publication orders were frequently used in combination with research funding, educational funding, prevention, or remedial orders. The authors discussed prerequisites for creative sentences in Canada, including that the corporate offender must accept responsibility for the offence and must be in a state of compliance with the environmental statute or regulation prior to the determination of the creative sentence; that the corporation cannot benefit from non-compliance with the law; and that the amount of the fine and funding for the creative sentencing project(s) must be significant and structured so as to be a deterrent to other potential offenders.[16]

Based on their review of federal and provincial legislation, the authors reported that "the largest group of potential orders set out in the statutes and used in practice, are orders to conduct specific projects of direct environmental benefit (whether remedial or preventive), usually by funding NGOs or government departments, and orders of a somewhat uncertain benefit to conduct research (again, often with educational NGO partners)."[17] Corporations fund these projects to satisfy the creative sentence. Projects are directed toward "achieving compliance with environmental standards through specific and general deterrence measures," specifically targeting both current and future environmental benefits. The types of sanctions that could be incorporated into creative sentences include prohibitions against specified activities, publication of facts pertaining to the offence, community service or actions intended to facilitate acceptable offender conduct, and funding for remedial action.

## Creative Sentencing in Alberta

In 2003, Susan McRory, the Environmental Coordinator, Special Prosecutions for Alberta Justice, and Lynda Jenkins, Environmental Prosecutor, reported that creative sentencing had "become a significant feature of almost every environmental prosecution in the province."[18] One early example, from 2003, is *R. v. Canadian 88 Energy Corp*. The oil company was charged with releasing a substance at a rate or amount that could cause a significant adverse effect to the environment pursuant to subsection 98(2) of the *Alberta Environmental Protection and Enhancement Act* (AEPEA),[19] and for the unlawful deposit of a deleterious substance into water, contrary to subsection 36(3) of the *Fisheries Act*.[20] The corporation pled guilty to both charges and the court imposed a global sentence of $154,650, which included $15,000 in fines and surcharges.[21] The balance of the financial penalty was divided equally between the provincial and federal offences, and most of the money paid by the corporation was deposited into the federal Environmental Damages Fund to "achieve remediation and restoration of damages to the natural environment in a cost-effective way."[22] The court noted that the corporation was a first-time offender, a "model corporate citizen" that had accepted full responsibility for the environmental damage throughout the proceedings, had spent $2.5 million to date on clean-up costs, and was expected to continue working with Alberta Environment[23] for the next ten years to monitor and remediate the area.[24] In this early case, most of the money paid by the corporation was directed toward improving the environment.

Today, under subsection 234(1) of *AEPEA*, the courts in the province can take an innovative approach to sentencing by ordering that funds be used to pay for specific types of projects to improve the environment. The sentencing judge will decide the appropriate penalty in the case, and then determine the amount of money to be allocated for the project(s) that will benefit the public and the environment to be funded by the corporate offender. As a general rule, corporations are not allowed to deduct the cost of remediation from the total penalty.[25] McRory has noted that the trend in the province "has been a 50/50 split between the fine and the creative sentence, as advocated by the provincial Crown," and that some of the requirements for creative sentences include the following: deterrence is the prime objective of the creative sentence; the order must be punitive; there must be a connection between the offence and the project(s) funded as part of the creative sentence; and the project(s) must truly address the wrong.[26] Creative sentencing guidelines provide that the prime beneficiary of a creative sentencing project(s) funded by a corporation "must be the public."[27] In 2012, Alberta Environment and Sustainable Resource Development (AESRD)[28] and the Alberta Department of Justice reported that for the purpose of clarifying administrative responsibilities, now once an order has been adopted by the court "it is the responsibility of the environmental investigations liaison to ensure the order is performed as outlined in the court document; the order can extend up to three years or can be extended with permission of the court."[29]

Often there is a lack of detailed information about the factors that are considered by corporations in deciding whether or not to participate in creative sentencing. Even though the following cases and associated orders have no precedential value, they do provide insight into the types of recent innovative sentences agreed to by corporations. The selected nine creative sentences were approved by the courts in Alberta during the period 2009–2013. As provided under the terms of the creative sentences, corporations are funding a variety of innovative projects, including research and education projects, habitat preservation, water quality monitoring and environmental improvement, student bursaries, and scholarships.

### *R. v. Suncor Energy* (2009)[30]—Research and Education to Avoid Repeating the Offence

Suncor Energy (Suncor), Canada's largest energy company, publishes an annual report on its environmental, social, and economic performance.[31]

Operations at the Suncor Firebag *in situ* oil sands facility started in December 2003. The corporation's original plant design included vapor recovery units (VRUs) on all process water tanks at the facility. The design plans were later changed to remove VRUs on the water tanks after experience with another project suggested they were not required. The design change was not incorporated into the project application that had been submitted to the provincial government. After an investigation by Alberta Environment, the company was charged under subsections 227(e) and (b) of *AEPEA*, for breaching a statutory authorization, for failing to install equipment to control emissions of a hazardous substance, and failing to report that the equipment had not been installed as required by the project approval. On April 2, 2009, the company pled guilty to the two counts and paid a $675,000 fine. In addition, as corporate executives were interested in how the company could avoid repeating the offences and as part of its corporate social responsibility program, Suncor paid $315,000 to the University of Calgary for researchers to undertake a regulatory compliance research and education project. The researchers wrote a case study and Executive Briefing that were distributed at a two-day workshop offered to industry executives, managers, and regulators.[32] Suncor representatives participated in the workshop. The research project funded under the creative sentence revealed a failure in project management oversight. Based on 46 interviews with Suncor employees, regulators, and lawyers who were aware of the circumstances surrounding the environmental offences, along with a review of the associated documentation, the university researchers identified the following three "root causes" of the environmental offences:

1. The corporation had a weak management of change process;
2. The corporation had weak operational compliance tracking;
3. The corporation exhibited a weak culture of compliance.[33]

The researchers also identified contextual factors that magnified the root causes of the environmental offence, including industry turbulence, new technology, and a shortage of qualified personnel.[34]

In addition to funding management research to minimize the risk that the corporation would commit the offence again, another factor in Suncor participating in the creative sentence was its commitment to corporate social responsibility (CSR).[35] Some Canadian corporations are more concerned about CSR than others. In light of media scrutiny of oil sands operations, some corporations in the extractive industries sector consider that environmental enhancement projects demonstrate CSR, and that the projects will support the social licence to operate over the long term. The International Institute for Sustainable Development states that "CSR promotes a vision of business accountability to a wide range of stakeholders, besides shareholders and investors. Key areas of concern for these corporations are environmental protection and the community and civil society in general, both now and in the future."[36] As part of its Report on Sustainability in 2009, Suncor Energy posted the following statement regarding the Firebag offences on its website:

> This incident should have never happened. We fell short of the expectations of regulators—and ourselves. There was a failure in management oversight, for which we take full responsibility. We have strengthened our project controls to prevent it from occurring again.[37]

This type of public admission and disclosure suggests that CSR was also a factor in the major energy corporation participating in the creative sentence. In addition to funding the regulatory compliance educational research project discussed above, pursuant to another term of the creative sentence, the corporation paid $75,000 into a college Endowment Fund to support an Environmental and Conservation and Sciences Program.

### *R. v. Syncrude Canada Ltd.* (2010)[38]—Habitat Preservation

Habitat preservation was another type of project funded under the creative sentence. The environmental prosecution in this case garnered national and international media attention in 2010. Syncrude, an oil sands mining company, was charged under subsection 5.1(1) of the *Migratory Birds Convention Act* (*MBCA*)[39] for depositing substances harmful to migratory birds and under section 155 of *AEPEA*, for "failing to keep or store a hazardous substance in a manner that avoids contact with animals," after approximately 1,600 migratory birds died after landing on a mine tailings pond that contained clays, silt, and residual amounts of hydrocarbons.[40] As the oil sands mine is located along a migratory bird route, based on an environmental impact study, the corporation was aware that birds could land on the tailings pond as with other lakes in the area. Syncrude had previously deployed scarecrows and propane cannons, and employed other bird deterrent practices in previous years. The corporation mounted a vigorous defence, but the court concluded that the corporation had failed to take adequate measures to deter the birds from landing on the tailings pond and ordered the corporation to pay a $300,000 fine under the *MBCA* and a $500,000 fine under *AEPEA*.[41] Pursuant to the terms of the creative sentence the corporation agreed to pay $2,200,000 to fund several projects that included a payment of $900,000 to the Alberta Conservation Association to purchase the Golden Ranches habitat.[42] In addition to funding habitat preservation, the corporation funded a $1,300,000 avian research project at the University of Alberta and paid $250,000 to fund curriculum development for a Wildlife Management Technician Diploma Program at a college in Fort McMurray, Alberta, to satisfy the conditions of the creative sentence.

### *R. v. Statoil Canada Ltd.* (2011)[43]—Online Training for Best Industry Practices to Avoid Future Prosecutions

In October 2011, Statoil Canada Ltd. pled guilty to contravening the "terms or conditions" of a Temporary Diversion Licence contrary to subsection 142(1)(e) of the Alberta *Water Act*.[44] A water use report submitted to Alberta Environment by the oil sands operator did not include an estimate of the volume of water that had been diverted for use in its drilling operations. The corporation admitted that the estimated volume of water that it had diverted daily had not been recorded, nor did its employees record the water level from the lake as required.[45] In addition, the corporation had not used the screen size stipulated in the licence, a provincial regulatory requirement designed to protect the fish population. The company was fined $5,000 and, as a term of the creative sentence, required to pay $185,000 to fund the development of an online training project called "Surface Water Diversion for the Oil and Gas Industry – Best Practices."[46] The purpose of the project was to "provide a clear and concise guide to surface water diversion" to educate oil and gas industry operators and reduce the possibility that Statoil and other industry members would commit the offence in the future.[47] It was a condition of the creative sentence that one of the project stakeholders, the Canadian Association of Petroleum Producers (CAPP),[48] host, along with Statoil, a learning presentation targeted at industry operators and include on its website an online portal for a period of three years from the date of the creative sentencing order.[49]

### *R. v. Devon Canada Corporation* (2011)[50]—Bursary for Students

During August 2011, Devon Canada Corporation was convicted under subsections 142(1)(i) and 142(1)(b) of the *Water Act*,[51] for not reporting a water crossing in its construction proposal for a pipeline. The oil company was subject to a global fine of $85,000, with $25,000 allocated to the fine and $60,000 paid to create a bursary for students in a Land and Water Resources diploma program at an Alberta college.

### *R. v. All-Can Engineering and Surveys Ltd.* (2012)[52]—Educating Industry Association Members

The engineering firm pled guilty to failing to provide information to the provincial government about a watercourse crossing required under subsection 142(1)(b) of the *Water Act*.[53] In addition to paying a fine of $10,000, under the terms of creative sentence, the company paid $40,000 into a trust account to fund a research project to be carried out by researchers at the University of Calgary, designed to increase compliance with the *Water Act* by industry members.[54] The research project included an incident investigation under which university researchers will "systematically gather and analyze information" regarding the events that led to the offence committed by the engineering firm, "for the purpose of identifying causes and making recommendations to prevent the incident from happening again."[55] In addition to data collection and synthesis, researchers will "develop best practices for ensuring environmental compliance."[56] The terms of the creative sentence require broad communication of the project findings to the provincial land surveying association.

### *R. v. Permolex Ltd.* (2012)[57]—Environmental Monitoring to Improve Water Quality

The corporation pled guilty to contravening a "term or condition" of an approval issued pursuant to AEPEA.[58] The approval required the corporation to discharge wastewater into the city sanitary sewer system in accordance with the municipal requirements and only emit effluent streams to the atmosphere from an ethanol scrubber exhaust vent indicated in the Permolex application. The corporation failed to comply with two conditions of the approval and pled guilty to both counts. The main reason the corporation did not comply with the above conditions was its failure to ensure that a qualified process engineer was working at its facility. The company addressed the problem by hiring a professional process engineer and agreeing to continue "to pay for the services of a qualified professional for the maximum time provided" under AEPEA, which was three years from the date of the order.[59] In addition to paying $50,000 in fines ($25,000 for each count), one condition of the creative sentence requires the corporation to pay $100,000 to fund the Red Deer River Storm Water Project.[60] One of the main objectives of the project was to improve the quality of the water in the river by implementing a new integrated water management approach under which the city would monitor water quality. Part of the funds paid by Permolex were used to pay a consulting company retained by the municipality to prepare a report that provided information on the chemical content and aquatic life present in the river, upstream and downstream from the municipal wastewater treatment plant. The $200,000, three-year project created by the municipal government to improve the quality of the river water was originally to be funded strictly by taxpayers. As a result of the corporate funding stipulated in the creative sentence, there was a significant reduction in the expense of the water management program to local taxpayers.

### *R. v. Stephen Brown* (2013)[61]—Environmental Consulting Companies, A Stop Order, and Article Publication in Weekly News

The withdrawal of water from unlicensed water bodies has the potential to injure ecosystems.[62] A large pipeline corporation was constructing a new pipeline in Alberta at an estimated cost of $1.8 billion. Several corporations and individuals were retained by the pipeline corporation to assist with the project. One of the individuals hired as a consultant on the project was Stephen Brown, the principal of Brownstone Environmental Services Ltd. Mr. Brown, who had experience with pipeline projects, was training to become a professional agrologist in BC. He had been working long hours and created a false Temporary Diversion Licence (TDL) to facilitate water extraction from a water body for the pipeline project. The "false TDL looked official on its face," and Mr. Brown "delivered a copy of the false TDL to the relevant pipeline company employee," who "sent a copy of the false TDL to an AESRD investigator who had requested it."[63]

After the deception was discovered by the large pipeline corporation and the environmental consulting company that had retained his firm, "Mr. Brown was terminated by the environmental consulting company."[64] Subsequently, Mr. Brown informed a pipeline corporation employee that "he blew it"[65] and provided the following statement to the AESRD investigator: "I just used a copy of the other ones that I had received on previous projects" (to create the false TDL)[66] He informed the AESRD investigator "that the decision to make the false document was his alone and that no one else was aware of what he had done."[67] As part of the AESRD investigation, a senior employee with the environmental consulting company, asked to comment about "the pressures faced by Mr. Brown," stated, "I think" people like Mr. Brown "are under quite a bit of pressure in the field to get things done quickly; the contractor wants to keep moving, and contractors are not always very good at thinking ahead. And so I think the contractor wasn't thinking far enough ahead about water, and they got to a point where they wanted water, and they wanted it now."[68] Mr. Brown pled guilty to Count 2 under section 142(1)(a) of the *Water Act* for providing a "false or misleading" document, and "all remaining charges against Mr. Brown and Brownstone Environmental Services Ltd." were withdrawn.[69]

Under the terms of the creative sentence, Mr. Brown was fined $1,000 and ordered to pay $9,000 to the RiverWatch Institute of Alberta, a charitable organization, to operate the RiverWatch Education Project. This project is designed to inform junior and senior high school students about the quality of river water and to motivate them "to protect and manage water quality for the benefit of wildlife, safe drinking water and recreation."[70] In addition, Mr. Brown was ordered "not to take any steps, for the period of one year, to pursue any designation" as a professional agrologist or agrology technologist in BC "or the equivalent professional designations in Alberta" and to "arrange for the publication of an article in the Environmental Services Association of Alberta's Weekly News" about the incident.[71] The creative sentence in this case was approved by the Provincial Court, as it satisfied the following "key criteria," and fell within the following creative environmental sentencing guidelines:

(1) There is a direct connection between the violation and the project;
(2) The project will benefit the environment;
(3) There is a geographic connection between the project and the offence;
(4) The project will benefit the public;
(5) There is no conflict of interest between the recipient of the funds, either the offender, the Crown, or the investigating agency; and
(6) The environmental enhancement project is to be carried out by a non-profit organization.[72]

### *R. v. Grizzly Oil Sands ULC* (2013)[73]—Habitat Improvement

The defendant oil sands exploration company, Grizzly Oil Sands ULC, failed to comply with the requirements of a temporary water diversion licence issued under the Alberta *Water Act*.[74] After conducting routine water use inspections regarding some of the company's exploration programs, provincial government inspectors questioned the validity of the information submitted on behalf of the company. Corporate executives were unaware that an independent contractor had prepared a false report to be submitted to the Alberta Government regarding the volume of surface water that had been diverted to carry out an exploration program. Immediately after learning that the contractor had prepared the false report, the services contract was terminated and the company reported the incident to the appropriate provincial government department. In 2013, the company pled guilty to contravening subsection 142(1) of the *Water Act* in light of the clear failure to satisfy the terms of the TDL. The Crown prosecutor and defence counsel made a joint submission to the Provincial Court for a creative sentence that provides funding for a habitat conservation project "to grow and establish plants of traditional aboriginal value in wetland habitat."[75] The Crown submitted that the project fell within the Guidelines for Creative Sentencing Projects, as it satisfied the following key criteria:

(1) There was a direct connection between the offence and the project;
(2) The project would benefit the public and produce concrete, tangible results;
(3) The functionally non-profit organization was the most qualified organization to carry out the project;
(4) There was no conflict of interest between the recipient organization, the corporate offender, the Crown, or the investigating agency.[76]

The court accepted the proposed creative sentence and, in addition to imposing a fine of $9,312, ordered the corporation to pay $90,688 into a trust account "for the sole purpose of funding the Wetland Boreal Plant Revegetation Project."[77] Another example of a case in which habitat restoration was funded pursuant to a creative sentence arose after Harvest Operations Corp. contravened subsection 109(2) of *AEPEA* by releasing or allowing the release of a substance into the environment in an amount, concentration, or level that might harm the environment.[78] The court ordered the payment of a $21,000 fine and a payment of $49,000 to Ducks Unlimited Canada to fund a wetland restoration project.[79]

#### *R. v. Plains Midstream Canada ULC* (2014)[80]—Habitat Improvement

The defendant company, Plains Midstream Canada ULC, owned and operated the Rainbow Pipeline.[81] The pipeline leaked 28,000 barrels of oil into a marshy muskeg area.[82] The court ruled that the company had failed to take all reasonable measures to repair, remedy, and confine the effects of the oil, contrary to section 112(1)(a)(i) of *AEPEA*. It therefore committed an offence contrary to section 227(j) of *AEPEA*.[83] In addition to imposing a fine of $225,000, the court ordered the company to pay an additional $225,000 to satisy a creative sentencing order that was jointly proposed by the Crown and defence counsel.[84] The proposed sentence included projects that were designed to conserve or enhance habitat in the Peace River area. It directed that funding would be provided: (a) to enhance access to Joker Lake, reducing the environmental impacts to the access points that anglers use; (b) to purchase, rehabilitate, and enhance the Reinwood conservation site near Deadwood; and (c) for other high-value riparian, lakeside, or marsh habitat conservation projects in the Peace River Area.[85]

The Crown submitted that the proposed creative sentence satisfied the main criteria in the guidelines for creative sentencing projects. The primary criteria included the following: a geographic connection between the offence and the creative sentencing projects; the projects would benefit the environment by conserving habitat with important ecological functions, such as filtering of water, retention of flood waters, and reduction in ecological effects of anglers accessing accessing fishing sites; and the projects would benefit the public by creating cleaner water supplies and habitat, and improve fisheries access.[86] There was no conflict of interest between the recipient of the creative sentencing funds (Alberta Conservation Association [ACA]) and the parties to the case.[87] To satisfy the creative sentencing order, the court ordered the company to deposit $225,000 into a trust account, which the ACA would use within three years to conserve habitat in the Peace River Area.[88] At the time of the sentence, the ACA was in the process of purchasing valuable and disappearing ecotypes in the province for conservation purposes.[89]

### *R. v. Sonic Oilfield Service Ltd.* (2015)[90]—Educational Waste Management Mobile Application

The company operated an oilfield trucking business in Alberta.[91] On June 9, 2011, a Sonic driver transported hydrocarbon condensate to one of its facilities and transferred the liquid to a storage tank.[92] In the process of discarding residual condensate, the liquid spilled onto an open industrial yard area at the facility.[93] A contract welder then inadvertently ignited condensate vapours, causing a flame-based explosion.[94] The Provincial Court of Alberta ruled that the company had disposed of the liquid waste contrary to section 176 of *AEPEA*, which requires waste to be disposed of properly in a container and transported to an appropriate waste treatment facilitiy.[95] The company also contravened section 227(j) of *AEPEA*.[96] In addition to requiring the company to pay a $50,000 fine, the court imposed a creative sentence pursuant to section 234(1) of *AEPEA*.[97] The court ordered the company to pay $200,000 to a local municipality, the City of Medicine Hat, to be held in trust to fund a "Safe Waste Mobile Application."[98] One of the conditions of the creative sentence was that a municipal general manager had to authorize all expenditures from the trust account.[99] In addition, the proposed web application would support Android and Apple mobile and tablet devices and be downloadable for free via online application stores.[100] Further, municipalities would be encouraged to provide links to the application as part of their general awareness and public outreach activities.[101] The application would be used to educate the public about the appropriate disposal of liquid waste.[102] Specifically, it would explain what happens to liquid wastes when they are improperly discharged in an urban setting, including the environmental impacts and impacts to municipal infrastructure related to those discharges.[103]

### *R. v. Canadian Natural Resources Limited* (2016)[104]—Research Project

Canadian Natural Resources Limited (CNRL) operates the Horizon Oil Sands Facility, north of Fort McMurray.[105] On January 24, 2009, the facility began producing synthetic crude oil.[106] Hydrogen sulfide ($H_2S$) is a hazardous substance extracted at the facility.[107] A sulfur recovery unit at the facility was designed to capture and convert $H_2S$ into less toxic substances.[108] In the event the equipment failed, a flare stack was to be employed to combust any excess $H_2S$.[109] On May 28, 2010, the sulfur recovery unit at the facility failed, and contrary to section 227(j) of *AEPEA*, the company did not immediately report the release to the provincial environmental department.[110] More than two years later, on August 2, 2012, the facility sulfur recovery unit failed again, contrary to a condition of the facility approval and section 227(e) of *AEPEA*.[111] As a result of the two statutory violations, the company paid a total financial penalty of $500,000; of that amount $425,000 was allocated to a creative sentencing project in which University of Calgary researchers would analyze the toxicological impact of different chemicals in the air in and around the area affected by the $H_2S$ release.[112]

The Crown submitted that the project fell within the guidelines for creative sentencing projects by meeting the following core criteria: The project would benefit the environment by: (a) determining if current air quality measurements generate sufficient data to perform human based toxicological research; (b) recommending what changes would be necessary to generate sufficient data or recommending what types of toxicological analysis can be undertaken using existing data; and (c) potentially undertaking further analysis to ascertain the potential human health aspects of chemicals in the air in and around Fort MacKay.[113] The project would benefit the public because this was the first case in which this type of human-based research would be undertaken in the area and province.[114] In addition, there was no reasonably perceived conflict of interest between the researcher and the parties to the case.[115] There was a geographic connection between the research project and the incident, as the $H_2S$ release occurred in the same region.[116] After approving the proposed creative sentence, the court ordered the company to deposit the research funds into an Alberta Energy Regulator trust account to be used for the purpose of funding the University of Calgary research project.[117]

### *R. v. Apache Canada Ltd.* (2016)[118]—Research Project

Apache Canada Ltd. owned and operated pipelines in Alberta.[119] On October 25, 2013,[120] and again on January 21, 2014,[121] pipelines operated by the company failed. The first pipeline failure resulted in the release of 1,813 cubic metres of oilfield-produced water, and the second pipeline failure facilitated the release of 1,978 cubic metres of produced water.[122] The company was charged with failing to protect a reinforced composite pipeline from damage on October 25, 2013, contrary to section 9(3) of the *Pipeline Rules*, thereby commiting an offence under section 52(2)(a) of the *Pipeline Act*.[123] The company was also charged with allowing a release into the environment on January 21, 2014 that "causes or may cause a significant adverse effect" contrary to section 109(2) of *AEPEA*.[124] This constituted an offence under section 227(j) of *AEPEA*.[125] The company pled guilty to both offences on September 30, 2016.[126]

The court ordered the company to pay a total financial penalty of $350,000; $160,000 allocated to the 2013 release and $190,000 for the second release.[127] A joint submission was made by the Crown and defence counsel for the company to fund a creative sentencing project called the "Use of Seed Priming and Biochar to Improve the Reclamation Performance of Alberta Native Species in Salt-Affected Soils" in the amount of $305,077.50[128] Alberta Innovates would be the organization that would carry out the research project, to be directed toward remediating salt-affected soil.[129] Salt water spills are a common problem at oil and gas wellsites in Alberta.

The Crown submitted that the project fell within the guidelines for creative sentencing projects by satisfying the following key criteria: there was a geographic connection, because the project would address remediation of salt-affected soils in the area affected by the offences, northwest Alberta;[130] the project would benefit the environment because it would improve scientific understanding of how salt affects soils at wellsites and how these soils can be more effectively remediated by using native plants than by sending the contaminated soil to a landfill;[131] the project would benefit the public by helping to ensure that less clean topsoil, which is a finite resource, will be needed to remediate recurring water pipeline breaks;[132] and there was no apparent conflict of interest between Alberta Innovates and the parties to the case.[133]

## Conclusion

There are a variety of factors that influence whether or not some corporate executives agree to creative sentences. Some executives are simply interested in making the environmental offence disappear and paying a fine. These executives may be concerned about publicity surrounding the offence and the additional legal costs of participating in a joint submission for a creative sentence. In other cases, executives have concluded that creative sentences afford an opportunity to reduce the risk that the corporation may repeat the offence and are interested in funding environmental enhancement projects that benefit the public and demonstrate corporate social responsibility.

Chief Justice Stuart has noted that professional condemnation of undesirable corporate activities can be a significant deterrent to corporations that commit environmental offences. Corporate legal expenses in proceeding to trial can be significant, and rather than just paying a fine some corporate executives would like to have some input as to how significant funds are spent and are interested in supporting environmental improvement projects. As was noted in *R. v. Keno Hill* and *R. v. Waters*, offender remorse is one of the factors to be considered in determining the amount of a fine, and remorse needs to be evaluated based on the offender's actions, not on its words. The reactions of corporate executives to the option of creative sentencing can also be influenced by the corporation's financial situation and corporate priorities, interest in minimizing the risk that the corporation may repeat the offence, and interest in CSR and the social licence to operate. Most of the corporations in Alberta that we have considered have substantial financial resources to fund creative sentencing projects, in particular for research and education.

Chief Justice Stuart has alluded to the role of incentives in encouraging environmental compliance. One incentive for corporations in the cases that have been discussed is minimizing corporate risk. In three of the eight cases in the following creative sentencing update table (Table 28.1), projects directed toward management research, regulatory compliance, and education have been funded. In addition to satisfying the minimum sentencing criteria developed by the provincial government, these projects incorporate a perceived corporate benefit, specifically minimizing the risk that the corporation will repeat the offence in the future. I submit that this is a factor which encourages corporate support for creative sentences that include this type of project.

**Table 28.1 | Alberta Creative Sentencing Update for Environment Offences**

| *Offence* | *Company* | *Fine* | *Project Funding* |
|---|---|---|---|
| *AEPEA*, ss. 227(e) & (b) | *R. v. Suncor Energy* (2009) | $675,000 | $390,000 - Education for Regulatory Compliance and Scholarship |
| *AEPEA*, s. 155; *MBCA*, s. 5.1(1) | *R. v. Syncrude Canada Ltd.* (2010) | $800,000 | $2,450,000 - Habitat preservation; research; and curriculum development |
| *Water Act*, ss. 142(1)(i) & 142(1)(b) | *R. v. Devon Canada Corporation* (2011) | $25,000 | $60,000 - Student bursary |
| *Water Act*, s. 142(1)(e) | *R. v. Statoil Canada Ltd.* (2011) | $5,000 | $185,000 - Education for Regulatory Compliance - Best Industry Practices |
| *AEPEA*, s. 227(e) | *R. v. Permolex* (2012) | $50,000 | $100,000 - Water quality monitoring |
| *Water Act*, s. 142(1)(b) | *R. v. All-Can Engineering and Surveys Ltd.* (2012) | $10,000 | $40,000 - Education for Regulatory Compliance |
| *Water Act*, s. 142(1)(a) | *R. v. Stephen Brown Brownstone Environmental Services Ltd.* (2013) | $1,000 | $9,000 - Stop order; Article publication in Alberta's Weekly News; and water education project |
| *Water Act*, s. 142(1) | *R. v. Grizzly Oil Sands ULC* (2013) | $9,312 | $90,688 - Plant revegetation and education project |
| *AEPEA*, ss. 112(1)(a)(i) & 227(j) | *R. v. Plains Midstream Canada ULC* (2014) | $225,000 | $225,000 - Habitat Conservation and Enhancement |
| *AEPEA*, ss. 176 & 227(j) | *R. v. Sonic Oilfield Service Ltd.* (2016) | $50,000 | $200,000 - Educational Waste Management Mobile Application |
| *AEPEA*, ss. 227(e) & (j) | *R. v. Canadian Natural Resources Limited* (2016) | $75,000 | $425,000- H2S Research Project |
| *AEPEA* ss. 109(2) & 227(j)<br>*Pipeline Act*, s.52(2)(a) & *Pipeline Rules* c. 9(3) | *R. v. Apache Canada Ltd.* (2016) | $44,922.50 | $305,077.50 - Reclamation of salt-affected soils research project |

As indicated in Table 28.1, under the terms of its creative sentence, Suncor Energy in 2009 funded a research and educational project to minimize the risk that the corporation would repeat the environmental offence, and to educate industry operators about the project results. In addition, the corporation created an endowment fund for an environmental education program consistent with its reported commitment to CSR and sustainability. In 2011, Statoil funded an online industry training project to foster increased environmental compliance and to reduce the risk that other industry members will commit the same offence in the future. All-Can Engineering & Surveys Ltd., in 2012, funded a research and education project with a similar objective to the one funded by Suncor Energy in 2009. The project is designed to identify the cause(s) of the environmental offence and to reduce the risk that the corporation and other industry members will commit the offence in the future. These research and education projects are beneficial to the corporations, the public, and the environment.

All of the cases considered in this chapter incorporate projects that contribute to an improved environment or programs designed to prevent environmental degradation. These types of projects can demonstrate corporate social responsibility, and therefore I submit that corporate social responsibility and the social licence to operate are other factors that encourage some corporations to participate in the creative sentencing option that may be available in some cases. Finally, the following economic factors may influence whether a corporation decides to just pay a fine(s) or pay both a fine and a financial penalty to fund environmental enhancement project(s) incorporated into a creative sentence: the financial resources of the corporation; trial costs; withdrawal of additional charges and avoiding the costs of additional litigation; the costs of participating in the development of a joint submission for the proposed creative sentence; potential maximum fine(s) for the offence(s); payment of a smaller fine for an offence along with a financial penalty paid to fund the project(s); the potential tax deductibility of project funding in creative sentences; and the inability of the corporation to deduct fines. Risk minimization, corporate social responsibility, and the economic factors that we have discussed explain why some corporations in Alberta are selecting this innovative sentencing option in some cases.

## NOTES

1 Dianne Saxe & Jackie Campbell, "Getting Creative with the Law" (16 April 2012) Water Canada at 1, online: <https://www.watercanada.net/feature/getting-creative-with-the-law/>.

2 *Ibid.*

3 *R v United Keno Hill Mines Ltd* (1980) 1 YR 299 (Terr Ct) [*Keno*].

4 RSC 1970 (1st Supp), c 28, s 6(1).

5 *Keno, supra* note 3, paras 12–13.

6 *Ibid,* para 17.

7 *Ibid,* paras 21–36.

8 SC 1994, c 22.
9 RSC 1985, c F-14.
10 SC 1999, c 33
11 Government of Canada, "Environmental Damages Fund: legal precedents" (accessed 9 February 2018), online: <http://www.ec.gc.ca/edf-fde/default.asp?lang=EN&n=F6B9CA63-1>.
12 *R v Van Waters & Rogers Ltd* (1998), 220 AR 315 (Prov Ct) [*Van Waters & Rogers*].
13 *Ibid*, paras 23–39.
14 Gordon Scott Campbell, "Fostering a Compliance Culture through Creative Sentencing for Environmental Offences" (2004) 9 Can Crim LR 1 at 19.
15 *Ibid* at 114–119.
16 E Hughes & L Reynolds, "Creative Sentencing and Environmental Protection" (2008) 19 J Envtl L & Prac 105–137.
17 *Ibid* at 131. The authors identified six categories in which the environmental creative sentences tend to fall: prohibition orders; publication orders; orders to conduct or fund research; orders to fund educational projects; prevention orders directed toward improvement of internal corporate operations; and remedial orders to fund specific environmental reclamation and improvement projects with non-governmental organizations (NGO) parties.
18 Environmental Law Centre News Brief, "Action Update, Creative Sentencing Part I – Overview" (2003) 18:2 News Brief at 8. Creative sentencing orders have been an option in Alberta since September 1993.
19 RSA 2000, c E-12; *R v Canadian 88 Energy Corp*, 2003 CarswellAlta 1547 (Prov Ct) at para 1 [*Canadian 88 Energy Corp*].
20 RSC 1985, c F-14.
21 *Canadian 88 Energy Corp*, *supra* note 19 at paras 40–41.
22 Appendix II to the Order.
23 Now Alberta Environment and Parks (AEP).
24 *Canadian 88 Energy Corp*, *supra* note 19 at para 5.
25 *VanWaters & Rogers Ltd*, *supra* note 12; *R v Chem-Security (Alberta) Ltd* (1998), 29 CELR (NS) 60 (Alta Prov Ct).
26 Environmental Law Centre, "Creative Sentencing, Part I – Overview, Creative Sentencing Workshop Part II" (2003) 18:3 News Brief at 8 and 10.
27 AESRD & Alberta Justice and Solicitor General, *Creative Sentencing in Alberta 2012 Report* at 4 [*2012 Report*].
28 Now Alberta Environment and Parks (AEP).
29 *2012 Report*, *supra* note 27 at 2.
30 Alberta Environment, "Enforcement Actions" at 10–12 (accessed 12 February 2018),, online: <http://aep.alberta.ca/about-us/compliance-assurance-program/environmental-protection-commission-reports/documents/Enforcement-2ndQuarterReport-2009.pdf>.
31 Suncor, "Presentations and Key Dates" (accessed 9 February 2018), online: <http://www.suncor.com/en/responsible/1434.aspx>.
32 F Bowen et al, "Lessons for Environmental Compliance From One Company's Creative Sentencing Case" (Presented at the Canadian Society for Unconventional Gas Conference, 19–21 October 2010) CSUG/SPE 138226 at 2–3.
33 *Ibid*.
34 *Ibid*.
35 The Kennedy School at Harvard University's Corporate Social Responsibility Initiative has defined corporate social responsibility (CSR) as follows: "corporate social responsibility encompasses not only what companies do with their profits, but also how they make them. It goes beyond philanthropy and compliance and addresses how companies manage their economic, social, and environmental impacts, as well as their relationships in all key spheres of influence: the community and the public policy realm."
36 International Institute for Sustainable Development (IISD), "IISD's Business and Sustainable Development: A Global Guide – Corporate Social Responsibility (CSR)" (accessed 9 February 2018), online: <http://www.iisd.org/business/issues/sr.aspx>.

37 Suncor Energy, "Firebag Control Orders" (accessed 12 February 2018), online: <http://sustainability.suncor.com/2009/en/responsible/1824.aspx>.

38 *R v Syncrude Canada Ltd*, 2010 ABPC 229 [*Syncrude Canada Ltd*].

39 SC 1994, c 22.

40 *Syncrude Canada Ltd, supra* note 38.

41 Borden Ladner Gervais, "Syncrude Sentenced $3 Million for Waterfowl Fatalities" (November 2010), online: Borden Ladner Gervais <http://blg.com/en/News-And-Publications/Documents/publication_1717.pdf>.

42 *2012 Report, supra* note 27, Appendix II at 12.

43 *R v Statoil Canada Ltd*, Order of JT Henderson (Alta Prov Ct, Edmonton), 31 October 2011 (accessed 12 February 2018), online: <http://aep.alberta.ca/about-us/compliance-assurance-program/compliance-enforcement/operations-division-prosecutions/documents/StatoilCanadaCSO-Oct31-2011.pdf>.

44 RSA 2000, c W-3.

45 *R v Statoil Canada Ltd*, Statement of Agreed Facts (2011), at 2 (accessed 12 February 2018), online: <http://aep.alberta.ca/about-us/compliance-assurance-program/compliance-enforcement/operations-division-prosecutions/documents/StatoilCanadaAgreedFacts-Oct31-2011.pdf>.

46 *2012 Report, supra* note 27, App A.

47 *Ibid.*

48 The industry association represents most of the major Canadian oil producing companies.

49 *2012 Report, supra* note 27, App A.

50 *Ibid* at 10.

51 Reported in the third quarter 2011, "Enforcement of the *Environmental Protection and Enhancement Act* and *Water Act.*"

52 *R v All-Can Engineering and Surveys Ltd*, Alberta Provincial Court, Criminal Division, Order Pursuant to Section 148(1) of the *Water Act*, 12 June 2012 at 1 (accessed 12 February 2018), online: <http://aep.alberta.ca/about-us/compliance-assurance-program/compliance-enforcement/operations-division-prosecutions/documents/AllCanCSO-Jun12-2012.pdf>.

53 *Ibid.*

54 *Ibid* at 2–4.

55 *Ibid* at 4.

56 *Ibid.*

57 *R v Permolex Ltd*, AB Prov Ct (Crim Div), Order Pursuant to Section 234(1) of the *Environmental Protection and Enhancement Act*, 18 April 2012 at 1 (accessed 12 February 2018), online: <http://aep.alberta.ca/about-us/compliance-assurance-program/compliance-enforcement/operations-division-prosecutions/documents/PermolexCSO-Apr18-2012.pdf> [*Permolex Ltd*].

58 Thereby committing an offence under s 227(e) of *AEPEA*.

59 *Permolex Ltd, supra* note 57 at 2.

60 *Ibid* at 2 and 4.

61 *R v Stephen Brown*, Order Pursuant to Section 148(1) of the *Water Act*, 26 June 2013 (accessed 12 February 2018), online: <http://aep.alberta.ca/about-us/compliance-assurance-program/compliance-enforcement/operations-division-prosecutions/documents/StephenBrownCSO-Jun26-2013.pdf> [*Stephen Brown*].

62 *Ibid.*

63 *R v Stephen Brown*, Agreed Statement of Facts (accessed 12 February 2018), online: <http://aep.alberta.ca/about-us/compliance-assurance-program/compliance-enforcement/operations-division-prosecutions/documents/StephenBrownAgreedFacts-Jun26-2013.pdf>.

64 *Ibid* at 7, para 36.

65 *Ibid.*

66 *Ibid* at para 37.

67 *Ibid* at para 38.

68 *Ibid* at para 39.

69 *Ibid* at para 40.

70 *Stephen Brown, supra* note 61, Sched A.

71 *Ibid* at 3.

72 *Stephen Brown, supra* note 61 at 2.

73 *R v Grizzly Oil Sands ULC*, Statement of Facts in Support of a Guilty Plea, 2013, online: <http://aep.alberta.ca/about-us/compliance-assurance-program/compliance-enforcement/operations-division-prosecutions/documents/GrizzlyOilSandsAgreedFacts-Mar27-2013.pdf>.

74 RSA 2000, c W-3.

75 *R v Grizzly Oil Sands ULC*, Order Pursuant to Section 148(1) of the *Water Act*, AB Prov Ct, Ft McMurray, 27 March 2013 (accessed 12 February 2018), online: <http://aep.alberta.ca/about-us/compliance-assurance-program/compliance-enforcement/operations-division-prosecutions/documents/GrizzlyOilSandsCSO-Mar27-2013.pdf>.

76 *Ibid* at 2.

77 *Ibid.*

78 *Ibid.*

79 *2012 Report*, *supra* note 27 at 10.

80 *R v Plains Midstream Canada ULC*, Order Pursuant to Section 234(1) of the *Environmental Protection and Enhancement Act*, AB Prov Ct, Red Deer, 10 July 2014 (accessed 28 February 2018), online: <http://aep.alberta.ca/about-us/compliance-assurance-program/compliance-enforcement/operations-division-prosecutions/documents/PlainsMidstreamCSO-Jul10-2014.pdf> [*Plains Midstream Canada ULC*].

81 *R v Plains Midstream Canada ULC*, Agreed Statement of Facts, AB Prov Ct, Red Deer, 3 June 2014 (accessed 28 February 2018), online: <http://aep.alberta.ca/about-us/compliance-assurance-program/compliance-enforcement/operations-division-prosecutions/documents/PlainsMidstreamAgreedFacts-Jun05-2014.pdf> at para 4.

82 *Ibid.*

83 *Plains Midstream Canada ULC*, *supra* note 80 at 1.

84 *Ibid* at 2.

85 *Ibid.*

86 *Ibid.*

87 *Ibid.*

88 *Ibid* at 2–3.

89 *Ibid* at Schedule A.

90 *R v Sonic Oilfield Service Ltd.*, Order Pursuant to Section 234(1) the Environmental Protection and Enhancement Act, AB Prov Ct, Medicine Hat, 20 March 2015 (accessed 28 February 2018), online: <http://aep.alberta.ca/about-us/compliance-assurance-program/compliance-enforcement/operations-division-prosecutions/documents/SonicOilfiedLtdFiledCSO-Mar-2015.pdf> [*Sonic Oilfield Service Ltd.*].

91 *R v Sonic Oilfield Service Ltd.*, Statement of Agreed Facts, Ab Prov Ct, Medicine Hat, 26 November 2014 (accessed 28 February 2018), online: <http://aep.alberta.ca/about-us/compliance-assurance-program/compliance-enforcement/operations-division-prosecutions/documents/RvSonicOilfieldStateFacts-Nov2014.pdf> at 2.

92 *Ibid.*

93 *Ibid.*

94 *Ibid* at 3.

95 *Sonic Oilfield Service*, *supra* note 90 at 1.

96 *Ibid.*

97 *Ibid* at 2.

98 *Ibid.*

99 *Ibid.*

100 *Ibid* at Appendix A.

101 *Ibid.*

102 *Ibid.*

103 *Ibid.*

104 *R v Canadian Natural Resources Limited*, Order Pursuant to Section 234(1) of the Environmental Protection and Enhancement Act, AB Prov Ct, Sherwood Park, 24 June 2016 (accessed 5 March 2018), online: <http://aep.alberta.ca/about-us/compliance-assurance-program/compliance-enforcement/operations-division-prosecutions/documents/CNRLcs01-June24-2016.pdf> [CNRL Order 1]; *R v Canadian Natural Resources Limited*, Order Pursuant to Section 234(1) of the Environmental Protection and Enhancement Act, AB Prov Ct, Sherwood Park, 24 June 2016 (accessed 1 March 2018), online:

<http://aep.alberta.ca/about-us/compliance-assurance-program/compliance-enforcement/operations-division-prosecutions/documents/CNRLcs02-June24-2016.pdf> [CNRL Order 2].

105 *R v Canadian Natural Resources Limited*, Agreed Statement of Facts, AB Prov Ct, Sherwood Park, 24 June 2016 (accessed 5 March 2018), online: <http://aep.alberta.ca/about-us/compliance-assurance-program/compliance-enforcement/operations-division-prosecutions/documents/CNRL-2010-AgreedFacts-Jun2016.pdf> at para 2.

106 *Ibid* at para 3.

107 *Ibid* at para 4.

108 *Ibid* at para 5.

109 *Ibid.*

110 Alberta Government, "Canadian Natural Resources Limited penalised $500,000 for hydrogen sulfide releases" (24 June 2016), online: <https://www.alberta.ca/release.cfm?xID=429942D1A0F1C-99A6-FF88-F72C01B8E70EE8D2>.

111 *Ibid.*

112 *Ibid.*

113 *Supra* note 104, CNRL Order 1 at 2–3; CNRL Order 2 at 2–3.

114 *Supra* note 104, CNRL Order 1 at 3; CNRL Order 2 at 3.

115 *Ibid.*

116 *Supra* note 104, CNRL Order 1 at 2; CNRL Order 2 at 3.

117 *Supra* note 104, CNRL Order 1 at 3; CNRL Order 2 at 3.

118 *R v Apache Canada Ltd.*, Sentencing Order, AB Prov Ct, Stony Plain, 30 September 2016 (accessed 6 March 2018), online: <http://www1.aer.ca/compliancedashboard/enforcement/201609-01_Creative SentencingOrder_Apache_Zama_2013-005.pdf> [Apache Sentencing Order 1]; *R v Apache Canada Ltd.*, Sentencing Order, AB Prov Ct, Stony Plain, 30 September 2016 (accessed 6 March 2018), online: <http://www1.aer.ca/compliancedashboard/enforcement/201609-02_Creative SentencingOrder_EPEA_Apache_2014-009.pdf> [Apache Sentencing Order 2].

119 *R v Apache Canada Ltd.*, Agreed Statement of Facts, AB Prov Ct, Stony Plain, 30 September 2016 (accessed 6 March 2018), online: <http://www1.aer.ca/compliancedashboard/enforcement/201609-01_AgreedStatementofFacts_Apache_2013-005.pdf> [Apache Facts 1] at para 2; *R v Apache Canada Ltd.*, Agreed Statement of Facts, AB Prov Ct, Stony Plain, 30 September 2016 (accessed 6 March 2018), online: <http://www1.aer.ca/compliancedashboard/enforcement/201609-02_AgreedStatementofFacts_Apache_2014-009.pdf> [Apache Facts 2] at para 2.

120 Apache Facts 1, *supra* note 119 at para 9.

121 Apache Facts 2, *supra* note 119 at para 13.

122 Alberta Energy Regulator, "News Release 2016-10-4: Apache pleads guilty after two pipeline failures" (accessed 6 March 2018), online: <https://www.aer.ca/about-aer/media-centre/news-releases/news-release-2016-10-04>.

123 Apache Facts 1, *supra* note 119 at para 1.

124 Apache Facts 2, *supra* note 119 at para 1

125 *Ibid.*

126 *Supra* note 119.

127 *Ibid.*

128 *Ibid.*

129 *Supra* note 118.

130 Apache Sentencing Order 1, *supra* note 118 at 2; Apache Sentencing Order 2, *supra* note 118 at 2.

131 *Ibid.*

132 Apache Sentencing Order 1, *supra* note 118 at 2–3; Apache Sentencing Order 2, *supra* note 118 at 2–3.

133 Apache Sentencing Order 1, *supra* note 118 at 4; Apache Sentencing Order 2, *supra* note 118 at 4.

# 29

# Environmental Non-Governmental Organizations and Creative Sentencing: Perspectives and Roles

CINDY CHIASSON

## Introduction

This chapter addresses the perspectives and roles of environmental non-governmental organizations (ENGOs) in relation to creative sentencing for environmental offences in Canada. It includes an initial overview of ENGOs and why they have a role in the enforcement arena, as well as a brief discussion of the scope of creative sentencing. The balance of the chapter covers two different aspects of ENGO involvement in creative sentencing: as monitor and "watchdog" of the effectiveness of environmental enforcement, and as a potential or actual recipient of proceeds of a creative sentence.

## ENGOs and Environmental Enforcement: The What and Why

The term "ENGO" is shorthand in the environmental sector (an area laden with jargon and acronyms) for "environmental non-governmental organization," a rather bureaucratic and awkward attempt to identify and categorize a range of organizations and interests that often defy categorization. In relation to environmental regulation, virtually anyone who is neither a regulator nor a regulated party could be an ENGO, though the term tends to refer to non-profit groups focused on some aspect of the environment.

While mainstream media and popular belief often depict Canadian ENGOs as highly sophisticated, well resourced, global activist conglomerates intent on blocking economic development, the actual context is far different.

**Table 29.1 | Geographic Area Served**

| *Geographic area served* | *Percentage of total Canadian ENGOs* |
|---|---|
| Local | 57% |
| Regional (within a province/territory) | 27% |
| One province/territory | 10% |
| More than one province/territory | 2% |
| National | 3% |

An extensive study carried out by Statistics Canada in 2003 shows a different and much more nuanced scenario.[1] Based on that data, there were estimated to be 4,424 environmental organizations active in Canada, which is 2.7 percent of the total number of non-profit organizations in Canada (161,227). As illustrated in table 29.1, the vast majority of these environmental organizations serve focused local interests.

For those organizations, the average annual revenue was $256,000, as compared to average annual revenue for Canadian non-profits in all sectors of $692,000. Nearly 70 percent of ENGOs reviewed in the study had no paid staff; half of staffed ENGOs had only 1–4 staff members.[2]

Environmental organizations also address a wide range of issues, though very few deal with the whole gamut of environmental matters within one organization. Alberta-specific surveying in 2003–4 showed that ENGOs in that province worked on wildlife and wilderness; water pollution; public land management; water quantity; climate change; habitat protection; and energy efficiency and conservation, among many other matters.[3]

There are a number of factors that support a role for ENGOs in relation to environmental enforcement. As discussed above, many deal specifically with local issues and thus have specialized interest, knowledge, and expertise to bring to bear in relation to offences within their geographic and subject areas. Among the broad range of Canadian ENGOs are at least half a dozen focusing on law as a means of environmental protection.[4] Canadians generally depend on non-profit organizations (usually non-governmental) to provide assistance to Canadian society as a whole.[5] In addition, citizens generally feel that opinions expressed by charities "on issues of public concern have value because they represent a public interest perspective."[6] It can be argued that in many instances, ENGOs act as a proxy for the public in addressing the public interest aspect of environmental issues.

## The Scope of Creative Sentencing

In considering the ENGO perspective on creative sentencing, one must be mindful that the scope of creative sentencing in environmental offences extends beyond monetary payments. Since 1993, Alberta courts have had broad discretion to impose orders in addition to prescribed fines or imprisonment for environmental convictions.[7] This can include:

- Prohibiting actions;
- Directing remedial or preventative action;
- Requiring publication or notification of conviction-related facts;
- Requiring deposit of security against compliance or reimbursement of government expenses related to the offence;
- Directing performance of community service; or
- Imposing any other conditions to secure good conduct and prevent other offences.

In addition to directing funds to various research, education, and restoration projects and requiring publication of apologies, the Alberta courts have more recently used this discretion to impose time-limited restrictions on the acquisition and use of specified professional designations by offenders in three separate convictions for providing false information.[8]

More recently, the federal government amended nine environmental Acts, providing the courts a similar range of powers to make additional orders at sentencing.[9] These amendments also create a common structured approach to assessing fines and provide enforcement principles and aggravating factors to be taken into account in setting penalties. The *Fisheries Act* has included powers enabling the courts to make additional orders at sentencing since 1991.[10]

## Assessing Enforcement Effectiveness

A key role that ENGOs can play in relation to creative sentencing and environmental enforcement is as a monitor and assessor of the success and effectiveness of enforcement efforts. In some instances this role may be very specific and localized, for example, where an ENGO is the complainant who has initiated the enforcement process and has a very direct interest in the outcome. This may arise from a "traditional" complaint to environmental regulators, direct citizen initiation of a regulatory investigation,[11] or bringing a private prosecution. In a private prosecution, it would be open to the ENGO as prosecutor to submit a creative sentencing proposal following a conviction, where enabled by the relevant legislation. In situations where the investigation and prosecution have been carried by the government, an ENGO could seek to provide relevant information on behalf of the environment for use at sentencing through contact with the prosecutor or investigators.

ENGOs may also have a broader, higher-level interest in monitoring and assessing the effectiveness of environmental enforcement, including creative sentencing. While the motivations for and uses of such assessments may be as diverse as the spectrum of Canadian ENGOs, likely purposes include measuring performance of the relevant environmental regulatory system determining the contribution of enforcement to environmental protection.

A key concern for ENGOs involved in these activities is access to relevant information and data, which can vary between jurisdictions and relevant legislation. For example, Alberta Environment and Sustainable Resource Development has a relatively broad approach to making environmental information publicly accessible, enabled by legislation and ministerial order.[12] However, information related to an open or ongoing investigation or proceeding cannot be publicly released.[13] Reporting of compliance and enforcement under the *Environmental Protection and Enhancement Act* and *Water Act* is publicly available on an annual (1993–2007) and quarterly (2002–present) basis.[14] These reports provide insight into enforcement action for a particular time period, but data has not been publicly aggregated to show trends over the longer term.

In relation to creative sentencing, Alberta has issued annual reports for the past two years to provide greater transparency and public accountability, on the basis that creative sentences divert funds that would otherwise flow to the province's general revenue.[15] These reports describe ongoing creative sentence projects and provide financial data on creative sentencing as a proportion of total fines assessed in relation to environmental offences. Since late 2011, the ministry also posts creative sentencing orders and related press releases on its website.[16] At the federal level, Environment Canada provides online links to press releases on convictions where fines are directed to the Environmental Damages Fund.[17] However, it is not clear whether this service provides information on all creative sentences issued under federal environmental legislation. Aggregated or cumulative data does not appear to be readily available.

## ENGOs as Beneficiaries of Creative Sentences

ENGOs can be more directly involved as beneficiaries of creative sentences. Keeping in mind the broad scope of legislated sentencing powers discussed above, ENGOs could receive benefit in non-monetary ways, such as through provision of goods or services. For example, creative sentences in Alberta have included the following:

- Directing an agricultural producer to provide turnips (valued at nearly $90,000) to the Edmonton Food Bank for distribution within Edmonton and to other northern Alberta food banks;[18]
- Requiring a convicted individual to perform 200 hours of community service for the public works department of a specified municipality;[19] and
- Directing a sod producer to provide sod (valued at approximately $55,000) to Habitat for Humanity and three municipalities in the region of the offence.[20]

However, payments of money under creative sentences have been the most common means of benefiting ENGOs and other organizations. The balance of this chapter will discuss two Canadian models for implementing monetary creative sentences and offer observations from the recipient of an early creative sentence.

## GRANT MODE

The Environmental Damages Fund (EDF) was created by the federal government in 1995 to provide a mechanism to distribute funds from creative sentences. It is a specified purpose account that is maintained apart from federal general revenues. Monies are directed to the EDF primarily through fines and other court-ordered payments but can also be contributed through negotiated settlements, such as Environmental Protection Alternative Measures under the *Canadian Environmental Protection Act, 1999* or voluntary payments.[21] As a result of amendments by the *Environmental Enforcement Act*, fines for convictions under nine different federal environmental statutes must now be credited to the EDF.[22] Though the bulk of funds flowing into the EDF are court-directed, it is the federal government, rather than the courts, that makes the ultimate decisions on payment of these funds. The courts have discretion to specify a person or organization to whom a fine should be paid from the EDF, but this takes the form of a recommendation to the Minister of Environment.[23]

Funds within the EDF are accessed by successful project applicants, similar to many other granting programs and bodies throughout Canada. The categories of eligible applicants include:

- Non-governmental organizations;
- Academic institutions;
- Aboriginal groups; and
- Provincial, territorial and municipal governments.

Ineligible groups can partner with eligible applicants to apply for funding, though offenders cannot apply for use of funds they paid.[24] Proposed projects must fit within one or more of these categories: restoration; improvement of environmental quality; research and development; and education and awareness. Restoration has been designated as the highest funding priority.[25] Funds are made available for applications on a geographic basis, usually linked to the specific province or territory from which a fine payment originated. Some funds are made available on a broader regional basis.[26] There are usually use restrictions imposed on the available funds, which indicate any parameters related to types of projects, subject matters or geographic siting. Successful project applicants must enter into a funding agreement with Environment Canada and must provide both activity and financial reporting during the project and at project completion.

### CASE-SPECIFIC COURT ORDER MODEL

In Alberta, the creative sentence has become a well-used tool in the environmental enforcement toolbox. Since 1996, 78 creative sentences have been imposed by the Alberta Provincial Court under the *Environmental Protection and Enhancement Act* and *Water Act*. A significant majority of these sentences have been monetary awards for a range of projects.

Guidelines for consideration and selection of creative sentencing projects were formalized in 2002.[27] They cover the following topic areas:

- Prerequisites;
- Aims and objectives of creative sentencing;
- Limitations on eligible projects;
- Limitations for eligible recipients; and
- Administrative limitations (conflict of interest; financial accountability).

Key elements include deterrence; punishment of the offender; and public benefit through either environmental improvement or reduction of risk to the public. There must also be a logical link between the offence and the project to ensure that the project benefits address the wrong caused by the offence. Geographic links are often considered, as well. Eligible recipients must be non-profit organizations, unless there is no non-profit capable of delivering the project under consideration. Recipients are investigated before sentencing with respect to their organizational viability and financial accountability, as well as to ensure there is no actual or perceived conflict of interest with the accused, the Crown or the investigating agency. Recipients sign an agreement with the Crown committing to fulfill obligations imposed in the sentencing order.[28]

An investigator within Alberta Environment and Sustainable Resource Development is responsible for the creative sentencing program and works closely with environmental prosecutors within Alberta Justice. The investigator researches possible projects for creative sentence consideration, investigates potential recipients, and maintains oversight and accountability of creative sentencing projects.

In practice, almost all creative sentencing projects have come before the Alberta courts as joint sentencing proposals submitted following a guilty plea. The broad types of projects that have been directed by creative sentence are as follows (in descending order):

- Education (public; professional/industry; post-secondary);
- Research (predominantly post-secondary);
- Publication of facts of offence or apology;
- Stop or compliance orders or similar restrictions on activities;
- Environmental improvement;
- Environmental restoration;
- Certification;
- Government reimbursement for investigation costs;
- Bursaries or scholarships;
- Victim surcharges;
- Community service;
- Provision of goods or services.

Commendable effort has been invested by the Alberta government in building and maintaining the creative sentencing program. The program was championed for nearly two decades by an environmental prosecutor and has had involvement and oversight by an environmental investigator for over a decade. There have been two workshops (2002 and 2013) with participants in the creative sentencing process to obtain feedback and improve the programs, as well as at least one survey of creative sentencing participants. In 2011, Alberta Environment and Sustainable Resource Development began steps to provide more public information on creative sentencing, including posting creative sentencing orders online and publishing annual creative sentencing reports.

## OBSERVATIONS OF A CREATIVE SENTENCE RECIPIENT

In late 1996, my organization, the Environmental Law Centre (ELC), became one of two recipients of Alberta's first creative sentence under environmental legislation. Dow Chemical Canada Inc. pled guilty to three offences under the *Environmental Protection and Enhancement Act* related to a leak of chlorofluorocarbons from its manufacturing facility near Fort Saskatchewan, Alberta.[29] In addition to imposing a $50,000 fine, the Provincial Court directed Dow to pay $75,000 into a trust account for the ELC to support a public education project on community-based air quality monitoring in Fort Saskatchewan and a further $75,000 into a separate trust account for the University of Alberta Faculty of Engineering to support an air quality research project.

The order was pleasant, though unanticipated, news to the ELC. There had been neither advance notice to the ELC nor any consultation by or discussions with the court or counsel involved. It is important to note that the project was not in any foisted on the ELC; it was part of a multi-module program that the ELC had been carrying out at the time. Until the court order, the Fort Saskatchewan module had been unfunded and the ELC had been pursuing various grant applications. It is likely that this project came to the attention of the Crown and defence counsel through a contact on the ELC board of directors who had links to Dow.

That there had been no pre-sentencing discussion with the ELC created some logistical challenges to be managed. The order directed an annual audit of financial records related to the trust account. To reduce expenses and maximize the amount of funds to be applied to the actual project work, the ELC had to work through the Crown and defence counsel to get permission from the court to have the ELC's annual organizational financial audit also encompass the audit of the trust account.

In addition, the amount ordered was actually more than had been budgeted to carry out the project. Faced with a surplus of funds at the end of project activity in Fort Saskatchewan, the ELC consulted with Crown and defence counsel and ultimately had defence counsel obtain a variation to the order allowing the surplus funds to be applied to an independent evaluation of all modules of the program. Because the ELC had not been a party to the original court order, we could not independently initiate either of these applications to vary the order.

Approximately five years after the project was completed, we discovered a communication gap between the ELC and Crown counsel. ELC management had directed staff carrying out the project to only refer to the funding as being from an order of the Provincial Court of Alberta, with no direct references to Dow. In the early 2000s, an Alberta Justice assessment report of creative sentencing indicated that the Crown felt the ELC project had been a failure, which was a shock to us, as the project had achieved the public education and outreach aims we had set. Follow-up with Crown counsel revealed that their assessment arose from the perception that the project had not provided a sufficient punitive element, likely due to our refraining from any direct mention of Dow's creative sentence in our public communications on the project.

It appears that these challenges, which are perhaps inevitable when being the first of any initiative, have since been addressed in Alberta's creative sentencing program. As discussed above, recipients of creative sentences are reviewed pre-sentence and must sign an agreement related to compliance with the anticipated order. ENGOs and other likely recipients are made aware in advance if their projects will be proposed as part of a creative sentencing order.[30] Sentencing orders also provide more direction in relation to project and financial reporting and no longer require audits of the trust funds. In relation to acknowledgement of funding sources, orders now generally provide that the final project report, which will be in the public domain, "will identify as the genesis of the fund, the conviction entered against [name of offender]."[31] One of the remaining challenges may be to find effective ways to bring ENGOs together with Crown and defence counsel and investigators to raise awareness of projects and initiatives meriting consideration for creative sentence support. The most recent workshop on creative sentencing advised the Alberta government to seek more project ideas from non-governmental organizations.[32]

## Conclusion

> The history of sentencing in environmental matters, particularly in this province [Alberta], has shown an increasing trend toward greater emphasis on the creative penalty. And in that regard, I tend to think of environmental prosecutions as essentially being in the forefront of restorative justice. In no area, either of criminal or quasi-criminal law, has there been such a thrust toward turning the penalty for

the wrongdoing into something that will actually do some good in and of itself, and in these environmental areas, particularly for the environment.[33]

As observed above in 2013 by Judge Jacques of the Alberta Provincial Court, creative sentencing has taken significant strides in entrenching a restorative aspect in environmental enforcement. Moving ahead, ENGOs have a continued and growing role to play. Their grassroots work, direct environmental experience, and resulting expertise all offer the enforcement process a valuable resource in ensuring positive results for the environment and the public interest. Involvement of ENGOs, both directly in implementation of creative sentences and as a means of bringing a public perspective to review, assessment, measurement, and improvement of environmental enforcement systems, can only help in meeting the increasing demand for social licence for activities that affect the environment.

## NOTES

1 National Survey of Nonprofit and Voluntary Organizations (Statistics Canada, 2003). Details on various reports related to this survey can be accessed online at Imagine Canada Research <http://sectorsource.ca/research-and-impact/sector-research/imagine-canada-research> under the heading "National Survey of Nonprofit and Voluntary Organizations."

2 Data from the National Survey of Nonprofit and Voluntary Organizations specific to environmental organizations was compiled in *A Profile of Environmental Nonprofit & Voluntary Organizations in Canada* (Toronto: Canadian Environmental Grantmakers Network, 2004).

3 *Maximizing Effectiveness: An Assessment of Environmental Priorities and Voluntary Sector Capacity Needs in Alberta* (Calgary: Alberta Ecotrust, 2004) at 14, online: Alberta Ecotrust <http://www.albertaecotrust.com/docs/maximizing-effectiveness-summary-2005.pdf>.

4 These include the author's organization, the Environmental Law Centre <http://www.elc.ab.ca/>, as well as Canadian Environmental Law Association <http://www.cela.ca/>; Ecojustice <http://www.ecojustice.ca/>; University of Victoria Environmental Law Centre <http://www.elc.uvic.ca/>; West Coast Environmental Law <http://www.wcel.org/>; and East Coast Environmental Law <http://www.ecelaw.ca/>.

5 *Talking About Charities 2013: Canadians' Opinions on Charities and Issues Affecting Charities* (Edmonton: The Muttart Foundation, 2013), online: The Muttart Foundation <https://www.muttart.org/wp-content/uploads/2015/11/3.-Talking-About-Charities-Full-Report-2013.pdf>. Ninety-three percent (93%) of those surveyed agree that charities are important to Canadians and eighty-eight percent (88%) agree that charities generally improve our quality of life: see *ibid* at 22, Fig 4.1.1. Note that not all Canadian ENGOs are charities; Alberta surveying showed

52% of surveyed ENGOs were registered charities. See *Maximizing Effectiveness*, *supra* note 3 at 14.

6 *Talking About Charities 2013*, *ibid* at 85–86.

7 *Environmental Protection and Enhancement Act*, RSA 2000, c E-12, s 234; *Water Act*, RSA 2000, c W-3, s 148.

8 *R v Brown*; *R v Buoy*; *R v Ulliac*. Details of these and other creative sentencing orders are available in *Creative Sentencing in Alberta: 2013 Report* (Edmonton: Alberta Environment and Sustainable Resource Development, 2014) at Appendix II, online: Alberta Environment and Sustainable Resource Development<http://aep.alberta.ca/about-us/compliance-assurance-program/creative-sentencing/documents/CreativeSentencingAlberta-2013.pdf>. Some Alberta creative sentencing orders can also be accessed online. See, e.g., the creative sentencing order in *R v Mather* (Alberta Provincial Court, 8 April 2013), online: Alberta Environment and Sustainable Resource Development <http://aep.alberta.ca/about-us/compliance-assurance-program/compliance-enforcement/operations-division-prosecutions/documents/MatherCSO-Apr08-2013.pdf>.

9 *Environmental Enforcement Act*, SC 2009, c 14. The Acts amended by this Act are: *Antarctic Environmental Protection Act*; *Canada National Marine Conservation Areas Act*; *Canada National Parks Act*; *Canada Wildlife Act*; *Canadian Environmental Protection Act, 1999*; *International River Improvements Act*; *Migratory Birds Convention Act, 1994*; *Saguenay-St Lawrence Marine Park Act*; and *Wild Animal and Plant Protection and Regulation of International and Interprovincial Trade Act*.

10 *Fisheries Act*, RSC 1985, c F-14, s 79.2.

11 In Alberta, citizens are able to trigger government investigation of environmental offences by filing a declaration: see *Environmental Protection and Enhancement Act*, *supra* note 7, ss 196–197.

12 *Environmental Protection and Enhancement Act*, *supra* note 7, s 35; *Water Act*, *supra* note 7, s 152.1; Ministerial Order 02/2010: "Designation of Public Information Under the *Environmental Protection and Enhancement Act*", online: Alberta Environment and Sustainable Resource Development <http://environment.alberta.ca/documents/Ministerial_Order_02-2010.pdf>.

13 *Environmental Protection and Enhancement Act*, *supra* note 7, s 35(9) and Ministerial Order 02/2010, *ibid*.

14 Online: Alberta Environment and Sustainable Resource Development, Annual and Quarterly Reports – Compliance Assessment Enforcement Reports <http://environment.alberta.ca/01292.html>.

15 See *Creative Sentencing in Alberta: 2012 Report* (Edmonton: Alberta Environment and Sustainable Resource Development, 2013) at 1, online: Alberta Environment and Sustainable Resource Development <https://open.alberta.ca/dataset/76948f36-d2c3-462c-b70f-20de6ee2e728/resource/91dbcbd9-fdd4-4ae9-8951-197fc2541cae/download/2013-creative-sentencing-report-2012-2013-03-14.pdf>. Also see *Creative Sentencing in Alberta: 2013 Report*, *supra* note 8.

16 These orders are usually summarized in the ministry's annual reports, such as the 2012 and 2013 reports cited in this chapter.

17 Online: Environment Canada, Environmental Damages Fund, Legal Precedents <http://www.ec.gc.ca/edf-fde/default.asp?lang=En&n=F6B9CA63-1>.

18 *R v Hillsight Vegetables Inc* (Alberta Provincial Court, 2005). See *Enforcement of the Environmental Protection and Enhancement Act and Water Act, 1 Oct 2005 – 31 Dec 2005* (Edmonton: Alberta Environment, 2006) at 10, online: Alberta Environment and Sustainable Resource Development <https://exts2.aep.alberta.ca/DocArc/

compliance/ComplianceReports/2005-10-2005-12-Quarterlyreport_Oct-Dec2005.pdf>.

19 *R v Wonnacott* (Alberta Provincial Court, 1998).

20 *R v The Manderley Corporation* (Alberta Provincial Court, 2005). See *Enforcement of the Environmental Protection and Enhancement Act and Water Act, 1 Apr 2005 – 30 Jun 2005* (Edmonton: Alberta Environment, 2005) at 11, online: Alberta Environment and Sustainable Resource Development <https://exts2.aep.alberta.ca/DocArc/compliance/ComplianceReports/2005-04-2005-06-QuarterlyReport_Apr-Jun2005.pdf>.

21 Online: Environment Canada, Environmental Damages Fund, Legal Community <http://www.ec.gc.ca/edf-fde/default.asp?lang=En&n=A82326FE-1#recommending>.

22 See *supra* note 9.

23 See, e.g., *Canadian Environmental Protection Act, 1999*, SC 1999, c 33, s 294.1(2).

24 See online: Environment Canada, Environmental Damages Fund, Potential Applicants <http://www.ec.gc.ca/edf-fde/default.asp?lang=En&n=C7C99D1F-1>.

25 See online: Environment Canada, Environmental Damages Fund <http://www.ec.gc.ca/edf-fde/default.asp?lang=En&n=BD1220D8-1>.

26 See online: Environment Canada, Environmental Damages Fund, Available Funds <http://www.ec.gc.ca/edf-fde/default.asp?lang=En&n=137DC913-1>.

27 Susan McRory & Lynda Jenkins, "Creative Sentencing: Part II – Outcome of Workshop" (2003) 18:3 Environmental Law Centre NewsBrief at 8, online: Environmental Law Centre <http://www.elc.ab.ca/Content_Files/Files/NewsBriefs/Vol.18No.32003.pdf>.

28 *Creative Sentencing in Alberta: 2012 Report*, *supra* note 15 at 4.

29 *R v Dow Chemical Canada Inc* (1996) 23 CELR (NS) 108 (Alta Prov Ct). Note that this reporting does not reproduce the actual creative sentence order.

30 Personal communication with Hanneke Brooymans, Environmental Investigations Liaison, Alberta Environment and Sustainable Resource Development (17 January 2014).

31 For an example, see the creative sentencing order in *R v Mather*, *supra* note 8.

32 *Creative Sentencing in Alberta: 2013 Report*, *supra* note 8 at 3.

33 Per Jacques J, Alberta Provincial Court, March 2013, as cited in *Creative Sentencing in Alberta: 2013 Report*, *ibid* at 2.

# 30

# Negotiating Sentences

PETER J. CRAIG

This chapter is admittedly not intended to be a treatise. It is primarily intended to highlight practical issues associated with negotiating sentences for environmental offences as a discussion guide for this broad topic among program attendees. The ancillary purposes are to assist practitioners in preparing for this process, and to provide a glimpse into the perspective of prosecutors in approaching particular cases.

## 1. The Legal Framework

### A. First Principles—The *Criminal Code*—Pertinent Sentencing Provisions

In Nova Scotia, by operation of our provincial *Summary Proceedings Act*, the provisions of the *Criminal Code* apply to the prosecution of all provincial regulatory statutes. Specifically, the sentencing factors/considerations set out in sections 718, 718.1 and 718.2 apply and are superimposed upon the contextual sentencing principles for particular kinds of regulatory offences. A similar regime exists in most other Canadian jurisdictions (i.e. an omnibus-form provincial statute that incorporates by reference the pertinent sections of the *Criminal Code* and effectively establishes that the governing substantive and procedural summary proceedings *Code* provisions apply to the prosecution of provincial offences).

I am often reminded by judges I appear before of these *Code* sentencing provisions and their application to regulatory offences. I have made the mistake of fixating, almost exclusively, on sentencing factors/considerations that have emerged from various regulatory cases, only later to be advised by the court that they have to be viewed through the lens of the *Code* sections as well. I can't emphasize enough that practitioners should never lose sight of this:

*Purpose*

718 The fundamental purpose of sentencing is to protect society and to contribute, along with crime prevention initiatives, to respect for the law and the maintenance of a just, peaceful and safe society by imposing just sanctions that have one or more of the following objectives:

(a) to denounce unlawful conduct;
(b) to deter the offender and other persons from committing offences;
(c) to separate offenders from society, where necessary;
(d) to assist in rehabilitating offenders;
(e) to provide reparations for harm done to victims or to the community; and
(f) to promote a sense of responsibility in offenders, and acknowledgment of the harm done to victims or to the community.

718.1 A sentence must be proportionate to the gravity of the offence and the degree of responsibility of the offender.

718.2 A court that imposes a sentence shall also take into consideration the following principles:

(a) a sentence should be increased or reduced to account for any relevant aggravating or mitigating circumstances relating to the offence or the offender, and, without limiting the generality of the foregoing,

  (i) evidence that the offence was motivated by bias, prejudice or hate based on race, national or ethnic origin, language, colour, religion, sex, age, mental or physical disability, sexual orientation, or gender identity or expression, or any other similar factor,
  (ii) evidence that the offender, in committing the offence, abused the offender's spouse or common-law partner,
    (ii.1) evidence that the offender, in committing the offence, abused a person under the age of eighteen years,

(iii) evidence that the offender, in committing the offence, abused a position of trust or authority in relation to the victim,

(iii.1) evidence that the offence had a significant impact on the victim, considering their age and other personal circumstances, including their health and financial situation,

(iv) evidence that the offence was committed for the benefit of, at the direction of or in association with a criminal organization, or

(v) evidence that the offence was a terrorism offence, or

(vi) evidence that the offence was committed while the offender was subject to a conditional sentence order made under section 742.1 or released on parole, statutory release or unescorted temporary absence under the *Corrections and Conditional Release Act*

shall be deemed to be aggravating circumstances;

(b) a sentence should be similar to sentences imposed on similar offenders for similar offences committed in similar circumstances;

(c) where consecutive sentences are imposed, the combined sentence should not be unduly long or harsh;

(d) an offender should not be deprived of liberty, if less restrictive sanctions may be appropriate in the circumstances; and

(e) all available sanctions, other than imprisonment, that are reasonable in the circumstances should be considered for all offenders, with particular attention to the circumstances of Aboriginal offenders.

## B. *The Environment Act* (N.S.) – Pertinent Sentencing Provisions

*Penalty*

159 (1) A person who commits an offence referred to in subsections 50(1), 61A(1), 61C(1), 67(1) or 68(1) or clauses 158(a), (e), (g) or (ga) is liable to a fine of not less than one thousand dollars and not more than one million dollars or to imprisonment for a period of not more than two years, or to both a fine and imprisonment.

(2) A person who commits an offence referred to in Section 32, subsection 50(2), Sections 55, 59 or 60, subsections 61A(2) or 61C(2),

Section 62, subsection 67(2), subsection 68(2), Sections 69, 71, 75, 76, 79, 83, 89, 115, 124 or 132 or clauses 158(b), (c), (d), (f), (h), (ha) or (hb) is liable to a fine of not more than one million dollars. . . .

(4) A person who commits an offence referred to in any other provision of this Act is liable to a fine of not more than five hundred thousand dollars.

*Section 99 offence*

159A (1) In this Section, "business" means

(a) a person authorized or entitled to carry on a trade, occupation, profession, service or venture with a view to a profit, including a partnership and a limited partnership; or

(b) a corporation.

(2) A business that commits an offence referred to in Section 99 is liable to a fine of not more than one hundred thousand dollars or the fine prescribed in the regulations.

(3) Notwithstanding clause 3(aj), a person, other than a business, who commits an offence referred to in Section 99 is liable to a fine of not more than ten thousand dollars or the fine prescribed in the regulations. (2006, c. 30, s. 47.)

161 Where a person is convicted of an offence under this Act and the court is satisfied that, as a result of the commission of the offence, monetary benefits accrued to the offender, the court may order the offender to pay, in addition to a fine under Section 159, a fine in an amount equal to the estimation of the court of the amount of those monetary benefits.

*Continuing offence*

162 Where an offence under this Act is committed or continued on more than one day, the person who committed the offence is liable to be convicted for a separate offence for each day on which the offence is committed.

*Liability of directors and officers*

164 Where a corporation commits an offence under this Act or the regulations, any officer, director or agent of the corporation who directed, authorized, assented to, acquiesced in or participated in the

violation of this Act or the regulations is guilty of the offence and is liable to the punishment provided for the offence, whether or not the corporation has been prosecuted.

*Court orders relating to penalty*

166 (1) Where a person is convicted of an offence under this Act, in addition to any other penalty that may be imposed pursuant to this Act, the court may, having regard to the nature of the offence and the circumstances surrounding its commission, make an order

- (a) prohibiting the offender from doing anything that may result in the continuation or repetition of the offence;
- (b) directing the offender to take any action the court considers appropriate to remedy or prevent any adverse effect that results or may result from the act or omission that constituted the offence;
- (c) directing the offender to publish, in the prescribed manner and at the cost of the offender, the facts relating to the conviction;
- (d) directing the offender to notify any person aggrieved or affected by the conduct of the offender, of the facts relating to the conviction, in the prescribed manner and at the cost of the offender;
- (e) directing the offender to post a bond or pay money into court in an amount that will ensure compliance with any order made pursuant to this Section;
- (f) on application to the court by the Minister within three years after the date of conviction, directing the offender to submit to the Minister any information with respect to the conduct of the offender that the court considers appropriate in the circumstances;
- (g) directing the offender to compensate the Minister, in whole or in part, for the cost of any remedial or preventive action that was carried out or caused to be carried out by the Government and was made necessary by the act or omission that constituted the offence;
- (h) directing the offender to perform community service;
  - (ha) directing the offender to pay to the Minister the costs incurred by the Minister in carrying out the investigation of the offence;

(hb) directing the offender to dispose of the litter in a manner and within the time prescribed by the Minister;

(i) requiring the offender to comply with any other conditions the court considers appropriate in the circumstances for securing the good conduct of the offender and for preventing the offender from repeating the offence or committing other offences.

The sentencing provisions of the Nova Scotia *Environment Act* are similar to those found in many other jurisdictions. Yet there are some very significant subtleties. The first can be found in section 159. In addition to the creative sentencing options set out in section 166, which are available for any offence under the *Act* or subordinate regulations, subsections 159(1) and (2) provide different "traditional" sentencing thresholds for the respective offences enumerated therein. The offences enumerated in subsection 159(1) draw potential maximum fines of one million dollars; carry minimum fines of one thousand dollars; and are the only offences for which imprisonment (up to two years) can be imposed, which can occur in conjunction with the fines. The offences enumerated in subsection 159(2) draw a maximum fine of one million dollars (without a prescribed minimum penalty), and custody is not an available option.

Subsection 159(4) sets out a maximum fine of five hundred thousand dollars for any other offence under the *Act* or regulations thereunder, and again, custody is not an available option.

Subsection 159A sets up a separate littering fine regime. A "business," which includes a certain type of person, is subject to a maximum fine of one hundred thousand dollars pursuant to subsection 159A(2). All other persons are subject to a maximum fine of ten thousand dollars pursuant to subsection 159A(3).

As a humble prosecutor, I, possibly like many of you, muse from time to time about the policy rationale behind this regime, which restricts custody to a small array of offences and sets up a four- or five-tier fine structure.

Section 161 empowers a sentencing judge to impose an additional fine to those set out in section 159 equal to the estimated amount of monetary benefit a defendant incurs by commission of an offence.

Section 166 sets out a very broad and robust range of creative sentencing options following conviction of any offence under the *Act* or subordinate regulations, which includes subsection 166(1)(i):

(i) requiring the offender to comply with *any other conditions the court considers appropriate in the circumstances* for securing the

> good conduct of the offender and for preventing the offender from repeating the offence or committing other offences. [emphasis added]

I would draw your attention to the wording in subsection (1) "in addition to any other penalty that may be imposed pursuant to this Act." Several Nova Scotia judges, quite properly in my respectful view, have interpreted this strictly. This has meant, in cases where the global sentence was heavily weighted towards creative sentencing, that a nominal fine(s) was/were imposed as well in order to comply with this precondition.

Prior to turning to the next topic, I feel I must acknowledge my own bias, lest I be viewed as a hypocrite: I am an unabashed proponent of and advocate for creative sentencing.

## 2. The Dialogue

To say the sentencing process is more art than science is not exactly relaying an insightful observation. I personally find the identification and application of notionally precedent sentencing decisions in environmental cases very challenging. To provide an example, the sentencing emphasis for separate defendants may be entirely different notwithstanding that they may be guilty of the same offence. In one case, the defendant may be a large, financially well-off company. In the next, the defendant may be a small, "mom & pop"-style corporate entity, barely surviving. In the next, it may involve an individual defendant (i.e. a real person), and one readily appreciates the range of financial wherewithal applicable here, which affects the viability and capacity to utilize various sentencing options in this context. Finally, superimpose on all these different scenarios an additional variable—whether your defendant is an incorrigible recidivist menace who has breached multiple administrative and court orders and otherwise been an enforcement nightmare for the investigators, OR whether your defendant has no negative enforcement history and is not "morally" culpable for a costly remediation event that culminated in a charge due to his/her/its status as an owner of property, perhaps solely. Finding precedent decisions, in my experience, on all fours with a present case has, indeed, been challenging.

I am always mindful of the purpose of the sentencing exercise in a regulatory prosecution. Environmental offences, like many others, are violations of public welfare legislation. I fully acknowledge the significance of deterrence, both general and specific in this context. But to my way of thinking, the focus of an environmental sentencing should be squarely placed on how deterrence is achieved, while at the same time addressing remediation causally connected to an offence, if applicable, and also promoting public or industry education and awareness that could change behaviour. I do not see these as mutually exclusive objectives.

So, how does all this theory manifest itself when dealing with environmental offence sentence negotiation? Although our provincial Minister of Finance may occasionally not be enamoured with my approach, I typically do not place primary emphasis on fine quantum. At least as far as I am aware, fine revenue, in this province (and likely others) goes directly into the general revenue stream. Accordingly, it is not, in effect, targeted in any responsive way to an environmental offence. I believe that a fine should always be a component of a global sentence package. However, my point is, how big should the fine piece of this global sentence pie be, and as a result, should counsel be fixating on fine quantum exclusively when discussing sentence? In jurisdictions like Nova Scotia that provide a broad array of creative sentence alternatives, are funds and human resources better directed elsewhere, particularly if there is an unresolved remediation problem or significant educational/awareness need tied to the root cause of an offence?

My general approach when considering sentence discussion with counsel is to first educate myself about the offence and the defendant, and my principal conduit in these respects is always the investigator. I lean heavily on investigators to school me about enforcement issues connected to a geographic area or industry sectors. I know few prosecutors positioned to gauge these things themselves, and I certainly include myself with the majority. I will provide an example to illustrate the exercise, and I will fudge a little bit of detail to protect identifying any individuals or entities.

Suppose you are a woe-begotten prosecutor who shows up for work one day and there is a multi–banker box file on your desk. It is a case involving the owner of a commercial premises that has its own onsite sewage disposal system. The corporate owner has been charged with an offence under the *Environment Act* for violating terms and conditions of its system approval. The particulars of the charge involve effluent exceedences outflowing into the lake adjacent to the property. The investigation reveals that, quite commonly, the owner hired a certified consultant to design, install, and secure approval for the system, and has further retained the consultant to monitor the system and forward to the department the quarterly produced effluent level data that is a further condition of the approval.

The owner, once charged, takes responsive action and corrects the problem. The principal of the company tells the investigator that everyone working in his industry essentially operates this end of their business the same way he does and virtually defers all compliance decisions and compliance filing responsibilities to consultants, for a commensurate fee, of course. The investigator tells you, the beleaguered prosecutor, when she calls you prior to the defendant's initial court date, that this is very typical, and, indeed, is something of a macro-enforcement/education issue. You, the noble warrior of justice, recognize that contracting out responsibility under the Act in this fashion certainly doesn't constitute due diligence, but you do also acknowledge the lesser degree of moral culpability on the part of this owner that the situation entails.

The defendant's counsel speaks to you on the arraignment date (i.e. the initial court appearance in answer to the charge). He is kicking the tires a little bit, and seeks your position on sentence if an early guilty plea is forthcoming. The parties agree to adjourn the defendant's plea for a month or so to allow discussions to occur in the interim.

You arrange a meeting with the investigator the following week. She elaborates on her case a little more. She has found the defendant, in the person of its principal, to have been very cooperative with the investigation and to have taken practical responsibility for the offence. What is more, this person is an active member of a *bona fide* provincial industry association that works periodically with the department and that encompasses most of the businesses carrying on similar operations in the province. The investigator elaborates further about the very tangible enforcement need to educate members of this industry about the practice of delegating statutory responsibility under the Act to consultants, which in her opinion is widespread and prevalent throughout the entire province.

You, the savvy prosecutor, quickly deduce that perhaps this is a case tailor-made for creative sentencing options. You kick this around some more with the investigator. She tells you that this industry association has an annual general meeting every spring that draws virtually all of the large number of its members together under one roof. Her department participates in some form of educational initiative at almost every one of these AGMs, which the department sees as a unique opportunity to get the most bang for its buck, and she is of the view that this would be an ideal forum for a creative sentence presentation about this case.

So, you, the not-so-commensurately-paid quasi–Minister of Justice, are now armed to discuss sentence further with the defendant's counsel. Prior to doing so, however, as you would for any type of offence, you research how similar offences have been treated by the courts in this province and throughout the country. This process quickly reveals that fines have been the overwhelmingly most common sentencing tool utilized, given that historically this was the only option available. Essentially, this process provides you with a broad fine range within which these precedent cases fell.

You then write the defendant's counsel and communicate your position on plea resolution and *joint* sentence recommendation. You use the fine range as a guide for the defendant's global financial penalty, so to speak, as you will be proposing several creative sentence initiatives for which there will be a hard cost to the defendant attached. You propose that the defendant:

- Fund a presentation at the industry association AGM in the amount of $5,000 that will reflect the circumstances of this offence. The form and content of the presentation will be mutually agreed on in advance as between the defendant and the investigating department, and will be presented by the principal of the company;
- Make a donation to a local Watercourse Preservation Society in the amount of $5,000;
- Publish the circumstances of the offence in a media outlet(s) mutually agreed as between the defendant and the department, with the content also to be mutually agreed, the total approximate cost of which shall be $5,000; and
- Pay a fine in the amount of $500.

Lest anyone get the wrong impression, the amounts noted above are not intended to reflect the actual fine range/global sentence package cost for an offence of this sort in this province, but are for illustration purposes only.

You will inevitably receive a call from defence counsel shortly following receipt of your letter wondering what all this means, and fairly inquiring about some of the logistics associated with these sentence initiatives. You will explain to counsel that the figures you have selected were not plucked out of thin air. Assuming counsel has researched the fine range, you will be able to easily demonstrate to your friend that the total cost associated with these initiatives falls well within the fine range for an offence of this nature, and also credits the defendant for the mitigation value of an early guilty plea.

As something of a carrot for the defendant, you mention to counsel, without holding yourself out as an authority on the following points by any means, that the defendant may be able to take accounting and tax benefits from a sentence structured in this fashion, as opposed to one that is predicated on a fine only. This is not a concern for you, as the global sentence range is maintained regardless of how a particular sentence is structured, and you urge counsel to have the defendant get advice from its professional financial advisors.

The next step in the process, of course, will be for defence counsel to confer with and advise the defendant, and receive instructions.

My experience with this negotiating process, and particularly utilizing creative sentencing, has been overwhelmingly positive. Counsel see that judges in this province appear to be embracing this exercise, notwithstanding that the process may entail some supervisory jurisdiction on their part through the life of the sentence order. My respectful observation is that judges view these types of sentences as more directly responsive to the offence, and more congruent with the sentencing principles for public welfare offences than sentences based on fines only.

So, the question becomes, why not approach the process this way?

# 31

# Creative Sentence Negotiation: Looking Beyond Deterrence

PAUL ADAMS

When sentencing for environmental offences, it is important to begin with a recognition that "regulatory offences and crimes embody different concepts of fault."[1] In the regulatory context, the primary focus is the protection and advancement of public and societal interests and values rather than punishment of the individual offender. Environmental protection legislation is "directed to the prevention of future harm through the enforcement of minimum standards of conduct and care."[2]

Deterrence has therefore become the paramount sentencing principle for environmental offences. Fines have been a primary mechanism by which deterrence is addressed, the idea being that a substantial monetary penalty makes it more cost-effective for the potential offender to meet the applicable standard of care. However, taking a fine-centric approach may represent a missed opportunity. An effective sentence can accomplish more than deterrence. It can educate as to the importance of the underlying regulatory purpose and make a tangible contribution to the preservation and enhancement of the environment. The creative sentencing tools available in environmental protection legislation recognize that potential. They allow a sentence to be both an effective deterrent and a meaningful contribution to attaining the regulatory goal.

In the context of negotiating sentences for environmental offences, it can be useful to shift the focus from the deterrent/punitive aspects of a sentence to the opportunity to contribute to and advance the regulatory purpose. First, it can frame the discussion in terms more amenable to the offender's interests and concerns. Second, and more fundamentally, it can produce sentences that have both a meaningful deterrent impact and an identifiable societal benefit.

## The Paramountcy of Deterrence

In *R. v. Hydro-Quebec*,[3] the Supreme Court of Canada emphasized the importance of environmental protection regulation:

> Whether viewed positively as strategies for maintaining a clean environment, or negatively as measures to combat the evils of pollution, there can be no doubt that these measures relate to a *public purpose of superordinate importance*, and one in which all levels of government and numerous organs of the international community have become increasingly engaged. In the opening passage of this Court's reasons in what is perhaps the leading case, *Friends of the Oldman River Society v. Canada (Minister of Transport)*, [1992] 1 SCR 3, at pp. 16–17, the matter is succinctly put this way:
>
> > The protection of the environment has become one of the major challenges of our time. To respond to this challenge, governments and international organizations have been engaged in the creation of a wide variety of legislative schemes and administrative structures.

Prosecutions and, in particular, the sentencing process have an expressive function with respect to societal values and goals.[4] As noted by the court in *R. v. Domtar*:[5]

> The 1989 unreported case of *R. v. Shamrock Chemicals Ltd.* makes it clear that, "Prosecutions also reinforce societal values" and that … the sentence is the most visible result of prosecution, the outcome by which the general public—rightly or wrongly—judges the success of a prosecution. Therefore, the outcome of the sentencing process is an important determinant of whether the public has respect for the legal system.

Given the "superordinate importance" of environmental protection and the imperative to reinforce that societal value, it is not surprising that courts have recognized the paramountcy of general deterrence when imposing sentences for environment offences.[6] The goal of sentencing in such cases "is to stop the polluting, repair any damage to the environment, warn others than such conduct will not be tolerated, and prevent repetition of such polluting practices."[7]

Environmental legislation is generally preventive in nature—designed to prohibit the creation of the risk of environmental harm. As noted in *R. v. Echo Bay Mines Ltd.*,[8] "we should always consider approaching the question of sentence not on what the damage in fact was, especially if it is minor, but on the potential for damage because the imposition of penalties is to ensure that the persons know that they must comply with the requirements of the law to avoid any potential harm."

In terms of quantifying an appropriate penalty, the well-established principle is that a fine must be substantial enough to effectively warn others that the offence will not be tolerated and not be so low as to appear to be the mere cost of doing business or a licence fee for illegal activity.[9] As noted in *R. v. Terroco Industries Ltd.*, with respect to an appropriate fine, "it should be such that it is cheaper to comply than to offend."[10]

When assessing the sufficiency of a sentence for deterrent purposes, the factors to be considered are equally well established. They include the nature of the environment; the extent of the injury; the criminality or blameworthiness of the conduct; the extent of attempts to comply; remorse; size of the corporation or offending party; profits realized by the offence; and the existence of any prior convictions.[11]

## An Opportunity to Do More

While fines have been a primary tool in addressing deterrence in sentencing for environmental offences, at least as far back as 1980 there has been a recognition that fines alone may not be the most effective means of correcting environmental harm and deterring future offences.[12] A "special approach" is required.[13] Some commentators have suggested that general deterrence and punishment should be secondary to remediation and rehabilitation in the regulatory context.[14] Others suggest that sentencing—particularly in the case of the corporate offender—"should look beyond deterrence and seize the opportunity for corporate rehabilitation and the broader public interest."[15] Whether or not such approaches are consistent with established sentencing principles, both recognize that focusing solely on deterrence may be a "missed opportunity"[16] to use the sentencing process to advance the underlying regulatory goal and associated societal interests.

In response, virtually all federal environmental legislation now includes a broad spectrum of "creative sentencing" tools to effectively address environmental offences. Some of the more commonly employed "creative sentencing" tools include prohibition orders, publication orders, orders to conduct or fund research, orders to fund educational projects, orders directed toward improvement of internal corporate operations and practices, and remedial orders funding specific environmental reclamation/improvement projects.[17]

These "creative sentencing" tools can and have been used to effectively address the paramount sentencing goal of deterrence. They also provide an opportunity to move beyond deterrence and make tangible contributions to the restoration, preservation, and enhancement of the environment. As noted by Hughes and Reynolds in their article "Creative Sentencing and Environmental Protection,"[18] "the potential is there, however, to use creative sentencing for larger goals of direct environmental benefit where the 'polluter pays.'"

## Negotiating a "Creative Sentence"

From the Crown perspective, when negotiating sentence for environmental offences, there are a number of considerations in determining the appropriateness of a "creative sentence."

Fundamentally, the global penalty must be sufficient to represent a meaningful deterrent both to the defendant and others. Beyond that, there must be a nexus or connection between the offence and the proposed creative sentencing measure—both with respect to the nature of the environmental harm and, preferably, the location where the offence occurred. The primary focus should be producing a tangible or identifiable societal benefit.

During sentence negotiation, framing the issue as an opportunity to contribute to and advance the regulatory purpose—rather than an exercise in deterrence and punishment—can be effective. In a sense, it allows the defendant to participate in and contribute to the achievement of the regulatory goal—environmental protection and enhancement. This can characterize the process in terms more amenable to the offender's interests and concerns. More fundamentally, it can produce sentences that have both a meaningful deterrent impact and a societal benefit.

There are many examples of this approach producing sentences that have meaningful deterrent value and tangible societal benefit. In the Atlantic region, several cases illustrate the point.

In *R. v. Corner Brook Pulp and Paper Ltd.*,[19] the defendant was charged with depositing a deleterious substance into waters frequented by fish contrary to subsection 36(3) of the *Fisheries Act*.[20] The charge related to the discharge of acutely lethal effluent from the company's pulp and paper mill into the adjacent marine environment (Humber Arm). There was evidence that the quality of the impacted marine environment had been seriously diminished by the ongoing effluent deposits. The "creative sentence" imposed on the defendant included a $500,000 fine; an order that $50,000 be directed to the Corner Brook Stream Development Corporation for purposes of related environmental restoration and enhancement projects; that $75,000 be directed to West Viking College in Corner Brook for the establishment of scholarships in its Resources Technology Program; and $125,000 be directed to Sir Wilfred Grenfell College, Memorial University, for the creation of scholarships in its Bachelor of Environmental Science Program. In addition, the defendant was ordered to complete the construction of an effluent treatment plant within a specified period. Satisfactory completion of the treatment effluent plant was secured by way of an "Irrevocable Letter of Guarantee" in the amount of $500,000 deposited with the presiding court.

In *R. v. City of Moncton,*[21] the City was charged with violating subsection 36(3) of the *Fisheries Act*. The charge related to the deposit of toxic leachate from a landfill site operated by the City into the adjacent Petitcodiac River. The "creative sentence" imposed included a $10,000 fine, an order that an additional $5,000 be directed to the Environmental Damages Fund[22] an order that an additional $25,000 be directed to the Jonathan Creek Committee to be used for purposes of restoration and enhancement of the impacted environment; and an order that the defendant implement all requirements of the "Jonathan Creek – Petitcodiac River Remedial Plan" within a specified period. The cost of implementation of the "Remedial Plan" was estimated at approximately $400,000.

In *R. v. Fox Harbour Developments Ltd.*,[23] the defendant was charged with two counts of carrying out works that resulted in the harmful alteration, disruption, and destruction of fish habitat contrary to subsection 35(1) of the *Fisheries Act*. The offence seriously damaged near-shore lobster habitat. The sentence imposed included a fine of $35,000; an order that an additional $130,000 be directed to DFO Oceans and Habitat Branch, to be used for the assessment, restoration, and enhancement of the lobster habitat impacted by the violation; and an order that an additional $15,000 be directed to DFO Conservation and Protection Branch for the conduct of educational seminars for students and industry representatives in the region in relation to conservation and protection of fish habitat.

More recently, in *R. v. Kelly Cove Salmon Ltd.*,[24] the defendant was charged with two counts of violating subsection 36(3) of the *Fisheries Act*. The offence involved the deposit of a toxic pesticide into the Bay of Fundy over an extended period during the course of the defendant's aquaculture operations. The sentence imposed included fines totalling $100,000; an order that $250,000 be directed to the University of New Brunswick for purposes of creating a "UNB Environmental Studies Scholarship"; an order that an additional $100,000 be directed to the University of New Brunswick and allocated by the "Dean of Science, Applied Science and Engineering" in support of environmental studies and research projects relating to the fishery and aquaculture industry in the Bay of Fundy Region; and an order that an additional $50,000 be directed to the Environmental Damages Fund for the restoration and enhancement of fish habitat in the impacted area.

In each of the above-noted cases, the sentences imposed were the result of negotiated sentence agreements that were jointly recommended to the sentencing court. All represent an attempt to set a meaningful deterrent in relation to significant environmental offences—while at the same time making a tangible contribution to the restoration and enhancement of the environment and its future protection. The idea was to look beyond deterrence to achieve an identifiable societal benefit.

## Conclusion

In my experience, approaching sentencing discussions as an opportunity rather than a blunt instrument has worked both from the Crown and defence perspective. Not surprisingly, it tends to produce agreement. More importantly, it results in sentences that enhance public confidence in the process by producing identifiable societal benefits, rather than simply directing monies to general government coffers.

Viewed as an opportunity to advance environmental stewardship as a "fundamental value"[25] in our society, a creative sentence can make contributions well beyond the deterrence and punishment of a particular offender.

### NOTES

1 *R v Wholesale Travel Group Inc*, [1991] 3 SCR 154 at para 219.
2 *Ibid* at para 219.
3 *R v Hydro-Quebec*, [1997] 3 SCR 213 at para 85 [*Hydro-Quebec*].
4 G Campbell, "Fostering a Compliance Culture Through Creative Sentencing for Environmental Offences" (2004) 9 Can Crim L Rev 1.
5 *R v Domtar*, [1998] OJ No 6408 (CJ) at para 5 [*Domtar*].
6 *Domtar, ibid* at para 4; *R v Cottonfelts* (1982), 2 CCC (3d) 287 at 295 (Ont CA) [*Cottonfelts*].
7 *R v Weldwood Canada Ltd*, [1999] BCJ No 2242 (Prov Ct) at para 34.
8 *R v Echo Bay Mines Ltd*, [1993] NWTJ No 44 at para 11.

9 *R v Terroco Industries Ltd*, [2005] ABCA 141 at para 60 [*Terroco*]; *Cottonfelts, supra* note 6.
10 *Terroco, ibid* at para 63.
11 *R v United Keno Hill Mines Ltd* (1980), 1 YR 299 (Terr Ct) [*United Keno Hill Mines*]; *Domtar, supra* note 5.
12 *United Keno Hill Mines, ibid.*
13 *Terroco, supra* note 9 at para 34.
14 S Verhulst, "Legislating a Principled Approach to Sentencing in Relation to Regulatory Offences" (2008) 12 Can Crim L Rev 281.
15 N Keith, "Sentencing the Corporate Offender: From Deterrence to Corporate Social Responsibility" (July 2010) 56 Crim LQ 294.
16 *Ibid* at 310.
17 EL Hughes & Dr LA Reynolds, "Creative Sentencing and Environmental Protection" (2009) 19:2 J Envtl L & Prac 105.
18 *Ibid.*
19 *R v Corner Brook Pulp and Paper Ltd*, Nfld Prov Ct, 14 May 1996.
20 RSC 1985, c F-14.
21 *R v City of Moncton*, NB Prov Ct., 2003.
22 The *Environmental Damages Fund* (EDF) is a special holding or trust account administered by Environment Canada. The EDF receives monies via court order made pursuant to sentencing provisions in various federal environmental legislation and allocates funds for purposes of environmental restoration, enhancement, and research projects. Eligible recipients include non-governmental organizations, universities, Aboriginal groups, and provinces, territories, or municipalities.
23 *R v Fox Harbour Developments Ltd*, NS Prov Ct, 2004.
24 *R v Kelly Cove Salmon Ltd*, NB Prov Ct, 2013.
25 *Hydro-Quebec, supra* note 3.

# 32

# The Law and Economics of Environmental Harm: A Primer and Update for Environmental Sentencing (PARTS I and II)

MARTIN OLSZYNSKI AND PETER BOXALL

Ever since Justice Stuart's landmark decision in *R. v. United Keno Hill Mines* (1980),[1] Canadian lawyers and judges have enjoyed a relatively stable list of factors to consider when determining the appropriate sentence to be imposed in the environmental law context. In at least one aspect, however, this longevity and stability can be misleading. I am referring here to the first couple of factors listed in the *United Keno Hill Mines* framework, namely, the nature and extent of environmental harm (both actual and potential).[2] As recently observed, and despite over 30 years of sentencing jurisprudence, the "difficulty of proving an ascertainable and quantifiable harm is present in most environmental cases."[3]

The purpose of this chapter, then, is to familiarize the judiciary and bar with the legal and economic dimensions of a relatively tried and tested approach to quantification that has yet to be successfully applied in the Canadian environmental sentencing context: environmental valuation, which can be described as simply economic valuation—"the valuation in monetary terms of items that people might care for"—applied to the natural environment.[4]

We begin by first providing some context: recent developments in both environmental economics and Canadian environmental law support a shift towards an economic approach to the quantification of environmental harm for the purposes of sentencing. Part II sets out the basic legal framework, while Part III sets out the basic economic concepts, principles, and methodologies of environmental valuation. Part IV consists of a case study. Finally, in Part V, we conclude by assessing the prospects of taking an economic approach to the quantification of environmental harm at this stage in Canadian sentencing law and the field of environmental economics.

## Part I: Recent Developments in Economics and Law[5]

### A. BRIEF HISTORY OF ENVIRONMENTAL VALUATION

Although often perceived as new, environmental valuation has actually been around since the 1950s.[6] One of the earliest examples (though still highly relevant, as further discussed below) was an attempt to quantify the value of some national parks in the United States (admission to which was free) using the costs that individuals incurred to visit such parks (e.g. for gas, hotels, food, etc.) as a proxy. This marked the beginning of what University of Alberta environmental economist Wiktor L. Adamowicz has described as the "travel cost valuation era."[7]

As is often the case in the environmental context, however,[8] it took a relatively catastrophic event—the 1989 running aground of the *Exxon Valdez* and subsequent oil spill—to really spur developments in this area, especially on the methodological side.[9] Indeed, one of the most well-known valuation studies to date is still the one done following the *Valdez* spill, which, using a then relatively controversial technique—contingent valuation—estimated environmental losses at a minimum of US$2.8 billion.[10]

Another significant boost for environmental valuation came in the late 1990s with the emergence of the "ecosystem services" paradigm,[11] now most commonly associated with United Nations' 2005 *Millennium Ecosystem Assessment Report* (MEA),[12] pursuant to which the natural environment is conceived as another form of capital (i.e. natural capital) that gives rise to the (largely free) flow of such goods and services as water purification, climate regulation, flood mitigation, etc.[13] Although it would be difficult to overstate the uniqueness and unprecedented success of the ecosystem services concept in furthering societal understanding of the numerous contributions made by functioning ecosystems to human health and prosperity,[14] the translation of those benefits into monetary terms is still very much an exercise in environmental valuation and has therefore further stimulated research in this area.

There are now in Canada several studies that have estimated the economic value of the natural environment. One of the first such studies was by Simon Fraser professor Nancy Olewiler, who in 2004 estimated the annual value of the Fraser River Valley's 40,000 hectares of wetlands at Can$231.7 million, primarily as a reflection of their "waste-treatment" services (and the uptake of agriculturally generated nitrogen and phosphorus in particular).[15] More

**Table 32.1: Recent Valuation Studies in Canada**

| *Focus of Study* | *For* | *Valuation (CDN)* |
|---|---|---|
| Mackenzie Region, NWT | Boreal Forest Initiative (2009) | $570.6 billion/year[a] |
| Credit River, ON | Pembina Institute and Credit Valley Conservation (2009) | $371 million/year[b] |
| Lower Mainland, BC | The Pacific Parklands Foundation (2010) | $5.4billion/year[c] |
| Polar Bear | Environment Canada (2011) | $6 billion/year[d] |
| Marine Mammals (inc. Beluga Whale) | Fisheries and Oceans Canada (2012) | $962 million/year[e] |
| Thousand Islands National Park | Statistics Canada (2013) | $12.5 million/year[f] |

a Mark Alnielski & Sara Wilson, *The Real Wealth of the Mackenzie Region* (Ottawa: Canadian Boreal Initiative, 2009), online: <http://www.borealcanada.ca>.

b Mike Kennedy & Jeff Wilson, *Natural Credit: Estimating the Value of Natural Capital in the Credit River Watershed* (Drayton Valley: Pembina Institute & Credit Valley Conservation, 2009), online: Pembina Institute <http://www.pembina.org>.

c Sara J Wilson, *Natural Capital in BC's Lower Mainland: Valuing the Benefits from Nature* (Vancouver: David Suzuki Foundation, November 2010), online: David Suzuki Foundation <http://www.davidsuzuki.org/publications/reports/2010/natural-capital-in-bcs-lower-mainland/>.

d ÉcoRessources Consultants, *Evidence of the Socio-Economic Importance of Polar Bears for Canada* (Ottawa: Environment Canada, 2011), online: <http://publications.gc.ca/site/eng/397569/publication.html>.

e PC Boxall et al, "Analysis of the economic benefits associated with the recovery of threatened marine mammal species in the Canadian St Lawrence Estuary" (2012) 36 Marine Policy 189–197.

f Statistics Canada, *Human Activity and the Environment: Measuring ecosystem goods and services in Canada* (Ottawa: Minister of Industry, 2013), online: <http://www.statcan.gc.ca/pub/16-201-x/16-201-x2013000-eng.htm>.

recently, both governments and non-governmental organizations (NGOs) have commissioned valuation reports for various ecosystem assets (see Table 32.1 above).

## B. RECENT CHANGES TO CANADIAN ENVIRONMENTAL LAW

As one might expect, growing societal recognition of the "true value of nature"[16] is being reflected in Canada's environmental laws. Probably the most significant development on this front was the passage in 2009 of the federal *Environmental Enforcement Act* (EEA).[17] The EEA amended—in a largely uniform way—the sentencing provisions of nine federal environmental statutes: the *Antarctic Environmental Protection Act*;[18] the *Canada National Marine Conservation Areas Act*;[19] the *Canada National Parks Act* (CNPA);[20] the *Canada Wildlife Act*;[21] the *Canadian Environmental Protection Act, 1999* (CEPA, *1999*);[22] the *International River Improvements Act*;[23] the *Migratory Birds Con-*

*vention Act, 1994* (*MBCA, 1994*);[24] the *Saguenay–St. Lawrence Marine Park Act*;[25] and the *Wild Animal and Plant Protection and Regulation of International and Interprovincial Trade Act* (*WAPPRITA*).[26]

While *CEPA, 1999*, the *MBCA, 1994*, and *WAPPRITA* are by far the more commonly prosecuted statutes of those amended by the *EEA*,[27] its new sentencing provisions were most recently considered in detail in *R. v. Decker* (2013)[28] in what appears to be the first reported sentencing decision for an offence under the *CNPA*.[29] The accused in that case was convicted of four violations for operating an all-terrain vehicle and a motor vehicle within the boundaries of Gros Morne National Park, off of any road and without a permit contrary to subsections 3(1) and 41(2) of the *National Parks Highway Traffic Regulations*,[30] and for removing flora (driftwood) from the park contrary to section 10 of the *National Parks General Regulations*.[31]

The court set out in detail the new sentencing scheme, which, as noted above, is more or less the same in each of the above-noted statutes (albeit tailored to the circumstances of each particular statute):

> The [*CNPA*] requires a sentencing judge to consider the principles of sentencing set out in sections 718.1 to 718.21 of the *Criminal Code* and a number of principles and factors specifically applicable to offences committed contrary to the [*CNPA*].
>
> Section 27.6 … indicates that the fundamental purpose of sentencing for these types of offences …
>
> … is to contribute to respect for the law establishing and protecting parks through the imposition of just sanctions that have as their objectives
>
> (a) to deter the offender and any other person from committing offences under this Act;
> (b) to denounce unlawful conduct that damages or creates a risk of damage to parks; and
> (c) to restore park resources.
>
> Section 27.7(1) … states that in addition to the principles and factors set out in the *Criminal Code*, in imposing sentence for breaches of the [*CNPA*] a sentencing judge must consider a number of additional principles…:

(a) the amount of the fine should be increased to account for every aggravating factor associated with the offence, including the aggravating factors set out in subsection (2); and
(b) the amount of the fine should reflect the gravity of each aggravating factor associated with the offence.

Section 27.7(2) ... deems certain circumstances to be an "aggravating factor" in sentencing:

(a) the offence caused damage or risk of damage to park resources;
(b) the offence caused damage or risk of damage to any unique, rare, particularly important or vulnerable park resources;
(c) the damage caused by the offence is extensive, persistent or irreparable;
(d) the offender committed the offence intentionally or recklessly;
(e) the offender failed to take reasonable steps to prevent the ... offence...;
(f) ... the offender increased revenue or decreased costs or intended to increase revenue or decrease costs;
(g) the offender committed the offence despite having been warned...;
(h) the offender has a history of non-compliance...;
(i) after the commission of the offence, the offender (i) attempted to conceal its commission, (ii) failed to take prompt action to prevent, mitigate or remediate its effects, or (iii) failed to take prompt action to reduce the risk of committing similar offences in the future.

Section 27.7(4) ... indicates that "damage" includes "loss of use value and non-use value."[32]

For those familiar with Canada's environmental sentencing jurisprudence, it should be clear that these provisions represent mostly a codification of the *United Keno Hill Mines* factors, albeit with some modification—the most relevant here being the inclusion of the economic terms "use value and non-use value" in the definition of "damage" (as referred to in factors (a)–(c)).

Although the evidence in *Decker* gave the court no cause to consider these terms in any further detail,[33] they are not unprecedented in Canadian environmental law. The Supreme Court of Canada had occasion to consider them in the context of civil liability in *Canadian Forest Products v. British Columbia* (*Canfor*).[34] In that case, the defendant company was found liable for negligently failing to extinguish a controlled burn. The provincial Crown sought both commercial damages and compensation for environmental damages, identifying several components of such loss:

> "Use value" includes the services provided by the ecosystem to human beings, including food sources, water quality and recreational opportunities. Even if the public are not charged for these services, it may be possible to quantify them economically by observing what the public pays for comparable services on the market …
>
> "Passive use" or "existence" [non-use] value recognizes that a member of the public may be prepared to pay something for the protection of a natural resource, even if he or she never directly uses it. It includes both the psychological benefit to the public of knowing that the resource is protected, and the option value of being able to use it in the future. The branch of economics known as "contingent valuation" uses survey techniques to attempt to quantify what the public would be prepared to pay to maintain these benefits [emphasis in original].[35]

In *Canfor*, however, the Crown did not actually adduce any evidence of such loss. Consequently, while the court did discuss in some detail the methods that could be applied in this context,[36] it ultimately dismissed this part of the claim.[37] We discuss the basic concepts, principles, and methods of environmental valuation in Part III. Part II sets out in further detail the applicable legal framework for the consideration of environmental harm in sentencing.

## Part II: The Legal Framework for Assessing and Quantifying Harm in Sentencing

While the SCC's decision in *Canfor* (and its relatively favourable disposition to the concepts and methods of environmental valuation in particular)[38] is plainly a relevant precedent, the assessment and quantification of environmental harm or damage (this chapter uses these terms interchangeably) in the sentencing context differs in at least two fundamental ways from the tort liability context: (1) the kinds of harm that matter; and (2) the applicable burden of proof.

## A. THREE KINDS OF HARM: ACTUAL, POTENTIAL-SPECIFIC, AND POTENTIAL GENERAL

It is probably now trite to state that in the context of environmental sentencing both *actual* and *potential* harm matter. As Stuart J. stated in *United Keno Hill Mines*,

> Extent of Injury. Penalties should reflect the degree of damage inflicted.... If the damage is irreparable, extensive, persistent or has numerous consequential adverse effects, the penalty must be severe. In some instances not only the actual damage caused but the potential damage that might have emanated from the polluter's activities must be considered.[39]

Over time, and seemingly as a result of Canadian courts' increasing focus on deterrence—both specific and general[40]—the consideration of *potential harm* has likewise taken on both specific and general dimensions. In the relatively recent (2011) case *R. v. Northwest Territories Power Corporation*, the court cited with approval several unreported decisions to explain this relationship as follows:

> As stated in *R. v. Shamrock*, an unreported case of the Ontario Provincial Offences Court on February 13, 1989, at page 7:
>
>> If public welfare offences are "preventative" and their purpose is to set high standards, no actual damage should be necessary to attract substantial penalties. The degree of risk or potential harm inherent in the activity should be the primary criterion for a substantial penalty, and actual harm an aggravating factor ...
>
> The issue of potential damages versus actual damage was also considered by the Nunavut Court of Justice in *R. v. City of Iqaluit*, Unreported Decision, August 8, 2002:
>
>> [6] There is no evidence in this case that the discharge of sewage in this case resulted in any fish kills or any other readily identifiable signs of environmental degradation. However, it is the potential for harm to the environment that is the gravamen of this offence. Actual damage where proved,

is an aggravating circumstance that would likely elevate the sentence that would otherwise be imposed …

> Many cases have stated that deterrence is the single-most important factor in sentencing environmental offenders. If the goals of sentencing in environmental cases are to "abate, mitigate and prevent", as indicated in the introductory remarks, *then a penalty which prevents a particular offender and other potential offenders from committing offences in the future is necessary in order to achieve the last of these goals.* [Emphasis added.][41]

With respect to the potential harm (risk of damage) *specific to the offence* before the court, the decision in *R. v. Terroco Industries Ltd.*[42] is perhaps the most instructive:

> The greater the potential for harm, the greater the warranted penalty. The potential for harm is informed by the probability of the risk, the nature of the product, the likely magnitude of damage if the risk materializes and the sensitivity of the site including its proximity to population and fragile environments [citations omitted].… Where there is potential for harm that is avoided by fortuitous circumstances, that potential is a relevant factor.[43]

Thus, the risk of damage specific to the offence appears to be primarily concerned with fortuitous intervening forces, or at least forces not attributable to the defendant's due diligence, but for which the actual environmental damage would likely have been greater. Returning to the *Decker* prosecution, one might imagine that Mr. Decker only narrowly and by chance avoided some rare or particularly unique flora in the area where the offence occurred. This specific risk of damage would also seem to be place-based; it is the risk of damage to the environment in the same place and under essentially the same conditions as where and when the offence occurred.

With respect to potential harm (risk of damage) from the regulated community more generally, two decisions under the *MBCA, 1994* provide good illustrations. In *R. v. Carriere,*[44] the accused were convicted of offences related to the illegal taking of approximately 170 birds. The court held that

> the actions of the accused have had no significant impact on the duck populations of either the Cumberland Marshes or the North

American continent as a whole. But this does not end the matter. Paragraph 13(4.1)(a) of the [*MBCA, 1994*] speaks not just of "harm" but also of the "risk of harm." I am of the view that while the actual harm caused by the accused at Mistik Lodge was small, *the risk of harm was significantly larger*.

> The sustained health of North America's wild duck population depends on the co-operation of the governments and peoples of three different countries.... That co-operation is not just restricted to the regulation of sport hunting, but regulation of sport hunting is key to maintaining duck populations. When one sees ducks in flocks exceeding a thousand birds, it may seem impossible that duck populations could be thinned by mere hunting. But duck hunters, particularly sport hunters, have the capacity to exert tremendous pressure. If every hunter took the view that he could double his legal limit, the annual duck hunt would potentially result in 30 million ducks killed. Perhaps the ducks could take this pressure for a short while. However, as the examples of the passenger pigeon and the whooping crane illustrate, sustained overhunting would likely lead to devastation. [Emphasis added.][45]

This approach was cited with approval in the relatively famous *Syncrude* prosecution (albeit in the consideration of due diligence):

> I doubt that the number of ducks lost on or about April 28, 2008 at the Aurora Settling Basin would have any significant impact on total duck populations and it may be a small number compared with the loss from hunting or total losses in industrial settings.... However, it is important to remember the purpose of the provincial and federal legislation. The legislation is designed to protect the environment and maintain migratory bird populations, respectively. As with most regulatory offences, the legislation is not just directed at the immediate and direct effect of the proscribed conduct but also at the potential harm if that conduct was widespread. See, for example: *R. v. Carriere*....[46]

Thus, the general risk of damage analysis attempts to extrapolate the conduct of the offender to the broader regulatory community. In *Carriere*, this meant other sports hunters. In *Syncrude*, the court seemed to contemplate other oil sands operators, or at least those whose operations entail the creation of tailings ponds. In some cases at least, the applicable legislative or regulatory scheme will define the relevant community; for example, for offences under the *Metal Mining Effluent Regulations*,[47] the relevant community would be all mining operations subject to those regulations. In contrast to the specific risk of damage, then, the general risk is not place-based but rather considers the environmental assets in question more broadly.

When considering both kinds of risk (specific and general), it may be useful to state these in the following terms borrowed from negligence law:

R = MP, where
R = Risk of damage (specific or general)
M = Magnitude of damage
P = Probability of occurrence

This formula captures most of the criteria set out by the court in *R. v. Terroco*, albeit in a more generalized way (e.g. it is not just applicable to "products" but could also apply to physical works or activities that have a direct impact on the environment). And while it is admittedly more complex than it may appear at first glance (in that both magnitude and probability can be further broken down into subcomponents), it is not being suggested here that surgical precision is required when considering the risk of damage—certainly the existing jurisprudence does not support such a standard.

### B. THE BURDEN OF PROOF: BEYOND A REASONABLE DOUBT

In contrast to the civil standard of a balance of probabilities, it is also well settled in Canada that an aggravating factor must be proven beyond a reasonable doubt and, further, that this burden of proof can create some difficulty in the environmental context.

The recent case of *R. v. Zellstoff Celgar Limited Partnership* (2012)[48] is illustrative. In that case, the Crown introduced evidence that the accused deposited approximately 500 million litres of effluent into the Columbia River that did not meet its permitted requirements for total suspended solids (TSS) and biological oxygen demanding (BOD), and some of which failed the 96-hour rainbow trout test.[49] While the court held that "the Columbia River must be considered an environmentally sensitive area" and that it "is a fish-bearing river" whose "denizens include endangered species"[50] and that harm from the deposit might appear self-evident,[51] the court nevertheless concluded that there was "actually no evidence of harm in this case, such that harm could be considered an aggravating factor on this sentence."[52]

**Table 32.2: Magnitude of Harm as a Function of Impact and Sensitivity**

| *Impact* | *Sensitivity of Environment or Ecosystem Asset* | | |
|---|---|---|---|
| | High | Moderate | Low |
| High | | | |
| Moderate | | | |
| Low | | | |

This left the question of potential harm. Here, too, the court concluded that it was "left with considerable doubt as to the degree to which the effluent that was discharged in the river … had a potential for harm or, if so, what the magnitude of the risk was. *It is clear in the authorities that the Crown must prove aggravating factors beyond a reasonable doubt, and in this case the Crown has not met that onus.*"[53]

Simply put, the Crown must introduce sufficient evidence of damage in order for the courts to rely on these aggravating factors in setting the appropriate fine, a task that admittedly poses some additional conceptual difficulties where the *risk of damage* (both specific but especially general) is concerned. Of course, this difficulty (of proving the existence of a risk—which is inherently uncertain—beyond a reasonable doubt) is not limited to an environmental valuation approach but rather has been present in each case since *United Keno Hill Mines.*

This difficulty would seem at least somewhat alleviated by the consistent adoption of the above-noted formula (R = MP) that, as noted above, could be further broken down into subcomponents. Thus, the magnitude of harm (M) could often be considered a function of the scale or degree of impact (low, moderate, high) and the sensitivity of the environment (e.g. a wetland or bog in a national park) or ecosystem asset (e.g. migratory birds) to disturbance (again low, moderate, high), as the following table sets out:

When considering the general risk of damage, the degree of impact could be further broken down by some estimate of the size of the regulated community (as the court seemed to do in *R. v. Carriere*): the larger the regulated community, the larger the potential impact associated with even individually minimal harm. For instance, when considering general deterrence in the context of an offence under the *MMER*, the number of mine operators in Canada would surely inform the magnitude of potential harm.

Similarly, the probability of occurrence (P) could be broken down into ranges: low (0–30%), moderate (30–60%), and high (60–100%). Generally speaking, one would expect the probability of damage to be greater when considering the specific risk of damage, especially where damage was avoided only by a fortuitous event, than when considering general risk. In this latter context, the Crown could perhaps rely on social science evidence or statistics on regulatory compliance to support its estimation. While none of these tools would lead to a determination of risk with exact precision, they would add some predictability and transparency to an exercise that—occasionally on fairly nebulous terms—has long since been and continues to be carried out in the sentencing context.

With respect to environmental valuation specifically, while even environmental economists would concede that their results are often marked with uncertainty, it may be useful to recall that some degree of uncertainty is endemic in environmental science and law generally,[54] and further—and perhaps most importantly—that, through the inclusion of "use and non-use value" in the definition of "damage," Parliament has clearly indicated that this kind of evidence should be considered for the purposes of environmental sentencing.

*(For Parts III, IV, and V, see chapter 33 by Professor Peter Boxall.)*

## NOTES

1 10 CELR 43 (Y Terr Ct) [*United Keno Hill Mines*].

2 *Ibid* at paras 11–13. According to Westlaw, *United Keno Hill Mines* has been judicially considered 71 times.

3 *R v Northwest Territories Power Corporation*, 2011 NWTTC 03 at para 89 [*Northwest Territories Power Corporation*]. See also *R v Terroco Industries Ltd*, 2005 ABCA 141 at para 47: "In many environmental offences, harm is not easily identified"; and *R v Zellstoff Celgar Limited Partnership*, 2012 BCPC 295 at paras 43–48 [*Zellstoff*].

4 WM Hanemann, "The Economic Conception of Water" in Peter P Rogers, M Ramón Llamas, & Luis Martinez-Cortina, eds, *Water Crisis: Myth or Reality?* (London: Taylor & Francis, 2006) 61 at 66.

5 Portions of this part of the chapter are adapted from Martin ZP Olszynski, "Environmental Damages after the Federal *Environmental Enforcement Act*: Bringing Ecosystem Services to Canadian Environmental Law?" (2012) 50:1 Osgoode Hall LJ 129 [Olszynski].

6 Wiktor L Adamowicz, "What's It Worth? An Examination of Historical Trends and Future Directions in Environmental Valuation" (2004) 48:3 Austl J of Agric Resource Econ 419 at 419 [Adamowicz].

7 *Ibid.*

8 See, e.g., Keith H Hirokawa, "Disasters and Ecosystem Services Deprivation: From Cuyahoga to the Deepwater Horizon" (2011) 74:1 Alta L Rev 547: "The idea that disasters incentivize changes in environmental law is well-settled.... [D]isasters provide an important and continuing point of reference by compelling us to revise our perceptions on the value of nature and natural processes."

9 Adamowicz, *supra* note 6 at 423.

10 Richard T Carson et al, "Contingent Valuation and Lost Passive Use: Damages from the Exxon Valdez Oil Spill" (2003) 25:3 Envtl & Resource Econ 257 at 278.

11 Gretchen Daily, *Nature's Services: Societal Dependence on Natural Ecosystems* (Washington, DC: Island Press, 1997) is widely regarded as the "breakthrough" work for ecosystem services theory and research.

12 See online: MEA <https://www.millennium assessment.org/en/index.html>.

13 The MEA adopted a broad definition of ecosystem services ("the benefits that humans derive from ecosystems"), which it divided into four categories: "Provisioning services are the products people obtain from ecosystems, such as food, fuel, fiber, fresh water, and genetic resources. Regulating services are the benefits people obtain from the regulation of ecosystem processes, including air quality maintenance … and water purification. Cultural services are the nonmaterial benefits people obtain from ecosystems through spiritual enrichment, cognitive development, reflection, recreation, and aesthetic experiences. Supporting services are those that are necessary for the production of all other ecosystem services, such as primary production, production of oxygen and soil formation." See MEA, *Ecosystems and Human Well-being: Current State and Trends Assessment*, vol 1 (Washington, DC: Island Press, 2005) at 29.

14 See Olszynski, *supra* note 5 at 134–135 and note 38.

15 Nancy Olewiler, *The Value of Natural Capital in Settled Areas of Canada* (Toronto: Nature Conservancy of Canada, 2004).

16 MEA, *Living Beyond Our Means: Natural Assets and Human Well-Being, Statement from the Board* (Washington, DC: MEA Board, 2005) at 5, online: MEA <https://www.millenniumassessment.org/documents/document.429.aspx.pdf>.

17 SC 2009, c 14 [*EEA*]. For a general overview of the *EEA*, see Olszynski, *supra* note 5 at 156–160; Penny Becklumb, *Legislative Summary: Bill C-16: Environmental Enforcement Act* (Ottawa: Library of Parliament, Parliamentary Information and Research Service, 2009); Environment Canada, *Backgrounder: Overview of the Environmental Enforcement Bill* (3 March 2009), online: Environment Canada <http://www.ec.gc.ca>.

18 SC 2003, c 20 [*AEPA*].

19 SC 2002, c 18 [*CNMCAA*].

20 SC 2000, c 32 [*CNPA*].

21 RSC 1985, c W-9 [*CWA*].

22 SC 1999, c 33 [*CEPA, 1999*].

23 RSC 1985, c I-20 [*IRIA*].

24 SC 1994, c 22 [*MBCA, 1994*].

25 SC 1997, c 37 [*SSLMPA*].

26 SC 1992, c 52 [*WAPPRITA*].

27 See Environment Canada's "Enforcement Notifications," online: <http://www.ec.gc.ca/alef-ewe/default.asp?lang=En&n=8F711F37-1>, for the most recent enforcement actions with respect to *CEPA, 1999* and *WAPPRITA*. It should also be noted that the *EEA* did not amend the *Fisheries Act*, RSC 1985, c F-14, which is by far the most commonly enforced federal environmental statute (especially ss 35 and 36). The *Fisheries Act* has been recently amended to reflect the higher fine regime put in place through the *EEA*, but it does not contain the same detailed sentencing provisions, including the definition of environmental damages.

28 2013 CanLII 58688 (Nfld Prov Ct) [*Decker*].

29 *Ibid* at para 23.

30 CRC, c 1126.

31 SOR/78-213.

32 *Decker*, *supra* note 28 at paras 10–15.

33 *Ibid* at para 26. The court notes, in contrast, a case where there was extensive damage caused by all-terrain vehicles; see *R v Lambe*, 2000 NFCA 23.

34 2004 SCC 38, [2004] 2 SCR 74 [*Canfor*].

35 *Ibid* at para 138. These terms are discussed in further detail in Part III.

36 *Ibid* at paras 142–143.

37 *Ibid* at para 153.

38 *Canfor*, *supra* note 34.

39 *United Keno Hill Mines*, *supra* note 1 at para 13.

40 *Northwest Territories Power Corporation*, *supra* note 3 at para 24: "The sentencing principle of deterrence is based on a model which punishes the offender sufficiently that he or she will not offend again (specific deterrence) and to such a degree that others who are in the same position as the offender was in, will not offend because they do not want to incur the same penalty (general deterrence)." See also Elaine L Hughes & Dr Larry A Reynolds, "Creative Sentencing and Environmental Protection" (2009) 19:2 J Envtl L & Prac 105 at 108.

41 *Northwest Territories Power Corporation*, *supra* note 3 at paras 39–42.

42 2005 ABCA 141.

43 *Ibid* at para 48, recently cited with approval in *Zellstoff*, *supra* note 3.

44 2005 SKPC 84, 272 Sask R 13 [*Carriere*].

45 *Ibid* at paras 45–46.

46 *R v Syncrude Canada Ltd*, 2010 ABPC 229, 53 CELR (3d) 196 at para 106.

47 SOR/2002-222 [*MMER*].

48 *Zellstoff*, *supra* note 3.

49 *Ibid* at para 43.

50 *Ibid* at para 44.

51 *Ibid* at para 45.

52 *Ibid*.

53 *Ibid* at paras 47–48. [Emphasis added.]

54 Daniel Farber, "Building Bridges over Troubled Waters: Eco-pragmatism and the Environmental Prospect" (2003) 87:4 Minn L Rev 852 at 855.

# 33

# The Law and Economics of Environmental Harm: A Primer and Update for Environmental Sentencing (PARTS III, IV and V)

PETER BOXALL AND MARTIN OLSZYNSKI

## Part III: Basic Concepts, Principles, and Tools for Environmental Valuation

The field of environmental valuation, a subdiscipline of environmental economics, has emerged in response to the need to develop monetary measures of changes in the provision of environmental goods and services. Although one cannot downplay the importance that damage assessment has played in the development of valuation methods, the field arose because of a need to develop monetized measures of environmental services for inclusion in formal cost/benefit analyses (CBA). The issue was that many resource development projects would have an impact on many environmental services that were not traded in formal economic markets. Hence attempting to estimate the economic values of these services would allow a more complete analysis of the benefits and costs arising from development or management changes of resources.

The concept of compensation for harm or damage to the environment, which in theory is a good that is "owned" by the collective or state, suggests that the responsible party should provide compensation equal to the damage in order to make the public "whole." While this appears to be a simple concept, in reality assessing environmental damages and determining appropriate levels of compensation is difficult. One reason is that economists view the environment as a resource or entity that provides a bundle of services to society. Relating the harm to physical changes in these service flows is a major challenge in determining compensation. The types of services can vary from place to place or ecosystem to ecosystem; the levels of use or enjoyment of the services can vary both spatially or temporally; and physical measurement of the service levels either before or after harm has occurred can be absent or expensive to implement. In addition, in many cases the environmental service flows may be beneficial to humans well away from the site or area damaged. Thus, the first challenge involves understanding the biophysical dimensions of changes in environmental quality caused by the harm.

The next set of challenges relates to translating the biophysical changes in goods and services affected by damages to measures of the value associated with these changes. This typically means that one needs to define the condition and value of the "base case," or in other words the condition of the environmental asset prior to the harm or damage taking place. This is needed to determine the situation before and after the environmental harm has taken place. In situations where this knowledge exists, economists have derived a number of approaches to develop monetary values of associated changes in service flows. Essentially what one needs are measures of the changes in human welfare (typically in monetary terms) arising from changes in environmental conditions. This can be straightforward to determine for environmental goods and services that are traded in markets (e.g. minerals, tourism, etc.). For example, one can assess changes in market values arising from changes in industrial production or costs resulting from environmental changes. If an environmental change impacts an industry or firm, changes in output levels resulting in lost profits, or input levels resulting in rising costs of production, can be directly assessed. However, many aspects of environment harm or damage involve changes in goods and services that are not traded in formal markets. Examples provided in the previous discussion (Part 1) involve such things as migratory birds, marine mammals, etc.

Environmental valuation basically involves two approaches: (1) identifying linkages between market goods and environmental goods and using these links to assess welfare changes associated with changes in environmental conditions; and (2) developing/creating hypothetical markets that incorporate environmental conditions and evaluating welfare changes using these hypothetical markets. Applying specific methodological approaches from these two categories always involves the assessment of a change in the "state of the world," which encompasses a change in environmental quality. Values expressed through market or near-market behaviour can include the purchase of individual or bundles of goods that are jointly related to the environmental change. These types of goods are referred to as "use" values, and the valuation methods employed to measure the values in an environmental context are called "revealed preference" methods, since "users" reveal their environmental preferences through their market behaviour or choices. The most common methods include a group of methods that have been applied to recreational use of the environment.

The first valuation approach, briefly referred to in Part I, is called the travel cost method, which involves revealing the value of recreation sites to visitors through the costs they pay travelling to sites. Since values of accessing sites are not revealed through entrance or access fees (which can be absent for many recreational areas), the total costs of access (both travel and entrance fees) approximate the "true price" of a visit. These methods would relate environmental quality changes to the responses of recreationists by examining changes in their levels of visitation. For example, given that X trips are made by recreationists to a park in a pristine state, damages to park quality would reduce the number of these trips to Y, and hence damages would be assessed through this reduction in visitation expressed using per-trip economic values.

Recent developments in the travel cost method, however, involve the construction of choice models, in which the actual attributes of recreation sites (including elements of environmental quality), in addition to travel costs, explain demand for the sites. These attributes can include man-made features such as campsites and roads, as well as environmental attributes such as forest conditions (species, age of trees, etc.), water clarity, etc.[1] Here an analyst develops a model that assesses the probability of visiting a particular site among a complex of sites as a function of these characteristics and travel costs. This allows assessment of changes in visitation as one or more attributes change at sites, and the model predicts where in the complex of sites a recreationist would go in response to the change. Thus this method allows a formal consideration of substitutes that can be used if an individual site is damaged. By relating changes in trip behaviour to travel costs, economic values can be estimated due to changes in one or more attributes across the complex of recreation sites as visitors pay more to access higher-quality sites farther from their homes to avoid the change in conditions.[2]

Another revealed preference approach involves statistical or econometric assessments of the variation in prices of properties in residential markets to evaluate changes in environmental quality. Since property prices are a function of the attributes associated with those properties, including environmental characteristics of the property or surrounding areas, the procedure "backs out" the value of the environmental asset by determining if its availability affects the sale price of an individual property. This approach, called the "hedonic price method," has been used to examine the values of positive or negative environmental amenities associated with properties.[3] In essence this intuition can be applied to most forms of economic transactions where attributes of the object purchased vary. For example, this includes hotel and tourism package prices. The method can also be used to examine the sensitivity of wage rates to changes in environmental or health-related characteristics.

In many cases, however, there is no observable behaviour that arises in response to an environmental quality change. For example, a local forest may support the existence of a rare and endangered species. Individuals may be concerned about the viability of this species, but there is no mechanism available through which they can pay for or vote to be taxed for actions to ensure its survival. This type of value is referred to as an "existence value," because while individuals may not go and view the species, or have any intention of "using" it, they nevertheless value its existence. Economists have broadened this concept to "passive use" value, which also includes possible future use and bequeathing use to future generations (passive use values are also considered non-use values in this case).

In cases where values associated with an environmental good or service are not associated with market purchases or behavioural trails, "stated preference" approaches are used to estimate passive use values. These methods utilize questionnaire surveys in which conversations with respondents are employed to estimate standard metrics of economic value—the "willingness to pay" (WTP) or the willingness to accept compensation (WTAC) in response to changes in environmental conditions. The most well known of these methods is "contingent valuation," in which a hypothetical referendum is introduced in the survey and respondents vote on accepting an environmental improvement in exchange for an increase in tax payments (hence an assessment of WTP). As noted in Part I, this method has a long history in the valuation of environmental harm, stemming from the 1989 Exxon *Valdez* oil spill in Alaska.[4]

The method has also been extended to include various attributes in a choice-modelling framework as mentioned above. Here, various "states of the world" are defined, based on changing levels in a set of attributes, and formed into sets of choices, and respondents are asked to choose among them. The attribute bundles include tax or income changes, and environmental quality changes are portrayed using adjustments in the attribute levels. The results permit a much richer understanding of preferences for environmental quality changes. The major difference between contingent valuation and the attribute-based choice modelling is that contingent valuation tends to focus largely on monetary factors.

Since actual environmental damages involve a change in conditions, determining the extent of economic harm also must involve assessing a change. Hence total values for some feature of the environment are not useful in the actual damage assessment context. Rather, one must use marginal economic values directly associated with the environmental quality change. This usually means that one must understand the before-the-damage conditions and compare this with the after-the-damage condition. Thus, utilizing the methods described above, for example in a recreation context, one must understand levels of visitation prior to the environmental damage. If one can forecast or determine a decrease in visitation levels, then this quantity of decrease must be multiplied by the per-trip economic value to assess the levels of damages. Alternatively, if a recreation choice model has been developed then one can measure the damages by changing the attributes at the damaged site, estimating the changes in visitation patterns, and calculating economic measures of damages based on these changes in trip patterns among the complex of substitute sites. Note that these procedures require knowledge of values or model development prior to the environmental harm taking place.

With respect to potential harm (risk of damage), economic damage assessments methods may not be *directly* useful in determining the level of compensation. Environmental valuation, however, is typically used to examine the benefits provided by environmental assets, not specifically in the economic assessment of damages. So these values could provide information to the judiciary on the magnitudes of undamaged environmental assets that might be useful in understanding the magnitudes of reductions in the value of services provided by damaged environmental assets. There is a growing literature that deals with transferring such estimates from one site to another, or from one type of use to another. The procedures for doing this are called "benefits transfer" and involve the direct transfer of a specific economic estimate (called a "unit value transfer") such as $/day. A more complicated transfer, called a "function transfer," can be performed by using the specific mathematical function developed for the original site or study. For example, if in study A an equation was developed that provided a benefit (damage) estimate then by using specific information available for study site B the values of the arguments of that equation that relate to site B are used in the equation for developing the new estimate.

Assuming there are a number of valuation projects undertaken that the judiciary can examine, it would be possible for potential damages to be assessed based on previous more formal damage assessments. A major issue, however, is that such a bank of specifically Canadian studies does not exist, nor have there been enough studies conducted in the country that would make such a bank worthwhile. Thus, one might have to turn to studies conducted in other parts of the world in order to learn something about potential damages in a Canadian context. One such database is the Environmental Valuation Resource Inventory (EVRI),[5] a database hosted and run by Environment Canada that contains a multitude of environmental valuation studies. The use of this database in a "damage transfer" process would mimic the benefits transfer approach.

## Part IV: A Case Study—Use and Non-Use Values Associated with the Wilmot River, PEI

As noted in the introduction to this chapter, an environmental valuation approach to quantifying harm has never been successfully carried out in the Canadian sentencing context. This is not to say, however, that such an approach has never been attempted. In this part, we consider one such attempt and then set out the kind of evidence that could have been introduced.

### A. *R. v. GEORGE M. CASELEY & SONS INC*[6]

The facts in this case are relatively straightforward. The accused, a potato producer, pled guilty to permitting a deleterious substance to enter waters frequented by fish, contrary to section 36(3) of the *Fisheries Act*,[7] following an incident whereby a rain squall caused runoff from two of his fields to reach the upper reaches of the Wilmot River. These fields had been sprayed the previous day with Azinphos-methyl, a pesticide that is extremely toxic to fish and other wildlife, which reached the Wilmot because the accused failed to ensure a sufficient buffer zone.[8] Subsequently, a total of 4,500 dead trout were collected from the Wilmot River.

In what appears to be the only reported case of its kind, the Crown called evidence in an attempt to show the "overall economic consequences of the offence," as follows:

> Lisa DeBaie, who is employed by the Federal Government with Environment Canada to study the economic impact of environmental issues, prepared a damage evaluation in relation to this matter. Ms.

DeBaie's report was filed as an exhibit on the sentencing hearing and Ms. DeBaie testified that the cost of the fish required to restock the Wilmot River is approximately $3,100. The cost of monitoring the recovery of the river is approximately $9,700 for a total of $12,800. The reliability of those figures is not in issue.

Ms. DeBaie then went on to attempt to quantify the more intangible losses which economists apparently believe occur from these kinds of events. Ms. DeBaie assigned a dollar value to the time spent by volunteers although they were unpaid. She assigned a dollar value to the work of government employees although no additional staff were hired as a result of this offence. She assigned a dollar value to the recreational enjoyment of individual fishers and multiplied it by the projected numbers of fishers who might be expected to use the Wilmot River, and multiplied that by the number of days that those individuals might have fished. This analysis of course assumes that none of those recreational fishers decided to fish elsewhere in Prince Edward Island. She estimated that total loss at up to $286,300.

Ms. DeBaie then attempted to quantify the total overall economic impact of resident, visiting non-resident Canadian, and visiting non-Canadian fishers not fishing on Prince Edward Island and in the case of non-residents, apparently not even visiting Prince Edward Island because of the closure of the Wilmot River to recreational fishing. Ms. DeBaie estimates that the total impact could be as high as $690,000 per year while the river remains closed.[9]

The court, however, rejected this evidence:

> The difficulty which the Court has with Ms. DeBaie's evidence is that it is for the most part not based on empirically grounded data. *There is no evidence of how many people fished the Wilmot River, on average, before its closure. There is no evidence that even one fisher stopped fishing in east Prince County because of the closure. There is no evidence that even one visitor failed to come to Prince Edward Island and fish because of the closure.*
>
> It may well be that the Province has suffered and will continue to suffer economic loss because of the closure of the Wilmot River and the impact on environmental tourism generally from pesticide-laced runoff and fish kills. *However, without evidence based on hard data,*

in the Court's view, Ms. DeBaie's conclusion must be regarded as speculation....

I therefore find the proven losses in this matter to be $12,800 for re-stocking and monitoring of the river's recovery. [Emphasis added.][10]

## B. QUANTIFYING DAMAGES: ACTUAL AND POTENTIAL (SPECIFIC AND GENERAL)

### (i) Actual Damages

*Caseley and Sons* highlights the importance of understanding baseline conditions prior to damages taking place, as well as having data on conditions following the incident. In particular, an analyst assessing damages would want information about the levels of use of the fishery as well as the condition of the fish populations prior to the incident taking place. Armed with this initial data, assessments of use levels following the damage would allow some understanding of the impacts of the damage on the use of the fishery. At the very least, being able to determine the level of reduction in fishing trips caused by the loss of trout, and using estimates from other fisheries of the economic value of a fishing trip through benefits transfer (perhaps using travel cost models), the analyst could develop *annual* estimates of the economic loss. Of course how long the damage to the fishery would last, and how quickly it would take fishers to return to former levels of use, would remain an open but important question in determining the total damage estimate over time.[11] These temporal considerations require reconnaissance of fisher efforts as well a biological knowledge on recovery.

In many cases there is existing data on use levels that has been collected for some other purpose. In the case of fisheries, for example, there are typically periodic creel surveys that are designed to estimate the annual levels of fish harvest. These surveys are designed and conducted by biologists who visit fishers on site, and the information collected is specifically used for biological purposes rather than determining use levels and associated economic values. This unfortunate but common situation requires intervention so that data collection efforts with a few modifications could be designed to serve multiple purposes, one of which could be developing estimates of the levels of use and the collection of information that might allow the development of travel cost models.

In addition to adjustments to systematic biological data collection, it is also possible to adjust other systems that collect data for the primary purpose of tracking revenues from users for auditing systems. These include park and campsite registrations as well as hunting and fishing licences. There has been research examining the utility of such systems for examining levels of use, determining where visitors come from, and for estimating travel costs with no or minor impact on their original intended purpose.[12] However, provincial and federal government agencies have not heeded calls by researchers to adjust such systems to incorporate these additional needs. It is also difficult to access such data under access to information legislation.

The comments above relate to "use values," which are easier to understand and estimate given sufficient data. However, significant challenges arise in determining the non-use values associated with some damage incident. Ideally an independent study of these values would be necessary, but this is difficult to see happening for two reasons. First, any study would have to be conducted *ex post* of the incident, and the results of such efforts could be influenced by knowledge of the incident. Thus, an *ex ante* study would be preferable, but it is difficult to predict where such studies would have to take place before damages occur. Second, estimating non-use values requires the use of stated preference methods as described in Part III above, and these are typically expensive to conduct.[13]

Despite considerable investments by Canadian resource management agencies in collecting biological data of relevance to environmental management, they have been reluctant to make similar investments in data collection efforts that could generate useful inventories of the use of environmental resources and to develop economic valuation information. This reluctance comes despite the need for this information in cost/benefit analyses of regulatory changes and in assessing environment harm and damage. The authors of this chapter are amazed at the myriad of requests for proposals that arise from government agencies to gather data on use and values despite the fact that this information simply does not exist in many cases. Funds for such contracts would be better spent in developing data collection systems and generating empirical economic valuation estimates.

### (ii) Risk of Damage (Specific)

Recalling the discussion in Part II, the focus of the inquiry here is to determine whether there was a real potential for greater environmental damage than actually occurred (e.g. the 4,500 dead trout). This analysis will be context specific; as in *Terroco*[14], the nature of the product (here a toxic insecticide that has since been slated for phase-out by the federal Pesticide Management

Regulatory Agency)[15] as well as the sensitivity of the receiving environment, here the Wilmot River, will be especially relevant.

For example, the Wilmot River is also salmon-bearing, at least of salmon at the juvenile stage and if only barely.[16] Consequently, the damage could have been greater if the event had occurred while salmon were spawning or juveniles were otherwise present. To determine the probability of such damage (*P*), it would be necessary to know the timing of spawning or juvenile presence generally and whether it could have overlapped with the timing of pesticide application in the potato-growing context. The magnitude (*M*) of the potential damage could be based on the number of salmon juveniles expected to be found in the Wilmot River at such a time.

A damage transfer approach would take estimates from a pollutant spill somewhere else in Canada (or North America or even possibly from around the world) that affected a recreational fishery and apply the findings to the Wilmot River case. Obviously, finding a fishery pollution impact case that can represent the Wilmot River situation as closely as possible would be preferable. So learning from cases where pollution impacts were known and assessed in economic terms would provide valuable information to the judiciary in understanding something about the potential risk of damage.

Alternatively, or at least in the meantime, environmental valuation could tell the court something about the value of Atlantic salmon generally against which to "benchmark" the risk of damage. For example, simply assessing the market value of fish filets killed in the Wilmot case would provide one simple measurable component of the overall impact of the pollution event. Other values of these fish and their use, however, would be much larger than this market food value—one recent study, for example, estimated that there is "over $105 million in public non-use value associated with wild salmon."[17] While the Wilmot River would represent only a tiny fraction of this value, it would nevertheless provide the court with some kind of benchmark for the purposes of quantifying this component of the risk of damage. It must also be recalled that potential harm to salmon is but one example and one component of the potential harm or risk of damage.[18]

#### (iii) Risk of Damage (General)

The focus of this inquiry is on the regulated community. Although this could be defined as broadly as all those persons or entities that are subject to the subsection 36(3) prohibition, a more useful category might be all PEI farmers who use pesticides on their crops, or perhaps all such farmers in the Maritimes.

Framed this way, the risk of general damage could be a function of the number of farmers and the amount of pesticides that they use on an annual basis. And while the probability of all such farmers ignoring appropriate buffers would be low, it does appear to be the case that fish kills like this one are actually not uncommon in PEI; according to one source found by the authors, there have been roughly 50 such fish kills in PEI in the past 50 years, or one per year.[19]

Here, again, in the absence of a damages transfer database, environmental valuation could tell the court something about the value of the environment or ecosystem asset at stake against which to benchmark the risk. Returning to the example of Atlantic salmon, even if the general risk of damage was deemed to be to only a fraction of a percent of the Atlantic salmon population (e.g. 0.1%), that still represents $105,000 in non-use values.

What this case study makes clear is that the risk of damage analysis, whether specific or general, is not limited the same way as the actual damage assessment analysis is, which is to say by the need for baseline information *prior to the incident*. The "risk of damage" assessment is hypothetical and, in the general risk context especially, is likely to take into account a considerably higher level of harm than the specific offence, such that the latter is not likely to affect the results of the former. Simply put, the absence of a baseline would not seem as problematic to this exercise as it is for actual damages. Thus, where the Crown deems it sufficiently important, it could elect to carry out a valuation study after the offence for the purposes of informing the general risk of harm analysis.

## Part V: Prospects for Environmental Valuation in Environmental Sentencing

It has now been a decade since the Supreme Court of Canada's decision in *Canfor*[20] and almost five years since the passage of the *EEA*, and there has yet to be a Canadian judgment—whether in the civil or regulatory context—that has seriously considered the loss of use and non-use values in the context of environmental damages.

It is clear that further development in this area, which the authors regard as necessary for the full consideration of environmental harm, will require considerable work and effort on the part of researchers, government agencies, and Crown prosecutors. The needed economic valuation information can only be provided from banks of sufficient data, which currently do not exist. Such data will need to be generated through developing new data collection efforts as well as adjusting existing data collection systems. Since sufficiently trained staff will be required to analyze and interpret this new data, regulatory agencies will need to add expertise beyond their traditionally trained environmental science staff.

Should agencies finally undertake expanding their expertise in this area, Canada's judiciary will also be challenged when it comes time to considering such evidence, although its existing track record for digesting complex scientific evidence suggests that it is entirely up to the task. Until then, it is apparent that the Canadian judges will have to continue to call on the Crown to collect and submit the necessary expert evidence, as was done in *R. v. United Keno Hill Mines*,[21] *R. v. Carriere*,[22] and numerous other cases, albeit it now with a shift towards economic quantification.

## NOTES

1 An example for Canadian wilderness recreation is: PC Boxall, DO Watson & J Englin, "Backcountry Recreationists' Valuation of Forest and Park Management Features in Wilderness Parks of the Western Canadian Shield" (1996) 26:6 Can J For Res 982 at 990.

2 Peter Boxall et al provide an example for the vandalism of Canadian Aboriginal rock paintings that were modelled as a recreation attribute: see "Valuing Aboriginal Artifacts: A Combined Revealed-Stated Preference Approach" (2003) 45:2 J Environ Econ Manage 213 at 230.

3 For example, Peter Boxall et al find that the presence of energy infrastructure developments within 4 km of a given country residential property depresses its sale price in Alberta: see "The Impact of Oil and Natural Gas Facilities on Rural Residential Property Values: A Spatial Hedonic Analysis" (2005) 27:3 Res Energy Econ 248 at 269; J Loomis and M Feldman uncover positive economic benefits for stabilizing lake levels of nearby properties in the US: see "Estimating the benefits of maintaining adequate lake levels to homeowners using the hedonic property method" (2003) 39:9 Water Res Research WES 2-1 at WES 2-6.

4 See Carson et al, "Contingent Valuation and Lost Passive Use: Damages from the Exxon Valdez Oil Spill" (2003) 25:3 Env Res Econ 257 at 286.

5 See online: <https:// https://www.evri.ca/en>.

6 (2004), 10 CELR (3d) 178, 241 Nfld & PEIR 194 [*Caseley & Sons*].

7 RSC 1985, c F-14.

8 Readers may be interested to know that, subsequent to the facts leading up to this case (2002), Azinphos-methyl's use has been slated to be phased out; see *Re-evaluation Decision Document*, RRD2004-05 (Ottawa: PMRA, 2004), online: <http://publications.gc.ca/site/eng/247893/publication.html>.

9 *Caseley & Sons*, *supra* note 6 at paras 9–11.

10 *Ibid* at paras 12–14.

11 This is a case of determining the "interim loss," which would involve the loss from the time of the incident to full recovery of the damages. This is discussed in some depth in CA Jones & KA Pease, "Restoration-Based Compensation Measures in Natural Resource Liability Statutes" (1997) 15 Contemp Econ Policy 111 at 122.

12 Such research has been conducted in Alberta for camping areas in the Rocky Mountain Foothills managed by the

provincial government: see PC Boxall, BL McFarlane & M Gartrell, "An Aggregate Travel Cost Approach to Valuing Forest Recreation at Managed Sites" (1996) 72:6 Forestry Chronicle 615 at 621. A similar report to Parks Canada's pointed out the potential use of their registration systems for similar purposes: see BF McFarlane, D Watson & PC Boxall, "Getting More from What We Have: The Case of Backcountry Permits" (2001) 9:3 Research Links 5 at 7.

13 It is estimated that the contingent valuation survey conducted to estimate the damages of the 1989 Exxon *Valdez* oil spill cost $3 million to implement. GC Harrison & JC Leahy, in "Must Contingent Valuation Surveys Cost So Much?" (1996) 31 J Env Econ Mgmt 79 at 95, discuss this and provide an alternative cheaper method. One would need to recognize that the survey expenditure level was high because the results were to be used in litigation around the damage assessment estimates. Stated preference surveys conducted by Boxall and colleagues typically cost in the range of $120,000–$150,000 each.

14 *R. v. Terroco Industries Ltd*, 2005 ABCA 141.

15 *Supra* note 8: "Based on a review of the available information, the PMRA has concluded that the use of azinphos-methyl and its associated end-use products in accordance with the current label directions entails an unacceptable risk of harm to agricultural workers pursuant to Section 20 of the PCP Regulations. Environmental concerns have also been identified...."

16 Department of Fisheries and Oceans (DFO), *Stock Status of Atlantic Salmon (Salmo Salar) in DFO Gulf Region (Salmon Fishing Areas 15 to 18)*, Canadian Science Advisory Secretariat Science Advisory Report 2012/040 (Ottawa: DFO, 2012), online: <http://www.dfo-mpo.gc.ca/csas-sccs/Publications/SAR-AS/2012/2012_040-eng.html>.

17 Gardner Pinfold, *Economic Value of Wild Atlantic Salmon* (Halifax: Atlantic Salmon Federation, September 2011), online: <http://www.asf.ca/gardner-pinfold-report.html>.

18 Revealing the numerous other benefits conferred on society by functioning ecosystems is the goal of the ecosystem services framework; for more on the potential to apply an ecosystem services framework to sentencing, see Martin Olszynski, "Environmental Damages after the Federal *Environmental Enforcement Act*: Bringing Ecosystem Services to Canadian Environmental Law?" (2012) 50:1 Osgoode Hall LJ 129.

19 *A Compiled History of PEI Fish Kills 1962–2011* (Belfast, PEI: Macphail Woods Ecological Forestry Project, 14 February 2013), online: <https://macphailwoods.org/wp-content/uploads/2013/02/History-of-Fish-Kills-PEI-.pdf>.

20 *Canadian Forest Products v. British Columbia*, 2004 SCC 38, [2004] 2 SCR 74.

21 (1980), 1 YR 299 (Terr Ct) at para 16.

22 2005 SKPC 84, 272 Sask R 13 at para 27.

SECTION 4

# Evidentiary Issues in Environmental Prosecutions and Hearings

# 34

# Proving Causation: Scientific Certainty vs. Legal Burden of Proof

DANIELLE MEULEMAN*

Neither law nor science operates in a world of absolutes. In the legal world we talk about proof in terms of standards—beyond a reasonable doubt, balance of probabilities—and tests for causation—but for, material contribution. In contrast, scientists use terms such as scientific method, uncertainty factors, statistical associations. At their core, both law and science rely on evidence, and, in the end, both law and science ultimately come to conclusions despite some amount of uncertainty. This chapter discusses the somewhat unique world of environmental law, where science often takes centre stage.

At the core of most environmental statutory regimes is the prohibition on the discharge of substances that have the potential to harm the environment and/or human health.[1] The definition of "substance" (also referred to as "contaminant," "pollutant," "material") is necessarily very broad and usually includes solids, liquids, gases, odours, heat, sound, vibration, etc. Therefore, evidence of the breach of these prohibitions rarely turns on the nature of the substance discharged. More often the debate focuses on proof that the substance *caused* an adverse effect that is prohibited.

## Do We Always Need Experts to Prove Causation?

Let's start with a look at Ontario's *Environmental Protection Act* (EPA), which has one of the most expansive definitions of "adverse effect" in Canadian legislation. Adverse effect is defined as one or more of:

* *The views presented in this chapter are my own and are not intended to represent the Province of Ontario, the Ministry of the Attorney General, or the Ministry of the Environment and Climate Change.*

(a) impairment of the quality of the natural environment for any use that can be made of it,
(b) injury or damage to property or to plant or animal life,
(c) harm or material discomfort to any person,
(d) an adverse effect on the health of any person,
(e) impairment of the safety of any person,
(f) rendering any property or plant or animal life unfit for human use,
(g) loss of enjoyment of normal use of property, and
(h) interference with the normal conduct of business.[2]

Keeping in mind this definition, you can see that sometimes proof of causation is very straightforward and requires nothing more than common sense. In the Supreme Court of Canada decision *Castonguay Blasting Ltd. v. Ontario (Environment)*,[3] the defendant was charged with failing to report the discharge of a contaminant into the natural environment that caused, or was likely to cause, an adverse effect.[4] The facts of the case were simple—the defendant was retained by the Ministry of Transportation to blast out a rock face allowing an adjacent highway to be widened. In the course of blasting, a series of rocks flew out of the controlled blast area onto a nearby residential property, causing property damage to the home and to the vehicle parked in the driveway. Luckily no one was injured. No expert witnesses were needed to prove the nature of the contaminant (the rocks were a solid), the adverse effects (damage to property, impairment of the safety of any person), or the cause of the adverse effects (the blast sent the fly rock through the air and the damage was caused by the impact of the rocks hitting the home and vehicle). If it looks like a duck and quacks like a duck, the courts are likely find it's a duck—no expert necessary.

Of course, many environmental cases are not so obvious and thus causation is more difficult to prove. Take the situation where someone is walking down the street and suddenly smells a chemical-type odour, feels irritation in her eyes, and suffers a gagging/coughing fit. She ducks (yes, I said duck) into her nearby car and after ten minutes or so feels fine again. While waiting in her car she reports the incident to the local Ministry of the Environment (MOE). An MOE officer later determines that a bath/shower manufacturer in the area reported a small processing upset that same afternoon that resulted in the discharge of excess styrene (an aromatic organic compound). Styrene is known to cause eye irritation and irritation of the nose/mouth upon inhalation. The company reported that the discharge was minimal and its employees didn't notice any impacts outside of the plant. All of this evidence seems to point to the discharge of styrene as the cause of the impacts on the passerby. But then again maybe not; perhaps this is an area with many industrial operations, any one of which could have discharged something that caused the impacts to this individual; perhaps she was hit with drifting ragweed pollen and had an allergic reaction; or perhaps she was coming down with a cold. Suddenly, the simple case is not so simple. Expert witnesses may be needed to provide evidence of wind direction, air dispersion modelling, a medical doctor to assess causation—to say nothing of the company's potential due diligence defence.

Governments often recognize the difficulties in proving causation with a sufficient degree of scientific certainty in the environmental context and may look simply to proof of causation. For example, the *Ontario Water Resources Act* prohibits the discharge of any material into or near water that may impair the quality of the water;[5] however, proof of the "impairment" is made more straightforward by a provision in the Act that provides that "the quality of water shall be deemed to be impaired" if any one of a number of criteria are met. These criteria include: that the material may cause a degradation in the appearance, taste, or odour of the water; a scientific test that is generally accepted as a test of aquatic toxicity indicates that the material is toxic; or a peer-reviewed scientific publication that indicates the material interference with organisms that are dependent on aquatic ecosystems.[6] Proof of these deeming provisions may still require an expert to testify that the material failed the toxicity test or to explain the peer-reviewed study, but there is no doubt that this is more straightforward than proof of *in situ* impairment.

## What About Proof of a Subjective Value?

Looking back at the definition of adverse effects in the EPA, you will see that the last two criteria are loss of enjoyment of normal use of property and interference with the normal conduct of business. These can be subjective criteria. Did the fly-rock incident in *Castonguay* prevent the nearby resident from sitting outside enjoying a BBQ while rocks were flying through the air? It's likely that the fly-rock event only lasted a minute—is this really an invasion of someone's use of their property that warrants sanction? Maybe this is an easier one to answer, but what about the impact of ongoing odours? While many odours are not actually harmful to someone's health (e.g. industrial compost operation odours or rendering plant) they can be very off-putting. Would you want to sit outside having a BBQ with friends in mid-July with a constant smell of rotting garbage nearby? Often MOE officers will "objectively" source and "quantify" the odour (rank it as the worst they have experienced/9 out of 10 in terms of intensity/they wouldn't sit outside while it was ongoing), and multiple lay witnesses may also provide evidence of their experiences with the odour. Often in these cases expert witnesses are not needed, but there is no doubt that we all bring our own subjective value systems into evaluation of these types of cases.

## What About Proof of the Exact Cause of a Breakdown that Resulted in a Discharge?

Industrial operations by their nature "discharge" to the natural environment, and sometimes things go wrong. Do we need to understand exactly what went wrong to prove that Company A was the source of the discharge of Pollutant X to the nearby river, resulting in fish kill? No, it is not always necessary to know the precise cause of the failure for the Crown to prove the *actus reus*; however, the defendant may want/need to understand the exact cause to prove that it was duly diligent. The leading case in this area is *R. v. Petro-Canada*, a 2003 case out of the Ontario Court of Appeal.[7] The facts of the *actus reus* in *Petro-Canada* are straightforward (gasoline spill from a pipe at a Petro-Canada facility), but neither the regulator nor the defendant knew the cause of the pipe failure. The court found that it was not necessary for the Crown to prove the precise cause of the failure to make out the offence *and* it was not incumbent on the defendant to likewise prove the precise cause to make out a due diligence defence; however, the court did concede that proof of due diligence would likely be made easier if the exact cause were known:

> For these reasons I do not think that the law requires the accused to prove precisely how the discharge came about—in this case precisely why the pipe failed—in order to avail itself of the due diligence defence. On the other hand, in a case where the accused can do this, it may be able to narrow the range of preventative steps that it must show to establish that it took all reasonable care. However where, as here, the accused cannot prove the precise cause of the pipe failure the due diligence defence is not rendered unavailable as a result. That being said, it must be emphasized that to invoke the defence successfully in such circumstances, the accused must show that it took all reasonable care to avoid *any* foreseeable cause. [Emphasis added.][8]

*R. v. Zellstoff Celgar Limited Partnership*[9] is another case from British Columbia that followed the Petro-Canada decision. In that case a pulp mill was charged with various offences related to discharge of "black liquor" into the Columbia River, including, under subsection 36(3) of *Fisheries Act*[10]—deposit of deleterious substance in water frequented by fish. There were two theories about the nature of the discharge—the Crown believed it was "black liquor soap" and the defendant put forward evidence that it was "dilute black liquor" (interestingly, it doesn't appear from the decision that any expert evidence was called by either party on this point—the evidence came from observations of Zellstoff Celgar's employees). In the end the court appeared to favour the evidence that this was black liquor soap but found that in any event it didn't really matter for proof of the *actus reus*—whichever derivative of black liquor, it was found to be deleterious to fish. In looking at due diligence, however, the court found that while the defendant was likely duly diligent if the discharge was dilute black liquor, it had not made out due diligence if the substance was black liquor soap.

> I cannot find on the evidence that the only probable cause of these offences lay with the state of the health of the [effluent treatment system ("ETS")]. I find there is compelling evidence to suggest the cause of the offences lay with Celgar's failure to follow its own procedures regarding a soap carryover. *As I cannot be satisfied that Celgar has proven the cause of the offence at issue, it follows that Celgar must show it acted with due diligence to prevent any foreseeable cause.* As it was obviously foreseeable that the introduction of weak black liquor soap into the ETS would cause a failure of the treatment system, I cannot be satisfied that Celgar has met its onus and shown that it exercised all reasonable care to prevent the commission of these offences. [Emphasis added.][11]

## Challenging Existing Legislation

Up to this point, I've mainly focused on the regulator's need to prove harm to make out an offence under environmental legislation. So let's switch gears a bit and discuss the scenario where someone wants to challenge an environmental law on the basis that it does not reflect the current state of science and in doing so may allow harm to the environment or human health. Environmental law doesn't generally seek to eliminate all discharges into the environment; rather it seeks to control them to ensure that where a discharge is permitted it will not result in harm. This can be done by legislation (a regulation that sets a limit on the amount/concentration of substance that can be discharged) or through a more tailored instrument, such as a site-specific approval that considers all of the discharges expected from a particular facility.[12] In my opinion, we should start from the proposition that legislation and regulatory guidelines are drafted in accordance with the current state of scientific knowledge. In Ontario all government ministries were required to put in place a Statement of Environmental Values (SEV) to record their commitment to the environment and to be accountable for ensuring consideration of the environment in their decisions. The Ontario Ministry of the Environment and Climate Change's SEV provides that the ministry use a precautionary, science-based approach in its decision making to protect human health and the environment.[13]

There have been a series of administrative appeals challenging renewable energy approvals issued to wind turbine farms in Ontario.[14] Most of the appeals are initiated by residents concerned that the noise limits and property setback limits for wind turbines established by regulation are not adequate to protect against harm to human health. These appellants have also sought to challenge these approvals on the basis that these limits violate their security of the person rights under section 7 of the Canadian *Charter of Rights and Freedoms.* In a decision from the Ontario Divisional Court (sitting on appeal of three such decisions of the Environmental Review Tribunal), *Dixon v. Ontario*, the court confirmed that the onus is on the appellants to prove the harm alleged, even where the appellants' assert that "science just doesn't know what is safe":

> 66 This brings us to the heart of the Appellants' s. 7 claims. They contend that unlike the certainty of scientific knowledge which surrounds the effects of the discharge of a contaminant such as mercury, when dealing with the effect of noise and vibrations from commercial wind farms we are dealing with "known unknowns". *The uncertainty of the state of scientific knowledge about the effects on human health of commercial wind farms, according to the Appellants, materially informs the analysis of the Charter adequacy of the review tests found in* EPA *ss. 142.1(3) and 145.2.1(2)*. Which leads, then, to the question of whether the statutory test adopted by the Legislature materially departed from the consensus scientific view about the impact of commercial wind turbines on human health....
>
> 75 On appeals such as these our Court can only consider a question of law; we cannot re-weigh or re-assess the evidence which was before

> the Tribunals or the factual findings they made. Our purpose in describing the expert evidence which was before the Tribunals on the issue of the impact of wind turbines on human health is a narrow one: *to identify that the Tribunals did not have before them expert evidence which seriously called into question the principle underpinning the EPA's renewable energy project regulatory regime* – i.e. that wind turbines which are set back 550m from a dwelling house and which do not generate noise levels in excess of 40 dBA at the lowest specified wind speed do not cause serious harm to human health based upon the current state of scientific knowledge. [Emphasis added.][15]

In attempting to prove harm to human health, individuals living near existing, operating wind turbine projects in Ontario gave evidence at each of the three tribunal hearings. All of the individuals believed that the turbines operating near their homes caused them to suffer from a range of health impacts (sleep disturbance, headaches, heart palpitations, and more); however, none of these claims was supported by expert medical or epidemiological evidence. In the end, all of the tribunal decisions found that the evidence of the lay witnesses alone, though sincere, was not sufficient prove that the turbines were the cause of the health impacts.

What if an appellant/applicant challenging environmental legislation does bring forward credible expert evidence? In *Millership v. Kamloops (City)*,[16] the appellant alleged that the City's addition of fluoride to the municipal drinking water supply caused him harm (fluorosis of his teeth as a teenager). Mr. Millership presented evidence from a number of experts in support of his position, including a medical doctor who concluded that fluoridation is "ineffective" and "dangerous to the health of consumers."[17] Likewise the City of Kamloops put forward expert evidence to the contrary, that fluoridation was safe and beneficial to the public. The British Columbia Supreme Court described the debate in the case as follows:

> In this case, there is a great deal of evidence from all parties dealing with the risks and benefits of publically fluoridated water. *There is a dispute between the parties whether fluoridation of public water has any benefits or clinically insignificant benefits*, and whether it poses risks including skeletal fluorosis, osteoporosis, hip fractures and cancer. [Emphasis added.][18]

The court in *Millership* sums it all up nicely: "Clearly this is a case where expert evidence is necessary."[19]

## NOTES

1 Ontario's *Environmental Protection Act*, RSO 1990, c E.19, s 14 [*EPA*] (I will use Ontario as the core example throughout this chapter, but each province has similar legislation).

2 *EPA*, s 1(1) "adverse effect."

3 *Castonguay Blasting Ltd v Ontario (Environment)*, 2013 SCC 52, [2013] 3 SCR 323 [*Castonguay*].

4 Contrary to s 15(1) of the *EPA*.

5 *Ontario Water Resources Act*, RSO 1990, c O.40, s 30(1) [*OWRA*].

6 *OWRA*, s 1(3).

7 [2003] OJ No 216 [*Petro-Canada*].

8 *Ibid* at para 20.

9 2012 BCPC 38 [*Zellstoff Celgar*].

10 RSC 1985, c F-14.

11 *Zellstoff Celgar*, *supra* note 9 at para 56.

12 See, e.g., s 9 of the *EPA*.

13 Government of Ontario, "Statement of Environmental Values: Ministry of Environment and Climate Change" (Environmental Registry, accessed 30 January 2018), online: <https://www.ebr.gov.on.ca/ERS-WEB-External/content/sev.jsp?pageName=sevList&subPageName=10001>.

14 Renewable Energy Approvals (REAs) are issued under s 47 of the *EPA*, and third parties are entitled to appeal REAs pursuant to s 142.1 of the *EPA*; appeals are heard by the Environmental Review Tribunal.

15 *Dixon v Ontario (Director, Ministry of the Environment)*, 2014 ONSC 7404 at paras 66, 75 [*Dixon*]; leave to appeal to the Ontario Court of Appeal was filed in January 2015.

16 2003 BCSC 82, aff'd 2004 BCCA 9 [*Millership*].

17 *Ibid* at para 70.

18 *Ibid* at para 63.

19 *Ibid* at para 64.

# 35

# Experts in Environmental Litigation

MARC McAREE, ROBERT WOON, AND ANAND SRIVASTAVA*

## Introduction

Environmental litigators find themselves embroiled in a world of disputes where science, engineering, and environmental law intersect. These disputes lead to environmental claims. Environmental litigators retain litigation experts. Experts help to decipher, untangle, and inform clients at the intersection of technical and legal issues. Litigators rely on experts because of their specialized expertise.

Environmental litigators depend on experts throughout the litigation process. Experts provide answers to everyday technical questions. They provide opinions. They write expert reports. Sometimes they testify. Environmental litigators know that a good expert can trump in a case while attacking or defending on issues of liability and damages.

Like any other evidence, an expert's evidence must be the subject of diligent scrutiny by the environmental litigator. Careful examination should not be limited to expert evidence submitted by opposing counsel. It must also apply to one's own expert and that expert's evidence. Environmental litigators must wade through the science to introduce into evidence supportable science, not junk science.

This chapter provides an overview of what environmental litigators should consider when counting on environmental experts in litigation. We examine what environmental litigators need to know about finding and retaining experts, the production of expert-generated documents, and the

* *The authors wish to thank Erin Garbett, an articling student at Willms & Shier Environmental Lawyers LLP, for her assistance in updating this chapter in 2018.*

requirements under Ontario's *Rules of Civil Procedure*[1] and the Law Society of Ontario's *Rules of Professional Conduct*.[2] We examine what opinions Canadian courts offer about the expected relationship between counsel and an expert, and alternative approaches to tendering expert evidence. Finally, we review the law about the admissibility of expert evidence, including how to establish and maintain an expert's credibility before and at trial.

## Pre-Trial

### THE LAW SOCIETY OF ONTARIO'S *RULES OF PROFESSIONAL CONDUCT*

The Law Society of Ontario's *Rules of Professional Conduct* require a lawyer to act with the requisite level of competence.[3] A competent lawyer is judged by his or her relevant knowledge, skills, and attributes.[4] A competent lawyer's use of experts is described in the Commentary to Rule 3.1-2 as follows:

> The lawyer should also recognize that competence for a particular task may require seeking advice from or collaborating with experts in scientific, accounting, or other non-legal fields, and, in such a situation, when it is appropriate, the lawyer should not hesitate to seek the client's instructions to consult experts.[5]

### RETAINING EXPERTS

Retaining the right expert is critical for any environmental litigator, and often for the outcome of the case itself. The expert should be qualified and have experience in the field of study generally and specifically relating to the issue about which the expert will opine.

#### Who Is an Expert?

Determining who is an expert in the eyes of the court is critical given the distinction between the role of a lay witness and expert witness at trial. As the authors of *The Law of Evidence in Canada* state:

> As a general rule, a witness may not give opinion evidence but may testify only to facts within her or his knowledge, observation and experience. It is the province of the trier of fact to draw inferences from the proven facts. A qualified expert witness, however may provide the trier of fact with a "ready-made inference" which the jury is unable to draw due to the technical nature of the subject matter.[6]

Defining who is an expert for purposes of testifying at trial is not so simple. The definition of an expert witness is not found in Ontario's *Rules of Civil Procedure*[7] or Ontario's *Evidence Act*.[8] The common law has broadly defined a properly qualified expert as "a witness who is shown to have acquired special or peculiar knowledge through study or experience in respect of the matters on which he or she undertakes to testify."[9]

In addition, the courts have created a distinction between experts hired prior to litigation and experts hired for the sole purpose of litigation. In *Continental Roofing Ltd. v. J.J.'s Hospitality Ltd.*, the Ontario Superior Court held that Rule 53.03 does not apply to experts involved with a matter prior to litigation.[10] In that case, the defendant retained a consultant to provide services to repair a roof. During the repair, the roof started to leak. The consultant conducted an inspection and recommended that the defendant hire another roofer to complete the repair. The court concluded that the consultant should not be regarded as an expert witness under Rule 53.03 because he was not retained for the sole purpose of providing expert testimony.[11] However, the court permitted the consultant to provide both factual and opinion evidence at trial.[12]

In *Westerhof v. Gee Estate* (*Westerhof*),[13] the Ontario Court of Appeal upheld the distinction between experts hired prior to litigation and experts hired for the sole purpose of litigation. The Ontario Court of Appeal helpfully created two categories of experts whose testimony is exempt from the application of Rule 53.03. First, Rule 53.03 will not apply to "participant experts" who are persons with "special skill, knowledge, training or experience" who testify about an opinion developed through observations of or participation in the events at issue, where the witness formed their opinion as part of the ordinary course of their skill, knowledge, training, and experience while observing or participating in such activities.[14] Second, Rule 53.03 will not apply to "non-party experts" where "the non-party expert has formed a relevant opinion based on personal observations or examinations relating to the subject matter of the litigation for a purpose other than the litigation."[15] The court in Westerhof was careful to emphasize that if a participant expert or non-party expert proffers opinion evidence extending beyond the scope of their personal observations or examinations, that witness must comply with Rule 53.03.[16]

### How to Find an Expert?

When in need of an expert, most environmental litigators refer to their own short list of known experts. These lists develop over years of practising in the field. However, it is not always the case that the very expert who is required is on the environmental litigator's shortlist. So, what happens when a litigator is new to environmental civil litigation, or not so new and requires expertise outside of his or her own shortlist?

One effective way to locate an expert is through referrals from other lawyers. This is common practice for lawyers and especially so from one lawyer to another in the same firm. Through referrals, lawyers learn about experts, including their expertise, work habits, and fee structures. A referral might not identify the right expert for the case, but may provide a good lead that gets the litigator to the right expert. Sometimes a lawyer may not know what type of expert he or she seeks until he or she starts the discussion with others in the same or similar field.

Online directories provide another useful method for locating experts. However, the reliability of these directories may be questionable and caution is required. Considerable due diligence on the part of the environmental litigator is required to ensure that the right expert is chosen to give the required opinion. Free directories such as ExpertLaw[17] and Expert Pages[18] provide American experts in real estate, engineering, and science disciplines. Legal associations also provide expert directories to their members such as the Ontario Trial Lawyers Association. Legal databases by Westlaw Canada or LexisNexis offer expert directories for a fee. The University of Toronto Blue Book[19] lists over 1,500 academic experts in many fields of study. Ryerson University provides a similar directory of its faculty.[20]

Finding the right expert with the right credentials, skills, and experience can tip the balance in a case. Many environmental disputes come down to a "battle of the experts." It is not necessarily the expert who is "right" that helps win a case, but rather the expert who sets forth the most plausible explanations and can best raise uncertainty about the other experts' theories. Considerable time and effort is required of the environmental litigator to search out, find, and retain the right person. That person must be articulate, confident, well-written, well-spoken, and available.

### How to Retain an Expert?

Environmental litigators should not overlook the importance of drafting a purposeful retainer letter. The retainer letter defines the relationship between the litigator and the expert. Litigators should be mindful that the contents of the retainer letter must be disclosed by the expert if the expert is to testify at trial.[21] Litigators need to balance between providing the expert with accurate and sufficient information to allow him or her to do his or her work while not providing irrelevant information. At a minimum, the litigator's retainer letter addressed to the expert should touch on the following topics:

CONFLICT OF INTEREST The litigator's retainer letter should confirm that the expert has completed a conflict of interest check. The letter should confirm that the expert is not aware of any conflict of interest in acting for and against parties to the litigation, and that there is no conflict relating to those properties that are the subject of the litigation.

BACKGROUND, PURPOSE, AND SCOPE OF WORK The litigator's retainer letter should include a recitation of the most salient background facts. The letter should set out the purpose for the expert's retainer and that the expert is being retained for the sole purpose of providing litigation support. The letter should also state that the expert is being retained by the litigator or law firm, and that the expert will be instructed by counsel. The letter should stipulate that the expert's advice and opinions will be utilized by the litigator in providing legal advice to the client. This is especially important if the litigator proposes to cloak the expert's work under privilege.

The expert's scope of work should be set out in the retainer letter in some detail. In some circumstances, the scope of work can be defined somewhat broadly, but not beyond the expertise of the expert. Additionally, the retainer letter may need to set out what the expert is not to opine about in the scope-of-work boundaries.

USE AND CONFIDENTIALITY The litigator's retainer letter should include a confidentiality provision. This is to ensure that all information exchanged and produced by the expert is kept physically separate and labelled "Privileged and Confidential." This applies to both hardcopy and electronic documents referred to and produced by the expert.

The retainer letter should identify when and how the expert is to communicate with the environmental litigator and/or the litigant. The retainer letter should state that the expert is to receive instructions only from instructing counsel. In addition, the letter should state that all findings, opinions, and conclusions are to be delivered by the expert exclusively to instructing counsel.

Finally, the retainer letter should identify who is responsible to pay the expert's accounts. Environmental litigators should note the presumption that the litigator is responsible for an expert's reasonable fees where the litigator instructs the expert to prepare material for litigation.[22] A litigator can rebut this presumption if the litigator specifies otherwise in the retainer letter.

### How Many Experts Can Each Litigant Retain?

Litigators must be selective about how many and which experts they intend to rely on at trial. In Ontario, parties are limited to calling three experts to testify at trial unless granted leave from the court.[23] Courts can also appoint additional experts on their own initiative.[24]

Justice Osborne's report for the Civil Justice Reform Project led to the 2010 reform of Ontario's *Rules of Civil Procedure*. In his report, Justice Osborne notes that the rule restricting three experts at trial is loosely enforced by the courts.[25] His Honour discusses the use of single-joint-expert systems in other judicial systems around the world.[26] Justice Osborne acknowledges that single joint experts may not be practical in most cases and may not save costs due to the retaining of "shadow" experts.[27] Although Justice Osborne did not recommend a mandatory use of joint experts in Ontario, he did recommend that parties consult early in the litigation process to discuss the prospect of jointly retaining a single expert.[28] We set out below a discussion about alternatives to the traditional use of experts.

Certainly, the use of competing experts will remain the norm unless and until the legislature amends the *Evidence Act*[29] or *Rules of Civil Procedure*[30] to adopt another approach or endorse alternative approaches. In the meantime, litigators should be mindful that the rule of three experts at trial is a prescribed limit and is enforceable in Ontario courts.

### Requirements under Ontario's Rules of Civil Procedure

The *Rules* govern how and when experts may be used in litigation.

EXPERT'S DUTY TO THE COURT All experts have a duty of loyalty to the court. Rule 4.1.01 states:

> (1) It is the duty of every expert engaged by or on behalf of a party to provide evidence in relation to a proceeding under these rules,
>
> (a) to provide opinion evidence that is fair, objective and non-partisan;
> (b) to provide opinion evidence that is related only to matters that are within the expert's area of expertise; and

(c) to provide such additional assistance as the court may reasonably require to determine a matter in issue.

(2) The duty in subrule (1) prevails over any obligation owed by the expert to the party by whom or on whose behalf he or she is engaged.

PARTY-APPOINTED EXPERTS Under Rule 53.03, a party may introduce expert evidence first by written report and then by oral testimony at trial.[31] The party must serve the expert's report on every opposing party within the time designations in the Rules. Under Rule 53.03(2.1), an expert's report shall include:

1. The expert's name, address and area of expertise.
2. The expert's qualifications and employment and educational experiences in his or her area of expertise.
3. The instructions provided to the expert in relation to the proceeding.
4. The nature of the opinion being sought and each issue in the proceeding to which the opinion relates.
5. The expert's opinion respecting each issue and, where there is a range of opinions given, a summary of the range and the reasons for the expert's own opinion within that range.
6. The expert's reasons for his or her opinion, including,

    i. a description of the factual assumptions on which the opinion is based,
    ii. a description of any research conducted by the expert that led him or her to form the opinion, and
    iii. a list of every document, if any, relied on by the expert in forming the opinion.

7. An acknowledgement of expert's duty (Form 53) signed by the expert.

Under Rule 53.03(3), an expert may not testify at trial on any issue not addressed in his or her report, except with leave of the court.[32]

COURT-APPOINTED EXPERTS The Rules also allow for the court to appoint an expert for the proceeding. Under Rule 50.06, the presiding pre-trial judge or master will consider the advisability of having the court appoint an expert. If no court-ordered expert is appointed at the pre-trial, the court may appoint an expert at trial under Rule 52.03. This can be done on motion by a party or by the judge's own initiative.

Any court-appointed expert will be given instructions by the court about the scope of their required report. The court may order the expert to inspect property or examine a party's physical or mental state as required. The parties to the action may be required to remunerate the expert as decided by the presiding judge at first instance.

In his summary of findings and recommendations, Justice Osborne notes that Rule 52.03 is "rarely used" by the court.[33]

Academic Nicholas Bala has advocated for increasing the use of Rule 52.03 to reduce costs and promote settlement between litigants.[34] Bala believes that lawyers are able to avoid obvious biases when hiring and instructing an expert. However, the broader paradigm of paying an expert for his or her opinion leads to subtle biases that may affect objectivity. Bala compares court-appointed experts to the financial sector's move to strengthen the independence of auditors and rating agencies.[35]

CONCURRENT EVIDENCE FROM EXPERTS The Rules provide that if an action is not settled at the pre-trial conference, the court may order a joint submission from any experts retained by the opposing parties.

Rule 50.07(1)(c) states:

> (1) If the proceeding is not settled at the pre-trial conference, the presiding judge or case management master may,
>
> ...
>
> (c) make such order as the judge or case management master considers necessary or advisable with respect to the conduct of the proceeding, including any order under subrule 20.05 (1) or (2).

Under Rule 20.05(2)(k), the court may order:

> (k) that any experts engaged by or on behalf of the parties in relation to the action meet on a without prejudice basis in order to identify the issues on which the experts agree and the issues on which they do not agree, to attempt to clarify and resolve any issues that are the subject of disagreement and to prepare a

joint statement setting out the areas of agreement and any areas of disagreement and the reasons for it if, in the opinion of the court, the cost or time savings or other benefits that may be achieved from the meeting are proportionate to the amounts at stake or the importance of the issues involved in the case and,

(i) there is a reasonable prospect for agreement on some or all of the issues, or
(ii) the rationale for opposing expert opinions is unknown and clarification on areas of disagreement would assist the parties or the court.

As we discuss below, Rules 50.07(1)(c) and 20.05(2)(k) are rarely used by the court.

## EXPERT DOCUMENTS

After the retainer is in place and instructions given, environmental experts typically produce lots of documentation, including communications to and from various stakeholders. This documentation may include work plans, field notes, correspondence, photographs, diagrams, charts, meeting notes, test results, draft reports, and final reports. The question is which of these materials are producible by parties in litigation and to what extent can privilege be exerted over the expert's work product during the litigation.

### Disclosure of Relevant Documents

Environmental litigants have broad disclosure obligations in civil actions. Rule 30.02(1) of the Ontario *Rules of Civil Procedure* states:

> Every document relevant to any matter in issue in an action that is or has been in the possession, control, or power of a party to the action shall be disclosed as provided in rules 30.03 to 30.10, whether or not privilege is claimed in respect of the document.[36]

In addition, there are specific rules that attach to experts that a litigant intends to call as a witness at trial. Rule 53.03(1) requires parties to produce a report for every expert called to testify at trial.[37] The report must be served not less than 90 days before the pre-trial conference.[38] Production must be made to every other party in the action. Rule 53.03(2.1) specifies the information that must be included in every expert report, including the factual assumptions, research, and documents that the expert relies on.[39] The rule also requires that the expert include a statement about their duty to the court. The expert must append to his or her report the instructions from the retaining party.

Commonly, during the earlier stages of litigation, parties will not produce an expert's report. As a result, Rule 31.06(3) is of particular importance for environmental litigators. The rule allows a party to request disclosure of the findings, opinions, and conclusions of experts to be relied on at trial.[40] Often a litigator will rely on this rule to try to obtain a sneak preview of the opposing expert's views. Most often, this is met with resistance.

### Assertion of Privilege

Rule 30.02(2) establishes that not every document that is discloseable must be produced if counsel asserts privilege over the document.[41] Typically, environmental litigators seek to cloak and protect an expert's file from production under litigation privilege.

"Litigation privilege is based upon the need for a protected area to facilitate investigation and preparation of a case for trial by the adversarial advocate."[42] This is commonly referred to as a "zone of privacy." The zone of privacy facilitates environmental litigators' preparation for trial through the use of experts.

In *General Accident Assurance Co. v. Chrusz* (Chrusz), the Ontario Court of Appeal stated:

> The "zone of privacy" is an attractive description but does not define the outer reaches of protection or legitimate intrusion of discovery to assure a trial on all of the relevant facts. The modern trend is in the direction of complete discovery and there is no apparent reason to inhibit that trend so long as counsel is left with sufficient flexibility to adequately serve the litigation client. In effect, litigation privilege is the area of privacy left to a solicitor after the current demands of discoverability have been met. There is a tension between them to the extent that when discovery is widened, the reasonable requirements of counsel to conduct litigation must be recognized.
>
> Our modern rules certainly have truncated what would previously have been protected from disclosure.[43]

The Court of Appeal in *Chrusz* adopted the "dominant purpose test." The test permits the assertion of privilege over documents created for the dominant purpose of litigation, actual or contemplated.[44] Applying the test, the court concluded that litigation privilege does not protect documents gathered or copied, where the original documents were not privileged.[45] Also at issue were communications and reports between an insurer's lawyer and the insurer's third-party claims adjuster. The court limited the extension of privilege to only those communications that occurred while the insurer contemplated litigation against the defendant.

Several years later, the Supreme Court of Canada affirmed the "dominant purpose test" in *Blank v. Canada*.[46] The court stated:

> ... the dominant purpose standard appears to me consistent with the notion that the litigation privilege should be viewed as a limited exception to the principle of full disclosure and not as an equal partner of the broadly interpreted solicitor-client privilege. The dominant purpose test is more compatible with the contemporary trend favouring increased disclosure.[47]

The court ruled that litigation privilege ends upon termination of the litigation that gives rise to the privilege.[48] The court noted that litigation privilege may extend beyond termination of the litigation where related litigation is pending or may reasonably be apprehended.[49] Related litigation can include separate proceedings that involve the same or related parties, arise from the same or related causes of action, or raise issues common to the initial action and share its essential purpose.[50]

In *Browne (Litigation Guardian of) v. Lavery*, the Ontario Superior Court noted that litigation privilege over a report is waived once it is delivered to the opposing party.[51] Later in *Lecocq Logging Inc. v. Hood Logging Equipment Canada Inc.*, the court held that a waiver over the expert's report served to remove any privilege that would otherwise extend to an expert's notes.[52]

In *Bazinet v. Davies Harley Davidson*, the Ontario Superior Court held that waiver of privilege over an expert's report includes a waiver over any other report relied on by the expert in preparing the expert's report.[53] In that case, the plaintiff provided an expert's report to a second expert. The court held that once the plaintiff relied on the second expert and produced the second expert's report, there was a waiver over the first expert's report.[54] Also, the opposing party was entitled to disclosure of the second expert's findings, opinions, and conclusions under Rule 31.06(3).

In *St. Onge v. St. Onge*, the court held that in the family law context, when a party authorized a medical expert to contact other medical experts for the purpose of completing an assessment, the party has waived their privilege attached to the contacted experts.[55] In this case, the applicant allowed a medical expert complete access to medical records created by other medical experts in order to complete a parenting capacity assessment. The court rejected an argument that the applicant's waiver was limited only to the medical expert's opinion.[56]

### Document Destruction Policies

Reliance on document destruction policies by experts to justify the deletion or shredding of documents in the expert's file has not been specifically addressed by the courts in Canada.

The destruction of file documents may give rise to ethical questions. First, destruction of documents often leads to more questions than answers about the motive behind and purpose for destroying documents. Second, it may be seen, or inferred, to be for some illegitimate or obfuscating purpose. Third, destruction of documents may be questionable where there is no "corporate destruction policy." The lack of a policy may give rise to inconsistency and a *laissez-faire* approach when the expert believes it is appropriate to destroy documents. Fourth, there may be a lack of application of what may otherwise be a good policy from file to file, and among experts even in the same organization. All of these issues can give rise to fodder for cross-examining an expert at trial.

Probably, the best approach is to not destroy any documents, or consistently apply a well-thought-out destruction policy throughout the organization and from file to file. Anything less can lead to an attack on the expert's credibility.

Regardless, environmental litigators and their clients cannot necessarily shield experts from disclosure of all information set out in deleted or shredded documents. In *Bookman v. Loeb*, the court ordered that a memorandum outlining counsel's instructions be produced if the instruction letters did not exist.[57] In addition, the Ontario Court of Appeal in *Conceicao Farms Inc. v. Zeneca Corp.* held that Rule 31.06(3) only requires production of information but not the actual document.[58]

#### NOTES

1 *Rules of Civil Procedure*, RRO 1990, Reg 194 promulgated under Ontario's *Courts of Justice Act* [*Rules*].

2 Law Society of Ontario, *Rules of Professional Conduct, Amendments based on the Federation of Law Societies*

*of Canada's Model Code of Professional Conduct* (Toronto: Law Society of Ontario, October 2014) [*Professional Conduct*].

3 *Ibid*, Rule 3.1-2.

4 *Ibid*, Commentary to Rule 3.1-2.

5 *Ibid.*

6 Alan W Bryant, Sidney N Lederman & Michelle K Fuerst, *Sopinka, Lederman & Bryant: The Law of Evidence in Canada*, 3d ed (Markham: LexisNexis Canada, 2009) at 771.

7 *Rules*, *supra* note 1.

8 *Evidence Act*, RSO 1990, c E-23, s 12 [*Evidence Act*].

9 *R v Mohan*, [1994] 2 SCR 9 at para 31 [*Mohan*].

10 *Continental Roofing Ltd v JJ's Hospitality Ltd*, 2012 ONSC 1751 at paras 40–43 [*Continental Roofing*].

11 *Ibid.*

12 *Ibid* at para 42.

13 2015 ONCA 206.

14 *Ibid* at para 60.

15 *Ibid* at para 62.

16 *Ibid* at paras 63–64.

17 Expert Law, online: <http://www.expertlaw.com>.

18 Expert Pages, online: <http://www.expertpages.com>.

19 University of Toronto, "Blue Book," online: <http://www.bluebook.utoronto.ca>.

20 Ryerson University, "Faculty Experts," online: <http://ryerson.ca/news/media/facultyexperts/index.html>.

21 *Rules*, *supra* note 1, Rule 53.03.

22 *1401337 Ontario Ltd v MacIvor Harris Roddy LLP*, 2011 ONSC 948 at para 27.

23 *Evidence Act*, *supra* note 8 at s 12.

24 *Rules*, *supra* note 1, Rule 52.03(1).

25 Hon Coulter A Osborne, "Civil Justice Reform Project – Summary of Findings & Recommendations" (2007) at 73 [*Osborne Report*], online: <https://www.attorneygeneral.jus.gov.on.ca/english/about/pubs/cjrp/>.

26 *Ibid* at 69–73.

27 *Ibid* at 72.

28 *Ibid* at 82.

29 *Evidence Act*, *supra* note 8.

30 *Rules*, *supra* note 1.

31 *Rules*, *supra* note 1, Rule 53.03.

32 *Ibid*, Rule 53.03(3).

33 *Osborne Report*, *supra* note 25 at 73.

34 Nicholas Bala, "Inside the Mind of an Expert," *The Lawyers Weekly* (15 February 2013) 10.

35 *Ibid.*

36 *Rules*, *supra* note 1, Rule 30.02(1).

37 *Ibid*, Rule 53.03(1).

38 *Ibid*, Rule 53.03(1).

39 *Ibid*, Rule 53.03(2.1).

40 *Ibid*, Rule 31.06(3).

41 *Ibid*, Rule 30.02(2).

42 *General Accident Assurance Co v Chrusz* (1999), 45 OR (3d) 321 at para 23 (CA) [*Chrusz*], citing RJ Sharpe, "Claiming Privilege in the Discovery Process" in *Law in Transition: Evidence*, LSUC Special Lectures (Toronto: De Boo, 1984) at 163.

43 *Chrusz*, *ibid* at paras 25–26.

44 *Ibid* at para 33.

45 *Ibid* at para 38.

46 *Blank v Canada (Department of Justice)*, 2006 SCC 39 at para 60 [*Blank*].

47 *Ibid.*

48 *Ibid* at para 36.

49 *Ibid* at para 38.

50 *Ibid* at para 39.

51 *Browne (Litigation Guardian of) v Lavery* (2002), 58 OR (3d) 49 at paras 18, 77 (Sup Ct J) [*Browne*] .

52 *Lecocq Logging Inc v Hood Logging Equipment Canada Inc* (2005), 14 CPC (6th) 287 at para 17 (Ont Sup Ct J).

53 *Bazinet v Davies Harley Davidson* (2007), 158 ACWS (3d) 561 at paras 32–34 (Ont Sup Ct J).

54 *Ibid* at para 26.

55 2017 ONCJ 156.

56 *Ibid* at para 76.

57 *Bookman v Loeb*, [2009] OJ No 2741, 2009 CarswellOnt 3796 at para 37 (Sup Ct J).

58 *Conceicao Farms Inc v Zeneca Corp*, 83 OR (3d) 792 at paras 14, 17, and 21 (CA).

# 36

# Communication Between Lawyers and Experts

MARC McAREE, ROBERT WOON, AND ANAND SRIVASTAVA*

## Introduction

Canadian case law on acceptable communication between lawyers and experts is unclear and lacking appellate review. The issue has most often arisen when a party seeks disclosure from an opposing party about communication with an expert or relating to an expert's draft report. The law of acceptable communication with an expert intersects with the law of disclosure and the law of privilege. Courts have had trouble balancing these interests and this, in turn, has led to mixed outcomes in the case law.

## Case Law Dating Back to 1979

In 1979, Justice Hart, speaking for the Nova Scotia Supreme Court, held in *T. Eaton Co. v. Neil J. Buchanan Ltd.*:

> It seems to me only logical that if the party wished to rely upon the testimony of its expert and was prepared to waive the privilege that he must also have intended to waive the privilege which extends to his discussions with the expert which form the basis of his report. Surely if a solicitor were called to testify as to an opinion given to his client he would have to reveal the facts related to him upon which the opinion was based. Similarly, in my opinion, an expert employed by the solicitor for the benefit of the party must, as an integral part of his

* *The authors wish to thank Erin Garbett, an articling student at Willms & Shier Environmental Lawyers LLP, for her assistance in updating this chapter in 2018.*

> evidence, be subject to crossexamination on the factual basis for his opinions, and this must be known to the party at the time the decision is made to waive the privilege and present the evidence.[1]

The Nova Scotia Supreme Court partially reversed its stance in 1992 with its judgment in *Crocker v. MacDonald.*[2] Justice Tidman, in reference to the above-mentioned excerpt, held:

> I agree with the logic of the statement, but in my view it does not extend the waiver of solicitor/client privilege to communications between counsel and the expert. While it may be necessary as stated by [Justice Hart] to require the expert to state what he was told of the facts upon which his opinion is based it is quite a different matter to require counsel to produce his correspondence to the retained expert.
>
> The correspondence may contain all kinds of information which counsel properly would not wish disclosed to the opposite party and for which purpose the solicitor/client privilege exists. There are many ways in which counsel can determine the alleged facts upon which the expert's opinion is based without requiring counsel's so-called retention letters.[3]

Case law around and immediately after *Crocker v. MacDonald* followed Justice Tidman's reasoning and did not require disclosure of correspondence between counsel and an expert. On a motion in *Mahon v. Standard Assurance Life Co.*, Master MacLeod of the Ontario Superior Court of Justice summarized the case law, in 2000, as follows:[4]

> [A] recent decision of this court on point to which I was referred was *Calvaruso v Nantais*[5] referring to *Bell Canada v Olympia & York.*[6] These cases are to the effect that the instructing letter to an expert is privileged. The same conclusion has been reached by the Nova Scotia Supreme Court Trial Division (*Crocker v MacDonald*)[7] and the B.C. Supreme Court (*Ocean Falls Corp. v Worthington (Canada) Inc.*).[8]

These issues were again addressed in 2002 by the Ontario Superior Court of Justice in *Browne (Litigation Guardian of) v. Lavery.*[9] On behalf of the court, Justice Ferguson held that any communication and possible improper modification of an expert's report should be tested in court by opposing counsel. This information would then speak to the weight the court should attribute to the expert report. The decision stated:

> An opinion can obviously be tested in many ways: by comparing the conclusion to the data relied on, by comparing the opinion to data which was available but not relied on, by considering whether the expert's opinion was influenced by the nature of the request of counsel or by information provided by counsel which was not relied on, and by considering whether the opinion was altered at the request of counsel—for instance, by removing damaging content.
>
> It is difficult to understand how a determination could be made as to what was influential. Would counsel decide? Why should this decision not be open to scrutiny? The expert might not realize or acknowledge the extent to which information provided has influenced his or her opinion.[10]

In addition, Justice Ferguson in *Browne* changed the court's position about the disclosure of information and instructions provided to an expert by counsel:[11]

> Any experienced counsel who has dealt with experts would appreciate how important it would be to know what the expert was instructed to do, what the expert was instructed not to do, what information was sent to the expert and the extent to which counsel instructed the expert as to what to say, include or omit in the report …
>
> In my view, the disclosure of this information would best enable an opposing counsel and the court to assess whether the instructions and information provided affected the objectivity and reliability of the expert's opinion. I also note there is much contrary opinion on this subject: e.g. *Mahon v Standard Life Assurance Co.*[12]

In *Flinn v. McFarland*,[13] Justice MacAdam, writing for the Nova Scotia Supreme Court in 2002, held that discussions of an expert with counsel about a draft report speak to the weight of the expert report. This approach is similar to the approach taken in *Browne*. Justice MacAdam stated:

> Clearly, the extent to which the final report of the expert may be the result of counsel's comments, is both relevant and entitled to be exam-

> ined by counsel for the defendants. This, however, does not extend to any earlier drafts the expert may have prepared which he, himself, may have amended, altered or revised in the course of considering the issues and his opinions. It is the fact the expert submitted a draft report to counsel for the plaintiff and then prepared a final report, that may or may not have been revised in accordance with suggestions by counsel for the plaintiff, that the defendants are entitled to pursue in examining the expert as to his opinions and the basis on which he reached his opinions, including to the extent the opinions offered are his or may be the consequence of suggestions by plaintiff's counsel.[14]

Justice MacAdam also agreed with the decision in *Browne* regarding disclosure:

> Whatever information and materials were provided to the expert must be disclosed. If this involves discussions with the party, counsel for a party or with a third party, it is, may be, or perhaps should have been, part of the informational basis used by the expert in reaching his conclusion, and must be disclosed.[15]

The only appellate guidance on these issues is the Ontario Court of Appeal's 2006 decision in *Conceicao Farms Inc. v. Zeneca Corp.*[16] The court limited the information and instruction given to an expert required to be disclosed to the following:

> [The required disclosure] clearly encompasses not only the expert's opinion but the facts on which the opinion is based, the instructions upon which the expert proceeded, and the expert's name and address. How far beyond this the right to obtain foundational information (as our colleague called it) extends, need not be determined here. Suffice it to say that we are of the view that it does not yet extend as far as is tentatively suggested in *Browne (Litigation Guardian of) v Lavery*.[17] We simply proceed on the basis that the rule entitles the appellant to obtain on discovery the foundational information for [the expert's] final opinion. As will become clear, we need not decide in this case the precise extent of the information that is discoverable.[18]

To date, the leading decision on these issues, *Moore v. Getahun* (*Moore*),[19] is the most far-reaching and clear.

## *Moore v. Getahun*

### BACKGROUND

Mr. Moore, then 21, was performing tricks on his motorcycle when he broke his arm. He visited a hospital seeking medical attention for his injury. The emergency room doctor attempted to realign Mr. Moore's arm and applied a full circumferential cast to his arm. The next day, in pain, Mr. Moore attended at a second hospital where the attending doctor diagnosed that Mr. Moore had compartment syndrome. Surgery averted further damage to Mr. Moore's arm. Mr. Moore brought a medical malpractice suit against Dr. Getahun, the initial emergency room attending doctor.

### THE DECISION AT TRIAL

The matter went to trial. In her trial decision,[20] Justice Wilson noted that one of the medical experts and counsel conferred about the experts' report. In fact, there was a telephone call that lasted about 90 minutes during which the expert doctor and counsel discussed the doctor's draft report. Justice Wilson declared that it was inappropriate for counsel to review draft expert reports. She wrote:

> I conclude that counsel's prior practice of reviewing draft reports should stop. Discussions or meetings between counsel and an expert to review and shape a draft report are no longer acceptable.[21]

### ISSUES WITH THE TRIAL DECISION

The Ontario Superior Court of Justice decision in *Moore* was not realistic in environmental litigation. Experts in litigation write technical, scientific reports. The experts are rarely, if ever, trained in law. Therefore, environmental counsel typically spend time engaging their experts throughout the litigation to ensure that the issues and scope of the expert report are clear and helpful to the decision maker.

In the Superior Court decision, the judge questioned an hour-and-a-half phone call between the defendant's lawyer and expert. During the call, the defendant's lawyer made "suggestions" for and "corrections" to the expert's draft report.[22] Justice Wilson raised concern about the expert's independence and integrity.[23] While the communication in *Moore* was viewed by the court as inappropriate, it was unfair and unhelpful to extend its application to a broad ban over all communications between counsel and an expert.

## THE DECISION OF THE ONTARIO COURT OF APPEAL

The Ontario Court of Appeal in *Moore* summarized its view of Justice Wilson's finding:

> The trial judge was obviously of the view that the then-current practice and the ethical rules and standards of the legal profession were inadequate to deal with the "hired gun" problem. Her solution was to strictly control discussions between expert witnesses and counsel and to require that all discussions be documented and subject to disclosure and production.[24]

In disagreeing with the trial judge, Justice Sharpe, writing for the Court of Appeal, cited three ways in which expert witness objectivity is fostered in the law and in practice:

> First, the ethical and professional standards of the legal profession forbid counsel from engaging in practices likely to interfere with the independence and objectivity of expert witnesses.
>
> ...
>
> Second, the ethical standards of other professional bodies place an obligation upon their members to be independent and impartial when giving expert evidence ...
>
> Third, the adversarial process, particularly through cross-examination, provides an effective tool to deal with cases where there is an air of reality to the suggestion that counsel improperly influenced an expert witness.[25]

In commenting on Justice Wilson's dictum about communications between expert witnesses and counsel, Justice Sharpe disagreed with the trial judge:

> Consultation and collaboration between counsel and expert witnesses is essential to ensure that the expert witness understands the duties reflected by rule 4.1.01 and contained in the Form 53 acknowledgement of expert's duty. Reviewing a draft report enables counsel to ensure that the report (i) complies with the *Rules of Civil Procedure* and the rules of evidence, (ii) addresses and is restricted to the relevant issues and (iii) is written in a manner and style that is accessible

> and comprehensible. Counsel need to ensure that the expert witness understands matters such as the difference between the legal burden of proof and scientific certainty, the need to clarify the facts and assumptions underlying the expert's opinion, the need to confine the report to matters within the expert witness's area of expertise and the need to avoid usurping the court's function as the ultimate arbiter of the issues.
>
> Counsel play a crucial mediating role by explaining the legal issues to the expert witness and then by pressing complex expert evidence to the court. It is difficult to see how counsel could perform this role without engaging in communication with the expert as the report is being prepared.
>
> Leaving the expert witness entirely to his or her own devices, or requiring all changes to be documented in a formalized written exchange, would result in increased delay and cost in a regime already struggling to deliver justice in a timely and efficient manner.[26]

The Court of Appeal proceeded to assess: (1) if there is an obligation to produce communications between counsel and expert witnesses, or (2) if such communications have the protection of litigation privilege.

The court stated the basic principle from *Blank v. Canada (Ministry of Justice)* (*Blank*),[27] that "[l]itigation privilege protects communications with a third party where the dominant purpose of the communication is to prepare for litigation."[28] The court in *Blank* refers to this principle as the "zone of privacy."[29]

Justice Sharpe wrote:

> In my view, the ends of justice do not permit litigation privilege to be used to shield improper conduct. As I have already mentioned, it is common ground on this appeal that it is wrong for counsel to interfere with an expert's duties of independence and objectivity. Where the party seeking production of draft reports or notes of discussions between counsel and an expert can show reasonable grounds to suspect that counsel communicated with an expert witness in a manner likely to interfere with the expert witnesses's duties of independence and objectivity, the court can order disclosure of such discussions.
>
> . . .

> Absent a factual foundation to support a reasonable suspicion that counsel improperly influenced the expert, a party should not be allowed to demand production of draft reports or notes of interactions between counsel and an expert witness.[30]

The Court of Appeal affirmed that the expert's report to be relied on at trial and other information mandated by Rule 53.03(2.1) of the Ontario *Rules of Civil Procedure* must be disclosed in the litigation.[31] This other information has been called "the foundational information" for the expert's opinion as referred to in *Conceicao Farms Inc. v. Zeneca Corp.*[32]

Rule 53.03(2.1) states:

> (2.1) A report provided for the purposes of subrule (1) or (2) shall contain the following information:
>
> 1. The expert's name, address and area of expertise.
> 2. The expert's qualifications and employment and educational experiences in his or her area of expertise.
> 3. The instructions provided to the expert in relation to the proceeding.
> 4. The nature of the opinion being sought and each issue in the proceeding to which the opinion relates.
> 5. The expert's opinion respecting each issue and, where there is a range of opinions given, a summary of the range and the reasons for the expert's own opinion within that range.
> 6. The expert's reasons for his or her opinion, including,
>    i. a description of the factual assumptions on which the opinion is based,
>    ii. a description of any research conducted by the expert that led him or her to form the opinion, and
>    iii. a list of every document, if any, relied on by the expert in forming the opinion.
> 7. An acknowledgement of expert's duty (Form 53) signed by the expert.[33]

On September 17, 2015, the Supreme Court of Canada denied leave to appeal the Ontario Court of Appeal's decision in *Moore*.[34]

## Jurisprudence since *Moore v. Getahun*

In the criminal matter *R. v. Colpitts*, defendants charged with fraud challenged the qualifications of a chartered accountant whom the Crown proffered as an expert on how stock market trading practices are used to artificially influence the price of publicly traded shares.[35] The proposed expert analyzed trading practices involving the shares of the defendant's corporation. The defendants argued that the proposed expert was not impartial, because he only reviewed the trading material provided to him by the Royal Canadian Mounted Police (RCMP), he relied primarily on the information and data that the RCMP provided to him without checking or assessing it for accuracy, and he did not seek additional information from the RCMP when such was warranted.[36] The Nova Scotia Supreme Court rejected the defendants' arguments. Relying on *Moore*, the court held that "[i]t is the role of all proposed experts to seek instructions from a party to the litigation. These types of contact do not equate to evidence of bias sufficient to finding the opinions inadmissible."[37]

In *Maxrelco Immeubles Inc. v. Jim Pattison Industries Ltd.*,[38] the Ontario Superior Court addressed whether a party is required to disclose the letter of instructions sent to its expert. Justice O'Bonsawin concluded that, absent a foundation to support a suspicion that counsel improperly influenced the expert, there was no obligation to produce the instruction letter.[39] Justice O'Bonsawin further held that Rule 53.03(2.1) was satisfied and the instruction letter was not required when the instructions provided to the expert are set out in the expert's report.[40] *Maxrelco* was subsequently followed in *Scaffidi Argentina v. Tega Homes Developments Inc.*[41]

In the family law matter *St. Onge v. St. Onge* (also discussed in chapter 35 of this volume, "Experts in Environmental Litigation"), the plaintiff moved for production of the defendant's experts' communication records.[42] The plaintiff argued that a letter from one of the defendant's experts to the plaintiff's expert disclosed an improper communication between the defendant's counsel and the defendant's expert.[43] The letter stated:

> I [defendant's expert] have been requested by Louise Morin, [the defendant's] lawyer, to provide you [plaintiff's expert] with confirmation that [the defendant] has been and is currently being treated by me for depression. . . .
>
> Ms. Morin also asked me to confirm that [the defendant] reported to me, prior to the allegations of sexual abuse of her children on December 30th, 2014, that she had been verbally and/or emotionally

> abused by [the plaintiff]. In that regard, I am enclosing a copy of a letter which I sent to Ms. Morin on May 13th, 2015 ...[44]

The plaintiff argued that the stated communication demonstrated improper influence by the defendant's counsel on the defendant's expert. The Ontario Court of Justice rejected the plaintiff's argument and held that the communication merely assisted the defendant's expert in providing relevant information to the plaintiff's expert.[45] The court declined to order production of the defendant's expert's communication records.

## Conclusion

Based on more recent cases, the law in Canada and Ontario is approaching clarity. *Conceicao Farms* provides appellate guidance that foundational information relating to the facts on which the expert opinion is based, instructions on which the expert proceeds, and the expert's personal details must be disclosed to opposing parties.

The Ontario Court of Appeal in *Moore* held that counsel and their experts are permitted to confer in a way that does not interfere with an expert's impartiality and meets the standards of conduct prescribed by both the expert's and counsel's respective professional regulating bodies. These communications do not need to be documented to avoid increased delay and cost. Cases since *Moore* have upheld the principles articulated by the Ontario Court of Appeal.

Counsel is to ensure that the expert (1) understands its legal duty to the court, (2) complies with applicable rules of procedure and evidence, (3) produces an opinion that is relevant to the issues in dispute, and (4) prepares a report that is comprehensible and useful to the court.

Communications between counsel and the expert will have the protection of litigation privilege unless there are reasonable grounds to suspect that counsel communicated with the expert in a way that is likely to interfere with the expert's duties of independence and objectively. Only "the foundational information" that supports and unpins the opinion must be disclosed, along with the expert's report to be relied on at trial.

### NOTES

1 *T Eaton Co v Neil J Buchanan Ltd* (1979), 31 NSR (2d) 135 at para 59 (CA), rev'd on a different point [1980] 2 SCR 228.

2 (1992), 116 NSR (2d) 181 at paras 21–22 (TD).

3 *Ibid.*

4 *Mahon v Standard Assurance Life Co*, [2000] OJ No 2042 at para 5 (Sup Ct J) [*Mahon*].
5 *Calvaruso v Nantais* (1992), 7 CPC (3d) 254 (Ont Gen Div).
6 (1989), 68 OR (2d) 103 (H Ct J).
7 [1992] NSJ No. 410 (NSTD).
8 (1985), 69 BCLR 124 (SC).
9 (2002), 58 OR (3d) 49 (Sup Ct J) [*Browne*].
10 *Ibid* at paras 58–59.
11 *Ibid* at paras 69–70.
12 (1999), 42 OR (3d) 641 (Ont CA)
13 2002 NSSC 272.
14 *Ibid* at para 9.
15 *Ibid* at para 17.
16 83 OR (3d) 792 (CA) [*Conceicao*].
17 *Browne, supra* note 9.
18 *Conceicao, supra* note 16 at para 14.
19 *Moore v Getahun*, 2015 ONCA 55 [*Moore*].
20 2014 ONSC 237.
21 *Ibid* at paras 50–52.
22 *Ibid* at para 47.
23 *Ibid* at para 50.
24 *Moore, supra* note 19 at para 45.
25 *Ibid* at paras 57, 60–61.
26 *Ibid* at paras 63–65.
27 2006 SCC 39 [*Blank*].
28 *Moore, supra* note 19 at para 68.
29 *Blank, supra* note 27 at para 34.
30 *Moore, supra* note 19 at paras 77–78.
31 *Ibid* at para 75.
32 *Supra* note 16 at paras 14, 16–17, 19, and 21.
33 *Rules of Civil Procedure*, RRO 1990, Reg 194 promulgated under Ontario's *Courts of Justice Act*, Rule 53.03(2.1).
34 [2015] SCCA No 119 (Ont CA).
35 2016 NSSC 219.
36 *Ibid* at para 32.
37 *Ibid* at para 33.
38 2017 ONSC 5836 [*Maxrelco*].
39 *Ibid* at para 37.
40 *Ibid* at para 38.
41 2017 ONSC 6530 [*Scaffidi*].
42 *St Onge v St Onge*, 2017 ONCJ 3729.
43 *Ibid* at para 53.
44 *Ibid* at para 52.
45 *Ibid* at para 55.

# 37

# Reporting Obligations to Third Parties

MARC McAREE, ROBERT WOON, AND ANAND SRIVASTAVA*

## Introduction

Environmental litigators commonly retain consultants to carry out environmental investigations. The outcome of these investigations can uncover environmental harms, including hazards and risks to public safety. Though retained by litigators under litigation privilege, these consultants may have an overriding obligation to report their findings to authorities or regulators.

## Engineers

In Ontario, engineers in the province are governed by the Association of Professional Engineers Ontario (PEO) under the *Professional Engineers Act*.[1] The PEO Code of Ethics imposes an obligation on engineers to act as faithful agents or trustees of their clients/employers, including keeping information confidential and avoiding or disclosing conflicts of interest.[2]

The Code of Ethics also creates a duty to the public and states that "a practitioner shall regard the practitioner's duty to public welfare as paramount."[3] Engineers can be disciplined by the PEO for professional misconduct, which includes "failure to act to correct or report a situation that the practitioner believes may endanger the safety or the welfare of the public."[4] This legal obligation is commonly referred to as the engineer's "duty to report."

The PEO encourages engineers to resolve conflicts by working with their client/employer to find acceptable solutions before reporting. Nevertheless, the PEO recognizes that conflicts can escalate. Accordingly, the PEO has outlined a reporting process for engineers.[5]

* *The authors wish to thank Erin Garbett, an articling student at Willms & Shier Environmental Lawyers LLP, for her assistance in updating this chapter in 2018.*

The process involves the PEO assisting the engineer and client/employer to find a resolution. Where the PEO believes a situation may endanger the safety or welfare of the public, the PEO will take action, including obtaining independent engineers to review the situation or requesting the client/employer to take all necessary steps. In certain circumstances, the PEO will report the risk to the appropriate government authorities.

Environmental litigators should strive for open avenues of communication with any engineer they retain. Hopefully, through open communication, these litigators can speak directly with an engineer who identifies a public safety issue and work toward finding an appropriate resolution before the engineer must report a dangerous situation. This approach to open communication may in some circumstances relieve the engineer of his or her initial inclination to report and potentially assist the client to mitigate a perilous situation.

## Geoscientists

Geoscientists in Ontario are governed by the Association of Professional Geoscientists of Ontario (PGO) under the *Professional Geoscientists Act, 2000*.[6] Similar to engineers, geoscientists have obligations to their clients/employers and the public.

The PGO Code of Ethics states that their public safety and welfare duty is paramount, just as in the case of engineers.[7] Geoscientists can be disciplined for professional misconduct, which includes "failing to correct or to report a situation that the member or certificate holder believes may endanger the safety or the welfare of the public."[8]

Again, environmental litigators should strive for good communication with any geoscientists that they retain. This may help to identify public safety risks and hopefully mitigate against the geoscientist having to report to a third party authority.

## Real World Experience

The authors report that during many years of retaining engineers and geoscientists it has not been necessary for an engineer or geoscientist to report to a government authority about a risk to public safety and public welfare. There have been infrequent circumstances where a conversation about reporting has taken place. Much advice about this issue has been provided to the authors' clients, but no reporting to a public authority has been made.

That said, the practice of environmental law is transforming, with much greater emphasis on risk assessment and human health effects. Certainly, since the passage of the 2011 amendments to the *Record of Site Condition Regulation*,[9] there has been greater movement afoot to assess risks, and particularly those that arise from vapour intrusion.

As we discover more about vapour intrusion and other not so obvious risks, more circumstances may arise where engineers and geoscientists feel compelled to focus on risks to safety and their duty to report. This may be an issue to more frequently broach with the client and engineer or geoscientist prior to and during environmental investigations.

## Procedural Alternatives in the Use of Experts In Environmental Litigation

The use of experts is adversarial, expensive, and may create bias. There are procedural alternatives that environmental counsel can consider when instructing experts. These alternatives present their own benefits and burdens. In some cases, an alternative approach may be more effective in an action than the traditional model.

### MANDATORY SINGLE EXPERTS

One alternative to the use of experts in litigation is to appoint a neutral single expert on any issue. This expert is then responsible to the court to provide an expert opinion on which opposing parties may rely. The single expert may be appointed jointly by the opposing parties or by the court. Neither party has the ability to submit additional expert evidence except with leave of the court. This approach is outlined in Ontario under Rule 52.03[10] and has been instituted as an option in the courts in the United Kingdom, Australia, and New Zealand.

#### Benefits and Drawbacks

One benefit of the single expert model is potential savings in time and costs of litigation. Multiple experts waste monetary resources leading up to trial and also consume valuable time at trial. In theory, single experts can aid the court and litigants and at less cost.

Further, while the *Rules of Civil Procedure* state that all experts have a duty to the court, single experts also eliminate any real or perceived bias that may limit party-appointed experts. Competent counsel will not influence a party-appointed expert's conclusions. However, counsel must still instruct and focus the expert.

Unlike party-appointed experts, single experts require agreed-upon instructions from opposing parties or the court. The instructions frame the evidence presented at trial and, as such, may be contested between the parties. Time and resources may be wasted at this stage if opposing counsel view the instructions to a single expert as a microcosm of the issues at trial.

Single experts also carry the burden of being the only expert opinion at trial on that issue. Should a single expert lose credibility with the court, there is no alternative opinion to consider. Likewise, there is no possibility for multiple expert opinions to confirm one another or highlight contested issues. It may be hard for the court to determine which issues within a single expert's report are integral to the action and which issues are benign.

### Applicability of the Single Expert Model in General Litigation

The applicability in Ontario of the single expert model was considered by the Honourable Coulter Osborne in the Civil Justice Reform Project.[11] Osborne believes that while the idea is good in theory, it will not work in practice in most cases.[12] Opposing parties often have different factual foundations on which an expert's report is based. For this reason, use of a single expert is evaluated on a case-by-case basis and is rarely used.[13] However, Osborne does not entirely support the current model either. He believes that trial judges should evaluate whether experts are retained unnecessarily when considering costs.[14]

In 2003, the Alberta Law Reform Institute (ALRI) considered the applicability of the single expert model in Alberta.[15] ALRI concluded that the model:

- may cause delay during the selection process of the single expert;
- may cause delay during the instruction process of the single expert; and
- may result in increased court applications from the above-mentioned processes.[16]

As a whole, ALRI concluded that switching to the single expert model would likely cause more problems than it would solve.[17] ALRI did not recommend the single expert model in Alberta.

In 2006, the British Columbia Civil Justice Reform Working Group did not recommend the single expert model in British Columbia.[18] The group recommended a similar approach to Ontario's Rules in which a judge may order a court-appointed single expert where appropriate.[19]

The United Kingdom's preferred single expert approach has had limited success. Since implementation, the model appears to have reduced the "hired gun" expert and their expert reports.[20] However, it may not reduce time or costs as litigants hire their own "shadow expert" to comment on the appointed expert's report.[21]

### Applicability of the Single Expert Model in Environmental Litigation

In Ontario, Rule 52.03,[22] as described above, permits a judge, on motion by a party or out of his or her initiative, to appoint a single expert. The rule is rarely used.

Osborne cautions against single experts where the factual foundations on which an expert's report are based are contested.[23] In environmental litigation, expert reports often pertain to contamination, mitigation, and remediation and should, in theory, be objective and non-partisan. The factual foundation on which experts rely (e.g. adjacent land uses, soil and groundwater data) should not be in dispute between the opposing parties, particularly where opposing environmental experts work side-by-side during the investigating, testing, and mitigating phases of the project. This is the ideal situation envisioned by Osborne for a single expert.

It is important to distinguish between known facts to ground an expert and legal liability (over which the parties will invariably disagree). A single expert can be instructed by both parties to make the relevant scientific conclusions based on the data available. The expert cannot make legal conclusions relating to intent, negligence, or statutory breaches.

A potential drawback of the single expert approach in environmental litigation is the unpredictability of having only one report govern the potential outcome of the litigation. For example, in soil and groundwater contamination litigation, objective data may be collected using boreholes and monitoring wells regarding contaminant concentration and groundwater levels. Based on this data, a conclusion about the source of the contamination or the groundwater flow direction is often not possible. At this stage, environmental experts may offer a subjective opinion—the strength of which depends on the objective data and its interpretation. Reasonable experts may arrive at different subjective opinions after looking at the same data.

This concern is not novel to environmental litigation, nor is it the only concern. It is representative of the larger debate about whether mandatory single experts are a benefit to the legal system.

## CONCURRENT EXPERT EVIDENCE

A second alternative is to have party-appointed experts produce concurrent evidence. In this practice, opposing parties commission and produce their own expert reports on a given issue. Once the reports are disclosed, counsel or the court may instruct the experts to meet independently and without prejudice.

As an outcome of this meeting, the experts identify areas of agreement, areas of disagreement, and each expert's reasons for any disagreement. Should the action proceed to trial, the experts may be examined independently or as a group to provide further reasoning in any areas of disagreement. The practice of producing concurrent expert evidence is also known informally as "hot-tubbing."

Ontario's *Rules of Civil Procedure* allow for, but do not mandate, the production of concurrent evidence.[24]

Hot-tubbing is a middle ground between true party-appointed experts and a mandatory single expert. Experts are still each appointed and instructed by one party. However, they are expected to discuss their findings with all other experts on the issue and expressly agree or disagree with one another.

### Benefits and Drawbacks

The benefits to producing concurrent evidence are potential savings in time and costs of the litigation as compared to the non-concurrent evidence model. By having the experts discuss their respective reports, the issues may be narrowed and focused. This saves resources in settlement negotiations or at trial and allows the parties and the court to more readily identify the "live" issues that will be determinative of the dispute.

An agreement to provide concurrent evidence allows experts to review the issues outside of the legal framework. Normally, experts are examined at trial by counsel with a specific legal agenda. At trial, experts do not have the floor to discuss their thoughts and opinions regarding how the conclusions of various expert reports interact with one another. When meeting outside of court, the experts may enter a cooperative environment that facilitates peer review and much more open dialogue.

Hot-tubbing also strengthens the most reasonable expert opinions. In the event of any disagreement, experts must either concede their position or defend their report. The justifications of each expert on areas of disagreement provide evidence of the strength of each expert's opinion. Expert opinions that are poorly supported will not fare well against the scrutiny of another expert. Put another way, this model provides a forum for the experts to directly respond to the opposing experts' reports and note any deficiencies and discrepancies.

Despite the benefits, the production of concurrent evidence also has drawbacks. Competent experts thoroughly research and prepare their reports. Such experts should consider all perspectives on an issue and arrive at the conclusion they believe the data best supports. A caucus of the experts may not lead to any changes in position. Each expert is entitled to hold his or her reasonable opinion. In this case, the production of concurrent evidence will not necessarily further the litigation and can be a waste of resources.

The production of concurrent evidence may be more applicable where the expert reports are centred on objective data. In cases where expert reports are based on subjective analyses, a hot-tub may serve only to illustrate that there is a broad range of viewpoints on a given issue. The concurrent evidence may not narrow or focus the issues.

Concurrent evidence favours confident, assertive, and persuasive experts. Courts and counsel must be careful to attribute weight based on the evidence presented and not the expert presenting the evidence. This concern also applies to non-concurrent expert testimony. However, under such circumstances, counsel have greater control over the expert's testimony.[25]

Concurrent evidence may also not decrease any partisanship or bias among experts, as they are still party appointed. No studies are known by the authors to have been undertaken to determine the relationship between hot-tubbing and bias.

### Applicability of Concurrent Evidence in General Litigation

As with mandatory single experts, the production of concurrent expert evidence is considered alternative because the practice is infrequently used in Ontario. Courts in Ontario may apply Rules 50.07(1)(c) and 20.05(2)(k) to order concurrent expert evidence at their discretion.

In *Glass v. 618717 Ontario Inc.*,[26] both parties submitted expert evidence regarding business valuation on a motion before Justice D.M. Brown of the Ontario Superior Court of Justice. Justice Brown held:

> Counsel for the plaintiffs and the [defendants] welcomed directions from me about further consultations and discussions between the experts.
>
> . . .
>
> . . . When both experts testify at trial I will want to gain a clear understanding of why their views about the fair market value of the

shares of those companies are so far apart. To assist me in gaining such an understanding and to focus clearly the business valuation issues for this trial, I direct John Seigel and Robert Martin, the authors of the PWC report, and Chris Nobes, the author of the Campbell Valuation Limited Critique Report, to meet and prepare a joint statement, signed by all of them, which clearly:

> i. identifies their areas of agreement in respect of the valuation of the common shares of the Pronorth Group of companies
> ii. identifies their areas of disagreement, and
> iii. explains in detail the reasons for any disagreements in their opinions.

Under Ontario's *Rules of Civil Procedure*, both sets of experts testify under the obligation to provide "opinion evidence that is fair, objective and *non-partisan*": Rule 4.1.01(1)(a). I expect their joint statement to provide me with *non-partisan* expert assistance in understanding why such divergent views appear to exist about the value of the common shares of what strike me as a pretty straight-forward group of commercial companies.[27] [Emphasis in original.]

Further into the trial, Justice Brown evaluated the merit of his earlier order:

> As noted earlier, in a mid-trial ruling I gave directions to the business valuators to meet and to prepare a joint statement in advance of their testimony. They did so. While the valuators were unable to develop a consensus range of share value, their Joint Statement proved of great assistance in identifying the areas of disagreement and the financial implications of those disagreements. I wish to thank Mr. Seigel and Mr. Nobes for their work in preparing the Joint Statement.[28]

Justice Brown, citing his earlier example of *Glass*, made identical orders for a joint statement from the experts in *Wood v. Arius3D Corp.*[29] and *Karrys Bros. Ltd. v. Ruffa.*[30]

In *Argo's Foods Inc. v. Economical Mutual Insurance Co.* (*Argo's Foods*), Justice C.D. Braid ordered experts engaged by the litigants to meet prior to trial and:

1. Identify the issues on which the experts agree and the issues on which the experts did not agree;
2. Attempt to clarify and resolve any issues that are the subject of disagreement; and
3. Prepare a joint statement setting out the areas of agreement and any areas of disagreement and the reasons for their disagreement.[31]

In *Argo's Foods*, the insured plaintiffs claimed against the defendant insurer for damage caused by windstorms. There was contradictory evidence before the court about whether the windstorms caused damage to the buildings used by the plaintiffs. The defendant insurer's experts concluded that the windstorms only damaged the buildings' roofs, while the insured plaintiffs' experts concluded that the windstorms damaged the entire buildings.[32]

The Federal Courts Rules allow for oral concurrent evidence at trial such that the experts are examined as a panel.[33] This approach has been used in the Federal Court in *Apotex Inc. v. AstraZeneca Canada Inc.*[34] and *Distrimedic Inc. v. Dispill Inc.*[35]

An order from the court is not required to produce concurrent evidence. Counsel may also direct the experts in an action to produce a joint statement if the parties believe it would be helpful or save resources. In *Livent Inc. (Special Receiver and Manager of) v. Deloitte & Touche*, Justice Gans scolded counsel in *obiter* for not using the hot-tub approach for the expert reports on damages.[36] Justice Gans held:

> I digress to observe that the complexity and confusion erupting from the banker's box of damage reports could have been more readily avoided had counsel directed their respective experts to engage in some early "hot tubbing," a concept which has not been met with favour from the Ontario bar though it has on occasion been ordered by this court. The resolution of certain evidentiary problems and factual disputes that disappeared during the course of the trial through the court-assisted conclusion of agreed statements of fact underscores why counsel should insist on more trial management, earlier and more often than a scant few weeks before trial.[37]

There is limited appellate guidance on the topic of expert hot-tubbing. In *Suwary (Litigation Guardian of) v. Women's College Hospital*,[38] the trial judge criticized the expert witnesses for not discussing their differences with one another prior to trial. The Court of Appeal held:

> We do not agree with the trial judge's criticisms of the expert witnesses in this case because they failed to meet with each other and review the issues prior to the trial. While it would no doubt be open to counsel to agree on such an approach, and while such an approach might well be desirable in some cases, that is a decision for counsel, not for the experts, to make.[39]

The onus rests on counsel to commission voluntary concurrent evidence, not the experts.

### Applicability of Concurrent Evidence in Environmental Litigation

Concurrent expert evidence remains untested (or, at least, unreported) in environmental litigation.

The technical, scientific data used to support expert reports in environmental litigation may be a good candidate for concurrent expert evidence. As discussed when considering mandatory single experts, the factual foundation on which environmental experts rely (e.g. adjacent land uses, soil and groundwater data, and the like) should not be in dispute between the opposing experts. This is particularly the case where opposing environmental experts work side by side during the investigating, testing, and mitigating phases of the project. If there is disagreement, it should pertain to the interpretation and conclusions drawn from the data. A hot-tub of experts to discuss, for example, the source of a contamination or available remedial options may narrow the issues, encourage settlement, or expedite the litigation. Without-prejudice meetings may facilitate peer review and collaboration among environmental experts.

The concerns of expert bias and an expert's unwillingness to consider another position are undoubtedly unknowns in any case. The effectiveness of concurrent evidence will vary on a case-by-case basis in environmental litigation, based on the issues and the particular experts involved. However, these concerns and potential isolated failures should not discourage a potentially useful practice.

## NOTES

1 RSO 1990, c P-28.

2 RRO 1990, Reg 941, s 77(3).

3 *Ibid*, s 77(2)(i).

4 *Ibid*, s 72(2)(c).

5 Association of Professional Engineers Ontario, *A Professional Engineer's Duty to Report* (Toronto: PEO, 2010).

6 SO 2000, c 13.

7 *Code of Ethics of Professional Geoscientists*, O Reg 60/01, s 5(2)(a).

8 *Disciplinary Matters – Complaints and Disciplinary Proceedings Relating to the Practice of Professional Geoscience*, O Reg 258/02, s 16(2)2.

9 O Reg 153/04 made under Ontario's *Environmental Protection Act.*

10 *Rules of Civil Procedure*, RRO 1990, Reg 194 promulgated under *Ontario's Courts of Justice Act*, Rule 52.03[*Rules*].

11 Hon Coulter A Osborne, "Civil Justice Reform Project – Summary of Findings & Recommendations" (200) [*Osborne Report*], online: <https://www.attorney general.jus.gov.on.ca/english/about/pubs/cjrp/>.

12 *Ibid* at 71–72.

13 *Ibid.*

14 *Ibid* at 72.

15 Alberta Law Reform Institute, *Expert Evidence and "Independent" Medical Examinations*, Consultation Memorandum No 12.3 (Edmonton: ALRI, 2003).

16 *Ibid* at 23.

17 *Ibid.*

18 Civil Justice Reform Working Group, British Columbia Justice Review Task Force, *Effective and Affordable Civil Justice: Report of the Civil Justice Reform Working Group to the Justice Review Task Force* (November 2006), online: <https://www2.gov.bc.ca/assets/gov/law-crime-and-justice/about-bc-justice-system/justice-reform-initiatives/cjrwg_report_11_06.pdf>.

19 *Ibid* at 14.

20 Robert Musgrove, "Lord Woolf's Reforms of Civil Justice: The Reforms, their Impact, and the Future for Civil Justice Reform in England and Wales" (Address to Advocates' Society Policy Forum, Toronto, 9 March 2006).

21 Lord Chancellor's Department, *Emerging Findings: An Early Evaluation of the Civil Justice Reforms: A Report* (London, UK: Lord Chancellor's Department, 2001) at paras 4.21–4.26, online: The National Archives <http://webarchive.nationalarchives.gov.uk/+/http://www.dca.gov.uk/civil/emerge/emerge.htm>.

22 *Rules*, *supra* note 10, Rule 52.03.

23 *Osbourne Report*, *supra* note 11 at 71–72.

24 *Rules*, *supra* note 10, Rules 20.05(2)(k), 50.07(1)(c).

25 Erik Arnold & Errol Soriano, "The Recent Evolution of Expert Evidence in Selected Common Law Jurisdictions Around the World," *The Lawyers Weekly* (23 January 2013) at 15.

26 2011 ONSC 2926 (Commercial List) [*Glass*].

27 *Ibid* at paras 24–26.

28 *Glass v 618717 Ontario Inc*, 2012 ONSC 535 at para 250.

29 2012 ONSC 5596 at para 8.

30 2014 ONSC 713 (Commercial List) at paras 19–21.

31 2016 ONSC 1169 at para 68.

32 *Ibid* at para 64.

33 *Federal Courts Rules*, SOR/98-106, s 282.1.

34 2012 FC 559 at para 6.

35 2013 FC 1043 at para 168.

36 2014 ONSC 2176, aff'd 2016 ONCA 11, rev'd on other grounds 2017 SCC 63.

37 *Ibid* at para 276.

38 2011 ONCA 676 [*Suwary*].

39 *Ibid* at para 114.

# 38

# Admissibility of Expert Evidence and Costs

MARC McAREE, ROBERT WOON, AND ANAND SRIVASTAVA*

## Introduction

The Supreme Court of Canada's judgment in *R. v. Mohan*[1] is the current leading authority on the admissibility of expert evidence. In *Mohan*, the court held that expert evidence should be admitted if the expert evidence is:

- relevant;
- necessary in assisting the trier of fact;
- absent of any exclusionary rule; and
- given by a properly qualified expert.[2]

The party tendering the expert bears the burden of meeting the four requirements in *Mohan*.[3] The *Mohan* test applies in both criminal and civil cases.[4]

### RELEVANCE

Relevance of an expert's evidence is a question of law to be decided by the presiding judge.[5] The evidence must not only be related to a fact in issue but also must be valuable to the trial. As described in *McCormick on Evidence*[6] and cited in *Mohan*, the value of the evidence must outweigh its impact on the trial process. In *Mohan*, the court held:

> Evidence that is otherwise logically relevant may be excluded on this basis, if its probative value is overborne by its prejudicial effect, if it

* *The authors wish to thank Erin Garbett, an articling student at Willms & Shier Environmental Lawyers LLP, for her assistance in updating this chapter in 2018.*

> involves an inordinate amount of time which is not commensurate with its value or if it is misleading in the sense that its effect on the trier of fact, particularly a jury, is out of proportion to its reliability.[7]

The ability for expert evidence to confuse or overwhelm a jury was questioned in *R. v. Melaragni*[8] and *R. v. Bourguignon*[9] and accepted in *Mohan* as being a factor in assessing the relevance of that evidence.[10]

### NECESSITY IN ASSISTING THE TRIER OF FACT

An expert's evidence must be necessary in order to "provide information 'which is likely to be outside of the experience and knowledge of a judge or jury.'"[11] This includes instances where the trier of fact is enabled by expert evidence to appreciate technical matters.[12] Likewise, the standard may also be described with a reverse onus—such that an ordinary person is unlikely to correctly judge the facts of the case if unassisted by an expert.[13]

Evidence is expert evidence not solely because it is presented by a well-qualified expert or presented with heavy technical wording. If an issue before the jurors does not require an expert, an expert's evidence may incorrectly influence the trier of fact.[14]

### ABSENCE OF ANY EXCLUSIONARY RULE

Expert evidence is not automatically admissible if it meets the other three criteria in *Mohan*. The expert evidence must also be admissible under the general law of evidence. If there is any applicable exclusionary rule, the expert evidence will be excluded despite being relevant, necessary, and provided by a properly qualified expert.[15]

### PROPERLY QUALIFIED EXPERT

A properly qualified expert is one who "is shown to have acquired special or peculiar knowledge through study or experience in respect of the matters on which he or she undertakes to testify."[16] Expertise is a relatively modest status that is achieved when the "expert witness possesses special knowledge and experience going beyond that of the trier of fact."[17]

In the 2015 case *White Burgess Langille Inman v. Abbott and Haliburton Co.* (*White Burgess*), the Supreme Court of Canada added an evaluation of the proposed expert's independence and impartiality to the "properly qualified expert" requirement of the *Mohan* test.[18] A discussion of the Supreme Court of Canada's analysis is set out below under "Credibility of Evidence."

## The Gatekeeper Function

In *Mohan*, the Supreme Court of Canada underlined the important role of trial judges in assessing whether otherwise admissible expert evidence should nonetheless be excluded based on a cost-benefit analysis.[19] *Mohan* did not explicitly address how the cost-benefit analysis fits into the overall analysis of expert evidence.

In 2009, the Ontario Court of Appeal's judgment in *R. v. Abbey* (*Abbey*) introduced clarity by dividing the assessment of expert evidence into two stages.[20] First, the party advancing expert evidence must meet the four requirements set out in *Mohan*. Second, if the requirements are met, the trial judge must decide if the evidence is "sufficiently beneficial" to the trial process.[21]

Justice Doherty described the function of the trial judge at the cost-benefit analysis stage as one of a "gatekeeper."[22] The Court of Appeal described the gatekeeper portion of the analysis as follows:

> The "gatekeeper" inquiry does not involve the application of bright line rules, but instead requires an exercise of judicial discretion. The trial judge must identify and weigh competing considerations to decide whether on balance those considerations favour the admissibility of the evidence. This cost-benefit analysis is case-specific and, unlike the first phase of the admissibility inquiry, often does not admit of a straightforward "yes" or "no" answer. Different trial judges, properly applying the relevant principles in the exercise of their discretion, could in some situations come to different conclusions on admissibility.[23]

Within this framework, the Supreme Court of Canada's concerns in *Mohan* about the jury being confused or overwhelmed can be considered outside of the four requirements. The trial judge must undertake his or her own discretionary cost-benefit analysis.[24] The costs and inherent risks of the admissibility of expert evidence include prejudice, confusion, and the consumption of time.[25] The benefit of the expert evidence is that the trier of fact is properly informed about an issue on which he or she does not have expertise. In addition, the trial judge must also consider the effect on the proper administration of justice of excluding expert evidence.[26]

In *White Burgess*, the Supreme Court of Canada adopted, with minor adjustments, the two-step process of qualifying experts as outlined in *Abbey*.[27] Justice Cromwell, on behalf of the court, held that:

> Consistent with the structure of the analysis developed following *Mohan* … the judge must still take concerns about the expert's independence and impartiality into account in weighing the evidence at the gatekeeping stage. At this point, relevance, necessity, reliability and absence of bias can helpfully be seen as part of a sliding scale where a basic level must first be achieved in order to meet the admissibility threshold and thereafter continue to play a role in weighing the overall competing considerations in admitting the evidence. At the end of the day, the judge must be satisfied that the potential helpfulness of the evidence is not outweighed by the risk of the dangers materializing that are associated with expert evidence.[28]

In the Ontario Court of Appeal's decision *Bruff-Murphy v. Gunawardena* (*Bruff-Murphy*),[29] the court reemphasized and provided guidance on the trial judge's gatekeeper role respecting proposed expert witnesses. In *Bruff-Murphy*, the plaintiff was injured in a car accident. The plaintiff sought to exclude evidence from one of the defendant's experts on the basis that the proposed expert was biased and that the proposed expert's report in essence existed to destroy the plaintiff's credibility.

At trial, the judge concluded that the defendant's expert could testify but was not permitted to testify on certain sections of his report. The trial judge also concluded that the expert could in no way testify about the plaintiff's credibility. However, the expert crossed the line and called into question the plaintiff's credibility.[30] Additionally, the expert had "torqued" testing results in order to produce "results that supported his conclusion."[31]

The Ontario Court of Appeal held that the trial judge appeared to have assumed that once the expert was qualified to give testimony, the trial judge's gatekeeper role ended. The Court of Appeal rejected this approach as an error of law and held:

> Where, as here, the expert's eventual testimony removes any doubt about her independence, the trial judge must not act as if she were functus. The trial judge must continue to exercise her gatekeeper function. After all, the concerns about the impact of a non-independent expert witness on the jury have not been eliminated. To the contrary, they have come to fruition. At that stage, when the trial judge recognizes the acute risk to trial fairness, she must take action.[32]

The Court of Appeal outlined several courses of action that the trial judge could have taken, including advising counsel that he was going to give either a mid-trial or final instruction that the expert's testimony would be excluded in whole or in part from the evidence, or could have asked for submissions from counsel on a mistrial.[33] The Court of Appeal concluded:

> The point is that the trial judge was not powerless and should have taken action. The dangers of admitting expert evidence suggest a need for a trial judge to exercise prudence in excluding the testimony of an expert who lacks impartiality before those dangers manifest.[34]

The Court of Appeal ordered a new trial. While the court acknowledged that generally the failure to object to a civil jury charge is "fatal to a request for a re-trial on appeal based on misdirection or non-direction," the expert's testimony resulted in a miscarriage of justice and a new trial was warranted.[35] Further, the court held that "given the importance of a trial judge's on-going gatekeeper role, the absence of an objection or the lack of a request for a specific instruction does not impair a trial judge's ability to exercise her residual discretion to exclude evidence whose probative value is outweighed by its prejudicial effect."[36]

The Court of Appeal's decision in *Bruff-Murphy* reinforces the importance of the trial judge's gatekeeper role in assessing expert evidence. The gatekeeper role continues even after an expert has been qualified to testify and does not depend on opposing counsel's objection or request for specific instruction.

## Junk Science

In recent years, some commentators have suggested that courts give too much weight and rely too heavily on expert evidence. The Supreme Court of Canada in *Mohan* stated:

> Dressed up in scientific language which the jury does not easily understand and submitted through a witness of impressive antecedents, this evidence is apt to be accepted by the jury as being virtually infallible and as having more weight than it deserves.[37]

Justice Sopinka also stated:

> In summary, therefore, it appears from the foregoing that expert evidence which advances a novel scientific theory or technique is

> subjected to special scrutiny to determine whether it meets a basic threshold of reliability and whether it is essential in the sense that the trier of fact will be unable to come to a satisfactory conclusion without the assistance of the expert.[38]

This was a stark warning to litigation counsel and the courts to judiciously assess their reliance on expert evidence. Courts have a role as gatekeeper to ensure junk science or pseudoscience is not entered into evidence at trial.

The approach taken by courts on junk science has largely been shaped by jurisprudence in the United States, specifically the *Daubert* trilogy. The *Daubert* trilogy comprises three US Supreme Court decisions: *Daubert v. Merrel Dow Pharmaceuticals Inc.*,[39] *General Electric Company v. Joiner* (*Joiner*),[40] and *Kumho Tire Company Ltd. v. Carmichael* (*Kumho*).[41]

In *Daubert*, the US Supreme Court considered the applicability of the "general acceptance" test with *Federal Court Rules* when admitting expert scientific testimony. The court concluded that the "general acceptance test" was not a precondition for the admission of scientific evidence under the *Federal Rules of Evidence*. Rather the *Federal Rules of Evidence* required a preliminary assessment about "whether the reasoning or methodology underlying the testimony is scientifically valid and of whether that reasoning or methodology properly can be applied to the facts in issue." The court identified a non-exhaustive list of factors for the assessment:

- whether the theory or technique can be (and has been) tested;
- whether the theory or technique has been subjected to peer review and publication;
- the known or potential rate of error and the existence and maintenance of standards controlling the technique's operation; and
- whether the theory or technique has been generally accepted by a relevant scientific community.

At issue in *Joiner* was the applicable standard of review for evidentiary rulings for expert scientific evidence. The US Supreme Court held that the "abuse of discretion" was the proper standard of review.

In *Kumho*, the US Supreme Court upheld the *Daubert* approach. This included "technical" or "other specialized" knowledge, such as engineering. The court reaffirmed that the list of factors in *Daubert* was not meant to be exhaustive and may not be applicable in all cases. The court identified examples where a subject has not been peer reviewed for lack of interest or where general acceptance may not be applicable because a discipline itself lacks reliability.

The Supreme Court of Canada in *R. v. J.-L.J.* adopted the *Daubert* list of factors.[42] The court cited *Mohan*, where the Supreme Court held that novel scientific theory or technique should be subject to "special scrutiny" and must meet a basic threshold of reliability.[43] Notably, in the criminal law context, the court in *R. v. J.-L.J.* was determining the admissibility of expert evidence relating to novel sexual assault testing. The court held that although the testing may be useful in therapy, it was not sufficiently reliable for use in a court of law.[44]

The Court of Appeal in *Abbey* offered a non-exhaustive broader list of questions that may be relevant and helpful in evaluating whether novel science expert evidence should be accepted:

- To what extent is the field in which the opinion is offered a recognized discipline, profession or area of specialized training?
- To what extent is the work within that field subject to quality assurance measures and appropriate independent review by others in the field?
- What are the particular expert's qualifications within that discipline, profession or area of specialized training?
- To the extent that the opinion rests on data accumulated through various means such as interviews, is the data accurately recorded, stored and available?
- To what extent are the reasoning processes underlying the opinion and the methods used to gather the relevant information clearly explained by the witness and susceptible to critical examination by a jury?
- To what extent has the expert arrived at his or her opinion using methodologies accepted by those working in the particular field in which the opinion is advanced?
- To what extent do the accepted methodologies promote and enhance the reliability of the information gathered and relied on by the expert?
- To what extent has the witness, in advancing the opinion, honoured the boundaries and limits of the discipline from which his or her expertise arises?
- To what extent is the proffered opinion based on data and other information gathered independently of the specific case or, more broadly, the litigation process?[45]

Environmental litigators should be aware of *R. v. J.-L.J.* and *Abbey*, especially where evolving and novel science is involved. The cases highlight why litigators must prudently examine the methodologies of opposing counsel's experts as well as their own experts. Litigators should determine if the expert is using widely accepted methods. Litigators should review the case law to assess if other courts have relied on the methods or techniques used by other experts in similar cases. Litigators need to be confident in their experts and the experts' methods and techniques.

## Credibility of Evidence

> With respect, the Court would find it very difficult to accept an explanation with regard to the cause of the landfill off-site odour from a lay person with absolutely no background or experience in waste management, landfill or environmental studies, over that of a well-known, knowledgeable and experienced waste management and landfill expert.[46]

An expert's experience and qualifications must provide a solid foundation and support for his or her credibility at trial. However, an expert's credibility is not infallible. Experts can lose their credibility faster than they earn it. Losing credibility reflects badly on the expert, the litigator who retains the expert, and the litigant who retains the litigator.

### INDEPENDENCE/BIAS

Experts are paid by the party that retains them. Naturally, experts want to ensure that their client is satisfied in order to continue with the current work and to secure future work. Lawyers are often instrumental in selecting and retaining expert witnesses. Some have been known to "shop around" for opinions they prefer and to apply gentle influence on the expert. Undoubtedly, these practices can impact an expert's credibility, with the court leaving the litigant to bear the brunt of the expert's loss of or perceived loss of independence.

In the context of a prosecution, the case of *R v. Commander Business Furniture Inc*[47] presents an example of a complete loss of credibility by the defendant's consultant who was tainted by the influence of the defendant (not counsel). The defendant operated a facility that spray painted office furniture. Neighbouring residents made numerous complaints about odours to the then Ontario Ministry of the Environment. The defendant retained a consultant to assess the odour problem and provide potential solutions. The defendant tried to rely on the consultant at trial to establish a due diligence defence. The Ontario Court of Justice found that the defendant instructed the consultant to change its recommendations.[48] The defendant wanted the consultant to recommend less expensive measures, though it was known by the defendant and consultant that the effectiveness of these less costly methods was limited. The court found that the expert's testimony, premised on the final report, was not a "credible professional opinion" given what the same consultant had said in earlier draft reports.[49]

In *WCI Waste Conversion Inc. v. ADI International Inc.* (*WCI Waste*), both defendants' experts lost credibility because of the defendants' influence in the preparation of the experts' reports.[50] The plaintiff and the defendant started a joint venture to construct and operate a composting facility. The plaintiff filed an action when the defendant later terminated the agreement and took over the facility. The defendant retained experts to opine on the design and operation of the facility.

Regarding one of the defendant's experts, the court found that the evidence contradicted the expert's claim that only he had authored his report. The court concluded that the defendant was "intricately involved in outlining, drafting, revising, and editing" the expert report.[51] The court stated, "[a]n expert report is only of benefit to the Court if it is independent and unbiased and is not unduly influenced by someone having a pecuniary interest in the contents of that report."[52]

After reviewing the draft reports of the other defendant's expert, the court found that the final report was altered to eliminate any matters that would reflect negatively on the defendant or positively on the plaintiff.[53] Comparisons of the draft reports indicated that a significant number of paragraphs were deleted or altered after the defendant reviewed the reports. The court concluded:

> … when the party engaging the expert seeks to control or direct or unduly influence the conclusions reached in the expert's report, that party has diminished the credibility and reliability of the report and of itself. When an expert succumbs to such influences, he or she compromises their own integrity and the report rendered is of little or no value.[54]

The challenge with the use of "hired guns" and "opinions for sale" was discussed in the *Osborne Report*.[55] Specifically, Justice Osborne wrote:

> The issue of "hired guns" and "opinions for sale" was repeatedly identified as a problem during consultations. To help curb expert bias,

> there does not appear to be any sound policy reason why the Rules of Civil Procedure should not expressly impose on experts an overriding duty to the court, rather than to the parties who pay or instruct them. The primary criticism of such an approach is that, without a clear enforcement mechanism, it may have no significant impact on experts unduly swayed by the parties who retain them.[56]

As a result, Ontario's *Rules of Civil Procedure* were amended based on Justice Osborne's recommendation to expressly impose a duty on experts.[57] The duty requires the expert to provide fair, objective, and non-partisan opinion evidence. The duty of the expert owed to the court is paramount to any obligation owing by the expert to his or her client/employer. In addition, the *Rules* now require that the expert acknowledge his or her duty to the court in his or her report.[58]

In *R. v. Inco*, the Ontario Superior Court of Justice held that the employment relationship or status of an expert vis-à-vis a party did not determine independence or impartiality.[59] In *Inco*, the defendant was charged with discharging untreated mine effluent into a watercourse. The trial judge declined to qualify an expert called by the then Ministry of the Environment for lack of independence with the Crown. On appeal, the court held that, before a witness can be rejected based on lack of independence, the court should conduct a *voir dire* hearing.[60] At the hearing, a judge can determine if the expert is in a co-venture with the party, or is acting as an advocate for the party.[61] A trial judge can also assess an expert's opinion based on how it is tested under cross-examination, the assumptions used, the disclosure of material facts, and the completeness and level of expertise.[62]

The court in *Abbey* did not address whether an expert's duty relates to admissibility of the evidence rather than simply to its weight. Further, if the expert's duty to the court goes to admissibility, there was no consensus about whether a threshold admissibility requirement existed respecting independence and impartiality.

In *White Burgess*, the Supreme Court of Canada added an evaluation of a proposed expert's independence and impartiality to the "properly qualified expert" element of the *Mohan* framework.[63] The court further held that there is a threshold admissibility respecting a proposed expert's duty of independence and impartiality to the court.

The independence and impartiality threshold is not onerous. The court in *White Burgess* held that "it will likely be quite rare" that a proposed expert's evidence would be ruled inadmissible for failing to meet it.[64] The court in *White Burgess* was careful, however, to state that "the expert's independence and impartiality should not be presumed absent challenge."[65] Rather, if an expert's independence and impartiality are not challenged, the expert's evidence will be admissible once an expert attests or testifies on oath recognizing and accepting their duty to the court.[66]

> A party who opposes the admission of expert evidence on the basis of bias must establish a "realistic concern" that the witness is unwilling or unable to comply with the duty of an expert.[67] The party proferring the expert evidence must rebut this concern on a balance of probabilities to satisfy the *Mohan* test.[68]

While an interest in or connection with the litigation does not automatically render the proposed expert evidence inadmissible, the court must consider whether the relationship or interest would result in the expert being unable or unwilling to carry out his or her primary duty to provide fair, non-partisan, and objective assistance.

In the criminal decision *R. v. Livingston*, the Crown sought to admit the evidence of Mr. Gagnon, a retired member of the Ontario Provincial Police (OPP) who was asked to participate in an OPP investigation as a technical analyst.[69] While Mr. Gagnon's role initially was limited to providing technical analysis of seized hard drives, his role quickly expanded. Mr. Gagnon provided technical input for an important Crown witness, attended an interview to provide assistance if technical issues arose, provided advice about the investigation's legal strategy, provided advice about a data preservation request, played a central role in processing an accused's Blackberry, recommended an additional charge be laid against the defendants, and participated in the execution of a search warrant. During a *voir dire*, the Ontario Court of Justice concluded that "[i]nstead of maintaining his distance and independence from the day-to-day activities of the [OPP] team, Mr. Gagnon did just the opposite" and that Mr. Gagnon "conflated the roles of expert and investigator."[70] After considering *White Burgess*, the court concluded that there was a realistic concern that Mr. Gagnon would be unable to provide independent, impartial, and unbiased evidence.[71] Further, the court held that the Crown did not rebut this concern on a balance of probabilities and failed to satisfy the "properly qualified expert" part of the *Mohan* test.[72] The court excluded Mr. Gagnon's evidence.

## EXPERT WITNESS CREDIBILITY AND COSTS

The issue of expert witness credibility and costs resulting from a sophisticated appellant's pursuit of an ill-founded appeal, where its expert professional engineer's opinions were held to be "fundamentally and irredeemably flawed,"[73] was the subject matter of *Seaspan ULC (formerly Seaspan International Ltd.) v. Director, Environmental Management Act*. This case was heard before the British Columbia Environmental Appeal Board. Applications for costs were decided on September 15, 2014.

Seaspan ULC (Seaspan) appealed a British Columbia Director's Order against Seaspan ULC and Domtar Inc. relating to contaminated land located adjacent to Burrard Inlet in North Vancouver, the location of Seaspan's Vancouver shipyard. Before the hearing, Seaspan filed its expert's report, in which its expert concluded that the tests did not indicate that the creosote plume was continuous from Parcel A to the Western Front. As the tribunal cited Seaspan's expert's opinion, "[i]n his professional opinion, the creosote contamination found in the Western Front more probably than not originated from the storage of creosote treated boomed timbers on the tidal flats of the Western Front." This opinion was in support of Seaspan's position that Seaspan was not responsible to remediate the entirety of this particular plume (although Seaspan did have responsibility to remediate other contamination at the site).

The hearing commenced before the board. Seaspan called its engineering expert to testify. The expert was qualified to "give opinion evidence as a professional engineer with respect to the cause or causes and delineation of creosote contamination in soil, groundwater and sediments at the subject site."[74] Seaspan's expert testified that he was aware of the duty of an expert as required in the *British Columbia Supreme Court Rules*. The expert's evidence-in-chief and cross-examination concluded at the end of day two of the hearing. It was expected that the expert would be subject to reexamination on day three. However, on day three, the board was presented with a copy of a letter advising that Seaspan was abandoning its appeals (except those relating to security and registration of a covenant). Following the collapse of the hearing, opposing counsel advised that they would consider applications for an order for costs. Meanwhile, the opposing parties were granted an order compelling the expert to produce his expert file.

The British Columbia Environmental Appeal Board posed two key questions: (1) What is the legal test to award costs? and (2) Should applications for costs be granted in the circumstances of this case?

After hearing submissions, the board posed these questions: "When does a party's behavior 'cross the line' to become a 'special circumstance'? At what point does it deserve to be punished? And, how does the Board ensure that the threshold is not too low, such that it results in a 'chill' on legitimate appeals and litigation strategies?"[75] The board held that the power to award costs is discretionary and that an award of costs will turn on the particular facts of the case.[76] The board's stated objective is to encourage responsible conduct throughout the appeal process and to discourage unreasonable and/or abusive conduct.[77] The board held that, "In other words, costs are punitive in nature: they are not compensatory, as in winner pays the losers' costs. Rather, they are intended to punish and deter unwanted conduct."[78] Finally, the board held that "[w]hen assessing whether or not to award costs, the Board will also weight the importance of ordering costs in the circumstances against the likelihood that an award of costs in those circumstances will have an unwanted 'chilling effect.'"[79] The board proceeded to review Seaspan's expert evidence presented during the hearing. The board held that:

- the expert's report is deceptive;
- the expert adopted an artificially technical definition of "contamination" in reaching his conclusions in the report by only including analytical results with recorded exceedances;
- once there is discovery of free product, the "discontinuous plume" theory that Seaspan adopted collapses and the expert's conclusion is completely discredited;
- the report was constructed such that a reader could not discern the unusual definition of contamination put forth by the expert;
- the expert's report contradicts the conclusions in previous reports even though the expert was instructed to assume that the previous reports correctly identified the nature and extent of creosote contamination in soil.[80]

As stated by the board, "Seaspan claims that it did not know, or could not have known, of the flaws in [its expert's] Report. The Panel disagrees. The Panel finds that Seaspan advanced a position that was fundamentally unsound from the outset, presumably, to avoid or lessen the costs of remediating the serious contamination at the Site."[81]

In the end, the board held that "this was more than a 'doubtful case.' Rather it was hopeless, and the theory advanced at the hearing should never have been pursued."[82] The board concluded that "[u]ltimately, the underlying theory of its case—the theory that it chose to pursue to a hearing—was so ill conceived that it crumbled almost immediately under cross-examination. Evidence that free phase DNAPL [dense non-aqueous phase liquid] creosote found in bore holes did not signify 'contamination' because of a lack of confirmatory test results was preposterous."[83]

As a deterrent, the board awarded costs in favour of the opposing parties. In addition, the board directed Seaspan to provide to the board, and to all other parties, submissions about the payment of the board's expenses.[84] On April 1, 2015, the board concluded that an award of the board's expenses was not justified.[85]

## FACTUAL ACCURACY AND CONFIRMING ASSUMPTIONS

Unlike some lay witnesses, experts are usually not present during the event that gives rise to the need for expert testimony. Accordingly, expert evidence usually comprises opinions formed on second-hand experiences. Experts base their opinions on factual information provided to the expert by others, and on assumptions that the expert draws. In an expert's report, the expert must provide his or her reasons for his or her opinions, including an outline of the factual assumptions upon which he or she bases his or her opinion.[86]

One can appreciate that expert opinions can only be as supportable as the facts upon which the expert bases his or her opinion. Litigators should ensure that their experts have all relevant background facts and other necessary information. This assures that the expert can assess the problem posed to them and provide an informed opinion. In *WCI Waste*, the defendant's expert was retained to provide recommendations about an aeration system at the waste facility. The expert relied strictly on information provided by the defendant. The expert failed to read or consider a 60-page manual that detailed the aeration control system.[87] As a result, the court held that the expert's recommendations for improving the system were already implemented and this substantially devalued the expert's testimony.[88]

In *Simpson v. Chapman* (*Simpson*), the plaintiff's expert was found by the court to have used the wrong methodology to assess if the site was contaminated.[89] The expert used a method that was not statutorily approved. The expert based the findings on this non-approved approach. The plaintiff's claim was dismissed because it failed to show that the property was contaminated as defined by provincial regulation.

*Simpson* demonstrates the importance for litigators of verifying with their experts the factual assumptions the experts make in providing the expert's opinion. This is especially relevant for environmental litigators where highly technical regulatory requirements are the law. One example of this is Ontario's *Record of Site Condition Regulation.*[90] Knowing the nature of the soil type, the land use, and other very specific aspects of the property can make a significant difference in the assessment of whether a property meets the Ontario Ministry of the Environment and Climate Change's *Soil, Ground Water and Sediment Standards.* Ensuring in advance that the expert is adopting correct methodologies and relying on correct standards (whether prescribed in law or not) can avoid an expert's fatal loss of credibility.

## Weight to be Afforded to Evidence

The Ontario Superior Court of Justice (Divisional Court), in *Ostrander Point GP Inc. v. Prince Edward County Field Naturalists* (Ostrander Point),[91] adopted the dictum of Justice Mohoney in *R. v. Capital Life Insurance Co.*:[92]

> In context, the court has said no more than what is trite law: the weight to be given expert evidence is a matter for the trier of fact and an expert's conclusion which is not appropriately explained and supported may properly be given no weight at all.

The Ontario Division Court in *Ostrander Point* held that it was up to the Environmental Review Tribunal to determine if the tribunal should rely on the expert medical doctor's theory about linking the medical symptoms complained of to the operation of the wind turbines. Not surprisingly, the court held that the tribunal's decision should be entitled to deference from the court.

### NOTES

1 [1994] 2 SCR 9 (SCC) [*Mohan*].
2 *Ibid* at paras 17–21.
3 *R v Terceira* (1998), 38 OR (3d) 175 (CA) aff'd [1999] 3 SCR 866.
4 *Drumonde v Moniz* (1997), 105 OAC 295 (CA).
5 *Mohan, supra* note 1 at para 22.
6 Edward Cleary, *McCormick on Evidence*, 3d ed (St Paul, MN: West Publishing, 1984) at 544.
7 *Mohan, supra* note 1 at para 22.
8 (1992), 73 CCC (3d) 348 at para 16 (Ont Gen Div).
9 [1991] OJ No 2670 (Gen Div).
10 *Mohan, supra* note 1 at para 22.
11 *Ibid* at para 26, citing Dickson J in *R v Abbey*, [1982] SCR 24 at para 44.
12 *R v Abbey*, [1982] 2 SCR 24.
13 *Kelliher (Village of) v Smith*, [1931] SCR 672 at para 17.
14 *Mohan, supra* note 1 at paras 25–27.
15 *Ibid* at para 30.
16 *Ibid* at para 31.
17 *R v Beland*, [1987] 2 SCR 398 at para 74.
18 2015 SCC 23.
19 *Mohan, supra* note 1 at para 22.
20 *R v Abbey*, 2009 ONCA 624 at para 76 [*Abbey*].

21 *Ibid.*
22 *Ibid* at para 78.
23 *Ibid* at para 79.
24 *Ibid* at para 89.
25 *Ibid.*
26 *Ibid* at para 93.
27 *Ibid* at para 22.
28 *Ibid* at para 54.
29 2017 ONCA 502.
30 *Ibid* at para 53.
31 *Ibid* at para 52.
32 *Ibid* at para 63.
33 *Ibid* at para 67.
34 *Ibid* at para 68.
35 *Ibid* at para 69.
36 *Ibid* at para 70.
37 *Mohan, supra* note 1 at para 23.
38 *Ibid* at para 32.
39 509 US 579 (1993) [*Daubert*].
40 522 US 136 (1997) [*Joiner*].
41 526 US 137 (1999) [*Kumho*].
42 2000 SCC 51 at para 33.
43 *Ibid* at para 35.
44 *Ibid.*
45 *Abbey, supra* note 20 at para 119.
46 *Ontario (Ministry of the Environment) v Sault Ste Marie (City)*, 2008 ONCJ 583 at para 91.
47 *R v Commander Business Furniture Inc* (1992), 9 CELR (NS) 185, 1992 CarswellOnt 222 (Ont Ct J) [*Commander*].
48 *Ibid* at paras 174–175, 188.
49 *Ibid* at para 194.
50 *WCI Waste Conversion Inc v ADI International Inc*, 2008 PESCTD 40, var'd 2011 PECA 14, leave to appeal to SCC refused (2012), 328 Nfld & PEIR 360 (note) [*WCI Waste*].
51 *Ibid* at paras 224–227.
52 *Ibid* at para 228.
53 *Ibid* at para 234.
54 *Ibid* at para 244.
55 Hon Coulter A Osborne, "Civil Justice Reform Project – Summary of Findings & Recommendations" (2007) at 75 [*Osborne Report*], online: <https://www.attorneygeneral.jus.gov.on.ca/english/about/pubs/cjrp/>.
56 *Ibid.*
57 *Rules of Civil Procedure*, RRO 1990, Reg 194 promulgated under Ontario's *Courts of Justice Act* at Rule 4.1 [*Rules*].
58 *Ibid* at Rule 53.03(2.1).
59 *R v Inco* (2006), 80 OR (3d) 594 at paras 42–45 (Sup Ct J).
60 *Ibid* at para 45.
61 *Ibid* at para 49.
62 *Ibid* at para 45.
63 2015 SCC 23 [*White Burgess*].
64 *Ibid* at para 49.
65 *Ibid* at para 47.
66 *Ibid.*
67 *Ibid* at para 63.
68 *Ibid.*
69 2017 ONCJ 645.
70 *Ibid* at paras 51, 64.
71 *Ibid* at para 68.
72 *Ibid* at para 68.
73 British Columbia Environmental Review Board, Decision Nos 2010-EMA-005(c) & 2010-EMA-006(c), 15 September 2014 at para 186.
74 *Ibid* at para 52.
75 *Ibid* at para 153.
76 *Ibid* at paras 162–163.
77 *Ibid* at paras 164.
78 *Ibid.*
79 *Ibid* at para 168.
80 *Ibid* at para 181.
81 *Ibid* at para 187.
82 *Ibid* at para 194.
83 *Ibid* at para 193.
84 *Ibid* at paras 216, 217.
85 *Seaspan ULC v British Columbia (Director, Environmental Management Act)*, [2015] BCWLD 3202 (EAB).
86 *Rules, supra* note 57, Rule 53.03(2.1).
87 *WCI Waste, supra* note 50 at para 212.
88 *Ibid* at paras 201–213.
89 *Simpson v Chapman*, 2009 BCPC 28 [*Simpson*].
90 O Reg 153/04 promulgated under the *Environmental Protection Act.*
91 2014 ONSC 974 (Div Ct), rev'd on other grounds 2015 ONCA 269.
92 [1986] 2 FC 171 at para 127 (Fed CA).

# 39

# Experts Only

JIM BUNTING, TERRI-LEE OLENIUK, AND SARAH POWELL

## Introduction

When you follow a guide off *piste* you are letting your guide take your life in their hands. Before doing so you will no doubt vet the qualifications of your guide to ensure that they have the necessary experience and skill to lead you safely down the mountain. The experience of the authors is, unfortunately, that many of our environmental and energy administrative tribunals do not apply the same rigour before admitting "expert" testimony into evidence before them. These administrative tribunals often follow what the Ontario Court of Appeal dubbed the "let it all in approach" when receiving expert testimony.[1] This approach has become so common that the authors noted during discussions with other counsel that some lawyers simply chose not to bother challenging the qualifications of an expert in administrative hearings.

This approach presents challenges for all parties. While the outcome is not as dramatic as falling into a chasm or being buried in an avalanche, the let it all in approach is of little to no value to administrative hearings, generally increases the complexity and cost of these hearings, and in some cases could have the effect of misleading the public.

This chapter reviews a few examples in which administrative tribunals have admitted expert evidence in circumstances where, in the respectful view of the authors, the evidence should have been refused or at the very least given no weight. In addition, the chapter briefly reviews other expert evidence issues that are unique to administrative tribunals. It then concludes with some recommendations for counsel and adjudicators to address the admissibility of proffered expert opinion evidence in a fair, efficient, and reasonable fashion.

It should be noted that it is not the intention of the authors to criticize prior decisions. The let it all in approach has likely evolved in an effort to be fair, efficient, and appeal-proof, in tribunal hearings where the strict rules of evidence do not apply and where public interest considerations are paramount. However, the authors suggest that this practice has downsides and the manner in which it is applied should be revisited

## Gatekeeper Function

Numerous papers address the law as it pertains to the admissibility of expert evidence. See, for example, "Admissibility of Expert Evidence and Costs,"[2] which discusses the critically important gatekeeper function that an adjudicator must exercise when expert evidence is tendered. This chapter does not cover that same ground; however, it is useful to briefly review the accepted legal principles regarding qualifying experts.

The role of the expert witness is to provide independent assistance by way of an objective, unbiased opinion in relation to matters within the expert's expertise. An expert witness should never assume the role of advocate and is less a "witness for a party" than a "witness for the court."[3] Where the expert assumes the role of an advocate, he or she can no longer be viewed as an expert in the legally correct sense.[4] It is up to the tribunal to consider whether the expert has the necessary expertise to express an opinion on a particular issue in the field (an expert witness may be properly qualified to provide an opinion on one issue but not another in the same field).

The importance of properly vetting proffered expert testimony cannot be overstated. Perhaps the most poignant illustration of the harm improper expert testimony can cause is found in the *Inquiry into Pediatric Forensic Pathology*.[5] This inquiry was commissioned in Ontario by the Honourable Stephen Goudge of the Ontario Court of Appeal in response to a number of wrongful convictions. The inquiry revealed that these wrongful convictions were due, in part, to the expert testimony of Dr. Smith, whom Justice Goudge described as follows:

> In the cases that led to the creation of this Inquiry, Dr. Charles Smith was allowed to give expert evidence in pediatric forensic pathology, often without challenge or with only limited review of his credentials. *He was an apparently well-accredited expert from a world-renowned institution. He was a commanding presence who often testified in a dogmatic style. The evidence at this inquiry demonstrated that the legal system is vulnerable to unreliable expert evidence, especially when it is presented by someone with Dr. Smith's demeanor and reputation.* An expert like this can too easily overwhelm what should be the gatekeeper's vigilance and healthy skepticism, as we have seen. In fact, as

we now know, Dr. Smith had none of the requisite training in forensic pathology and no reliable scientific basis for many of his opinions.[6] [Emphasis added.]

The inquiry lists a number of the ways in which Dr. Smith's expert testimony was faulty, including that Dr. Smith:

a) Failed to understand that his role as an expert was not to assist his client in advancing their case, but to assist the court.
b) Failed to acknowledge the limits of his expertise. Justice Goudge commented that "[e]xpert witnesses are called to the court to speak to the issues that involve their expertise. They are not given free rein to discuss other matters on which they happen to have an opinion."
c) Provided inappropriate unscientific evidence by referring to his own personal experiences or impressions.
d) Provided opinions that were speculative, unsubstantiated and not based on scientific findings.
e) Used loose and unscientific language that carried a risk of misinterpretation.
f) Failed to testify at all times with the candour required of an expert.[7]

The case of Dr. Smith provides warning flags for a trier of fact to watch for, but it also establishes the crucial importance of properly assessing expert testimony in order to avoid the risk of the expert advocate unwittingly influencing the trier of fact without a proper foundation.

## Rules of Different Tribunals Regarding Expert Testimony

### ALBERTA UTILITIES COMMISSION

The Alberta Utilities Commission (AUC) is not bound by the rules of evidence applicable to judicial proceedings.[8] However, while it has some flexibility to determine the admissibility and weight of evidence, it "cannot ignore the principles that underlie the formal rules of evidence."[9] The AUC has discretion to refuse evidence that it considers inherently flawed.[10] That said, administrative tribunals may admit any material as evidence that is "logically probative."[11] The AUC has described its approach to evidence as follows:

> The Commission may hear any evidence introduced that may be relevant, decide what evidence is relevant and what is not, decide what

part of the evidence is to be accepted and what part rejected, weigh the evidence that it accepts and where there are conflicts in the evidence decide which evidence is more likely to be true, and come to reasonable conclusions based on such evidence. Its overriding duty is to observe the principles of procedural fairness. This requires listening to and acting fairly regarding all parties, and giving each party a fair opportunity to respond to and contradict adverse testimony or information presented at hearing.[12]

Unlike in a court proceeding, the AUC has acknowledged that its proceedings are not matters between two or more competing parties to determine who wins and loses.[13] With respect to expert evidence, the AUC has proceeded as follows:

a) Consider whether the evidence is relevant.
b) If so, consider whether the evidence is opinion evidence related to a specialized or technical field and whether the person giving the opinion is qualified to do so because of expertise.
c) If so, consider the weight to be given to the evidence based on, *inter alia*: (i) the independence and objectivity of the expert witness; and (ii) the extent the witness was acting as an advocate for a client.[14]

The AUC requires expert witnesses to restrict their opinion evidence to issues or matters "within their area of expertise." Where experts testify on matters beyond the limits of their expertise, the AUC: (i) gives the evidence the weight of lay witness opinion; and (ii) prefers the evidence of any other expert witnesses qualified to give evidence in that area. Questions about the scope of a witness' evidence vis-à-vis the area in which the expert was qualified and the weight of that witness' opinion are considered by the AUC during the proceeding.

In a recent proceeding, the AUC advised all parties that it *would not* be necessary for counsel to request that their respective witnesses be qualified as "expert" witnesses with regard to their pre-filed written evidence or testimony in the proceeding. It stated:

> [T]he Commission has generally allowed witnesses, whether qualified as experts or not, to provide opinion evidence where relevant to the scope of a proceeding. The value ascribed to such evidence is a question of weight, which is a function of the professional qualifications,

> specialized knowledge, experience, relevant publications, industry recognition and independence of the witness.
>
> Given the above, the Commission is currently considering whether its current practice of qualifying expert witnesses is necessary or efficient. The elimination of the need to qualify witnesses as experts may streamline proceedings and avoid possible disputes over the "expert" designation, while continuing to allow parties to focus on the issue of the weight that should be accorded by the Commission to a party's evidence in the circumstances.
>
> The Commission is interested in using this proceeding as an opportunity to assess an alternative to the usual procedures for qualifying expert witnesses. To that end, the Commission has directed the writer to advise all parties that it will not be necessary for counsel to request that their respective witnesses be qualified as "expert" witnesses with regard to their pre-filed written evidence or testimony in this proceeding.[15]

Essentially, the AUC's recent approach is not to act as a gatekeeper of any sort but to focus instead solely on the weight it gives expert evidence. Further discussion of the AUC's approach to expert evidence is provided later in the case study portion of this chapter.

### ONTARIO ENVIRONMENTAL REVIEW TRIBUNAL

The Ontario Environmental Review Tribunal (ERT) *Rules of Practice and Practice Directions* contain "Practice Directions for Technical and Opinion Evidence." This Practice Direction explains the role and procedure to be followed by both "expert or opinion witnesses" and "technical witnesses." The rules pertaining to expert or opinion witnesses are substantively the same as the common law rules for an expert witness. A "technical witness" under the Practice Direction is described as follows:

> Many witnesses, particularly government employees, appear before the Tribunal to give evidence of scientific and technical observations, tests, measurements, and estimates. While these witnesses are often not considered experts who interpret scientific and technical evidence and provide opinions, they collect, compile, and to some extent interpret, information that is essential to the Tribunal's understanding of the issues and often forms the basis for expert opinion evidence. In this Practice Direction, these witnesses are referred to as "technical

witnesses" and the scientific and technical information they convey is referred to as "technical evidence".[16]

The Practice Directions set out the purpose and role of both the expert and technical witness, including describing the requirements to be followed in preparing any expert report. That Practice Direction provides as follows in circumstances where requirements under the Practice Direction are not adhered to:

> If this Practice Direction is not complied with, the Tribunal may:
>
> (a) decline to accept the opinions or evidence of an otherwise qualified witness;
> (b) admit the evidence, but accord it little weight;
> (c) adjourn the date of the Hearing until such time as this Practice Direction is complied with;
> (d) note the conduct of the witness and subject the witness to adverse comment in its decision;
> (e) report a breach of professional standards of conduct, an attempt to mislead, incompetence or negligence, extensive violation of this Practice Direction, or serious interference with the Tribunal's process to the professional association or licensing body responsible for compliance with standards of conduct; and/or
> (f) order that costs be paid forthwith by the Party who retained or employed the witness.[17]

## NATIONAL ENERGY BOARD

Interestingly, the National Energy Board (NEB) allows for a person to participate in a hearing as an expert intervenor *not* affiliated with any potentially affected party.

The *Jobs, Growth and Long-term Prosperity Act* came into force in July 2012 and amended the *National Energy Board Act* (NEB *Act*).[18] One of the amendments was the addition of section 55.2, which establishes what discretion the NEB has with respect to granting participation rights or "standing" for certain NEB proceedings. Section 55.2 provides:

> 55.2 On an application for a certificate, the Board shall consider the representations of any person who, in the Board's opinion, is directly affected by the granting or refusing of the application, *and it may consider the representations of any person who, in its opinion, has relevant*

*information or expertise*. A decision of the Board as to whether it will consider the representations of any person is conclusive.[19] [Emphasis added.]

The NEB has indicated that these changes assist it with collecting information that the NEB considers to be relevant to its mandate and the application before it.[20]

In determining whether an applicant has relevant information or expertise, the NEB considers whether the applicant has met the onus of showing possession of relevant information or expertise. In terms of its role as a gatekeeper, the NEB uses an Application to Participate process to determine who should be granted standing in a hearing. The application is generally a four-page form that the person fills out, and there is no other qualification process.

In its section 55.2 Guidance, the NEB included the following considerations to explain how it determines whether a person has relevant information:

a) The source of the person's knowledge (for example, local, regional or Aboriginal);
b) The extent to which the information is within the project scope and related to the list of issues; and
c) How much value the information will add to the Board's decision or recommendation.

The same section 55.2 Guidance states that the NEB may consider the following factors when deciding if a person has relevant expertise:

a) The person's qualifications (for example, the person has specialist knowledge and experience);
b) The extent to which the person's expertise is within the project scope and related to the list of issues; and
c) How much value the information will add to the Board's decision or recommendation.[21]

In a recent ruling the NEB had the following comments regarding its assessment of applicants who claim to have "relevant information or expertise":

> The Board also considers whether the relevant information or expertise being offered will add value to the Board's assessment. The

> Board is an expert tribunal with decades of experience in assessing applications for projects under its jurisdiction in the Canadian public interest, and the Board employs this expertise when assessing completed ATP forms.[22]

The NEB's ruling on participation determines whether a person meets the test for having relevant information or expertise and, if so, whether the person can participate as an intervenor or a commentor. It is important to note that if a person is granted standing as an intervenor they have full participatory rights and can bring motions, file evidence, make information requests of the proponent and other intervenors, and make argument.

This approach is challenging, as the NEB's recent rulings on participation have not provided any guidance regarding the area of expertise that the expert is qualified to opine on, the rationale applied by the NEB to determine whether such expertise is helpful, or the value that the NEB places on such evidence. In addition, it is not apparent why the NEB, an expert tribunal with decades of experience in assessing applications for projects under its jurisdiction in the Canadian public interest, would determine that such expertise is necessary.

In addition to granting persons with relevant expertise standing as intervenors, the NEB's Participant Funding Program provides intervenors with the opportunity to apply for financial assistance to intervene in proceedings. The maximum amount of funding is $12,000 for individual intervenors.[23] The NEB's Participant Funding Program Guide details how to apply for funding to hire experts.[24] Recently, the NEB granted $1,790 in participant funding for travel to a hearing for an intervenor who was granted standing based on "relevant expertise."[25]

## Case Discussion

Refusing to admit expert testimony when a witness clearly lacks expertise is generally not a difficult task. The battle lines with regard to expert testimony are usually drawn around the scope of expertise and whether the expert in question is independent or impartial. The following case examples illustrate some of the issues faced by administrative tribunals.

### THE ARMOW WIND DECISION[26]

A recent hearing before the ERT in connection with an appeal from the approval of the Armow Wind renewable energy project serves as a good discussion point. In this case, the appellant tendered Rick James as an expert witness in the area of acoustics. Mr. James had testified before the ERT in at least three prior proceedings before the Armow Wind appeal. His independence had been challenged in the K2 Wind appeal, which was heard a few months before the Armow Wind proceeding, but the ERT in that case did not provide any reasons analyzing the challenge to Mr. James' qualifications and independence. In contrast, the ERT in Armow Wind addressed the challenge to Mr. James' qualifications and independence.

By way of context, in the Armow Wind proceeding, as a matter of efficiency, Mr. James' qualifications and independence were challenged as part of his cross-examination on the substance of his opinion, and there was not a separate *voir dire* to consider the admissibility of his evidence. This obviously impacts the manner in which a tribunal discharges its gatekeeper function, as the tribunal will hear the evidence before ruling on its admissibility.

The evidence established the following in respect of Mr. James' independence:

(a) Since 2005, Mr. James, has represented clients in about 30 different matters and not one client he has represented has supported the development of wind turbines.
(b) Mr. James was a founding member and current member of the board of directors of the Society for Wind Vigilance, which had publicly called for "a moratorium on further industrial wind development."
(c) Mr. James agreed that through his work with the Society for Wind Vigilance he is "*advocating*" against the development of wind projects close to homes.
(d) While Mr. James testified that he is not against all wind projects, just projects that are too close to homes, he testified that he has never seen a project in Ontario that he would consider safe and he does not know what a safe setback distance would be for a wind turbine.

In addition to the facts above that have had an impact on Mr. James' independence, cross-examination revealed a number of other instances where Mr. James, in the view of the authors, failed to comply with the requirements necessary for proper and admissible expert testimony. Of particular note, Mr. James provided (or at least attempted to provide) an opinion outside his area of expertise (acoustics), including testimony about the physiological response of the human body to certain types of noise and about the merits of an epidemiological study. Mr. James offered an opinion in these areas despite confirming that he is not qualified to provide a medical opinion as a doctor would and that he is not an expert in statistics or epidemiology.

Mr. James also used unscientific and alarmist statements during the course of his testimony. For example, he acknowledged that he had previously testified in a proceeding in Michigan where he described the noise from a small non-industrial wind turbine as "like being on the battleship in World War II with a Kamikaze pilot coming towards you." Similarly, in his testimony before the ERT:

a) Mr. James testified that low frequency sound and infrasound from wind turbines occurs in the one hertz range and that sources of noise in the natural environment that generate frequencies in that same range are things like earthquakes, tsunamis and tornadoes. He conceded, however, that waves crashing on a beach generate noise close to that same range.
b) Mr. James described bursts of elevated infrasound as being "like a gunshot". He conceded, however, that he could instead have testified that these sound bursts were very short like "a snap of the fingers" or "a tap of the foot".[27]

The ERT considered all of Mr. James' evidence and found that he met the requisite qualifications to provide opinion evidence on matters related to acoustics and noise control engineering and wind turbines. The ERT held, however, that his evidence "on other matters, including health effects of wind turbines and epidemiology, would be excluded from consideration."[28] This was, in the view of the authors, correct. Mr. James had sufficient experience to be qualified in the area of acoustics, but he was not qualified to testify in the other areas.

The major contention with Mr. James' evidence, however, was whether he was sufficiently independent to be permitted to give expert testimony. On the issue of Mr. James' objectivity and impartiality, the ERT found as follows:

> The evidence about Mr. James' independence is equivocal. Some aspects of his evidence were selective and he was not entirely forthcoming about the actual state of the science with respect to wind turbine noise. His failure to modify his witness statement after it was shown to be inaccurate through cross-examination in a previous Tribunal hearing shows carelessness, at a minimum. His use of alarmist language may indicate that he is acting more as an advocate than as an objective

> and independent expert. While all of these factors could influence the weight to be given to his evidence, the Tribunal does not consider that his evidence is so tainted that it should be excluded entirely.[29]

In the view of the authors, the ERT correctly noted that there were issues with Mr. James' independence. However, having made the findings it did about Mr. James' independence, the ERT could have gone further and found that even if his evidence was admitted it would be afforded little to no weight. In the view of the authors, in the absence of independence, the evidence of an expert cannot be trusted and there is a risk—as illustrated by the case of Dr. Smith—that the opinion evidence is not fair or balanced and could be misleading.

Put simply, whether an expert is independent and impartial is not something that should be "equivocal." If there are serious issues and concerns about an expert's independence that evidence either should not be admitted at all or it should be given little to no weight.

### THE PLATINUM PRODUCE DECISION[30]

In another appeal from a renewable energy approval, the ERT permitted the appellant, Platinum Produce, the right to deliver an expert report of Dr. Robert McMurtry in reply to certain evidence led by the approval holder. Dr. McMurtry had previously testified in a number of renewable energy approval appeals and expressed an opinion about the alleged harms to human health caused by wind turbines.

Although Dr. McMurtry's opinion in this appeal ultimately ended up being of no consequence, because it was premised on incorrect assumptions, it is concerning to the authors that Dr. McMurtry's opinion was considered at all in the circumstances of this case. In this regard, numerous facts raised questions about the independence of Dr. McMurtry, including his involvement as the founding chair of the Society for Wind Vigilance and his involvement as an incorporating director of the Alliance to Protect Prince Edward County (APPEC), an organization whose mission statement suggests there is "no location in the County that is appropriate for a wind turbine development." These concerns about independence were exacerbated by the manner in which Dr. McMurtry prepared his expert report for this appeal. In particular, the ERT made the following evidentiary findings:

> [97] On cross-examination Dr. McMurtry acknowledged that he did not draft his reply witness statement and that the witness statement should be corrected to state his opinion that it is "more probable than

not" the Project will cause serious harm to human health of the workers. He also failed to provide a signed "Acknowledgement of Expert's Duty" form prior to giving his evidence.

Stated plainly, Dr. McMurtry did not draft his expert report, he did not appear to have read the report before it was served and filed, the report was wrong in that it overstated the opinion Dr. McMurtry held, and Dr. McMurtry did not at any time sign an acknowledgement of expert's duty in connection with his testimony as required under the applicable Practice Direction.

In the circumstances of this case, it is the respectful view of the authors that Dr. McMurtry lacked the necessary level of independence and impartiality for his evidence to be given any weight at all by the ERT.

## TRANSALTA ENFORCEMENT PROCEEDINGS

In December 2014, the AUC commenced the hearing for Proceeding No. 3110.[31] The proceeding involved an investigation by the Market Surveillance Administrator (MSA) of timed outages and related trading at certain coal-fired generating units operated by TransAlta Corporation (TransAlta). In its application, the MSA relied on a report by Dr. Matt Ayres, Deputy Administrator and Chief Economist of the MSA. The MSA also proffered Dr. Ayres as an expert witness in the hearing before the AUC.

Dr. Ayres played a leading role in the MSA's two-year investigation of TransAlta, which ultimately led to the hearing. Over the course of the investigation, Dr. Ayres: (i) authored/signed the initial notice of investigation; (ii) interviewed TransAlta staff; (iii) was the contact person at the MSA for correspondence with TransAlta; (iv) was in contact with and guided MSA staff; and (v) authored a report the MSA relied on in the application.

In a *curriculum vitae* filed with the AUC, Dr. Ayres described his role with the MSA as including: (i) leading a team of economists and other staff in providing expert analysis of market rules, market monitoring activity, and investigations; and (ii) providing expert evidence in AUC proceedings on MSA matters.

TransAlta did not challenge the qualification of Dr. Ayres as an expert prior to the hearing. In its written submissions, however, TransAlta argued that the AUC should reject Dr. Ayres' evidence or give it little weight. In support of this position, TransAlta relied on the fact that Dr. Ayres was the lead investigator into the allegedly impugned conduct and that he had a vested interest in the outcome of this proceeding. According to TransAlta, Dr. Ayres was not independent and, as a result, his evidence was unreliable.

The MSA filed its reply argument on February 19, 2015[32] and submitted that Dr. Ayres is an expert. According to the MSA, his full-time job is to monitor the Alberta market, and the assumptions he employed were derived both from his extensive experience in the Alberta market and his education in economics. The MSA argued that Dr. Ayres is: (i) independent of any market participant; and (ii) serves only the legislative mandate of the MSA and the development of a fair, efficient, and openly competitive market in Alberta.[33] It went on to suggest that preventing an expert body with a statutory mandate and requirement to bring matters before the AUC from utilizing that expertise in performing its statutory mandate due to "bias" is without foundation.[34]

## BLUEARTH RENEWABLES BULL CREEK WIND PROJECT[35]

In June 2012, 1646658 Alberta Ltd. ("BluEarth"), a wholly owned subsidiary of BluEarth Renewables Inc., filed an application with the AUC to construct and operate the Bull Creek Wind Project, which included 46 wind turbines with 2.5-megawatt capacity. The AUC received objections to the project, including a number from members of the Killarney Lake Group (KLG), which was made up of of nearby landowners.

A key issue in the proceeding was whether operation of the project may cause adverse health effects for nearby residents, including those with preexisting medical conditions. Eight expert witnesses filed reports and testified on this topic in the proceeding. The record before the AUC on this topic was considerable. In addition to the expert reports, numerous medical, epidemiologic, and acoustic studies and reports were referenced or filed in the proceeding.[36]

On January 15, 2013, the KLG filed a request for advanced funding that included funding for nine expert witnesses. In Decision 2013-0261, the AUC awarded advanced costs of $142,109.50 to the KLG with respect to legal and consulting fees.[37]

The AUC ruled on the qualifications of expert witnesses three days prior to the oral hearing.[38] In doing so, it noted the following legal principles regarding expert witnesses:

- *Independent and unbiased expertise* – An expert witness should provide independent assistance to the Court by way of objective unbiased opinion in relation to matters within his expertise. Expert witnesses are held to a high standard and must fully disclose the kind of relationships and history that might lead to concerns about bias.

Such a finding would generally lead to an adverse inference on the impartiality and character of that expert witness

- *Scope of expertise* – Aspects of experts' evidence that extend beyond the limits of their expertise should be given the weight of a lay witness rather than the weight of a properly qualified expert in these areas.
- *Expert not advocate* – An expert witness should never assume the role of advocate.

The AUC indicated that the fact that an expert is permitted to give evidence on a particular point is not a determination by the AUC of the credibility or weight to be accorded to that evidence.[39] Below is a summary of issues that were raised regarding some of the individuals tendered as experts.

### Expert as Advocate

KLG experts Dr. Carl Phillips, Dr. Christopher Hanning, and Mr. James were all affiliated with the Society for Wind Vigilance ("Society"), in the capacity of either a board member or scientific advisor. During the hearing, Dr. Phillips, Dr. Hanning, and Mr. James did not dispute that the Society's own press release indicates that it supports "a moratorium on further industrial wind development."[40] In addition, the majority of the reports and studies cited in support of the KLG expert's positions regarding the effects of wind turbine noise on health were either authored by or peer reviewed by Society members and advisors – Phillips, Hanning, James, Nissembaum, Krogh, Horner, Aramini, Salt, Shepherd, and Thorne.

Dr. Hanning testified with respect to his involvement with the Society.[41] The only paper that Dr. Hanning authored regarding the effects of wind turbines was co-authored by Drs. Aramini and Nissenbaum. Dr. Hanning testified that Dr. Aramini is a scientific advisor for the Society, while Dr. Nissenbaum sits on the Society's board of directors.[42] Mr. James is one of the founders and is a board member of the Society. He noted that the Society was formed by a group of professionals, as a forum to review and provide white papers on wind turbine noise and health effects, and, curiously, to provide personal protection for its members against lawsuits.[43]

### Expert Is Unlicensed Physician

The KLG also sought to rely on the expert evidence of Dr. Sarah Laurie. Dr. Laurie practised as a rural general physician for a short time but had not practised medicine for over 11 years and was, at that time, not a licensed physician. In her expert report, Dr. Laurie discussed her role as Chief Executive Officer of the Waubra Foundation, an Australian organization whose goal is to facilitate properly conducted, independent multidisciplinary research into the health problems identified by residents living near wind turbines. Dr. Laurie has previously testified on behalf of opponents of wind farm projects in other jurisdictions.[44]

### Expert Opining Outside Area of Expertise

Noise levels were crucial to the hearing. Dr. Adrian Upton, qualified as a neurologist, described AUC Rule 012 (which governs noise from facilities, measured cumulatively with noise from other facilities) as an "arbitrary assessment of what range of noise is acceptable."[45] In addition, Dr. Upton was unable to provide any detail regarding how the references he provided in his opening statement supported his opinion regarding the effects of wind turbine noise on sleep and health.

### AUC Findings

The AUC was not prepared to disregard the evidence provided by the KLG experts solely because they are members of the Society or a similar organization, nor was it prepared to disregard the evidence provided by the applicant's witnesses because they have previously testified on behalf of other wind developers. It indicated that while such affiliations are a factor that the AUC may take into account when assessing each expert's objectivity, it must consider a number of other factors when determining the overall weight to give each expert's evidence. In the AUC's view, the best place for this analysis is within the decision where the expert's evidence is discussed.[46]

The AUC concluded that Dr. Laurie lacked the necessary skills, experience, and training to comment on the interpretation of epidemiologic studies or the interpretation of acoustical studies and reports. The AUC gave little weight to this aspect of Dr. Laurie's evidence.[47]

In the AUC's view, Dr. Upton did not appear to have specialized knowledge or experience specifically with respect to wind turbines and their health effects. The AUC also held that Dr. Upton appeared to be unfamiliar with the qualifications of some of the authors of the reports he relied upon in forming his opinion on the health impacts of wind turbines or whether the reports he referenced were published or peer reviewed. The AUC took this apparent unfamiliarity with the subject into account when it weighed Dr. Upton's evidence regarding the general health impacts of wind turbines on nearby residents.[48]

The AUC found that Dr. Phillips provided evidence that was consistent with his expertise, and that Dr. Phillips attempted to provide his evidence in an objective manner. The AUC observed that Dr. Phillips was far less definitive in his oral testimony than he was in his written evidence with respect to many of his conclusions. This suggested to the AUC that Dr. Phillips retained some flexibility in his views regarding the health effects associated with wind turbines. Despite these findings, the AUC gave little weight to Dr. Phillips' specific conclusions regarding the project's health effects on nearby residents. First, Dr. Phillips provided little rationale for his predictions regarding the number of people who would experience health effects from the project. Second, Dr. Phillips confirmed that his conclusions were not based upon any particular adverse event reports, and, in fact, he had not reviewed any adverse event reports in the preparation of his written evidence. Third, Dr. Phillips confirmed that the data he looked at was not organized in a systematic way and that he did not break down the data to determine a dose-response relationship between wind turbine operation and the symptoms he described. Fourth, Dr. Phillips conceded that he had not specifically defined the population upon which his conclusions were based.[49]

Despite these findings, costs were nonetheless awarded for the participation of these experts in excess of $20,000.

## Conclusion/Recommendations

There is no one size fits all approach that can be applied to expert evidence submitted before administrative tribunals. In some instances, the breadth and volume of the evidence submitted will be such that it is most appropriate to consider and rule on qualifications and independence before hearing testimony on the opinion in issue. There will also be circumstances where the evidence, if admitted, could be sufficiently prejudicial or complex that the administrative tribunal should decide in advance whether it is prepared to hear that evidence before ruling on qualifications and independence. Finally, there will be cases where a form of the "let it all in" approach is most efficient. This will be in circumstances where receiving the evidence will not substantially lengthen the hearing and the administrative tribunal is situated to hear the evidence without being misled by it.

It is up to counsel and the administrative tribunal to carefully consider each situation and decide which approach to follow. What is clear, however, is that many administrative tribunals must do more than just "let it all in." Where opinion evidence is offered by an individual who does not have the requisite qualifications, independence, or impartiality, the administrative tribunal should make that finding and refuse to accept the evidence on that basis or afford the evidence little to no weight. In addition, in certain administrative tribunals where cost awards are granted or participant funding is awarded, properly excluding experts at the outset (instead of taking a let it all in approach and then giving little to no weight to their evidence) would promote efficiency and cost effectiveness for all parties.

In conclusion, when it comes to discharging its gatekeeper function, it matters less how a particular administrative tribunal does it and more that it is done.

## NOTES

1 *Johnson v Milton (Town)*, 2008 ONCA 440, 91 OR (3d) 190 at para 46.

2 Chapter 38 in this volume.

3 *1159465 Alberta Ltd v Adwood Manufacturing*, 2010 ABQB 133 at para 2.11.

4 *Perricone v Baldassarra* (1995), 7 MVR (3d) 91 at 99 (Ont Gen Div).

5 *Inquiry into Pediatric Forensic Pathology in Ontario Report* (Toronto: Ministry of the Attorney General, 2008) (Commissioner: the Honourable Stephen T Goudge) vol 3 [The Goudge Inquiry] (accessed 5 February 2018), online: <http://www.attorneygeneral.jus.gov.on.ca/inquiries/goudge/report/v3_en_pdf/Vol_3_Eng.pdf>.

6 The Goudge Inquiry, *ibid* at 470.

7 The Goudge Inquiry, *ibid* at 17–19.

8 *Alberta Utilities Commission Act*, SA 2007, c A37.2, s 20. This reflects the common law position that administrative tribunals are not bound to apply strict rules of evidence, unless expressly prescribed. Tribunals are entitled to act on any evidence that is logically probative: *Alberta (Workers' Compensation Board) v Appeals Commission*, 2005 ABCA 276 at paras 63–64 [*WCB*].

9 AUC Decision 2011-436: AltaLink Management Ltd and EPCOR Distribution & Transmission Inc – Heartland Transmission Project, Application No 1606609, Proceeding ID No 457, 1 November 2011 at para 82 [Heartland Transmission Project], aff'd on other grounds 2012 ABCA 378. See also AUC Decision 2012-303: ATCO Electric Ltd – Eastern Alberta Transmission Line Project, Applications No 1607153 and No 1607736, Proceeding ID No 1069, 15 November 2012 at para 96 [ATCO Electric Ltd], where the AUC qualified this statement by adding the underlined: "While this allows the Commission some flexibility to determine what evidence to admit and what weight to give the evidence it admits, it cannot ignore the principles of procedural fairness that underlie the formal rules of evidence."

10 *Lavallee v Alberta (Securities Commission)*, 2010 ABCA 48 at paras 16–17 [*Lavallee*] (interpreting a similar section of the Securities Act, RSA 2000, c S-4). Leave to appeal to SCC was dismissed in *Lavallee v Alberta (Securities Commission)*, [2010] SCCA No 119.

11 *WCB*, *supra* note 8 at para 63, citing *TA Miller Ltd v Minister of Housing and Local Government*, [1968] 1 WLR 992 at 995 (CA); *Trenchard v Secretary of State for the Environment*, [1997] EWJ No 1118 at para 28 (CA); and *Bortolotti v Ontario (Ministry of Housing)* (1977), 15 OR (2d) 617 (CA).

12 AUC Decision 2012-104: Milner Power Inc – Complaint by Milner Power Inc Regarding the ISO Transmission Loss Factor Rule and Loss Factor Methodology, Application No 1606494, Proceeding ID No 790, 16 April 2012 at para 200 [Milner Power Inc]. The commission cited the following authorities: *Kane v University of British Columbia*, [1980] 1 SCR 1105 at 1112–13; *Mooring v Canada (National Parole Board)*, [1996] 1 SCR 75; and *Lavallee*, *supra* note 10.

13 ATCO Electric Ltd, *supra* note 9 at para 87; Heartland Transmission Project, *supra* note 9 at para 73; AUC Decision 2012-327: AltaLink Management Ltd – Western Alberta Transmission Line Project, Application No 1607067, Proceeding ID No 1045, 6 December 2012 at para 140.

14 Heartland Transmission Project, *supra* note 9 at para 96.

15 Proceeding 2739, Application No 1609784, correspondence dated 18 June 2014.

16 Ontario Environmental Review Tribunal, *Rules of Practice and Practice Directions* (12 September 2016), online: <http://elto.gov.on.ca/tribunals/ert/guides-rules/> at 46.

17 Ontario Environmental Review Tribunal, *ibid* at 50.

18 *Jobs, Growth and Long-term Prosperity Act*, SC 2012, c 19, Division 2.

19 *National Energy Board Act*, RSC 1985, c N-7, s 55.2.

20 NEB, Trans Mountain Pipeline ULC (Trans Mountain) – Application for the Trans Mountain Expansion Project (Application), 16 December 2013, and Ruling on Participation (Ruling), 2 April 2014.

21 NEB, "Section 55.2 Guidance – Participation in a Facilities Hearing" (22 March 2013).

22 NEB, "Ruling on Participation and Updated Timetable of Events in the Application for the Line 9B Reversal and Line 9 Capacity Expansion Project" at 3.

23 NEB, "Participant Funding Program," online: <http://www.neb-one.gc.ca/prtcptn/hrng/pfp/prtcpntfndngprgrm-eng.html>.

24 NEB, *Participant Funding Program Guide* (13 July 2017, accessed 5 February 2018), online: <https://www.neb-one.gc.ca/prtcptn/hrng/pfp/prgrmgd-eng.html>.

25 NEB, "Allocation of Funds for Participation in the Public Hearing for Trans Mountain Expansion" (17 February 2015, accessed 5 February 2018), online: <http://www.neb-one.gc.ca/prtcptn/hrng/pfp/llctnfnd/trnsmntnxpnsn-eng.html>.

26 *Kroeplin v Director, Ministry of the Environment*, [2014] OERTD No 24, 88 CELR (3d) 1 [*Kroeplin*].

27 Mr. James' Evidence, 9 January 2014, Transcript, 364–366, Compendium, vol 1, tab E.

28 *Kroeplin*, *supra* note 26 at 86.

29 *Kroeplin*, *ibid* at 86.

30 *Platinum Produce Company v Director, Ministry of the Environment*, Case No 13-096 [*Platinum*].

31 The AUC has not rendered its decision in respect of Proceeding No 3110.

32 Reply Argument of the Market Surveillance Administrator, Application No 1610350, Proceeding No 3110 [Reply Argument].

33 Reply Argument, *ibid* at para 132.

34 Reply Argument, *ibid* at para 136; see AUC Decision 3110-D02-2015 Market Surveillance Administrator allegations against TransAlta Corporation et al., 18 September 2015.

35 AUC Decision 2014-040: 1646658 Alberta Ltd., Bull Creek Wind Project (20 February 2014) [Decision].

36 Decision, *ibid* at para 365.

37 AUC Decision 2013-026: 1646658 Alberta Ltd – Bull Creek Wind Project – Advance Funding, Application No 1608556, Proceeding ID No 1955, 31 January 2013.

38 Ruling on the Qualification of Expert Witnesses in Proceeding ID No 1955.

39 Ruling on the Qualification of Expert Witnesses in Proceeding ID No 1955; AUC Advance Costs Decision 2013-026 at 6.

40 The Society for Wind Vigilance, News Release, "The Society for Wind Vigilance Announces First International Symposium" (17 July 2010, accessed 5 February 2018) online: <http://www.windvigilance.com/news/the-society-for-wind-vigilance-announces-first-international-symposium>.

41 Transcript, vol 6, 1426.

42 Transcript, vol 6, 1447.

43 Transcript, vol 8, 1738.

44 Decision, *supra* note 35 at para 309.

45 Transcript, vol 8, 1833.

46 Decision, *supra* note 35 at para 52.

47 Decision, *ibid* at para 375.

48 Decision, *ibid* at para 373.

49 Decision, *ibid* at paras 369 and 383–386.

# 40

# An Overview of Expert Evidence in Canada

GARY A. LETCHER AND ANDREA C. AKELAITIS

## Opinion Evidence: Not Just the Facts

The justification for admitting opinion evidence is to explain complexity. As it has evolved, however, the purpose of explaining substantive complexity has introduced considerable procedural complexity into the trial process. As set out in the leading decision of *R. v. Mohan*:[1]

> Admission of expert evidence depends on the application of the following criteria:
>
> (a) relevance;
> (b) necessity in assisting the trier of facts;
> (c) the absence of any exclusionary rule;
> (d) a properly qualified expert.

Our Canadian courts are not entirely comfortable with expert opinion evidence. The Supreme Court of Canada has repeatedly cautioned that vigilance must be undertaken to ensure that the potential "mischief" of expert evidence does not overwhelm the benefits to the trier of fact. Indeed, the focus of the court's analysis in *Mohan* was on the dangers that expert evidence can bring to the adjudicative process. In *R. v. D.D.*,[2] Major J., said this:

> In Mohan, Sopinka J. stated that the need for expert evidence must be assessed in light of its potential to distort the fact-finding process. . . .

The potential for expert evidence to overwhelm the process is likely even greater in an administrative tribunal setting, where many environmental issues are heard.

As it has evolved, and as discussed below, there are now three categories of opinion evidence: expert scientific evidence, expert non-scientific evidence, and lay opinion evidence.

## The Big Four

Adducing expert evidence in the environmental law context requires careful focus on four issues:

- Selecting the precise question with respect to which the opinion is sought;
- Ensuring that the expert is qualified with respect to that precise question;
- Determining the assumptions necessary to underpin the opinion and ensuring that those assumptions can be proven; and
- Ensuring that the expert opinion meets the requirements of admissibility (the *Mohan* factors as they have evolved).

We will address each of these in turn.

### SELECTING THE QUESTION

For the most part, environmental law issues are statute driven. That is the case in environmental prosecutions, in environmental assessment litigation, and in statute-based contaminated sites litigation. As such, the first question for counsel is what statutory requirements must be established (or disproved) and what, if any, expert evidence, if available, may be helpful in order to meet that burden of proof. The earlier that this process occurs the better.

### QUALIFICATIONS

One of the *Mohan* factors deserves particular early consideration. This is, it is not enough that the person selected to provide an opinion is an expert in his or her field. It is necessary to establish that the person providing the opinion is an expert in the precise discipline or area of knowledge with respect to which the opinion is directed. (An expert hydrogeologist experienced with groundwater flow dynamics may well not be an expert in toxicity issues related to that groundwater.)

### ASSUMPTIONS

An opinion based on a set of assumptions may be completely rejected if the assumptions underlying the opinion are not proven. In the recent BC Environmental Appeal Board case, *Seaspan ULC v. Director, Environmental Management Act*,[3] in which a number of assumptions on which the expert relied were upset on cross-examination, the board recounted that the expert "at the conclusion of his cross-examination ... conceded that if any of the information he considered in reaching his conclusion was incomplete, or if any of the assumed facts were incorrect, then at the very least, he would have to reconsider his opinion."[4] In that case the expert was not re-examined.

### ADMISSIBILITY

In 2014, in *R. v. Sekhon*,[5] the Supreme Court of Canada again reviewed the admissibility factors contained in *R. v. Mohan*:

> *A. Requirements for Expert Opinion Evidence*
> [43] As set out *R. v. Mohan*, [1994] 2 SCR 9, at pp. 20–25, and affirmed in *R. v. J.-L.J.*, 2000 SCC 51, [2000] 2 SCR 600, and *R. v. D.D.*, 2000 SCC 43, [2000] 2 SCR 275, the admission of expert evidence depends on the following criteria: (1) relevance; (2) necessity in assisting the trier of fact; (3) the absence of any exclusionary rule; and (4) a properly qualified expert.
>
> [44] With respect to the "relevance" criterion, *Mohan* states that the judge must conduct a cost-benefit analysis to determine "whether its value is worth what it costs" (p. 21, quoting *McCormick on Evidence* (3rd ed. 1984), at p. 544). The cost-benefit analysis requires the judge to balance the probative value of the evidence against its prejudicial effect (*Mohan*, at p. 21).
>
> [45] As for the "necessity" criterion, *Mohan* holds that "[i]f on the proven facts a judge or jury can form their own conclusions without help, then the opinion of [an] expert is unnecessary" (p. 23, quoting Lawton L.J. in *R. v. Turner*, [1975] 1 QB 834, at p. 841). The Court went on to note that the concern "inherent in the application of this criterion [is] that experts not be permitted to usurp the functions of the trier of fact" (p. 24).
>
> [46] Given the concerns about the impact expert evidence can have on a trial—including the possibility that experts may usurp the role of the trier of fact—trial judges must be vigilant in monitoring

and enforcing the proper scope of expert evidence. While these concerns are perhaps more pronounced in jury trials, all trial judges—including those in judge-alone trials—have an ongoing duty to ensure that expert evidence remains within its proper scope. It is not enough to simply consider the *Mohan* criteria at the outset of the expert's testimony and make an initial ruling as to the admissibility of the evidence. The trial judge must do his or her best to ensure that, throughout the expert's testimony, the testimony remains within the proper boundaries of expert evidence. As noted by Doherty J.A. in *R. v. Abbey*, 2009 ONCA 624, 97 OR (3d) 330, at para. 62:

> The admissibility inquiry is not conducted in a vacuum. Before deciding admissibility, a trial judge must determine the nature and scope of the proposed expert evidence. In doing so, the trial judge sets not only the boundaries of the proposed expert evidence but also, if necessary, the language in which the expert's opinion may be proffered so as to minimize any potential harm to the trial process. A cautious delineation of the scope of the proposed expert evidence and strict adherence to those boundaries, if the evidence is admitted, are essential.... [Emphasis added; citations omitted.]

[47] The trial judge must both ensure that an expert stays within the proper bounds of his or her expertise and that the content of the evidence itself is properly the subject of expert evidence.

## THE COURT AS GATEKEEPER

In *R. v. Abbey*,[6] the court set out a two-step process for the assessment of expert evidence based on the criteria set out in the *Mohan* case. This two-step process has been described as a "rules-based" analysis under the first step (the four criteria for admission of expert evidence in *Mohan*) and under the second step focuses on the court's role as a gatekeeper.[7] It is at the gatekeeper phase of the inquiry where the court considers the cost-benefit analysis. The cost-benefit analysis also requires the consideration of the probative value of the evidence versus its prejudicial effect to the hearing.

It is important to note that the 2014 decision of the Supreme Court of Canada in *R. v. Sekhon*, referred to above, can be read to say that the "gatekeeper" function, or cost-benefit analysis, is not a separate step in the assessment of the admissibility of expert evidence but is considered within the relevance and necessity steps in the *Mohan* criteria.

## Novel Scientific Theory or Technique

### GENERAL PRINCIPLES OF ADMISSIBILITY: RELIABILITY

In *R. v. Mohan*, the Supreme Court of Canada considered expert opinion evidence in the context of a novel scientific theory or technique. The Supreme Court of Canada held that a novel scientific theory or technique is subject to special scrutiny and must satisfy a basic threshold of reliability:

> Expert evidence which advances a novel scientific theory or technique is *subjected to special scrutiny to determine whether it meets a basic threshold of reliability* and whether it is essential in the sense that the trier of fact will be unable to come to a satisfactory conclusion without the assistance of the expert. The closer the evidence approaches an opinion on an ultimate issue, the stricter the application of this principle.[8] [Emphasis added.]

In *R. v. Mohan*, the Supreme Court of Canada did not create a specific test with respect to the admissibility of novel scientific evidence or techniques. Rather, the court set out the criteria to distinguish opinion evidence that is sufficiently reliable and necessary to assist the trier of fact from those opinions that are unnecessary, unreliable, or incompatible with the litigation process. In other words, novel scientific evidence or techniques are subject to the same criteria for admissibility as other expert evidence but with a particular focus on reliability. In *R. v. J.(J.-L.)*, the Supreme Court of Canada confirmed this approach and stated as follows:

> Mohan kept the door open to novel science, rejecting the "general acceptance" test formulated in the United States in *Frye v. United States*, 293 F. 1013 (D.C.) CIR. 1923, and moving in parallel with its replacement, the "reliable foundation" test more recently laid down by the US Supreme Court in *Daubert v. Merrell Dow Pharmaceuticals, Inc.*, and 509 US 579 (1993).[9]

The Supreme Court of Canada in *R. v. J.(J.-L.)* then went on to determine that a trial judge could evaluate the reliability of novel science or techniques on the basis of the factors identified in the US *Daubert* case. These factors are:

1. Whether the theory or technique can be and has been tested;
2. Whether the theory or technique has been subjected to peer review and publication;
3. The known or potential rate of error or the existence of standards; and
4. Whether the theory or technique used has been generally accepted.[10]

## NOVEL NON-SCIENTIFIC EVIDENCE

Both *Abbey* and a recent BC Court of Appeal decision (*R. v. Aitken*[11]) discuss the application of the reliability criteria in the context of novel non-scientific expert evidence. In *Abbey*, the court recognized that the Daubert factors are not essential to the reliability inquiry where the evidence is based on specialized knowledge acquired through training or experience in a particular discipline. *Abbey* was considering the admissibility of expert opinion evidence of a sociologist who was an expert in urban street gang culture in Canada. The court found that the expert's opinion "could not pass scientific muster." However, the court found that the expert's opinion "flowed from his specialized knowledge gained through extensive research, years of clinical work and his familiarity with the relevant academic literature."[12]

The court in *Abbey* then went on to determine that, with respect to non-scientific expert evidence:

> Scientific validity is not a condition precedent to the admissibility of expert opinion evidence. Most expert evidence routinely heard and acted upon in the courts cannot be scientifically validated. For example, psychiatrists testify to the existence of various mental states, doctors testify as to the cause of an injury or death, accident reconstructionists testify to the location or cause of an accident, economists or rehabilitation specialists testify to future employment prospects and future care costs, fire marshals testify about the cause of a fire, professionals from a wide variety of fields testify as to the operative standard of care in their profession or the cause of a particular event. Like Dr. Totten, these experts do not support their opinions by reference to error rates, random samplings or the replication of test results. Rather, they refer to specialized knowledge gained through experience and specialized training in the relevant field. To test the reliability of the opinion of these experts and Dr. Totten using reliability

factors referable to scientific validity is to attempt to place the proverbial square peg into the round hole.[13]

It is often said that much of what environmental engineers do is as much an art as a science. An example might be a hydrogeologist making an inference as to groundwater flow path. The "art" aspect of the environmental expert evidence may arise from the expert's experience while the "science" part is the application of scientific principles in methodology. As discuss in *Abbey*, both types of expert evidence are admissible if otherwise falling within the *Mohan* criteria.

## Particular Issues Relating to Objectivity

The Rules of Procedure in many of the provinces mandate objectivity on the part of the expert providing opinion evidence. For instance, Rule 11-2 of the *British Columbia Supreme Court Rules* provides that in giving an opinion to the court, an expert has a duty to assist the court and is not to be an advocate for any party. The Rule then goes on to require the expert to certify in their report that they are aware of the duty and have made the report in conformity with that duty and will give their oral or written testimony in conformity with that duty.

The independence issue is often just below the surface in many environmental contests given the different and sometimes overlapping roles played by environmental experts. The same person may have done the work (remediated the contaminated site) and assisted counsel in preparing to cross-examine, and may be proffered to provide expert evidence on the substantive issue.

Two appellate level decisions, one from Ontario and one from Nova Scotia, discuss the issues of objectivity, independence, and impartiality with respect to expert evidence. The appeal of the Nova Scotia Court of Appeal decision *Abbott and Haliburton Company v. WBLI Chartered Accountants*[14] was dismissed by the Supreme Court of Canada.[15] Both decisions take a less than strict view of issues relating to the "independence" of an expert.

The Nova Scotia decision found that issues related to "independence or even objectivity" go to weight rather than admissibility.[16] The court found that "it is when a court is satisfied that the evidence is, in fact, so tainted by bias or partiality, so as to render it of no or minimal assistance, it can be excluded."

The Ontario Court of Appeal decision, *Moore v. Getahun*,[17] to the relief of the Ontario Bar, made this finding:

> I reject the trial judge's proclamation that the practice of consultation between counsel and expert witnesses to review draft reports must end.

## Lay Opinion Evidence

In *Giczi v. Kandola* (the "Bette Midler Case"),[18] Sigurdson J., in the context of somewhat colourful facts, discussed the principles surrounding the admission of lay opinion evidence and held that witnesses from the entertainment field could provide admissible lay opinion "comparing the plaintiff to other tribute performers generally, Bette Midler tribute singers, or Bette Midler." The court referred to the leading authority on this point, *R. v. Graat*.[19] In *Graat*, this is what was said by the court:

> The judge in the instant case was not in as good a position as the police officers or Mr. Wilson to determine the degree of Mr. Graat's impairment or his ability to drive a motor vehicle. The witnesses had an opportunity for personal observation. They were in a position to give the Court real help. They were not settling the dispute. They were not deciding the matter the Court had to decide, the ultimate issue. The judge could accept all or part or none of their evidence....
>
> I accept the following passage from Cross as a good statement of the law as to the cases in which non-expert opinion is admissible.
>
> > When, in the words of an American judge, "the facts from which a witness received an impression were too evanescent in their nature to be recollected, or too complicated to be separately and distinctly narrated", a witness may state his opinion or impression. He was better equipped than the jury to form it, and it is impossible for him to convey an adequate idea of the premises on which he acted to the jury:
> >
> > "Unless opinions, estimates and inferences which men in their daily lives reach without conscious ratiocination as a result of what they have perceived with their physical senses were treated in the law of evidence as if they were mere statements of fact, witnesses would find themselves unable

to communicate to the judge an accurate impression of the events they were seeking to describe." There is nothing in the nature of a closed list of cases in which non-expert opinion evidence is admissible. Typical instances are provided by questions concerning age, speed, weather, handwriting and identity in general [at p. 448]."[20]

## Something to Think About

One can easily form the view that the practice in Canadian trial courts and administrative tribunals with respect to the treatment of opinion evidence is not entirely in accord with the Supreme Court of Canada jurisprudence. The gatekeeper function for the most part is an open gate. Too often the cost-benefit of admitting expert evidence into the hearing process results in a net deficit. Also too often the question of whether the probative value is worth the cost is not fully addressed.

While expert evidence may be more likely to be useful in the litigation of environmental issues—given the technical overlay—careful thought should be given to whether the expert is actually explaining a complexity that the judge or the board could not on its own determine (especially in the case of expert tribunals).

Stepping back and reminding ourselves of basic principles, we see that the essential purpose of expert evidence is to explain complexity to the trier of fact while trampling as little as possible in the area of the determination of the ultimate issue and avoiding the role of an advocate. Necessity, within the principles set out in *Mohan*, can justify an expert providing a "ready made inference," particularly where the added ingredient provided by the expert is sourced from experience and not just the application of scientific principles. Is a "ready made inference" provided by an expert "necessary" in many environmental cases? As discussed in *Sekhon*, the court (or tribunal) must control the expert evidence sought to be adduced so that the evidence does not overwhelm the adjudicative process. While it may be tempting to leave it to an expert to opine on what essentially is the ultimate issue, is it necessary in the sense of no other practicable way of determining the issue?[21]

### NOTES

1 [1994] 2 SCR 9 at para 17.
2 [2000] SCJ No 44 at para 48.
3 2010-EMA-005 and 006.
4 *Ibid* at para 88. See also *Gregory v Insurance Corp of British Columbia*, 2010 BCSC 651.

5 [2014] 1 SCR 272 at paras 43–47.

6 2009 ONCA 624.

7 See *R v Aitken*, [2012] BCJ No 632, where the BC Court of Appeal summarized this two-step process for the assessment of expert evidence at paras 71 to 80 [*Aitken*].

8 [1994] SCJ No 36 at para 28.

9 *R v J(J-L)*, [2000] SCJ No 52 at para 33.

10 *Ibid.*

11 *Aitken*, *supra* note 7.

12 *R v Abbey*, [2009] OJ No 3534 at para 108.

13 *Ibid* at para 109

14 2013 NSCA 66; *Abbott and Haliburton Co. v White Burgess Langille Inman*, 2015 SCC 23, [2015] 2 SCR 182.

15 The appeal was heard on 7 October 2014 and judgment has been reserved.

16 See also *Conseil Scolaire Francophone de la Colombie-Britannique v British Columbia (Education)*, 2014 BCSC 851.

17 2015 ONCA 55 at para 66; see also *Westerhof v Gee Estate* 2015 ONCA 206 and *White Burgess Langille Inman v Abbot and Haliburton Co.*, 2015 SCC 23.

18 2014 BCSC 508.

19 [1982] 2 SCR 819.

20 *Ibid* at 836–37.

21 See, for example, the class action lawsuit for decreased property values as a result of soil contamination, *Smith v Inco Ltd*, 2009 CanLII 63374, where the court found that while the expert evidence was helpful to the court, it was not necessary for the fair determination of the issues. In this case the court found the evidence was primarily a compendium of factual research and not opinion evidence.

# 41

# Issues Respecting Expert Advisors, Expert Witnesses, and Retaining Counsel

NICHOLAS R. HUGHES AND MONIKA A. SAWICKA*

## Introduction

Retaining an expert is an integral part of a litigation or advisory practice. The relationship between the expert and counsel is complex and multifaceted, as both have their own roles, obligations, and limitations during the course of a litigation file.

An early assessment of your needs for expert assistance and the role you want your experts to play is essential to advancing your client's interests. As with all facets of litigation, complex ethical and professional issues arise in respect of your choices and dealings with your experts. Such issues often touch on disclosure requirements and privilege and whether the expert or counsel breached their corresponding obligations. As noted in the authorities, the last thing counsel needs in advancing their clients' cause is for counsel's dealings with its experts to become the focal point of a trial.

This chapter will attempt to address some of these issues and offer practical guidance on how to address them.

## The Expert Advisor vs. the Expert Witness

### ROLE OF THE EXPERT ADVISOR

The role of the expert as an "advisor" is to advise counsel on technical matters in order to assist counsel to build his or her case. Experts in this role investigate

* *These materials were prepared by Nicholas R. Hughes and Monika A. Sawicka, with special thanks to Ailbish Skinner, Articling Student, of McCarthy Tétrault LLP, Vancouver, BC.*

facts, issues, and causal relationships and relate their analysis to counsel's legal theory. In essence, the expert advisor is a member of the litigation team who assists counsel in understanding and advancing the case.

For an expert retained solely as an advisor, and who does not depart from that role, all communications between the expert and counsel and all documents created, produced, or assembled by counsel or the expert for the "dominant" purpose of aiding in the conduct of litigation are protected by litigation privilege. Accordingly, retaining an expert advisor on a complex case, such as a construction dispute or a medical malpractice action, may be very beneficial, as the expert will be able to advise counsel on the technical issues of the case without fear of the communications and opinions being disclosed to the opposing party.

## ROLE OF THE EXPERT WITNESS

Rule 11-2(1) of the British Columbia *Supreme Court Civil Rules*[1] codifies the duty of expert witnesses as follows: in giving an opinion to the court, an expert has a duty to assist the court and is not to be an advocate for any party. By way of comparison, Rule 4.1 of the Ontario *Rules of Civil Procedure*[2] states that the expert witness must provide: fair, objective, and non-partisan evidence; opinion evidence that is related only to matters that are within the expert's area of expertise; and such additional assistance as the court may reasonably require to determine the matter in issue. Equally, the Alberta courts have recognized that an expert witness should strive to be impartial and independent, and should not be an advocate for either party.[3] In essence, irrespective of the jurisdiction, the expert witness's duty is to be objective and impartial and to assist the court, not its client or counsel.

The privilege and disclosure implications surrounding the expert witness are more complex than that of the expert advisor. Once the expert's opinion is disclosed to be relied upon as evidence in court, the litigation privilege over the expert's files is waived. The privilege is waived by either the voluntary disclosure of the opinion or because of the court's need to properly assess credibility and reliability of the opinion.

## THE DISTINCTION BETWEEN THE ROLES

The distinction between an expert advisor and an expert witness, and the privilege and disclosure implications associated with each, was well described in *Vancouver Community College v. Phillips, Barratt* (*Vancouver Community College*),[4] a 1987 decision of the British Columbia Supreme Court (BCSC). Mr. Justice Finch stated as follows:

> *So long as the expert remains in the role of a confidential advisor, there are sound reasons for maintaining privilege over documents in his possession. Once he becomes a witness, however, his role is substantially changed. His opinions and their foundation are no longer private advice for the party who retained him. He offers his professional opinion for the assistance of the court in its search for the truth.* The witness is no longer in the camp of a partisan. He testifies in an objective way to assist the court in understanding scientific, technical or complex matters within the scope of his professional expertise. He is presented to the court as truthful, reliable, knowledgeable and qualified. It is as though the party calling him says: "Here is Mr. X, an expert in an area where the court needs assistance. You can rely on his opinion. It is sound. He is prepared to stand by it. My friend can cross-examine him as he will. He won't get anywhere. The witness has nothing to hide." [Emphasis added.][5]

## THE EXPERT IN A DUAL ROLE

Practitioners in British Columbia generally advise against retaining of one expert who will fill both roles as an advisor and expert witness. The primary reason for this advice is Rule 11-6(8)(b), which establishes that prior to the expert testifying, privilege over the expert's file will be lost. Rule 11-6(8)(b) requires the disclosure, if requested by a party of record, of the contents of the expert's file relating to the preparation of the opinion set out in the expert's report.

In *Conseil scolaire francophone de la Colombie-Britannique v. British Columbia (Education)* (CSF),[6] the BCSC further explained the disclosure principles under Rule 11-6(8)(b):

> With regard to the scheme of [Rule] 11-6(8), I note that [Rule] 11-6(8)(a) enumerates a number of documents that must be served on a requesting party immediately, namely written statements or statements of facts on which the expert based his or her opinion; records of independent observations made by the expert in relation to the report; data compiled by the expert in relation to the report; and the results of any tests conducted by the expert or inspections conducted by the expert. *Rule 11-6(8)(a) thus already requires production of the observations and analysis underlying the expert's opinion. Rule 11-6(8)(b) should therefore be read as requiring production of something more than the underpinning of the report.*

My interpretation of [Rule] 11-6(8)(b) thus takes a middle road between the broad scope of disclosure at common law and the narrow view asserted by the plaintiffs. *As I see it, on request pursuant to [Rule] 11-6(8)(b), an expert must produce the contents of the expert's file that are relevant to matters of substance in his or her opinion or to his or her credibility unless it would be unfair to do so.* [Emphasis added.][7]

Even earlier than the CSF case, *Vancouver Community College* established that an expert loses privilege immediately on entering the witness box. As stated by Justice Finch:

> *When an expert witness who is not a party is called to testify, or when his report is placed in evidence, he may be required to produce to counsel cross-examining all documents in his possession which are or may be relevant to matters of substance in his evidence or to his credibility, unless it would be unfair or inconsistent to require such production.* Fairness and consistency must be judged in the circumstances of each case. If those requirements are met, the documents are producible because there is an implied intention in the party presenting the witness's evidence, written or oral, to waive the lawyer's brief privilege which previously protected the documents from disclosure. [Emphasis added.][8]

That the expert produce "all documents in his possession" has been followed in subsequent cases, including in *Delgamuukw v. British Columbia*:

> Thus the present law requires an expert witness who is called to testify at trial to produce all documents which are or have been in his possession, including draft reports (even if they come from the file of the solicitor with annotations) and other communications which are or may be relevant to matters of substance in his evidence or his credibility unless it would be unfair to require production. It is a presumption of law that solicitor's privilege is waived in respect to such matters of substance, etc., when the witness is called to give evidence at trial.[9]

As a result of the difficulties associated with one expert acting as both an advisor and witness, and in particular those involving the loss of privilege over the expert's file, practitioners in British Columbia have in some cases retained two experts—one as an advisor and one as an expert witness. Where only one expert is retained, counsel should conduct discussions with the expert in such a way that the risk of disclosure is minimized. Without commenting on the probity of this practice, some practitioners advise their experts not to commit their views to writing until asked to do so.[10]

Having said this, according to Justice Finch, the skilled expert can indeed, with the assistance of counsel, fill both roles of advisor and witness successfully:[11]

> I do not think there are, or should be, any limitations on the pre-opinion, or pre-trial, exchanges between counsel and their expert advisors [...] I do, however, think that when the decision is made to adduce the experts opinion into evidence, either orally or in writing, counsel must anticipate the prospect of a thorough cross examination, and decide whether the anticipated good will outweigh the possible bad. *The trustworthy expert will not be uncomfortable about disclosing his pre-trial communication with counsel. Nor will counsel be embarrassed if his communication were directed towards refining an objective opinion based upon reasonable factual assumptions.* [Emphasis added.]

## Obligations of Experts and Counsel

### CONSEQUENCES WHERE EXPERTS BREACH THEIR DUTIES

In circumstances where an expert does not conform to the standards expected of the expert, the court may: (i) refuse to admit the expert's report; or (ii) penalize the party or the counsel tendering the expert through an award of special costs. An award of special costs against counsel for a party will only be awarded in circumstances in which the court views the conduct of the party or counsel as reprehensible. Examples of circumstances giving rise to these outcomes are illustrated by the cases below.

#### Inadmissibility of Report

The examples discussed below are provided in chronological order and not in order of significance. It should be noted that there are few reported decisions on the exclusion of expert reports. This reflects the reality that orders excluding such evidence are generally made orally during a trial. As a result, the following are mere examples of cases where experts have been found not to have provided unbiased assistance to the court.

In *Coulter (Guardian ad Litem of) v. Ball*,[12] an expert opinion was challenged on the grounds of bias. The trial judge concluded that the expert report was argumentative, evasive, and not the sort expected from an expert endeavouring to assist the court. In the result, the trial judge concluded the expert was acting as an advocate for the defence and accordingly his opinions could not be relied on. The judge, however, did not find that tendering the report was intended to mislead the court, and therefore the use of the expert did not constitute conduct warranting a costs penalty.

The following two cases involve situations where the excessive use of bolded fonts to emphasize conclusions provided indicia that the expert tendered was acting as an advocate.

In *Warkentin v. Riggs*,[13] the expert used bold font to highlight words and phrases in the report that benefited the plaintiff's claim and supported his diagnosis. Matters contrary to the plaintiff's claim or that did not support his diagnosis were either omitted or presented in non-bolded font. The trial judge found the report amounted to an advocacy piece and ruled the report inadmissible. The court concluded that the report was likely to distort the fact-finding function for the trier of fact and, therefore, its prejudicial effect far outweighed its probative value.

Similarly, in *Turpin v. Manufacturers Life Insurance Company*,[14] the plaintiffs objected, among other things, to the fact that an expert report did not comply with requirements established by the Supreme Court Civil Rules, and that the expert was acting as an advocate for a party. The court's findings in this regard were based on the author's use of bold and italicized font in the report. The court held that the report did not comply with the requirements (i.e. the report did not list every document relied upon in the opinion) and that the use of emphasis is not to be encouraged and may have been introduced by counsel's letter of instructions. The report was held to be inadmissible.

In *Maras v. Seemore Entertainment Ltd.* (*Maras*),[15] the court held that a particular expert's report suffered from a number of deficiencies that resulted in it not being admitted. The deficiencies cited included:

(1) the report contained many pages of comments on, and summaries of, various records and reports the expert reviewed, which were neither necessary nor of assistance to the jury unless there was a specific purpose for doing so which related to the opinion;
(2) what constituted facts, assumptions, and opinions were not clearly identified; and

(3) the report contained certain "editorial comments," which should, at the very least, have been linked to an assumed fact and/or the expert's opinion.

### Cost Awards

The following examples of cases in which costs penalties were imposed for experts departing from their obligations are also listed in chronological order and not necessarily in order of significance.

In *Heppner v. Schmand*,[16] the BC Court of Appeal approved an award of special costs where the insurer, despite previous judicial criticism of the same practice, repeatedly introduced similar engineering opinions on behalf of its insured defendants.

In *Jayetileke v. Blake*,[17] the plaintiff sought costs because the defendant called an expert witness who had been branded as an advocate in prior cases, and whose conduct in the trial was deserving of rebuke. The court awarded special costs against the defendant, as the defendant's expert witness, among other things:

(1) had a history before the courts where his evidence was rejected and his objectivity called into question;
(2) was an advocate, argumentative, defensive, non-responsive, and prone to rambling discourses that were not relevant to the questions posed in cross-examination;
(3) displayed an alarming inability to appreciate his role as an expert and the accompanying privilege to provide opinion evidence;
(4) was asked to leave the courtroom so that counsel could argue about questions to be put to him, but was seen peeking into the courtroom and listening to the discussion; and
(5) defence counsel was alive to the expert's propensity to abuse the role of an expert.

In *Bailey v. Barbour*,[18] the court awarded costs against counsel for calling an unqualified and biased expert witness. The subject expert's initial evidence under cross-examination conveyed an involvement in the proceeding beyond that expected of an expert witness. The court found that the expert was biased and effectively acted as co-counsel and advocate and that having the expert testify was wasted trial time. Ultimately, the court held that the calling of the expert by the lawyer, knowing of the expert's lack of objectivity, was enough to warrant an award of personal costs against the lawyer. In its reasons, the court highlighted the following:

> Similarly, it defies common sense and reason to accept that a lawyer who receives an email from his expert that refers to another expert's report as a 'load of bs', and further states that 'my guess is that he is never given expert evidence in court before, and Izaak has not told him that he cannot protect him from cross-examination. He thinks that he can get away with this crap', could fail to recognize that the expert was too personally involved to objectively comment upon the other expert's methodology and conclusions … the Court can reach no conclusion other than that [the lawyer] was aware, or should have been, that [the expert] had taken on a role beyond that of an expert witness.
>
> … the decision to provide the Court with expert testimony is part of the role of the lawyer having carriage of the matter, and his or her professional expertise should include an understanding that it undermines the integrity of the justice system to direct a biased expert to step into the witness box … [The lawyer] cannot shield himself from costs where he has acted in a manner that is contrary to the administration of justice. Accordingly, I must find that it is [counsel] who caused the unnecessary waste of costs.[19]

In *Seaspan* ULC *v. Director, Environmental Management Act*,[20] the British Columbia Environmental Appeal Board (the board) awarded costs against an appellant, despite its policy to only award costs in "special circumstances." The special circumstances justifying an award of costs require a party's behaviour to be reprehensible. After hearing submissions on the question of costs, the board ordered the appellant to pay the respondent and third parties their costs. In doing so, the board was critical about many aspects of the appellant's expert's opinion and about the dealings between the expert and counsel. The board's concerns included that:

(1) the expert's conclusion had changed from a previous draft that stated that contamination "could have" resulted from a particular source to an opinion in the final draft that "more probably than not" the contamination resulted from that source;

(2) the original question posed to the expert had been whether the contamination "could have originated" from a particular source,

whereas the question posed for the final report had morphed to what was "the cause of the contamination" (with no corresponding additional analysis being conducted by the expert);

(3) on counsel's directions, the expert did not address in his report significant evidence that contradicted his opinion;
(4) the expert in direct examination changed his position on a material aspect from his written opinion without explaining to the panel that he had done so, let alone explaining why.

The board concluded that the expert's opinion was deceptive, that he had ignored relevant data (including ignoring data on the instructions of counsel), and that the opinions were such that his report was "fundamentally unsound and irredeemably flawed." In issuing an award for costs, the board also held that the expert's client bore responsibility for advancing a position that was "ill conceived," "preposterous," and "should never have been pursued."

## THE LAWYER'S ROLE IN ASSISTING AN EXPERT IN PREPARING THE REPORT

### General Practice

In assisting an expert in preparing his or her report, counsel should:[21]

(1) ensure the expert's retainer letter does not suggest the desired opinion;
(2) ensure the expert receives an objective set of facts;
(3) limit communications between counsel and expert while the expert is reviewing the facts and formulating the substance of his or her opinion;
(4) discuss the expert's views orally before he or she provides anything in writing;
(5) limit the number of drafts provided to counsel;
(6) keep counsel's editing of the report to a minimum.

Despite these points of caution, the courts have permitted certain involvement from counsel, as discussed in the cases below.

### Case Law

In *Vancouver Community College v. Phillips, Barratt*,[22] disclosure of the expert's working files demonstrated that the expert revised his opinion several times at the suggestion of counsel. The court ultimately held the revisions went beyond mere clarification and the opinion was rejected. Finch J. stated as follows:

I in no way wish to condemn the practice of an expert's editing or rewriting his own reports prepared for submission in evidence, or for that matter, prepared solely for the advice of counsel or litigants. Nor do I wish to condemn the practice of counsel consulting with his experts in the pre-trial process while 'reports' are in the course of preparation. It is, however, of the utmost importance in both the rewriting and consultation processes referred to that the expert's independence, objectivity and integrity not be compromised. I have no doubt that in many cases these ends are achieved, and counsel and experts alike respect the essential boundaries concerning the extent to which a lawyer may properly discuss the expert's work product as it develops towards its final form.

Regrettably, in this case, the boundaries were not observed. I cannot avoid saying that generally counsel participated far too much, and inappropriately, in the preparation of [Mr. A's] reports. [Mr. A] willingly permitted such participating by counsel and seriously compromised the objectivity of his opinions. Counsel suggested, and [Mr. A] agreed to, many additions and deletions to his report. These suggestions went far beyond statements concerning factual hypotheses, their evidentiary foundation, the definition of issues, or other matters on which counsel might properly have advised or commented. Rather, the suggestions went to the substance of [Mr. A's] opinions and the way in which they were expressed. The suggested changes were all one way.[23]

In *William et al. v. British Columbia et al.*,[24] the court stated as follows with respect to the expert's file and counsel's involvement therein:

The exchange of correspondence between counsel and [the expert] contained unfortunate language which left open the argument that counsel dictated the opinion required and [the expert] complied with the dictates of counsel. Counsel's editing of the report left open a similar argument. Counsel should strive, at all times, not to place themselves in the position where their conduct becomes a focal point of the court's concerns.

In *Medimmune Ltd. v. Novartis Pharmaceuticals, UK Ltd. & Anor*,[25] the England and Wales High Court noted that expert witnesses may require a "high level of instruction by the lawyers" and "considerable assistance from the lawyers drafting their report" in highly technical areas such as patent law. Despite this, the court cautioned that lawyers must always keep the expert's need to remain objective at the forefront.

In *Maras*, the court directed plaintiff's counsel to review the deficient expert reports with the expectation that the length of the reports could be considerably shortened and accordingly made more accessible to the jury. The court further stated that counsel has a role in helping experts to provide a report that satisfies the criteria of admissibility and quoted Justice McColl in *Surrey Credit Union v. Willson*:[26]

> There can be no criticism of counsel assisting an expert witness in the preparation of giving evidence. Where the assistance goes to form as opposed to the substance of the opinion itself no objection can be raised. It would be quite unusual in a case of this complexity if counsel did not spend some time in the preparation of witnesses before they were called to give evidence. It is no less objectionable to engage in the same process where the witness to be called is an expert. Indeed had the process been followed here much of the objectionable material might have been avoided.[27]

In *Moore v. Getahun*,[28] at issue was the preparation of expert reports in the context of a medical malpractice action. The trial judge held it was improper for counsel to assist an expert witness in the preparation of the expert's report. During cross-examination at trial, the expert indicated he had sent a draft of one of his reports to the appellant's counsel for review. The expert testified he had produced his final report following an hour and a half conference call with counsel. The trial judge expressed concern over the call and asked the expert to organize his file in chronological order and to provide the court with draft reports. The judge also directed the appellant's counsel to provide the court with all instructing letters and records of any conference calls. Subsequently, the expert's draft reports were reviewed in detail and the notations and changes made as a result of discussing the draft reports with the appellant's counsel were scrutinized. Ultimately, the trial judge rejected the expert's evidence, as she concluded there had been significant changes as a result of discussions with counsel and the expert's duty of impartiality was breached.

The issue on appeal was whether the trial judge erred in her treatment of the appellant's expert opinion evidence by criticizing the appellant's counsel for discussing with an expert witness the content of his draft report. The Ontario Court of Appeal accepted that consultation between counsel and expert witnesses in the preparation of reports, within certain limits, is necessary to ensure the efficient and orderly presentation of expert evidence and the timely, affordable, and just resolution of claims. In addition, the court held the changes to the expert's draft report could be described as relatively minor, editorial, and stylistic modifications intended to improve the clarity of the reports. The court held there was no evidence of any significant change in substance or anything to indicate that either counsel or the expert did anything improper or that the expert's report reflected anything other than his own genuine and unbiased opinion.

Ultimately, the Ontario Court of Appeal held the trial judge erred in holding it was unacceptable for counsel to review and discuss the draft expert reports. In its reasons, the Ontario Court of Appeal emphasized that reviewing a draft report enables counsel to ensure that the report: (i) complies with the rules of civil procedure and the rules of evidence; (ii) addresses and is restricted to the relevant issues; and (iii) is written in a manner and style that is accessible and comprehensible.

## The Retainer Letter

### GENERAL PRACTICE

When dealing with experts the importance of the retaining letter cannot be overstated. The retainer letter governs the relationship between the expert, counsel, and retaining party. Accordingly, its terms must be carefully considered and tailored to the particular case, the expert at hand, and the specific role that the expert is expected to play. At the very least, the retainer letter for an expert witness should include clarity on the following:

(1) the question or issues the expert is expected to address;
(2) the expert's obligations to the court;
(3) the facts and assumptions the expert is expected to rely on; and
(4) the materials the expert is entitled to rely on in formulating his or her opinion.

In addition to the foregoing, counsel should address with the expert, perhaps outside the retainer letter, the following issues:

(1) expectations about confidentiality and dealing with persons adverse in interest;

(2) the principles governing the admissibility of expert reports under the rules of civil procedure and the legal limits on expert testimony;
(3) the preservation and disclosure of the expert's file, including, notes, working papers, drafts, and correspondence; and
(4) a fee arrangement, which must not include an "incentive" or "contingency" agreement.

### WHEN THE EXPERT HAS A DUAL ROLE

The retainer letter may be slightly more complex if one expert is retained as both an expert advisor and expert witness. In this circumstance, the letter should clearly state that the retainer is for two separate services, namely that the expert is to provide (1) advice and consulting services and (2) opinions. Some practitioner's instruct their experts to keep two separate files for the expert's two separate roles. It is unclear from the authorities whether by doing so a party can resist the disclosure of their expert's "advisory" files once the expert is tendered as an expert witness.

#### NOTES

1 BC Reg 168/2009.
2 RRO 1990, Reg 194.
3 *IFP Technologies (Canada) v Encana Midstream and Marketing*, 2014 ABQB 470.
4 [1987] BCJ No 3149 [*Vancouver Community College*].
5 *Ibid* at para 27
6 2014 BCSC 741.
7 Ibid at paras 41 and 44
8 *Vancouver Community College, supra* note 4 at para 34.
9 1988 CanLII 3195 at para 11 (BCSC).
10 *Expert Evidence in British Columbia Civil Proceedings* (Vancouver: Continuing Legal Education Society of British Columbia, 2011).
11 LSG Finch, "The Court's Perspective" in *Experts and Experts Reports* (Vancouver: Continuing Legal Education Society of British Columbia, 1988).
12 [2003] BCJ No 1804.
13 2010 BCSC 1706.
14 2011 BCSC 1159.
15 2014 BCSC 1109 [*Maras*].
16 (1998), 59 BCLR (3d) 336 (CA).
17 2010 BCSC 1478.
18 2014 ONSC 3698.
19 *Ibid* at paras 45 and 46
20 Decision Nos 2010-EMA-005(c) and 2010-EMA-006(c).
21 Nevin Fishman, *Preparation of the Expert Report – How Much Input from Counsel?* (Vancouver: Continuing Legal Education Society of British Columbia, 2009).
22 [1988] BCJ No 710.
23 *Ibid* at paras 33 and 34
24 2005 BCSC 131 at para 34.
25 [2011] EWHC 1669 at para 110 (Pat).
26 1990 CanLII 1983 (BCSC).
27 *Maras, supra* note 15 at para 90.
28 2015 ONCA 55.

# 42

# Continuity of Evidence and Remediation Advice for Investigators: Some Brief Comments

JOHN D. CLIFFE, Q.C., AND JOHN S.G. CLARK*

In any environmental incident, two vital matters that investigators, first responders, and legal counsel must be mindful of, are continuity of the evidence gathered and timely remediation of the environment.

## Continuity of Evidence

My comments are from an enforcement and prosecutorial perspective.

### "CONTINUITY" ORDINARILY DEFINED

The plain and ordinary definition of the word "continuity" is a "connection uninterrupted; cohesion; close union of parts."[1] "Continuity" is also defined as "the state of being continuous; uninterrupted succession."[2]

### "CONTINUITY" IN THE LEGAL CONTEXT: GENERALLY

The issue of continuity, or what is sometimes referred to as "continuity of possession" or what some American jurisdictions have termed "chain of custody," arises when real evidence, including articles of physical evidence, is tendered in legal proceedings such as a trial.

Watt's Manual of Criminal Evidence, 2013, defines real evidence to include

** Mr. Cliffe will address "Continuity of Evidence" and Mr. Clark will address "Remediation Advice for Investigators." The statements, opinions, and views of the writers herein are solely those of the writers and are not those of or reflective of either Cliffe Tobias, Barristers & Solicitors, the Federal Department of Justice and/or the Government of Canada.*

> any evidence that conveys a relevant *first-hand sense impression* to the trier of fact. In other words it appeals to the trier of fact to use their own senses to make observations and draw conclusions, rather than being told about the object by a witness … [and it] is unlimited in its variety. It includes, but is not limited to production of articles, observations of demeanor or appearance of witnesses, taking a view, and audio or videorecordings. It may be direct or circumstantial in nature.[3]

The introduction of real evidence, including physical evidence (articles of all kind), as exhibits at trial requires a foundation of admissibility laid by the testimony of witnesses or admissions at trial made by the accused. A proper foundation rests on three points.[4]

One, the proposed exhibit must have relevance to the proceedings. In other words, it has probative value in proving a fact in issue. Two, it is what it purports to be and accordingly is authentic and/or identifiable. Three, a witness or witnesses must verify the authenticity or otherwise identify the proposed exhibit.

Continuity is relevant to the above second point. In this regard, it must be shown, for example, that the proposed exhibit is the same one that was seized[5] or received during the investigation; if its source is relevant, that it came from the particular source;[6] it has not been tampered with;[7] or its chemical composition if relevant has not been altered, contaminated, or modified in any manner prior to its forensic analysis.[8] Accordingly, evidence being *viva voce* evidence is required to prove continuity unless, as stated above, an admission of proof of continuity is made by the accused.

It is trite to say that the evidentiary onus of proof of continuity is on the party tendering the proposed exhibit. In the case of an exhibit tendered by the prosecution it is upon the Crown, who has the overarching onus of proving its case against the accused beyond a reasonable doubt, to establish continuity of the proposed exhibit.

A failure to prove continuity can have adverse and drastic consequences, the most serious of which is that the proposed exhibit is found by the court to be inadmissible. If the exhibit is found admissible, however, the court may rule that the exhibit and any collateral evidence such as analytical results pertaining to the exhibit may have little evidentiary value or what is termed "little weight."

For example, in the context of a drug prosecution the failure to prove continuity of a sample of the seized drug has been commented upon as follows:

> Where the continuity of possession has been broken, and where the evidence gives rise to a reasonable apprehension the exhibit may have become contaminated, the courts have generally resolved any doubt on the issue in favour of the accused.... None the less, such doubts must be based on reasonable grounds and not a mere 'fantasy of the mind' ...[9]

That said, the courts have on occasion relaxed the requirements for strict proof of continuity. For example, in the case of continuity of a proposed exhibit whose chemical composition is relevant, the courts have held that continuity need only be established with respect to the period from the time of seizure or receipt to the completion of analyses.

It has also been long recognized that, depending on the facts of the case (including evidence of various precautionary measures), gaps in continuity are permissible where it is highly unlikely that any alteration, contamination, or modification occurred.[10] For example, such a gap where precautionary measures have been taken and the means by which proposed exhibits are transported are viewed as trustworthy, such as by mail and/or commercial delivery by bus, truck, and aircraft, has not been problematic.

### CONTINUITY IN THE ENVIRONMENTAL CONTEXT: GENERALLY

Given that most environmental investigations involve the collection of samples of pollutants and/or impacted environment, including waters, fish, and wildlife and that prosecutions of same involve tendering evidence of such samples and the results of their forensic analyses (chemical composition, fish bioassay testing, etc.), the issue of continuity is a live one at trial unless there is an admission by the accused. Of course, and as stated above, other items of physical evidence gathered during the investigation and to be tendered at a trial will attract the requirement to prove continuity with respect to those items.

An environmental prosecution should never be lost on the basis of failure to prove continuity!

It has been my experience that most government environmental protection agencies have internal procedures governing continuity of collected evidence and that such procedures are followed such that continuity is frequently admitted by the accused. However, there are exceptions, which will be addressed in oral presentation.

As the collection of samples such as those mentioned above is such an integral part of an environmental investigation I will focus my comments regarding continuity to that form of real evidence.

## WHEN CONTINUITY IS ENGAGED IN THE ENVIRONMENTAL CONTEXT

In government environmental protection agencies, the question commonly asked is "are we taking legal samples or non-legal samples." The answer dictates whether continuity has to be established by the investigator.

The difference is based on whether the sample and its results are to further a criminal investigation of the environmental incident and subsequently be used in legal proceedings, hence the word "legal." The reference to "non-legal" is to what is sometimes termed "routine sampling" by the agency for compliance purposes, which does not require the rigours of continuity.

This difference and what is entailed by it, including continuity, are aptly described in the *Interpol Environmental Security Sub-Directorate Pollution Crime Forensic Investigation Manual, 2014* (the *Interpol* Manual), and as follows:

> The distinction between legal sampling and routine sampling is the ability to prove in court the chain-of-custody of a sample. This is the practice of ensuring security of the sample so that no one has an opportunity to tamper with or otherwise alter the sample or the results. The prevention of tampering involves the placement of seals on the sample container and locking the sample in storage, shipping containers and/or vehicles in such a manner so that no one other than the documented sample handlers has direct access to the samples.... Legal sampling involves approximately 30% more effort to carefully handle and document the samples and evidence. Laboratories require additional security procedures and may charge up to 50% more for handling legal samples and providing special legal reports. [Emphasis added.][11]

When specifically legal sampling should be undertaken may be dictated by an agency's internal sampling policies and procedures or by decision in the moment by management staff or individual investigators. The *Interpol* Manual recommends that legal sampling should be conducted in the following circumstances:

- When you strongly suspect a violation may have or is occurring for which an enforcement action and/or a penalty is likely to apply;
- Spills or environmental accidents;
- When you have no previous knowledge about compliance history;
- There is unlikely to be a subsequent chance to collect a sample or the cost/logistics of collecting a subsequent sample are prohibitively high.

## ESTABLISHING AND PROVING CONTINUITY OF LEGAL SAMPLES

It is trite to say that the investigator who conducts legal sampling will have control at least in part over continuity of those samples. Other agency staff may be involved in subsequent handling of the sample containers and as a result be in control of continuity.

Leaving aside sampling procedure and its conduct, continuity may comprise requirements for sample containers appropriate and specific to the type of samples being taken, including appropriate lids and lid liners for the containers; sufficient detailed and lasting labels affixed, marked, and/or scratched on the sample container to later permit authentication and identification in court; seals sufficiently affixed to the sample container such that the seal must be destroyed to open the container, thereby confirming whether someone has had access to the container; interim storage before being transported to the forensic laboratory; use of a lockable shipping container to store the sample containers for transport; transport to or arranging transportation to the forensic laboratory for analyses and testing; taking photographs or video to record the continuity process; completed detailed documentation, usually on a specific agency continuity form, recording all dealings with the sample containers (and/or shipping container storing the sample containers); making detailed notes of the sampling and continuity thereafter.[12]

In addition, there is the continuity process followed at the forensic laboratory, which includes receipt of the sample containers and interim storage prior to and during analyses.

Unless there is an admission made by the accused of proof of continuity, counsel tendering legal samples and their analytical results as exhibits at trial must prove it. As a result counsel must know and understand the continuity process followed by the investigator, other agency staff, and the forensic laboratory so counsel can gather and present the evidence of it in an organized and cohesive manner.

## Remediation Advice for Investigators

My interest in this subject arose from a series of courses John Cliffe and I worked on. We spoke at several dozen multi-day environmental enforcement workshops across the country. Early on we realized we needed to address this, as investigators consistently brought up a variety of fascinating real life scenarios on this subject.

Besides addressing the queries of the investigators, we found there were several reasons for providing legal advice on this subject, including:

- Cleanup is always a good idea. Our assumption, which seemed to be shared by many, was that it is always in the Crown's interest, the public interest, and the interest of the accused to restore, remediate, and/or protect the environment as well and as quickly as is feasible;
- The Crown should not get in the way. It would be detrimental to the Crown's case to have any suggestion that an investigation in any way hampered remediation efforts; or that greater harm to the environment resulted because an investigation complicated remediation works of the accused;
- Uncertainty due to investigation. Some accused have stated in court, or otherwise, that they would have quickly cleaned up a site, or significantly lessened the environmental impact of works, but no one in authority ask them to do so; and in the circumstances of uniformed officers attending their premises, they did not want to take any steps without specific direction. One can easily imagine circumstances where it would look (and be) unreasonable if the Crown did not take immediate steps to remediate harm;
- Timing. Many types of environmental impacts benefit significantly from prompt cleanup efforts. If the harm is left to be dealt with by way of a court order, adverse environmental effects may be greater or last longer;
- All this goes to sentencing; any efforts, successes, or lack thereof by the accused will be relevant to any sentences or orders imposed upon conviction. In some cases complete and timely restoration may be a factor in the Crown not proceeding with charges.

## WHAT SHOULD INVESTIGATORS AND THEIR LEGAL COUNSEL BEAR IN MIND REGARDING REMEDIATION?

Who is the accused and what is the accused doing? The first matter an investigator should confirm is if the accused has already undertaken all reasonable remediation efforts. Many larger companies or public utilities will have the mandate and resources to undertake remediation efforts at the earliest reasonable time. Investigators can often quickly determine if a corporate accused is taking all such steps. If this is the case, remediation issues will likely not be relevant to investigative efforts.

How complex is the problem? Often, devising measures to protect or remediate the environment is more complicated than lay people appreciate. There are many sites and many environmental problems that cannot be feasibly remediated and that will only be made worse by human efforts. Providing advice to an accused that makes a site worse will be detrimental to both the environment and a potential prosecution.

How sophisticated is the accused? Sometimes the offence at issue is at least in part due to the lack of expertise or care of the accused. Investigators should consider whether it makes sense to have this particular accused, corporate or otherwise, undertake delicate remedial efforts.

Use of experts? If the circumstances are beyond the capabilities of the investigators and/or the regulators, they may be able to use experts within their ministry, or who are known to their ministry. Conversely, investigators can suggest, encourage, or in some cases direct an accused to obtain appropriate expertise to provide a remediation or cleanup plan.

### INVESTIGATORS AND THEIR LEGAL COUNSEL NEED TO BE CLEAR AS TO THE CROWN'S POSITION.

The following is noted:

- Investigators should leave no doubt that their actions will not hamper remediation efforts. If this is an issue, investigators must secure the most important and time-sensitive physical evidence (e.g. samples; photographs; taking measurements; identifying individuals) and leave witness interviews until they will not impact remediation efforts;
- Investigators should document their remediation advice. For example, this can be done by using emails to confirm onsite recommendations and suggestions;
- Provide complete cleanup advice. In my experience DFO officers have a practice of sending cleanup advice letters soon after attending an impacted site. The letters explicitly confirm that the advice does not entail a promise of avoiding prosecution, nor are the cleanup or remediation recommendations and suggestions to be considered a threat of prosecution. The letters can provide and document the best advice of the regulator as to how to remediate the impacted environment;
- Issue a Direction. Various environmental acts allow regulators to issue directions to remediate. Where applicable, this practice can have environmental and legal benefits.

Where potential accused comply with such directions and mitigate environmental harm, this action will at least go to sentencing, and place an accused in a more sympathetic light in a prosecution. In some cases significant remedial efforts may influence the Crown not to proceed with a prosecution.

Conversely, if a statutory direction is not complied with, this may result in further charges brought by the Crown. A prosecution for failure to comply with such a direction is typically easier to prove in court, as due diligence will rarely be an issue.

## DID THE REGULATOR MAKE A DEAL?

What are the legal consequences if a regulator, or government expert, or an investigator implies that charges will go away if everything is cleaned up? To my knowledge, the Crown does not have a position as to whether this is an appropriate practice. However, if such comments are made, and an accused does undertake the requested cleanup efforts, it would appear to be problematic for the Crown to continue to prosecute, as the accused would likely raise a good argument that to do so would be an abuse of process for which a judicial stay of proceedings is warranted.

## HOW LONG WILL THE CLEANUP TAKE?

Sometimes remediation planning, discussions, and works can take place over several years. Investigators and their legal counsel should remain aware of the applicable statutory limitation periods under which the Crown can bring charges. The regulator may find itself statute barred if remediation works never eventually take place or continue for an unreasonable period of time.

We hope that the above comments are helpful.

### NOTES

1 Virginia S Thatcher & Alexander MacQueen, eds, *The New Webster Encyclopedic Dictionary of the English Language* (New York: Avenel Books, 1984) at 185.
2 *Webster's Dictionary For Everyday Use* (Florida: PSI Associates, 1988) at 85.
3 *Ibid* at 82–83.
4 Lee Stuesser, *An Advocacy Primer*, 3d ed (Toronto: Thomson Carswell, 2005) at 228 [Stuesser].
5 Bruce A MacFarlane, *Drug Offences in Canada* (Toronto: Canada Law Book, 1979) at 305 [MacFarlane].
6 *R v Andrade* (1985), 18 CCC (3d) 41 at 61 (Ont CA).
7 Stuesser, *supra* note 4 at 228.
8 MacFarlane, *supra* note 5 at 305–306.
9 *Ibid* at 306.
10 *Ibid* at 307–308.
11 *Ibid* at 105.
12 *Ibid* at 106–111.

# 43

# Proving the Right to Be Heard: Evidentiary Barriers to Standing in Environmental Matters

ADAM DRIEDZIC

## Introduction

"Standing" is the legal status necessary to receive a hearing from a court or an administrative board or tribunal (a "tribunal"). In 2014 the Environmental Law Centre in Edmonton completed a major review of standing in environmental matters from which this chapter is derived.[1]

Evidence is rarely treated as its own topic with respect to standing. Most courts, legislatures, academic commentators, and law reform institutes have been more focused on the legal tests for standing. Yet, facts are very important to individual determinations of standing under these tests. The core issue in environmental matters is that the traditional approach to standing was developed by the common law courts in the context of the adversarial litigation system. Many tests for standing require evidence of personal interests and harm to those interests, whereas in environmental matters the interests are often collectively held and the harm to those interests is indirect. There are uncertainties about what must be proven, who should bear the burden of proof, what the standard of proof should be, and whether standing should be determined as a preliminary matter separate from the merits of the substantive claims. These issues can be acute at environmental tribunals, where the proceedings are not litigation and the rules of evidence need not apply.

Case law on standing at environmental tribunals is sparse, but evidentiary issues are central and trends are emerging. Courts in multiple provinces are following the tests articulated by legislatures for standing at administrative hearings, but are intervening against tribunals that create unnecessary evidentiary and procedural barriers. They are also beginning to articulate concerns with fairness, access to justice, and with upholding the mandates of tribunals. This suggests that a cohesive jurisprudence on standing at tribunals may be within reach.

## The Evidentiary Issues

The evidentiary issues in standing are similar at courts and tribunals despite the different mandates of these institutions. These issues are not really about the sufficiency of facts upon which to base environmental decisions. They are about rules and practices that make it hard to show sufficient facts to trigger hearings. These issues can be understood as: what must be proven; who should bear the "burden of proof"; what the appropriate "standard of proof" should be; and whether standing should be determined as a preliminary matter.

### WHAT MUST BE PROVEN?

What must be proven to establish standing is dependent on how the legal tests for standing are articulated. Many tests are notoriously vague and provide minimal guidance to decision makers. These tests require that persons be "directly affected," "adversely affected," "aggrieved," or suffer a particular "prejudice."[2] The leading academic commentary has called these tests a "semantic wasteland," a criticism that has been noted by the Federal Court and Federal Court of Appeal.[3]

An additional problem in public law matters is that the legal tests for standing favour private property and economic interests. They may even imply a need to show possible causation of harm to those interests. Requirements for harm to personal interests create disproportionate barriers to standing in environmental matters because the interests at stake are often collectively held and the impacts on those interests are often indirect.

### THE BURDEN OF PROOF

The burden of proving standing is on the person seeking standing. This appears uncontentious but it is not. Law reform commissions in multiple jurisdictions have proposed tests that resemble a presumption of standing in public law matters.[4] This presumption would be rebuttable by specific arguments against standing, such as the need to conserve judicial resources. Likewise, the Manitoba Public Interest Law Centre once proposed that environmental reviews should allow all persons to make their submissions subject to requirements for relevance and tribunal authority to take efficiency measures.[5] The

University of Victoria Environmental Law Centre has expressed concern with the tribunal process of placing the burden of proving standing on persons harmed by pollution rather than requiring persons seeking to pollute to show that they will not cause harm.[6] Some tribunals already offer a rebuttable presumption of standing, for example to landowners within a set distance from proposed industrial projects.[7]

All of these examples of presumptive standing would put focus on the substantive issues instead of the interests of the parties. They could reduce disputes about standing and ensure that reasons for denying standing are based on real circumstances rather than hypothetical ones.

### THE STANDARD OF PROOF

The standard of proof for determining standing is often lower than the "balance of probabilities" standard that must be met to prove civil claims. The appropriate standard is sometimes stated as a *prima facie* case. This low standard of proof emphasizes the distinction between standing and the merits of substantive claims, and is warranted where standing is determined as a preliminary matter.

### PRELIMINARY DETERMINATIONS OF STANDING

Standing may be determined as a preliminary matter, but need not be. The tension is between the efficiency of preliminary determinations and the risk of dismissing meritorious claims without the full evidence available.[8] To resolve this tension, multiple law reform reports recommend determining standing as a preliminary matter, using relaxed tests for standing.[9]

## Standing in the Courts

Common law tests for standing and determinations of standing under those tests frequently merge questions of law, fact, and judicial policy. The two key tests in public law matters are the English "public nuisance rule" and the Canadian development of "public interest standing." The "public nuisance rule" provides that the appropriate plaintiff to enforce public rights is either the Attorney General or someone with the Attorney General's consent.[10] Private citizens who lack consent can only enforce public rights if their own private rights have also been harmed or if they have suffered harm that is different from that suffered by the general public. This rule is constantly criticized as ineffective for environmental matters, but it persists.[11] "Public interest standing" is a late 20th-century Canadian development that diverges from the historic public nuisance rule in limited circumstances. This discretionary form of standing is granted to uphold the role of the courts in scrutinizing legality. To date, it has been made available to challenge the constitutionality of legislation and the legality of administrative action. The test considers whether there is a "serious issue" suitable for judicial determination, whether the plaintiff is "directly affected" or demonstrates a "genuine interest," and whether the proposed litigation provides a reasonable and effective means for the issue to be heard by the courts.[12]

The largest evidentiary barrier to common law standing is what must be proven to pass the public nuisance rule. The courts are inconsistent on whether the harm suffered by private citizens must be different from the general public "in kind" or "in degree."[13] It is possible that the required factual circumstances could be more extreme than those required to initiate private litigation.

If the issues are ones for which public interest standing is available then the courts have eliminated the evidentiary barriers. The Supreme Court of Canada (SCC) has not provided much help in this endeavour. SCC cases on public interest standing are all non-environmental matters and most feature directly affected plaintiffs, so the SCC has provided minimal guidance on what amounts to a "genuine interest." Consequently, some early environmental cases in the lower courts diverged on what must be proven. The British Columbia Supreme Court (BCSC) required some difference from the general public.[14] In contrast, the Alberta Court of Queen's Bench (ABQB) held that the interest could be shared by thousands of others.[15] Eventually the lower courts established objective indicators of "genuine interest" in environmental matters that are fairly consistent across jurisdictions. The most important indicators are the purpose of environmental organizations and their record of involvement in the issues or subject matter.[16] The records of members, directors, or affiliates of organizations can be probative as well.[17] Prior participation or activities related to the dispute can help establish an interest, but their absence does not hurt.[18] The BC courts have weighted geographic proximity to environmental impacts, but only in cases where this has assisted persons seeking standing.[19] The Federal Court has found geographic proximity to be fairly irrelevant due to the interconnectedness and complexity of modern society.[20] The Federal Court's approach somewhat resembles the manner in which interveners are screened, where the court looks for "experience" or "expertise" to help resolve the issues.[21]

In non-environmental matters, the SCC has denied public interest standing multiple times because of the existence of other possible means for the issue to be litigated.[22] This jurisprudence was criticized for reliance on hypothetical circumstances, theoretical fears, and latent ideology over reality.[23] In 2012, the SCC deliberately lowered this barrier by considering the practical reality of equivalent litigation occurring and the appropriateness of public interest plaintiffs.[24] This development has been lauded by advocates in non-environmental disciplines.[25] However, it may have minimal effect on environmental matters. Standing in environmental matters is rarely ever denied due to other means for issues to be litigated, because often no one is more directly affected or able to litigate than the public interest organization.

The "burden of proof" on the plaintiff remains uncontested in the jurisprudence despite the above commentary to the effect that this practice is questionable. The "standard of proof" is rarely articulated, but it is fairly low. Usually the plaintiff must simply show some facts to establish their "genuine interest." In contrast, their opponents must prove on a "balance of probabilities" that there is no arguable case. For example, the Federal Court of Appeal has held that standing should only be used to discourage meddlers and not to pre-emptively determine that litigation has no cause of action.[26] This indicates a difference between standing in public law matters and attempts to bring private law claims against government, as in the latter case the threshold issue may be the existence of a cause of action.

The courts may determine standing as a preliminary matter if the issues, evidence, and arguments available provide a sufficient understanding of the interest being asserted.[27] Commitment to this practice varies by jurisdiction. The Federal Court consistently makes preliminary determinations, and if standing is granted then it ceases to be an issue. Some cases from Alberta and British Columbia note that it may be necessary to determine standing through hearings on the full evidence and merits of substantive claims.[28] Overall, the largest barrier to standing in environmental litigation is not evidentiary but rather the limited legal issues for which public interest standing is available.

## Standing at Tribunals

Standing at tribunals has received less attention than standing in the courts, but this is changing. The analysis must begin with an understanding that tribunals are not courts. Tribunal hearings may resemble litigation due to evidence and argument from the parties, but this resemblance is superficial.[29] Courts must establish the facts of past events to decide legal disputes between the parties in a yes–no manner. Tribunal hearings rarely involve legal disputes between the parties, and even if so there are further public interests at stake.

Tribunal decisions must look to the future, which favours a range of reasonable outcomes.

Another key difference is that tribunals have no inherent jurisdiction to hear issues or grant standing. Tribunal authority to determine standing must come through ordinary legislation. There are countless legislated models, ranging from completely open standing to the exclusion of everyone except for categorized rights holders. The implication of legislated mandates is that tribunal determinations of standing have sometimes been treated as questions of "law and fact" on the basis that the relevant policy is that of the legislature.[30] Whether tribunals can grant common law public interest standing is a separate issue tackled elsewhere by the Environmental Law Centre and others.[31]

The evidentiary issues common to courts and tribunals can be aggravated by tribunal procedure. Persons seeking standing may be inexperienced and may face tight deadlines on which to file written statements or forms. Even if the parties submit sworn affidavits there may be no hearing on standing, prehearing conferences, or opportunities to challenge contrary evidence. Determinations of standing may be issued through letters to the parties or through decision documents that rely on the paper submissions.

There are few cases on standing at environmental tribunals, but evidentiary issues are often central to these cases. Most of the following examples from Alberta, British Columbia, and Ontario concern air emissions. This affirms the challenge created by collective interests and indirect impacts.

## REGULATORY BOARDS IN ALBERTA

Several striking examples of high evidentiary barriers come from regulatory boards in Alberta. Standing at these tribunals is provided to persons who may be "directly and adversely affected" by proposed energy and utility projects. Determinations of standing to intervene in the regulatory decision are made as a preliminary matter through letters to the persons seeking standing. The Alberta Court of Appeal (ABCA) treats determinations of standing by these tribunals as a question of "law and fact," requiring a legally recognizable interest and evidence that it may be affected.[32] The tribunals show preference for property and economic interests. Historically the ABCA has upheld denials of standing to more indirect interests.[33] The court only requires a *prima facie* case of adverse effects.[34] However, it can find that this low standard is not met, even in cases featuring geographically proximate property and economic interests.[35]

Since 2009 the ABCA has shown propensity to intervene where the tribunals create evidentiary barriers beyond those required by legislation. Three key cases concern the same group of landowners exposed to health risks from proposed sour gas wells. The tribunal in question is a recently defunct Energy Resources Conservation Board. In *Kelly v. Alberta* (*Kelly #1*), the ABCA overturned a denial of standing and ordered the tribunal to grant standing and hold a hearing.[36] The tribunal had produced a model of airborne gas which indicated that the landowners resided in a zone where there was a risk of life-threatening and possibly irreversible health effects in the event of a gas release. This geographic proximity created a right to be consulted by the proponent company under a standardized regulatory directive issued by the tribunal. The ABCA held that a person with this right to be consulted qualified as directly and adversely affected for the purpose of standing. The court rejected the tribunal's interpretation of the standing test as requiring that a person show that they may be affected to a greater or different degree than the general public.

After *Kelly #1*, the tribunal changed its airborne gas model in a manner that excluded the landowners from this zone of high risk, claiming a technical error in the prior model. In *Kelly v. Alberta* (*Kelly #2*), the landowners resided within a lower risk zone where persons would be advised to evacuate or take shelter in the event of a gas release.[37] The tribunal denied standing due to inadequate evidence supporting a claim that the landowners' existing medical conditions would be aggravated by the gas. It also stated that risk of evacuation was not an "adverse" effect because evacuation is a benefit. The ABCA rejected the tribunal's findings on both points, holding that the right to intervene was designed for persons with "legitimate concerns" to have input into decisions "that will have a recognizable impact on their rights."[38]

The ABCA continued to overturn the tribunal in a third case concerning intervener costs.[39] After being ordered to grant standing in *Kelly #1*, the tribunal held a hearing, but it denied intervener costs under a semantically narrower test that required a directly and adversely affected interest in "land." The ABCA found that the landowners were eligible for costs despite this different test. Again it emphasized the role of hearings in the regulatory process. Most notably it articulated a view of regulatory proceedings as not purely win-lose or adversarial in the manner of litigation.

The *Kelly* cases are significant in several regards. Foremost, they concern a regulatory board making original decisions in the public interest. This context is even less like litigation as compared to quasi-judicial appeals tribunals. Concerning what must be proven, the court definitely focused on individual interests, but it rejected requirements to be differently affected from the general public. The court never questioned that the interveners must prove their standing, but it might have sensed a moving goalpost. In *Kelly #1*, the tribunal created requirements beyond the legislation while ignoring participation rights in its own regulations. Following the case, it shifted its own hypothetical model rather than acknowledging real impacts on people. In *Kelly #2*, the tribunal's requirements practically resembled "toxic tort" litigation where plaintiffs must prove that specific pollution causes their individual health problems. This can be impossible to prove in a full trial with tested expert evidence, let alone through a preliminary determination on paper submissions. The standard of proof implied by the tribunal was higher than the legislated requirement that one "may" be affected, so the court properly focused on the existence of a risk of harm.

## APPEALS TRIBUNALS IN ALBERTA

In multiple cases since the mid-1990s, the Alberta courts have considered whether community activists pass a "directly affected" test for standing at appeals tribunals. Two foundational cases concern a now-defunct public health tribunal.[40] In both cases the ABCA upheld denials of standing by the tribunal, finding that the test required personal rather than communal interests. This authority was followed by the ABQB in *Kostuch v. Alberta* to uphold a denial of standing by the current Alberta Environmental Appeals Board.[41] The court held that there must be a causal connection between these personal interests and the matter under appeal. In the subsequent case of *Court v. Alberta* it overturned a denial of standing by this tribunal, holding that the effects on personal interests need not be different in kind from any other Albertan or user of the area.[42] The court held that standard of proof only requires a *prima facie* case that interests may be affected, not that they be affected. It found that the tribunal imposed an unreasonable test and evidentiary requirements that were inconsistent with the participatory role envisaged by the legislation. It also held that standing should be determined as a preliminary matter. The case centred on an area landowner concerned with emissions from a cement plant. The tribunal had determined standing with the merits of the substantive issues at the end of the proceedings. The effect of this practice was to dismiss the appeal for no standing, even though by that point in proceedings the tribunal had recognized concerns with the decision being appealed. In a 2013 case, the ABQB found that the tribunal had no jurisdiction to grant common law public interest standing.[43] Multiple environmental organizations and individuals sought to appeal the legality of a decision to the tribunal, which it could have heard but for lack of standing.

The Alberta appeals tribunal cases suggest that the courts and tribunals are struggling to articulate what must be proved to pass the "directly affected" test. The cases also illustrate how these tests make it hard for tribunals to follow the accepted practices of low standards of proof and preliminary determinations. They further suggest that evidentiary barriers to standing can exceed those to the substantive claims. If the substantive issue is with the legality of a decision but one must be "directly affected," then more facts may be required to prove standing than to settle the substantive issues.

## THE BRITISH COLUMBIA ENVIRONMENTAL APPEAL BOARD

Some of the most recent and principled judicial statements on standing at tribunals concern the requirements to be "aggrieved" for standing at the British Columbian Environmental Appeals Board. In the 2014 case of *Gagne v. Sharpe*, the BCSC overturned a denial of standing to six individuals, a local environmental organization, and a regional environmental organization who were all seeking to challenge an emissions permit for a metal smelter.[44] Reasons for the decision included breach of fairness, an overly high standard of proof, and an unnecessary requirement that members of incorporated groups be individually aggrieved.

The tribunal in question granted standing to two local residents but denied standing to the individuals and organizations based in the broader geographic region. Standing was determined as a preliminary matter on written submissions. The appellants requested a pre-hearing conference and particulars on the issues concerning standing, but the tribunal denied these requests. After the written submissions were filed, the tribunal requested extra material from the permit holder in relation to determining standing. The appellants were not notified of this event or provided an opportunity to respond. The tribunal's procedural manual stated that the tribunal could obtain information not tendered by the parties, but before considering such information it must give all parties notice and opportunities to respond. The manual also stated that persons involved in the process could expect these procedures to be followed.

While this was not clear from the decision, the information that was provided after the written submission deadline was the permit holder's environmental report. This material was known to the appellants and likely in their possession, but it was not yet filed into evidence and might have been challenged by the appellants if there was a hearing.

The BCSC found that there was a strong duty of fairness owed to persons seeking standing, that the tribunal breached its own procedural rules, and that there was a legitimate expectation that these rules be followed. It also found that the tribunal imposed the standard of proof of a "balance of probabilities." This standard was too rigorous for a preliminary determination because definitive proof of harm was unnecessary and tribunals should not consider the substantive merits at this stage. The court justified a low standard of proof based on risk that meritorious arguments could be foreclosed, the short timelines, the unavailability of expert evidence, the lack of a pre-hearing, and the lack of identified specific concerns with standing. It further held that incorporated environmental organizations may qualify for standing as persons without having to show that their members would have standing.

*Gagne* is significant for articulating common law principles and judicial policy concerns with "access to justice" in a review of standing under a legislated test. In that regard it goes beyond looking at standing as question of law, fact, and policy of the legislature.

Unfortunately *Gagne* does not settle what must be proven. The court believed that the requirement to be "aggrieved" was broad enough to include environmental organizations that lacked specific property and economic interests, but it admitted that they may face challenges. It also provided an *obiter dictum* opinion that public interest standing was not available at this tribunal. The case further illustrates how the ability of tribunals to forego the formal rules of evidence can occasionally be a barrier to standing.

### THE ONTARIO ENVIRONMENTAL REVIEW TRIBUNAL

The Ontario Environmental Review Tribunal provides an important contrast between standing and the substantive issues. Provincial legislation in the form of an *Environmental Bill of Rights* provides rights to third parties to appeal specific decisions to the tribunal.[45] The legislation creates a two-step process where "any person" with an interest in the decision has standing, but they must then pass a test for leave to appeal to the tribunal on the substantive issues.[46] The interest requirement is sufficiently relaxed to provide standing to environmental groups, but the requirements for leave to appeal are stringent. The tribunal must refuse leave to appeal unless there is good reason to believe that a decision was unreasonable and that it could result in significant environmental harm.[47] Early tribunal decisions differed on the standard of proof for establishing this harm, but the tribunal has settled on only requiring a *prima facie* case.[48]

In *Dawber v. Ontario*, the Ontario Divisional Court upheld the tribunal's decision to grant standing and leave to appeal to groups and individuals opposed to a waste incineration permit.[49] The interests required for standing were met by persons who filed written submissions on the permit decision and persons who resided sufficiently close to the site, even though some lived on an island several kilometres away. Despite this relaxed approach, not all persons showed sufficient evidence to establish an interest. The court held that the test for leave to appeal was stringent and created a presumption against leave. It noted that the requirements for an unreasonable decision and significant environmental harm must both be met or leave must be denied. However, it found that this barrier was "not insurmountable." Evidence of the reasonableness of the decision and the likelihood of environmental harm included environmental policies that legislation required the decision maker to consider. The questions of reasonableness and likely harm were not limited to whether the permit complied with regulations. Mere regulatory compliance did not establish that environmental harm would not occur, the decision maker had power to make permits more stringent than the regulations, and the tribunal could look to other environmental policies. The court also held that the standard of proof for preliminary determinations of standing and leave to appeal was lower than a balance of probabilities.

The Canadian Environmental Law Association stated that *Dawber v. Ontario* should clarify the grounds for appeal that the tribunal may favour, but it questioned the extent to which the legislation has facilitated access to justice or impacted environmental decisions.[50] The number of third party appeals will remain minimal without legislative change, because the need to show evidence of unreasonableness and potential harm will result in most applications being dismissed. Records of the tribunal and the provincial Environment Commissioner affirm that third party appeals are very infrequent.[51]

The evidentiary requirements for leave to appeal practically combine the need to establish multiple substantive claims in litigation and regulatory proceedings. Finding that a decision is unreasonable would typically be the finding of a substantive judicial review hearing. Finding the chance of significant environmental harm would typically be the finding of an environmental assessment review. It is quite striking that both are needed simply to get a hearing under environmental rights legislation.

### TRENDS IN THE TRIBUNAL CASES

The above cases illustrate several trends. One is that there is no cohesive jurisprudence or leading authority on standing at tribunals, as each court is narrowly focused on the legislation and tribunal in question. Many cases may have limited application to those regimes. Nonetheless the similarities are apparent.

The litigation always concerns vague tests, many of which are interpreted more restrictively than is necessarily required from the face of the legislation. Often the tribunals struggle to articulate the interests and impacts that must be proven to pass these tests. The articulated requirements and findings of fact might really depend on a tribunal's latent receptivity to holding hearings.

The practice of placing the burden of proof on the person seeking standing is not challenged, which suggests that use of an adversarial litigation model is being taken for granted. All of the above tribunals and even some courts have struggled to maintain low standards of proof even if they theoretically favour this practice. Standing is very hard to settle as a preliminary matter using informal approaches to evidence because the tests promote a conflation of standing with the merits of the substantive claims.

On one hand the courts are finding that the legislature can dictate the test for standing at tribunals. On the other hand they are articulating concerns with fairness, access to justice, and the mandate of tribunals. In response the courts are proving willing to intervene in unnecessary evidentiary and procedural barriers created by the tribunals. They are also willing to uphold tribunal decisions to grant standing and to hear appeals even if the tests are stringent.

## Conclusion

Standing remains a contentious issue in environmental matters. Many of the evidentiary issues transcend the difference between courts and administrative tribunals, but the institutional responses have been very different. Where the courts find issues for which public interest standing is available, they have reduced the evidentiary barriers to standing by using objective indicators of genuine interest and a policy-driven approach to assessing the appropriate means to hear the issues.

In contrast, evidentiary issues are widespread at environmental tribunals that use models of standing borrowed from the adversarial litigation system. Litigation is increasing and the trend is towards judicial intervention into evidentiary barriers created by tribunals. The real need is for legislative reform to provide standing tests that fit tribunal mandates, but there are opportunities to challenge and improve tribunal practice through the courts. If advocates and adjudicators are attuned to these trends, then a principled and cohesive jurisprudence on standing at tribunals is increasingly possible.

### NOTES

1 Adam Driedzic, *Report on Standing in Environmental Matters* (December 2014) [unpublished, archived at Environmental Law Centre, Edmonton, Alberta] [*Standing in Environmental Matters*].

2 Thomas A Cromwell, *Locus Standi: A Commentary on the Law of Standing in Canada* (Toronto: Carswell, 1986) [*Locus Standi*].

3 *Friends of the Island Inc v Canada (Minister of Public Works)*, [1993] 2 FCR 229 at para 79 [*Friends of the Island*], citing *Locus Standi, ibid*; *Irving Shipbuilding Inc v Canada (Attorney General)*, 209 FCA 116 at para 33 [*Irving Shipbuilding*], citing *Locus Standi, ibid*; *Air Canada v Toronto Port Authority*, 2010 FC 774 at para 64 [*Toronto Port Authority*], citing *Irving Shipbuilding*; *Public Mobile Inc v Canada (Attorney General)*, 2011 FC 130 at para 71, citing *Irving Shipbuilding*.

4 Australian Law Reform Commission, *Standing in Public Interest Litigation*, ALRC Report 27 (Sydney: ALRC, 1985), updated by Australian Law Reform Commission, *Beyond the Door Keeper: Standing to Sue for Public Remedies*, ALRC Report 78 (Sydney: ALRC, 1996) at para 5.28 [Australian Commission]; Ontario Law Reform Commission, *Report on the Law of Standing* (Toronto: OLRC, 1989) at 107 [Ontario Commission].

5 Byron Williams, "Public Interest Standing in Public Review Processes" (Paper delivered at the Canadian Conference of Administrative Tribunals, Calgary, 15 May 2012) [unpublished].

6 Mark Haddock, *Environmental Tribunals in British Columbia* (Victoria: University of Victoria Environmental Law Centre, 2011) at 32 [*Tribunals in British Columbia*].

7 Alberta Utilities Commission, Bulletin 2010-04, "Heartland Transmission Project Notice of Enhanced Participation Process" (20 January 2010, accessed 18 December 2017), online: <https://www.alberta.ca/release.cfm?xID=276704ca630be-ca3c-4933-5b10f10ae6bf2e28>.

8 *District of Kitimat v Alcan Inc*, 2005 BCSC 44 at paras 3–4 [*Kitimat*].

9 *Standing in Environmental Matters*, *supra* note 1; Australian Commission, *supra* note 4 at paras 5.30–5.32.

10 Ontario Commission, *supra* note 4 at 10.

11 Jenny Scott, "Directly Affected and the Alberta Public Health Advisory and Appeal Board: Can the Public Nuisance Rule Survive?" (1996) 6 JELP 275 [Public Nuisance Rule]; Australian Commission, *supra* note 4 at paras 4.11, 4.15 and 5.8; Ontario Commission, *ibid* at 16.

12 *Canada (Attorney General) v Downtown Eastside Sex Workers United Against Violence Society*, [2012] 2 SCR 524 at para 37, Cromwell J [*Downtown Eastside*].

13 Ontario Commission, *supra* note 4 at 15.

14 *Society for the Preservation of the Englishman River Estuary v Nanaimo (District of)*, [1999] BCJ No 370 at para 41[*Englishman River*].

15 *Reese v Alberta*, 11 Admin LR (2d) 265, 85 Alta LR (2d) 153 at para 30 [*Reese*].

16 *Sierra Club of Canada v Canada (Minister of Finance)*, [1999] 2 FC 211 at para 52 [*Sierra Club*]; *MiningWatch Canada v Canada (Minister of Fisheries and Oceans)*, 2007 FC 955 at paras 179–80 [*MiningWatch*]; *Chetwynd Environmental*

*Society v Dyer*, [1995] 13 BCLR (3d) 338 at para 34 [*Chetwynd*]; *Reese*, *supra* note 15 at para 26.

17 *Great Lakes United v Canada (Minister of the Environment)*, 2009 FC 408, [2010] 2 FCR 515 [*Great Lakes United*]; *West Kootenay Community EcoSociety v Her Majesty the Queen*, 2005 BCSC 744 at para 34 [*West Kootenay*]; *Reese*, *supra* note 15 at paras 39–45; *Sierra Club*, *supra* note 16 at paras 58–68; *MiningWatch*, *supra* note 16 at paras 2 and 180.

18 *Sierra Club*, *supra* note 16 at para 68; *West Kootenay*, *supra* note 17 at paras 31–35; *Chetwynd*, *supra* note 16.

19 *Chetwynd*, *supra* note 16; *West Kootenay*, *supra* note 17 at paras 31–32 and 34.

20 *Sierra Club*, *supra* note 16 at paras 62–68.

21 *Sierra Club*, *ibid* at para 52.

22 *Canadian Council of Churches v Canada (Minister of Employment and Immigration)*, [1992] 1 SCR 236 [*Canadian Council*]; *Hy and Zel's Inc v Ontario (Attorney General), Paul Magder Furs Ltd v Ontario (Attorney General)*, [1993] 3 SCR 675 [*Hy and Zel's*].

23 Peter Bowal & Mark Cranwell, "Persona Non Grata: The SCC Further Constrains Public Interest Standing" (1994) 33 Alta L Rev 192; Russell Binch, "The Mere Busybody: Autonomy, Equality and Standing" (2002) 40 Alta L Rev 367; Scott Fairley, "Is the Public Interest Falling from Standing? Two Recent Comments from the Supreme Court of Canada" (1993) 11 The Philanthropist 28.

24 *Downtown Eastside*, *supra* note 12 at para 51.

25 Jane Bailey & Angela Chaisson, "On Being Part of the Solution: Public Interest Standing after SWUAV SCC" (2012) 1 Canadian Journal of Poverty Law 121.

26 *Moresby Explorers Ltd v Canada (Attorney General)*, 2006 FCA 144 at para 17 [*Moresby Explorers*].

27 *Finlay v Canada (Minister of Finance)*, [1986] 2 SCR 607 at para 20 [*Finlay*].

28 *Reese*, *supra* note 15 at para 47; *Kitimat*, *supra* note 8 at paras 3–4.

29 Robert MacCaulay & James Sprague, *Hearings Before Administrative Tribunals*, 2d ed (Toronto: Carswell, 2002) [*Administrative Tribunals*].

30 *Dene Tha' First Nation v Alberta (Energy and Utilities Board)*, 2005 ABCA 68 at paras 9–12, leave to appeal to SCC dismissed [2005] [*Dene Tha'*]; *Friends of Athabasca Environmental Association and Edmonton Friends of the North Environmental Society v Public Health Advisory and Appeals Board*, 1996 ABCA 11 at paras 5–8 [*Friends of Athabasca*]; *Canadian Union of Public Employees, Local 30 v WMI Waste Management of Canada Inc*, 1996 ABCA 6 at paras 14–19 [*WMI*].

31 Adam Driedzic, "Can Administrative Agencies Grant Common Law Public Interest Standing?" 39-3 LawNow, Special Report: Public Interest Standing (Jan/Feb 2014, accessed 22 December 2017), online: <https://www.lawnow.org/administrative-agencies-public-interest-standing/>; Adam Driedzic, "Environmental groups denied standing on water appeals" (25 April 2013, accessed 22 December 2017), online: Environmental Law Centre <http://elc.ab.ca/environmental-groups-denied-standing-to-challenge-water-licensing/>; Shaun Fluker, "No Public Interest Standing at the Alberta Environmental Appeals Board" (15 February 2013, accessed 22 December 2017), online: <http://ablawg.ca/2013/02/15/no-public-interest-standing-at-the-alberta-environmental-appeals-board/>.

32 *Dene Tha'*, *supra* note 30.

33 *Sawyer v Alberta (Energy and Utilities Board)*, 2007 ABCA 297.

34 *Whitefish Lake First Nation v Alberta (Energy and Utilities Board)*, 2004 ABCA 49 at para 22.

35 *Cheyne v Alberta (Utilities Commission)*, 2009 ABCA 348 [*Cheyne*]; *Prince v Alberta (Energy Resources Conservation Board)*, 2010 ABCA 214.

36 *Kelly v Alberta (Energy Resources Conservation Board)*, 2009 ABCA 349 [*Kelly #1*].

37 *Kelly v Alberta (Energy Resources Conservation Board)*, 2011 ABCA 325 [*Kelly #2*].

38 *Ibid* at para 26.

39 *Kelly v Alberta (Energy Resources Conservation Board)*, 2012 ABCA 19.

40 *Friends of Athabasca*, *supra* note 30; *WMI*, *supra* note 30.

41 *Kostuch v Alberta (Director, Air & Water Approvals Divisions, Environmental Protection)*, 35 Admin LR (2d) 160, 182 AR 384, 21 CELR (2d) 257 at paras 16–18.

42 *Court v Alberta Environmental Appeal Board*, 2003 ABQB 456 at para 69.

43 *Alberta Wilderness Association v Alberta (Environmental Appeals Board)*, 2013 ABQB 44.

44 *Gagne v Sharpe*, 2014 BCSC 2077, 247 ACWS. (3d) 4, 89 Admin. L.R. (5th) 306.

45 Richard Lindgren, "Third Party Appeals Under the Environmental Bill of Rights in the Post-Lafarge Era: The Public Interest Perspective" (Presentation delivered to the Ontario Bar Association, 2 February 2009) [archived at Canadian Environmental Law Association] [Third Party Appeals]; Richard Lindgren, "Statutory Environmental Rights: Lessons Learned From Ontario's Experience" (Paper prepared for the Renewing Environmental Law Conference, Vancouver, 3–4 February 2011) [archived at Canadian Environmental Law Association [Environmental Rights].

46 *Environmental Bill of Rights, 1993*, SO 1993, c 28, ss 38(1) and 41.

47 *Ibid*, s 41.

48 Third Party Appeals, *supra* note 45.

49 *Dawber v Ontario (Director, Ministry of the Environment)* (2008), 36 CELR (3d) 191 (Ont Div Ct), upholding *Dawber v Ontario (Ministry of the Environment)*, [2007] OERTD No 25, 28 CELR (3d) 281 [*Dawber* Tribunal Decision].

50 Third Party Appeals, *supra* note 45 at 26; Environmental Rights, *supra* note 45 at 14.

51 *Application for Review: Filed Pursuant to Section 61 of the Environmental Bill of Rights, 1993: Re: Environmental Bill of Rights* (21 December 2010, accessed 22 December 2017), online: <http://www.cela.ca/sites/cela.ca/files/761.Application_for_Review_of_the_EBR.pdf>; Environment and Land Tribunals Ontario, *Annual Reports and Statistics* (accessed 22 December 2017), online: <http://elto.gov.on.ca/tribunals/arb/resources/annual-reports-statistics/>.

# 44

# The Challenges of Gathering Expert Evidence by Private Individuals

ASHA JAMES

## Introduction

What good is it to members of the public, ordinary men of ordinary means, to have the right to commence appeals of certain types of environmental projects if the costs of experts make it prohibitive to mount an effective case? This chapter addresses the issues faced by ordinary citizens who dare to challenge multi-million dollar energy projects on the basis that the project has the potential to cause harm to the health of the litigant and/or harm to the natural environment.

Specifically, this chapter will address the role experts play generally in the litigation process, but more specifically, the role that expert witnesses play in appeals before Environmental Tribunals. As a lawyer practising in Ontario, I have had the privilege of acting for ordinary citizens, most living in rural environments, before the Ontario Environmental Review Tribunal (ERT) on appeals of renewable energy projects.

Given the nature of these appeals, as explored in detail below, the expert becomes a vital component of the appeal, not only in the giving of evidence but also in the preparation for the hearing by educating the lawyer about the very complicated technical issues at play.

Currently, the regulatory process in place for these types of appeals in Ontario makes it virtually impossible for citizens of ordinary means to meaningfully participate in the hearing process. Sadly, the appellant is faced with a monumental mountain to climb to be successful on an appeal, a mountain that, financially, they just can't afford.

## The Role of an Expert Witness

What is the role of an expert? Generally, an expert is defined as a person possessing certain specialized knowledge, training, education, skill, and/or experience that goes beyond the knowledge of ordinary members of the general public. In the most simplistic form, in legal proceedings, we rely on experts to explain to the trier of fact that which lies outside our general realm of understanding.

If that is the role of the expert, what is the role of an Environmental Tribunal? An Environmental Tribunal is a body with specialized knowledge about the issues it decides. Basically, we expect that the tribunal has a unique understanding about the issues that come before it.

Often I have clients ask, "If the tribunal has specialized knowledge about environmental issues, why do I need an expert for my case?" The answer, at least in Ontario, is quite simply, that you cannot win without one.

People think of an expert witness as someone who testifies at a trial or hearing to help one side or the other prove its case. An expert witness is typically seen as testifying on behalf of one party or the other to support that party's version of the case. But in actuality, that is not the job of an expert. An expert is supposed to come to a hearing as an independent third party to provide the trier of fact with an explanation and opinion about complex technical issues that are beyond the general knowledge of most people. An effective expert witness can take technical jargon and explain it in a way that a person of ordinary intelligence can understand.

For decades, courts have provided guidance on the role an expert should play in legal proceedings. In the case of *R. v. Abbey*, Mr. Justice Dickson (as he then was) commented on the role that experts play in the trial process.

> With respect to matters for special knowledge, an expert in the field may draw inferences and state his opinion. An expert's function is precisely this: to provide the judge and jury with a ready-made inference which the judge and jury, due to the technical nature of the facts, are unable to formulate. An expert's opinion is admissible to furnish the Court with scientific information which is likely to be outside the experience and knowledge of a judge or jury. If on the proven facts a judge or jury can form their own conclusion without help, then the opinion of the expert is unnecessary.
>
> An expert witness, like any other witness, may testify as to the veracity of facts of which he has first-hand experience, but this is not

> the main purpose of his or her testimony. An expert is there to give an opinion. And the opinion more often than not will be based on second-hand evidence.[1]

In essence, the evidence of an expert acts as an exemption to the rule against hearsay evidence.

### USE OF THE EXPERT WITNESS IN PREPARATION FOR TRIAL

In addition to providing evidence on behalf of a party, experts can be invaluable as an aid in reviewing expert reports received from the opposing party, and can assist in the understanding of certain legislation and technical requirements (such as regulatory regulations for renewable energy projects) and in preparing for cross-examination of the expert witnesses retained by the opposing side. In an appeal before an environmental tribunal, the lawyer representing the private citizen has to become, in essence, an expert with respect to the issues that are being raised before the tribunal in order to be able to present his or her client's case to its best advantage and to conduct creditable cross-examinations. For these reasons, it can be very useful to have an expert witness attend at the hearing, particularly when the opposing party's expert is giving his or her evidence.

The ability to have your expert attend the hearing has the benefit of being an onsite resource for the lawyer during the presentation of the evidence and the cross-examination of opposing experts.

## The Ontario Experience at Tribunal Appeals of Renewable Energy Projects

### THE TIME FRAME FOR THE EXCHANGE OF DOCUMENTS

The Ontario Environmental Tribunal Rules of Procedure for appeals of renewable energy products sets out the time frame for the exchange of documents, including the exchange of any expert reports that will be relied upon during the course of the hearing. Pursuant to the Tribunal Rules as of the writing of this chapter, expert reports are to be filed within 5.5 weeks after the filing of the appeal and within 2.5 weeks after the parties exchange all relevant documents in their possession.[2]

This expedited time frame makes it extremely difficult for an appellant to retain an expert to assist at a hearing. In essence, the time frame makes it so that an individual appellant would actually have to engage an expert prior to a proponent receiving government approval for the project. The expedited timeline for appeals of renewable energy projects, in essence, acts as a barrier to individual appellants being able to engage experts to support in their appeal of a project.

Imagine that one day you receive notice that a high-rise building is going to be built on your quiet residential street between your house and the house of your neighbour. Common sense tells you that building something so large in your area will block your access to sunlight in your home, which will, as a consequence, kill all the plants in your garden that you have worked at nurturing meticulously for the last ten years. On top of that, the building produces some level of noise that will keep you awake at night, and everyone knows that prolonged periods of deprived sleep are harmful to your health. So you decide that you don't want this building going up by your home. This is going to affect your health and your natural environment and you decide that you are going to oppose this project. Now, the body that determines approvals for these high rise buildings tells you that if you want to oppose the building you have to file expert reports that relate to how the loss of sunlight will affect your garden and to what degree it will be affected. You will need expert reports about the potential effect of any noise related to the building and how that noise will affect your health. To top it off, you will be required to find an expert, gather this information, and provide a report within six weeks.

This is a daunting task for the well resourced, never mind those of us who can barely scrape together enough money to hire a lawyer to assist us in the process. This expedited process forces many appellants into a corner, and they have to figure out ways to mount a credible appeal with very limited expert assistance, or even worse, without the assistance of any expert at all.

## CAN YOU WIN WITHOUT AN EXPERT?

Recently, there have been a number of cases in Ontario where appellants have challenged the approval of renewable energy wind projects on the basis that the project as approved will cause serious harm to the health of appellant. In attempting to prove their case, many appellants have called the evidence of individuals who have lived in close proximity to wind turbines and claim that after the turbines became operational they began experiencing adverse health effects.

The evidence before various tribunals has been that the wind turbines caused these witnesses to experience sleep disturbances, nausea, dizziness, and cognitive difficulties, feeling vibrations in their body, increased blood pressure, and increased levels of stress.[3]

Despite evidence that these symptoms were never present prior to operation of the turbines, the Ontario Environmental Tribunal has consistently held that this evidence is not sufficient to prove causation and that expert evidence is required to show a causal link between the claimed symptoms suffered from the wind turbines and the wind turbines themselves. In *Kawartha Dairy*, the tribunal stated:

> ... the question is whether the subjective symptoms reported ... are sufficient to establish that night-time noise emissions pose a likelihood of harm, or actual harm, to his health or the health of the members of his family. While the Tribunal gives due weight to Mr. Hornibrook's subjective report of the symptoms he and his family have experienced, as an evidentiary matter, the Tribunal cannot simply assume that he is correct in his assertion that various members of his family suffer from a sleep disorder, aggravation of Crohn's disease, cognitive impairment, or depression. Confirmation of those conditions requires the diagnostic skills of a qualified health professional. Similarly, the Tribunal also cannot simply assume that Mr. Hornibrook is correct in his assertion that sleep disruption resulting from the night-time noise emissions is an operative cause of these conditions, to the extent that they do exist. Accordingly, in weighing the evidence, the Tribunal finds that it can only consider the problems reported by Mr. Hornibrook as subjectively reported symptoms.[4]

However, recently Health Canada released its Study Summary, which found a statistical association between wind turbine noise and annoyance. The Study Summary also found a statistical association between annoyance and a number of self-reported and measured endpoints, including but not limited to: blood pressure, migraines, tinnitus, dizziness, scores on the PSQI, and perceived stress, and measured hair cortisol and systolic and diastolic blood pressure.[5]

The results of the Health Canada study are consistent with the evidence of those living in close proximity to wind turbines in respect of the adverse health effects that they suffer, and have been subsequently considered regarding this evidence and the causation issue.[6]

### THE ABILITY TO RETAIN AN EXPERT

As outlined above, the Ontario Environmental Tribunal is a very specialized tribunal that addresses matters only pertaining to environmental issues. The tribunal has specialized knowledge about the issues that come before it. In Ontario, pursuant to the *Environmental Protection Act*, an appellant can appeal the approval of a renewable energy project on only two grounds:

> **142.1** (1) This section applies to a person resident in Ontario who is not entitled under section 139 to require a hearing by the Tribunal in respect of a decision made by the Director under section 47.5. 2009, c. 12, Sched. G, s. 9.
>
> *Same*
>
> (2) A person mentioned in subsection (1) may, by written notice served upon the Director and the Tribunal within 15 days after a day prescribed by the regulations, require a hearing by the Tribunal in respect of a decision made by the Director under clause 47.5 (1) (a) or subsection 47.5 (2) or (3). 2009, c. 12, Sched. G, s. 9.
>
> *Grounds for hearing*
>
> (3) A person may require a hearing under subsection (2) only on the grounds that engaging in the renewable energy project in accordance with the renewable energy approval will cause,
>
> (a) serious harm to human health; or
> (b) serious and irreversible harm to plant life, animal life or the natural environment.[7]

Given that the tribunal requires expert evidence for an appellant to successfully discharge their burden of proof on an appeal, the next question is where one can find such an expert. Due to the specialized nature of the issues before the tribunal, the pool of experts with the specific knowledge of the issues in play is very limited. When combined with the fact that many of the experts who have this specific knowledge have already been engaged by renewable energy developers, the pool of possible experts becomes even smaller.

Appellants are faced with the daunting task of finding an expert, educating them on the issues, retaining them, and receiving a comprehensive expert opinion all within five weeks of the issuing of the renewable energy approval. The time constraints make it virtually impossible. My office has had a number of experts indicate that they would be interested in assisting in the matter but the expedited timelines make it virtually impossible for them to participate.

The other response that we have received is that due to the time constraints, the cost of a report can be triple what it would be if the expert were to have two to three months to review all the documentation and provide an opinion. Given the opportunity, an appellant would be best advised to call experts in the fields of sleep disturbances, epidemiology, public health, psychology, public policy, hydrology, engineering, acoustics, biomechanics, veterinary medicine, and an environmentalist.

The only way an appellant could mount the kind of case that might lead the tribunal to find in their favour would be to engage experts prior to an approval being granted. There are not very many citizens who can undertake to spend tens of thousands of dollars on experts without being certain that an approval would be granted.

## Access to Justice

The Ontario process for appeals of renewable energy projects acts as a bar to access to justice for an appellant of average financial means. Generally, appellants commence these claims because they believe that the project will cause harm to their health and the environment. These beliefs are not unfounded, as evidenced by the Health Canada Study Summary, which has not been given much weight by the ERT. However, the current appeals process makes it very difficult for appellants to meaningfully participate in the process.

Recently, there has been a shift in the justice community, and recognition that the issues of access to justice require national discussion and a coordinated action strategy. The recent report *Access to Civil & Family Justice: A Roadmap for Change*, by the Honourable Justice Thomas Cromwell of the Supreme Court of Canada, calls for a culture shift in the way the courts approach the issue of access to justice. The report calls for new ways of thinking, imagination, and reform, to be aimed at concrete improvement. Justice Cromwell states that "it is time to move away from old patterns and old approaches."[8]

The report encourages courts to aim for a justice system that is "timely, efficient, effective, proportional and just." In doing so, Cromwell J highlights that the system was, in fact, created for litigants, and that it is in place to serve the public. Calling for a culture shift in the way courts approach access to justice, Justice Cromwell's first guiding principle for change is the need to put the public first:

> The focus must be on the people who need to use the system. This focus must include all people, especially members of immigrant,

> aboriginal and rural populations and other vulnerable groups. Litigants, and particularly self-represented litigants, are not, as they are too often seen, an inconvenience; they are why the system exists.[9]

In other words, according to Justice Cromwell, the principle of access to justice thus requires us to be mindful of those who need the system. The costs of hiring experts and the tribunal's insistence that they are necessary to have even the smallest glimmer of hope on an appeal make the tribunal process cost prohibitive for many appellants and leave many out in the cold without the opportunity to seek justice on issues that affect their life, their health, and their environment.

The role of the expert in these tribunal hearings needs to be seriously reconsidered, because, as things currently stand, appellants are not in a position to retain experts to assist in their case because of the high costs, and therefore, the tribunal, in essence, becomes a rubber stamp of approval for these projects.

### NOTES

1 *R v Abbey*, [1982] 2 SCR 24 at paras 44–45.

2 Environmental and Land Tribunals Ontario, *Rules of Practice and Practice Directions of the Environmental Review Tribunal* (Toronto: 12 September 2016), Appendix A.

3 See *Drennan v Director (Ministry of the Environment)*, [2014] OERTD No 10; *Alliance to Protect Prince Edward County v Ontario (Ministry of the Environment)*, [2013] OERTD No 40 [*Ostrander*]; *Dixon v Director, Ministry of the Environment*, [2014] OERTD No 5; *Bovaird v Director (Ministry of the Environment)*, 2013 CarswellOnt 12680.

4 *Kawartha Dairy Ltd v Director (Ministry of the Environment* (2008), 41 CELR (3d) 184 at para 21 [*Kawartha Dairy*].

5 Health Canada, "Wind Turbine Noise and Health Study: Summary of Results" (6 November 2014, accessed 19 February 2018), online: <http://www.hc-sc.gc.ca/ewh-semt/noise-bruit/turbine-eoliennes/summary-resume-eng.php>.

6 The Health Canada study has been referred to in several ERT hearings, including: *Dingeldein v. Ontario (Director, Ministry of the Environment and Climate Change)*, [2015] OERTD No 32; *Hirsch v. Ontario (Environment and Climate Change)*, [2016] OERTD No 6; *Mothers Against Wind Turbines Inc. v. Ontario (Director, Ministry of the Environment and Climate Change)*, [2015] OERTD No 19; *Clarington Wind Concerns v. Ontario (Director, Ministry of the Environment and Climate Change)* [*Clarington*], 2015 CarswellOnt 12289; and SR *Opposition Corp. v. Ontario (Environment and Climate Change)*, [2015] OERTD No. 61, 100 CELR (3d) 212.

The tribunal has consistently followed *Dixon v. Director, Ministry of the Environment*, [2014] OJ No 6170, where the Divisional Court stated that it was not the intention of the Health Canada summary to address causation. Limitations of the Health Canada Summary described in *Dixon* were affirmed in *Bryce v. Ontario (Director, Ministry of the Environment and Climate Change)*, 2016 ONSC 4191; the ERT has also stated that the Health Canada Summary does not constitute sufficient evidence to establish that the Health Test has been met (*Mothers Against Wind Turbines* at para 200). The ERT has also criticized the fact that the Health Canada summary has not been peer reviewed (*Clarington* at para 52). In the many tribunal hearings in which the summary was cited, it was not found that the summary provided sufficient evidence that annoyance associated with wind turbine noise would cause serious harm to human health in the context of those projects (*Clarington* at para 52). An association is not sufficient to permit an inference of causation (SR *Opposition Corp.* at para 30).

7 *Environmental Protection Act*, RSO 1990, c E.19.

8 Action Committee on Access to Justice in Civil and Family Matters, *Access to Civil & Family Justice: A Roadmap for Change* (Ottawa: October 2013), online: <http://www.cfcj-fcjc.org/sites/default/files/docs/2013/AC_Report_English_Final.pdf>.

9 *Ibid* at 7.

# 45

# The Challenges in Using Aboriginal Traditional Knowledge in the Courts

DAVID LAIDLAW

Aboriginal traditional knowledge has governed Aboriginal Peoples'[1] relationships with themselves and their world since time immemorial. But recognition of that knowledge within Canadian society, and in particular the legal system, is problematic. Canada's Assembly of First Nations (AFN) describes three definitions of *Aboriginal Traditional Knowledge* (ATK):

> Aboriginal Traditional Knowledge is not a concept that is easily defined or categorized. However, it can be generally described as the customary ways in which aboriginal peoples have done or continue to do certain things or activities, as well as the new ideas or ways of doing things that have been developed by Aboriginal peoples which respect their traditions, cultures and practices. Many of these customary ways have been passed on from generation to generation and are considered sacred. This unique body of knowledge is culturally based, context specific, holistic and differs from nation to nation.
>
> The Royal Commission on Aboriginal People (1996) has also described indigenous knowledge as "oral culture in the form of stories and myths, coded and organized by knowledge systems for interpreting information and guiding action … a dual purpose to manage lands and resources and to affirm and reinforce one's relationship to the earth and its inhabitants."
>
> ATK can also be seen as the summation of all knowledge, information, and traditional perspectives relating to the skills, understandings, expertises, facts, familiarities, justified beliefs, revelations,

and observations that are owned, controlled, created, preserved, and disseminated by a particular Indigenous nation. ATK is comprised of a holistic body of knowledge and it remains the sole right of the community to determine what knowledge establishes their ATK.

It is important to note that these are general definitions and do not necessarily reflect or conform to the definitions held by ATK holders.[2]

The entry points for ATK in Canadian courts can be grouped into three categories:

(1) Court review of government or board rulings under legislation referencing ATK;
(2) Court review under the doctrine of the Crown's duty to consult and accommodate Aboriginal Peoples; and
(3) Aboriginal rights claims, Aboriginal title, and criminal defence of wildlife charges.

## Packaging ATK

Despite admonitions from the highest authority in *Delgamuukw v. British Columbia*,[3] lower courts have been and continue to be reluctant to accept and consider ATK. There may be many reasons for this, including the oral transmission nature of ATK, which runs afoul of the hearsay rule, reluctance to accept ATK particularly if it conflicts with Western scientific evidence, and the observational nature of ATK evidence, which Aboriginal Peoples traditionally are reluctant to generalize. Further, while courts and tribunals may follow the standard or revised evidentiary rules (e.g. *Delgamuukw*), the definitional issues, oral transmission, and observational nature risks that information being given little weight.

In response to this attitude, Aboriginal litigants have resorted to studies of ATK such as traditional land use studies, historical studies, etc., and have engaged experts in related fields to collect and opine on them.[4] With few actual experts in ATK, this second-hand collection of ATK by way of expert reports risks the attendant misunderstandings and issues.[5] While a tradition has arisen in Aboriginal litigation since *Delgamuukw* to present an Aboriginal Peoples elder's evidence first,[6] ATK, if it is included, has been generally packaged by experts. This is an expensive and cumbersome process leading to some situations where relevant ATK is not advanced, including those involving financial constraints or confidentiality concerns.

## Court Review of Government or Board Rulings under Statutes that Reference ATK

There are two categories of legislation referencing ATK: general legislation and Implementing Legislation that approves Comprehensive Land Claim Agreements[7] and establishes a number of institutions [Boards] to provide for the Aboriginal joint management of land planning, environmental protection, development approval, land and water rights, wildlife conservation, and other matters. These Boards may be directed in that legislation to consider ATK and will implicitly consider ATK due to their Aboriginal membership. Boards can make recommendations to government, have decision-making powers, and make rules of procedure for the consideration and protection of ATK. Board rules of procedure and First Nation government processes will not be separately considered in this chapter.

Only two of the 28+ Canadian statutes that reference ATK in the environmental context[8] define what that term means: the Nunavut *Wildlife Act*, which incorporates Inuit traditional knowledge,[9] and the *Yukon Environmental and Socio-economic Assessment Act*, which defines traditional knowledge as:

> the accumulated body of knowledge, observations and understandings about the environment, and about the relationship of living beings with one another and the environment, that is rooted in the traditional way of life of first nations.[10]

Statutes referencing ATK fall into several categories: environmental protection,[11] environmental assessment,[12] oceans,[13] land and marine conservation areas,[14] wildlife,[15] forest conservation,[16] species protection[17] including migratory birds,[18] surface and water rights in the North,[19] land planning in Northern Ontario, Nunavut, and Eastern Manitoba,[20] nuclear waste disposal,[21] and game conservation plans under Modern Land Claim Agreements that include the British Columbia governments as well as Canada.[22]

### BEARERS OF TRADITIONAL KNOWLEDGE

The common formulation in statutes is Aboriginal traditional knowledge or First Nations and Métis communities traditional ecological knowledge;[23]

however, some use community knowledge[24] in addition, or in one case local knowledge,[25] as a replacement. The local or community knowledge formulations are undefined but will allow consideration of non-Aboriginal knowledge under those statutes. Only the Ontario *Endangered Species Act*[26] defines "aboriginal" by reference to section 35(2) of the *Constitution Act, 1982*.[27]

It is noteworthy that the *Oceans Act* speaks only of traditional ecological knowledge,[28] while the *Canada National Marine Conservation Areas Act* includes Aboriginal traditional ecological knowledge as a subcategory of traditional ecological knowledge.[29]

In terms of combining scientific knowledge and ATK, Alberta's *Environmental Protection and Enhancement Act* has an "Indigenous Wisdom Advisory Panel" to advise Alberta's Chief Scientist, responsible for monitoring and reporting on Alberta's environment, as to the incorporation of ATK into the governing science.[30] The balance of ATK legislation is silent in this regard.

In terms of rights to or authority to advance ATK, the relevant Aboriginal group would generally hold such knowledge, as an Aboriginal right on a communal basis as outlined by the Supreme Court of Canada (SCC) in *Behn v. Moulton Contracting Ltd.*[31] One aspect of ATK is its diffuse nature, with some knowledge being restricted to certain families and held in confidence within that Aboriginal subgroup.[32] This may accord with the SCC's statement in *Behn* that:

> It will suffice to acknowledge that, despite the critical importance of the collective aspect of Aboriginal and treaty rights, rights may sometimes be assigned to or exercised by individual members of Aboriginal communities, and entitlements may sometimes be created in their favour. In a broad sense, it could be said that these rights might belong to them or that they have an individual aspect regardless of their collective nature. Nothing more need be said at this time.[33]

Thus, identifying relevant ATK may require additional enquiries, beyond the general knowledge of the Aboriginal group, as to who may hold additional knowledge.

Holders of ATK may be reluctant to disclose that information in a public fashion. There are provisions in ATK legislation that could protect the confidentiality of ATK, such as section 42(6)(b) in the *First Nations Oil and Gas Environmental Assessment Regulations*, section 10.2(c) of the *Species at Risk*

*Act*, which allows only permitted information to be shared, the Northwest Territory's *Wildlife Act*, section 168(1)(b), and *Yukon Environmental and Socio-economic Assessment Act*, section 121(a). Agreements or court orders could also be structured to protect ATK, but without them holders of confidential ATK may be reluctant to advance it.

## STATUTORY PREAMBLES AND PURPOSE SECTIONS

In *Quebec (Attorney General) v. Moses*,[34] the Supreme Court of Canada, in interpreting statutory preambles, noted that section 13 of the federal *Interpretation Act* provides "[t]he preamble of an enactment shall be read as a part of the enactment intended to assist in explaining its purport and object."[35] Thus, although "a legislative preamble will never be determinative of the issue of legislative intent since the statute must always be interpreted holistically, it can nevertheless assist in the interpretation of the legislature's intention."[36]

References to ATK in the preamble of federal legislation include: *Canadian Environmental Protection Act, 1999; Canada National Marine Conservation Areas Act; Species at Risk Act;* and, provincially, *Ontario's Climate Change Mitigation and Low-carbon Economy Act*; and territorially in Yukon's *Parks and Land Certainty Act* and *Species at Risk (NWT) Act*. The ATK provisions in the preambles for the ATK legislation have yet to receive judicial consideration, although other components, such as the precautionary and polluter pay principles,[37] have informed the interpretation of legislation.

In *Moses*, legislative purpose statements were described as "[t]he most direct and authoritative evidence of legislative purpose."[38] Purpose statements referencing ATK are found in Ontario's *Great Lakes Protection Act, 2015*, the *Wildlife Act*,[39] and Yukon's *Forest Resources Act*, but those purpose statements have yet to be judicially considered.

The *Canadian Environmental Assessment Act* (CEAA) contains an ATK purpose statement in section 4 that has yet to receive judicial consideration.[40] The predecessor legislation[41] contained a similar purpose statement in section 4 that did not refer to ATK and was the subject of varying interpretations. In *Environmental Resource Centre v. Canada (Minister of Environment)*, a 2001 decision, the Federal Court said:

> Section 4 imposes no duties on the MOE [Minister of the Environment] nor does it state how she is to discharge her duties under the Act. It is a statement of general principle. The MOE does not breach

> this section and the submissions alleging an error of law in relation to section 4 are without foundation.[42]

However, in *Union of Nova Scotia Indians v. Canada (Attorney General)*, a 1996 decision in the Aboriginal context, the Federal Court said:

> The applicants also urge that the Ministers were required to conduct a careful and reasonable assessment of the project in light of para. 4(a) of the CEAA which specifies, among other purposes of the Act, "to ensure that the environmental effects of projects receive careful consideration before responsible authorities take actions in connection with them". I accept that standard as consistent with the purposes and the processes established by the Act.[43]

It is arguable that in the Aboriginal context *CEAA* would, given the purpose statement, invite greater court scrutiny of government decisions with contrary ATK. This contention is supported by *Moses*, which involved a decision as to applicability of *CEAA* under the James Bay Land Claim Settlement, and where the Supreme Court of Canada said:

> [45] Accordingly, unlike the Quebec Court of Appeal, I do not believe the correct outcome here is to substitute the Section 22 Treaty procedure in place of the statutory procedure required by the *CEAA*. The *CEAA* procedure governs but, of course, it must be applied by the federal government in a way that fully respects the Crown's duty to consult the Cree on matters affecting their James Bay Treaty rights in accordance with the principles established in *Haida Nation v. British Columbia (Minister of Forests)*, ... *Taku River Tlingit First Nation v. British Columbia (Project Assessment Director)*, ... and in *Mikisew Cree First Nation v. Canada (Minister of Canadian Heritage.* [citations omitted][44]

It should be noted that the current federal policy, the Updated Guidelines for Federal Officials to Fulfill the Duty to Consult (2011) states that:

> The environmental review process is generally viewed by Aboriginal groups and third parties ... as the most effective method managed

by the Crown to identify environmental effects of proposed activities and related changes.[45]

Ontario's *Endangered Species Act*[46] purpose statement in section 1, aside from the ATK aspect, was considered by the Ontario Court of Appeal in 2016 in *Wildlands League v. Ontario (Natural Resources and Forestry)*,[47] when it upheld a regulation permitting interference with listed species. Likewise, the *Yukon Environmental and Socio-economic Assessment Act* purpose statement in section 5, aside from the ATK aspect, was interpreted to uphold the Yukon Final Agreement in that a project approval did not carry over to the regulatory process and overrule the Water Board's licensing decision.[48] The purpose statement in section 4 of the *Migratory Birds Convention Act, 1994*[49] was interpreted straightforwardly in *Animal Alliance of Canada v. Canada (Attorney General)*.[50]

The federal *Species at Risk Act* (SARA) contains a purpose section 6, which does not explicitly reference ATK but provides:

> 6. The purposes of this Act are to prevent wildlife species from being extirpated or becoming extinct, to provide for the recovery of wildlife species that are extirpated, endangered or threatened as a result of human activity and to manage species of special concern to prevent them from becoming endangered or threatened.[51]

This purpose statement has been interpreted in *Adam v. Canada (Environment)*.[52] *Adam* was a judicial review application on a decision statement by the Minister of the Environment to not include Alberta woodland caribou on a list of species at risk. The Federal Court said:

> Given all of the information that was specifically addressed in the Decision, it was not a reviewable error for the Minister to have failed to have specifically addressed the objectives of the SARA in his Decision. In my view, the manner in which the Decision addressed the relevant scientific and other information in the Certified Record was not inconsistent with the purposes of the SARA, [in section 6].[53]

The implication was that if the minister had not addressed that information in his decision that would be a reviewable error, and indeed by failing to address an emergency request without justification the minister committed a reviewable error.[54] It is noteworthy in *Adam* that pursuant to ATK the "First Nations

Applicants have voluntarily stopped hunting boreal caribou, in an attempt to address the current threat to the caribou's survival and recovery."[55]

Purpose statements in ATK legislation that do *not* refer to ATK include Alberta's *Environmental Protection and Enhancement Act*[56] section 2, which was interpreted as involving "balancing sensitive environmental concerns with general economic well being and social needs of the Province of Alberta."[57] It also affected the contentious issue of standing in interpreting Alberta's environmental legislation requiring a person be "directly and adversely affected."[58] Other ATK Acts that contain purpose statements that do *not* refer to ATK include the *Canada National Marine Conservation Areas Act*,[59] Nova Scotia's *Endangered Species Act*,[60] New Brunswick's *Species at Risk Act*,[61] Ontario's *Far North Act, 2010*,[62] the *Species at Risk (NWT) Act*,[63] Nunavut's *Wildlife Act*,[64] and Yukon's *Forest Resources Act*[65] and have not received court review.

## DUTY STATEMENTS

The *Canadian Environmental Protection Act, 1999* has a duty statement in section 2(1) that says:

> 2 (1) In the administration of this Act, the Government of Canada shall, having regard to the Constitution and laws of Canada and subject to subsection (1.1),
>
> (a) exercise its powers in a manner that protects the environment and human health, applies the precautionary principle that, where there are threats of serious or irreversible damage, lack of full scientific certainty shall not be used as a reason for postponing cost-effective measures to prevent environmental degradation, and promotes and reinforces enforceable pollution prevention approaches;
>
> ...
>
> (i) apply knowledge, including traditional aboriginal knowledge, science and technology, to identify and resolve environmental problems;
>
> ...

In *Great Lakes United v. Canada (Minister of the Environment)*, this duty section was interpreted to require the minister to include the mining industry information on waste rock and tailings disposals on site in the *National Pollutant Release Inventory* (NPRI) established by the minister to provide an inventory of pollutants released into the environment.[66] The ATK duty in section 2(1)(i) was not an issue in that case, but the possibility remains that this may require ATK consideration in a proper case.

## PERMISSIVE LEGISLATION

The importance of preambles and purpose and duty statements come from the nature of ATK legislation. Most of the ATK legislation is phrased *permissively*, either by giving discretion to government to consider ATK or confining ATK to an advisory role.

In the maritime context, ATK is limited to educational purposes. The *Oceans Act*, section 42(j), says the minister *may* "conduct studies to obtain traditional ecological knowledge for the purpose of understanding oceans and their living resources and ecosystems." In the *Canada National Marine Conservation Areas Act*, section 8(3) says Canada "*may* conduct scientific research and monitoring and carry out studies based on traditional ecological knowledge, including traditional aboriginal ecological knowledge, in relation to marine conservation areas." (Emphasis added.)

In *CEAA*, the only reference to ATK is in section 19(3), where:

> 19(3) The environmental assessment of a designated project *may* take into account community knowledge and Aboriginal traditional knowledge. [Emphasis added.]

This is contrast to section 19(1), where:

> 19(1) The environmental assessment of a designated project *must* take into account the following factors:
>
> (*a*) the environmental effects of the designated project …
>
> …
>
> (*j*) any other matter relevant to the environmental assessment … [Emphasis added.]

The *First Nations Oil and Gas Environmental Assessment Regulations*, section 11(1), lists factors that must be considered, and section 11(2) says, "The environmental assessment *may* also consider community knowledge and aboriginal traditional knowledge." The *Nuclear Fuel Waste Act* Advisory Council, members of whom should have expertise in ATK, merely advise the minister.

Manitoba's *The East Side Traditional Lands Planning and Special Protected Areas Act* indicates in section 10(4) that the planning council *may* apply traditional knowledge. Alberta's *Environmental Protection and Enhancement Act*, section s 15.3(1), involves at best a second-hand incorporation of ATK into the governing scientific standards. The Ontario *Far North Act, 2010*, section 6 reads, "First Nations *may* contribute their traditional knowledge and perspectives on protection and conservation for the purposes of land use planning under this Act," but there is no direction on the usage of that information. The *Great Lakes Protection Act, 2015* and the *Climate Change Mitigation and Low-carbon Economy Act* in Ontario are similar.

That being said, particularly when developments are undertaken within the traditional areas of Aboriginal peoples,[67] in practice some consideration is given to ATK under the doctrine of the Crown's duty to consult and accommodate First Peoples discussed below.

## SPECIES AT RISK ACTS

The federal *Species at Risk Act* (SARA), and provincial equivalents, represent a special case. The general scheme under SARA is the listing of at-risk species in various categories by way of committees established for that purpose. The listing of a species can change, and if it meets a standard of endangerment that status will engage mandatory plans to curtail exploitation or habitat destruction or enhance recovery.

In SARA, the preamble takes notice of ATK when it says, "the traditional knowledge of the aboriginal peoples of Canada should be considered in the assessment of which species may be at risk and in developing and implementing recovery measures." SARA establishes a *Canadian Endangered Species Conservation Council* (CESPCC) in section 7 composed entirely of government ministers or their delegates.[68] The role of the CESPCC is to "provide general direction on the activities of COSEWIC [Committee on the Status of Endangered Wildlife in Canada], the preparation of recovery strategies and the preparation and implementation of action plans" and to coordinate government activities.[69] SARA directs the creation of a "National Aboriginal Council on Species at Risk [NACSR], consisting of six representatives of the aboriginal peoples"[70] who would presumptively consider ATK, but the role of NACSR is *limited to advising* the government's CESPCC.

The minister, after consulting with the CESPCC, may create a public "stewardship action plan that creates incentives and other measures to support voluntary stewardship actions taken by any government in Canada, organization or person."[71] That stewardship action plan is educational and must include commitments to, among other things, "methods for sharing information about species at risk, including community and aboriginal traditional knowledge, that respect, preserve and maintain knowledge and promote their wider application with the approval of the holders of such knowledge, with other governments and persons."[72]

Section 14 establishes a "Committee on the Status of Endangered Wildlife in Canada" (COSEWIC). The functions of COSEWIC include periodically assessing the status of species[73] at risk, identifying the existing or potential threats, and classifying each species as extinct, extirpated, endangered, threatened, of special concern, or not at risk.[74] COSEWIC "must carry out its functions on the basis of the best available information on the biological status of a species, including scientific knowledge, community knowledge and *aboriginal traditional knowledge*,"[75] including a finding of insufficient knowledge.[76] Members of COSEWIC "must have expertise drawn from a discipline such as conservation biology, population dynamics, taxonomy, systematics or genetics or from community knowledge or *aboriginal traditional knowledge* of the conservation of wildlife species."[77] COSEWIC must establish a "subcommittee specializing in *aboriginal traditional knowledge*"[78] whose chairperson and members will be appointed by the minister after consultation with Aboriginal groups that she considers appropriate.[79] COSEWIC has approved *Aboriginal Traditional Knowledge: Process and Protocols Guidelines* (2010) that include four Guiding Principles, the last of which directs "equal recognition and value with western Science and Community Knowledge"; however, they are only guidelines.[80]

Thus, under *SARA*, aside from membership requirements, ATK consideration is confined to an advisory role to COSEWIC, albeit a prominent one. Provincial legislation generally follows the same model as *SARA*.[81]

## MANDATORY LEGISLATION

Implementing legislation can mandate consideration of ATK, and implicitly acknowledges its relevance in the Aboriginal composition of the resulting Boards:

- Nunavut Agreement: Nunavut's Territorial *Wildlife Act*, with its explicit description of Inuit ATK and its application; the *Nunavut Waters and Nunavut Surface Rights Tribunal Act* in section 119, where "due regard and weight shall be given to Inuit culture, customs and knowledge" and the *Nunavut Planning and Project Assessment Act*, section 103(3) ("must take into account any traditional knowledge").

- Yukon Umbrella Agreement: In the *Forest Resources Act*'s section 1(1), "forest resource management" is the *practical* application of scientific, biological, social, cultural, and economic information and traditional knowledge of First Nations; *Parks and Land Certainty Act* preamble: to "establish protected areas based on available traditional knowledge"; *Environment Act*, section 53: "partnership with Yukon First Nations using knowledge"; and the *Yukon Environmental and Socio-economic Assessment Act*'s explicit definition in 2(1), YESAA Board's rules on integration, treatment, and confidentiality of ATK in section 33, and section 39 equal treatment.
- Gwich'in, Sahtu Dene and Metis, Inuvialuit, Déline and Tåîchô Agreements: Northwest Territories' *Wildlife Act*'s Principles; *Surface Rights Board Act* section 32(b) (hearings *must* take into account any relevant Aboriginal traditional knowledge); and the *Mackenzie Valley Resource Management Act* (established Land and Water boards who shall consider ATK in section 60.1(b) with Environmental Impact Board considering cumulative impacts using ATK in addition to other informant in section 115.1).

Implementing legislation for modern land claims settlements can mandate consideration of ATK, especially with respect to wildlife management plans with the provincial parties.[82]

## CONSIDERATION OF ATK

Whether framed in a mandatory or permissive fashion, there is little statutory guidance for courts as to the relevance, weight, or evidentiary standards regarding ATK. The *Nunavut Waters and Nunavut Surface Rights Tribunal Act*, section 119 ("due regard and weight") and the *Nunavut Planning and Project Assessment Act*, section 103(3) ("must take" ATK into account) have not received judicial consideration to date.

The *Yukon Environmental and Socio-economic Assessment Act* [YESAA] contains ATK consideration directions that have received judicial consideration. In *White River First Nation v. Yukon Government*,[83] sections 39 and 74(1) of YESAA were considered. Section 39, entitled General Requirement, provides:

> 39 A designated office, the executive committee or a panel of the Board shall give full and fair consideration to scientific information, traditional knowledge and other information provided to it or obtained by it under this Act.

and section 74(1) provides:

> 74 (1) A decision body considering a recommendation in respect of a project shall give full and fair consideration to scientific information, traditional knowledge and other information that is provided with the recommendation.

At issue in *White River* was the March 19, 2012, Tarsis Resources Ltd. ("Project Proponent") approval for a Mining Land Use Approval permit under YESAA for a Quartz Exploration Project (the "White River Project") on lands claimed by the White River First Nation ("First Nation"). That application, under YESAA regulations, was directed to a Designated Office for evaluation. That Designated Office, after appropriate consultation with the Project Proponent and First Nation under section 39 of YESAA, issued an Evaluation Report, dated July 30, 2012, recommending that the White River Project not be allowed to proceed because it would have significant adverse effects both on wildlife and wildlife habitat (specifically the Chisana Caribou Herd) and on traditional land use and culture of the First Nation—effects that could not be mitigated. The Evaluation Report was forwarded to a Decision Body, in this case the Director of Mineral Resources (the "Director"), who met once with the First Nation to review the Evaluation Report on August 21, 2012.[84] The Director issued a Decision Document on September 5, 2012 on the basis that the impacts of the White River Project could be mitigated.[85]

Justice Veale found that the First Nation members, in the meeting with the Director, were asked in effect if they agreed with the negative Evaluation Report—to which they naturally agreed.[86] The Director knew on August 16, 2012, *prior to the meeting*, that it had contrary scientific information from telemetry as to the stability of the Chisana Caribou herd and *they did not disclose that information* to the First Nation. That scientific information ultimately formed the basis for rejection of the Evaluation Report in the Decision Document.[87]

Justice Veale contrasted the conduct of the Decision Body in *Liard First Nation v. Yukon Government and Selwyn Chihong Mining Ltd*,[88] wherein that

Decision Body closely monitored the submissions to the Designated Office and exchanged drafts of the Decision Document with the affected First Nation. In *White River* it was argued that the Decision Body had behaved similarly, but Justice Veale rejected this argument, saying:

> However, here the consideration was not full and fair. The First Nation should have had the opportunity to put forward a technical expert, challenge the telemetry data, and present their traditional knowledge. Fairness and the honour of the Crown require that the First Nation be given an opportunity and time to put forward their view when the Decision Body, as here, is contemplating a decision completely at odds with the one that was rendered after an in-depth consultation process.[89]

Noting the significance of Decision Document in the *YESAA* process, Justice Veale quashed the Director's Decision Document. Justice Veale was careful to not direct any specific result or comment on the appropriate weight to be given to ATK—just the lack of consideration.[90] However, as a consultation and accommodation case it may be significant in that *lack of consideration of ATK may be dishonourable on its own.*

While Board Rules can provide guidance as to ATK reception, in their absence recourse to the court's administrative law concepts such as natural justice, proper reasons, etc., may be the only mechanisms to advance ATK consideration in the courts under ATK legislation.

## ATK AND THE CROWN'S DUTY TO CONSULT AND ACCOMMODATE

The Crown's duty to consult and accommodate with Aboriginal Peoples is well established as part of Canadian law that governs decisions regarding matters that affect Aboriginal rights, lands, and interests.[91] The leading authorities include *Haida Nation v. British Columbia (Minister of Forests)*,[92] *Taku River Tlingit First Nation v. British Columbia (Project Assessment Director)*,[93] *Mikisew Cree First Nation v. Canada (Minister of Canadian Heritage)*,[94] and *Beckman v. Little Salmon/Carmacks First Nation*.[95] Together these cases make it clear that governments owe a duty to consult and accommodate Aboriginal Peoples' interests prior to making any government decisions that would impact them. There are Aboriginal consultation policy instruments in every Canadian jurisdiction that provide direction to governments as to the existence of that duty, the acceptable delegation of procedural aspects to project proponents, and standards of consultation and accommodation with Aboriginal Peoples in order to satisfy this duty.[96]

In the process of consultation with governments under this doctrine, Aboriginal Peoples will deploy ATK to persuade governments about the seriousness of a claim and the impact of the proposed decision. If Aboriginal Peoples are dissatisfied by the actions of government, recourse may be had to the courts. In those proceedings, analogies from administrative law are applicable and the standard of review would focus on the process:

> Should the government misconceive the seriousness of the claim or impact of the infringement, this question of law would likely be judged by correctness. Where the government is correct on these matters and acts on the appropriate standard, the decision will be set aside only if the government's process is unreasonable.[97]

As noted in the *Alberta First Nations Consultation & Accommodation Handbook* (2014) (*Handbook*), litigation of this type is expensive and potentially futile, such that Aboriginal Peoples may be unwilling to engage in court proceedings.[98] A good example of ATK playing a role in consultation litigation is *West Moberly First Nations v. British Columbia (Chief Inspector of Mines)*.[99] In that case a permit for coal mining exploration was quashed when it interfered with critical habitat of caribou that the West Moberly First Nation had, in accordance with its ATK, suspended hunting.[100]

A further barrier to court consideration of ATK arises through the operation of the environmental assessment process under CEAA, which is considered by the federal government to be the "best process" to satisfy the Crown's duty.[101] CEAA defines environmental impact in section 5(1)(a) and (b) as including the usual impacts on the environment but goes on in section 5(1)(c) to say:

> (c) with respect to aboriginal peoples, an effect occurring in Canada of any change that may be caused to the environment on
>
> (i) health and socio-economic conditions,
> (ii) physical and cultural heritage,
> (iii) the current use of lands and resources for traditional purposes, or

(iv) any structure, site or thing that is of historical, archaeological, paleontological or architectural significance.[102]

This definition of environmental impact allows for the permissive consideration of ATK in section 19(3) of *CEAA*.[103] Projects such as oil sands mines, mines, hydropower dams, interprovincial pipelines, etc., that engage federal jurisdiction[104] will be subject to *CEAA*. On major projects, *CEAA* provides for Joint Review Panels (JRPs) negotiated with provinces to reduce potential regulatory overlap. These JRPs will hold hearings and make decisions as to the environmental impact of a designated project and project conditions and submit their recommendation to the government, with cabinet making the final decision.

The mandates of JRPs are open for public comment, but the template for Aboriginal issues appears to be fixed.[105] This mandate is described in *Council of the Innu of Ekuanitshit v. Canada (Attorney General)*[106] as the JRP providing Aboriginal Peoples with the opportunity to present their perspective on the following matters:

- Their traditional ecological knowledge about environmental effects of the Project;
- The effect that environmental change caused by the Project may have on the current use of lands and resources for traditional purposes;
- The nature and scope of their … asserted Aboriginal rights or treaty rights, the potential impacts of the Crown's activities in relation to the Project on those rights and the appropriate measures to avoid or mitigate those impacts.[107]

However, the JRP's mandate excluded any determinations or interpretations as to:

- the validity or strength of any Aboriginal group's claims to Aboriginal rights or title;
- the scope or nature of the Crown's duty to consult Aboriginal persons or groups;
- whether the provincial or federal government had satisfied that duty; and
- any interpretation of the [relevant] Land Claims Agreement[108]

The court characterized this, saying, "In other words, the Joint Review Panel could not determine the strength of the Innu of Ekuanitshit's claim to Aboriginal rights or the scope of the duty to consult but was to consider the Project's impacts on their claimed rights."[109] An argument can be made that despite limited mandate, JRPs are *effectively* ruling on the existence and strength of Aboriginal rights or title in balancing the "benefits vs the costs."

In any case, JRPs are ruling on ATK, and the court in *Ekuanitshit* deferred to the JRP's determinations.[110] The use of JRP panels to conduct Crown consultation and accommodation further distances court consideration of ATK, as courts are restricted by administrative doctrines of jurisdictional legality and reasonability of outcomes.

## ABORIGINAL RIGHTS, ABORIGINAL TITLE, AND CRIMINAL DEFENCE OF "WILDLIFE CHARGES"

In civil litigation to determine constitutional Aboriginal rights or Aboriginal title, ATK plays a significant role in courts' findings—by their very definition.

In the leading case of *R v. Van der Peet*,[111] Justice Lamer for the SCC said that Aboriginal rights are activities that "must be an element of a practice, custom or tradition integral to the distinctive culture of the aboriginal group claiming the right,"[112] being practised in a current form that relates to the original practice prior to European contact.[113] The pre-contact way of life is ATK in the broadest sense.

In *Delgamuukw*, Aboriginal title was described by Justice Lamer, for the majority, as a unique (*sui generis*) fusion of common law and Aboriginal legal systems.[114] ATK plays a role in any finding of Aboriginal title by evidencing the necessary exclusive occupation[115] and the qualification as to use representing Aboriginal Peoples' attachment to land.[116]

As noted in its trial decision,[117] ATK was deployed in the first declaration of Aboriginal title in the recent SCC case *Tsilhqot'in Nation v. British Columbia*.[118]

Much of the modern Aboriginal constitutional jurisprudence has come from the defending Aboriginal Peoples from "wildlife charges."[119] The first decision of the SCC interpreting Aboriginal rights, *R v. Sparrow*,[120] had its origins in criminal charges under the *Fisheries Act*, as did the *Van Der Peet* decision and *R v. Adams*.[121] ATK played a role in those cases—by establishing Aboriginal rights to hunt and fish. As Aboriginal law doctrines have developed, most wildlife statutes have acknowledged exemptions for Aboriginal Peoples' rights,[122] but ATK still plays a role in defining Aboriginal rights.

**Table 45.1**

| *Legislation* | *ATK Preamble/ Purpose* | *Formulation* | *Use* | *Mandatory* |
|---|---|---|---|---|
| *Canadian Environmental Protection Act, 1999*, SC 1999, c 33 | Preamble<br>Duty 2(1)(i) | traditional aboriginal knowledge | s 2(1)(i) apply knowledge, including traditional aboriginal knowledge, science and technology, to identify and resolve environmental problems;<br>247 alternative qualification for Review Officers | may |
| *Canadian Environmental Assessment Act*, 2012, SC 2012, c 19 | Purpose 4(1)(d) | community knowledge and Aboriginal traditional knowledge | 19(3) EA may take into consideration | may |
| *First Nations Oil and Gas Environmental Assessment Regulations*, SOR/2007-272 | | community knowledge and aboriginal traditional knowledge | 11(2) environmental assessment may also consider | may |
| *Oceans Act*, SC 1996, c 31 | | traditional ecological knowledge | s 42(j) Minister may conduct studies to obtain | |
| *Canada National Marine Conservation Areas Act*, SC 2002, c 18 | Preamble | traditional ecological knowledge | 8(1)(3) may conduct studies | may |
| *Nuclear Fuel Waste Act*, SC 2002, c 23 | | traditional aboriginal knowledge | s 8(2)(b.1) members of advisory council shall have expertise in | shall |
| *Species at Risk Act*, SC 2002, c 29 | Preamble | scientific, community and aboriginal traditional knowledge | 10(c) Stewardship Plan<br>15(2) COSEWIC must classify best information<br>16(2) COSEWIC qualification<br>18(3) Aboriginal Traditional Knowledge Subcommittee | shall |
| *Endangered Species Act*, 2007, SO 2007, c 6 | Purpose 1.1 | scientific information, including information obtained from community knowledge and aboriginal traditional knowledge | 3(4)(b) COSSARO qualification<br>5(3) COSSARO shall classify species best<br>48(e) COSSARO subcommittee | shall |
| *Species at Risk Act*, SNB 2012, c 6 | | scientific knowledge, community knowledge and aboriginal traditional knowledge | 10(1)(b) COSSAR qualification<br>15(2) COSSAR shall classify species best | shall |

**Table 45.1 | *continued***

| *Legislation* | *ATK Preamble/ Purpose* | *Formulation* | *Use* | *Mandatory* |
|---|---|---|---|---|
| *Endangered Species Act*, SNS 1998, c 11 | | scientific information and traditional knowledge as documented in peer reviewed status reports | 10(2) Group to make decision on best information | shall |
| *Species at Risk (NWT) Act*, SNWT 2009, c 16 | Preamble | Aboriginal traditional knowledge, community knowledge and scientific knowledge | 17(2) SARC make decision best information<br>18(2) SARC qualification<br>30(4) Species status reports | shall |
| *Endangered Species Act*, SNL 2001, c E-10.1, s 6(2) | | scientific knowledge, traditional ecological and local ecological knowledge | 6(2) SSAC make decision best information<br>12(1) SSAC shall consult with info holders | shall |
| *Environmental Protection and Enhancement Act*, RSA 2000, c E-12 | | traditional ecological knowledge | s 15.3(1) Indigenous Wisdom Panel to provide advice to Chief Scientist on integration | may |
| *The East Side Traditional Lands Planning and Special Protected Areas Act*, CCSM c E3 | | traditional knowledge | 10(4) planning council may apply traditional knowledge | may |
| *Far North Act*, 2010, SO 2010, c 18 | | First Nations traditional knowledge | 6 First Nations may contribute [for] land use planning | may |
| *Great Lakes Protection Act*, 2015, SO 2015, c 24 | Purpose 1(2)5 | traditional ecological knowledge | 28(1) First Nations and Métis communities ... may offer<br>28(2) Minister shall take into account for strategy | shall |
| *Climate Change Mitigation and Low-carbon Economy Act*, SO 2016, c 7, | Preamble | traditional ecological knowledge | 7(2) if First Nations and Métis communities offer traditional ecological knowledge the Minister shall take into consideration with respect to the [Climate change] action plan | shall |

**Table 45.1 | *continued***

| *Legislation* | *ATK Preamble/ Purpose* | *Formulation* | *Use* | *Mandatory* |
|---|---|---|---|---|
| IMPLEMENTING LEGISLATION: NUNAVUT AGREEMENT | | | | |
| *Wildlife Act*, SNu 2003, c 26 | | s 8 has extensive Inuit ATK definitions | | shall |
| *Nunavut Waters and Nunavut Surface Rights Tribunal Act*, SC 2002, c 10 | | Inuit culture, customs and knowledge | 119 due regard and weight shall be given to Inuit culture, customs and knowledge | shall |
| *Nunavut Planning and Project Assessment Act*, SC 2013, c 14, | | traditional knowledge or community knowledge | 103(3) must take into account any traditional knowledge or community knowledge provided to it. | shall |
| IMPLEMENTING LEGISLATION: GWICH'IN, SAHTU DENE AND METIS, INUVIALUIT, DÉLINE AND TÅÎCHÔ AGREEMENTS | | | | |
| *Wildlife Act*, SNWT 2014, c 31 | Principles 2(1)(d) & (e) | traditional, scientific and local knowledge<br>2 (2) "local knowledge" includes a person's knowledge about wildlife or habitat acquired through experience or observation; | 2(1)(e)<br>168 (1)(b) provides ATK confidentiality | shall |
| *Mackenzie Valley Resource Management Act*, SC 1998, c 25 | | traditional knowledge and scientific information | 60.1(b) Land and Water boards shall consider<br>115.1 Environmental Impact Board shall consider<br>146 Cumulative impact monitor | shall |
| *Surface Rights Board Act*, SNWT 2014, c 17 | | Aboriginal traditional knowledge | 11(2) alternate Board qualification,<br>s 32 (b) hearing shall take into account any material that it considers relevant, including Aboriginal traditional knowledge<br>s 90 (c) rules on confidentiality decisions on | shall |

**Table 45.1 | *continued***

| *Legislation* | *ATK Preamble/ Purpose* | *Formulation* | *Use* | *Mandatory* |
|---|---|---|---|---|
| IMPLEMENTING LEGISLATION: YUKON UMBRELLA AGREEMENT | | | | |
| *Forest Resources Act*, SY 2008, c 15 | Purpose 6(2) Forest plan comply with | traditional knowledge of First Nations | 1(1) "forest resources management" is the practical application of scientific, biological, social, cultural and economic information and traditional knowledge of First Nations | shall |
| *Parks and Land Certainty Act*, RSY 2002, c 165 | Preamble | traditional knowledge, local knowledge and scientific information | Preamble "(e) to establish protected areas based on available traditional knowledge, local knowledge and scientific information" | shall |
| *Environment Act*, RSY 2002, c 76 | | traditional knowledge of Yukon First Nations | 48(1) (b) shall incorporate into Status report<br>51(2) Educational materials<br>53 partnership with Yukon First Nations using knowledge | shall |
| *Yukon Environmental and Socio-economic Assessment Act*, SC 2003, c 7 | Purpose 5(2)(g) | Defined 2(1) traditional knowledge means the accumulated body of knowledge, observations and understandings about the environment, and about the relationship of living beings with one another and the environment, that is rooted in the traditional way of life of First Nations. | Yukon Environmental and Socio-economic Assessment Board (Board)<br>33 Board shall make rules<br>(a) integration of scientific information, traditional knowledge<br>(b) determination of traditional knowledge confidentiality<br>(c) the handling of information to prevent its disclosure<br>39 Board shall give full and fair consideration to scientific information, traditional knowledge and other information | shall |

**Table 45.1 | *continued***

| *Legislation* | *ATK Preamble/ Purpose* | *Formulation* | *Use* | *Mandatory* |
|---|---|---|---|---|
| *Tsawwassen First Nation Final Agreement Act*, SBC 2007, c 39 | | | Schedule – Chapter 10 Wildlife Management Plans para 43 Provincial Minister will take into account Tsawwassen First Nation ATK | shall |
| *Maa-nulth First Nations Final Agreement Act*, SBC 2007, c 43 | | | Schedule – Chapter 23, para 23.10.1 "consult with applicable Maa-nulth [FN] ATK." | shall |
| *Migratory Birds Convention Act, 1994*, SC 1994 | Article II amended to say "long-term conservation of migratory birds … shall be managed in accord with the following conservation principles:<br>…<br>Means to pursue these principles may include, but are not limited to:<br>…<br>Use of aboriginal and indigenous knowledge, institutions and practices" | | | |

## NOTES

1 In this chapter this term refers to First Nations, Inuit, and Métis Peoples.

2 Aboriginal Traditional Knowledge and Intellectual Property Rights (2011: AFCN, Ottawa) at 3, online: <http://www.afn.ca/uploads/files/env/atk_and_ip_considerations.pdf> (accessed 14 November 2017). This has been implemented in a Resolution ATK & Intellectual Property Rights (2011), online: <http://www.afn.ca/2011/06/15/atk-intellectual-property-rights/> (accessed 14 November 2017).

3 *Delgamuukw v British Columbia*, [1997] 3 SCR 1010, 153 DLR (4th) 193 [*Delgamuukw*] at para 84 ("adapt the laws of evidence so that the aboriginal perspective on their practices, customs and traditions and on their relationship with the land, are given due weight by the courts"); see also para 87.

4 *Tsilhqot'in Nation v British Columbia*, 2007 BCSC 1700, Executive Summary: "Evidence was tendered in the fields of archeology, anthropology, history, cartography, hydrology, wildlife ecology, ethnoecology, ethnobotany, biology, linguistics, forestry and forest ecology."

5 For an elaboration on the difficulties these experts face, see Arthur Ray, *Telling It to the Judge: Taking Native History to Court* (Montreal: McGill-Queen's University Press: 2011) ch 8 at 145 to 159.

6 *Ibid* at 28.

7 Reference Map (2016), online: <https://www.aadnc-aandc.gc.ca/DAM/DAM-INTER-HQ-AI/STAGING/texte-text/mprm_pdf_modrn-treaty_1383144351646_eng.pdf>.

8 Search terms *indigenous traditional knowledge, Aboriginal traditional knowledge, traditional knowledge, community knowledge,* and *local knowledge* conducted on 19 November 2017. We have limited this discussion to the environment, but note that this search flagged legislation relating to *human* health, social work, and customary election codes under the *Indian Act*, RSC 1985, c I-5.

9 *Wildlife Act*, SNu 2003, c 26, s 8, has extensive Inuit ATK definitions. Per s 5(2) and (3), this implementing legislation

is subject to the *Agreement between The Inuit of The Nunavut Settlement Area and Her Majesty The Queen in Right of Canada* (1993) signed 25 May 1993, online: <http://publications.gc.ca/site/eng/9.644783/publication.html> with a list of amendments at <https://www.aadnc-aandc.gc.ca/eng/1100100030970/110010003097> [Nunavut Agreement]. The Nunavut Agreement created the Territory of Nunavut, prevails over all legislation in Nunavut, and continued the Nunavut Wildlife Management Board and Nunavut Species at Risk Committee.

10 *Yukon Environmental and Socio-economic Assessment Act*, SC 2003, c 7, s 2(1). This implementing legislation, and all other Yukon legislation in this chapter, is subject to and interpreted in accordance with the *Umbrella Final Agreement Between the Government of Canada, the Council for Yukon Indians and the Government of the Yukon* (1993), online: <http://www.aadnc-aandc.gc.ca/eng/1100100030607/1100100030608> [Yukon Umbrella Agreement] under s 4. The Yukon Umbrella Agreement forms the basis for standardized Land Claims Settlement Agreements. See *Traditional Territories of Yukon First Nation*, online: <http://www.env.gov.yk.ca/maps/media/uploads/pdf-maps/Traditional_Territories_ENV.020.02.pdf>.

11 *Canadian Environmental Protection Act, 1999*, SC 1999, c 33, Preamble, and Duty of the Government of Canada in s 2(1)(i) to "apply knowledge, including traditional aboriginal knowledge, science and technology, to identify and resolve environmental problems"; and s. 247 (alternative qualification for Review Officers that consider appeals from persons under an environmental order); *Environment Act*, RSY 2002, c 76, s 47 (tri-annual State of the Environment Report intended to establish early warning, baseline determinations, and ongoing accountability of the ministry), and under s 48(1)(b) *shall* "incorporate the traditional knowledge of Yukon First Nation members as it relates to the environment"; under s 51(2) educational materials should include the same; and s 53 speaks of partnership with First Nations, including using their knowledge and experience; *Environmental Protection and Enhancement Act*, RSA 2000, c E-12, s 15.3(1) (Indigenous Wisdom Panel to provide advice to Alberta's Chief Scientist on incorporating "traditional ecological knowledge" into the science program); *Great Lakes Protection Act, 2015*, SO 2015, c 24, s 1(2)¶5 ("promoting the consideration of traditional ecological knowledge") and ss 28(1) (First Nations and Métis communities that have a historic relationship with the Great Lakes–St. Lawrence River Basin may offer their traditional ecological knowledge), 28(2) (minister shall take that into account for strategy); *Climate Change Mitigation and Low-carbon Economy Act*, SO 2016, c 7, Preamble and s 7(2) (if First Nations and Métis communities "offers its traditional ecological knowledge to the Minister, the Minister shall take into consideration the role of traditional ecological knowledge with respect to the [Climate change] action plan").

12 *Canadian Environmental Assessment Act, 2012*, SC 2012, c 19, s 52 [*CEAA*]; s 19(3) (may take into account "community knowledge and Aboriginal traditional knowledge" in conducting environmental assessments), as well as *First Nations Oil and Gas Environmental Assessment Regulations*, SOR/2007-272, s 11(2); notably, s 42(6)(b) protects "information whose disclosure would result in the public becoming aware of aboriginal traditional knowledge that a first nation has always treated in a confidential manner"; *Yukon Environmental and Socio-economic Assessment Act, supra* note 10, s 2(1) (definition), s 33 (integration and handling), and s 39 ("shall give full and fair consideration to scientific information, traditional knowledge and other information").

13 *Oceans Act*, SC 1996, c 31, s 42(j) (Minister may "conduct studies to obtain traditional ecological knowledge for the purpose

of understanding oceans and their living resources and ecosystems")

14 *Parks and Land Certainty Act*, RSY 2002, c 165, Preamble: "(e) to establish protected areas based on available traditional knowledge, local knowledge and scientific information"; and *Canada National Marine Conservation Areas Act*, SC 2002, c 18, Preamble and s 8(3) (the government may establish facilities to "conduct scientific research ... and carry out studies based on traditional ecological knowledge, including traditional aboriginal ecological knowledge, in relation to marine conservation areas").

15 *Wildlife Act*, SNu 2003, *supra* note 9; *Wildlife Act*, SNWT 2014, c 31; s 2(1)(d) (traditional Aboriginal values and practices in relation to harvesting and conservation of wildlife are to be recognized and valued); (e) (best available information, including traditional, scientific and local knowledge to be used is to be used in the conservation and management of wildlife and habitat); s 2(2) (in para (1)(e), "local knowledge" includes a person's knowledge about wildlife or habitat acquired through experience or observation); s 168(1)(b) (if the information is traditional knowledge and an Aboriginal organization requests that it not be disclosed). The Northwest Territories have entered into the Gwich'in, Sahtu Dene and Metis, Inuvialuit, Déline, and Tåîchô Agreements (online: <https://www.aadnc-aandc.gc.ca/eng/1100100030598/1100100030599>) that govern in the case of conflicts.

16 *Forest Resources Act*, SY 2008, c 15, s 1(1): "forest resources management" means the practical application of scientific, biological, social, cultural, and economic information and traditional knowledge of First Nations to the management of forests; this is subject to the Yukon Umbrella Agreement.

17 *Species at Risk Act*, SC 2002, c 29, Preamble; s. 10.2(c) (Stewardship Action Plan must include "methods for sharing information about species at risk, including community and aboriginal traditional knowledge, that respect, preserve and maintain knowledge and promote their wider application with the approval of the holders of such knowledge, with other governments and persons"); A Committee on the Status of Endangered Wildlife in Canada (COSEWIC) is established in s 14, and members can include holders of "aboriginal traditional knowledge of the conservation of wildlife species." Under s 15(2), COSEWIC must operate on the "best available information on the biological status of a species, including scientific knowledge, community knowledge and aboriginal traditional knowledge." COSEWIC must establish an Aboriginal Traditional Knowledge subcommittee in s 18.

Provinces have similarly structured Acts: *Endangered Species Act, 2007*, SO 2007, c 6; *Species at Risk Act*, SNB 2012, c 6, s 10(1)(b) (alternate qualification for Committee); ss 15(2), 18(2)(b) (Aboriginal traditional knowledge of the conservation of wildlife species); *Endangered Species Act*, SNS 1998, c 11 (where species list changes based on "scientific information and traditional knowledge as documented in peer reviewed status reports"); *Species at Risk (NWT) Act*, SNWT 2009, c 16, s 17(2) ("[Committee] shall carry out its functions on the basis of the best available information, including Aboriginal traditional knowledge, community knowledge and scientific knowledge"); *Endangered Species Act*, SNL 2001, c E-10.1, s 6(2) ("[Committee] shall base its decisions on the best scientific knowledge available to it and on traditional ecological and local ecological knowledge about a species").

18 *Migratory Birds Convention Act, 1994*, SC 1994, c 22, amending the Migratory Bird Treaty (1918) to provide in art II that conservation principals include "aboriginal and indigenous knowledge, institutions and practices."

19 *Nunavut Waters and Nunavut Surface Rights Tribunal Act*, SC 2002, c 10, s 119 ("due regard and weight shall be given to

Inuit culture, customs and knowledge"); *Mackenzie Valley Resource Management Act*, SC 1998, c 25, ss 60.1, 115.1, and 146 (cumulative impact, joint-management Land and Water Boards shall consider Aboriginal traditional knowledge); *Surface Rights Board Act*, SNWT 2014, c 17, s 11(2) (alternate Board Membership qualification), s 32(b) (hearing shall take into account any relevant Aboriginal traditional knowledge), s 90(c) (rules on confidentiality decisions on Aboriginal traditional knowledge).

20 *Far North Act, 2010*, SO 2010, c 18, s 6 (First Nations "may contribute their traditional knowledge and perspectives on protection and conservation for the purposes of land use planning under this Act"); *Nunavut Planning and Project Assessment Act*, SC 2013, c 14, s 103(3) ("must take into account any traditional knowledge or community knowledge provided to it"); and *The East Side Traditional Lands Planning and Special Protected Areas Act*, CCSM c E3, s 10(4) ("a planning council may apply traditional knowledge in relation to" plans in areas where First Nations traditionally used lands).

21 *Nuclear Fuel Waste Act*, SC 2002, c 23, s 8(2)(b.1) (members of advisory council "reflects expertise in traditional aboriginal knowledge").

22 *Tsawwassen First Nation Final Agreement Act*, SBC 2007, c 39, Sched, c 10, cl 43, where the provincial minister in approving Wildlife Harvest Plans will take into account scientific *and* Aboriginal traditional knowledge of "Wildlife populations, numbers, health, distribution and methods for managing Wildlife." See also CQLR, c M-35.1.2, r 1 for Quebec's *New Relationship with the Crees of Québec* (2014).

23 See *supra* note 11, *Great Lakes Protection Act, 2015*, and *Climate Change Mitigation and Low-carbon Economy Act* (2016).

24 *Supra* note 12: *CEEA*, s 19(3); *First Nations Oil and Gas Environmental Assessment Regulations*, s 11(2); *supra* note 17: *Species at Risk Act*, SNB 2012, ss 15(2), 18(2); *Endangered Species Act, 2007*, SO 2007, ss 1, 5(3), and 48(f); *Species at Risk Act*, SC 2002, Preamble, ss 2(1) status report, 15(2), and 16(2); *Species at Risk (NWT) Act*, s 17(2); *supra* note 20: *Nunavut Planning and Project Assessment Act*, s 103(3).

25 *Wildlife Act NWT*, *supra* note 15.

26 Ontario *Endangered Species Act*, *supra* note 17 at s 2 (1).

27 *Constitution Act, 1982*, Sched B to the Canada Act 1982 (UK), 1982, c 11 [*Constitution*].

28 *Oceans Act supra* note 13. This may be a reference to the long history of non-Aboriginal fisheries.

29 *Canada National Marine Conservation Areas Act*, *supra* note 14. It is interesting that the maritime regimes speak of *ecological* knowledge as opposed to environmental knowledge. The recent Ontario strategy legislation, *Great Lakes Protection Act, 2015*, and *Climate Change Mitigation and Low-carbon Economy Act* (2016), does as well.

30 See *Environmental Protection and Enhancement Act*, *supra* note 11, s 15.3(1). See also *Yukon Environmental and Socio-economic Assessment Act*, *supra* note 10, s 33(a), where the Yukon Environmental and Socio-economic Assessment Board has the power to make rules respecting the integration of science and traditional information. Other board rules may call for this.

31 *Behn v Moulton Contracting Ltd*, [2013] 2 SCR 227, 2013 SCC 26 at para 33 [*Behn*].

32 This was part of the problem in *Ktunaxa Nation v British Columbia (Forests, Lands and Natural Resource Operations)*, 2017 SCC 54 at paras 35–38. For an inadequate analogy consider the idea of a "favourite fishing hole" where the location is kept secret and only disclosed in confidence to other "proper" persons.

33 *Behn*, *supra* note 31 at para 37.

34 *Quebec (Attorney General) v Moses*, [2010] 1 SCR 557, 2010 SCC 17 [*Moses*].

35 *Interpretation Act*, RSC 1985, c. I-21. The *Interpretation Act*, RSNWT 1988, c I-8, s

11, and *Interpretation Act*, RSY 2002, c 125, s 8 are identical. Ontario's *Legislation Act, 2006*, SO 2006, c 21, Sched F, s 69 is similar.

36 *Moses supra* note 34 at para 101.

37 *Syncrude Canada Ltd v Canada (Attorney General)*, 2014 FC 776 at para 48, aff'd *Syncrude Canada Ltd v Canada (Attorney General)*, 2016 FCA 160; see also reference in *114957 Canada Ltée (Spraytech, Société d'arrosage) v Hudson (Town)*, [2001] 2 SCR 241, 2001 SCC 40 at paras 30–32 [*Spraytech*]. As to the polluter pays principle see *Imperial Oil Ltd v Quebec (Minister of the Environment)*, [2003] 2 SCR 624, 2003 SCC 58 at para 23.

38 *Moses* supra note 34 at para 101.

39 SNWT 2014, c 31.

40 *Supra* note 12, s 4. But see *Canada (Minister of the Environment) v Bennett Environmental Inc*, 2005 FCA 261 at para 63. See also Considering Aboriginal traditional knowledge in environmental assessments conducted under the *Canadian Environmental Assessment Act* – Interim Principles, online: <https://ceaa-acee.gc.ca/default.asp?lang=En&n=4A795E76-1> [*CEAA* Interim Principles].

41 *CEAA*, SC 1992, c 37, s 4. That purpose statement omitted ATK.

42 *Environmental Resource Centre v Canada (Minister of Environment)*, 2001 FCT 1423 at para 141.

43 *Union of Nova Scotia Indians v Canada (Attorney General)*, 1996 CanLII 11847, 122 FTR 81 at para 67 (cited to FTR) [*Union of Nova Scotia Indians*]. That standard was met in the case.

44 *Moses supra* note 34 at para 45.

45 *Aboriginal Consultation and Accommodation - Updated Guidelines for Federal Officials to Fulfill the Duty to Consult (March 2011)* (Minister of the Department of Aboriginal Affairs and Northern Development Canada, Ottawa: 2011) at 25, online: <http://www.aadnc-aandc.gc.ca/DAM/DAM-INTER-HQ/STAGING/texte-text/intgui_1100100014665_eng.pdf>.

46 *Supra* note 17, s 1.

47 *Wildlands League v Ontario (Natural Resources and Forestry)*, 2016 ONCA 741 at paras 16–17 and 91–99.

48 *Western Copper Corporation v Yukon Water Board*, 2011 YKSC 16 at paras 119–126.

49 *Supra* note 18, s 4.

50 *Animal Alliance of Canada v Canada (Attorney General)*, [1999] 4 FCR 72, 1999 CanLII 8154.

51 *Supra* note 17, s 6.

52 *Adam v Canada (Environment)*, 2011 FC 962 [*Adam*].

53 *Ibid* at para 65.

54 *Ibid* at paras 66–67.

55 *Ibid* at para 33.

56 *Supra* note 11, s 2, and in s 40 (purpose of environmental assessment process).

57 *Castle-Crown Wilderness Coalition v Alberta (Director of Regulatory Assurance Division, Alberta Environment)*, 2005 ABCA 283 at para 55.

58 *Court v Alberta Environmental Appeal Board*, 2003 ABQB 456 at para 76.

59 *Supra* note 14, s 4.

60 *Supra* note 17, s 2. There are no court cases from Nova Scotia considering this section. In *Western Canada Wilderness Committee v British Columbia (Ministry of Forests)*, 2003 BCCA 403, the court commented on Nova Scotia's inclusion of the precautionary principle. See also *Spraytech, supra* note 37.

61 *Supra* note 17, s 2.

62 *Supra* note 20, s 1.

63 *Supra* note 17, s 9.

64 *Supra* note 9, s 8.

65 *Supra* note 16, s 6(2).

66 *Great Lakes United v Canada (Minister of the Environment)*, [2010] 2 FCR 515, 2009 FC 408 at paras 199–202.

67 It has been estimated that some 75% of Canada's planned megaprojects ($100M+) will be in the Treaty 8 area.

68 *SARA*, note 17, s 7.

69 *Ibid*. Quotation edit to expand acronym in the legislation.

70 *Ibid*, s 8.1. Acronym added by way of edit in quotation.

71 *Ibid*, s 10.1.

72 *Ibid*, s 10.2(c).

73 *Ibid*, s 2(1) ("status report" means a report, prepared in accordance with the requirements of regulations made under subsection 21(2), that contains a summary of the best available information on the status of a wildlife species, including scientific knowledge, community knowledge, and Aboriginal traditional knowledge).

74 *Ibid*, s 15(1).

75 *Ibid*, s 15(2). Emphasis added.

76 *Ibid*, s 15(1)(1)(ii).

77 *Ibid*, s 16(2). Emphasis added.

78 *Ibid*, s 18(1). Emphasis added.

79 *Ibid*, s 18(3).

80 *Aboriginal traditional knowledge: process and protocols guidelines* (2010), online: <https://www.canada.ca/en/environment-climate-change/services/committee-status-endangered-wildlife/aboriginal-traditional-knowledge.html>.

81 See *supra* note 17.

82 *Tsawwassen First Nation Final Agreement Act*, SBC 2007, c 39, Sched, c 10, Wildlife Management Plans, para 43 (provincial minister will take into account Tsawwassen First Nation ATK); *Maa-nulth First Nations Final Agreement Act*, SBC 2007, c 43, Sched, c 23, para 23.10.1 ("consult with applicable Maa-nulth [FN] ATK").

83 *White River First Nation v Yukon Government*, 2013 YKSC 66 [*White River*].

84 *Ibid*, required under YESAA, s 74(2): "A decision body considering a recommendation in respect of a project shall consult a first nation for which no final agreement is in effect if the project is to be located wholly or partly, or might have significant adverse environmental or socio-economic effects, in the first nation's territory."

85 *Ibid*, paraphrased from paras 1–3 and 44–53.

86 *Ibid* at para 112.

87 *Ibid*, paraphrased from paras 56–73.

88 *Liard First Nation v Yukon Government and Selwyn Chihong Mining Ltd*, 2011 YKSC 55 at paras 25–37 [*Liard*].

89 *White River, supra* note 83 at para 123. See at para 112: "While s. 74(2) is drafted somewhat narrowly in that respect, I rely on the *Haida Nation, Taku River Tlingit* and *Rio Tinto* cases to find that it nonetheless requires an exchange or dialogue that gives the First Nation some meaningful input into the decision-making process."

90 *Ibid* at para 106; and regarding exchanging Draft Decision Documents, paras 109 and 122.

91 Canadian Institute of Resources Law, Occasional Paper #44 *Alberta First Nations Consultation & Accommodation Handbook* (2014) [*Handbook*], online: <http://dspace.ucalgary.ca/jspui/bitstream/1880/50216/1/ConsultationHandbookOP44.pdf>; see also Chris W Sanderson, QC, Keith Bergner & Michelle S Jones, "The Crown's Duty to Consult Aboriginal Peoples: Towards an Understanding of the Source, Purpose, and Limits of the Duty" (2011–2012) 49 Alta L Rev 821.

92 *Haida Nation v British Columbia (Minister of Forests)*, 2004 SCC 73, [2004] 3 SCR 511 [*Haida*].

93 *Taku River Tlingit First Nation v British Columbia (Project Assessment Director)*, 2004 SCC 74, [2004] 3 SCR 550 [*Taku River*].

94 *Mikisew Cree First Nation v Canada (Minister of Canadian Heritage)*, 2005 SCC 69, [2005] 3 SCR 388 [*Mikisew*].

95 *Beckman v Little Salmon/Carmacks First Nation*, 2010 SCC 53 [*Beckman*].

96 *Handbook, supra* note 91. See generally Part 3 and Appendix 4A & 4B. YESAA is in effect a legislated framework for satisfying the Crown's duty to consult and accommodate in the Yukon see: *Liard, supra* note 88 at 113 and *White River, supra* note 83 at 96–112

97 *Handbook, supra* note 91 at 1.3; the cited quote is from *Haida, supra* note 92 at para 60.

98 *Ibid*.

99 *West Moberly First Nations v British Columbia (Chief Inspector of Mines)*, 2011

BCCA 247, leave refused 2012 CanLII 8361 (SCC).

100 *Ibid* at para 26.

101 *Supra* note 44.

102 *CEAA*, supra note 12, s 5. Provincial Environmental Assessment legislation does not include similar provisions.

103 *Ibid*, s 19(3).

104 Often historically under the *Fisheries Act*, RSC 1985, c F-14, but this has changed.

105 Recent JRPs include the same language: Jackpine Mine Expansion Joint Review Panel Agreement, section 6; the Enbridge's Northern Gateway Pipeline Joint Review Panel Agreement, section 8; and the JRP for the New Prosperity Mine Report (2013) included the original Terms of Reference limiting the consideration of validity or strength, online: <https://ceaa-acee.gc.ca/050/documents/p63928/95631E.pdf> at 258.

106 *Council of the Innu of Ekuanitshit v Canada (Attorney General)*, 2014 FCA 189; leave refused 2015 CanLII 10578 (SCC) [*Ekuanitshit*].

107 *Ibid* at para 93.

108 *Ibid* at para 97.

109 *Ibid* at para 98.

110 *Ibid* at paras 101–102. The decision to not contest the specific findings of the JRP was fatal in that case, but it may have been influenced by the lack of funding to conduct studies to advance proper ATK: see paras 114 to 118.

111 *R v Van der Peet*, [1996] 2 SCR 507, 137 DLR (4th) 289 [*Van der Peet*]. The companion decisions in *R v NTC Smokehouse Ltd*, [1996] 2 SCR 672, 137 DLR. (4th) 528, and *R v Gladstone*, [1996] 2 SCR 723, 137 DLR (4th) 648 [*Gladstone*] were similar "harvesting" cases decided at the same time, but they all applied the *Van der Peet* test.

112 *Van der Peet, ibid* at para 46.

113 In *R v Sappier; R v Gray*, 2006 SCC 54, [2006] 2 SCR 686, the SCC dealt with some confusion that had arisen with the application of the *Van der Peet* test. As to the distinctive test, the enquiry into culture (at para 45) "is really an inquiry into the pre-contact way of life of a particular aboriginal community, including their means of survival, their socialization methods, their legal systems, and, potentially, their trading habits."

114 *Delgamuukw, supra* note 3 at paras 110–112.

115 *Ibid* at para 143.

116 *Ibid* at para 117; also see paras 128 to 130.

117 *Supra* note 4.

118 *Tsilhqot'in Nation v British Columbia*, 2014 SCC 44.

119 Every Species at Risk Act, Wildlife Act, or Fisheries Act proscribes some form of hunting or fishing. One can speculate that the lower evidentiary standard of reasonable doubt may be a factor in the framing of Aboriginal rights.

120 [1990] 1 SCR 1075, 70 DLR (4th) 385 [*Sparrow*].

121 [1996] 3 SCR 101, 138 DLR. (4th) 657 [*Adams*].

122 For example, *SARA*, s 3.

# 46

# Privilege in Environmental Enforcement

ERIN EACOTT

## 1. Privilege 101—Its Purpose

In both prosecutions and civil litigation there is a basic rule regarding disclosure of evidence. In prosecutions, the rule is that an accused has a right to all relevant information regarding the prosecution so that the accused can make full answer and defence. For civil litigation, the axiom is that all relevant evidence should be available to the parties in the litigation.

Privilege is an exception to these rules because it precludes obtaining and/or tendering relevant evidence. Privilege has been found by the courts to apply in situations where disclosure of the relevant information would cause serious harm to people, the judicial process or the public's interest. From a prosecution perspective, these are situations where the need to protect the information outweighs the accused's right to full answer and defence.

## Types of Privilege Found in Environmental Enforcement

This article discusses the several key types of privilege that are encountered in environmental enforcement, namely:

- Informer Privilege
- Investigative Technique
- Ongoing Investigation
- Third Party *Privacy* (not privilege)

* *Counsel, Public Prosecution Service of Canada, Regulatory and Economic Crime Team, Edmonton, Alberta.* *Any views or opinions expressed in this article are solely those of the presenter and are in no way to be taken as the view, policy or opinion of the Attorney General of Canada, the Director of Public Prosecutions or the Public Prosecution Service of Canada.*

- National Interest Privilege
- Cabinet Confidences
- Solicitor-Client Privilege
- Work Product/Litigation Privilege

Informer privilege and solicitor-client privilege are the two main types of class privilege. This means there is a *prima facie* presumption of inadmissibility of relevant information.

The other types of privilege listed above are types of case-by-case privilege. This means there is a *prima facie* presumption of admissibility. For the information in a particular case to be inadmissible, it must meet a common law test, such as the Wigmore test. In general, the tests balance the interests in keeping the relevant information secret with the accused's right to make full answer and defence (or in the civil context, in the party's interest in full disclosure).

Many of the types of case-by-case privilege, such as investigative privilege, fall under the category of public interest privilege, whereby it is in the public's interest to keep the information secret. Public interest privilege is protected by both common law and section 37 of the *Canada Evidence Act*.

The remainder of this article briefly discusses each of the above listed types of privilege, in order of how they may be encountered over the course of an environmental investigation through to a prosecution.

## INFORMER PRIVILEGE

Informer privilege arises when a person has provided information to officers about an investigation and the person wishes to remain anonymous.

The purpose of informer privilege is two-fold. First, it protects people who have provided information to officers. Second, it encourages people to come forward to the police with information regarding offences.[1]

Informer privilege is only granted by the Crown. It is not granted to every witness who wishes their identity to remain a secret. Once granted, only the informant can waive the privilege.

In order to protect informer privilege, prosecutors redact all information from disclosure that could identify an informant. In some cases, even indicating the existence of an informant can identify them.

In environmental enforcement, investigations often commence as a result of a tip by a member of the public, for example that a spill has occurred or wildlife has been killed or injured. In some cases, the tipster wishes to remain anonymous. This anonymity can be especially important in rural areas where a limited number of people may have witnessed the incident. In some cases, it is the employee of the company that committed the offence who provides the tip, and the employee is concerned that they might lose their job as a result. Such whistleblower cases are an example of where simply indicating the existence of an informant could identify him or her (the offending company could, for instance, go on a hunt to identify the employee).

There are several ways that members of the public can provide tips of environmental offences. Crime Stoppers is one example. In addition, each province has its own environmental violation hotline. Such hotlines are anonymous and a type of informer privilege. Even the tip sheet recorded by the person who took the hotline call is protected by informer privilege.[2]

### INVESTIGATIVE TECHNIQUE

An investigative technique used by officers is privileged where disclosure of the technique would undermine the use of the technique in current and future investigations. Investigative technique is an example of case-by-case privilege. The court must balance whether the interests in keeping the technique secret override the accused's right to full answer and defence.

Investigative technique privilege arises in environmental enforcement, particularly in wildlife trafficking. It often results in the sealing of an Information to Obtain a Search Warrant (i.e. the contents of the Information to Obtain remain sealed in court and unavailable to the public or the individual upon whom the Search Warrant is executed). An example of investigative technique which may be deemed privileged in wildlife trafficking is the type of undercover vehicle used.

### ONGOING INVESTIGATION

Information about an ongoing investigation by officers is privileged where its disclosure would undermine the investigation. For example, people might destroy evidence if they know the details of the investigation.

Ongoing investigation is an example of case-by-case privilege. The court must balance the public interest in disseminating information on the investigation with the importance of keeping investigative information secret.

There are many reasons for information in an ongoing investigation to be privileged. For instance, disclosure may:

i) Result in the destruction of evidence and/or lack of cooperation by witnesses;
ii) Breach the rights of the individual being investigated. They are innocent until proven guilty;
iii) Breach privacy rights of third parties;
iv) Contaminate the minds of potential witnesses and/or jurors.

(There have been cases where police have revealed too much information about an investigation thus resulting in the trial being moved from the jurisdiction where the offence occurred.[3])

Civil actions against police have been successful where police provided investigative information to the public, particularly where charges did not result from the investigation. Police have been held liable for damages for adverse publicity, loss of business and damage to reputation.[4]

*R. v. Trang* is a helpful case regarding privilege for investigative technique and ongoing investigation.[5]

## THIRD PARTY PRIVACY

Third party privacy is not a type of privilege. However, it is important in all prosecutions, including environmental prosecutions, and serves a similar purpose.

The Crown protects third party privacy by redacting personal information from disclosure provided to the accused. For example, core personal information redacted for third parties, such as witnesses, includes home addresses, phone numbers, driver's licences, dates of birth, and social insurance numbers.

It is beyond the scope of this chapter to address third party records (documents). For further information on protecting the privacy and confidentiality of third party records, see the Supreme Court of Canada cases of: *R. v. O'Connor*,[6] *R. v. Mills*,[7] and *R. v. McNeil*.[8]

## NATIONAL INTEREST PRIVILEGE

National interest privilege exists where disclosure of information could affect international relations, national defence or national security.

National interest privilege is protected by section 38 of the *Canada Evidence Act* and applies to criminal and civil trials, as well as federal tribunals. National interest privilege is a type of case-by-case privilege. The relevant test for inadmissibility under s.38 of the *Canada Evidence Act* is set out in *R. v. Ribic.*[9]

Cases involving radioactive materials which have potential environmental and human health impacts are a potential example of where information could be deemed to be privileged for national defence/security.

### CABINET CONFIDENCES

Documents of the Privy Council (this includes the Prime Minister's Cabinet) are privileged. This includes memorandums with proposals/recommendations; discussion papers providing background, analysis or policy options; records to brief Ministers; and draft legislation.

Section 39 of the *Canada Evidence Act* protects Cabinet confidences. Section 39 indicates that the privilege is automatic. Where a Minister or the Clerk of the Privy Council certifies in writing that the information is a confidence of the Privy Council, then the disclosure of the information is refused without examination or hearing by the court. There are exceptions to the privilege of Privy Council documents. For instance, Privy Council documents more than 20 years old are not privileged.

Cabinet confidences are more likely to arise in civil and administrative environmental law matters, such as judicial review. However, they can arise in environmental prosecutions. In one environmental prosecution, I requested documents to assist in understanding the reasons why environmental legislation was drafted that way it was. I wanted the information for the purposes of sentencing so that I could better explain the harm of the offence (failure to provide documents) to the court. I was advised that I could not obtain certain documents because they were Cabinet confidences.

### SOLICITOR-CLIENT PRIVILEGE

Solicitor-client privilege is communication between a solicitor and client for the purpose of seeking or giving legal advice which is intended to be confidential. Not all communications between counsel and client are privileged. Only communications that relate to the provision of confidential legal advice are privileged. Solicitor-client privilege can only be waived by the client. If the client causes the communication to be disclosed to a third party, solicitor-client privilege is deemed to be waived.[10]

Solicitor-client privilege is arguably the most frequent privilege encountered in environmental enforcement. Communications between Crown counsel (such as Public Prosecution Service of Canada counsel, Provincial Justice counsel, Department Legal Services Unit (DLSU) counsel) and an investigative agency is privileged.

During investigation of environmental offences, officers frequently encounter communications between the offender and their counsel or between a third party (witness) and their counsel for the purpose of seeking or giving confidential legal advice.

### Solicitor-Client Privileged Documents and Execution of a Search Warrant—What Happens?

If solicitor-client privilege documents are found during the execution of a search warrant, what happens? There is no statutory process that sets out what an officer should do if solicitor-client privilege documents are found during the execution of a search warrant. There are cases that provide some guidance. Practically speaking, where solicitor-client privilege documents are found (and the location being searched is not a law office[11]), the following occurs:

1. At the time of the execution of the search warrant, the individual being searched makes a claim of solicitor-client privilege over document(s); or, the officer doing the search believes document(s) may be solicitor-client privileged;
2. The officer places the document(s) in a sealed envelope and labels it;
3. At the completion of the search, the officer takes the sealed envelope to Queen's Bench/Superior Court;
4. Defence counsel attends Queen's Bench/Superior Court to review and release to the officer any documents that are not solicitor-client privileged. Defence counsel will usually divide the documents into three groups: documents that are clearly solicitor-client privileged, documents that are not solicitor-client privileged, and documents that are potentially solicitor-client privileged;
5. Defence counsel brings an application to have the court review the remaining documents for a determination of solicitor-client privilege. This should be defence counsel's application. However, in cases where defence counsel has been slow or unreceptive in bringing the application, the Crown has brought it. The party claiming privilege has the onus of proof on a balance of probabilities. The Court usually reviews each document.

This process is slightly different when dealing with electronic seizures by warrant. Officers will often seize a computer or a mirror image that they have made of a hard drive. Officers then search the computer or image offsite, using search terms relevant to the warrant. They make copies of the relevant documents (electronically or as printouts) for the investigation.

There can be claims that solicitor-client privilege documents exist on the computer or image. There are several options to deal with these solicitor-client privilege claims. The option used is often chosen by agreement of Crown and defence counsel.

First, the computer or image can be sealed and taken to Queen's Bench/Superior Court to later be reviewed onsite by defence counsel accompanied by an officer. This option is not practicalwhere the computer or image containes a large amount of material to be reviewed. In addition, Queen's Bench/Superior Court often does not have a lot of secure storage space and so is not keen to receive computers.

Second, the computer or image are not sealed. The investigating officer searches the computer or image offsite for documents relevant to the warrant. Alternatively, an officer independent from the investigation (e.g. from another agency such as the RCMP, or a retired RCMP officer) does the search. The officer can then make a copy of, and retain for the investigation, the relevant documents that are *not* potentially solicitor-client privileged. Alternatively, the officer can print relevant documents *including* those that are potentially solicitor-client privileged, seal them, and take them to Queen's Bench/Superior Court for review and/or a privilege application by defence counsel.

## CLAIMS OF SOLICITOR-CLIENT PRIVILEGE: CHOOSE YOUR OWN ADVENTURE

Imagine that you are defence counsel for an oil company that is being investigated for an oil spill under the *Fisheries Act* and under your applicable provincial environmental act. The investigating officers kindly advise that they will be executing a Search Warrant on the oil company later this week. As defence counsel, you think that some of the documents relevant to the search warrant are solicitor-client privileged. Here is where you get to "choose your own adventure". On the day the officers arrive to execute the warrant, you claim solicitor-client privilege over which of the following:

a) *All* of the documents related to the oil spill incident;

b) Several previously existing documents that you had the vice-president of the oil company send to you by email the previous day;
c) The oil company's internal investigation report of the oil spill incident;
d) Documents which are confidential legal advice between a lawyer and the oil company;
e) Some combination of the above.

The following part of this chapter discusses each of the options a) thru d) above.

**a) *All* of the documents related to the oil spill incident:**

It is not appropriate to claim solicitor-client privilege over all of the documents related to an incident or investigation. Defence counsel in past environmental investigations have attempted to do this. It is like trying to throw a magic cloak of privilege over all of the documents. But no such magic cloak exists. Solicitor-client privilege only applies to documents related to seeking or giving confidential legal advice. Throwing the magic cloak of privilege over all of the documents is contrary to the administration of justice. It results in boxes of documents to syphon through in Queen's Bench/Superior Court. This takes a lot of time and expense, and the court does not have space to securely store such large amounts of documents.

During the execution of a search warrant, there may be a large group or category of documents that defence counsel, or the alleged offender, have not had time to review and for which they are uncertain whether solicitor-client privilege may apply. It is prudent to claim solicitor-client privilege over this large group of documents, and then later attend at Queen's Bench/Superior Court to review and make a determination. This is not an infrequent occurrence, and it is very different than attempting to throw a magic cloak of privilege over all of the documents.

**b) Several previously existing documents that you had the vice-president of the oil company send to you by email the previous day:**

Pre-existing documents are not made privileged just by virtue of being passed to a lawyer (see *Kilbreath v. Saskatchewan (Attorney General)*[12]). I have witnessed such attempts in environmental enforcement cases. It may be that some of the documents sent to you by email are legitimately solicitor-client privileged, but they would not be made so simply by being sent to you.

#### c) The oil company's internal investigation report of the oil spill incident:

A company's internal investigation report of an incident under investigation may or may not be solicitor-client privileged. It depends upon the purpose for which the report was created. Internal investigation reports, also known as environmental audits, are often done by a company after an incident. The primary purpose of the report is usually to determine what happened and how to make changes to prevent a future incident. A company's written procedures often require that an internal investigation report be done following an incident. An internal investigation report does not become solicitor-client privileged by simply being sent to a lawyer, or by simply marking the report as solicitor-client privileged. I have seen both such attempts in environmental enforcement cases.

To be solicitor-client privileged, internal investigation reports need to be created for a purpose of seeking or giving legal advice. This need not be the exclusive purpose, but must be at least one of the purposes of the report. It is not enough for a lawyer to tell a company, "you need to do an internal investigation report". This does not make the report solicitor-client privileged. The lawyer actually needs to do something with, or intend to do something with, the report related to providing confidential legal advice to the company. Once the report is shared with a third party, the solicitor-client privilege is deemed to be waived.

#### d) Documents which are confidential legal advice between a lawyer and the oil company:

This is the only option from a) thru e) above where an appropriate claim of solicitor-client privilege is obvious: documents are solicitor-client privileged where they are for the purpose of seeking or giving confidential legal advice.

### WORK PRODUCT/LITIGATION PRIVILEGE

*Work product privilege* attaches to the work product of Crown counsel in criminal and regulatory (including environmental enforcement) proceedings. Work product privilege includes documents such as Crown counsel's interviews, memorandum, correspondence, briefs, and records of phone conversations. When preparing for trial, Crown counsel may discover new evidence, for instance when speaking with a witness, and all new evidence must be disclosed. Such a disclosure obligation means that work product privilege is a little narrower than litigation privilege.

*Litigation privilege* is the same type of privilege as work product privilege, but litigation privilege exists in the civil realm and applies to counsel for the alleged offender in criminal and regulatory offences. Litigation privilege attaches to documents and communications prepared or gathered by counsel, or under counsel's direction, for the "dominant purpose" of anticipated litigation. For litigation privilege to apply to a document, litigation cannot be one of the purposes or even the substantial purpose for the creation of the document; litigation must be the dominant purpose of its creation.[13]

Communications and documents related to settlement negotiations fall under work product and litigation privilege.

### Communication between Lawyer and Expert Witness

The Ontario Court of Appeal case of *Moore v. Getahun*[14] holds that communications between counsel and an expert, including draft reports, are covered by litigation privilege, as long as the communications do not interfere with the expert's independence and objectivity. All of the "foundational information" upon which the expert's opinion is based must be disclosed. I would argue that the principles outlined in this case apply equally to Crown counsels' communications with expert witnesses in criminal and regulatory cases, including environmental enforcement.

The Court of Appeal explained that lawyers' communication with experts in civil cases is crucial in developing expert reports that "are comprehensible and responsive to the pertinent legal issues in the case."[15] This applies equally in environmental investigations and prosecutions. In environmental investigations and prosecutions, scientific experts are used to convey complicated evidence. These experts are usually unfamiliar with the legal system and have never written an expert report for court or testified. Crown counsel need to openly discuss and review draft reports with expert witnesses to ensure that their opinions are clear, understandable by a lay person and will assist the Court. As described by the Ontario Court of Appeal, disclosure of such communications would:

- "inhibit careful preparation" of expert witnesses and their reports;
- "discourage participants from reducing preliminary or tentative views to writing, a necessary step in the development of a sound and thorough opinion";[16] and

- "would also encourage the use of those expert witnesses who make a career of testifying in court and who are often perceived to be hired guns likely to offer partisan opinions, as these expert witnesses may require less guidance and preparation."[17]

### Reports Generated by or for the Offender

In environmental investigations, officers often wish to seize reports, such as expert reports or internal investigation reports, generated by or for a company following an environmental incident for which it is being investigated. Such reports are not protected by litigation privilege if the reports were obtained by the company for determining what happened in the incident and improving the company's practices. The reports *are* protected by litigation privilege if the reports were obtained by the company for the dominant purpose of anticipated litigation.18

In my experience with environmental enforcement, defence counsels' claims of litigation privilege over internal investigation reports seized during search warrants are usually retroactive attempts to apply litigation privilege to the reports. The reports were truly done on the basis of internal procedures which required the report to be done to determine what happened in the incident and to make improvements. At the time the reports were done, they were not done for the dominant purpose of potential litigation.

If a document is prepared in the ordinary course of business, such as pursuant to corporate policy, or would have come into existence despite the anticipated litigation, litigation privilege does not apply, even if one of the document's purposes is anticipated litigation.[19]

## Conclusion

In conclusion, there are many types of privilege that can arise in environmental enforcement from an investigation through to a prosecution. This article addresses some but not all of the possible types of privilege that can arise. The most common types of privilege in environmental enforcement are ongoing investigation, solicitor-client privilege and work product or litigation privilege. For a thorough review of privilege, see the periodical by R. Hubbard., S. Magotiaux and S. Duncan, *The Law of Privilege in Canada,* Canada Law Book.

## NOTES

1 *R v Leipert*, [1997] 1 SCR 281 (SCC).

2 *Ibid.*

3 *R v Feeney*, 1998 CarswellBC 347 (SC).

4 See for example, *Uni-Jet Industrial Pipe Ltd v Canada (Attorney General)* (2001), 156 Man R (2d) 14; 2001 MBCA 40.

5 *R v Trang* (2002), 168 CCC (3d) 145 (ABQB).

6 [1995] SCJ No 98.

7 [1999] 3 SCR 668.

8 2009 SCC 3.

9 *R v Ribic* (2003), 185 CCC (3d) 129, [2005] 1 FCR 33 (FCA), leave to appeal to SCC refused 185 CCC (3d) 129n. This test is nicely summarized in Robert W Hubbard, Susan Magotiaux & Suzanne M Duncan, *The Law of Privilege in Canada* (Toronto: Canada Law Book, 2006) (2 vol looseleaf) at 4.130.

10 *R v Lavallee*, [2002] 3 SCR 209; *Canada v Solosky* (1979), 50 CCC (2d) 495 (SCC).

11 Where the location being searched is a law office, the steps to be taken are clearly set out in *R v Lavallee, ibid*; and *Maranda v Richer*, [2003] 3 SCR 193 (SCC).

12 *Kilbreath v Saskatchewan (Attorney General)*, 2004 SKQB 489.

13 The leading case on litigation privilege is *Blank v Canada (Department of Justice)*, 2006 SCC 39. See also *Lizotte v Aviva Insurance Company of Canada*, [2016] 2 SCR 521.

14 *Moore v Getahun*, 2015 ONCA 55 (CanLII) at paras 50-78.

15 *Ibid* at para 62.

16 *Ibid* at para 71.

17 *Ibid* at para 65.

18 But see *R v Bidzinski et al*, 2007 MBQB 138. *Bidzinski* holds that documents made in reasonable anticipation of a civil litigation are not protected by litigation privilege for the purposes of production in a criminal investigation. In *Bidzinski*, the Manitoba Queen's Bench found that written witness statements taken in anticipation of civil litigation were not protected by litigation privilege when seized during a criminal investigation because the civil proceeding and criminal proceeding were not related.

19 See for example, *Transalta Corporation v Market Surveillance Administrator*, 2015 ABQB 180.

# 47

# Judicial Notice of Climate Change

BRENDA HEELAN POWELL

## Introduction

Recent catastrophic weather events provide tangible evidence of the detrimental impacts of climate change.[1] The Intergovernmental Panel on Climate Change (IPCC), which was formed in 1988 by the World Meteorological Organization and the United Nations Environment Programme, has concluded that global warming is unequivocally happening.[2] Furthermore, the IPCC has noted that anthropogenic greenhouse gas emissions (GHGs) are extremely likely to be the cause of global warming.

Despite these developments, there remains a good portion of the Canadian population that denies climate change is happening.[3] In the United States, Senator Jim Inhofe—a member of the Senate Environmental and Public Works Committee—is a high-profile climate change denier and author of *The Greatest Hoax: How the Global Warming Conspiracy Threatens Your Future.* As an illustration of his disbelief in climate change, in early 2015, he tossed a snowball in the Senate as his evidence that global warming is a hoax.[4] Similarly, President Donald Trump has repeatedly expressed skepticism about the existence of climate change.[5]

So, how have the courts responded in light of the strong scientific consensus regarding climate change and a somewhat skeptical public? Climate change litigation is still fairly novel in Canada, the United States, and abroad. Despite its nascent stage, several courts have been sufficiently satisfied with the state of climate change science to take judicial notice of climate change as a matter of fact.

## What *Is* Judicial Notice?

Judicial notice is a procedural mechanism that "allows uncontroversial facts to be established without evidentiary proof."[6] This means that a judicially noticed fact is not subject to the usual processes for testing evidence such as sworn evidence and cross-examination. While judicial notice contributes to the efficiency of court processes by eliminating the formal requirements for submitting evidence, courts use it in a limited manner due to concerns about fairness and accuracy.[7]

The Supreme Court of Canada (SCC) has provided clear direction on the appropriate use of judicial notice in its decisions in *R. v. Find*[8] and *R. v. Spence*.[9] In *R. v. Find*, the SCC stated that:[10]

> Judicial notice dispenses with the need for proof of facts that are clearly uncontroversial or beyond reasonable dispute. Facts judicially noticed are not proved by evidence under oath. Nor are they tested by cross-examination. Therefore, the threshold for judicial notice is strict: a court may properly take judicial notice of facts that are either: (1) so notorious or generally accepted as not to be the subject of debate among reasonable persons; or (2) capable of immediate and accurate demonstration by resort to readily accessible sources of indisputable accuracy.

The SCC provided further elaboration on the appropriate use of judicial notice in *R. v. Spence*. It confirmed that use of judicial notice is only acceptable for facts that are notorious or generally accepted by reasonable persons, or capable of demonstration by referring to easily accessible sources of indisputable accuracy (otherwise referred to as the "Morgan criteria" by the court).

With respect to whether a fact is notorious or generally accepted by reasonable persons, the court established an informed reasonable person test. It stated:[11]

> I believe a court ought to ask itself whether such "fact" would be accepted by reasonable people who have taken the trouble to inform themselves on the topic as not being the subject of reasonable dispute for the particular purpose for which it is to be used, keeping in mind that the need for reliability and trustworthiness increases directly with the centrality of the "fact" to the disposition of the controversy.

Further, the SCC indicated that the appropriate use of judicial notice depends upon whether a fact is adjudicative or non-adjudicative. The centrality of the fact to disposition of the matter is also relevant as to whether or not judicial notice is appropriate. As the SCC explained:

> No doubt there is a useful distinction between "adjudicative facts" (the where, when and why of what the accused is alleged to have done) and "social facts" and "legislative facts" which have relevance to the reasoning process and may involve broad considerations of policy: Paciocco and Stuesser, at p. 286. However, simply categorizing an issue as "social fact" or "legislative fact" does not license the court to put aside the need to examine the trustworthiness of the "facts" sought to be judicially noticed.
>
> ... the permissible scope of judicial notice should vary according to the nature of the issue under consideration. For example, more stringent proof may be called for of facts that are close to the center of the controversy between the parties (whether social, legislative or adjudicative) as distinguished from background facts at or near the periphery. To put it another way, the closer the fact approaches the dispositive issue, the more the court ought to insist on compliance with the stricter Morgan criteria.[12]

The SCC established that, with respect to judicial notice, the appropriate approach is to apply the Morgan criteria regardless of the type of fact sought to be judicially noticed. If the Morgan criteria are met, then the fact can be judicially noticed. If the Morgan criteria are not met and the fact is adjudicative, then the fact will not be judicially noticed.

However, when dealing with social facts or legislative facts, the Morgan criteria may not necessarily be conclusive. The SCC stated that "[o]utside the realm of adjudicative fact, the limits of judicial notice are inevitably somewhat elastic."[13] As the legislative or social fact approaches the central issue, the Morgan criteria have more weight in determining acceptability of judicial notice. In the context of climate change litigation, it is likely that the purpose for which climate change science is adduced will dictate the willingness of the courts to accept it as a matter of judicial notice.

## Judicial Notice of Climate Change

Despite strong scientific consensus, there remains public debate on the existence and cause of climate change. However, this debate is not taking place in the courts.[14] While there is still substantial public skepticism in some sectors of society, most courts (at least in the United States) have been sufficiently satisfied with the state of climate change science to take judicial notice of climate change as a matter of fact. Climate change debates in the courts tend not to be centred on its existence or its cause but rather on its impacts.[15]

## BRIEF OVERVIEW OF CLIMATE CHANGE LITIGATION

An assessment of climate change litigation in the United States and internationally was conducted by the United Nations Environment Programme in cooperation with the Columbia Law School's Sabin Center for Climate Change (UN-Sabin Assessment).[16] As of March 2017, climate changes cases "had been filed in 24 countries (25 if one counts the European Union), with 654 cases filed in the U.S. and over 230 cases filed in all other countries combined."[17] With respect to non-US litigation, Australia has seen more cases (80) than any other country and Canada has seen 13 cases filed as of March 2017.[18] Overall, the UN-Sabin Assessment found that both the number of cases and the number of countries where cases have been filed have grown in the past few years.

The UN-Sabin Assessment found that:

> Recent judicial decisions and court filings reveal several trends in regards to the purposes of climate change litigation. Five such trends are described here: holding governments to their legislative and policy commitments; linking the impacts of resource extraction to climate change and resilience; establishing that particular emissions are the proximate cause of particular adverse climate change impacts; establishing liability for failures (or efforts) to adapt to climate change; and applying the public trust doctrine to climate change.[19]

An earlier assessment of climate change litigation done by Wilensky found:

> Climate change litigation across the world does not lend itself to one consistent narrative. Most litigation surrounding climate change has involved tactical suits aimed at specific projects or details regarding implementation of existing climate policies. Beyond that, jurisdictions vary widely in terms of the amount, nature, and relative success of climate change litigation.[20]

In the United States, Wilensky found that climate change litigation is used strategically in driving the course of climate change regulation. In other parts of the world, climate change litigation has been aimed at specific projects or at details regarding implementation of existing climate change policies.

## THE CANADIAN EXPERIENCE

As can be seen in the foregoing, climate change litigation has not yet established a strong foothold in Canada. A review of the Columbia Law School's Sabin Center for Climate Change database indicates that there have been approximately 13 cases in Canada dealing with climate change matters. Despite the sparsity of climate change litigation in Canada, there have been instances where the courts have taken judicial notice of climate change science.

In *Citizens for Riverdale Hospital v. Bridgepoint Health Services*,[21] the Divisional Court of the Ontario Superior Court considered an appeal from a decision of the Ontario Municipal Board, which had reviewed and approved planning decisions made by the City of Toronto. One ground for appeal was that the board erred in law when it determined that the plan and zoning bylaw amendments conformed with objectives and policies regarding the environment and carbon dioxide ($CO_2$) emissions. Ultimately, the court found no reason to doubt the correctness of the board's decision in this regard.

In making its decision, the court made the following statement:

> I do, however, agree that the issue of $CO_2$ emissions is an important environmental concern to all members of the public, and in particular, those persons who live in the nearby vicinity where the construction and demolition will take place.

The court explicitly accepted that climate change is an important environmental issue. This means that, at least implicitly, the court accepted that climate change science is sufficiently established as to accept the fact of climate change and the significance of $CO_2$ emissions as a matter of judicial notice.

The Federal Court made an even stronger statement in *Syncrude Canada Ltd. v. Attorney General of Canada*.[22] In this case, a provision of the federal *Renewable Fuel Regulations* made pursuant to the *Canadian Environmental Protection Act, 1999* was subject to a constitutional challenge. This provision required that diesel fuel produced, imported, or sold in Canada contain at least 2 percent renewable fuel. In its challenge, Syncrude argued that the dominant purpose of the impugned provision was to regulate non-renewable resources and promote the economic benefits of protecting the environment and to create a demand for biofuels in the Canadian marketplace. In essence, Syncrude argued that the provision was not a constitutionally sound use of the federal criminal law power, as any prohibition of harm was merely ancillary.

The Federal Court upheld the constitutionality of the impugned provision. In response to Syncrude's assertion that the production and consumption of petroleum fuels are not dangerous and do not pose a risk to human health or safety, the court stated:

> [83] … there is a real evil and a reasonable apprehension of harm in this case. The evil of global climate change and the apprehension of harm resulting from the enabling of climate change through the combustion of fossil fuels has been widely discussed and debated by leaders on the international stage. Contrary to Syncrude's submission, this is a real, measured evil, and the harm has been well documented.

In affirming the decision of the Federal Court, the Federal Court of Appeal stated:

> [62] It must be recalled that it is uncontroverted that GHGs are harmful to both health and the environment and as such, constitute an evil that justifies the exercise of the criminal law power.

The *Syncrude* decision reaffirms the view previously expressed by Canadian courts that protection of the environment is a valid criminal purpose.[23] The court clearly accepts that, as a matter of judicial notice, climate change is actually happening.

### THE US EXPERIENCE

By far, the bulk of climate change litigation worldwide has been generated in the United States. American courts have taken judicial notice of several aspects of climate change science. This includes acknowledgement of the link between GHGs and climate change, the mechanism of climate change (i.e. the greenhouse effect), and the general impacts of climate change.

There are examples of judicial notice of climate change science by the American courts dating back to the 1990s. The *City of Los Angeles v. National Highway Traffic Safety Administration Center for Auto Safety*[24] decision involved a challenge to the decision of the National Highway Traffic Safety Administration's refusal to prepare an environmental impact statement covering its Corporate Average Fuel Economy standards for model years 1987–1988 and

1989. Ultimately, the court held that the challenge failed on its merits. However, in reaching this determination, the court clearly stated that "[n]o one disputes the causal link between carbon dioxide and global warming."[25]

A 2007 decision—*Massachusetts v. EPA*[26]—has become the leading climate change case in the United States. In this case, a group of states petitioned for *certiorari* that the EPA had abdicated its responsibility under the *Clean Air Act* to regulate four greenhouse gases. The questions before the US Supreme Court were whether the EPA had statutory authority to regulate GHGs emanating from new motor vehicles and, if so, were the EPA's stated reasons for not doing so justified. The court determined that, under the *Clean Air Act*, the EPA had the authority to regulate GHGs from new motor vehicles. Further, the court concluded that the EPA failed to provide reasoned explanation for its refusal to regulate GHGs from new motor vehicles. In reaching its decision, the Supreme Court stated:[27]

> A well-documented rise in global temperatures has coincided with a significant increase in the concentration of carbon dioxide in the atmosphere. Respected scientists believe the two trends are related. For when carbon dioxide is released into the atmosphere, it acts like a ceiling of a greenhouse, trapping solar energy and retarding the escape of reflected heat. It is therefore a species – the most important species – of a "greenhouse gas".

Further, the Supreme Court found that the EPA did not dispute the causal connection between man-made GHGs and global warming. It also found that "[t]he harms associated with climate change are serious and well recognized."[28] The harms identified by the court included retreat of mountain glaciers, reduction in snow cover, earlier spring melting, and accelerated rate of rise of sea levels.

The aspects of climate change science judicially noticed in the *Massachusetts v. EPA* decision were referenced by the US Supreme Court in *American Electric Power v. Connecticut.*[29] In this case, the plaintiffs filed nuisance actions against five major power companies, which were the largest greenhouse gas emitters in the United States. The plaintiffs sought a cap on GHGs to be set for each power company. In this case, the court held that the *Clean Air Act* and actions by the EPA pursuant to that Act displaced any common law rights to seek abatement of GHGs from power plants.

In making its decision, the Supreme Court referred to its previous comments on climate change science in the *Massachusetts v. EPA* decision.[30] In particular, the court noted that GHGs cause the greenhouse effect and that GHGs have been elevated to unprecedented levels almost entirely by human activity. The court also noted the impacts of climate change such as melting ice caps, rising sea levels, hurricanes, and floods.

Judicial notice of climate change science was also taken in *Green Mountain Chrysler v. Crombie.*[31] In this case, a variety of motor vehicle manufacturers challenged Vermont's adoption of GHGs regulations for new motor vehicles. The court upheld Vermont's plan to adopt such regulations. According to Haughey, the "*Massachusetts* case was vital in the *Green Mountain Chrysler* case because factual findings regarding the reality of global warming and the legitimacy of deeming [greenhouse gases] as pollutants under the [*Clean Air Act*] – the same under which Vermont's new regulations were developed – bolstered Vermont's defense in this case."[32]

Indeed, the court refers to the statement in *Massachusetts v.* EPA that the "harms associated with climate change are serious and well recognized" and include rises in sea levels, irreversible changes to ecosystems, reduced snowpack, and increased spread of disease.[33] As stated by the court:[34]

> In Massachusetts v. EPA, the Supreme Court recognized for the first time the phenomenon of global warming and its potentially catastrophic effects upon our environment. The Supreme Court described human-generated contributions to global warming, including carbon dioxide emissions from motor vehicles.

The decision in *Green Mountain Chrysler v. Crombie* provides another example of American courts taking judicial notice of several aspects of climate change science, including the causal link between human cause GHGs and climate change, and the significant environmental impacts of climate change.

The decision in *Massachusetts v.* EPA was also noted by the court in *Coalition for Responsible Regulation v.* EPA,[35] which opened its decision with the following:[36]

> We begin with a brief primer on greenhouse gases. As their name suggest, when released into the atmosphere, these gases act "like the ceiling of a greenhouse, trapping solar energy and retarding the escape of reflected heat." *Massachusetts v* EPA, 594 U.S. at 505, 127 S.Ct. 1438. A wide variety of modern human activities result in greenhouse gas emissions; cars, power plants, and industrial sites all release significant amounts of these heat-trapping gases. In recent decades "[a]

well-documented rise in global temperatures has coincided with a significant increase in the concentration of [greenhouse gases] in the atmosphere." *Id.* At 504-05, 127 S. Ct. 1438. Many scientists believe that mankind's greenhouse gas emissions are driving this climate change. These scientists predict that global climate change will cause a host of deleterious consequences, including drought, increasingly severe weather events, and rising sea levels.

In 2014, a New York court took judicial notice of climatological records in *Wohl v. City of New York.*[37] This case involved an action by homeowners to recover damages to their premises and personal property caused by flooding during a severe rainstorm and by backing-up of the public sewer during Hurricane Irene. In the course of its decision, the court took judicial notice of climatological reports issued by the National Data Centre in New Jersey. The court concluded, as a result of the facts accepted through judicial notice, that the city was subjected to an inordinate amount of rainfall and that the flooding was due to the rainfall rather than improper design, inspection, or maintenance of the sewer system.

A 2017 decision in a class action case, *Cole v. Collier,*[38] took judicial notice of certain impacts of climate change. In this case, the plaintiffs sought relief from prison conditions existing during heat waves. In considering the impacts on prisoners, the court stated that "[t]he Court and the parties have no way of knowing when a heat wave will occur, but it is clear that one will come."[39] In a footnote to this statement, the court stated:[40]

> The Court takes judicial notice that "climate scientists forecast with a high degree of confidence that average temperatures in the U.S. will rise throughout this century and that heat waves will become more frequent, more severe, and more prolonged." Daniel W. E. Holt, Heat in U.S. Prisons and Jails: Corrections and the Challenge of Climate Change, Columbia Law School Sabin Center for Climate Change Law, (August 2015), https://web.law.columbia.edu/sites/default/files/microsites/climate-change/holt_-_heat_in_us_prisons_and_jails.pdf.

While not a case of judicial notice, the comments of a Massachusetts District Attorney in dealing with criminal charges against climate protesters who used a lobster boat to stop a coal shipment to a power station are noteworthy.[41] In

2014, Massachusetts District Attorney Samuel Sutter dropped criminal conspiracy charges against two climate activists. In so doing, he stated that climate change is "one of the gravest crises our planet has ever faced" and that "the political leadership on this issue has been sorely lacking."

Along the same line of reasoning, there are several examples of climate change protestors claiming a necessity or justification defence to criminal charges (with varying degrees of success).[42] In one such case, *Iowa v. Pearson*,[43] a person was charged with trespassing. The defendant argued that she was not guilty of trespass because her actions were justified as she was protesting the construction of a pipeline that will contribute to climate change (under Iowa law, a person is not guilty of trespass if he or she can demonstrate justification). Ultimately, Pearson was found guilty, but the court's instructions to the jury included the following:

> You are instructed that the court has taken judicial notice of the following:
>
> ...
>
> 2. When fossil fuels are burned to generate electricity or to power our cars a gas known as carbon dioxide or $CO_2$ is released into the atmosphere where it traps heat. $CO_2$ is considered a greenhouse gas. Accumulation of greenhouse gases is a contributing factor to climate change.
> 3. The State of Iowa, through one of its agencies, the Department of Natural Resources, or DNR has issued a statement relative to the impact of climate change on the State of Iowa as indicated in Exhibit 20 which has been admitted.
>
> ...
>
> These items are regarded by the court to be facts, you may, but are not required to, accept these facts to be true.

Although the justification defence was not successful in this particular case, the court decisively accepted climate change science without requiring expert evidence or cross-examination.

## THE INTERNATIONAL EXPERIENCE

While not as extensive as that in the United States, there has been more experience with climate change litigation internationally than in Canada. In the international arena, climate change litigation has typically been aimed at challenging specific projects or at the implementation of existing climate change policies.[44] Several examples of courts taking judicial notice of the fact of climate change can be found in Australia and New Zealand.

In Australia, the Victorian Civil and Administrative Tribunal (VCAT) considered a challenge to a planning scheme amendment that facilitated the continued operation of a power station.[45] The decision to allow the amendment was challenged on the ground that the planning panel failed to consider the environmental effects of GHGs resulting from continued operation of the power plant. Ultimately, the VCAT found that the planning panel had made an error by failing to allow and consider evidence related to the issue of GHGs.

In determining that GHGs were relevant to the planning scheme amendment, the VCAT stated:

> It is to be observed that a planning scheme may be made to further the objective of "maintaining ecological processes"; and, further, "to balance the present and future interests of all Victorians". These are broad words. Ecological processes include processes within the atmosphere of the earth, including its chemistry and temperature. Many would accept that, in present circumstances, the use of energy that results in the generation of some greenhouse gases is in the present interest of Victorians; but at what cost to the future interests of Victorians? Further the generation of greenhouse gases from a brown coal power station has the potential to give rise to "significant" environmental effects. Hence I think it follows that a planning scheme could contain a provision directed at reducing the emission of greenhouse gases from a coal burning power station – not only to maintain an ecological process, but to balance the present and future interests.[46]

In making this statement, the VCAT accepted several aspects of climate change science as a matter of judicial notice. Firstly, the VCAT accepted the connection between GHGs and climate change. Secondly, the VCAT acknowledged climate change as a significant environmental issue. Lastly, the VCAT recognized the long-term impact of GHGs on future generations.

Another example of judicial notice in the international arena can be found in a New Zealand immigration tribunal decision.[47] In this case, a Tuvalu family appealed a denial of New Zealand resident visas for its family members. The family argued that, if its family members were deported, they would be at risk of suffering the adverse impacts of climate change in Tuvalu, an island nation experiencing the detrimental effects from sea level rise due to climate change. The Immigration and Protection Tribunal found exceptional circumstances of a humanitarian nature that justified allowing the family to remain in New Zealand. These circumstances included the presence of extended family in New Zealand, the family's integration into New Zealand society, and the best interests of the children.

The tribunal did not determine whether or not climate change provided a basis for granting resident visas in this case. However, the tribunal stated:

> As for the climate change issue relied on so heavily, while the Tribunal accepts that exposure to the impacts of natural disasters can, in general terms, be a humanitarian circumstance, nevertheless, the evidence in appeals such as this must establish not simply the existence of a matter of broad humanitarian concern, but that there are exceptional circumstances of a humanitarian nature such that it would be unjust or unduly harsh to deport the particular appellant from New Zealand.[48]

This statement provides a clear example of a decision maker accepting the relationship between climate change and natural disasters as a matter of judicial notice.

In a similar case—*Teitiota v. Minister of Innovation and Employment*[49]—a person sought leave to appeal a decision of the Court of Appeal that had denied leave to appeal to the High Court against a decision of the Immigration and Protection Tribunal. The Immigration and Protection Tribunal had determined that Teitiota did not fit either the Refugee Convention or New Zealand's protected person jurisdiction. Teitiota was seeking such status on the grounds that his homeland (Kiribati) was suffering the effects of climate change. The Court of Appeal denied leave to appeal. The court found that, while Kiribati undoubtedly faces challenges, there is no evidence that the Kiribata government is not taking steps to protect its citizens from the effects of environmental degradation and therefore Teitiota does not face "serious harm" if returned. The court stated that the decisions in this case "do not mean that environmental degradation resulting from climate change or other natural disasters could never create a pathway into the Refugee Convention or protected person jurisdiction."[50] This statement implies that the court accepts the relationship between climate change and adverse environmental and human impacts.

Perhaps one of the most significant decisions in climate change liability, on an international scale, is the decision in *Urgenda Foundation v. The State of the Netherlands (Ministry of Infrastructure and the Environment).*[51] In this case, the Hague District Court required the Dutch government to take action to ensure that Dutch GHGs are at least 25 percent lower than 1990 levels by 2020.[52] In making its decision, the court made considerable reference to the climate change science released by the IPCC and found that:

> the possibility of damages for those whose interests Urgenda represent, including current and future generations of Dutch nationals, is so great and concrete that given its duty of care, the State must make an adequate contribution, greater than its current contribution, to prevent hazardous climate change.[53]

The court concluded that, as a matter of legal protection and in accordance with its duty of care, the Dutch government must do more to avert the imminent danger caused by climate change.

Similar arguments were successfully made in *Leghari v. Federation of Pakistan*.[54] In this case, the petitioner was an agriculturist and a citizen of Pakistan who challenged the "inaction, delay and lack of seriousness on the part of the Federal Government and the Government of the Punjab to address the challenges and to meet the vulnerabilities associated with Climate Change."[55] The petitioner argued that climate change is a serious threat to water, food, and energy security, which undermines the constitutional and fundamental right to life. In making its decision, the court stated:

> Climate Change is a defining challenge of our time and has led to dramatic alterations in our planet's climate system. For Pakistan, these climatic variations have primarily resulted in heavy floods and droughts, raising serious concerns regarding water and food security. On a legal and constitutional plane this is clarion call for the protection of fundamental rights of the citizens of Pakistan, in particular, the vulnerable and weak segments of the society who are unable to approach this Court.[56]

In this case, the court ultimately found that the state's delay in implementing a climate change framework offended the fundamental rights of Pakistan's citizens. The decision reveals the court's acceptance of climate change science, particularly the environmental and human impacts of climate change.

It should be noted that a very similar action is ongoing in the United States wherein the applicants are suing the government for violation of the public trust for failing to take steps to reduce, and in fact contributing to, the impacts of climate change.[57] This action aligns with other recent US climate change decisions based upon the notion of public trust.[58]

## Looking Ahead

Although climate change litigation is in its infancy in Canada,[59] there are already examples of Canadian courts taking judicial notice of climate change science. Further, as novel climate change litigation gains momentum, the judiciary's treatment of climate change science is becoming increasingly important.

The purpose for which climate change science is adduced will dictate the willingness of courts to accept it as a matter of judicial notice. Climate change science introduced for non-adjudicative purposes, such as in social or legislative contexts, is likely to receive judicial notice. However, climate change science introduced for adjudicative purposes, such as the demonstration of actual harm, is likely to be subject to traditional evidential requirements.

Where climate change science is subject to traditional evidential requirements, the courts must proceed with some measure of reasonable flexibility. As stated by McLeod-Kilmurray:

> Scientific expertise and uncertainty should not be an excuse for courts to abdicate their legal duties, and should not be used as tools to hide policy preferences or to deny justice to those most seriously affected by environmental harm.[60]

Consequently, while judicial notice of climate change science may not be appropriate in all circumstances, the courts should remain alert to the fact that significant scientific consensus on the existence, mechanisms, and impacts of climate change is already reasonably established.

#### NOTES

1 See IPCC, 2012, *Managing the Risks of Extreme Events and Disasters to Advance Climate Change Adaptation.* A Special Report of Working Groups I and II of the Intergovernmental Panel on Climate Change (ed by Christopher B. Field et al), which "focuses on the relationship between climate change and extreme weather and climate events, the impacts of such events, and the strategies to manage the associated risks" (p viii).

2 IPCC, Climate Change 2014: Synthesis Report: Summary for Policymakers (ed by the Core Writing Team, Rajendra K. Pachauri & Leo Meyer).

3 According to Forum Research Inc, Toronto, Canada (19 July 2014), 13% of the Canadian population is comprised of climate change deniers.
4 Senator James Inhofe, *The Greatest Hoax: How the Global Warming Conspiracy Threatens Your Future*, (Washington, DC: WND Books, 2012). For the snowball incident see <http://www.washingtonpost.com/blogs/the-fix/wp/2015/02/26/jim-inhofes-snowball-has-disproven-climate-change-once-and-for-all/>. In our view, Senator Inhofe's action is evidence of his conflation of the concepts of weather and climate change.
5 See Dylan Matthews, "Donald Trump has tweeted climate change skepticism 115 times. Here's all of it." (1 June 2017), online: <https://www.vox.com/policy-and-politics/2017/6/1/15726472/trump-tweets-global-warming-paris-climate-agreement>.
6 Elizabeth F Judge, *Curious Judge: Judicial Notice of Facts, Independent Judicial Research, and the Impact of the Internet*, SSRN Scholarly Paper (Rochester, NY: Social Science Research Network, 1 July 2012), online: <http://papers.ssrn.com/abstract=2195327> at 327.
7 *Ibid.*
8 *R v Find*, [2001] 1 SCR 863 [*Find*].
9 *R v Spence*, [2005] 3 SCR 458 [*Spence*].
10 *Find*, *supra* note 8 at para 48.
11 *Spence*, *supra* note 9 at para 65.
12 *Ibid* at paras 57 to 63.
13 *Ibid* at para 63.
14 Michael Gerrard, "Court Rulings Accept Climate Science" (2013) 250:52 New York Law Journal
15 Michael A. Zody, "Climate Science in the Courts: Scientific Consensus makes for a Strong Adversary" (December 2009) Climate Change, Sustainable Development, and Ecosystems Committee Newsletter of the American Bar Assn Section of Environment, Energy, and Resources.
16 Michael Burger and Justin Gundlach, *The Status of Climate Change Litigation – A Global Review* (United Nations Environment Programme, May 2017) [Burger & Gundlach]. For a similar, earlier publication see Meredith Wilensky, *Climate Change Litigation in the Courts: An Assessment of Non-U.S. Climate Litigation* (Columbia Law School Sabin Center for Climate Change, 2015) [Wilensky]. See also David Markell and J.B. Ruhl, "An Empirical Assessment of Climate Change in the Courts: A New Jurisprudence or Business as Usual?" (2012) 64 Florida L Rev 15; and David Markell and J.B. Ruhl, "An Empirical Survey of Climate Change Litigation in the United States" (2010) 40 Environmental Law Reporter 10644
17 See Burger & Gundlach, *supra* note 16 at 10.
18 See Burger & Gundlach, *ibid* at 11–12.
19 See Burger & Gundlach, *ibid* at 14.
20 Wilensky, *supra* note 16 at page 41.
21 *Citizens for Riverdale Hospital v Bridgepoint Health Services*, 2007 CanLII 23599 (Ont Div Ct).
22 *Syncrude Canada Ltd v Attorney General of Canada*, 2014 FC 776, aff'd 2016 FCA 160. It should be noted that commentary on this case is adopted from a blog post dated 1 October 2014 titled "Facts, Reasons and Environmental Evils: Recent Canadian Environmental Law decisions" on the Environmental Law Centre's blog.
23 See, e.g., *R v Hydro-Quebec*, [1997] 3 SCR 213.
24 *City of Los Angeles v National Highway Traffic Safety Administration Center for Auto Safety* (1990), 912 F 2d 478 (US CA, DC Cir).
25 *Ibid* at para 76.
26 *Massachusetts et al v Environmental Protection Agency et al*, (2007) 27 S Ct 1438 (US SC)
27 *Ibid* at 1446.
28 *Ibid* at 1455.
29 *American Electric Power, Inc v Connecticut et al*, 564 US No. 10-174 (US SC, 2011).
30 *Ibid* at 1–3.

31 *Green Mountain Chrysler v Crombie*, Case No 2:05-cv-302 (US Dist Ct Vermont, 2007) [*Crombie*].

32 Addie Haughey, "Green Mountain Chrysler Plymouth Dodge Jeep v. Crombie" (2007) 8:1 Sustainable Development Law & Policy 72 at 72.

33 *Crombie*, *supra* note 31 at 98.

34 *Ibid* at 238.

35 *Coalition for Responsible Regulation v EPA*, 684 F 3d 102 (2012).

36 *Ibid* at 114.

37 *Wohl v City of New York*, NY Slip Op 51618 (SC, 2014).

38 *Cole v Collier*, Civil Action No 4:14-cv-1698 (Dist Ct, SD Texas, 2017).

39 *Ibid* at 67.

40 *Ibid.*

41 See online: <http://www.bostonglobe.com/metro/2014/09/08/activists-drops-charges-case-blocked-coal-shipment-power-plant/sUpBpGxzxAz3E2Vr5RFQQM/story.html>.

42 See, e.g., *People v Shalauder* (NYC Crim Ct, No 2014NY076969, 5 March 2015), a case in which climate change protestors claimed the necessity defence. While this defence was ruled out, the court did take judicial notice of climate change: see <https://www.newyorker.com/news/news-desk/climate-change-activists-consider-the-necessity-defense>. Similar attempts to use a necessity defence have been made in Minnesota: see <https://insideclimatenews.org/news/16102017/climate-change-activists-arrest-pipeline-shutdown-necessity-defense>. See also Tiffany Challe, "Minnesota and Washington Courts Said Climate Protesters Could Present Necessity Defense at Trial; Protester Found Guilty of Criminal Mischief and Trespass After North Dakota Court Denied Permission to Present Necessity Defense" (7 November 2017) in November 2017 Updates to the Climate Change Charts, Climate Law Blog, online: <http://blogs.law.columbia.edu/climatechange/2017/11/07/november-2017-updates-to-the-climate-case-charts/>.

43 *Iowa v Pearson*, Criminal No SMCR505323 (Iowa Dist, 2017).

44 Wilensky, *supra* note 16.

45 *Australian Conservation Foundation et al v Minister for Planning* (2004, Victorian Civil and Administrative Tribunal).

46 *Ibid* at para 43.

47 *Re: AC (Tuvalu)* (Immigration and Protection Tribunal New Zealand), [2014] Case 501370-371. See also the companion case, *Re: AD (Tuvalu)* (Immigration and Protection Tribunal New Zealand), [2014] Case 800517-520, which deals with the family's refugee claim.

48 *Re: AC (Tuvalu)*, *ibid* at para 32.

49 *Teitiota v Minister of Innovation and Employment*, [2015] NZSC 107 (20 July 2015)

50 *Ibid* at para 13.

51 *Urgenda Foundation v The State of the Netherlands (Ministry of Infrastructure and the Environment)*, 2015, C/09/456689/ HA ZA 13-1396, online: <http://uitspraken.rechtspraak.nl/inziendocument?id=ECLI:NL:RBDHA:2015:7196&keyword=urgenda>. See also Brenda Heelan Powell, *Exciting Developments in Climate Change Action* (30 June 2015), Environmental Law Centre blog, for a brief summary of this decision, online: <https://environmentallawcentre.wordpress.com/2015/06/30/exciting-developments-in-climate-change-action/>.

52 *Urgenda Foundation*, *ibid.*

53 *Ibid* at para 4.89.

54 *Leghari v Federation of Pakistan* (2015), WP No 25501/2015 (4 September 2015) and (14 September 2015) (*Leghari #1* and *Leghari #2*, respectively). See also *Thomson v Minister for Climate Change Actions*, CIV 2015-485-919, [2017] NZHC 733, wherein a judicial review of the government's response to climate change, in particular the adequacy of targets for reducing greenhouse gas emissions, was unsuccessful.

55 *Leghari #1, ibid* at para 1.

56 *Ibid* at para 6.

57 *Juliana ex rel Loznak v United States of America*; see Complaint for Declaratory and Injunctive Relief filed 12 August 2015, online: <http://ourchildrenstrust.org/sites/default/files/15.08.12YouthComplaintAgainstUS.pdf>. An application to dismiss the action was denied in November 2016 (see *Juliana v US*, Case No 6:15-cv-01517-TC (Dist Ct, Oregon, 10 November 2016). The action is under case management and updates are available at <https://www.ourchildrenstrust.org/us/federal-lawsuit>.

58 See a discussion of these US cases, along with the *Urgenda Foundation* decision, in Jessica Wentz, *Failure to Take Climate Action Is Not Only Morally Wrong, It's Illegal* (30 November 2015), Climate Change Blog, Sabin Center for Climate Change Law, online: <http://blogs.law.columbia.edu/climatechange/2015/11/30/failure-to-take-climate-action-is-not-only-morally-wrong-its-illegal/>.

59 For discussion of challenges associated with climate change litigation in Canada, see *Climate Change Litigation* by the University of Victoria, Environmental Law Centre, online: <http://www.elc.uvic.ca/associates/documents/Climate-Change-Dec3.07.pdf>. Challenges include forum issues, duty of care, causation, and apportionment of liability. See also Martin Olszynski, Sharon Mascher & Meinhard Doelle, "From Smokes to Smokestacks: Lessons from Tobacco for the Future of Climate Change Liability," online: <https://papers.ssrn.com/sol3/papers.cfm?abstract_id=2957921>.

60 Heather McLeod-Kilmurray, "Placing and Displacing Science: Science and the Gates of Judicial Power in Environmental Cases" (2009) 6:1–2 UOLTJ 25 at para 82.

# SECTION 5

# Inspections and Enforcement Issues: On-site and in Court

# 48

# The Art of Responsive Regulation: How Agencies Can Motivate Regulated Firms to Become Virtuous

JAMES FLAGAL

## Introduction

The power of a regulatory agency to conduct inspections is a fundamental feature of every regulatory scheme. This power gives a designated agency official the authority to enter and inspect private property without the occupier's consent and without a court warrant or order. These powers provide the authority for officials to take certain actions as part of the inspection, including requiring the production of certain documents or information or seizing things that afford evidence of an offence.[1] Without such powers, a regulatory agency would be unable to carry out its mandate of protecting the public interest by ensuring that regulated actors comply with the requirements of a regulatory scheme.

Inspections are often the primary point of contact between a regulated actor and the agency. They are also serve as the backbone of every agency's compliance and enforcement program, which at its core seeks to answer two very basic questions that ultimately inform how to allocate scarce agency resources: "who to inspect"; and "how to respond when a violation is detected." The effectiveness of an agency's compliance and enforcement program that address these two core regulatory functions can be measured on three levels:

(a) *from the perspective of the regulated firm*—Does the program motivate the regulated firm to become "virtuous," by voluntarily adopting self-audit functions that seek to identify and correct violations without the need for agency intervention?

(b) *from the perspective of the regulated sector*—Do other regulated firms in that sector believe that investing in self-auditing functions is in their self-interest?

(c) *from the perspective of the public*—Does the program instill greater public confidence that the agency is an effective regulator, is acting to protect the public interest and is not subject to regulatory capture?

This chapter seeks to examine these questions, with a focus on the Ontario Ministry of Environment and Climate Change's (MOECC) compliance and enforcement program. The first section of the chapter discusses how courts have considered inspection provisions in light of section 8 of the *Charter* and ends with a description of the way inspection powers in provincial environmental protection statutes are circumscribed to be consistent with section 8 and designed to satisfy other policy objectives. The second section briefly introduces the theory of responsive regulation and the regulatory pyramid and discusses some of the insights that literature suggests for what makes an effective compliance and enforcement policy—namely to what extent the policy motivates regulated firms in a particular sector to become and remain "virtuous" by adopting self-auditing functions. The final section describes the MOECC's compliance and enforcement program, including how it determines which regulated actors to inspect and how a response to a contravention is formulated, and ends with observations that responsive regulation theory would suggest for the MOECC program.

## Inspections and Section 8 of the *Charter*

Soon after the introduction of the *Canadian Charter of Rights and Freedoms*, courts were confronted with challenges to regulatory inspection provisions and asked to consider whether they were consistent with section 8 of the *Charter*. When the decision *of Hunter v. Southam*[2] was rendered, there was some doubt that such regulatory inspection powers would survive *Charter* scrutiny. In *Hunter* the court was asked to consider provisions under the federal *Combines Investigation Act* that authorized inspectors, after obtaining prior authorization from a designated official, to enter private premises and seize documents. The powers were held to be inconsistent with section 8 of the *Charter* for the reason that they did not provide a prior authorization procedure before a search of the premises could be undertaken. According to the Supreme Court of Canada (SCC), there were two defects in the provisions that authorized the exercise of the search powers under the Act. First, the official who provided prior authorization was not sufficiently independent of the responsible regulatory agency. Second, the search powers were not appropriately circumscribed by only authorizing searches where there were reasonable and probable grounds that an offence had been committed.

For some time after the decision in *Hunter*, there was a question as to how the SCC would treat regulatory inspection provisions that authorized entry without prior authorization from an independent official and without reasonable and probable grounds that an offence had been committed. However, in decisions that followed *Hunter*, the SCC began to signal that a more flexible standard must be applied when determining whether a regulatory inspection provision authorized unreasonable searches, contrary to section 8 of the *Charter*. They agreed that a regulatory inspection was a search for the purposes of section 8 of the *Charter*—but they held that an inspection was not an unreasonable search if the statute clearly authorized the entry and the provisions authorizing the entry were appropriately circumscribed given the regulatory context. In other words, the court recognized that applying the *Hunter* standard to regulatory inspection would be impractical because of the central role they play in regulatory schemes: As La Forest J. observed in *Thomson Newspapers*:

> In many cases, this regulation must necessarily involve the inspection of private premises or documents by agents of the state. The restaurateur's compliance with public health regulations, the employer's compliance with employment standards and safety legislation, and the developer's or homeowner's compliance with building codes or zoning regulations, can only be tested by inspection, and perhaps unannounced inspection, of their premises. Similarly, compliance with minimum wage, employment equity and human rights legislation can often only be assessed by inspection of the employer's files and records.[3]

Even if inspections may ultimately lead to enforcement actions, including prosecutions, this does not take away from their predominant purpose of being one of compliance. As the court noted in *Comité paritaire de l'industrie de la chemise v. Potash; Comité paritaire de l'industrie de la chemise v. Sélection Milton*:

> *The underlying purpose of inspection is to ensure that a regulatory statute is being complied with.* It is often accompanied by an information

> aspect designed to promote the interests of those on whose behalf the statute was enacted. *The exercise of powers of inspection does not carry with it the stigmas normally associated with criminal investigations and their consequences are less draconian. While regulatory statutes incidentally provide for offences, they are enacted primarily to encourage compliance.* It may be that in the course of inspections those responsible for enforcing a statute will uncover facts that point to a violation, but this possibility does not alter the underlying purpose behind the exercise of the powers of inspection. The same is true when the enforcement is prompted by a complaint. Such a situation is obviously at variance with the routine nature of an inspection. However, a complaint system is often provided for by the legislature itself as it is a practical means not only of checking whether contraventions of the legislation have occurred but also of deterring them. [Emphasis added.][4]

The italicized portion of the above extract from the *Potash* decision seems to presage the jurisprudence that would develop in later years under section 8 of the *Charter*, where the courts sought to place limitations on the use of regulatory inspection powers to gather evidence for a regulatory prosecution. Specifically, the passage hints at the "predominant purpose" test that was later adopted by the leading case on this issue—*R v. Jarvis*.[5] This chapter will not delve into that issue or the jurisprudence, as it is canvassed in the chapter by my colleague Paul McCulloch (see chapter 52, "Environmental Investigations: A Government Perspective").

There are several factors a court will consider when determining if an inspection provision is constitutionally valid and authorizes reasonable search and seizures in the circumstances, namely:

- (a) the context of the power (whether it is criminal, quasi-criminal, or regulatory);
- (b) the intrusiveness of the search power;
- (c) the reasonable expectation of privacy in the property searched; and
- (d) the purposes of the power.

The focus of the inquiry, then, is whether the legislation in question strikes the appropriate balance between a person's reasonable expectation of privacy and the state's interest in ensuring it can effectively administer and enforce the regulatory scheme in question to protect the public interest. The courts have repeatedly recognized that persons engaged in regulated activity have a reduced expectation of privacy and for that reason will not apply the *Hunter* standard to regulatory inspection provisions.[6]

However, even if the courts were not prepared to apply the prior authorization requirement set out in *Hunter* to regulatory inspections, they continued to scrutinize those provisions under section 8 of the *Charter* to determine whether the powers were appropriately circumscribed given the public purpose of the regulatory regime and the expectation of privacy by those being regulated. For example, in *Johnston v. Minister of Ontario (Minister of Revenue)*[7] the Court of Appeal for Ontario struck down the inspection provisions in Ontario's *Tobacco Tax Act* because they authorized a warrantless search of any commercial motor vehicle regardless of whether the vehicle was connected with the trade of tobacco or any reasonable grounds that the commercial vehicle contained evidence of a contravention of the Act. Arbour J.A. observed:

> For a random search to be reasonable under s. 8, even in a case where the privacy interest affected is minimal, it has to be established that such a random search is the least intrusive method available to provide for adequate enforcement of the regulatory scheme.

Section 156 of the *Environmental Protection Act*[8] sets out the inspection authority of provincial officers under that Act and is typical of inspection provisions found in many MOECC-administered statutes. The power provides provincial officers, who are designated by the minister, to enter property without consent and without a warrant or court order, but the power is circumscribed in several important respects so that it is consistent with section 8 of the *Charter*. The following are the constraints that are typically imposed on the exercise of an inspection authority and other policy issues that typically arise in the drafting of inspection provisions:

- The power to inspect can only be exercised at "reasonable times."
- A provincial officer can only enter a place if he or she has a "reasonable belief" that a thing or activity that is subject to the Act can be found in that place. For instance, the provincial officer can enter into a place if he or she has reasonable belief that the place is required to be subject to an approval under the Act.

- Officers are required to identify themselves and explain the purpose of their entry.
- In 1998, the inspection provisions in the *Environmental Protection Act* and the *Ontario Water Resources Act*[9] (OWRA) were re-introduced and structured to separate in one subsection the places a provincial officer could enter and in a separate subsection what things a provincial officer could do after entering a place. Because the provision was structured in this fashion, the Court of Appeal for Ontario held that the MOECC could not rely on its inspection powers to make telephone inquiries—inquiries could only be made as part of an inspection of a place. Those statutes have since been amended to include an express authority for provincial officers to make telephone inquiries.[10]
- Force cannot be used to execute an inspection. If an occupant refuses to allow a provincial officer to enter to a place, even though the provincial officer has lawful authority to exercise the entry, the only recourse is to obtain a court inspection order under section 158 of the *EPA* or to refer the matter to the Investigations and Enforcement Branch on the grounds that the person obstructed the provincial officer in carrying out his or her duties under the Act.[11]
- The inspection powers cannot be used to enter any room that is used as a dwelling. A dwelling can only be inspected pursuant to a court inspection order under section 158. When drafting legislative provisions concerning inspection orders or warrants issued by the court, it is appropriate to expressly provide that if the application for the inspection order or warrant concerns the inspection of a dwelling the application should expressly advise the court of this.[12]
- More current provisions concerning regulatory inspections provide that where an entry is exercised and property is damaged as a result of the inspection, the officer must restore the property to the condition it was in prior to the entry.[13]
- Inspection provisions often expressly permit the officer to be accompanied by another person who has expert or special knowledge that is related to the purpose of the entry.[14]
- Most inspection provisions under provincial environmental protection statutes permit inspections without giving the occupant prior notice of the inspection (otherwise known as unannounced inspections). However, recently, in response to stakeholder concerns, some MOECC Acts that are to be administered locally require that prior

reasonable notice of the entry be given to the occupant. An exception is provided where the officer reasonably believes that a contravention has occurred and that entry without reasonable notice is necessary to prevent or reduce environmental harm. There should be careful consideration before imposing a notice requirement on the power of entry, particularly if it is determined that unannounced inspections are necessary to effectively regulate the regulated actors that will be subject to the regulatory scheme.[15]

- Some recent statutes have required that officers must complete a training course—the requirements of which are prescribed by the regulations—before exercising an entry power. This was included in recent MOECC statutes that were to be administered locally, largely at the request of the agricultural sector in response to their concerns that local officers entering agricultural operations understand how to deal with risks related to biohazards at an agricultural operation.[16]

## Responsive Regulation and the Regulatory Pyramid

The theory of "responsive regulation" and the "regulatory pyramid" was first introduced by Ayres and Braithwaite in their seminal book *Responsive Regulation*.[17] The theory was advanced to bridge the divide between the two competing regulatory theories that emerged during the 1980s. The first believed that a strict enforcement approach was necessary to deter regulated actors from violating the law. The second competing theory took the opposite view, calling for the use of persuasion as the primary compliance tool. However, critics charged that this was just another call for deregulation. Advocates of this theory asserted that strict enforcement was counterproductive because it undermined the potential for a cooperative relationship between regulated actors and the regulator and diminished a regulated firm's motivation to adopt self-auditing functions. Ayres and Braithwaite attempted to bridge these two disparate theories through the conception of the regulatory pyramid—suggesting that an agency's compliance and enforcement program must incorporate aspects from both theories and be calibrated so that it directs the appropriate response given the circumstances of a particular case. In the words of Baldwin and Black:

> The crucial question for Ayres and Braithwaite was "When to punish; when to persuade?" Their prescription was a 'tit for tat' or responsive approach in which regulators enforce in the first instance by

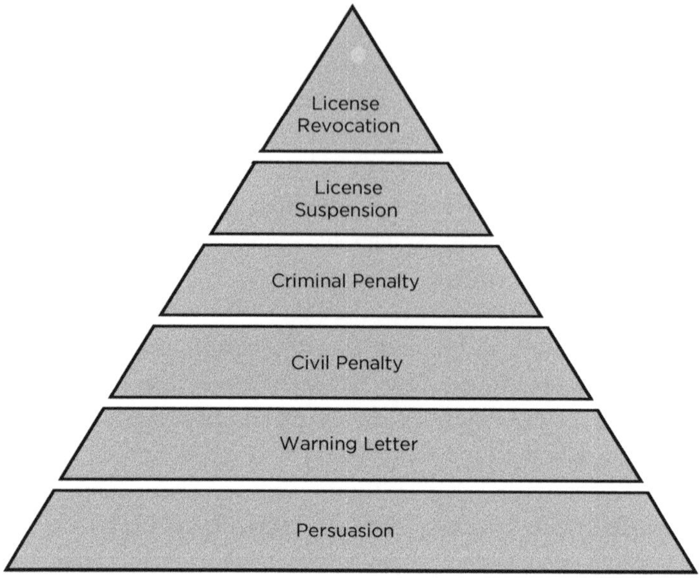


**Figure 48.1 | Example of a Regulatory Pyramid** (*Source*: Update of I. Ayres and J. Braithwaite. 1992. *Responsive Regulation: Transcending the Deregulation Debate*, p. 35)

> compliance strategies, but apply more punitive deterrent responses when the regulated firm fails to behave as desired. Compliance, they suggested, was more likely when a regulatory agency displays an explicit enforcement pyramid – a range of enforcement sanctions extending from persuasion, at its base, through warning and civil penalties up to criminal penalties, license suspensions and then license revocations. Regulatory approaches would begin at the bottom of the pyramid and escalate in response to compliance failures. There would be a presumption that regulation should always start at the base of the pyramid.[18]

Three types of regulated actors are suggested by the theory:

(a) the *virtuous firm*: a firm that genuinely desires to identify and self-correct violations without any agency intervention;
(b) the *rational firm*: a firm that generally only complies if they believe there will be a financial consequence to non-compliance and therefore may require some form of agency response where a

violation is detected in order to deter it from future non-compliance; and finally

(c) the *incapacitated firm*: no matter what amount of financial penalty a regulatory agency may impose for non-compliance, this type of firm simply does not have the capacity to or simply refuses to comply; accordingly, the agency must consider elevating its response to the top of the pyramid and withdrawing the firm's licence to engage in the regulated activity.

The goal of responsive regulation is to try to cultivate a regulatory environment where regulated firms are motivated to become and remain virtuous: where the firm's front line staff and management assume the mentality that it is their duty to establish and maintain appropriate self-auditing functions such as environmental management systems to ensue compliance, rather than waiting for these violations to be discovered through an inspection. The goal, then, is to design policies that allow inspectors to calibrate their response to violations, knowing when to escalate their response so that it sends the appropriate signal to the violator and to the other regulated firms in that sector. The foundation of the approach is dialogue with the regulated firm and escalating the response only reluctantly when the tools at the base of the pyramid fail and, once compliance has been achieved, de-escalating the agency response back to the base of the pyramid. As Braithwaite notes: "The pyramid is firm yet forgiving in its demands for compliance. Reform must be rewarded just as recalcitrant refusal to reform is ultimately punished."

The regulatory pyramid approach to regulation only works effectively if the agency demonstrates that it is willing and able to escalate its enforcement response to the very top of the pyramid and to revoke a firm's licence to engage in a regulated activity—the ultimate penal consequence. If the regulated community begins to suspect that this threat of escalation is a hollow one and that the agency would never exercise this power of last resort, the regulatory pyramid approach is undermined and there will be little motivation on the regulated community to comply.

> The logic of regulatory pyramids relies on the peak of the pyramid to activate these compliance principals. The peak of the pyramid represents the ultimate constraint on pursuing a course of action that is in breach of the rules. Providing it is a credible sanction, that is, those being regulated believe that the regulator can and will use this power,

> it serves a number of functions. In a societal sense, it signals the seriousness of a breach of rules. It reminds those being regulated of their obligations and of course of action they should pursue, as agreed in the social compact at the base of the pyramid. Should social pressures fail, economic pressures come into play. It is costly to escalate to the top. It is rational for the regulatee not to carry the costs of non-compliance, and return to a cooperative stance at the base of the pyramid that respects the law sooner rather than later.[19]

Agencies in many jurisdictions have sought to integrate a version of the regulatory pyramid into their compliance and enforcement policies. For instance, many regulatory agencies in Australia have adopted a version of the enforcement pyramid, and the effectiveness of those policies has been discussed at length.[20] One challenge, however, in adapting the regulatory pyramid approach for environmental protection regimes is that a broad range of activities subject to an environmental protection law may not require a licence from the agency. Rather, the law may simply impose operational requirements on the activity or the activity may only be subject to some form of a general pollution prohibition. Further, many regulators are moving toward reducing the range of activities that are subject to a licensing scheme, requiring instead that such activities simply register on a government registry and setting out operational rules that must be followed for regulated firms in that sector (often called a "permit by rule approach").[21] Without the authority to suspend or revoke a licence, and left essentially with the power to impose monetary penalties such as fines to respond to violations, such agencies may face unique challenges in adopting an effective regulatory pyramid approach. In other words, can the regulatory pyramid approach work effectively if the regime does not provide the regulator with a mechanism to suspend or permanently shut down a regulated firm's operations, something that is inherent in a licensing scheme?

One can easily question the assumptions underpinning the regulatory pyramid approach—for instance, what levels of non-compliance will the approach condone before violators are penalized? Will this approach ultimately undermine the public perception that the agency is being a firm and effective regulator? Does the approach downplay the risks posed by a contravention? What about the charges that this approach may give rise to too much potential for an appearance of regulatory capture? For instance, instruments made or issued under provincial environmental protection statutes, such as regulations or approvals, that impose pollution discharge standards, generally require a regulated actor to report to the ministry any instances where those discharge standards are exceeded. This is also true of pollution incidents that breach the general pollution prohibition. This form of self-reporting is a cornerstone of environmental protection legislation. Indeed, environmental protection legislation could not operate without such self-reporting obligations. The SCC has held that imposing an obligation on a regulated actor to self-report a contravention as part of a larger regulatory scheme does not offend the *Charter*'s guarantee in section 7 against self-incrimination.[22] One might think—where a regulated firm violates something as significant as a pollution discharge standard or a general pollution prohibition—shouldn't that generally be followed up with a swift enforcement response that involves some form of penalty both from a specific and general deterrence perspective? Wouldn't the public interest and the protection of the environment demand such a firm response?

However, there is some evidence to suggest that an overly aggressive enforcement policy may be counterproductive and undermine a regulatory environment that motivates regulated actors to become and remain more "virtuous." In one study that analyzed data over a ten-year period from US industrial facilities subject to the *Clean Air Act*, it was observed that an enforcement response that relied on penal threats often did not produce the desired outcome—that a regulated firm would carry through on promises to institute a self-auditing function. Instead the authors postulated that in many instances the threat of a penalty created an adversarial relationship between the regulated actor and the agency, undermining past cooperative dealings and negatively affecting the morale of front line staff and management and their motivation to voluntarily identify and correct violations. The study found that the critical motivator for regulated actors to become or to remain virtuous was for the agency to ensure close surveillance—meaning a robust inspection regime. Close surveillance tells the regulated firm that its efforts at self-auditing are being closely watched and signals to other firms that investing in self-auditing functions is a sound choice because their competitors are also being closely monitored. As the authors of the study, Short and Toffel, note:

> [We] demonstrate that there are important distinctions between the effects of sanctions and surveillance on organizational behaviour that are not fully captured by either deterrence theory or the organizational literature on social control and cooperation. Although coercive regulatory threats appeared to have dampened intrinsic motivations to self-regulate, surveillance had the opposite effect. Disclosing

> facilities in heavily monitored industries were more likely than those in less monitored industries to follow through on their commitment to self-regulate. Furthermore even direct surveillance of individual facilities promoted effective implementation of self-regulation.[23]

Since its introduction, many scholars have expanded on the foundation of responsive regulation, including Professor Malcolm Sparrow, in his *Regulatory Craft*.[24] Sparrow calls for a pragmatic approach to compliance and enforcement policy and suggests three core elements to reform:

(1) *A clear focus on results*: The focus of an agency's compliance regime should be on defined outcomes and not merely on process outputs(i.e. counting how many types of inspections or enforcement actions have been taken and whether there is an increase or decrease in those numbers from one year to the next); rather the focus should be on developing meaningful performance measures to determine if the chosen outcomes are being met;

(2) *The adoption of a problem-solving approach*: The identification of important risks or patterns of non-compliance to help explain how an agency's scarce resources will best be allocated to achieve the desired outcomes. Sparrow emphasizes that there should be tailor-made solutions for each problem, and he also stresses the need to retain the appropriate balance in enforcement policy—one that "enhances the agency's enforcement sting while using enforcement actions economically and within the context of coherent enforcement strategies."

(3) *An investment in collaborative partnerships*: Engaging in an open dialogue with all stakeholders to identify a shared purpose through collaborative agenda setting and prioritization—meaning the process of problem identification should be done by the agency in an open and transparent manner.[25]

It is beyond the scope of this chapter to delve deeply into Sparrow's approach, as he is the first to acknowledge that his problem-solving approach to regulation is extremely difficult to implement. The next section will return to the two core questions that animate every agency's compliance and enforcement regime—with a focus on the MOECC's program—namely, how does the MOECC decide who to inspect; and when a provincial officer detects a violation during an inspection, how does the provincial officer formulate his or her response. The section will conclude with some observations about the MOECC's program based on the insights that responsive regulation and the regulatory pyramid have suggested make for an effective regulator.

## What Lessons the MOECC's Compliance Program Can Learn from Responsive Regulation

The Ministry of Environment and Climate Change (MOECC) regulates a wide range of sectors, from drinking water systems to waste disposal sites and waste management systems, industrial, commercial and municipal sewage works, pesticide applications, and point source air discharges. Some of the more significant statutes that engage the MOECC in compliance and enforcement activities include the following:

- *Environmental Protection Act*
- *Ontario Water Resources Act*
- *Pesticides Act*
- *Safe Drinking Water Act*
- *Toxics Reduction Act*
- *Nutrient Management Act* (the MOECC has responsibility for the compliance and enforcement provisions of this Act)

In a typical year, the ministry conducts between 3,000 and 4,000 proactive (or planned) inspections across a range of program areas that fall within its mandate and approximately 350 reactive inspections (in response to an incident). In the fiscal year 2014/15, a total of 4,033 inspections were completed. The ministry's Operations Division (OD), the division that is responsible for compliance and enforcement within the ministry, assigns each program area to an OD Region or branch. See table 48.1 (next page).

Using a risk-based approach, each year the program leads determine which regulated firms should be subject to planned inspections. Firms are ranked and selected based on an analysis of potential impacts to human health and the environment in addition to the firm's compliance history. The source protection planning process that was introduced by the *Clean Water Act* provides a good example of how risk is incorporated into the planning process for proactive inspections.[26] Source protection plans are required to identify the areas where a specific type of activity, such as the operation of a waste disposal site, is considered to be a significant risk to a municipal drinking water source.

**Table 48.1**

| *OD region* | *Regulatory Program* |
|---|---|
| Central | Hazardous Waste<br>Non-Hazardous Waste<br>Brownfields<br>Properties of Environmental Concern |
| West Central | Air |
| Southwest | Agriculture<br>Permits of Take Water<br>Surface and Groundwater |
| Eastern | Pesticides<br>Water Wells<br>Aggregates |
| Northern | Communal Sewage<br>Industrial Sewage<br>Mining |
| Sector Compliance Branch | Vehicle Emissions<br>Renewable Energy<br>EASR and Toxics Audits |

OD will use this information to give priority to those firms whose operations are located within significant threat areas. There is a delicate balance for program leads, when planning proactive inspections for a given year, between identified local priorities and the program priorities being set centrally within the ministry.

The ministry's Compliance Policy[27] governs how the ministry responds when it finds a violation, including during both a proactive or reactive inspection. My colleague Fred Maefs' chapter in this volume, "Anatomy of a Compliance Regime: Initiation of Action" (chapter 50) describes the elements of that policy. The focus of discussion here will be on the Informed Judgment Matrix (IJM) and the case-specific considerations set out in the Compliance Policy—because they direct how a provincial officer is required to formulate his or her response to an incident[28] and determine whether a "voluntary" or "mandatory" abatement approach is appropriate in the circumstances. "Voluntary abatement" means using the tools at the base of the regulatory pyramid, including "persuasion" or a "warning letter"—in other words, allowing for a dialogue with the regulated actor before an incident is elevated to a "mandatory abatement" response. "Mandatory abatement" means using statutory enforcement powers to compel compliance, and those tools include orders, a ticket issued under Part I of the *Provincial Offences Act*,[29] amending an approval for the site if one exists, or referring the matter to the Investigations and Enforcement Branch for a possible laying of charges to commence a prosecution under Part III of the *Provincial Offences Act*. It also includes the issuance of an environmental penalty order (EP), which is a type of administrative penalty but is only available to be used against facilities in one of the nine industrial sectors listed in the environmental penalty regulations and only in relation to contraventions specified in those regulations (largely contraventions related to unlawful discharges from those facilities to land or water).[30]

### CASE-SPECIFIC CONSIDERATIONS (EXAMPLES)

- Is there public concern about the incident?
- Is the regulatee someone with whom we can work to achieve a positive outcome?
- Did the regulatee disclose the incident voluntarily? Did the responsible person cooperate?
- How swiftly did the regulatee respond?
- Did their actions effectively resolve the incident and prevent its recurrence?
- Given the sophistication of the regulatee, would education and outreach be more effective to assist the person in understanding, managing, and complying with ministry legislation?
- Was the incident the result of gross negligence and/or deliberate actions by a responsible person?

Where a provincial officer detects an incident, that officer is required to determine, using the IJM, whether the incident falls within Category I, II, or III. This is based on assessing (on the y axis of the IJM) the compliance history of the regulated actor and (on the x axis of the IJM) the environmental/health impacts of the incident. Case-specific considerations can then be applied to determine whether the category of the incident should be escalated or de-escalated. Once an incident is classified into a category, the policy sets out the following responses for each category:

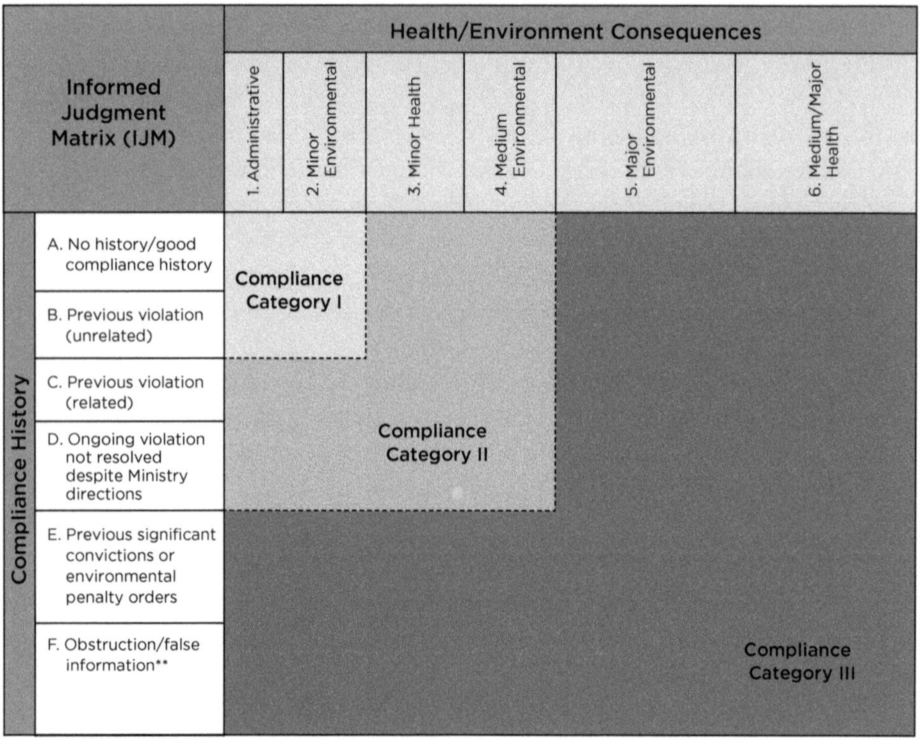


Figure 48.2

- *Category I:* Voluntary compliance—including education and outreach, though mandatory abatement actions such as orders or referrals to IEB may be considered.
- *Category II*: Stronger mandatory application of tools such as orders are recommended, and an IEB referral should be considered.
- Category *III*: Mandatory tools strongly recommended, and the incident must be referred to IEB.

Figure 48.3 sets out the decision tree a provincial officer is directed to follow when detecting an incident during an inspection. After the appropriate response is chosen (whether voluntary or mandatory abatement), the provincial officer is required to follow up to determine if the incident has been resolved. At all stages of the response the provincial officer is directed to document his or her decisions. Where a voluntary abatement approach is taken, and the

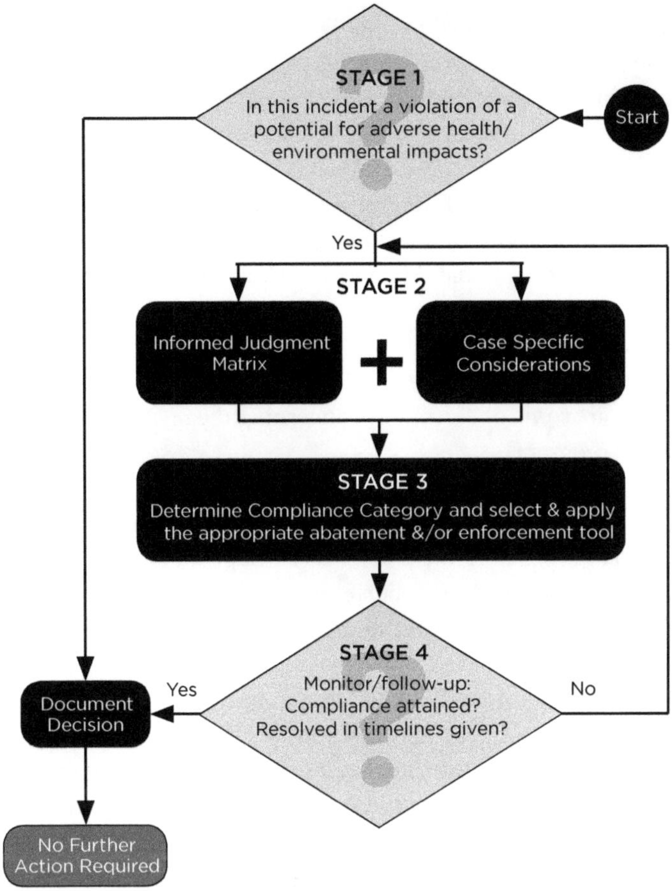


**Figure 48.3**

regulated firm enters into a voluntary abatement plan to resolve the incident, the policy provides that unsatisfactory progress shall not be tolerated beyond six months (180 days). Where voluntary abatement efforts are not working to resolve an incident, the response must be escalated to a mandatory abatement response.

It is worth mentioning the compliance and enforcement scheme under the *Safe Drinking Water Act*, because unlike in other MOEC statutes, a regulation[31] under that Act prescribes the minimum frequency of inspections for municipal drinking water systems and for labs and when a mandatory abatement response must be taken to deal with certain types of contraventions under that

Act. The Act also establishes a Chief Drinking Water Inspector and requires the chief to publish an annual report that describes the results of inspections of municipal drinking water systems and labs and the level of compliance found at those facilities. All of these features were incorporated into the *Safe Drinking Water Act*[32] to satisfy the recommendations of the Walkerton Inquiry Report.[33] In that report, Mr. Justice O'Connor set out many detailed recommendations for a *Safe Drinking Water Act*, including recommendations about compliance and enforcement under that Act and what matters should be prescribed by the law—matters that are, under other MOECC statutes, left entirely to the discretion of the MOECC.

Drawing on the responsive regulation literature canvassed in the second section, here are some observations concerning the MOECC's compliance and enforcement program:

1. *Establish clear outcomes for each program area to guide inspection planning and compliance and enforcement actions*: Through an annual integrated planning process, the program leads currently establish a set of goals for each program area, and identify the priorities that will be the focus for the coming year and the results to be achieved. After these strategic directions are established, the program leads then work with each region to determine which regulated actors should be the target of proactive inspections. The development of the strategic direction guides the integrated planning process for a program area, including setting goals and identifying priorities for a given period, and would benefit in several ways if it were done in a more open and transparent manner involving the participation of regulated actors and other stakeholders. First, providing this opportunity for a dialogue would assist in obtaining buy-in from regulated actors to the ministry's priorities and would help leverage such partnerships. Further, engaging in the integrated planning exercise in a more open fashion would enable regulated actors across the sector to understand where their self-auditing efforts should be focused and the ministry rationale behind the two fundamental decisions of "who to inspect" and "how to respond." Finally, conducting this planning exercise in a more open and transparent manner will help build public confidence in the MOECC as an effective regulator.

2. *Regular reporting for each program area on compliance and enforcement outcomes*: Responsive regulation cautions against too much of a focus on tracking agency outputs as a performance measure; for instance, tracking whether the

number of prosecutions has increased or decreased from one year to the next. At a minimum, each program area should report to the public at regular intervals on the number of proactive and reactive inspections conducted during the reporting period, the occasions when voluntary versus mandatory abatement was used to resolve an incident, the number of incidents that were resolved successfully without the need for escalation, and the type of abatement responses used (warnings, voluntary abatement plans, orders, prosecutions). The ministry currently releases annual "environmental compliance reports" that describe incidents where air or water discharge standards are exceeded and what follow-up action was taken to respond to the incident.[34] Going beyond the mere exercise of "bean counting," however, effective reporting would measure agency performance against a set of performance measures and assess whether established outcomes are being achieved. Public reporting is also important, as it allows an agency to highlight the tools it has employed in the program area during the reporting period to achieve outcomes, including any targeted inspection programs, compliance assistance programs, and programs designed to incentivize regulated firms in that sector to adopt self-auditing functions. Even more importantly, regular public reporting for each program area would allow the ministry to demonstrate that it is capable of escalating enforcement responses up the regulatory pyramid when necessary, including highlighting cases where approvals have been suspended or revoked.

3. *Motivate regulated actors to adopt self-auditing functions*: In most types of MOECC approvals, such as approvals for waste disposal sites, the approval holder is required to prepare an annual report that includes a requirement to report any incidents of non-compliance and how the incident was resolved. Similarly, under the *Safe Drinking Water Act*, municipal drinking water system operators are required to prepare annual reports documenting any violations, the duration of the violation, and what actions were taken to correct the violation.[35] Recently, a regulation under the *EPA* has required that a third party be retained to certify the accuracy of a compliance report.[36] Another regulation under the *EPA* that requires specific industrial facilities to prepare spill prevention and contingency plans requires an officer or director of the regulated firm to make a written statement, as part of an annual report, affirming that the plans comply with the regulation. Are regulated firms that are compelled by law to document violations and how they are resolved more inclined to adopt and maintain effective self-auditing functions? Do facilities that are compelled by law to monitor their own compliance have higher rates of compliance as a

result of these legal obligations? Finally, to what extent are compliance reporting obligations audited by the regulator? These questions deserve examination because the trend has been to legally compel these self-auditing functions, and it would be valuable to know to what extent these requirements result in higher compliance rates.

Beyond compelling self-audits by law, the ministry has developed softer approaches to motivate the adoption of self-auditing functions. Under the Environmental Penalty program, a violator is given an automatic reduction to a penalty if the violator can demonstrate that, at the time of the contravention, it had an environmental management system in place that meets the requirements of the regulation. In July 2004 the ministry adopted the *Environmental Leaders Program*,[37] a program that promised a regulated firm certain benefits such as assured turnaround times on approval decisions if the regulated firm agreed to certain conditions, including having an environmental management system in place. Finally, as part of the integrated planning process, a program area may develop a compliance promotion project to encourage regulated firms to adopt self-auditing functions. How these compliance promotion projects are communicated to regulated firms can have significant bearing on their success.[38] Programs that recognize the importance of self-auditing functions and motivate regulated firms to adopt self-auditing functions are critical from the perspective of responsive regulation. Since the regulator cannot be at all places at all times to detect violations, the agency's compliance and enforcement approach must send the appropriate signals that the virtuous firms in a sector will be recognized and rewarded.

4. *A call for greater use of administrative penalties to supplement the MOECC's regulatory pyramid*: Administrative penalties are simply the authority of an agency to impose a monetary penalty on a violator without having to use a court process such as a prosecution or a civil action. Administrative penalties have a long tradition in a broad range of regulatory contexts (including environmental protection) in the United States and in other jurisdictions, but they have not been adopted widely in Canada until quite recently, with the exception of specific regulatory contexts such as taxation and aeronautics. This means the only way the MOECC can impose a monetary penalty for a violation is by commencing a prosecution. There are many downsides to an over-reliance on prosecutions. First, investigations and prosecutions are very resource-intensive. Consequently, prosecutions are not suitable for penalizing violations of a minor nature. Second, the monetary penal consequence

resulting from a prosecution is imposed long after the contravention has been detected, sometimes up to two years following the detection. Indeed, for the ministry, often the only mandatory abatement response available to deal with violations that aren't suitable for prosecution is a provincial officer issuing a contravention-based order,[39] which often is simply an order requiring the regulated firm to comply with a legal requirement the firm was supposed to comply with in the first place. In other words, an order power without a concomitant administrative penalty power greatly hampers the leverage of the agency in compliance negotiations with a regulated firm.

Take, for example, a routine proactive inspection of a regulated firm that uncovers a long list of violations. Most of those violations may be classified as minor or administrative in nature, such as failures to report, document, or monitor—violations that from an agency resource perspective are not appropriate to be pursued through prosecution. When the inspection report is given to the regulated firm with the list of violations, beyond a referral to IEB the only other mandatory abatement tool that a provincial officer has to compel compliance is a contravention-based order. With a properly tailored administrative penalty scheme, the monetary consequences of non-compliance for the regulated firm would be far more manifest and urgent. Unlike fines that are set by courts on the facts based on the particular case, administrative penalties are set in a far more predictable and transparent manner. They also can be tailored to reward certain behaviour, such as providing reductions for firms that have environmental management systems in place, or provide for significant reductions or even cancelled penalties if violations are corrected within a specified time. Moreover, unlike prosecutions, most administrative penalty schemes are based on absolute liability—the steps a violator took to prevent a violation are considered in determining the penalty amount and not as a defence. Reliance wholly on strict liability offences to monetarily penalize violators may motivate regulated firms not to be as forthcoming to investigators about what steps they took to prevent a violation, on the grounds that this may unduly prejudice their due diligence defence in any potential prosecution.

After introducing enabling legislation in 1998 for administrative penalties, in 2002 the ministry consulted on draft administrative penalty regulations for a very broad range of contraventions, but not for serious matters such as unlawful spills.[40] However, the government of the day never pursued the proposal after encountering intense pressure from the regulated community, which opposed giving the ministry the authority to penalize violators and felt that the proposal would create an adversarial relationship between the MOECC's

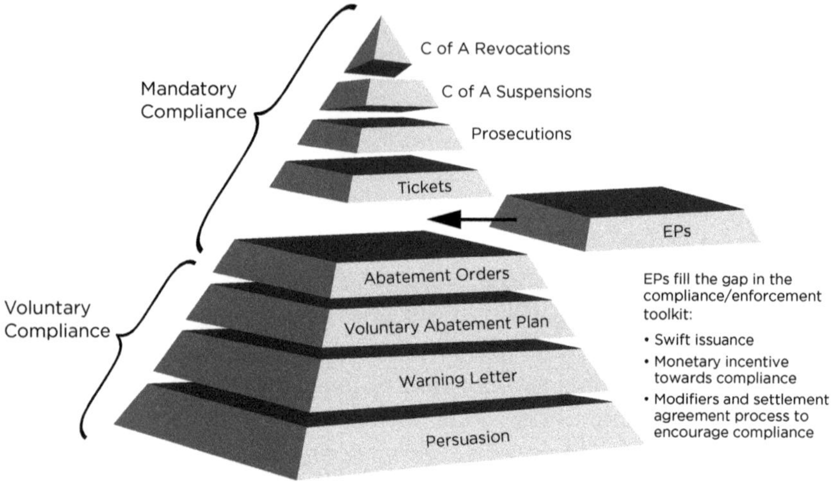


**Figure 48.4 | How environmental penalties (EPs) fill the gap in the ministry's compliance toolkit** (*Source*: Adapted from: M. K. Sparrow, *The Regulatory Craft* [Bookings CEC, 2000])

abatement staff and regulated firms—a relationship they felt had always been a cooperative one. In 2005, however, in response to a series of spills to the St. Clair River from industrial facilities in the Sarnia area, the government passed legislation to replace the 1998 administrative penalty provisions with a new type of administrative penalties called "environmental penalties" (EPs). Unlike the older provisions, which were designed to deal with violations of a minor nature, these new administrative penalties were designed specifically to deal with contraventions of a serious nature, such as unlawful spills. For example, the new provisions allow a person to be prosecuted for a contravention even in cases where an administrative penalty has been imposed and paid. Further, the maximum penalty amount for EPs was increased ten-fold. However, environmental penalties are only available for specific types of industrial facilities and only in relation to contraventions that relate to unlawful discharges to land and water. The MOECC needs a broad-based administrative penalty tool to respond to violations—one that will allow it to reserve prosecutions for the most serious types of violations. The diagram above (Figure 48.4) was used by the ministry when environmental penalties were introduced to explain the gap in the regulatory pyramid EPs were designed to fill. That gap continues to exist in the many program areas where EPs are not available.

Mastering the art of being an effective regulator is an exceedingly difficult balancing act. The simple decision of determining what regulated firms to inspect and how to respond to a violation is fraught with difficult choices about how to best expend scarce agency resources. An agency often has to navigate between competing and sometimes contradictory pressures, addressing the need to be responsive to local concerns while dealing effectively with priorities being set by its leadership. The foremost message from responsive regulation is simple: pragmatism—the need to identify problems and find solutions by methodically setting goals and developing performance measures to achieve results. It means a commitment and an investment in gathering and analyzing data on an agency's decisions and actions to figure out in a systemic way what works and what doesn't. And it also means planning and reporting on compliance and enforcement activities in as open and transparent a manner as possible in order to command confidence from the individual regulated firm, from the other firms in that sector, and from the public at large.

## NOTES

1 See s 156 of the *Environmental Protection Act*, RSO 1990, c E.19 [*EPA*] as an example of a general inspection power commonly found in environmental protection statutes in Ontario. Section 156 includes the power to require the production of documents: see s 156(2)(g). See s 160 of the *EPA* as an example of a provision that authorizes seizures during an inspection.

2 [1984] 2 SCR 145.

3 *Thomson Newspapers Ltd v Canada (Director of Investigation and Research, Restrictive Trade Practices Commission)*, [1990] 1 SCR 425 at 507.

4 [1994] 2 SCR 406 at 421.

5 *R v Jarvis*, [2002] SCJ No 76.

6 *BC Securities Commission v Branch*, [1995] 2 SCR 3.

7 75 OR (2d) 558 (CA).

8 *EPA*, *supra* note 1..

9 RSO 1990, c O.40 (*OWRA*).

10 *R v Crompton* (2005), 78 OR (3d) 135 (CA). In 2009, to respond to that court decision, s 157.0.1 was added to the *EPA* and s 15.0.1 was added to the *OWRA* to expressly provide authority for provincial officers to make telephone inquiries.

11 See s 184 of the *EPA*; s 184(1) provides that "No person shall hinder or obstruct any provincial officer or employee in or agent of the Ministry in the performance of his or her duties under this Act."

12 As an example of this, see s 26 of the *Lake Simcoe Protection Act, 2008*, SO 2008, c 23, specifically s 26(19).

13 *Ibid*, s 26(25).

14 See *ibid*, s 26(9).

15 See *ibid*, ss 26(11)–(12). The inspection power in the *Clean Water Act, 2006*, SO 2006, c 22, also contained a notice requirement: see s 62 of that Act. Other provincial statutes that deal with environmental protection matters also contain notice provisions that predate their introduction in MOECC statutes, such as the *Conservation Authorities Act*, RSO 1990, c C.27, ss 28(20)–(22), and the *Niagara Escarpment Planning and Development Act*, RSO 1990, c N.2, s 28. Often these notice constraints are placed in statutes

that are to be administered by local bodies as opposed to provincial bodies. In his report following the Walkerton Inquiry, Mr. Justice O'Connor spoke about the importance of ensuring that unannounced inspections be authorized in the legislation that was to regulate drinking water systems. He made a number of important recommendations concerning compliance and enforcement under his proposal for a *Safe Drinking Water Act*. See Part Two, Report of the Walkerton Inquiry, ch 13, in particular 452–455 at 454: "The Ministry of Environment's inspection program for municipal drinking water systems should consist of a combination of announced and unannounced inspections. The inspector may conduct unannounced inspections when he or she deems it appropriate and least once every three years, taking into account such factors as work priority and planning, time constraints, and the record of the operating authority."

16 See s 26(7) of the *Lake Simcoe Protection Act, 2008*—a similar training requirement appears in the *Clean Water Act, 2006*. Note that the inspection authority in the *Clean Water Act* is very similar to that in the *Lake Simcoe Protection Act* (LSPA), and the very recently passed *Great Lakes Protection Act, 2015*, SO 2015, c 24, largely adopts by reference the inspection provision in the LSPA, as both statutes contain a regulation-making authority governing activities in shoreline areas and adjacent to wetlands.

17 I Ayres & J Braithwaite, *Responsive Regulation* (Oxford: University Press, 1992).

18 Robert Baldwin & Julia Black, *Really Responsive Regulation*, LSE Law Society and Economy Working Papers 15 (London, UK: London School of Economics & Political Science Law Dept, 2007). See also John Braithwaite, "The Essence of Responsive Regulation, Fasken Lecture" (2011) 44 UBC L Rev 475.

19 M Ivec and V Braithwaite (2015), *Applications of Responsive Regulatory Theory in Australia and Overseas: Update* (Canberra: Regulatory Institutions Network, Australian National University), online: <http://regnet.anu.edu.au/sites/default/files/publications/attachments/2015-05/Occasional%2520Paper%252023_Ivec_Braithwaite_0.pdf> at 7.

20 See Ivec & Braithwaite, *ibid*.

21 See, e.g., changes made to the *Environmental Protection Act* and the *Ontario Water Resources Act* that introduced the "modernization of approvals program," wherein activities that were subject to the requirement of a MOECC approval would now be exempt from such requirements and instead required to register on the Environmental Activity and Sector Registry (EASR); see in particular Part II.2 of the *EPA*. A description of the program can be found online: <https://www.ontario.ca/page/environmental-approvals> (accessed 6 February 2018).

22 *R v Fitzpatrick*, [1995] 4 SCR 154.

23 Jodi Short & Michael Toffel, "Making Self-Regulation More Than Merely Symbolic: The Critical Role of the Legal Environment," Georgetown Public Law and Legal Theory Research Paper No 11-14 (2010) 44 Admin Sci Q 361 at 388.

24 Malcolm K Sparrow, *The Regulatory Craft: Controlling Risks, Solving Problems and Managing Compliance* (Washington, DC: Brookings Institution Press, 2000).

25 See *ibid*, discussion of the three core elements in particular ch 7, "Elements of Reform."

26 *Clean Water Act, 2006*, *supra* note 15, ss 26 and following.

27 *Compliance Policy: Applying Abatement and Enforcement Tools* (May 2007), online: <https://www.ontario.ca/page/compliance-policy-applying-abatement-and-enforcement-tools>.

28 "Incident" is defined in the Compliance Policy not only to be a contravention but incidents not involving a contravention where an activity has the potential to result in an adverse impact. The reason

for this is that the ministry's abatement powers are not only available when a contravention is found; the ministry is also is given preventive measure order powers so that it does not have to wait for a breach of the general pollution prohibition to intervene: see, e.g., ss 18 and 157.1 of the *EPA*.

29 RSO 1990, c P.33.

30 See s 182.1 of the *EPA* and s 106.1 of the *OWRA* and the regulations made under those sections (O Reg 222/07 and O Reg 223/07).

31 See O Reg 242/05 (Compliance and Enforcement).

32 SO 2002, c 32.

33 The Honourable Dennis R O'Connor, *A Strategy for Safety Drinking Water, Report of the Walkerton Inquiry, Part Two* (Toronto: Queen's Printer for Ontario, 2002).

34 See Government of Ontario, "Environmental Compliance Reports" (accessed 6 February 2018), online: <https://www.ontario.ca/data/environmental-compliance-reports>.

35 See O Reg 170/03 (Summary Reports for Municipalities), Sched 22 made under the *Safe Drinking Water Act*, SO 2002, c 32.

36 See O Reg 298/12 (Collection of Pharmaceuticals and Sharps – Responsibilities of Producers), s 9.

37 Ministry of the Environment, Environmental Innovations Branch, *A Framework for Ontario's Environmental Program* (July 2004).

38 Agencies have found that the very manner in which an agency seeks to communicate with a regulated firm to induce the firm to identify and correct violations can have a significant impact on whether the firm will follow through—the area is sometimes called "Communications for Compliance"—see, e.g., Scott Killingsworth, "Modeling the Message: Communicating Compliance Through Organizational Values and Culture" (2012) 25 Geo J Leg Ethics 960.

39 See, as an example of a provincial officer contravention-based order, s 157 of the *EPA*.

40 The draft regulations were proposed under the *Environmental Protection Act*, the *Ontario Water Resources Act* and the *Pesticides Act*. See Government of Ontario, "Regulation Proposal Notice" (Environmental Registry, accessed 6 February 2018), online: <https://www.ebr.gov.on.ca/ERS-WEB-External/displaynoticecontent.do?noticeId=MTMxNzQ=&statusId=MTMxNzQ=>.

# 49

# Regulatory Inspections: A Private Practitioner's Perspective

KATIA OPALKA

Individuals and businesses with questions pertaining to regulatory development or methods of how to comply with Environment and Climate Change Canada administered legislation should consult legal expertise with experience in environmental legislation.

ENVIRONMENTAL ENFORCEMENT WEB PAGE, ENVIRONMENT AND CLIMATE CHANGE CANADA, 2 JANUARY 2016

## Introduction

If, in the 1970s, Canada had followed the United States and adopted federal environmental laws requiring standard setting and enforcement for pollution control, and containing citizen suit provisions allowing NGOs and others to force the federal government to comply with those laws, the courts could now play a vital role in helping the country achieve long-term environmental goals by keeping political opportunism at bay.[1] And if Canada had a federal environmental policy agenda, built around federal standard setting and oversight and provincial and territorial implementation—which it does not—the courts could, as they do in the United States, provide a valuable safeguard against federal regulatory overreach, weighing in on the constitutionality of environmental protection rules made by the federal government under its authority to, say, regulate interprovincial commerce or navigation.[2]

And were the federal government of Canada inclined to use the courts to protect biological diversity on Canadian soil, then there would be a large body of contemporary jurisprudence, as there is in the United States,[3] describing the reach of federal conservation authority on non-federal land. Indeed, policy makers in Canada have long known that land use planning is the means by which conservation goals are achieved.[4] The Policy for the Management of Fish Habitat (1986)[5] and the federal Water Policy (1987)[6] pretty much say so. Unfortunately, Canada gave up on integrated land use planning in the late 1990s,[7] and as in other parts of the Constitution,[8] in the absence of litigation, there is nothing to force the parties back to the table. None of these policy failures can be addressed at a project level without the risk of government being ordered to indemnify aggrieved investors.[9]

What has this got to do with regulatory inspections and the courtroom, you may ask. My point is that there is rarely a connection, in Canada, between environmental regulatory inspections and the courts, and one of the reasons therefor is that in Canada governments don't normally use the courts to achieve compliance with environmental laws.[10]

## Inspections

Now for inspections.[11] A business can be taken off guard by an environmental regulatory inspection. The owners may not know that the operations are subject to environmental controls, perhaps on the mistaken assumption that the business is grandfathered. Or a neighbour may have called authorities to report a release to the environment coming from a facility, a release of which company employees or management may, as yet, be unaware. Or maybe it's a spot check. But it can also be routine, or triggered by an application to install new pollution control equipment, or increase production levels, or transfer the company's assets to a new owner.

In all cases, an inspection is an act by which the state reminds a landowner or the operator of a business that ownership or occupancy of land is subject not only to common law rules of tort, such as the rule that if you cause a nuisance you are liable to pay compensation to those whom you owe a duty of care and who have suffered harm attributable to your breaching that duty, but also to statutory rules such as the prohibition on unauthorized releases of contaminants to the environment. The arrival of an inspector can also be a reminder that governmental authorizations aren't always a shield against liability, whatever you may have thought.[12]

Whatever the reason behind the inspector's presence in the lobby, an inspection is likely to feel like a medical exam: intrusive, unpleasant, and somehow unfair. You'd rather not have to go through with it. You ask yourself if everyone has to put up with this. You may feel anger mixed with resentment, especially if the inspector appears to be younger than your grandchildren and seems to understand not a word of what you're saying. You probably wonder if you are being given the same treatment as your neighbours and competitors, especially if you are foreign or from out of province. The fact is, your feelings are valid, and the government knows it.

First, there is no common law duty to enforce the law, but if the government chooses to enforce, then there are rules on how that needs to be done in order to avoid government civil liability.[13] Predictability and fairness are two important considerations in this regard.

Second, while the common law and the laws of Canada may not require enforcement to occur, Canada has an obligation to enforce its environmental laws under a side agreement to the North American Free Trade Agreement (NAFTA). Since others will talk to you about the common law, the Charter, and the Criminal Code, and because it's important, I've chosen to focus on free trade.

## Environmental Measures Conditioned by Trade Agreements

Canada and its provinces do not argue about jurisdiction over environmental protection only.[14] Among many other things, they fight about jurisdiction to implement the terms of international treaties. So, for example, when Canada negotiates a trade agreement with one or more countries, the provinces will take the position that they are not bound by that agreement on matters under their jurisdiction until they say so.[15] If the treaty contains undertakings relating to environmental protection and conservation, you can see how matters can get muddled.[16] You would think that if an environmental problem is serious enough to warrant a global, regional, or bilateral treaty, then the federal government would have authority to require the provinces to step up and ensure compliance or get out of the way.[17] Yet only the courts can say for sure, and even on the bench, there has been considerable disagreement.[18]

The difference between trade agreements and environmental agreements is that in the former, the focus is on reducing barriers to the free flow of goods, services, and even capital, while in the latter, the objective is generally to slow down or reverse the loss of biological diversity or control pollutants. One is a green light, the other is red; in the words of the Beatles, "you say stop and I say go." So it should come as no surprise that in international business circles, much of environmental law is shrugged off as protectionism, thinly disguised.[19] It follows that when you read the dispute resolution provisions of trade agreements, you learn that when a foreign investor challenges an environmental measure adopted by a party to such an agreement, the tribunal set up to look into the matter will be hearing arguments on, first, whether the measure really is about protecting the environment and, second, whether it affects local and foreign companies equally. Third, even if it really is about protecting the environment and applies to everyone equally, the tribunal will examine whether the measure has the effect of expropriating the foreign investor without compensation and runs contrary to assurances made by the host government upon which the foreign investor relied in making its investment decision. Every litigator should know this. Trade law is a treasure trove.

Normally, it is trade agreements that speak to environmental agreements. Near the beginning, you are told that nothing in the trade agreement takes away from the obligations of the parties under the following environmental agreements: [...]. Deeper in the text, trade agreements often specify that when countries make environmental laws, they should endeavour to do so in the least trade restrictive manner possible. And when they enforce those laws, they must treat local and foreign companies in like manner, they should not use non-enforcement of environmental laws as a means of attracting or retaining investment, and if an environmental measure amounts to expropriation, then indemnification must be paid. Insofar as a sudden, overwhelming concern for the environment not infrequently coincides with the realization that a project that was supposed to be a vote getter is actually guzzling political capital,[20] you may say that trade agreements help keep decision makers honest by making governments pay damages to aggrieved investors.

## Recessions, Free Trade, and Federal Facilities Enforcement

Canada's experience with negotiating free trade agreements centres on the Canada–US agreement, followed by NAFTA.[21] The relevant time period is from the recession in the early 1980s to the recession of the 1990s.[22] Not surprisingly, this was also the period when Canada made its best efforts to get its act together on environmental protection. Indeed, "[i]n the post-Cold War world, free trade plus sustainable development was supposed to achieve, for all of us, what regular capitalism and communism hadn't: an improvement in the human condition motored by self-interest and conditioned by ecological constraints."[23]

So, aside from issuing policy mentioned earlier on fish habitat protection and water resources conservation, in 1988, Canada adopted the *Canadian Environmental Protection Act*, a legislative *fourre-tout* for dealing with federal environmental responsibilities. Canada then created a Canadian Council of

Ministers of the Environment (CCME) to work on aligning Canada's jurisdictions on all things environmental.[24] In 1992, Canada was the first of the treaty's signatories to ratify the United Nations Convention on Biological Diversity;[25] in 1993, Canada entered into the North American Agreement on Environmental Cooperation (NAAEC),[26] and in 1994, Canada's provinces entered into the Internal Trade Agreement,[27] which, among other things, gives people and provinces standing to challenge a province's relaxation of environmental controls in cases where this is done to attract or retain investment.[28]

In the NAAEC, which was signed to placate a very wary US Congress, the countries of North America promised each other to effectively enforce their environmental laws through appropriate governmental action, and they defined enforcement as including, among other things, inspections (see Article 5 of the NAAEC, reproduced in Annex A to this paper, "NAAEC Part II – Obligations"). I believe that the obligations found in the NAAEC explain much of what has happened in Canadian environmental law and policy since the mid-1990s. Below I'll identify some of the information I rely on.

In 2002, Fisheries and Oceans Canada and Environment Canada made public a compliance and enforcement policy for the habitat protection and pollution prevention provisions of the federal *Fisheries Act*.[29] The policy document states:

> One of the principal tools available to the federal government to ensure sustainable fisheries for Canadians is the *Fisheries Act*. The *Act* provides the legal basis for protecting and conserving fish and fish habitat. Specifically, the habitat protection and pollution prevention provisions of the *Fisheries Act* include sections 20 through 22, 26 through 28, 30, 32, and 34 through 42, and are intended to protect fish and fish habitat from harm caused by physical alteration or pollution (a synopsis of these sections is presented in Annex A). These provisions are an important component of the federal government's overall environmental protection program.
>
> However, laws and regulations are not sufficient in themselves; they must be administered and enforced in a fair, predictable, and consistent manner. Those who administer the laws and those who must comply with them need to understand how the government intends to achieve compliance with the legal requirements. For these reasons, this *Compliance and Enforcement Policy* has been developed for the habitat protection and pollution prevention provisions of the *Fisheries Act*.

> ...
>
> This *Compliance and Enforcement Policy* lays out general principles for application of the habitat protection and pollution prevention provisions of the *Fisheries Act.* The *Policy* explains the role of regulatory officials in promoting, monitoring and enforcing the legislation. It is a national *Policy* which applies to all those who exercise regulatory authority, from Ministers to enforcement personnel.
>
> The *Policy* explains what measures will be used to achieve compliance with the *Fisheries Act* habitat protection and pollution prevention provisions. It sets out principles of fair, predictable, and consistent enforcement that govern application of the law, and responses by enforcement personnel to alleged violations. This *Policy* also tells everyone who shares a responsibility for protection of fish and fish habitat—including governments, industry, organized labour and individuals—what is expected of them.[30]

You can see how this policy is relevant to regulatory inspections. It tells the regulated community that inspections will be part of an overall plan, that regulatees will know what is expected of them, and that government enforcement activity will be fair, predictable, and consistent.

The *Fisheries Act* was gutted in a budget rider in 2012,[31] and it's not clear where the enforcement policy stands. But that doesn't mean that we can't glean information from the document itself and statements made about the policy more than 20 years ago, for example, in this excerpt from a speech given by Environment Canada's head of enforcement at an international conference in 1992:[32]

> In addition to the Canadian Environmental Protection Act, environment [*sic*] Canada enforces the pollution prevention provisions of the Fisheries Act. That act is probably Canada's first environmental statute, and has been in force since 1868. The purpose of the statute is to protect fish, fish habitat and human use of fish. One of the strongest provisions to achieve that statutory objective is the prohibition against the deposit, into waters where fish are found, of any substance that is harmful to fish. Like CEPA, the Fisheries Act states, in section 2, that the federal government is subject to the act and all its regulations.
>
> So, the concept of federal law applying to Canada's federal government is not new in Canadian law. But what is new is that in 1988 the minister of environment announced the intention of his department

to treat the public sector, that is, government, the same way as the private sector in terms of enforcement of Environmental law. The minister believed that the federal government must be exemplary in its environmental behavior and specifically committed the government of Canada to that goal.

> Consequently, in July 1988, environment [*sic*] Canada published its enforcement and compliance policy for the Canadian Environmental Protection Act, which provided equal treatment in enforcement to both government and non-government regulatees. The soon to be published compliance policy for the habitat protection and pollution prevention provisions of the Fisheries Act takes the same approach.

Give this some time to sink in. Now take a moment to enter "federal facilities enforcement" into Google.

Making information available to the public has never been our government's strong suit,[33] so you can understand why Canadian government websites are relatively empty on all things environmental, including enforcement.[34] Luckily, the same does not hold true in the United States

The US EPA and FWS (Fish and Wildlife Service) enforce the law against the federal government of the United States, notably because they are directed to do so by presidential fiat.[35]

According to the NAAEC, inspections are enforcement. For details on how governments plan and carry out inspection programs, google "US EPA inspections." We know from the NAAEC that enforcement needs to occur and it needs to be fair. If the law is not enforced against government, then enforcement is not fair if it is done against industry. One of the ways to prevent enforcement from occurring is by not exercising the power to regulate. So, for example, the federal government has not issued regulations under the *Canadian Environmental Protection Act* requiring federal facilities to assess and clean up their contaminated sites, including those that might be contaminating waters frequented by fish, even though in 2002, the Office of the Auditor General of Canada issued a report containing the following recommendation and response:[36]

> 2.71 *Recommendation*. Environment Canada should develop a clear, mandatory requirement for federal organizations to clean up or manage their contaminated sites.

> *Environment Canada's response.* The Department does not accept this recommendation at this time. It does not propose to develop a mandatory instrument under the *Canadian Environmental Protection Act* (CEPA) at this time. Environment Canada views Treasury Board Policies as mandatory. Departments are making progress and significant investments are being made. The Department will continue to monitor progress on the implementation of the Treasury Board policy and will explore the development of CEPA instruments.

If federal facilities are not required by law to clean up their contaminated sites, it would seem unfair to force industry to do so.

Fast forward to the US presidential elections in 2008. The Democratic candidates made statements to the press about reopening NAFTA, notably to bring the terms of the NAAEC into the trade agreement itself, to make them enforceable.[37] Then in 2009, the federal government of Canada made sweeping amendments to its environmental laws to toughen the enforcement provisions and put more tools in the toolbox, including adding a system of administrative penalties.[38] Quebec followed suit in 2011.[39]

These developments are instructive. First, the timing of these systematic changes to Canadian environmental laws is in keeping with what I said earlier about recessions being good for environmental law in Canada. 2008 was a disastrous year for the American economy. It was therefore not surprising that NAFTA would take a beating during the primaries and that environmental law enforcement by the US's NAFTA partners would come under scrutiny. I have heard it said that the changes to Canadian legislation that were brought into force in 2009 had been in the works for a long time, the implication being that they were in no way related to statements coming from US presidential candidates in 2008 about reopening NAFTA. I do not doubt that Canada had been working on these amendments for quite a while. All I'm saying is that US pressure might have had something to do with getting them across the finish line.

## Conclusion

To enforce a law fairly, you need to have the ability to detect non-compliance and you need a range of measures for dealing with violations appropriately. There is no point in inspecting facilities when the only tool you have for dealing with violations is prosecution.[40] In the vast majority of cases, prosecution is too blunt a tool. Administrative penalties, issued like parking tickets, are usually more fitting.[41] Also, for chronic offenders, levying administrative penalties repeatedly allows you to build a case file that you can later table with the Department of Justice along with a recommendation that charges be laid.

So you would think that by forcing us to upgrade our environmental laws, NAFTA has been good for the environment in Canada. Well, it's not that simple. Remember that the provinces don't like federal interference on environmental matters. And remember that the NAAEC obligation is only to enforce the laws you've got; repeal the laws and the obligation becomes less burdensome.[42] In the period 2010–2012, the federal government rolled back federal environmental laws drastically, shrinking the territorial scope of application and refocusing the statutes as natural resource management laws.[43] By doing so, the prime minister called the provinces' bluff. Generally speaking, each province can now protect its environment as much or as little as it likes.[44] The prime minister even hinted that henceforward, any penalties the federal government has to pay because of a failure by a province to meet commitments under international agreements entered into by Canada may be deducted from the province's transfer payments.[45]

The approach described above is fiscally advantageous for the federal government at two levels. First, the federal balance sheet is not thrown off by a province's actions, because although the federal government is still on the hook vis-à-vis its treaty partners, it can set off the penalty when making transfer payments to the offending province. Second, the relative absence of federal environmental law requirements means that the problem of nonenforcement against federal facilities is resolved: the law is not being enforced unfairly because, more often than not, it simply doesn't apply. This shields the federal government from civil liability and, significantly, rules out the problem of having to account for extremely onerous environmental liabilities in the financial statements of the Government of Canada, something that is required under accounting principles to which Canada subscribes.[46]

To wrap up, then: governmental inspections are key to environmental law enforcement, but to withstand judicial scrutiny, they need to be part of a coherent, defensible system. We can thank our biggest trading partner for pushing us to make such a system. As for the fact that our response has been to dismantle federal environmental laws, we have only ourselves to blame.[47]

## ANNEX A | NORTH AMERICAN AGREEMENT ON ENVIRONMENTAL COOPERATION | PART II - OBLIGATIONS

### Article 2: General Commitments

1. Each Party shall, with respect to its territory:

(a) periodically prepare and make publicly available reports on the state of the environment;
(b) develop and review environmental emergency preparedness measures;
(c) promote education in environmental matters, including environmental law;
(d) further scientific research and technology development in respect of environmental matters;
(e) assess, as appropriate, environmental impacts; and
(f) promote the use of economic instruments for the efficient achievement of environmental goals.

2. Each Party shall consider implementing in its law any recommendation developed by the Council under Article 10(5)(b).

3. Each Party shall consider prohibiting the export to the territories of the other Parties of a pesticide or toxic substance whose use is prohibited within the Party's territory. When a Party adopts a measure prohibiting or severely restricting the use of a pesticide or toxic substance in its territory, it shall notify the other Parties of the measure, either directly or through an appropriate international organization.

### Article 3: Levels of Protection

Recognizing the right of each Party to establish its own levels of domestic environmental protection and environmental development policies and priorities, and to adopt or modify accordingly its environmental laws and regulations, each Party shall ensure that its laws and regulations provide for high levels of environmental protection and shall strive to continue to improve those laws and regulations.

### Article 4: Publication

1. Each Party shall ensure that its laws, regulations, procedures and administrative rulings of general application respecting any matter covered by this

Agreement are promptly published or otherwise made available in such a manner as to enable interested persons and Parties to become acquainted with them.

2. To the extent possible, each Party shall:

(a) publish in advance any such measure that it proposes to adopt; and
(b) provide interested persons and Parties a reasonable opportunity to comment on such proposed measures.

### Article 5: Government Enforcement Action

1. With the aim of achieving high levels of environmental protection and compliance with its environmental laws and regulations, each Party shall effectively enforce its environmental laws and regulations through appropriate governmental action, subject to Article 37, such as:

(a) appointing and training inspectors;
(b) monitoring compliance and investigating suspected violations, including through on-site inspections;
(c) seeking assurances of voluntary compliance and compliance agreements;
(d) publicly releasing non-compliance information;
(e) issuing bulletins or other periodic statements on enforcement procedures;
(f) promoting environmental audits;
(g) requiring record keeping and reporting;
(h) providing or encouraging mediation and arbitration services;
(i) using licenses, permits or authorizations;
(j) initiating, in a timely manner, judicial, quasi-judicial or administrative proceedings to seek appropriate sanctions or remedies for violations of its environmental laws and regulations;
(k) providing for search, seizure or detention; or
(l) issuing administrative orders, including orders of a preventative, curative or emergency nature.

2. Each party shall ensure that judicial, quasi-judicial or administrative enforcement proceedings are available under its law to sanction or remedy violations of its environmental laws and regulations.

3. Sanctions and remedies provided for a violation of a Party's environmental laws and regulations shall, as appropriate:

(a) take into consideration the nature and gravity of the violation, any economic benefit derived from the violation by the violator, the economic condition of the violator, and other relevant factors; and
(b) include compliance agreements, fines, imprisonment, injunctions, the closure of facilities, and the cost of containing or cleaning up pollution.

**Article 6: Private Access to Remedies**

1. Each Party shall ensure that interested persons may request the Party's competent authorities to investigate alleged violations of its environmental laws and regulations and shall give such requests due consideration in accordance with law.

2. Each Party shall ensure that persons with a legally recognized interest under its law in a particular matter have appropriate access to administrative, quasi-judicial or judicial proceedings for the enforcement of the Party's environmental laws and regulations.

3. Private access to remedies shall include rights, in accordance with the Party's law, such as:

(a) to sue another person under that Party's jurisdiction for damages;
(b) to seek sanctions or remedies such as monetary penalties, emergency closures or orders to mitigate the consequences of violations of its environmental laws and regulations;
(c) to request the competent authorities to take appropriate action to enforce that Party's environmental laws and regulations in order to protect the environment or to avoid environmental harm; or
(d) to seek injunctions where a person suffers, or may suffer, loss, damage or injury as a result of conduct by another person under that Party's jurisdiction contrary to that Party's environmental laws and regulations or from tortious conduct.

**Article 7: Procedural Guarantees**

1. Each Party shall ensure that its administrative, quasi-judicial and judicial proceedings referred to in Articles 5(2) and 6(2) are fair, open and equitable, and to this end shall provide that such proceedings:

(a) comply with due process of law;
(b) are open to the public, except where the administration of justice otherwiserequires;
(c) entitle the parties to the proceedings to support or defend their respectivepositions and to present information or evidence; and
(d) are not unnecessarily complicated and do not entail unreasonable charges or time limits or unwarranted delays.

2. Each Party shall provide that final decisions on the merits of the case in such proceedings are:

(a) in writing and preferably state the reasons on which the decisions are based;
(b) made available without undue delay to the parties to the proceedings and,consistent with its law, to the public; and
(c) based on information or evidence in respect of which the parties were offered the opportunity to be heard.

3. Each Party shall provide, as appropriate, that parties to such proceedings have the right, in accordance with its law, to seek review and, where warranted, correction of final decisions issued in such proceedings.

4. Each Party shall ensure that tribunals that conduct or review such proceedings are impartial and independent and do not have any substantial interest in the outcome of the matter.

**NOTES**

1 See, e.g., *Massachusetts v Environmental Protection Agency*, 549 US 497 (2007); Kernaghan Webb, "Gorillas in the Closets? Federal-Provincial Fisheries Act Pollution Control Enforcement" in P Fafard & K Harrison, *Managing the Environmental Union* (Montreal & Kingston: McGill-Queen's University Press, 2000) 163–207.

2 See Ann Althouse, "Enforcing Federalism After *United States v Lopez*" (1996) 38 Ariz L Rev 793; Eugene A Forsey, "Powers of the National and Provincial Governments" in *How Canadians Govern*

*Themselves*, 9th ed (Ottawa: Parliament of Canada, 2016, accessed 15 February 2018), online: <http://www.lop.parl.gc.ca/About/Parliament/senatoreugeneforsey/book/chapter_3-e.html>.

3 See United States Environmental Protection Agency, "About Waters of the United States" (accessed 17 January 2016), online: <https://www.epa.gov/wotus-rule/about-waters-united-states>; United States Environmental Protection Agency, "Clean Water Rule Litigation Statement" (accessed 15 February 2018), online: <https://19january2017snapshot.epa.gov/cleanwaterrule/clean-water-rule-litigation-statement_.html>. See also RT, "US House votes to block clean water rule as Flint scandal grows" (15 January 2016, accessed 15 February 2018), online: <https://www.rt.com/usa/329117-congress-clean-water-flint/>.

4 See, e.g., Government of Alberta, "A Policy for Resource Management of the Eastern Slopes" (1984, accessed 15 February 2018), online: < https://open.alberta.ca/publications/0864990677>; compare to original, 1977 version of same policy, referenced here (accessed 15 February 2018): <http://www.keepersofthewater.ca/keystonecaribou-documents.pdf>. See also Alberta, "Importance of Mountain Headwaters to Alberta" (INARCH Inaugural Workshop, October 2015, accessed 15 February 2018), online: <http://www.usask.ca/inarch/InauguralWorkshopOct2015/S1_Diiwu.pdf>.

5 Department of Fisheries and Oceans Canada, *Policy for the Management of Fish Habitat*; online: (2001, accessed 15 February 2018), online: <http://www.dfo-mpo.gc.ca/Library/23654.pdf>.

6 Government of Canada, "Water governance: Federal policy and legislation (accessed 15 February 2018), online: <https://www.ec.gc.ca/eau-water/default.asp?lang=En&n=E05A7F81-1>.

7 Agriculture and Agri-Food Canada, "National Ecological Framework" (accessed 15 February 2018), online: <http://sis.agr.gc.ca/cansis/nsdb/ecostrat/index.html>. That said, the 2012 *Canadian Environmental Assessment Act*, adopted in a budget rider, talks about "regional studies" (see *Canadian Environmental Assessment Act, 2012*, SC 2012, c 19, ss 73–77).

8 *Delgamuukw v British Columbia*, [1997] 3 SCR 1010 at para 186.

9 Paul Withers, CBC News Nova Scotia, "Feds appealing NAFTA tribunal decision of Nova Scotia quarry project" (20 August 2015, accessed 15 February 2018), online: <http://www.cbc.ca/news/canada/nova-scotia/feds-appealing-nafta-tribunal-decision-of-nova-scotia-quarry-project-1.3196817>.

10 See Andy Blatchford, "Environment Canada investigates many, but convicts few," *The Globe and Mail* (6 February 2011, updated 26 March 2017, accessed 15 February 2018), online: <http://www.theglobeandmail.com/technology/science/environment-canada-investigates-many-but-convicts-few/article565185/>. See also Katia Opalka & Johanna Myszka, "Sustainability and the Courts: A Snapshot of Canada in 2009" (2009) 10 J Sust Dev Law & Pol 59.

11 See Scott Jacobs & Cesar Cordova, "Good Practices for Regulatory Inspections: Guidelines for Reformers" (prepared for the World Bank Group, December 2005, accessed 27 January 2017), online: <http://www.fao.org/3/a-at377e.pdf>.

12 See *St Lawrence Cement Inc v Barrette*, [2008] 3 SCR 392 at para 95; Mark A Geistfeld, "Tort Law in the Age of Statutes" (2014) New York University Public Law and Legal Theory Working Papers, Paper 452 (accessed 15 February 2018), online: <http://lsr.nellco.org/nyu_plltwp/452>.

13 See *Kamloops v Nielsen*, [1984] 2 SCR 2 at 13; *Laurentide Motels Ltd c Beauport (Ville)*, [1989] 1 RCS 705.

14 See *R v Hydro-Québec*, [1997] 3 SCR 213.

15 See, e.g., Sue Bailey, "Newfoundland and Labrador says it won't participate in ongoing trade talks," *The Globe and Mail* (19 January 2015, updated 25 March 2017, accessed 15 February 2018), online: <http://www.theglobeandmail.com/news/politics/newfoundland-and-labrador-says-it-wont-participate-in-trade-agreements/article22519888/>.

16 Laura Barnett, "Canada's Approach to the Treaty-Making Process" (Background Paper 2008-45-E, rev 6 November 2012) at s 4.3 "Working with the Provinces" (accessed 15 February 2018), online: Library of Parliament Research Publications <http://www.parl.gc.ca/content/lop/researchpublications/2008-45-e.htm#a13>.

17 See *Canadian Environmental Protection Act, 1999*, SC 1999, c 33, provisions on international air pollution and international water pollution, which allow the federal government to step in and regulate if a province fails to control a pollution source that is causing pollution outside Canada or causing Canada to violate a commitment under an international agreement. But see United Nations Environment Programme "PCBs Overview" (accessed 15 February 2018), online: <http://chm.pops.int/Implementation/PCBs/Overview/tabid/273/Default.aspx>; ici Radio-Canada, "L'incendie des BPC de Saint-Basile-Le-Grand, 25 ans plus tard" (23 August 2013, accessed 15 February 2018), online: <http://ici.radio-canada.ca/regions/Montreal/2013/08/23/001-25-ans-catastrophe-saint-basile-le-grand.shtml>; and Marie-Ève Maheu, "*Entreposage illégal de* BPC *à Pointe-Claire: Québec veut récupérer 4 millions*" (5 March 2015, accessed 15 February 2018), online: <http://ici.radio-canada.ca/nouvelle/709852/entreposage-illegal-bpc-pointe-claire-avis-hypothque-legale-ministere-environnement>.

18 *R v Crown Zellerbach Canada Ltd*, [1988] 1 SCR 401.

19 See Daniel C Esty & Maria H Ivanova, "Globalization and Environmental Protection: a Global Governance Perspective" (Prepared for Global Environmental Governance: the Post-Johannesburg Agenda, Yale Center for Environmental Law and Policy, New Haven, CT, 21 July 2004, accessed 15 February 2018), online: <http://citeseerx.ist.psu.edu/viewdoc/download?doi=10.1.1.596.4578&rep=rep1&type=pdf>.

20 Jane Taber, "New Brunswick, Alberta join forces to push Energy East pipeline," *The Globe and Mail* (30 October 2015, accessed 15 February 2018), online: <http://www.theglobeandmail.com/news/politics/new-brunswick-alberta-join-forces-to-push-energy-east-pipeline/article27054317/>; Keith Brooks, "Time for Kathleen Wynne to take a stand against Energy East," *The Star (Toronto)* (24 January 2016, accessed 15 February 2018), online: <http://www.thestar.com/opinion/commentary/2016/01/24/time-for-kathleen-wynne-to-take-a-stand-against-energy-east.html>.

21 John Ibbitson, "After Twenty-Five Years, Free Trade Deal with U.S. has Helped Canada Grow Up," *The Globe and Mail* (29 September 2012, accessed 15 February 2018), online: <http://www.theglobeandmail.com/report-on-business/economy/after-25-years-free-trade-deal-with-us-has-helped-canada-grow-up/article4576313/?page=all>.

22 Armine Yalnizyan, Canadian Centre for Policy Alternatives, "Exposed: Revealing Truths About Canada's Recession" (29 April 2009, accessed 15 February 2018), online: <https://www.policyalternatives.ca/publications/reports/exposed-revealing-truths-about-canadas-recession>.

23 Katia Opalka, "Sustainable Development, NAFTA and Water" in Kinvin Wroth &

Hoi Kong, eds, *Sustainable Development and NAFTA* (Cambridge, UK: Cambridge University Press, 2015) 204.

24 See CCME, "Guide to the Canada-Wide Accord on Environmental Harmonization" (29 January 1998, accessed 15 February 2018), online: <http://www.ccme.ca/files/Resources/harmonization/guide_to_accord_e.pdf>. See also Canadian Environmental Law Association, "Federal-Provincial Harmonization Accord" (Office of the Auditor General of Canada, Petition No 10, 22 January 1998, accessed 15 February 2018), online: <http://www.oag-bvg.gc.ca/internet/English/pet_010_e_28706.html>.

25 *Convention on Biological Diversity*, 29 December 1993, 1760 UNTS 79.

26 See Auditor General of Canada, "Canada's Support For and Commitment to the North American Agreement on Environmental Cooperation" (Petition No 166, 4 April 2006, accessed 15 February 2018), online: <http://www.oag-bvg.gc.ca/internet/English/pet_166_e_28901.html>.

27 Canadian Free Trade Agreement (accessed 15 February 2018), online: <http://www.ait-aci.ca/>.

28 *Ibid*, ch 17.

29 Environment and Climate Change Canada, *Compliance and Enforcement Policy for the Habitat Protection and Pollution Prevention Provisions of the Fisheries Act*, 2002, online: <https://www.canada.ca/en/environment-climate-change/services/environmental-enforcement/publications/compliance-enforcement-policy-fisheries-act.html>.

30 *Ibid* at 1.

31 See Elizabeth May, "Bill C-38, The Environmental Destruction Act," *The Tyee* (10 May 2012, accessed 15 February 2018), online: <http://thetyee.ca/Opinion/2012/05/10/Bill-C38/>. See also Gloria Galloway, "Controversial Changes to Fisheries Act Guided by Industry Demands," *The Globe and Mail* (5 August 2013, accessed 15 February 2018), online: <http://www.theglobeandmail.com/news/politics/fisheries-act-change-guided-by-industry/article13606358/>.

32 See Paul Cuillerier, Director Office of Enforcement, Environmental Protection, Environment Canada, "Enforcement of Canadian Laws of Environmental Protection as Applied to Federal Facilities" (1992, accessed 15 February 2018), online: International Network for Environmental Compliance and Enforcement (INECE) <https://www.inece.org/library/show/57aa1ed107163>.

33 See Office of the Information Commissioner of Canada, "Open Information" (ch 6) in *Stopping the erosion of access to information in Canada – The Information Commissioner's recommendations to modernize the Access to Information Act* (31 March 2015, accessed 15 February 2018), online: <http://www.oic-ci.gc.ca/eng/communique-de-presse-news-releases-2015_1.aspx>. See also Gloria Galloway, "Information Commissioner Takes Tories to Court Over Long-Gun Data," *The Globe and Mail* (23 June 2015, accessed 15 February 2018), online: <http://www.theglobeandmail.com/news/politics/judge-orders-ottawa-to-hand-over-gun-registry-data/article25072076/>.

34 Environment and Climate Change Canada, "Environmental Enforcement: responsibilities and activities" (accessed 15 February 2018), online: <https://www.ec.gc.ca/alef-ewe/default.asp?lang=En&n=C3039403-1>.

35 See, e.g., United States of America – Government Services Administration, "Executive Order 13186 – Responsibilities of Federal Agencies to Protect Migratory Birds" (10 January 2001, accessed 15 February 2018), online: <http://www.gsa.gov/portal/content/101570>.

36 2002 October Report of the Commissioner of the Environment and Sustainable Development, ch 2—The Legacy of Federal

Contaminated Sites,online: <http://www.oag-bvg.gc.ca/internet/English/parl_cesd_200210_02_e_12408.html>.

37 See Doug Palmer, "Clinton, Obama threat to end NAFTA alarms business," *Reuters* (27 February 2008, accessed 15 February 2018), online: <http://www.reuters.com/article/us-usa-politics-nafta-idUSN2744905320080227>; Alex Spillius, "Barack Obama wants to reopen NAFTA," *The Telegraph* (18 February 2009, accessed 15 February 2018), online: <http://www.telegraph.co.uk/news/worldnews/barackobama/4685362/**Barack-Obama-wants-to-reopen-NAFTA**.html>; and Alexander Panetta, "Obama's NAFTA promise resurfaces; Harper spokesperson denies renegotiations," *The Canadian Press* (18 February 2014, accessed 15 February 2018), online: Huffington Post <http://www.huffingtonpost.ca/2014/02/18/barack-obama-nafta-tpp_n_4810868.html>.

38 Penny Becklumb, "Legislative Summary of Bill C-16, Environmental Enforcement Act" (1 April 2009, accessed 15 February 2018), online: Library of Parliament Research Publications <http://www.lop.parl.gc.ca/About/Parliament/LegislativeSummaries/Bills_ls.asp?lang=E&ls=c16&Parl=40&Ses=2&source=library_prb>.

39 See Québec, "*Loi modifiant la Loi sur la Qualité de l'environnement afin d'en renforcer le respect*" (accessed 15 February 2018), online: Ministère du Développement durable, de l'Environnement et de la Lutte contre les changements climatiques <http://www.mddelcc.gouv.qc.ca/lqe/>.

40 Dick Martin, Secretary, Canadian Labour Congress, Evidence to the House of Commons Standing Committee on Environment and Sustainable Development in Parliament of Canada, *ENSU Committee Meeting* (19 February 1998, accessed 15 February 2018), online: <http://www.parl.gc.ca/HousePublications/Publication.aspx?Language=e&Mode=1&Parl=36&Ses=1&DocId=1038418>.

41 See, e.g., "Policy on Civil Penalties – EPA General Enforcement Policy – GM 21" (16 February 1984, accessed 15 February 2018), online: US Environmental Protection Agency <https://www.epa.gov/enforcement/policy-civil-penalties-epa-general-enforcement-policy-gm-21>.

42 See NAAEC, art 3 and Annex 41; and Québec, Décret 930-96, "*CONCERNANT l'Accord intergouvernemental canadien concernant l'Accord nord-américain de coopération dans le domaine de l'environnement entre le gouvernement du Québec et le gouvernement du Canada*" (22 July 1996, accessed 15 February 2018), online: Publications du Québec <http://www2.publicationsduquebec.gouv.qc.ca/dynamicSearch/telecharge.php?type=1&file=26030.PDF>.

43 Elizabeth May, "Bill C-38 – The Environmental Destruction Act," *The Tyee* (10 May 2012, accessed 15 February 2018), online: <http://thetyee.ca/Opinion/2012/05/10/Bill-C38/>.

44 Quebec National Assembly, "Point de presse de M. David Heurtel, ministre du Développement durable, de l'Environnement et de la Lutte contre les changements climatiques" (25 September 2014, accessed 15 February 2018), online: <http://www.assnat.qc.ca/fr/actualites-salle-presse/conferences-points-presse/ConferencePointPresse-17903.html>.

45 See Bertrand Marotte & John Ibbitson, "Provinces on hook in future trade disputes," *The Globe and Mail* (26 August 2010, updated 27 March 2017, accessed 15 February 2018), online: <http://www.theglobeandmail.com/report-on-business/provinces-on-hook-in-future-trade-disputesharper/article1378647/>. See also Scott Sinclair, Canadian Centre for Policy Alternatives, "130 million NAFTA payout sets troubling precedent" (22 March 2011, accessed 15 February 2018), online: <https://www.policyalternatives.ca/

publications/commentary/130-million-nafta-payout-sets-troubling-precedent>.

46 See Paul M Kazenski, Casualty Actuarial Society, "Recognition, Measurement and Disclosure of Environmental Liabilities" (1994, accessed 15 February 2018), online: <https://www.casact.org/pubs/forum/94sforum/94sf367.pdf>. See also Financial Reporting and Assurance Standards Canada, "Liability for Contaminated Sites" (accessed 15 February 2018), online: <http://www.frascanada.ca/standards-for-public-sector-entities/projects/completed/item55574.aspx>.

47 See Eugene Lee & Anthony Perl, *The Integrity Gap: Canada's Environmental Policy and Institutions* (Vancouver: UBC Press, 2003). See also West Coast Environmental Law Association, "In Wake of Systemic Dismantling of Canada's Environmental Laws, Political Parties Vie for Environmental High Ground" (Media Release, 14 October 2015, accessed 15 February 2018) online: <http://www.marketwired.com/press-release/media-release-in-wake-systemic-dismantling-canadas-environmental-laws-political-parties-2063782.htm>.

# 50

# Anatomy of a Compliance Regime: Initiation of Action—A Regulator's Perspective

FRED MAEFS*

## Principal Legislation

In Ontario, the Ministry of the Environment and Climate Change (MOECC) mainly regulates compliance by the administration of five provincial statutes:

- *Environmental Protection Act* (EPA)[1]
- *Ontario Water Resources Act* (OWRA)[2]
- *Nutrient Management Act* (NMA)[3]
- *Pesticides Act* (PA)[4]
- *Safe Drinking Water Act* (SDWA)[5]

The MOECC appoints two different types of provincial officers to regulate compliance with these statutes: inspectors and investigators. The two types of provincial officers have two very different roles and as a result are granted very different powers.

According to the MOECC's Compliance Policy Applying Abatement and Enforcement Tools:

> *6. Violations: Identification and Response*
> Violations of legislation or incidents with potential to adversely affect human health or the natural environment are identified by Ministry staff through a variety of channels:

* *The views presented in this paper are my own and are not intended to represent the Province of Ontario, Ministry of the Attorney General, or the Ministry of the Environment and Climate Change.*

- Pollution incident reports (e.g., complaints from private individuals)
- Spill reports
- Notifications from the regulated community
- Response inspections
- Planned risk based inspections
- Mandatory inspections
- Adverse water quality incidents
- Report submissions
- Ministry audits and investigations
- Application to investigate under the Environmental Bill of Rights
- Information furnished by other agencies[6]

There are two primary courses of action that may be taken to address an incident that involves a violation. One is the abatement approach, where measures are taken to bring about and to maintain compliance or to prevent, reduce, or eliminate the risk of adverse impact to human health or the natural environment. The second is enforcement, which involves prosecuting the responsible person who has committed an offence. These two courses of action may proceed in parallel to respond to an incident. For instance, in response to a severe spill that results in adverse impacts to the natural environment, the ministry may issue a control document to ensure the responsible person is under a legal obligation to remediate the impacts, and the ministry may also commence an investigation to determine if the person should be prosecuted.

When an incident does not involve a violation but has the potential to adversely affect human health or the natural environment, abatement tools such as the request for an abatement plan or the issuance of a preventive measures order may be used to resolve the incident."[7]

## Inspection vs. Investigation

As noted in the decision in *R. v. Soviak*:

> As a matter moves from an administrative regulatory/auditing function towards a criminal, quasi-criminal investigation, the rules of engagement change and the procedures for obtaining evidence are also subject to change.[8]

## INSPECTIONS

Provincial officers carrying out inspections have very wide-reaching powers. In exercising those powers, it is up to them to determine compliance with applicable environmental rules and regulations. It is not predominantly about collecting evidence. If non-compliance is found, the provincial officer, or inspector, may take various steps, such as issuing an administrative order to ensure compliance. The powers are so far-reaching that inspection powers are known as "super powers," allowing the officer to carry out an inspection in the absence of consent or any judicial authorization. For example, the inspector may enter property, seize items, take samples, question employees, and make other inquiries.[9] In general, the powers of inspection are consistent with the inspector making a physical inspection, including making reasonable inquiries, orally or in writing. Depending on the nature of the subject matter of the inspection, specific protocols may apply, such as those under the SDWA.

In 2005, the Ontario Court of Appeal ruled that inspection powers did not include permitting the officer to make an inquiry by a telephone call.[10] The powers were amended in 2010 to permit telephone inquiries.[11] Environmental legislation also makes it an offence to hinder or obstruct a provincial officer in the performance of his or her duties, provide false or misleading information, or refuse to furnish any provincial officer with information required.[12]

The MOECC's Compliance Policy sets out the steps to be taken in addressing a potential environmental violation.[13] At stage one, a determination must be made as to whether the incident is a violation, or has the potential for adverse health/environmental impacts. If the answer is yes, then the inquiry moves to stage two. At this stage the inspector considers all of the relevant information, including the potential health and environmental consequences arising from the incident, the compliance history of the facility or person involved, and specific considerations to be made with regard to this incident. The inspector will apply an "Informed Judgment Matrix" in an effort to determine what steps to take. This will be included with an assessment of case-specific considerations in assessing the severity of the incident. At stage three, the inspector will determine what compliance category to apply and select and implement the most appropriate abatement and/or enforcement tools. In stage four, the inspector will monitor the situation to determine whether or not compliance has been obtained and, if so, whether it was resolved in the timelines given by the officer. A determination will then have to be made as to whether further steps need to be taken or no further action is required. While considering what abatement responses may be required, the inspector will also consider whether or not a referral to the MOECC's Investigations and

Enforcement Branch (IEB) will be warranted in order for an investigation to be carried out.

According to the policy, there are specific types of abatement and enforcement tools available.

### Education and Outreach

The inspector may consider meeting with the parties to analyze the consequences of the incident in question and work to prevent a reoccurrence through education and outreach.

### Issue/Amend an Authorizing Document

If the party in question has received prior authorization from the MOECC in the form of a document issued pursuant to environmental legislation, the inspector may consider whether that authorization needs to be amended or whether another type of authorization is required under the circumstances.

### Notice of Violation

The inspector or other appropriate employee of the MOECC may put the party on notice either in writing or verbally of a violation arising from the incident. This Notice of Violation is not considered an offence and is intended to address only minor violations.

### Abatement Plan

The inspector may either in writing or verbally advise the party in question that it is incumbent to develop an Abatement Plan within a specified time period to correct the violation or put preventative measures in place.

### Control Documents (Orders)

The inspector may issue a formal order setting out the obligations on a party to take corrective action or implement procedures. The order will include timelines within which the items must be complied with. The party in question may request that it be reviewed by a director, which is usually the Director of the Regional Office. There is also a right of further review of the director's order by way of appeal of the decision to the Environmental Review Tribunal.

### Environmental Penalty Order

Both the *EPA* and the *OWRA* provide for the issuance of an Environmental Penalty Order in addressing specific types of violations at specified types of facilities.

### Suspension/Revocation/Refusal of an Authorizing Document

If it is determined that an authorizing document has been breached or that the issuance of an authorizing document should be refused, the director may suspend, revoke, or refuse an authorizing document. Such a decision may be appealed to the Environmental Review Tribunal.

### Program Approval

The party in question may develop an outline of abatement activities to be undertaken in addressing the matter at issue. The Program Approval will be subject to agreement with the plan by the ministry.

### Enforcement

PART I OF THE *PROVINCIAL OFFENCES ACT* If the potential offence is relatively minor, the inspector may issue an Offence Notice, also known as a Ticket or a Summons. The Offence Notice or Summons must be issued no later than 30 days after the date of the alleged offence. The maximum fine that may be imposed is $500. The issuance of an Offence Notice or Ticket results in a prosecution in Provincial Offences Court. The party may choose to plead guilty and pay the designated fine, plead guilty with an explanation, or request a trial. A Part I Summons, on the other hand, establishes no set fine and requires both the party and the ministry to go to Provincial Offences Court for a trial.

PART III OF THE *PROVINCIAL OFFENCES ACT*: THE ISSUANCE OF FORMAL CHARGES Where the matter has been referred to the IEB, an investigation will be conducted. If it is determined that there are reasonable and probable grounds that an offence has been committed, the investigator may lay charges in the form of a Part III Information under the *Provincial Offences Act*. The laying of charges will result in a prosecution being conducted by Crown counsel on behalf of the MOECC before a Justice of the Peace in Provincial Offences Court.

### Public Reporting

The ministry will keep the public advised of environmental compliance activities to assure members of the local community that environmental laws are being complied with. Information for these activities may be accessed on the ministry's internet site at http://www.ene.gov.on.ca.

## INVESTIGATIONS

A provincial officer appointed as an investigator, on the other hand, will conduct a search for evidence of an offence. Parties under investigation have rights pursuant to the *Canadian Charter of Rights and Freedoms*. The powers of an investigator are more limited. For example, the EPA merely states that "a provincial officer may investigate offences under this Act and may prosecute any person whom the provincial officer reasonably believes is guilty of an offence under this Act."[14]

The purpose of an investigation is to determine if the possibility for penal liability exists. Predominantly an investigation is about gathering evidence to determine whether "reasonable and probable grounds" exist, and if so, laying charges under the appropriate environmental legislation. An investigator cannot use the super powers of an inspector and will require judicial pre-authorization such as a search warrant to enter premises or demand documents, unless consent is granted or exigent circumstances are present.

In general, any evidence obtained in an inspection prior to the onset of the investigation can be accessed by the investigator. After the onset of the investigation, only information that is exculpatory or obtained without the use of inspection super powers may be obtained.

### Investigations and Enforcement Branch—Referral and Intake

The MOECC's Investigations and Enforcement Branch has a standard operating procedure in evaluating the significance of incidents referred by Abatement for investigations.

PRE-REFERRAL Provincial officers who have carried out an inspection and identified a potential violation may consider referring the matter for an investigation. The decision whether or not to refer a matter will be based on legislative requirements, and the process referred to earlier as set out in the *Compliance Policy Applying Abatement and Enforcement Tools*. The officer may also consider involving the IEB while an inspection is ongoing if immediate action is required.

REFERRAL A referral by Abatement to the IEB will include such information as the observations that have been recorded in the course of the inspection, an index of relevant documents or approvals, and the party's compliance history over the past three years.

Once the information has been screened by a senior IEB Supervisor, the case will then be categorized in a range from Category A, very high priority and a high complexity, to Category E, which is non-prosecutorial investigations. The designation of the appropriate category will determine the priority of the investigation and the resources required.

## The Evolution of the Distinction between Inspections and Investigations

Courts have always tried to differentiate between "regulatory" offences and "criminal" offences. The high-water mark was established in the 1978 decision of the Supreme Court of Canada, *R. v. Sault Ste. Marie (City)*, which set out three categories of offences—two of which were simply "regulatory" in nature.[15]

The distinction began to become less clear as:

- Regulatory penalties increased;
- The number of regulated entities expanded; and
- Legislation imposed a greater impact on the rights of regulated entities.

## The Decision in *R. v. Inco Ltd.*

In *R. v. Inco Ltd.*, the Ontario Court of Appeal ruled that an inspection becomes an investigation when "an inspector under a regulatory regime possesses reasonable and probable grounds to believe that an offence has been committed."[16] It may have been challenging to establish when an inspector, untrained as an investigator, would have determined the existence of "reasonable and probable grounds."

### THE CURRENT STATE OF THE LAW: *R. V. JARVIS* AND *R. V. LING*

In the companion cases of *R. v. Jarvis*[17] and *R. v .Ling*,[18] the Supreme Court of Canada ruled that what is relevant is a determination of the "predominant purpose" for which the public official has entered onto property and/or made demands for information.

Both cases were based on inquiries by Canada Customs and Revenue Agency (CCRA). Just as with the inspectors and investigators of the MOECC, the CCRA has two distinct branches, the Audit Branch and the Special Investigations Unit. The cases arose out of initial inquiries by the Audit Branch into the activities of taxpayers. In the course of inquiries, auditors became increasingly aware that the taxpayers might have been involved in fraudulent activities. The question then became when an audit had turned into an investigation seeking evidence with penal ramifications. The Supreme Court of Canada stated that the determination as to whether or not the audit had "crossed the line into an investigation" would be a fact-based decision in each case.

In *Jarvis*, the court stated:

> In our view, where the predominant purpose of a particular inquiry is the determination of penal liability, CCRA officials must relinquish the authority to use the inspection and requirement powers under secs. 231.1(1) and 231.2(1). In essence, officials "cross the Rubicon" when the inquiry in question engages the adversarial relationship between the taxpayer and the state. There is no clear formula that can answer whether or not this is the case. Rather to determine whether the predominant purpose of the inquiry in question is the determination of penal liability, one must look to all factors that bear upon the nature of the inquiry.[19]

Seven factors for determining the predominant purpose of the inquiry were set out in *Jarvis* as follows:

> (1) Did the authorities have reasonable grounds to lay charges? Does it appear from the record that a decision to proceed with a criminal investigation could have been made?
> (2) Was the general conduct of the authorities such that it was consistent with the pursuit of a criminal investigation?
> (3) Had the auditor transferred his or her files and materials to the investigators?
> (4) Was the conduct of the auditor such that he or she was effectively acting as an agent for the investigators?
> (5) Does it appear that the investigators intended to use the auditor as their agent in the collection of evidence?
> (6) Is the evidence sought relevant to liability generally? Or, as is the case with evidence as to the *mens rea*, is the evidence relevant only to penal liability?
> (7) Are there any other circumstances or factors which can lead the trial justice to the conclusion that the compliance audit had in reality become a criminal investigation?[20]

As pointed out in *Lowe*[21]:

> It can be difficult to differentiate between when the inspection ends and the investigation begins, in fact, in some cases both can be carried out at the same time, as long as the purpose of the continuing inspection is for the predominant purpose of inquiring into or

determining the extent of compliance only and not for the purpose of gathering further evidence to prove the observed crime, then it is an inspection.

### DOES THE "PREDOMINANT PURPOSE" TEST APPLY TO PROVINCIAL REGULATORY INSTITUTIONS?

*Jarvis* and *Ling* arose under the federal *Income Tax Act*. However, the Supreme Court specifically noted that the seven factors referred to would have to be applied in the context of other provincial or federal departments, even if they have different organizational structures.

The court noted that there may well be other provincial or federal departments that have different organizational settings, which in turn may mean that the above-noted factors, as well as others, will have to be applied in those particular contexts.

Both the MOECC and CCRA have separate branches that carry out audit/inspection and investigation functions.

## Conclusion

In the event of potential non-compliance with environmental legislation, the MOECC has numerous responses available to consider in light of the specific circumstances. The focus is on determining the details of the incident, applying whatever immediate response is appropriate, and working with parties involved to remediate and prevent a reoccurrence and, if necessary, consider enforcement action. The wide-ranging powers available permit the MOECC to address any adverse event in an ongoing effort to protect the natural environment.

#### NOTES

1 *Environmental Protection Act*, RSO 1990, c E.19.
2 *Ontario Water Resources Act*, RSO 1990, c O.40.
3 *Nutrient Management Act*, SO 2002, c 4.
4 *Pesticides Act*, RSO 1990, c P.11.
5 *Safe Drinking Water Act*, SO 2002, c 32.
6 Ontario Ministry of the Environment and Climate Change, *Compliance Policy Applying Abatement and Enforcement Tools*, May 2007, online: <https://www.ontario.ca/page/compliance-policy-applying-abatement-and-enforcement-tools#section-5>.
7 *Ibid* at s 6.
8 *R v Soviak*, [1997] OJ No 1215 (Prov Div) at para 134.
9 For example, see s 156 of the *EPA*.
10 *R v Crompton Co /CIE* (2005), 78 OR (3d) 135 (CA).
11 Section 157.01(2) of the *EPA*.
12 Section 184 of the *EPA*.
13 *Compliance Policy*, *supra* note 6 at s 8.
14 Section 5(5) of the *EPA*.

15 *R v Sault Ste Marie (City)*, [1978] 2 SCR 1299 at para 60.

16 *R v Inco Ltd* (2001), 54 OR (3d) 495 (CA) at para 33.

17 *R v Jarvis*, [2002] 3 SCR 757 [*Jarvis*].

18 *R v Ling*, [2002] 3 SCR 814.

19 *Jarvis*, *supra* note 17 at para 88.

20 *Ibid* at para 94.

21 *R v Lowe*, [2007] NJ No 456, 280 Nfld & PEIR 331 (Prov Ct) at para 23.

# 51

# Collecting Essential Evidence for Environmental Investigations and Prosecutions: Approaches to Legal Strategy and Associated Issues

JACK D. COOP

## 1. Introduction

Environmental investigations and prosecutions can be daunting, even for the most experienced environmental practitioner. The variety of fact situations, offences, expert evidence, and law that may be brought to bear in any particular case can be expansive and challenging. At every stage of the process, the effective management, control, collection, evaluation, and presentation of evidence is critical to a positive outcome. This chapter provides an overview of one practitioner's recommended "best practices" with respect to many of these evidentiary activities.

We begin in Part 2 by providing a legal context for environmental offences and the evidentiary implications of the laddered enforcement approach common to most public welfare regimes. In Part 3 we examine the key evidence that is required by one's client in order to "stop a prosecution before it starts"—in a nutshell, how clients can avoid the commission of environmental offences by achieving due diligence. In Part 4, we review, in some detail, strategic legal approaches for responding to the many evidentiary issues raised by an environmental investigation. In Part 5, we move out of the investigatory phase and into the pre-trial and trial phase that follows the laying of charges. Here, we examine the strategic legal issues that arise, from an evidentiary perspective, as one deals with the Crown prosecutor pre-trial, or otherwise prepares for trial.

We hope that by the time you reach the conclusion of this chapter in Part 6, your thinking will have been stimulated, you will be asking lots of new questions, and you will feel even more prepared for your next case.

## 2. Background on Environmental Offences—Evidentiary Implications

### A. THE LADDER OF ENFORCEMENT—ITS EVIDENTIARY IMPLICATIONS

All environmental regulators adopt a stepped or laddered approach to enforcing compliance.[1] For practical purposes, this means:

STEP 1 - VOLUNTARY ABATEMENT As a first step, regulators will almost always attempt to achieve compliance through "voluntary abatement." The regulator (abatement officers, inspectors) uses "suggestions" to persuade companies to voluntarily comply with statutory prohibitions, regulatory limits, and approval requirements. The value of this approach is that it saves both the regulated party and the regulator enforcement costs.

STEP 2 - APPROVALS As a second step, legislation sometimes requires regulated parties to obtain approvals or permits for a wide variety of activities (air emissions, water emissions, handling of waste). These approvals and permits often have detailed, legally binding terms and conditions.

STEP 3 - ADMINISTRATIVE ORDERS As a third step, discretionary decision makers (director or minister) may exercise their broad statutory powers to require mandatory compliance through orders. Usually, such orders can be appealed to an expert tribunal or court. If they are not appealed, they remain legally binding and impose absolute liability.

STEP 4 - ENVIRONMENTAL PENALTIES As a fourth step, discretionary decision makers can impose "environmental penalties" or "administrative monetary penalties" upon parties out of compliance with the law. Such penalties impose absolute liability fines for violations of environmental legislation. On their appeal, often a reverse onus is imposed (appellant must disprove that offence occurred).

STEP 5 - QUASI-CRIMINAL INVESTIGATION & PROSECUTION As a fifth and final step, where voluntary abatement, approvals, orders, and environmental penalties have failed to secure the required behaviour of the regulated party, the regulator may resort to investigation and prosecution. The investigation is one in which the predominant purpose is to collect evidence for the purpose of acquiring reasonable and probable grounds sufficient to lay charges, and to create a "Crown Brief" of evidence that may be used by the Crown prosecutor to prove those charges beyond a reasonable doubt. These are generally "strict liability" offences, in which the Crown needs only prove the "*actus reus*" of an offence beyond a reasonable doubt, namely, that a statutory prohibition (e.g. causing an "adverse effect"), regulatory limit, order, or approval has been violated. In such a prosecution, the accused can negate an offence by proving "due diligence" (i.e. non-negligence), on a balance of probabilities. If the accused is convicted, the court may impose substantial penalties, including multi-million dollar fines and/or imprisonment and disgorgement of profit.

The focus of this chapter is preferred strategies around the collection of evidence when one's client is involved in this fifth and last step—an investigation and prosecution. However, one must remember that a good legal strategy requires consistent approach throughout all aspects of regulation (from Step 1 through to and including Step 5).

The significance of being at Step 5 is that your client is already in a situation where the regulator has concluded that Steps 1 to 4 are inadequate because of the gravity or persistence of your client's non-compliance. The regulator perceives your client as a serious offender who needs a heavy stick to achieve compliance.

The consequence is that it may be an uphill battle to persuade the ministry to return to Steps 1–4. However, you may be able to do so by:

- Demonstrating and documenting your client's environmental management system (EMS) and due diligence;
- Establishing with evidence your client's *bona fides* with the ministry;
- Responding carefully and diligently to inspections and investigations, in a manner that provides evidence that has been demanded but controls its flow;
- Demonstrating with evidence that your client has fixed the problem so that it will never occur again.

Note that the above actions can also be taken proactively—prior to any prosecution—to completely avoid (a) non-compliance, (b) investigation and (c) prosecution.

### B. EVIDENTIARY IMPLICATIONS OF PUBLIC WELFARE LAW

The defence of due diligence has been defined by the Supreme Court in *Sault Ste. Marie* as follows:

> The defence will be available if the accused reasonably believed in a mistaken set of facts which, if true, would render the act or omission innocent, or *if he took all reasonable steps to avoid the particular event.* [Emphasis added.][2]

For our purposes, the significance of this definition is that:

(1) The Crown assumes that an accused was negligent (not duly diligent) and failed to take all reasonable steps, i.e. that there will be evidence in the Crown Brief confirming same;

(2) The investigator will seek evidence to prove an accused's negligence, for inclusion in the Crown Brief;

(3) You must independently assess whether there is evidence proving, on a balance of probabilities, that the accused was duly diligent, i.e. not negligent. Applying the test in *Sault Ste. Marie*, and the long list of cases in which the defence basic test has been adumbrated,[3] you must determine whether your client took all reasonable steps to avoid the particular *actus reus* in question; and

(4) An accused must put in place systems to prove it will be duly diligent going forward, and provide you with evidence that it has done so.

## 3. Legal Strategy for Stopping a Prosecution before It Starts

### A. MOST IMPORTANT STEP—CLIENT MUST ACHIEVE (AND CREATE EVIDENCE OF) DUE DILIGENCE.

The number one strategy for avoiding investigation and prosecution is to assist your client in avoiding the commission of an offence by achieving due diligence. I often do this by providing to my clients the following list of factors that a court will weigh and balance when assessing due diligence. These are taken from the *Commander Business* decision:[4]

1. the nature and gravity of the adverse effect;
2. the foreseeability of the effect, including abnormal sensitivities;
3. the alternative solutions available;

4. legislative or regulatory compliance;
5. industry standards;
6. the character of the neighbourhood;
7. what efforts have been made to address the problem;
8. over what period of time, and promptness of response;
9. matters beyond the control of the accused, including technological limitations;
10. the skill level expected of the accused;
11. the complexities involved;
12. preventive systems;
13. economic considerations; and
14. actions of officials.

The difficulty is that there are literally hundreds of court decisions discussing how these factors should be interpreted and applied. So, at most, discussing these factors with a client will only provide them with a general idea of what they need to do.

### B. DUE DILIGENCE THROUGH AN ENVIRONMENTAL MANAGEMENT SYSTEM

Probably the most constructive advice that one can give to a client is to focus the discussion on factor number 12—preventive systems. This turns the client's mind to whether they can actually prevent all future non-compliance—i.e. offences—by having a proper EMS in place, one that is vigorously and fully implemented. In my experience, this advice provides clients with the biggest "bang for the buck," since the cases are fairly clear that the essence of due diligence is being able to prove that one has a "system" in place to avoid committing offences.

So, for example, in *Bata*,[5] the court observed that for an accused to establish due diligence, it "must establish that they exercised all reasonable care by establishing a *proper system* to prevent commission of the offence and by taking reasonable steps to ensure the effective operation of the system."

According to *Bata*, a proper EMS must include:

- a reasonable and realistic corporate policy;
- an adequate commitment of resources;
- no omissions in identifying environmental impacts within the organization's control; and
- up-to-date legal requirements.

So do not be afraid to ask your client whether it has evidence that it has an EMS in place that meets these minimum requirements.

Similarly, in *Courtaulds Fibres*,[6] the court observed:

> Reasonable care and due diligence do not mean superhuman efforts. They mean a high standard of awareness and decisive, prompt and continuing action. To demand more, would, in my view, move a strict liability offence dangerously close to one of absolute liability.

The court in *Syncrude*[7] put it in these terms:

> To meet the onus, Syncrude is not required to show that it took all possible or imaginable steps to avoid liability. It was not required to achieve a standard of perfection or show superhuman efforts. It is the existence of a "proper system" and "reasonable steps to ensure the effective operation of the system" that must be proved.

More generally, the key elements of due diligence will require evidentiary proof that:

- An adequate system was properly implemented;
- There has been compliance with reasonable industry standard;
- There was no feasible alternative;
- The contraventions were not reasonably foreseeable; and
- The activities in question were conducted by competent personnel within the scope of their employment.

Occasionally, clients will ask whether implementing ISO 14001 is the solution. ISO 14001 is often viewed as the Cadillac of EMSs. However, in *Zelstoff*,[8] the defendant was convicted of discharging effluent into the Columbia River despite the fact that it had ISO procedures in place to prevent the discharge. Why? Because the defendant failed to follow those ISO procedures. This underscores the fact that no matter how sophisticated a client's EMS, one must "use it or lose it"—an EMS system must be diligently followed to afford evidence of a defence.

To conclude, an EMS alone does not equal due diligence. To achieve due diligence, your client must vigorously implement the EMS. This includes: ensuring the EMS is documented and followed; regular training; and conducting spot checks, keeping records, and acting promptly to rectify deficiencies.

Also, it must also be remembered that an EMS system is a double-edged sword. EMS documentation can also provide evidence to the regulator of non-compliances, declining environmental performance, and third party complaints/claims.

## C. DUE DILIGENCE OF DIRECTORS AND OFFICERS

It has become quite common in recent years that whenever charges are laid against a corporation, similar charges will also be laid against its directors and officers (D&Os). In the past, this was based upon aiding and abetting provisions, or situations in which corporations were closely held such that by definition the actions of the corporation were also the actions of its "controlling mind."

More recently, even the directors and officers of large, publicly held corporations will be subjected to charges. This may be a function of the fact that specific D&O liability provisions have become pretty much ubiquitous in all environmental legislation.

For example, under the *Canadian Environmental Protection Act, 1999*:

> If a corporation commits an offence under this Act or the regulations, any officer, director or agent of the corporation who directed, authorized, assented to, acquiesced in or participated in the commission of the offence is a party to and guilty of the offence, and is liable to the punishment provided for the offence, whether or not the corporation has been prosecuted or convicted.[9]

Similarly, under Quebec's *Environmental Quality Act*, directors and officers of a corporation are deemed to have committed a corporation's offence unless they can establish that due diligence was exercised and all necessary precautions taken to prevent offence.[10]

Under Ontario's *Ontario Water Resources Act* and *Environmental Protection Act*, directors and officers have a duty to take all reasonable care to prevent the corporation from discharging a contaminant.[11] There is also a reverse onus that shifts to directors or officers an obligation to demonstrate that they have discharged this duty.[12] Moreover, directors and officers may be found guilty of an offence whether or not the corporation is prosecuted or convicted.[13]

Generally, directors and officers can only avoid prosecution by establishing that they have, each of them, personally exercised due diligence. That is, they need to be able to answer each of the following questions (taken from *Bata*)[14] with a "yes":

- Did the board of directors establish a pollution prevention "system" for the company—an EMS?
- Does the EMS ensure proper supervision? Inspection? Improvement in business methods? Compliance with industry standards? Compliance with environmental laws?
- Did the directors exhort those they controlled or influenced to implement EMS?
- Did directors ensure officers report back periodically to the board on the operation of the system, and ensure that the officers are instructed to report any substantial non-compliance to the board in a timely manner?
- Did the directors review environmental compliance reports provided by the officers or consultants? Place reasonable reliance on those reports?
- Did the directors substantiate that the officers are promptly addressing environmental concerns brought to their attention by government agencies or other concerned parties, including shareholders?
- Are the directors aware of the standards of their industry and other industries that deal with similar environmental pollutants or risks?
- Did the directors immediately and personally react when they noticed the system had failed?

Therefore, as legal counsel to an accused director or officer, one should ask what evidence your client has to prove the desired "yes" answers to each of the above questions, to the satisfaction of the investigator, Crown counsel, or the court.

## 4. Legal Strategy for Responding Effectively to an Investigation—How to Manage the Evidence?

### A. WHAT IS AN INVESTIGATION?

Prosecutions begin with investigation by a ministry investigator (in Ontario, from the ministry's Investigation & Enforcement Branch, or "IEB"). Clients need to understand that an investigator is not there to assist the client in abating a compliance problem. The presence of an investigator means the client is already at "Step 5," so the investigator's predominant purpose is typically to collect evidence in order to lay charges and prosecute.[15]

The evidence sought by an investigator includes witness statements, documents in the client's possession, actual samples taken, and the personal observations and photographs of the investigator. This evidence goes into a "prosecution brief" that is given to the ministry prosecutor (Crown counsel) and will form the basis of the Crown's proof of charges. If this evidence is not provided by the client "voluntarily," the investigator cannot rely on statutory inspection powers but rather must obtain and execute a search warrant in order to compel disclosure.[16]

The primary difficulty facing most clients is that abatement "inspections" (which can properly rely upon statutory inspection powers) may occasionally transform into investigations that lead to the laying of quasi-criminal charges when, during an inspection, the inspector acquires evidence which affords him or her "reasonable and probable grounds" (RPG) to believe an offence has been committed, begins collecting evidence for the purpose of prosecution, and effectively becomes an agent of a quasi-criminal investigation.[17] For practical purposes, this means that clients cannot let their defences down just because the government employee initially enters the premises as an "inspector."

## B. WHAT CAN AN INVESTIGATOR DO?

Matters are complicated by the fact that an investigator can access and make use of any incriminating information collected by an inspector prior to the inception of the quasi-criminal investigation.[18] Again, this reinforces that clients should be advised that they cannot let their defences down just because they are responding to an "inspection."

Once an investigation is underway, the inspection can continue in parallel, but the inspector can no longer share fruits of her inspection with the "investigative side."

Moreover, in the context of an investigation, an accused's rights under section 7 (liberty) and section 8 (privacy) of the *Charter* are engaged. As a consequence, the investigator cannot compel disclosure of evidence through the use of an inspector's statutory "inspection" powers, even when demanding information or documents from third parties.[19] The investigator needs either consent or a search warrant.

As a result, an investigator cannot use the following statutory inspection powers during an investigation:

- Enter a building
- Excavate (with a duty to restore the property to its previous condition)
- Require the operation of any machinery
- Examine, record, or copy documents or data, in any form and by any method

- Photograph/videotape the condition of operations
- Remove documents/data from the premises
- Make reasonable inquiries of any person, orally or in writing (includes an interview).[20]

However, she can do many of these things with a search warrant.

Moreover, an investigator may have the power to seize (without warrant or court order) anything produced or in "plain view" if he reasonably believes it is evidence of an offence.[21] Clients should be cautioned against leaving sensitive or incriminating documents in plain view.

Both an inspector and an investigator may have the power to issue an order prohibiting entry to prevent the destruction of evidence of an offence or discharge causing an adverse effect.[22] Clients should be cautioned to take steps to preserve evidence so that such an order is unnecessary.

## C. QUESTIONS FOR THE INVESTIGATOR

So when an agent of the regulator comes knocking, without a search warrant, the client's first task is to determine if they come in the capacity of an inspector, entitled to rely on statutory inspection powers, or as an investigator. A good starting point is to ask the officer:

(a) Does she have RPG to believe that an offence has been committed?
(b) Is she doing an investigation or inspection?
(c) Is the client is compelled to answer her questions and provide evidence, or is its cooperation entirely voluntary?

The agent will likely give one of two possible answers:

- She may admit that she has RPG, is conducting an investigation, exercises no statutory powers, and is completely reliant on voluntary cooperation.
- She may say she has no RPG (or is "not yet sure" about RPG), is inspecting, is relying on statutory inspection powers, and that compliance is mandatory.

If the first answer is given, the client can ask the investigator for more time in which to obtain legal advice before making a decision on whether to cooperate.

If the second answer is given, the client is typically under a statutory duty to answer questions and not obstruct the inspection.[23]

## D. WHAT IS OBSTRUCTION?

Generally, it is a statutory offence to obstruct a provincial officer (e.g. inspector or abatement officer) in the performance of his or her statutory duties.[24] Hereinafter, provincial officer is referred to as "officer" or "PO."

Under Ontario's *EPA*, for example, one cannot:

- "Hinder or obstruct" the officer in the performance of his/her duties;
- Submit "false or misleading information in any statement, document or data"; or
- "Refuse to furnish" the officer with information required for purposes of the Act or its regulations.[25]

"Obstruction" means making it more difficult for the PO to carry out his or her statutory duties.[26] Obstruction need not be a positive action. It can amount to simply failing to do something that the officer requests.[27] So clients need to know that they are obligated to cooperate and provide information reasonably required by an officer who is an inspector or abatement officer, but not a warrantless investigator.

Specifically, with respect to requests for an interview, clients need to know that it is not obstruction to:

- Refuse to give a voluntary interview to an investigator, during an investigation;
- Ask to have a lawyer present during an interview (however, the inspector may exclude the company lawyer during the interview of an employee);
- Ask to have your management point person (e.g. Accident Coordinator) present during an interview.

Moreover, under most environmental statutes, the officer may not exclude the lawyer of the person being interviewed. Individuals have a right to have their own lawyer present even during an inspection interview.[28]

Clients also need to be aware that there is no such thing as confidential, "off the record" discussion with the inspector/investigator. All information provided is with prejudice. Regarding warrantless or warranted requests for documents and information, it is not obstruction to:

- Provide only the documents requested; and
- Answer only questions asked.

## E. HOW TO HANDLE CONFIDENTIAL INFORMATION

It is also not obstruction to protect privileged and confidential information. Clients need to know that, presumptively, "privileged and confidential" documents include:

- Those marked "privileged and confidential";
- Communications between a company and its lawyers for the purpose of obtaining legal advice or for the purpose of pending/contemplated litigation. Note that lawyers include in-house counsel and external counsel; and
- Consultant reports prepared for your lawyers at your request.

If the inspector demands that you produce privileged and confidential communications, clients need to know that they should:

- Provide them in a sealed envelope marked privileged and confidential;
- Keep the originals or at least copies of the documents provided; and
- A court will then decide (on motion) if the regulator can look at them.[29]

## F. HOW TO HANDLE A SEARCH WARRANT OR INSPECTION ORDER

In Ontario, a search warrant for investigation and seizure must be obtained from justice of the peace (JP) under section 158 of the *Provincial Offences Act.*[30] To obtain such a warrant, the investigator must have RPG that an offence has been committed. In addition, a search warrant: can only be used at the location expressly authorized; expires within 15 days of issue; and must be executed between 6 a.m. and 9 p.m. Before challenging a search warrant on any of these grounds, clients would do well to obtain legal advice.

Under section 163.1 of the EPA, an investigator can obtain an order from a JP authorizing the use of a tracking or other device, if she has RPG that an offence has been committed.

However, an investigator does not need a search warrant or inspection order in "exigent circumstances"—i.e. where it is impractical to obtain a search warrant. A statutory precondition to such a search and seizure is that the investigator have RPG that one of two kinds of offences are being committed:

- Discharge of a contaminant causing an adverse effect, or
- An offence relating to hazardous waste or hauled liquid industrial waste.[31]

In carrying out warrant/order, the officer may "use such force as is reasonably necessary"[32] and may call for assistance from the police.[33]

## G. AVOIDING THE DISRUPTION OF SEARCH WARRANT EXECUTION

Investigators are often content to receive documents voluntarily, so they can avoid the time and cost associated with obtaining and executing a search warrant. Clients should work with their environmental lawyer to:

- communicate with the investigator;
- narrow down the documents requested to a specific list;
- provide only the listed documents; and
- avoid providing unnecessarily incriminating documents.

In the result, your clients may be able to avoid the disruption associated with the execution of search warrant, including the wholesale seizure of all files, seizure of confidential information, and seizure of computers required by the client for ongoing operations.

## H. THE VALUE OF AN INVESTIGATION PROTOCOL AND CHECKLIST

Clients may be able to avoid business disruption, self-incrimination, and loss of important evidence through the early adoption and implementation of an investigation "Protocol and Checklist." If obtained from your lawyer and implemented well in advance of any inspection or investigation, such a Protocol and Checklist can offer valuable guidance on how employees and management should respond to an investigation.

Typically, the Protocol and Checklist will cover:

- What the company's receptionist/security should do upon an investigator's arrival;
- Who will be the point person to coordinate the company response (escort the investigator throughout the premises, answer questions, obtain documents);
- What information should be obtained from the investigator, for example: name, ID, purpose (routine audit vs. whether RPG),

person(s) the investigator wishes to meet, whether the visit is supported by a search warrant, a copy of the search warrant, supporting information.

It should also cover the role of management before, during, and after the visit, including advice to management on:

- How and when to involve the company lawyer;
- How to evaluate the search warrant and determine if there is compliance;
- How to observe and guide the investigator's search without obstructing it;
- How to make a complete documentary record of the search (admissions of investigator, notes, duplicate samples, and photos) that can used in your defence;[34] and
- How to control documentary disclosure and defuse a potentially disruptive search by voluntarily providing documents to the regulator.

On the subject of interviews, the Protocol and Checklist will address:

- How to defer potentially incriminating interviews until employees are properly represented by independent legal counsel and given an informed choice on whether they want to be interviewed;
- How employees and management should answer questions;
- How to handle and safeguard documentary disclosure;
- How to conduct an exit interview of the investigator; and
- What commitments you should and should not make to the investigator.

If you do not have a standard precedent for such a Protocol and Checklist, speak to an environmental lawyer who does.

### I. EMPLOYEE INTERVIEWS?

Employee interviews can expose a company and its directors and officers to serious liability, especially if the employee is without a lawyer and unprepared. Employee statements may be adopted by the court as admissions of the company, and may be admitted into evidence without even calling the employees as witnesses at trial.[35]

In addition, there is a real risk that a scared employee may be more inclined to point fingers at management or other employees. This is not a desirable outcome from the company's perspective.

The employee's fear may be well-founded if an employee is suspected of committing an offence and could be charged personally. Even if the employee is not a suspect, she or he may become one as a result of the interview.

As a result, an employee has a right to remain silent and should be advised of that right by the investigator. Unfortunately, not all investigators are forthcoming with this warning, so that responsibility may fall upon your corporate client or you.

Since all interviews during an investigation must be given voluntarily, employees should be given the right to seek legal advice before agreeing to an interview, and an opportunity to have their own lawyer present at the interview.

If an employee is not part of the company's management, I will often recommend that the company facilitate (i.e. pay for) the retainer of independent legal counsel for the employee. This avoids many of the above problems, mitigating employee fears, ensuring the employee receives independent legal advice, and ensuring the employees do not automatically volunteer to give interviews. It also avoids the conflict of interest problem that can arise where a company lawyer represents both the company and the employee, and the employee ultimately testifies against the company.[36]

The independent legal counsel can act for all employees, if they agree to a joint retainer. She can also communicate closely with the company lawyer, and take the advice of the company lawyer, should she agree with it. However, she will give her advice to any employees in complete confidence.

In instances where an employee is a part of company management, and their interests are aligned, the company lawyer can usually represent both the company and the employee, and attend the employee interview on the company's behalf.

## 5. Legal Strategy for Responding Effectively to a Prosecution—How to Manage the Evidence

If you are retained after charges are laid, the effective defence of an environmental prosecution will generally reflect a number of "best practices" relating to the collection and disclosure of evidence. These best practices have as their object not only the favourable settlement of the matter (withdrawal of some or all charges; plea to some charges; agreed fine) but also effective representation at trial. The "best practices" include:

### A. WITNESSES

If an investigation is ongoing after charges have been laid, continue to control the number of witnesses made available to an investigator, and prepare the witnesses. Do not personally attend witness interviews by the Crown if you plan to be the trial lawyer. Never offer up your employees to an investigator on company time or as a representative of the company. Never arrange employee interviews. Always clarify that the employee does not speak for the company.[37]

### B. EMPLOYEES

As noted earlier, ensure that employees are onside and feeling protected with independent legal representation.[38] Circle the wagons with them, and their legal counsel, in terms of their right to refuse an interview where the investigator has no statutory power to compel an interview. Conduct your own interview of employees in the presence of their legal counsel.

### C. CROWN DISCLOSURE

Always demand full Crown disclosure. Include not only a generic request but also a specific request that highlights the weaknesses in the Crown's case, and the evidence you anticipate may be exculpatory of your client. Not only is Crown disclosure essential to proper case preparation and constitutionally required,[39] it can also force Crown counsel to confront evidence that he or she may not have noticed during charge screening, which can result in the withdrawal of charges or a favourable plea.

### D. LIMITATION PERIODS

One can occasionally get all charges withdrawn based on a limitations defence. If any of the charges cover offence dates that are outside the Crown's limitation period for laying charges,[40] demand disclosure of documentation you either know or suspect may be in the Crown's possession that would prove the ministry knew about the offence so long ago that the limitation period expired before charges were laid.

### E. CLIENT DISCLOSURE

As defence counsel, you must obtain full documentary disclosure from your own client and analyze it carefully to prepare a tentative "theory of the case." It is not possible to assess whether your client has a due diligence defence without undertaking this important step.

## F. MISSING CLIENT DISCLOSURE

If your client's disclosure is obviously missing critical pieces of evidence that should be in your client's possession (and this is frequently the case), you need to ask your client to find the missing evidence for you. You do not want evidentiary surprises during discussions with the Crown, or when your client is on the witness stand, in court.

## G. CO-DEFENDANTS

In most prosecutions, you will want to "circle the wagons" with co-defendants and their legal counsel. Invoke common interest privilege. Agree not to give interviews or provide additional evidence to the investigator/Crown in which co-defendants point fingers at each other. Agree on defects in the Crown's case. Agree on a strategy that presents a united front to the Crown.

## H. CROWN IMMUNITY AGREEMENT

On occasion there will be cases in which it does not make sense to "circle the wagons" with co-accused persons. These are cases in which your client was a genuine victim of illegal conduct by a co-accused, despite taking all reasonable steps to avoid the commission of an offence. In such a case, which is admittedly rare, it may be preferable to enter into a Crown immunity agreement with Crown counsel. Under such an agreement, your client agrees to provide evidence to the Crown in exchange for complete or partial immunity from prosecution.[41]

## I. ANALYSIS OF THE CROWN'S CASE

A critical step in the defence of environmental charges is to review the Crown disclosure you have received to determine:

(a) Whether the Crown can prove *actus reus* beyond reasonable doubt (and whether there is a reasonable prospect of conviction);
(b) Whether your client can establish a defence of due diligence on balance of probabilities;
(c) Whether the Crown has been misled by co-defendants, and this requires correction; and
(d) Whether the Crown is missing exculpating evidence that is in your client's possession, which may lead the Crown to drop a charge, or reduce a requested fine.

### J. OBTAIN NEW EVIDENCE WHERE NECESSARY

Where both your client and the Crown are missing critical pieces of evidence, good defence counsel will consider whether it is important to go out and find, or generate, new evidence by:

- (a) Tasking the client to make inquiries and collect new documentation and evidence;
- (b) Directly seeking out and interviewing new witnesses yourself; and
- (c) Retaining a trial expert(s) to provide new opinion evidence that tests or challenges the Crown's expert evidence.

### K. EDUCATE THE CLIENT ON DUE DILIGENCE

We have discussed the elements of due diligence earlier in this chapter. In my experience, and depending upon the level of sophistication of your client, it is often a necessary precondition to the successful collection of available and new evidence under steps E, F, and G, above, to educate your client about the meaning of "due diligence." Without undertaking this important educational step, many clients will not be able to self-assess whether they have such evidence in their possession, will not be able to provide you with this evidence, and will not know that they need to take active steps to generate new evidence on the subject.

### L. DUE DILIGENCE "AFTER THE FACT"

If it should turn out that your client has no arguable due diligence evidence (because, for example, there were certain reasonable steps it could have taken, but did not take, to avoid the commission of the offence), it is extremely important to the effective defence of a case to determine whether your client has rectified the problem by undertaking these reasonable steps after the offence occurred. Your key question for the client will be: "What steps have you taken since the alleged offence occurred to ensure that similar offences do not happen again in the future?"

If inadequate steps have been taken, you should counsel your client to take immediate steps in this regard. You may need to provide your client with access to expert resources to accomplish this objective. If your client has not obtained an environmental compliance report in some time, complete with recommendations on what steps that should be taken to rectify non-compliance (covering all steps, whether immediate, systemic, policy manual, procedural, monitoring, reporting, training, or management), now is the time to do so. I will often recommend that the client commission such a report through legal counsel, so it can be protected by solicitor-client privilege until such time as a decision is made to disclose it to the Crown.

In the case of a particular offence the client believes may evidence larger, systemic problems, I will often recommend that more than one report be commissioned: one that is responsive to the particular offence in question, suitable for disclosure to the Crown; and another, often larger report, that looks at non-compliance throughout the client's facility, which is kept confidential and not disclosed to the Crown. The latter sort of report is used by the client internally to correct existing problems without bringing them to the Crown's attention.

In the case of compliance reports suitable for disclosure to the Crown, while such evidence is "after the fact" and therefore does not support a due diligence defence, it will be critical to satisfying the Crown that there is no need for deterrence through a high fine.[42]

### M. REASONABLE PROSPECT OF CONVICTION

Complete your own analysis of whether, in light of all the available evidence, there is a reasonable prospect of conviction. This requires finalizing your analysis of the Crown's case, per item I above. What is required here is an honest and unvarnished assessment of these critical issues, which can be shared with the client and can form the basis for obtaining instructions from your client and holding settlement discussions with the Crown (or trial preparation). Jettison unrealistic and unprovable defences that will only clutter your case, cost your client, irritate the Crown, and bemuse the court.[43]

### N. COMMUNICATION WITH CROWN

Open the lines of communication with Crown counsel. Meet with Crown counsel. Find out what plea and penalty Crown counsel wants and why. Provide additional evidence and argument to Crown counsel in support of your client's position on plea and penalty. This requires your judgment as to whether it will be more effective and in your client's best interest to disclose additional evidence and arguments upfront, or to "keep your powder dry" for trial.[44]

### O. SETTLEMENT

Most environmental prosecutions settle. This is true for a number a reasons.

First, it is true because the likelihood of conviction is high. Generally, charges are only laid after the Crown brief of evidence is subjected to charge screening by Crown counsel, that is, is carefully reviewed and a conclusion reached that there is "reasonable prospect of conviction," and that it is "in the public interest" to prosecute.[45]

Second, it is often more costly to defend than to settle. Clients are first and foremost businesses, and with your help they will carefully evaluate whether it makes monetary sense to fight a case at trial to avoid a fine or obtain a reduced fine. In addition to the immediate cost of settling, a client will need to weigh the cost of agreeing to a conviction, thereby exposing itself to the risk of an increased minimum fine for a second or subsequent offence.

Third, the Crown will occasionally lay charges that are duplicative,[46] or more commonly will lay multiple counts of the same charge in relation to different time periods in which the same offence was committed.[47] Crowns may advise that they did so out of an abundance of caution, but it cannot be ignored that these practices tend to strengthen the Crown's hand during settlement discussions. As a result of these practices, the Crown may be willing to withdraw some charges if an accused pleads to a more limited number of "representative charges." The Crown may also show some flexibility on quantum of fine, especially where defence counsel can establish an arguable defence of due diligence, or due diligence "after the fact."

Counsel must carefully document in writing any settlement reached with the Crown. Documentation may include one or more of the following, depending on the case: (a) Minutes of Settlement, (b) Exchange of letters or emails, (c) Agreed Statement of Facts, (d) Agreed Submissions as to Penalty, and (e) Crown Agreement Granting Immunity from Prosecution. Agree on as much as possible, and leave the rest for submissions to the court.

## P. TRIAL

Where no settlement can be reached, prepare for trial. Evidentiary considerations and issues arise at every step of trial preparation.

For example, it is common to prepare a trial brief that contains all relevant legal documents, including the Information, court orders, legal memos, and case law. However, the trial brief also needs to include all of the Crown's evidence that has been disclosed to an accused, including (but not limited to) the Crown Brief that gave rise to the laying of charges. The Crown's evidence will include all investigation materials, police notes, witness statements, expert reports, demonstrative evidence, official documents (e.g. approvals, searches of records), demonstrative evidence, and relevant government correspondence.

Defence counsel must also prepare, either as part of the trial brief or as a separate "trial book," his or her work-product in preparation for trial. A typical trial book would include a list of all key "to do" action items by defence counsel, an opening statement, the elements of each offence accompanied by defence counsel's "theory of the case" with respect to each element, an exhibit list, notes for any motions, notes on key evidence the defence intends to present, a closing statement, and so on.

It is also critical to trial preparation that defence counsel prepare any motions that he or she contemplates as likely at trial, whether for the commencement of trial or during its course, whether brought by an accused or by the Crown. These typically would include motions to:

- obtain an order for further and better Crown disclosure;
- strike an information for delay;[48]
- obtain a change of venue;
- quash an Information due to invalidity or irregularity;
- strike out charges on account of duplicity or multiplicity;
- amend charges;
- order the joinder of charges;
- order the severance of co-accuseds;
- exclude witnesses;
- exclude evidence;
- adjourn;
- obtain a directed verdict; and
- obtain a court order declaring a mistrial.

You will need to support most of these motions[49] with affidavit or *viva voce* evidence that is prepared well in advance of the motion.

Finally, a key to effective trial preparation is the preparation of your own witnesses. In the case of factual lay witnesses, the most important goal will be to refresh the witness's memory of the relevant facts. Usually, one would prepare a witness statement or "will say" with the assistance of the witness, to ensure there is a clear and common understanding of the witness's intended testimony. Counsel should speak with the witnesses and review the facts of the case and have them review their prior statement before testifying.

In the case of expert witnesses, one would normally obtain an expert report from the witness, for the same reason. Defence counsel may provide appropriate input into such a report, subject to procedural guidelines.[50]

## 6. Conclusion

In this chapter, we have attempted to outline some effective legal strategies for the management, control, collection, evaluation, and presentation of evidence at every stage of an environmental prosecution—its investigation, pre-trial process, and trial. We hope that our review has cemented in the reader's mind the critical importance of carefully formulating an evidentiary strategy for the defence of such cases. We also hope that it stimulates the reader to reconsider their own "best practices," and to dig deeper into the rich case law and practice associated with regulatory litigation generally, and environmental defence work in particular. Ideally, you will be asking lots of new questions, and you will feel even more prepared for your next case.

### NOTES

1 See, e.g., Ontario Ministry of the Environment and Climate Change, *Compliance Policy Applying Abatement and Enforcement Tools*, May 2007, online: <https://www.ontario.ca/page/compliance-policy-applying-abatement-and-enforcement-tools#section-5>.

2 *R v Sault Ste Marie (City)* (1978), 40 CCC (2d) 353 (SCC) at 373–374.

3 See, e.g.: *R v Wholesale Travel Group Inc* (1991), 67 CCC (3d) 193 (SCC); *Lévis (City) v Tétreault*, [2006] 1 SCR 420; *R v Commander Business Furniture Inc* (1992), 9 CELR (NS) 185 (Ont CJ, Prov Div), aff'd 22 WCB (2d) 526 (Gen Div) [*Commander Business Furniture*]; and *R v Courtaulds Fibres Canada* (1992), 9 CELR (NS) 304 (Ont CJ, Prov Div) [*Courtaulds Fibres Canada*], to name but a few.

4 *Commander Business Furniture*, *ibid* at para 87.

5 *R v Bata Industries Ltd* (1992), 7 CELR (NS) 245 (Ont CJ, Prov Div) at para 41 [*Bata Industries*].

6 *Courtaulds Fibres Canada*, *supra* note 3 at para 39.

7 *R v Syncrude Canada Ltd*, 2010 ABPC 229 at para 99.

8 *R v Zellstoff Celgar Limited Partnership*, 2012 BCPC 38.

9 *Canadian Environmental Protection Act, 1999*, SC 1999, c 33, s 280 [*CEPA*].

10 *Environmental Quality Act*, RSQ, c Q-2, s 115.40.

11 *Ontario Water Resources Act*, RSO 1990, c O.40, s 116(1) [*OWRA*]; *Environmental Protection Act*, RSO 1990, c E.19, s 194 [*EPA*].

12 *OWRA*, s 116(2.1); *EPA*, s 194(2.1).

13 *OWRA*, s 116(3); *EPA*, s 194(3).

14 *Bata Industries*, *supra* note 5.

15 *R v Jarvis* (2002), 169 CCC (3d) 1 (SCC) [*Jarvis*]; and *R v Ling* (2002), 169 CCC (3d) 46 (SCC).

16 *Ibid.*

17 *Jarvis*, *supra* note 15 at para 94.

18 *Supra* note 15.

19 *Ibid.*

20 See, e.g., s 156 of the *EPA*, *supra* note 11.

21 Although in *Safety Kleen Canada Inc v Canada* (1991), 7 CRR (2d) 299 (Ont CJ (Gen Div)) at 307, the court held that there is no "plain view" principle for provincial offences where a search is conducted under warrant, this decision may be in doubt based on the Supreme Court of Canada ruling in *R v Macooh*, [1993] 2 SCR 802. See also *R v Busat* (2006), 274 Sask R 1 (QB). Statutes may expressly empower an inspector to seize evidence of an offence in plain view: see s 160 of the *EPA*.

22 For example, see s 156.4 of the *EPA* and s 57(6) of the Ontario *Occupational Health and Safety Act*, RSO 1990, c O.1 [*OHSA*].

23 See, e.g., s 184 of the *EPA*.

24 *EPA*, s 184. *OHSA*, s 62(1).

25 *EPA*, *ibid.*

26 *R v Tortolano* (1975), 28 CCC (3d) 562 (Ont CA); *R v Yussuf*, 2014 ONCJ 143; and *R v Clare* (2014), 115 WCB (2d) 383 (Ont CJ), aff'd 2015 ONCJ 341.

27 *R v O'Hara* (1993), 10 CELR (NS) 112 (NS Prov Ct).

28 *EPA*, s 156(4).

29 *Provincial Offences Act*, RSO 1990, c P.33, s 160.

30 *Ibid*, s 158.

31 *EPA*, s 161.

32 *EPA*, s 163.

33 *EPA*, s 166.

34 It is critical that sampling evidence be collected by qualified consultants, who take "legal samples" under seal, so that an unbroken chain a custody/continuity can be proven at trial, establishing that the laboratory results tendered pursuant to the relevant statutory provisions in fact relate to the material sampled. See, e.g.: *R v Metalore Resources Ltd*, 2012 ONCJ 518; and *R v Unitec Disposals Inc* (1994), 14 CELR (NS) 78 (Ont CJ (Prov Div)), to name only a few cases.

35 *R v Syncrude Canada Ltd*, [2010] AJ No 421 (Prov Ct).

36 Remember that it is generally a bad idea for the company lawyer to represent employees in an investigative interview. If the employee is subsequently called as a Crown witness to testify against the company, you may be disqualified from acting for the company, i.e., acting against your former client. See *R v Laidlaw Environmental Services (Sarnia) Ltd* (1996), 19 CELR (NS) 42, aff'd 23 CELR (NS) 1 (Ont CJ, Gen Div) [*Laidlaw Environmental Services*].

37 For a classic example of defence counsel violating most of these best practices, see *R v Syncrude Canada Ltd*, 2010 ABPC 123.

38 *Laidlaw Environmental Services*, *supra* note 36.

39 It is constitutionally required under s 7 of the *Charter* to enable an accused to make "full answer and defence." See *R v Stinchcombe*, [1991] 3 SCR 326.

40 The limitation period for prosecutions under most of Ontario's environmental laws is two years from the date of the offence, or from when the provincial officers first knew about it, whichever is later. See s 195 of the *EPA* and 94 of the *OWRA*.

41 See, e.g., online: <http://www.ppsc-sppc.gc.ca/eng/pub/fpsd-sfpg/fps-sfp/tpd/p3/ch03.html>.

42 The leading case on sentencing in Ontario is *R v Cotton Felts Ltd* (1982), 2 CCC (3d) 287 (Ont CA), which ruled that the primary purpose of sentencing in all regulatory offences is "deterrence." Of course, there are many other factors a court is mandated to consider: see, e.g., s 188.1 of the *EPA* for a list of such factors.

43 See, e.g., *R v Syncrude Canada Ltd*, 2010 ABPC 229, the newsworthy "oil ducks" prosecution in Alberta. Here, the defendant advanced a multitude of defences, arguing not only due diligence but also impossibility of compliance, act of God, abuse of the approvals process, officially induced error, and that the infraction was *de minimis*. The court rejected all six defences, and convicted.

44 In civil litigation, there is an obligation upon every party to disclose to the party opposite all relevant documentary evidence in their "power, possession and control," as well as an obligation to make full oral disclosure during

examinations-for-discovery. By contrast, in a quasi-criminal prosecution, only the Crown is obligated to disclose. An accused is under no disclosure obligation, and is free to "keep its powder dry" and to surprise Crown witnesses with undisclosed evidence at trial. In practice, however, "keeping your powder dry" generally only promotes one thing—it ensures that a matter will proceed to trial. As a result, this practice is usually not in your client's best interests. If your client has cogent evidence of due diligence, give it to the Crown. Most Crowns will be reasonable and (with the advice of the investigator) will try to evaluate it objectively and do what is right and fair. Give them a chance to exercise prosecutorial discretion in your client's favour.

45 See, e.g., Province of Ontario, Ministry of Attorney General, *Crown Policy Manual* (21 March 2005), Charge Screening, online: <https://www.attorneygeneral.jus.gov.on.ca/english/crim/cpm/2005/ChargeScreening.pdf>.

46 For example, the Crown may lay duplicative charges for polluting under s 14 of the *EPA* and s 30 of the *OWRA*, or for failing to notify the ministry of a discharge/spill under ss 13 and 92 of the *EPA*. These extra charges may not withstand a motion to strike based upon the rule against multiple convictions set out in *R v Kienapple*, [1975] 1 SCR 729, but they still serve the Crown as fodder for negotiation.

47 For example, when charging an accused with operating a waste transportation system without a required approval, it is common for the Crown to lay multiple counts of the same charge for every period of days within a given year in which the illegal system was allegedly operated.

48 Previously referred to as an "*Askov*" motion; now, more likely a "*Jordan*" motion, after the recent Supreme Court of Canada decision in *R v Jordan*, 2016 SCC 27, [2016] 1 SCR 631. For cases going to trial in the provincial court (which would include all environmental prosecutions), the SCC established a presumptive ceiling of 18 months from the charge to the actual or anticipated end of trial, failing which the charges will be struck out for delay. This protects the s 11(b) *Charter* right of an accused person "to be tried within a reasonable time."

49 Obviously not all motions require evidence from the accused—e.g., a motion for a directed verdict is based entirely upon the evidence submitted by the Crown in its case.

50 *Moore v Getahun*, 2015 ONCA 55; see also *White Burgess Langille Inman v Abbott and Haliburton Co*, [2015] 2 SCR 182.

# 52

# Environmental Investigations: A Government Perspective

PAUL McCULLOCH

Environmental regulatory regimes in Canada typically include offence provisions that can result in significant penalties such as fines, payments into funds, issuance of court orders, and even prison terms for individuals. The purpose of these penalties is to enforce compliance with the regulatory requirements through general deterrence.[1] Nevertheless, the enforcement agency still bears the burden of demonstrating that the perpetrator committed the impugned act. An effective investigation that collects the necessary evidence is therefore a key element of any enforcement action that leads to the imposition of a penalty. This chapter explains the difference between an investigation and an inspection in a regulatory context, describes the investigation process, and reflects upon recent cases that have addressed the inspection versus investigation divide.

## Inspections and Investigations

There are a variety of tools available to enforcement agencies to promote environmental protection. Education and outreach, voluntary compliance, standards and requirements imposed through regulations or permits/approvals/licences, warnings or notices of non-compliance, orders, administrative penalties, and finally prosecutions are all part of the agency's arsenal. Furthermore, the various tools are not mutually exclusive. An agency may either proceed in a stepwise fashion, starting with voluntary compliance and progressing to stricter means if the response is not satisfactory, or it may pursue two courses of action at the same time, such as issuing an order and also commencing an investigation.

An inspection is conducted to determine compliance with applicable regulatory requirements. It may lead to any one of the responses described above being used, or the suspension or revocation of a permit/approval/licence, in addition to referring a matter for investigation. The first contact between the regulated community and an enforcement agency often occurs through an inspection.

Environmental officers generally have a broad range of powers to carry out inspections that permit them to enter any place, including private property (except, in most cases, dwellings), without a warrant to make and record observations, take samples, gather information, make inquiries, and request and copy documents as long as doing any of these things is consistent with the purposes of the authorizing statute.[2] These powers have been upheld as not violating sections 7 and 8 of the *Charter* that protect against self-incrimination and unreasonable searches and seizure, for a number of reasons:

- There is a relatively low expectation of privacy for activities that are subject to state regulation[3]
- A less stringent standard can be applied because a regulatory regime does not carry the same moral reprimand and stigma that accompanies *Criminal Code* offences[4]
- Actors that voluntarily participate in the regulated activity must accept the corresponding terms and conditions.[5]

Inspections may be initiated for a number of different reasons, including:

- Routine inspections (announced or unannounced)
- Random stop programs
- Response to complaints
- Follow-up on self-reporting
- Specific incidents such as a spill or process upset
- Information provided by a whistleblower.

The common element is that the initial purpose is not to decide whether to lay charges. Rather, the inspector is initiating the inspection to determine whether the operation is out of compliance and, if so, to decide upon an appropriate course of action. While the officer may have a suspicion prior to arrival that he or she will find the facility to be out of compliance, this is not in itself sufficient to convert an inspection into an investigation.[6] The officer will not be in a position to decide what course of action should be taken until completing at least the initial inspection. Furthermore, while an opposing relationship may exist between the officer and the facility owner or operator (simply referred to as the "facility" for the remainder of this paper), the relationship is not necessarily adversarial. In many cases, an officer may work constructively with the facility to provide guidance on how to come into compliance.

An investigation, on the other hand, has a much more focused purpose. The main if not sole purpose of an investigation is to gather evidence to determine whether enforcement action should be taken that will result in penal consequences, usually by laying charges. At this point, the relationship between the investigator and the facility has become adversarial.[7]

There is no simple line that clearly delineates between an inspection and investigation. The determination requires a contextual analysis taking into account a number of factors as described in the Supreme Court of Canada (SCC) decision *R. v. Jarvis*. In that case, the defendant was audited by Revenue Canada (as it then was) for income tax compliance purposes and was then later investigated for tax evasion. Audits and investigations were conducted by two separate branches within Revenue Canada. At issue was what information the investigation branch could use that was collected by the audit branch. The SCC listed the following factors, which have been paraphrased below:[8]

- Reasonable grounds
    - Did the authorities have reasonable grounds to lay charges?
    - Does it appear that a decision to proceed with an investigation that could lead to penal consequences could have been made?

- General conduct
    - Was the general conduct of the authorities such that it was consistent with the pursuit of penal consequences?

- Referral to investigator
    - Had the inspector transferred his or her files and materials to the investigator?

- Inspector acting as agent for investigator
    - Was the conduct of the inspector such that he or she was effectively acting as an agent for the investigator?

- Does it appear that the investigator intended to use the inspector as an agent in the collection of evidence?

- Relevance of information/evidence
    - Is the evidence sought relevant to liability generally?
    - Is the evidence relevant only to penal liability? (e.g. motive, intentions, due diligence)

- Other circumstances
    - Any other facts that could lead the trial judge to the conclusion that the inspection had in reality become an investigation?

In Ontario, similar to Revenue Canada, the Ministry of the Environment and Climate Change has created separate administrative branches for regional inspectors (called environmental officers) and investigators that report to separate directors. However, other enforcement agencies, such as the Ontario Ministry of Labour, do not use this administrative structure. In that situation, an enforcement officer must "wear two hats," so to speak, and make the determination as to the point at which an inspection has turned into an investigation. The factors listed above will need to be reformulated in the case of an enforcement agency that does not split its enforcement officers between separate inspection and enforcement roles.

The distinction between an inspection and an investigation can be further complicated when there is a need for follow-up compliance inspections and/or continuing offences are occurring. In these situations, there can be a legitimate justification for enforcement officers to carry out further inspections even if there is an ongoing investigation. A common example is where an inspector conducts an inspection, determines that the operation is out of compliance, and issues an order to the facility that sets out steps that must be taken to come into compliance, but an investigation is also commenced to determine whether charges should be laid with respect to the initial non-compliance. Follow-up inspections may be undertaken to determine whether the order is being complied with. During these inspections, additional information may be gathered that is also relevant to the investigation. Where the enforcement officer was able to demonstrate that there was a valid purpose to the follow-up inspections to determine compliance with the orders, in at least one case, it was found that there was no *prima facie* evidence of a *Charter* breach.[9]

## The Investigation Process

At the point that an investigation is commenced, the investigator enters into a more adversarial relationship with the facility. For this reason, unlike in an inspection, the courts have determined that an investigator cannot rely upon the regulatory inspection powers to collect evidence. Rather, the investigation will be governed by more stringent requirements in determining whether any *Charter* rights were violated.[10]

Nevertheless, an investigation can still be effectively carried out, only using different techniques. Much of the evidence obtained during an investigation consists of information generated during the inspection stage. The inspector will provide the evidence along with a statement and his or her notes, which often form the foundation of an investigator's case. There is nothing prohibiting an investigator from making use of evidence obtained through the proper exercise of inspection functions.[11] An investigator can then pursue other sources of information as described below.

### EVIDENCE FROM OTHERS THAN THE FACILITY WHO ARE WILLING TO VOLUNTARILY COOPERATE

Basic investigative work includes interviewing and obtaining documentary evidence such as photographs from people other than the facility who will voluntarily provide such evidence, including:

- Victims or complainants
- Eyewitnesses
- Neighbours
- Employees
- Subcontractors
- Other agencies.

However, people are not always willing to cooperate. In particular, employees often do not wish to speak to an investigator out of loyalty to their employer or perhaps fear of reprisals despite the statutory protections that are provided.[12]

### EVIDENCE GENERATED BY THE FACILITY PRIOR TO THE INVESTIGATION

Environmental regulatory regimes generally require facilities to report key information to the regulator that may eventually be available to the investigator.

This information can provide important evidence for the investigator's case. Examples include:

- Applications for licences/approvals/permits, which often include supporting studies or engineering evaluations
- Reports such as environmental assessments, annual reports, or logbooks
- Monitoring data required to be kept by regulations or administrative instruments.

### SURVEILLANCE

When a suspected offence is ongoing, an investigator may engage in direct surveillance of the facility. Following trucks is a common example.

### DETERMINING THE LEGAL ENTITY

Where the facility is not an individual, an investigator must request business documents to determine the legal entity to charge. Searches for corporate profile reports, business name registrations, and partnership documents may be required depending upon the case. It is also helpful to obtain business records such as invoices to determine the specific legal entity that is responsible. This can be especially important when a number of related corporate entities such as parent and subsidiary companies are part of the operation. Where subcontractors are involved, it will be necessary to obtain contracts to establish the respective roles and responsibilities.

### RETENTION OF EXPERTS

Many of the more serious environmental offences involve discharges that cause or may cause an adverse effect. The investigator must demonstrate that the discharge in fact meets this requirement. This may require an expert opinion to be obtained.

The investigator must do so in a manner that does not contradict the expert's primary obligation to the court to provide impartial evidence. The investigator must clearly articulate the subject matter of the requested opinion, must detail what information was provided to the expert, and must be open to accepting the opinion of the expert whether it supports the laying of charges or not. Needless to say, the investigator cannot unduly influence the expert in any way. In many cases, the investigator will use government-employed scientists and engineers whom the courts have determined can be qualified as expert witnesses.[13] However, an investigator may also retain outside experts if internal expertise is not available.

### VOLUNTARY STATEMENTS BY OR ON BEHALF OF THE ACCUSED

Despite the fact that a facility or its employees are not required to provide any information to an investigator, they may voluntarily do so in any event. There are a number of reasons for this, including to:

- Convince the investigator that it did not commit the offence
- Provide evidence that the facility exercised due diligence
- Avoid being the subject of a search warrant
- Demonstrate cooperation with the investigation, which can be a mitigating factor at the penalty stage if convicted.

### SEARCH WARRANTS AND INSPECTION ORDERS

Where an investigator cannot obtain necessary information through any of the techniques described above, or where the investigator may have reason to believe that evidence may possibly be tampered with or destroyed in the near future, the main alternative is to obtain a search warrant. The onus is on the investigator to demonstrate under oath to a justice that reasonable grounds exist justifying a search of a place for evidence as to the commission of an offence.

Some environmental statutes also provide authority for the court to issue an investigative procedure order empowering an investigator to go beyond simply conducting a search and also utilize other investigative techniques or procedures to obtain evidence. In Ontario, environmental investigators have used this authority to conduct site visits to make detailed observations of a facility accompanied by an expert to assist the expert in rendering an opinion. However, an inspection order cannot be used to compel a facility or its employees to answer questions without explicit statutory authority.[14]

In Ontario, once an environmental investigation is complete, and if it is determined that charges are warranted, the environmental investigator compiles the evidence into a Crown Brief. The brief also includes a statement by the investigator describing the steps taken in the investigation in order to provide the necessary context and substantiate basic investigative principles such as the voluntariness of statements and continuity of evidence. The brief is submitted to ministry's prosecution department, which is a seconded legal services branch within the Ministry of the Attorney General to obtain legal advice on whether a reasonable prospect of conviction exists in accordance with the ministry's Charge Screening Practice Memorandum.

## Recent Cases Interpreting Section 8 of the *Charter* and Inspections

It is sometimes asserted by facilities that their section 8 *Charter* rights were violated on the basis that the evidence was obtained through an inspection that in fact had become an investigation. These arguments rely upon the *Jarvis* case, decided in 2002, for the proposition that a prosecution cannot use evidence obtained using inspection powers where the predominant purpose of the enforcement officer is to gather evidence for penal purposes. However, more recent decisions have indicated that the court will take a contextual approach in assessing the purpose or justification for carrying out the inspection.

In *R. v. Nolet*,[15] the SCC analyzed a search using a "continuing regulatory purpose" test. In that case, a police officer stopped a transport trailer for a valid regulatory purpose—to conduct an inspection pursuant to the provincial highways Act. The officer observed that the truck had an expired fuel sticker and lacked a valid provincial licence and that there were inconsistent entries in the driver's logbook. These infractions justified a further search of the truck's cabin, which led to the discovery of over $100,000 in small bills, which in turn led to the discovery of a hidden compartment containing a significant quantity of marijuana. The court permitted the cash and marijuana to be entered as evidence by having regard to the manner in which the search progressed on a step-by-step basis and determining that the search was reasonable at each step. The fact that the police officer was also extremely interested in whether there might be contraband did not by itself render the search unconstitutional. The more important question was whether there was a legitimate regulatory purpose for proceeding to each stage of the search. In reaching its decision in *Nolet*, the SCC distinguished the *Jarvis* case as applying where there is a clear distinction between a "civil audit" on the one hand and an investigation that may result in penal remedies on the other. The police officer in *Nolet* was always in an adversarial position with the defendant, which is a wholly different situation.

Before even claiming a breach of section 8 of the *Charter*, the onus is on the defendant to first demonstrate that it had a right to privacy. The right to privacy was fairly clear in the *Jarvis* case, where personal banking records were obtained. For environmental offences, there are many situations where the facility has a very limited right to privacy. For example, lakes and rivers or the surrounding air comprise a shared part of the natural environment. Even when samples are taken from the discharge point that may be on the facility's property, an argument can be made that there is a highly diminished privacy interest in the facility's use of the shared environment, especially a commercial or industrial facility. Therefore, even where an inspector may have made a determination that a matter may be referred for investigation, he or she may still be able to collect evidence from the natural environment without violating any *Charter* rights.

This proposition is supported by the case of *R. v. Mission Western Developments Ltd.* Department of Fisheries and Oceans officers conducted a warrantless inspection at a vacant commercial property that was intended for redevelopment. While there was a fence around the property, the gate was not locked. The inspectors entered through the gate and observed that alterations had been made along a fish-bearing creek that runs across the back of the property. The BC Court of Appeal, in denying leave to appeal, agreed with the appeal court justice that "owners of property subject to a high degree of regulation – such as property zoned for commercial development – cannot expect to sustain an expectation of privacy which forecloses the statutory powers of inspection of relevant regulatory authorities."[16]

These more recent decisions indicate that the determination as to whether a regulatory inspection violates section 8 of the *Charter* will be very fact-specific. At one end of the spectrum, an inspector carrying out a routine inspection with no prior expectation of what he or she may find has broad powers to carry out a warrantless inspection. At the other end, an investigator whose sole purpose is to decide whether or not to lay charges cannot generally use regulatory inspection powers or an inspector as an agent to obtain the necessary evidence. However, there will be a wide variety of situations in between that must be evaluated on a case-by-case basis. The courts do appear to be willing to give a fair amount of latitude to enforcement officers that are carrying out inspection functions in good faith. Conversely, any evidence of bad faith will be a significant factor against the Crown.

## NOTES

1 *R v Jarvis*, [2002] SCJ No 76, [2002] 3 SCR 757 at para 55 [*Jarvis*]; See also *R v Wholesale Travel Group Inc*, [1991] SCJ No 79.

2 For example, see s 156 of the Ontario *Environmental Protection Act*, RSO 1990, c E.19.

3 *Comité paritaire de l'industrie de la chemise v Potash*, [1994] SCJ No 7 at paras 8–13 and 60–67.

4 *Thomson Newspapers Ltd v Canada (Director of Investigation and Research, Restrictive Trade Practices Commission)*, [1990] SCJ No 23 at para 139; *Goodwin v British Columbia (Superintendent of Motor Vehicles)*, 2015 SCC 46 at para 60. For a more general discussion of the distinction between criminal and regulatory offences, see *Wholesale Travel Group Inc*, *supra* note 1.

5 *R v Fitzpatrick*, [1995] SCJ No 94.

6 *Jarvis*, *supra* note 1 at para 90.

7 *Ibid* at para 93.

8 *Ibid* at para 94.

9 *R v Demolition and Recycling*, [2009] OJ No 5318 at paras 23–40.

10 *Jarvis*, *supra* note 1 at para 96.

11 *Ibid*, at para 95.

12 See, e.g., ss 104 to 116 of the Ontario *Environmental Bill of Rights, 1993*, SO 1993, c 28, or s 174 of the Ontario *Environmental Protection Act*.

13 *R v Inco*, [2006] OJ No 1809; but see *Ontario (Ministry of Labour) v Advanced Construction Techniques Ltd*, [2015] OJ No 6130 for a case where a government engineer became too involved in the investigation to be qualified as an unbiased expert. For a more recent example in a criminal context, see *R v Livingston*, 2017 ONCJ 645.

14 *Branch v Ontario (Minister of the Environment)*, [2009] OJ No 45.

15 *R v Nolet*, 2010 SCC 24.

16 *R v Larsen*, 2012 BCCA 167 at para 28.

# 53

# Recapitulation and Alternatives: Lessons Learned from a Hypothetical Case Study

JENNIFER FAIRFAX*

## Overview

The lessons learned from prior environmental cases, in the context of inspections through to investigations and prosecutions, are likely endless. This chapter uses a hypothetical case study[1] as the lens through which to showcase some key lessons learned or "best practices" in working with regulators to bring a site into environmental compliance in difficult circumstances.

## Hypothetical Fact Scenario

A company involved in the gold mining industry owns a mine site located in Remoteville, Canada. The company is in financial distress and the mine is in a non-operating, care and management state. During care and management, the staff at the mine is greatly reduced, leaving only a few individuals to handle the day-to-day management. Although the mine is not operating, the tailings ponds on the site continue to accumulate water, due in part to ongoing precipitation that mixes with the tailings. The height of the water in the tailings ponds is close to exceeding the legal limit, and, with the approaching spring thaw, there is a potential risk that the tailings will overflow and discharge into the natural environment.

* *Jennifer would like to thank her colleague, Patrick Welsh, an associate in Osler's Litigation and* REAL *Groups, for his assistance in reviewing and editing this chapter, and for providing his insights.*

Both provincial and federal inspectors conduct inspections and request updates on the status of the ponds, but, because of the company's financial distress, communications with the regulators have broken down. Orders are issued to lower the water levels in the tailings ponds to a safe level. To comply with the orders and in an effort to lower the water levels, the company attempts to treat the water before releasing it to the environment, but discovers after the fact that the released water has failed the toxicity tests required pursuant to the *Metal Mining Effluent Regulations* (MMERs).[2] Although the water repeatedly failed the toxicity tests, the company has continued to release it to the environment in an effort to continue to lower the water levels.

Due to the sudden onslaught of inclement weather, an inadvertent spill of 100,000 cubic metres of tailings water occurs, and is not noticed by staff for many hours. It is possible that a nearby fish-bearing creek is impacted by the spill. Once noticed, it is reported to the appropriate authorities. The company experiences delays in its attempts to repair the tailings pond and remediate the natural environment, and does not follow the protocols outlined in its environmental management system (EMS) and emergency response plan relating to spills. An inspector visits the sites and documents are voluntarily provided.

At some point, the inspection turns into an investigation. The inspector, wearing the hat of an investigator, requests interviews with employees, audio-records the interviews, and requests the production of further documentation, all of which is voluntarily provided in an attempt to cooperate with the investigation. The employee interviews are scheduled through the company representative and legal counsel, during company hours and on the company premises. Company legal counsel remains throughout the interviews.

Deeming the information provided by the company insufficient, the investigator arrives unannounced and without warning at the mine site, with police officers and a search warrant, seizing both specified documents and all documents in plain view, including potentially privileged records. The investigator insists that the search can continue as long as it takes to complete—to midnight or beyond. A prosecution is subsequently commenced against the company for the release of water that failed the required toxicity tests and for the spill of 100,000 cubic metres of tailings water to the environment, using the employee interviews as admissions against the company. While the investigation and prosecution are ongoing, the company continues to experience regular visits and requests for updates from the local inspector in order to continue to ensure the mine site, while in care and management, is in compliance.

## Lessons Learned and Best Practices

### 1. RELATIONSHIP WITH REGULATORS MUST NOT BE ALLOWED TO BREAK DOWN

A breakdown in communications with regulators—where there is a perception that the company is no longer being transparent in disclosing information to the regulators, in keeping the regulator updated, and in otherwise responding to questions—is often a red flag for more problems to come. If an inspector does not believe a company is being proactive and responsive, then the inspector will think it is necessary to move from voluntary abatement to mandatory compliance.

All jurisdictions take a laddered approach to enforcing compliance, with the first rung on the ladder being voluntary abatement, in which regulators work to persuade companies to voluntarily comply with statutory prohibitions, regulatory limits, and approval requirements. If voluntary abatement is not seen to be working, regulators will begin to use the compulsory enforcement tools available to them, including the broad statutory power of issuing orders or directions, forcing compliance.[3] Once you are in the territory of the regulator issuing orders, it is an uphill battle (but not impossible) to convince the regulator to return to voluntary compliance.

If a positive working relationship can be maintained with the regulator, through an assigned, direct line of contact at the company working collaboratively with the abatement officer or inspector on solutions to achieve compliance, the abatement officer or inspector will want to continue to work with the company.

Examples of best practices include the following:

- Assign one reliable, direct point of contact at the company to respond to an inspector or abatement officer's questions and requests for updates in a timely manner, who can develop a relationship of trust with the regulator. A company would be well served by proactively seeking out an open relationship with the applicable inspector or abatement officer;
- Respond to inquiries and suggestions promptly and fully;
- Proactively update the inspector or abatement officer, without waiting for questions, on the status of the facility and its EMS;
- Establish open lines of communication with the abatement officer. Set up a written protocol for these communications, with weekly or monthly touch-points or "check-ins," as needed. If the manager

assigned to regularly communicate with the inspector or abatement officer is not engendering the inspector's confidence, assign a new manager to that role;

- Take action and be seen to be taking action—continuous voluntary abatement and improvement measures where needed. If the company takes a positive, voluntary abatement step, update the regulator on the step taken;
- Report all discharges or spills, and, when in doubt, report;
- Generally, be a good corporate citizen;
- If the company is planning to cease operations, even on a temporary basis, as with a mine entering a care and management stage, reach out proactively to the regulator, and request a meeting in person to explain the situation, to assure the regulator that environmental obligations will be abided by during the cessation, and ask the regulator if it has any questions or particular concerns that it would like to see addressed. Use open communications to ward off the possibility of a knee-jerk reaction from the regulator, such as an order, as a result of concerns that the company is not addressing environmental matters or is walking away from the site. In our experience, this transparency has resulted in a cooperative relationship, in which the regulators suggested making practical amendments to the company's mining permits to reduce the required monitoring and sampling for the duration of the care and management period, with specific requirements for if and when the mine resumed operations.

In a nutshell, the regulator does not need to be treated as a company's "enemy" but as someone who can work with the company to achieve workable solutions.

### 2. DUE DILIGENCE MUST BE ACHIEVED AND SEEN TO BE ACHIEVED—PAPER, PAPER, PAPER

All environmental practitioners speak of the importance of due diligence. Due diligence is not merely about doing appropriate due diligence; it is about being seen to be doing appropriate due diligence. As lawyers, we continually advise companies to "paper" what they are doing—to create a clear paper trail to demonstrate that the company was duly diligent at all times, before the incident, during the incident, and after, to demonstrate to the regulator that the company did everything reasonable to prevent the incident but also everything reasonable to minimize the potential adverse effects and to prevent the incident from happening again.

As the Supreme Court of Canada stated in *R. v. Sault Ste Marie*,[4] an accused may have a due diligence defence if it can prove, on a balance of probabilities, that it had (i) a reasonable belief in a mistake in fact which, if true, would render the act or omission innocent, or (ii) "exercised all reasonable care by establishing a proper system to prevent commission of the offence and by taking reasonable steps to ensure the effective operation of the system. The availability of the defence to a corporation will depend on whether such due diligence was taken by those who are the directing mind and will of the corporation, whose acts are therefore in law the acts of the corporation itself."[5] However, as the court in *R. v. Bata Industries* recounted, "[t]he cases interpreting the phrase 'all reasonable care' indicate that the wording does not require that all steps be taken, only those that could be reasonably expected in the circumstances. The case law makes no distinction between 'all reasonable care' and 'reasonable care'. The degree of reasonable care to be exercised is dependent upon the circumstances of the case."[6]

One key element of a due diligence defence will be whether the company in question had a proper EMS and whether that EMS was implemented and followed—that is, whether reasonable steps were taken to ensure the effective operation of whatever system the company had in place.[7] If such an EMS is not in place, or is not followed, a company may be hard-pressed to prove it was duly diligent.

In the above hypothetical case study, would a regulator or the courts consider that the company was duly diligent? On the one hand, the company continued to try to abide by its environmental obligations, and was working to address environmental risks. On the other hand, although it was foreseeable that, during a non-operating state, environmental incidents could still occur, the company reduced its staff to a number that apparently could not cope with the workload required to ensure the safety of the mine during care and management. Moreover, when the incident occurred, the company, despite having an EMS and emergency response plan in place, failed to adhere to its EMS and did not act quickly enough to remediate the situation.

As this hypothetical case study shows, having an EMS in place does not guarantee that, when an incident occurs, the company will be found to have been duly diligent. Additionally, EMS and emergency response plans must be comprehensive and be able to capture potentially harmful activities that are within the reasonable scope of the company's business. For example, in *R. v. Canadian Tire Corp.*,[8] the company was convicted of importing banned

CFCs in bar fridges for resale. Although the company had in place an EMS, the EMS did not ensure only CFC-free fridges would be imported. As a result, the EMS was not comprehensive and did not address all areas of potential non-compliance. Therefore, a company's EMS needs to be continually reviewed and updated, the employees need to be regularly trained in the procedures outlined in the EMS, and the company should, among other things, conduct spot checks to ensure that the EMS is followed.

### Reasonable Care and Due Diligence Do Not Mean Superhuman Efforts or Perfection

It is important to remember that, as found in *R. v. Courtaulds Fibres,*[9] "[r]easonable care and due diligence do not mean superhuman efforts. They mean a high standard of awareness and decisive, prompt and continuing action. To demand more, would ... move a strict liability offence dangerously close to one of absolute liability."[10] The court in *R. v. Syncrude*[11] adopted these trite principles of due diligence and stressed that Syncrude was "not required to show that it took all *possible or imaginable* steps to avoid liability, and was not required to achieve a standard of perfection"; rather, "[t]he conduct of the accused is assessed against that of a reasonable person in similar circumstances."[12]

What constitutes "all reasonable care in the circumstances" demands an examination of various factors; there is no single comprehensive list of appropriate considerations for all cases. Every case must be decided on its own facts. In *R. v. Commander Business Furniture Inc.* (*Commander Furniture*),[13] the court provided a lengthy list of factors that could be taken into consideration to determine the defence of due diligence:

1) the nature and gravity of the adverse effect;
2) the foreseeability of the effect, including abnormal sensitivities;[14]
3) the alternative solutions available;[15]
4) legislative or regulatory compliance;
5) industry standards;
6) the character of the neighbourhood;
7) what efforts have been made to address the problem;
8) over what period of time, and promptness of response;
9) matters beyond the control of the accused, including technological limitations;
10) skill levels expected of the accused;
11) complexities involved;
12) preventative systems;

13) economic considerations;
14) actions of officials.[16]

Considering the element of financial distress in our hypothetical case study, it is important to consider to what extent courts take a company's financial situation into consideration when assessing due diligence. The court in *Commander Furniture* examined the relevant economic considerations (factor 13 above) and ultimately concluded that, while cost alone cannot be determinative of due diligence, "the economics of various alternative solutions is one consideration which must be weighed along with all the other factors in assessing due diligence."[17] However, as eloquently put by the court in *Bata Industries* in its sentencing decision, the paramount objective of environmental protection must be heeded: "[t]he message they receive from this sentence must be that even in this bleakest of financial times, the environment must not be a sacrificial lamb on the altar of corporate survival."[18]

Generally, courts will take a pragmatic approach in applying economic considerations in assessing whether the due diligence standard was met in the circumstances—by acknowledging that economic factors cannot be ignored or else the examination of due diligence will lack the required "air of reality." That said, courts will strive to balance the need to protect the environment and the costs of those protective measures. The former will generally outweigh the latter when the potential harm to the environment is grave. The court in *Commander Furniture* explained the analysis as follows:

> In my view, the degree of control that an accused can exercise over a problem must have an air of reality and therefore must include some consideration of cost. The cases generally accept that industrial standards are relevant in determining what steps are reasonable. In my view, economic factors are fundamental to determining what a particular industry will adopt as its standard. If industrial standards are relevant then so too must be economic considerations.
>
> Having said that, economic concerns must be properly balanced against other factors. For example, phasing in an operational change which will both protect the environment and the economic viability of a company may be duly diligent in all the circumstances. It is difficult to imagine that any industrial standards or reasonable person would support a non-phased-in approach which would destroy a company when a realistic phased-in timely approach would have reasonable success over a reasonable period of time and thereby accommodate

> both interests. On the other hand, if a phased-in approach that complied with the industry standard would destroy the environment or cause a risk of serious harm, no cost would be too great. The degree or level of harm or adverse effect must therefore be reasonably balanced with economic considerations and the other factors set out earlier for a due diligence defence.[19]

In our hypothetical case study, the company is striving to abide by its environmental obligations in very difficult circumstances, where it simply does not have the funding or resources to implement all possible corrective or alternative measures, nor does it have time on its side with the approaching spring thaw. As a result, the company chooses what it views as the feasible solution in the circumstances to bring the site into compliance: treating and releasing the water to the environment. The treatment system, however, does not work as expected and is, ultimately, not enough to prevent an inadvertent spill in extreme weather. Whether this would be enough to constitute due diligence in the circumstances would be the subject of close scrutiny.

### The Teachings of Syncrude

VEERING FROM A COMPANY'S ESTABLISHED PROCEDURES AND REDUCING STAFF AND RESOURCES CAN BE VIEWED AS A LACK OF DUE DILIGENCE The case of *R. v. Syncrude Canada Ltd.* (*Syncrude*)[20] provides an apt example of what type of conduct a court could consider to demonstrate a failing in due diligence, judging the accused "on the basis of the information available to it at the time of the alleged offence."[21] In *Syncrude*, the company was convicted for failing to store hazardous substances away from animals and migratory birds, and failing to take reasonable steps to deter birds from landing in its tailings ponds, which resulted in the death of 1,600 birds.

The ultimate question for Syncrude was whether it took all reasonable steps to ensure that waterfowl would not be contaminated in its tailings pond.[22] And the ultimate issue was with Syncrude's lack of a proper preventive system. The existing documents outlining the procedures for preventive measures were not comprehensive, and Syncrude had significantly cut back in previous years on the number of bird deterrents. Specifically, Syncrude had a Waterfowl Protection Plan with employees tasked to the Bird and Environmental Team (BET), but the employees had no formal training in dealing with wildlife and there was no formal schedule for the deployment of deterrents to birds landing in the tailings. In fact, resources and deterrents available for the BET team's use were not as strong as in prior years, and staff had been significantly reduced.[23]

As a result, Syncrude was sentenced to pay a total of $3 million in a combination of fines and payments to conservation organizations.[24] Thus, with respect to our hypothetical case study, a court would scrutinize whether the company's reductions in staff, while the site is in care and management, is a factor supporting a lack of due diligence.

### A Recent Lesson in Tailings Due Diligence

A COMPANY "IN OVER ITS HEAD" A recent October 2015 decision by the New Brunswick court, *R. v. Stratabound Minerals Corp.*,[25] provides an example of the application of due diligence principles in a similar situation to our hypothetical case study. Stratabound was having financial difficulties and facing dissolution. It also faced a situation where the treatment system for the mining effluent was not working and toxicity tests were failing, but the ponds were dangerously increasing in water levels. To prevent an overflow, Stratabound deliberately released about 2 million litres of treated water, in the face of repeated, consecutive toxicity test failures that had not been redressed. The release again proved fatal to fish. The court explained the situation as follows:

> On May 16th, Stratabound notified Environment Canada that their holding cells, polishing pond and the open pit were reaching a critical stage, that they were almost full of rain water. At this sentencing hearing, the Stratabound representative related to the Court that the problem emanated from a significant rainfall amount over the course of three days in May of 2013. On May 24th, due to the anticipated heavy rain forecasted for the weekend, Stratabound was under pressure to discharge mine effluent in order to increase their on-site storage capacity. Failure to do so would risk the possibility of an uncontrolled overflow from the open pit. Environment Canada, as mentioned, had been notified of the situation. Stratabound told them they were to release effluent on May 24th. On that day, the mine was inspected in order to ensure compliance with the MMER's. Mine effluent was observed leaving the property in the eastern corner of the site via a drainage ditch adjacent to the previous pit location at the lower sump area. This effluent was being discharged into a marsh which eventually led to the Portage River. Mine effluent samples were collected by Environment Canada inspectors at this location. The volume of deleterious effluent discharged from the mine site on May 24th was not quantified but tests were conducted on the samples collected. At full

strength, the effluent was highly toxic to fish. Even when diluted to 6.25 percent, it was considered a deleterious substance as 60 percent of exposed fish died in that diluted concentration.[26]

The court convicted and sentenced Stratabound Minerals to a fine of about $75,000 for breaches of the *MMERs* and the *Fisheries Act*, including the unlawful deposit of mine effluent on three occasions. The fine imposed could have been much higher had the amended minimum/maximum fine structure of the current *Fisheries Act* applied (as the events in question occurred before the amendments).[27] Although no actual proof of harm to the environment had been demonstrated, the potential for harm was significant, and that was enough to justify the conviction.

The *Stratabound Minerals* decision provides a lens through which to study how prosecutors and courts generally approach these types of cases, and the types of factors they take into consideration in sentencing. The court found the company negligent, but not reckless. The company did not deliberately set out to harm the environment; rather, the acts "arose in the context of a company without a great deal of experience in actual mining operations, strenuously attempting to raise needed funds to further their continuing mining exploration activities and getting caught up in something beyond their ability to rectify."[28] In short, according to the court, the company simply could not cope.[29] The decision highlights that inexperience, a lack of preparedness, a lack of foresight, and a lack of funds can create the perfect storm when grappling with "the enormous job" of protecting the environment.

Some take-aways from the *Stratabound Minerals* decision are as follows:

- *Unexpected or extreme weather will not excuse a lack of due diligence*: As the court stated, "[i]t is of no consequence that the water was polluted prior to their starting up operations. It is also of no consequence that more rain fell than could have been predicted during their mining operations. The vagaries of nature do not excuse non-compliance with strict regulatory directives intended to protect our environment."[30]
- *A lack of preparedness and inexperience is not necessarily an excuse*: A company is generally expected to have the necessary expertise to operate, and if they don't have this expertise, the company can hire experts to assist. Companies need to recognize when they are "in over their heads" and get help: "Undoubtedly Stratabound was

aware of its responsibilities in regards to water treatment. They attempted to comply with them. They were communicating with the on-site Environmental Monitoring and Compliance Officer who was actually at the mine site. They attempted to correct the problem. They utilised the chemicals destined to manage the settling process and modify the pH content of the water at the site prior to discharge, but these chemicals did not correct the toxic metals content in the effluent. To use the vernacular, in my opinion they were simply 'in over their heads' and couldn't cope. I would classify this offence as one of negligence and disregard brought about by lack of experience and lack of prudence."[31]

- *No proof of actual harm to the environment is needed for a conviction*: "To summarize then, Stratabound, a company experienced in the mining industry but relatively inexperienced in actual mining operations, committed a serious offence by discharging mining effluent that had the potential to be very harmful to the environment. No actual proof of harm has been demonstrated or alleged."[32]

As outlined above in discussing the factor of economic considerations addressed in *Commander Furniture*, a company's finances or financial distress will be considered by the courts when examining due diligence, but a lack of funds does not necessarily excuse a violation of environmental obligations. Financial distress can, however, also be a factor taken into account in sentencing. The court in *Stratabound Minerals* confirmed that the "financial position of the company is always taken into consideration by the Court in sentencing, as part of a group of factors considered."[33]

Recognizing that Stratabound was in financial distress, the court still held that the principle of general deterrence—sending a message to other mining companies in similar situations—justified imposing the fine in the circumstances. Although the company was on the financial brink and a fine against the company might not achieve much as far as the company was concerned, the polluter pays principle prevailed: "The message must be clear: flagrant abuse of the environment resulting in harm or potential harm is not to be tolerated because the protection of the environment is essential to the health and well-being of all creatures and plants living on this planet. Polluters must pay for the cost of their illegal actions."[34]

It is possible a court could deem the company in our hypothetical fact scenario as "in over its head," akin to Stratabound Minerals, since the company could not fix the water treatment system or arrive at an alternative solution, and continued to release water, knowing that it was likely toxic.

### Lessons Learned from Mount Polley

NEW RECOMMENDATIONS COULD AFFECT FUTURE STANDARDS OF CARE FOR DUE DILIGENCE On December 17, 2015, the Chief Inspector of Mines for British Columbia's Ministry of Energy and Mines (MEM) completed its 16-month investigation into the August 4, 2014 tailings pond breach at the Mount Polley Mine in BC and released its investigation decision.[35] The Mount Polley breach released 10 million cubic metres of water and 4.5 million cubic metres of sediment into Polley Lake, triggering an environmental emergency situation.

The Chief Inspector determined that MEM would not prosecute the Mount Polley Mining Corporation (MPMC) for violations of environmental legislation.[36] MEM's investigation team had conducted approximately 100 interviews and had reviewed over 100,000 pages of documents going back to 1989; it was the largest and most complex investigation ever conducted in BC.[37]

Although MEM found that MPMC had conducted inadequate water management in respect of its tailings pond, had failed to conduct adequate studies and site investigations of the perimeter embankment foundation for the tailings pond, and had failed to operate using best available practices, operations of the mine site were not, at the time, in contravention of any regulation, in part because there were no specific guidelines or regulatory requirements in place for water management at mine sites. The Chief Inspector of Mines concluded that "weak practices ... do not constitute a legal contravention of existing mining legislation."[38]

Although the Mount Polley tailings breach did not result in a MEM prosecution, the Chief Inspector of Mines made 19 recommendations directed at mining operators, the mining industry, professional organizations, and the government regulators to prevent such incidents in the future and "to build a safer, more sustainable industry."[39] The BC government worked with industry and professional organizations to incorporate the recommendations into the *Health, Safety and Reclamation Code for Mines in British Columbia* released in spring 2017.[40] The recommendations formed the foundation for the new *Code* and provide a guide for best practices.

Some of the key recommendations include:

- All mines with tailings storage facilities (TSFs) will be required to have a designated mine dam safety manager and a designated individual to oversee the mine's water balance and water management plan. "[A]ny mine with a tailings storage facility (TSF) should have a qualified individual designated as a mine safety manager responsible for oversight of planning, design, operation, construction and maintenance, and surveillance of the TSF, and associated site-wide water management."[41]
- Mines with TSFs will be required to have water management plans designed by a qualified professional;
- The mine manager should ensure that the operation, maintenance, and surveillance manual for the TSFs, required by BC's Health, Safety and Reclamation Code for all impoundments, adheres to applicable Canadian Dam Association and Mining Association of Canada guidelines;
- The mine manager must ensure that the Mine Emergency Response Plan adheres to applicable regulations, is maintained on a regular basis to ensure currency, incorporates appropriate response measures to emergencies, including those involving the TSF, and is written and distributed in such a format as to serve as a procedural guide during an emergency or other event;
- All mine personnel should be educated in the recognition of conditions and events that could impact TSF safety or contravene applicable permit conditions and regulations;
- Independent technical review boards will be required for all mines with TSFs;
- The Association of Professional Engineers and Geoscientists of BC, the Mining Association of Canada, and the Canadian Dam Association should update and strengthen guidelines and standards of practice, including those specific to TSF design and management, dam safety, and construction;
- The regulator should consider and incorporate as appropriate guidelines from these external associations, as applicable;
- The regulator should establish a dedicated investigation, compliance, and enforcement team within MEM, led by a new deputy chief inspector of mines;
- To strengthen records management and improve openness and transparency around design, construction, and operation, the

government will establish a formal documentation management system for all TSFs from development to post-closure; and
- The stakeholders should foster innovations in the mining sector that improve current technologies in tailings processing, dewatering, and discharge water treatment.[42]

Of interest, in June 2016, the Mount Polley Mine resumed operations, following authorizations from the Ministry of Energy and Mines and Ministry of Environment. In October 2016, Mount Polley submitted its long-term water remediation plan permit amendment application, which was approved by the Ministry of Environment on April 7, 2017 after a public review process.[43] The company reported its progress on its remediation plans at a community meeting in BC, and a human health risk assessment was accepted by the Ministry of Environment and an ecological risk assessment was in the process of being finalized as of November 21, 2017.[44]

Moreover, in October 2016, "frustrated by what it perceived to be inaction or slow action on the part of the BC government," MiningWatch Canada laid a private information against Mount Polley and the Province of British Columbia, charging them with a number of offences under the *Fisheries Act*.[45] In January 2017, the federal Crown obtained a stay of these proceedings pursuant to section 579(1) of the *Criminal Code*.[46]

### Due Diligence—Looking Forward

Companies, like the mining company in our case study, will be judged against their knowledge and the industry standards in place at the time of the incident in question. However, the fallout from Mount Polley may affect the assessment of the standard of care that a reasonable person must meet in the circumstances going forward. The Mount Polley recommendations may be seen as new standards mining companies should meet to demonstrate due diligence, both within BC and beyond. To what extent the recommendations will be adopted remains to be seen. Mining companies, however, should pay heed to some of the recommendations and consider to what extent the best practices or principles espoused in the recommendations can be adopted.

Regardless of the particular industry, the first line of offence is a good defence—if you are thinking about how to be duly diligent and what constitutes reasonable steps in the circumstances, remember to ensure a sufficient paper trail of due diligence is readily available for disclosure to the regulator when needed.

## 3. Know the Difference between Inspections and Investigations and How It Impacts Rights

The company in the above case study entered the murky waters of an inspection-turned-investigation. It is important to understand the difference between an investigation and an inspection and how this could impact a company's rights. An inspection, on the one hand, requires cooperation—a company cannot obstruct an inspector or abatement officer carrying out his or her inspection powers. In Ontario, it is an offence to obstruct a provincial officer in the performance of his or her statutory duties.[47]

On the other hand, during an investigation, a company has certain rights that it would not otherwise have during an inspection, including the right, should it want to assert it, not to cooperate. Key to an investigation is its purpose: an investigation is undertaken when the investigator has reasonable and probable grounds to believe that an offence has occurred and the investigator is seeking to gather evidence of that offence.[48]

Added to the confusion is that inspections can become investigations and lead to a prosecution when, during an inspection, a provincial officer acquires evidence that gives her "reasonable and probable grounds" to believe an offence has been committed. Another difficulty arises from the fact that an investigator can access and make use of any incriminating information previously collected, prior to the commencement of the investigation, by an inspector. However, once an investigation is underway, the inspection can continue in parallel but the inspector can no longer share the fruits of the inspection with the "investigative side."[49]

In contrast to inspectors, investigators cannot use statutory "inspection" powers (i.e. to enter buildings, examine records, take samples) without consent or a search warrant. Once armed with a search warrant, the investigator can generally seize anything permitted by the warrant, but also anything in "plain view" if she reasonably believes it is evidence of an offence.[50] As a result, companies should take care not to leave sensitive or potentially incriminating or otherwise sensitive or confidential documents in plain view.

A simple way to deal with this confusion, when asked by an environmental officer to consent to or otherwise schedule a visit to the facility, is to ask the officer if the visit is for the purpose of an inspection or an investigation. In other words, ask the officer if she has reasonable and probable grounds to believe that an offence has been committed, if she is doing an investigation or inspection, and if you are compelled to answer her questions. It is also advisable

**Table 53.1**

| *Inspections* | *Investigations* |
|---|---|
| Carried out by an inspector or PO (abatement officer) | Also carried out by an inspector or PO (but with MOECC, usually former police officer or trained investigator from IEB) |
| Compliance oriented and information gather - used to conduct field audits, secure evidence at scene, achieve immediate "voluntary compliance,, issue orders, impose administrative penalties, issue *POA* "tickets" | To investigate violations of legislation and lay quasi-criminal charges |
| No warrant is necessary where the predominant purpose of the visit is an "inspection" | Generally, warrant is required if the predominant purpose of the visit is an "investigation" |
| PO relies on their statutory inspection powers to tour premises, demand documents and interview witnesses | PO must caution witness that they could be charged; once cautioned, no obligation to give statement/documents - no statutory investigation powers |

to contact your lawyer, whether in-house or external counsel, to get advice on how to respond to the officer.

Other chapters in this section of the volume discuss in some depth the differences between inspections and investigations, and the powers available to environmental officers during the conduct of each. Table 53.1, above, is a summary table that explains, at a high level, the differences between inspections and investigations.

In our hypothetical case study, it appears that the mining company did not treat the inspections any differently than the investigation, which may not have served the company well in preventing the investigation from escalating.

## 4. Know the Consequences of Employee Interviews so You Can Make an Informed Decision

If an inspector or investigator asks to interview an employee, it is important to understand the potential consequences of that interview so that you can make an informed decision as to how that interview should be conducted, and, in the context of an investigation, whether it should happen at all. Employee interviews can expose a company and its directors and officers to serious liability.

Also, the employee could be suspected of committing an offence, or become a suspect at a later point, and could be charged personally and, as such, needs to understand those potential consequences. The investigator should appropriately caution the employee in such a situation.

Given the potential conflicts of interests between employees and the company, the biggest mistake companies can make is to try to "go it alone" without legal advice from a lawyer who has specialized environmental expertise. From the moment the accident or potential violation occurs, or the investigator comes knocking, the company should get legal advice on how best to respond. Every fact situation is different, but your lawyer can make sure you follow the lessons learned from other cases.

Your lawyer can assist you in dealing with the investigator by:

- Communicating with the investigator directly, which allows the company to avoid admissions and strategic errors such as consenting to "voluntary" interviews unless compelled or properly prepared;
- Underscoring with the investigator how seriously the company is treating the event under investigation;
- Gathering the company's defences and advocating the company's position with the investigator from day one;
- Convincing the investigator that the company was duly diligent;
- Convincing the investigator that even if the company was not duly diligent, the company no longer needs to be deterred with a fine because the problem has been corrected;
- Organizing and controlling the company's disclosure to the investigator;
- Organizing and controlling the company's interviews given to the investigator;
- Arranging independent legal counsel for employees and ensuring the independent legal counsel is properly briefed;
- If charges are laid, reaching a reasonable settlement with the Crown prosecutor, if a settlement is in the company's best interests.

The case of *R. v. Syncrude Canada Ltd.*[51] provides yet another set of "lessons learned" in the murky territory of employee interviews. Investigators obtained several statements from individuals identified as employees of Syncrude. Only the company was charged, and a *voir dire* was held to determine the admissibility of a statement made by the employees as evidence against the company.

The court ruled that, in order for such a statement to be admitted as the company's statement, the statement must have been made by a person who was an agent or employee of the company at the time it was made and the statement must have been made within the scope of the agent or employee's authority.[52] The defence had submitted that since the employee had never been told that his statement could be used as a statement of the company, the statement could not be used as evidence of the company's operating mind.

The court concluded that there was evidence on a balance of probabilities that the person interviewed was an employee of Syncrude at the time the statement was made and that the statement was reasonably related to the discharge of his duties for Syncrude. The court also concluded that the statements were reliable, adopting the principle that it is unlikely that an agent, while still employed by the principal, would make statements against the principal's interests unless it were true.[53] As such, the statement was admissible against the company without the Crown having to call the employee to testify.

Understanding what was allowed to happen in *Syncrude* assists in distilling the lessons learned. The court arrived at its conclusion to admit the employee's statement as the company's statement, in part, because of the following factors:

- The employee interview was arranged by representatives of Syncrude, including Syncrude's legal counsel.
- Syncrude's legal counsel was present during the interview (which was formal and recorded) and signed a document acknowledging that an investigation was underway and that she acted as counsel for both Syncrude and the employees.
- Syncrude had been formally notified by letter that Alberta Environment was undertaking an investigation, and was aware of the purpose of the meetings and interview requests. The employee, management, and corporate legal counsel knew that the interview was part of the investigation, with potentially serious consequences for Syncrude.[54]

Significantly, the court dismissed the defence's complaint that the investigators never cautioned or warned the employee that his statements could be used as evidence against the company or treated as the company's statement.[55] Rather, the court relied on the fact that there was no evidence the employee or corporate counsel was ever told that the statement would *not* be used as a statement of the company.

In dismissing this complaint, the court concluded that the confession rule in criminal matters (i.e. the rule that statements must be freely and voluntarily made with the absence of inducements, policy trickery, threats, or promises) does not apply directly or by analogy to determine the admissibility of admissions of a corporation. According to *Syncrude*, there is no authority to suggest that the rule applies to an admission attributed to a corporation. Unlike an individual, a corporation does not have the benefit of the right to life, liberty, or security of the person under section 7 (and its guarantee of the right to silence) or the right against self-incrimination under section 11(c) of the *Canadian Charter of Rights and Freedoms*.[56]

The treatment of employee statements as statements attributable to the corporate accused fits within the legislative scheme for environmental offences. In most environmental legislation, such as the *Fisheries Act*, offences committed by an employee or agent of the corporation are sufficient proof of the offence by the employer, principal, and owner. Statements made by an employee or principal are attributable to the corporate accused.[57]

In our hypothetical scenario, the mining company permitted the investigator to interview and audio-record its employees, in the presence of company legal counsel during company hours and on company premises, similar to what was done in *Syncrude*. Should a court deem the employees to be agents of the company and acting within the scope of their employment or authority, then a court would likely similarly permit these employee interviews to be tendered as statements of the company in a prosecution. Knowing the potential end game before allowing such employee interviews is critical to making an informed choice regarding next steps.

## 5. When the Investigator Shows Up with a Search Warrant—Be Ready

In the above case study, the execution of the search warrant was unexpected, particularly when the company had been cooperative with the investigator prior to the search. However, once a search is underway, the company cannot obstruct or impede the search, and must let it proceed. To minimize the disruption of such a search warrant and to protect their legal rights, companies need to be ready in advance for the possibility of a search warrant by working with its personnel and legal counsel to ensure that everyone knows what can happen and what should not happen during a search, and the limits of an investigator's search warrant powers. In my colleague Mr. Coop's chapter

(chapter 51), he outlines in some detail the protocol and checklists that a company can implement to assist in getting them ready for the possibility of search warrant.

In Ontario, for instance, it is important to understand that a warrant for such an environmental search must be obtained from a justice of the peace under section 158 of the *Provincial Offences Act*, and that the Act, like the *Criminal Code*, contains certain inherent limitations in the scope of authority granted by the warrant. For instance, the warrant must be executed between 6 a.m. and 9 p.m.[58] If an officer is ignoring these rules, it is important to get a lawyer involved to speak to the officer and ensure the officer is following the law in conducting the search and paper your objections on the conduct of the search. Be mindful of the limits placed on officers carrying out such warrants, and speak to your lawyer.

Also, one should verify that the warrant has not expired. An expired warrant should be treated as of no force or effect, and a new valid search warrant has to be obtained.[59]

If the officers purport to bend the rules applicable to search warrants, paper in writing your objections relating to the way in which the warrant was conducted, so that you can raise the appropriate objections in court should the matter proceed to prosecution.

It is also helpful to ask the officers to provide the company with a copy of the sworn information or supporting affidavit that was submitted when the warrant was taken out. Sometimes this request is denied. If the information is not made available when the warrant is served and the officer refuses to provide the information to you, have a search done of the court file. If the court file is sealed, consider bringing a motion for a court order that a copy of the information or affidavit be unsealed and be made available.[60]

The seizure of potentially privileged documents presents a challenge. Generally speaking, it is good advice to inform the officers, upon their arrival with the warrant, of the names of the law firms and lawyers, and in-house counsel, working with the company, so that documentation involving those law firms or lawyers can be protected from disclosure. Follow up this information with a written letter setting out the assertions of privilege, requesting that any such documents not be seized, and, if seized, demanding that they be placed under seal and not opened or read by anyone at the regulator or any third party. If the officers proceed to seize privileged documents, again paper the objections in writing to the seizure, identifying the seized privileged items where possible, and ask that they remain sealed and not be opened or read. Also, request that the seized privileged items be returned to the company as soon as possible, and, if they are not returned, ultimately seek a final ruling from a court regarding their privileged status, if necessary.

## Conclusion

Using the lens of the hypothetical case study, the object of this chapter was to outline some key lessons learned or best practices, based on some high-profile cases and developing standards, particularly in the mining context. Of course, one cannot purport to deal with the endless array of lessons learned and the thousands of cases dealing with environmental violations and due diligence. This chapter provides the "tip of the iceberg," and hopefully piques your interest in the complex issues presented when a company grapples with the regulator and deals with inspections, investigations, and prosecutions.

### NOTES

1 This case study is hypothetical, melding some of the facts from real environmental cases, either prosecuted to conclusion or currently under investigation, including the *Syncrude* "oily ducks" prosecution, the Mount Polley regulatory investigations, *R v Bloom Lake General Partner Ltd*, 2014 CarswellQue 14668, and *R v Stratabound Minerals Corp*, [2015] NBJ No 282 (Prov Ct) [*Stratabound Minerals*], among others.

2 *Metal Mining Effluent Regulations*, SOR/2002-222 [*MMERs*], enacted pursuant to the *Fisheries Act*, RSC 1985, c F14.

3 See, e.g., Ontario Ministry of the Environment and Climate Change, *Compliance Policy Applying Abatement and Enforcement Tools*, May 2007, online: <https://www.ontario.ca/page/compliance-policy-applying-abatement-and-enforcement-tools#section-5>. See also Environment and Climate Change Canada, *Compliance and Enforcement Policy for the Habitat Protection and Pollution Prevention Provisions of the Fisheries Act*, 2002, online: <http://www.ec.gc.ca/alef-ewe/default.asp?lang=en&n=D6B74D58-1>.

4 *R v Sault Ste Marie*, [1978] 2 SCR 1299 [Sault Ste Marie].

5 *Ibid* at 1331, as repeatedly cited in various cases, including *R v Bata Industries Ltd*, 1992 CanLII 7721 [*Bata Industries*].

6 *Bata Industries, ibid.*

7 *Ibid*. In *Bata*, the court found a failing in due diligence, since "Bata did not establish a proper system to prevent the commission of the offence, nor did they take reasonable steps to ensure the effective operation of whatever system they had. They simply allowed the barrels to sit, rust and eventually disintegrate."

8 *R v Canadian Tire Corp Ltd*, 2004 CanLII 4462 (ONSC).

9 *R v Courtaulds Fibres* (1992), 76 CCC (3d) 68, [1992] OJ No 1972 (Prov Ct).

10 *Ibid* at paras 7–8. The court found Courtaulds Fibres to have been duly diligent: "Admittedly, this was an aging plant, and needed immediate attention. No one could seriously suggest that all of the environmental ills of this Company could be addressed in 11 months. However, I conclude that such a period, given the continuing, and earnest, and widespread efforts of the Company to

address its environmental problems, does prove that the Company used all reasonable care, and exercised due diligence with reference to the spills we are dealing with. Reasonable care and due diligence do not mean superhuman efforts. They mean a high standard of awareness and decisive, prompt, and continuing action. To demand more, would, in my view, move a strict liability offence dangerously close to one of absolute liability."

11 *R v Syncrude*, 2010 ABCP 229 [*Syncrude Trial Decision*].

12 *Ibid* at para 99.

13 *R v Commander Business Furniture Inc* (1992), 9 CELR (NS) 185 at 212 (Ont CJ, Prov Div), [1992] OJ No 2904 at 19 (QL) [*Commander Business Furniture*].

14 As the court in *Syncrude Trial Decision* stated, a person "is only required to take steps to avoid that which it can reasonably foresee" (para 120).

15 As the court in *Syncrude Trial Decision* explained, "Reasonableness of care is often best measured by comparing what was done against what could have been done. The reasonableness of alternatives the accused knew or ought to have known were available is a primary measure of due diligence. To successfully plead the defence of reasonable care the accused must establish on a balance of probabilities there were no reasonable feasible alternatives that might have avoided or minimized injury to others" (para 116, citing *R v Gonder* (1981), 62 CCC (2d) 326; 1981 CarswellYukon 8 (Y Terr Ct) at para 25).

16 *Commander Business Furniture, supra* note 13 at 19 (QL). See also *Syncrude Trial Decision, supra* note 11 at para 100. Regarding the last factor ("actions of officials"), the court in *Commander Business Furniture* explained as follows at 23 (QL): "In my view, the advice, actions of lack thereof, and opinions of government officials are factors to consider in assessing the accused's knowledge of the problem and the solutions. However, the responsibility to know the subject matter and take reasonable and timely action still rests upon the accused. Similarly, it is my opinion that where advice, actions and opinions of consultants or experts have been sought, they are a factor to consider in assessing the accused's knowledge. However, the accused alone is still expected to acquire an appropriate level of expertise in the circumstances and to act with due diligence. An accused cannot hide behind one opinion in the face of other reliable evidence which reasonably leads to a contrary conclusion."

17 *Ibid* at 21 (QL).

18 *Ibid* citing *Bata Industries, supra* note 5.

19 *Ibid* at 22 (QL) (emphasis added). At p 20 (QL), the court quoted from John Swaigen in *Regulatory Offences in Canada: Liability and Defences* (Toronto: Carswell, 1992) at 119, in support of its position that economic factors are relevant: "Certainly, a company cannot choose to deliberately violate a law, regardless of the harsh economic impacts that may result from compliance. *However, the cost of taking steps to prevent violations can be taken into account in determining the standard of care required to establish due diligence.* A distinction may be drawn between commencing an activity knowing that it may entail a risk of non-compliance, and continuing an activity commenced without such awareness once the possibility of non-compliance becomes apparent. In the latter case, it is suggested that the assessment of the reasonableness of ceasing the activity may involve a balancing of the potential harm to the public or the environment from continuing the activity, and the harm to the enterprise from ceasing it. Some industrial processes cannot be shut down suddenly without risk of injuring employees, destruction of large quantities of product or raw materials, damage to equipment, or lengthy delay in recommencing operation. Once a person knows that his activities are violating the law, or is forewarned of the likelihood that these activities will culminate in violations, there is a heavy

onus on that person to make whatever expenditures are needed to cease or prevent violations. *But the amount of money that must be spent depends on how foreseeable and serious the harm is. The costs incurred to anticipate and prevent violations is proportional to the risk. The higher and more foreseeable the risk, the greater the expenditures the public may reasonably expect an enterprise to incur to reduce, or eliminate it, and vice versa*" [Emphasis added.]

20 *Syncrude Trial Decision, supra* note 11.

21 *Ibid* at para 96, citing *R v MacMillan Bloedel Ltd*, 2002 BCCA 510.

22 *Ibid* at para 101. There was no evidence of any mistake of fact in Syncrude's situation; the court found that Syncrude should have known that the proscribed conduct would occur as it was reasonable foreseeable that birds could land in the tailings pond (para 97).

23 *Ibid* at paras 23–28.

24 *R v Syncrude Ltd* (22 October 2010), St Albert No 09015792226P1 (Alta Prov Ct, Crim Div).

25 *Stratabound Minerals, supra* note 1.

26 *Ibid* at para 17.

27 As a result of the *Environmental Enforcement Act*, the *Fisheries Act* and other federal Acts were amended to include stiffer minimum and maximum fines. For instance, for a breach of the *Fisheries Act*, a corporation could face a minimum fine of $500,000 and a maximum fine of $6 million for an indictable offence, or a minimum fine of $100,000 and a maximum fine of $4 million on summary conviction: s 40(2).

28 *Stratabound Minerals, supra* note 1 at para 23.

29 *Ibid.*

30 *Ibid.*

31 *Ibid* at paras 25–26.

32 *Ibid* at paras 47–48.

33 *Ibid* at para 41.

34 *Ibid* at paras 41–42.

35 Decision and Reasons for Decision of the Chief Inspector of Mines on whether to submit a Report to Crown Counsel to assess if charges should be laid and a prosecution commenced for contravention of the Mines Act, Chief Inspector of Mines, signed 8 December 2015, online: <http://mssi.nrs.gov.bc.ca/1_CIMMount Polley/T0229_TAR431_ANALYSIS_ Decision%20DocumentCIM_ 20151208.pdf>.

36 *Ibid* at 1. The British Columbia Conservation Officer Service (COS) is still conducting its investigation into the Mount Polley accident, based on compliance with the Ministry of Environment legislation, and it is possible that the COS investigation may find non-compliance that warrants a prosecution. Environment Canada also opened an investigation on 4 August 2014, which is being conducted jointly with the British Columbia Ministry of Environment, COS, and the Major Investigations Unit. Environment Canada's investigation focuses on alleged violations of the *MMERs* and the *Fisheries Act.*

37 Ministry of Energy and Mines, News Release, "Government takes action on Chief Inspector of Mines' Recommendations" (17 December 2015) at 1 [*News Release*], online: <https://news.gov.bc.ca/ releases/2015MEM0030-002119>.

38 *Ibid, Backgrounder 1, Findings of the Chief Inspector*, at 1–2. In summary, the Chief Inspector of Mines' decision found that MPMC "failed to effectively manage water at the mine site and in the TSF. An adequate water management plan did not exist, there was no qualified individual responsible for water balance in the TSF, and MPMC did not adequately characterize the risk of surplus supernatant water, which had been compounding since the mine reopened in 2005."

39 *News Release, supra* note 37 at 1.

40 *Health, Safety and Reclamation Code for Mines in British Columbia* <https://www2.gov.bc.ca/assets/ gov/driving-and-transportation/ transportation-infrastructure/ contracting-with-the-province/

documents/12811-2018/t3-10-health-safety-and-reclamation-code-for-mines-in-british-columbia-2008.pdf> (this Code was released in June 2017, between the writing of this chapter and the publishing of this volume).

41 *Ibid, Backgrounder 2*, Chief Inspector of Mines' recommendations at 1 [*Backgrounder 2*].

42 *News Release, supra* note 37 at 1–2. For all recommendations see *Backgrounder 2, ibid* at 1–3.

43 Government of British Columbia, Ministry of Environment, "Long Term Water Management Plan Approve for Mount Polley" (7 April 2017, accessed 24 January 2018), online: <https://news.gov.bc.ca/releases/2017ENV0038-001156>.

44 Quesnel Cariboo Observer, "Mount Polley Shares Remediation Plans in Williams Lake" (21 November 2017, accessed 24 January 2018), online: <https://www.quesnelobserver.com/news/mount-polley-shares-remediation-plans-in-williams-lake/>.

45 *Lapointe v Mount Polley Mining Corp*, 2017 BCPC 140 at para 1.

46 *Ibid.*

47 For example, see s 184 of Ontario's *Environmental Protection Act*, RSO 1990, c E.19. "Obstruction" means making it more difficult for the provincial officer to carry out his or her statutory duties; it need not be a positive action. It can be failing to do something that the provincial officer requests.

48 Stanley D Berger, *The Prosecution and Defence of Environmental Offences* (Toronto: Canada Law Book, 2015) at 3-56 to 3-58 and 3-62.

49 Berger, *ibid* at 3-58.

50 See, e.g., s 160 of Ontario's *Environmental Protection Act, supra* note 46.

51 *R v Syncrude Canada Ltd*, 2010 ABPC 123 (Alta Prov Ct) [*Syncrude – Admissibility Decision*].

52 *Ibid* at para 20.

53 *Ibid* at para 39.

54 *Ibid* at para 10.

55 Investigators acknowledged that they did not warn the employee during the interview that his statements would be regarded as the statements of Syncrude.

56 *Syncrude – Admissibility Decision* at paras 28–33, citing *Irwin Toy Ltd c Quebec (Procureur general)*, [1989] 1 SCR 927 at para 96; *BC (Securities Commission) v Branch*, [1995] 2 SCR 3 at paras 39–40. A British Columbia court recently agreed that the confessions rule does not apply to corporate admissions: *R v Gwaii Wood Products Ltd*, 2015 BCPC 248 at para 9.

57 For example, see s 78.3 of the *Fisheries Act*; *R v Gwaii Wood Products Ltd*, 2015 BCPC 292 at para 61.

58 *Provincial Offences Act*, RSO 1990, c P.33, s 158(3). *Criminal Code of Canada*, RSC 1985, c C-46, s 488 states that "a warrant issued under section 487 or 487.1 shall be executed by day," and day is defined as "the period between six o'clock in the forenoon and nine o'clock in the afternoon of the same day." However, a search warrant "authorize[ing] [the police] to enter the said place or premises between the hours of 5:15 p.m. on Aug. 10, 2002 to 8:00 p.m. on Aug. 10, 2002" does not necessarily mean the police must vacate the premises by 8:00 p.m. if their search is not completed. They must enter during the time specified and can then remain a reasonable time to complete their search and seizure: *R v Cardinal*, [2003] BCJ No 2598, 2003 BCSC 158.

59 A search warrant on which the date has expired cannot be revived by the police officer requesting and the justice granting a change of date on the warrant. The officer's only recourse is to apply for a new warrant: *R v Jamieson*, [1989] NSJ No 158, 48 CCC (3d) 287 (CA).

60 At common law, access to the search warrant information, since it is a judicial act, is a presumptive right once the search warrant has been executed and a seizure made: *Nova Scotia (Attorney General) v MacIntyre*, [1982] SCJ No 1, 65 CCC (2d) 129 (SCC).

# 54

# Anatomy of a Compliance Regime: Recapitulation and Alternative Lessons from the United States

JONATHAN LEO

## Introduction

The modern US federal pollution control laws enacted in the period from the late 1960s to the early 1980s are examples of "cooperative federalism," a constitutional legislative regime in which Congress explicitly authorizes a federal executive branch agency—here, the US Environmental Protection Agency (EPA)—to address the statutorily determined need to protect public health and safety and the environment from specified dangers by controlling their sources. The federalism is "cooperative" because it relies on supervised delegation by the EPA to the states, which in turn can or must develop corresponding statutory and regulatory regimes to assist the EPA's achievement of national standards by enforcing compliance within their own borders.[1] One of the central enforcement mechanisms of the federal and authorized state programs is the regulatory agency's issuance of an operating permit to every business whose activities are covered by the law. The operating permit's conditions include, *inter alia*, compliance with all applicable state laws and regulations as well as facility-specific compliance conditions required by the agency.

### GENERAL REGULATORY AUTHORITY TO INSPECT AND ENFORCE ENVIRONMENTAL COMPLIANCE

One of the core elements of these federal and authorized state enforcement programs is the authority of regulatory agency personnel, upon presentation of credentials, to enter a facility at "reasonable times" or "during regular business hours" to conduct a compliance inspection. These inspections can include the examination and copying of any records required to be maintained by the business (including any accidental release and mitigation programs, or spill prevention and control programs), the inspection of any pollution control and process equipment, and the sampling of any discharge or emission.[2] These sections authorizing a right of entry and inspection also include a "catch-all" clause stipulating that the "[the business] shall provide such other information as the administrator may reasonably require,"[3] which is understood to permit consensual employee interviews.

After an inspection is concluded, environmental regulatory agencies have a variety of progressively more intrusive enforcement tools to employ in the discharge of their mandate to protect public health and safety and the environment. These include:

- letters sent to facilities by agency program managers requesting specific information about production and waste generation and management processes, including a request to sample or test air emissions and/or discharges to water and soil;[4]
- administrative subpoenas, administrative search warrants, and/or compliance orders to compel facilities to grant access for site inspections, to produce records and present witnesses to testify under oath, and to comply with particular permit or regulatory requirements;
- imminent and substantial endangerment orders designed to immediately abate more serious releases of pollutants or contaminants to the environment;
- civil enforcement lawsuits, brought by United States attorneys for the Department of Justice (DOJ) against corporations and individuals to obtain penalties and injunctive relief to abate ongoing violations of law, including compliance with imminent and substantial endangerment orders; and
- criminal actions, including use of criminal search warrants, brought by United States attorneys for the DOJ against corporations and individuals where violations of law are "knowing," "negligent," or "willful."[5]

States with federally authorized environmental compliance and enforcement programs have similar ranges of information-gathering powers and administrative, civil, and criminal enforcement authorities.[6]

## THE CALIFORNIA INVESTIGATIVE SUBPOENA

In California, regulatory agencies and their prosecuting attorneys have an additional statutory investigative tool that is unmatched in any federal environmental statute. The investigative subpoena (IS) authorizes the "head of a department" (including the state attorney general and, when investigating *Unfair Competition Law* violations, county district attorneys) to inspect and copy records, promulgate interrogatories, and compel the sworn testimony of corporate witnesses as part of an investigative inquiry *in the absence of any formal proceeding or lawsuit.*[7] Any business association receiving an IS must designate and produce a "person most qualified" (PMQ) to testify regarding the matters on which examination is requested in the IS. While there are procedural requirements for proper service of process and geographical limits on where the PMQ must provide testimony, the statute is silent regarding the right of the PMQ to be represented by counsel during the taking of testimony, and both the attorney general and district attorneys have advised respondents in these proceedings that they have no right to obtain copies of either the transcripts of their testimony or the documents shown to them by prosecuting attorneys during questioning. To date, courts have accepted the analogy that the IS is like a grand jury proceeding, in which neither witnesses nor targets (if they waive their constitutional right against self-incrimination) have the right to counsel.

If a business believes that the IS compels disclosure of information that is confidential or a trade secret, the PMQ has the burden of producing sufficient evidence to persuade a court that the trade secret's or confidential business information's value to the business outweighs the agency's need for the information.[8] The refusal to respond or provide adequate responses to an IS can only be enforced by an order to show cause, accompanied by an order compelling the respondent to appear at the show cause hearing. The show cause hearing is limited to evaluating the adequacy of the IS by the standards of the three-part test described above.[9] If any constitutional objections based on the Fourth Amendment's proscription of unreasonable searches and seizures or the Fifth Amendment's privilege against self-incrimination are not raised in the show cause hearing, they will result in a waiver. A respondent who refuses to comply with an order to compel will be subject to contempt, but the order to compel is directly appealable as a final judgment, and no sanction can be imposed on a respondent for refusing to respond until and unless a court order to do so is upheld on appeal.[10] (For examples of successful uses of the Investigative Subpoena, see Appendix A, *infra*, for chart of "California Multi-Jurisdictional/

Multi-Facility Civil Environmental Settlements (January 1, 2009 through August 2014)," embedded in Schmall and Endemann paper, at fn. 9.)

## THE COSTS OF NON-COMPLIANCE AND THE INCENTIVES FOR INTERNAL CORPORATE ENVIRONMENTAL MANAGEMENT PROGRAMS

Clearly, regulatory agency personnel can obtain evidence of a business's non-compliance with permit conditions and other regulatory or statutory obligations at *any* stage of their information-gathering process. They are trained to determine the significance of that evidence from their evaluation of a number of variables, including: the seriousness of any actual or threatened environmental or public health endangerment; the degree to which the violation is accidental, negligent, or intentional; the duration of the particular violation; the past compliance history of the business or facility; the degree to which the facility culture, and the larger corporate culture of which it is a part, have internalized a regulatory compliance ethic into their business production and management attitudes and practices; and the cooperative or combative attitudes of the facility's staff and management. Accordingly, evidence of relatively non-serious violations discovered during routine regulatory agency inspections may be resolved immediately with a small fine, whereas more serious violations can result in the agency's issuance of an order for administrative penalties, a civil enforcement order, or a referral to the DOJ, the state attorney general, or a county district attorney, for civil and/or criminal prosecution charging the business entity and/or individual employees and officers.

The enforcement sections of the major federal environmental statutes provide less than crystal clarity regarding which kinds of acts and omissions will result in criminal, civil, or administrative proceedings, and, in many cases, the same action can be enforced by any one of those three alternatives. The exercise of prosecutorial discretion ultimately determines whether there will be a criminal prosecution, but for businesses and their counsel, this uncertainty only creates anxiety about whether, when, and what kind of enforcement hammer will hit them.[11]

Independently enforceable corrective action orders are the "compliance-forcing" components of the administrative, civil, or criminal enforcement proceedings. They can require completion of such corrective actions as remedial investigations, feasibility studies, and remedial action plans, including the installation of groundwater monitoring wells to permit verification of contamination source elimination and containment of contaminant migration.

Alternatively, corrective action orders may require the repair or replacement of inefficient process and/or pollution-control equipment that has caused or contributed to spills or releases of pollutants whose concentration levels exceed state and/or federal standards, and they can require installation of more stringent leak or spill-detection systems. Every corrective action order imposes a compliance schedule for completion of each of its elements and typically provides that the issuing and enforcing agency may impose penalties for the respondent's failure to meet specified deadlines.

Since businesses have to allocate whatever financial and human resources are necessary to comply with these kinds of corrective action orders without interrupting their daily operations to meet production quotas and revenue projections, they must usually hire a professional environmental engineering and consulting firm with a proven track record both in performing the required corrective actions and working effectively with the regulatory enforcement agency in charge. In order to maximize their control over the later production or discovery of the consultant's reports and notes, businesses facing these enforcement orders should have special environmental outside counsel hire the consulting firm under a contract which provides that the consulting firm is performing work and generating reports for outside counsel because of actual or anticipated litigation and is, therefore, subject to the attorney-client privilege.

One of the most effective ways for businesses to limit the substantial costs of responding to enforcement orders and litigation over environmental violations is to develop, institutionalize, and regularly fine-tune an internal corporate environmental compliance management program. These kinds of programs will include the kind of internal environmental compliance audit practices that EPA, the DOJ, and many state attorney generals and environmental agencies have come to expect from the regulated community.

## Internal Corporate Environmental Compliance Management Programs and the EPA's Audit Policy

The EPA first published an Environmental Auditing Policy Statement in 1986 in an effort to respond to the rapid growth of voluntary environmental audit policies and practices that had already taken root in certain sectors of the regulatory community. A Price-Waterhouse study in 1995 found that more than 90 percent of businesses operating in such heavily regulated industries as petroleum refining and chemical manufacturing had already adopted some form of regular self-auditing procedures.[12]

In 1995, the EPA issued its first final Audit Policy,[13] supplemented 13 months later by its "Audit Policy Interpretive Guidance,"[14] a 40-page document that, for the first time, articulated the EPA's commitment to providing limited enforcement leniency to businesses that discovered violations voluntarily, disclosed them promptly, corrected them quickly, and took serious action to prevent recurrences. A new final Audit Policy, which superseded the 1995 policy, was issued in 2000 and remains in effect, with some modifications, today.[15]

The 2000 EPA Audit Policy encourages self-policing, self-disclosure, and prompt self-correction of environmental violations and, for companies that meet the conditions of the policy, offers the following four incentives: (1) the EPA will not seek any gravity-based penalties for entities that self-disclose and meet all nine policy conditions, including "systematic discovery," although it retains the discretion to recover the "economic benefit" civil penalty component;[16] (2) gravity-based penalties will be reduced by 75 percent where the disclosing entity does not detect the violation through systematic discovery but meets all of the other policy conditions; (3) when a disclosure that meets the terms and conditions of the policy results in a criminal investigation, the EPA "will generally not recommend criminal prosecution for the disclosing entity, although the Agency may recommend prosecution for culpable individuals and other entities;"[17] and (4) the EPA—in a reaffirmation of its policy since 1986—will not routinely request copies of audit reports from disclosing entities in order to trigger further enforcement investigations.

Of the nine Audit Policy conditions that must be fulfilled in order for the EPA to agree to the waiver of all gravity-based penalties for self-disclosing entities, the five most important are: (1) the "systematic discovery" of the violation, (2) the identification of the violation "voluntarily" and not by some government-required procedure, (3) disclosure to the EPA within 21 days after discovery, (4) correction of the violation followed by certification of correction to all appropriate agencies within 60 days, and (5) prevention of any recurrence by making improvements in the entity's environmental management system. Policy benefits are not available for violations that result in serious actual harm to the environment, that may have presented an imminent and substantial endangerment to public health or the environment, or that violate the specific terms of any order, consent agreement, or plea agreement.[18]

Also, the EPA remains adamantly opposed to legislation in certain states that creates a statutory privilege for environmental audits and also provides immunity from certain kinds of enforcement against companies that meet the law's audit requirements. In the words of the 2000 Audit Policy, "Audit privilege and immunity laws are unnecessary, undermine law enforcement, impair protection of human health and the environment, and interfere with the public's right to know of potential and existing environmental hazards."[19]

Businesses with internal environmental compliance management programs, whether or not through an ISO-14001–certified environmental management system,[20] benefit from institutionalizing a strategy for voluntary disclosure and prompt corrective action of environmental violations. They recognize both the importance of, and the vigilance required to implement and maintain, an internal audit program that has the support of every level of the corporate organization, even in the face of business interruptions, customer dissatisfaction, and the need for new kinds of collaboration among normally independent business units. A 2010 Harvard Business School empirical analysis found that facilities that made voluntary disclosure of violations were able to obtain a 17 percent reduction in the likelihood of being inspected, compared to facilities that failed to take advantage of the EPA Audit Policy.[21]

On September 9, 2015, the DOJ dramatically increased the incentives for corporations to establish and diligently maintain an internal environmental compliance management program that incorporates an effective self-audit component. On that date, Deputy US Attorney General Sally Yates issued a memorandum titled "Individual Accountability for Corporate Wrongdoing" (Yates Memo). The Yates Memo is applicable to all future investigations of corporate wrongdoing as well as to investigations pending as of September 9, 2015 to the extent practicable. Its primary purpose is to "fully leverage the resources [of the DOJ] to identify [and pursue] culpable individuals at all levels in corporate cases."[22] Even attorneys who regard the Yates Memo as primarily a restatement of existing practice consider the fact of its issuance as highly significant.[23]

## The Yates Memo and the US Attorneys' Manual

The Yates Memo amends provisions of the "Principles of Federal Prosecution of Business Organizations" in Title 9 (Criminal) of the *United States Attorneys' Manual* (*USAM*), as well as the "Compromising and Closing" provisions of Title 4 (Civil) of the *USAM*.[24] Its primary contribution to the policies governing federal criminal and civil prosecution of business organizations is to withhold the extension of *any* "cooperation credit" as a mitigating factor in cases where DOJ is investigating business organizations for possible indictment or prosecution, *unless* the corporation completely discloses to DOJ all relevant facts about individual misconduct.[25]

The *USAM* advises federal prosecutors, during the conduct of an investigation, to consider ten factors when making the determination whether and what kind of charges to bring and when negotiating plea, settlement, and other agreements. Six of those ten factors are directly related to the considerations that underlie corporate environmental compliance management programs, and they are also found in the EPA's Audit Policy. They are: (1) the pervasiveness of wrongdoing within the corporation, including the complicity in, or the condoning of, the wrongdoing by corporate management (*USAM* 9-28.500); (2) the corporation's history of similar misconduct, including prior criminal, civil, and regulatory enforcement actions against it (*USAM* 9-28.600); (3) the corporation's willingness to cooperate in the investigation of its agents (*USAM* 9-28.700); (4) the existence and effectiveness of the corporation's pre-existing compliance program (*USAM* 9-28.800); (5) the corporation's timely and voluntary disclosure of wrongdoing (*USAM* 9-28.900); and (6) the corporation's remedial actions, including any efforts to implement an effective corporate compliance program or to improve an existing one, to replace responsible (i.e. culpable) management, to discipline or terminate wrongdoers, to pay restitution, and to cooperate with the relevant government agencies (*USAM* 9-28.1000).

The employees of every regulated business need to understand that, when agency personnel arrive outside the facility's gate to request access to perform an inspection, those inspectors, their agency managers, the agency's in-house counsel, and the federal law enforcement authorities to whom the agency's in-house counsel may refer violations for civil or criminal prosecution, will each be judging the potential culpability of the business and its employees by reference to those enforcement decision-making factors.

The Yates Memo, and now the *USAM* as well, directs the DOJ to pursue individual civil and criminal corporate wrongdoing in accordance with six guidelines:

(1) To be eligible for any cooperation credit under the Principles of Federal Prosecution of Business Organizations, the company must completely disclose to the DOJ all relevant facts about individual misconduct.
(2) Both criminal and civil corporate investigations should focus on individuals from the inception of the investigation.
(3) Criminal and civil attorneys handling corporate investigations should be in routine communication with one another.

(4) Absent extraordinary circumstances, no corporate resolution will provide protection from criminal or civil liability for any individuals.
(5) Corporate cases should not be resolved without a clear plan to resolve related individual cases before the statute of limitation expires, and declinations as to individuals in such cases must be memorialized.
(6) Civil attorneys should consistently focus on individuals as well as the company, and evaluate whether to bring suit against an individual based on considerations beyond that individual's ability to pay.[26]

In its discussion of the general principle of cooperation credit, the *USAM* states that "a company is not required to waive its attorney-client privilege and attorney work product protection in order satisfy this threshold,"[27] and it further states that "prosecutors should not ask for such waivers and are directed not to do so."[28] "The extent of the cooperation credit earned will depend on all the various factors that have traditionally applied in making this assessment (e.g. the timeliness of the cooperation, the diligence, thoroughness and speed of the internal investigation, and the proactive nature of the cooperation).[29]

When Donald Trump was inaugurated as the 45th President of the United States, Sally Yates became the Acting Attorney General. Ten days later, on January 20, 2018, President Trump fired Ms. Yates for "insubordination," following her instruction to the DOJ not to enforce or defend Trump's Executive Order 13769, temporarily banning the admission of refugees and barring all travel from seven Muslim-majority countries. Her replacement, and the current Deputy Attorney General, Rod Rosenstein, has not publicly indicated any intention to reverse the DOJ's corporate enforcement policies as set out in the Yates Memo and its revisions to the US Attorneys' Manual.

## The Regulatory Inspection, Employee Interviews, and Attorney-Client Privilege Issues

The Yates Memo's emphasis on identifying and pursuing culpable individuals in both civil and criminal corporate prosecutions, and the policies it prioritizes to achieve that goal, have potentially dramatic, but as yet untested, consequences for the criminal and civil enforcement of federal environmental laws in the United States in at least the following contexts: (1) the strategies and tactics employed by corporations and their employees in preparing for and responding to environmental regulatory inspections; (2) the corporation's preparation for employee interviews in internal and regulatory agency investigations, including whether and when to provide employees with independent counsel; (3) the relations between the corporation and its employees; and (4) the extent of government scrutiny of corporate assertions of attorney-client privilege used to justify the refusal to produce requested information.[30]

## THE REGULATORY AGENCY INSPECTION AND THE ROLE OF CORPORATE COUNSEL

During each of the five years from 2009–2013, the EPA conducted, on average, 20,000 non-*CERCLA* facility inspections and 200–300 multiple-day, multimedia civil investigations, from which approximately 3,000 civil enforcement cases were filed. The overwhelming majority of all facility inspections involve only one or two civil investigators; less than 1 percent involve enforcement attorneys. Most inspections are unannounced because agency staff, not surprisingly, wants to obtain a real-time "snapshot" of how each particular regulated entity operates its business. All inspections, except for those conducted pursuant to a search warrant, require the consent of facility management, even though virtually every regulated facility's operating permit requires it to allow access at "reasonable times" or "during regular business hours" so that regulatory agency staff can evaluate compliance status. The reasons for warrantless (i.e. regular) inspections are several: a routine check on compliance with permit conditions and regulations; a referral from other agencies about possible violations of laws and regulations outside the jurisdiction of the referring agencies; citizen complaints; follow-ups on earlier inspections and information request letters; and annual or biennial program effectiveness assessments.[31]

Warrantless facility inspections, whether by the EPA or California environmental regulatory agencies, usually involve two inspectors, who, upon arrival, present their credentials, and request access and to speak with the "person in charge." The inspection begins with the lead inspector conducting an "opening conference," where the inspector explains the purpose and scope of the inspection so that the facility's managers can better assist the inspectors and warn about construction areas or other potential safety issues on site.[32] During the opening conference, inspectors will also identify particular facility records they want to inspect and/or copy before they leave. (The company must provide the government with copies and retain all originals for its own records.) Inspectors may take photographs of process and pollution-control equipment, as well as liquid and soil samples at any location on or off the property where it is safe to do so. Normally, inspectors will provide the facility with splits of all physical samples they take, but the facility staff should nonetheless make a specific request for these items.[33]

One or more facility personnel must always accompany the inspectors while they are on the business premises, and some agencies require that facility personnel accompany their inspectors during every part of the inspection, both to "oversee" the inspection and to answer any questions the inspectors may have as and when they arise.[34] Facility personnel must sometimes walk a fine line between ensuring that the inspection stays within its announced scope and does not improperly disrupt or interrupt the facility's business operations, and constraining the inspectors' activities to an extent that could be construed as obstruction of justice.[35] During the "closing conference," the inspectors usually provide an overview of their observations and identify specific deficiencies that need attention. Since everything mentioned during a closing conference (along with much more that is not mentioned) will become part of the agency's final inspection report, the facility needs to understand and respond to the particulars of every identified deficiency (whether communicated orally or in writing) so that, when the final report is issued, the facility's responses and comments will demonstrate how quickly and effectively it took necessary corrective action.

An increasing number of high-value-penalty enforcement cases arise from so-called "dumpster dives," where agency inspectors wait just beyond the property line of the target facility to intercept private waste-hauling trucks that have completed pickups from the facility, before the facility's waste is commingled with that from later-serviced facilities. It is established federal and California state judicial precedent that neither individuals nor organizations have any legitimate expectation of privacy in the trash they make available for removal by local government or private haulers, so these "dumpster dives" do not violate the Fourth Amendment's proscription on unreasonable searches and seizures.[36]

During the majority of warrantless agency inspections, the presence of corporate counsel (whether in-house or outside) is unnecessary and may also give inspectors the false impression that the business has something to hide. However, in the unusual situation where three or more inspectors are present, or if the inspection involves more than one regulatory agency, or if the business really *does* have something to hide, then it is advisable for outside counsel to be present.[37] Before that "moment of truth" ever occurs, in-house and outside counsel need to have removed as many attorney-client privileged and attorney work product documents as possible from facility files, and any privileged information that must be or is kept at the facility must be segregated and properly marked, in order to minimize or eliminate the possibility that a facility employee may unwittingly disclose it. If, under extraordinary circumstances, outside counsel *must*, but cannot, be present during a warrantless inspection (either because he or she is too far away or the inspectors refuse to wait), counsel must consider the pros and cons of informing agency inspectors either directly or through the agency's counsel that—until and unless outside counsel can be physically present—the corporation withholds its consent to any inspection, including the interviewing of any employees.

If the inspection is authorized by a search warrant, particularly a criminal warrant, facility employees or counsel must copy the warrant without delay so that they can familiarize themselves with the scope of inspection and the seizure of documents and objects that the warrant authorizes. Here, the presence of outside counsel is particularly critical, but government investigators are not required by law to wait for corporate counsel before proceeding to execute the warrant. If they refuse to wait, corporate counsel needs to make a record of formally objecting to the execution of the warrant in his or her absence, and also needs to assert attorney-client privilege and attorney work product protection over all covered documents and information. To the extent that any such documents are kept at the facility and have been properly marked and segregated, corporate counsel, assisted by facility personnel, can identify them to the investigators in advance.[38]

The ideal arrangement is for outside counsel to be notified immediately of the presence of inspectors with a search warrant, so that counsel can speak directly with them to learn the scope and details of the warrant and obtain their agreement either to delay warrant execution until counsel arrives or, at least, to conduct employee interviews only in the presence of outside counsel at an approved later time or date. If outside counsel cannot get the investigators to delay the warrant execution until counsel arrives, then counsel must at least try to get the investigators to agree that they will not interview employees unless he or she can be present.[39] Since that may not be possible, outside and in-house corporate counsel need to have earlier informed all facility employees that, under these circumstances, they have the right to request that they be interviewed in the presence of corporate counsel or, where appropriate, their own independent counsel. Most of all, facility employees need to hear from corporate counsel that, if and whenever they are interviewed by government agency personnel, they need to cooperate fully, tell the truth, and only provide information that is specifically requested.

## EMPLOYEE INTERVIEWS AND ATTORNEY-CLIENT PRIVILEGE ISSUES[40]

Every regulated business should establish policies for responding to governmental agency inspections and investigations. These policies should address the role of in-house counsel in advising and preparing employees for interviews by, and interactions with, government agency personnel. Whether or not it is required by formal corporate policy, in-house counsel should also develop checklists or guidelines that clearly instruct employees what they should do and whom within the company they should notify when inspectors appear at the company gate or office door to inspect with or without a warrant.

In-house counsel must ensure employees understand that, while they have the right to refuse to be interviewed by government investigators, the company asks that they agree to be interviewed, and that they answer all questions truthfully and without speculating or providing any information not requested. In-house counsel should also tell employees that they have the right, but not the obligation, to speak with in-house counsel before the interview takes place, that they have the right to have counsel present with them when the government interview is conducted, and that the counsel who accompanies them can be in-house counsel or, if appropriate, their own independent counsel.

In addition to, and separate from, the advice that in-house counsel should give to all employees as described in the preceding paragraph, and whether in-house counsel plans to interview an employee pursuant to an internal corporate investigation or audit or, instead, intends to advise the employee of his or her rights in connection with an interview to be conducted by a government agency investigator, in-house counsel must provide every employee with a particular advisement or warning required by the Supreme Court's decision in the *Upjohn* case.[41] The traditional *Upjohn* warning includes the following elements: in-house counsel represents the company and does not represent the employee individually or personally; the interview, if internal, is being conducted to gather information to provide legal advice to the company for business purposes; all communications between in-house counsel and the employee are protected by the attorney-client privilege, but that privilege is held by the company alone and not by the employee; the company alone may elect to waive the privilege and disclose some or all of its communication with the employee to third parties (including the government), without notifying the employee in advance; and the employee is requested and expected to maintain all information discussed as confidential.[42]

The scope of the *Upjohn* warning is greater when in-house counsel is interviewing the employee pursuant to an internal investigation than it is when in-house counsel is advising a corporate employee about his or her rights in a potential interview by a government investigator as part of a facility inspection or a broader external investigation. This is because, in the context of the internal corporate investigation, in-house counsel must not only make sure that the employee knows and understands that in-house counsel (or an outside corporate counsel acting with the approval and knowledge of in-house counsel) represents the corporation and not the employee but must also determine whether the employee's and the corporation's interests are so actually or potentially adverse that counsel should further affirmatively warn the employee that he or she should be represented by his or her own, independent counsel and *not* by the corporation's counsel.

Although not required by law or judicial decision, it is advisable for corporate counsel to at least make contemporaneous notes of the extent and content of each *Upjohn* warning given, if not also to memorialize every *Upjohn* warning in writing, rather than to rely on oral communication alone. If the warning is later found to have been inadequate, the consequences can include loss of the privilege, financial exposure to the company, and discipline of corporate counsel.[43]

In the wake of the Yates Memo and the DOJ's new policy to focus on individual culpability from the inception of all criminal and civil investigations (see discussion above), the interests of the corporation and its individual employees are likely to conflict earlier and more often. This increased tension arguably renders the traditional, "bare bones" *Upjohn* warning inadequate, and, as noted above, may require a more forceful warning that the corporation's and the employee's interests may or actually do conflict, and that the employee is advised to consult independent counsel in order to protect his or her interests.

It bears repeating that, if in-house or outside corporate counsel knows that a particular employee may have personal knowledge of, or have been involved in, corporate wrongdoing related to an anticipated or ongoing investigation, counsel should seriously giving an *Upjohn* warning to such an employee that explicitly states that the employee's and the corporation's interests are adverse in certain respects and, therefore, the employee's interests can only be represented by his or her own independent counsel. The corporation will likely have to bear the cost of paying for personal counsel for such employees.

Effectively, the recent changes in DOJ enforcement policy with respect to corporate civil and criminal investigations incentivize each of the corporation and its employees to "give up" the other to government investigators at the earliest opportunity in order to protect their own interests: the corporation, because its chance for *any* cooperation credit to mitigate a penalty or fine imposed after a final judgment of civil liability or even a criminal conviction depends on its prompt disclosure of the identity of employees who were involved in or bore some responsibility for the misconduct being investigated; and the employees, because the earlier they inform the government about their knowledge of the corporation's misconduct, the greater the likelihood both that they will get "whistleblower protection" from being fired or otherwise discriminated against by their corporate employer and that their early cooperation will mitigate any penalty they might otherwise receive if they are ultimately found personally liable for the misconduct.

For employees, the consequences of failure or refusal to cooperate with reasonable internal investigations (whether conducted by in-house or outside counsel or both) can be dramatic, as illustrated by a recent decision from the Second Circuit Court of Appeals. In *Gilman v Marsh & McLennan Cos.* (*Gilman*),[44] the New York State attorney general indicted the corporate employer for allegedly fraudulent business practices and antitrust violations, based on the identification of two employees of Marsh & McLennan Cos. (Marsh) as co-conspirators in a "bid-rigging" scheme with AIG, another insurance company. Marsh expanded its pre-existing internal investigation to focus on those two employees, Gilman and McNenney (who were also officers of the corporation), and suspended them both, with pay, pending the outcome of that internal investigation. Even though Marsh requested that Gilman and McNenney sit for interviews with the company's outside counsel, and warned that they would be fired if they refused, both employees refused to cooperate, and Marsh fired them. When they sued Marsh for wrongful termination, both the trial and the appellate courts ruled against them. The Second Circuit held that the corporation was entitled to seek information from its own employees about suspicions of on-the-job criminal conduct; could take measures to protect its standing with investors, clients, employees and regulators; and had a duty to its shareholders to investigate any potentially criminal conduct by its employees that could harm the company. Additionally, the Second Circuit held that the employees had a duty to their corporate employer to disclose information they had about the attorney general's allegations. Because the Second Circuit held that Gilman and McNenney had been terminated "for cause," they lost their entitlement to all unvested stock benefits and severance pay.[45]

In the *Gilman* case above, the two corporate officers who were fired "for cause" for refusing to cooperate with the corporation's internal investigation had been earlier identified as "co-conspirators" in a bid-rigging scheme with AIG, so their leverage with either their employer or the New York State attorney general was virtually non-existent. Most corporate employees who learn about corporate misconduct *do* have a choice of either speaking out or remaining silent. For those who choose to speak out, most federal environmental statutes have "whistleblower" provisions that protect employees from being discharged or discriminated against for assisting the enforcement of environmental laws.[46]

As noted earlier, both the Yates Memo and the *USAM* explicitly mention the sacrosanct nature of the attorney-client privilege and attorney work product doctrine, although the *USAM* recognizes that "a wide range of commentators and members of the American legal community and criminal justice system have asserted that [the DOJ's] policies have been used, either wittingly or unwittingly, to coerce business entities into waiving attorney-client privilege and work-product protection."[47]

The DOJ's policy to "identify and pursue culpable individuals at all levels in corporate cases" means that corporations now must become even more alert to the need to take prompt action in response to the acquisition of facts that should reasonably alert them to the possibility of individual employee wrongdoing. The corporation must quickly identify, evaluate, and act on the earliest indications of potential civil or criminal liability, such as the receipt of any kind of government subpoena, request for information, notice of violation, or notice to comply; efforts by government agents to speak to employees or executives; reports or allegations of corporate wrongdoing by employees who may become whistleblowers; and any information revealed through such internal and regulatory compliance functions as auditing, "ordinary course" reports, and mandatory reporting obligations. If the corporation deliberately or negligently fails to promptly investigate evidence or allegations of non-compliance or legal violations, it can subject itself and its relevant officials to even greater liability.

The more varied the advice provided to companies by their in-house counsel, the greater the chance that the line between business and legal advice can become blurred and otherwise attorney-client privileged communications can become discoverable. When, for example, in-house counsel provides advice to the corporation about its environmental compliance history, and suggests recommendations for changes in compliance policies and/or procedures, there is likely to be some discussion of the costs and benefits associated with those recommendations. (Where in-house counsel is also an officer of the corporation, such as a Vice-President for Environmental Affairs, the blurring of distinctions between business and legal advice can be even more common.) To the extent possible, in-house counsel should avoid talking about the business aspects of corporate environmental compliance when the primary purpose of the advice concerns the details of particular environmental investigations and inspections, and should avoid discussing the details of particular environmental investigations and inspections when the primary purpose of the advice concerns the business aspects of the corporation's environmental compliance history, policies, and procedures. This distinction is likely to be as awkward to achieve in practice as it is to articulate in principle.

Corporations with robust internal environmental compliance management systems are more likely to recognize the kinds of facts and circumstances that can form the basis for civil and criminal enforcement. They are also more likely to promptly engage counsel expert in the law and ethics of internal investigations as well as the complexities of environmental laws and regulations to guide them through the intricacies of deciding whether and how to make early disclosure to the government of facts relevant to individual employee culpability without waiving critically important privileges and protections.[48]

## NOTES

1 In some cases, such as the *Clean Air Act* (42 USC § 7410), states are required to enact EPA-approved plans to implement, maintain, and enforce the EPA's national primary and secondary ambient air quality standards (NAAQS) for each air quality control region within their borders. In other cases, such as the *Resource Conservation and Recovery Act* (RCRA) (42 USC § 6926), any state that seeks to administer and enforce a "hazardous waste program" must obtain the EPA's approval for one that is "substantially equivalent" to the EPA's own permitting and enforcement regime for hazardous waste treatment, storage, and disposal facilities.

2 *Comprehensive Environmental Response, Compensation and Liability Act of 1980* (CERCLA or Superfund), 42 USC §§ 9604(e)(2), (3); *Clean Air Act*, 42 USC § 7414(a); RCRA, 42 USC § 6927(a).

3 *Clean Water Act*, 33 USC § 1318(a)(A)(5).

4 The CERCLA § 104(e) information request letter requires an initial response but also creates a continuing obligation to supplement the questions with fresh answers as situations at the facility change over time. Failure to respond, a response in bad faith, or a misrepresentation

of information creates civil liability. Examples of emissions-and-discharge sampling and testing request letters can be found in the *Clean Air Act*, the *Clean Water Act*, and RCRA.

5 *Clean Air Act*, 42 USC § 7413; *Clean Water Act*, 33 USC § 1319; *RCRA*, 42 USC § 6928; *Emergency Planning and Community Right-to-Know Act of 1986* (*EPCRA*), 42 USC § 11045; *Surface Mining Control and Reclamation Act* (SMCRA), 30 USC §§ 1268, 1271; *Safe Drinking Water Act*, 42 USC § 300h-2.

6 If a business is facing civil or criminal litigation based on non-compliance that is actionable under both federal and state law, its counsel should determine whether the enforcing agency will consider a settlement that resolves the business's liability under both federal and state law for any charges that could be brought arising out of the enforcement action's operative facts. This kind of resolution can prevent simultaneous or subsequent duplicative enforcement proceedings and dramatically reduce costs to the business.

7 *California Government Code*, §§ 11180–11191 (1921, as amended in 2003). The minimum requirements of an IS for purposes of document production and witness testimony are determined by a three-part test: (1) the investigation must be within the general authority of the issuing department; (2) the information sought by the IS must be "reasonably relevant" to the investigation, although the department is not required to make any showing of good or probable cause; and (3) the information sought must not be too indefinite.

8 If the company and its PMQ are concerned that the IS calls for production of confidential business information or trade secret data, they *must* assert that claim and withhold production at the earliest opportunity, or they may be held to have waived the right to claim protection from disclosure of such information at a later date. During execution of search warrants, a company must also be prepared to make such a claim or risk waiving the right to its later assertion. In search warrant contexts, however, if the government team executing the warrant is aware that there may be attorney-client privileged, trade secret, and/or confidential business information documents that are otherwise covered by the scope of the warrant, it may ask the magistrate approving the warrant to designate an attorney to accompany the team, personally review all files and documents as to which such privileges or claims are made by the company, copy them, and remove them in a marked and sealed envelope for the court to review *in camera* at a later, special hearing, where the company will have the opportunity to persuade the court not to order production of the documents to the government.

9 See *supra* note 7.

10 See generally Deborah J Schmall & Buck B Endemann, "Investigative Subpoenas Wielded by California Prosecutors" (Paper delivered at the State Bar of California Environmental Law Section Annual Yosemite Conference, 2014).

11 See David M Uhlmann, "Prosecutorial Discretion and Environmental Crime" (August 2015) 45 Env L Rep 10801. In the enforcement sections of the major federal environmental statutes, Congress made only limited distinctions between acts that could result in criminal, civil, or administrative enforcement. The same violation can often give rise to criminal, civil, *or* administrative enforcement. In some cases, the charging language in the enforcement statutes will distinguish between conduct that is "knowing," "negligent," "intentional," and "wilful," while in other cases (*CERCLA* or Superfund, for example) the statute provides a "strict liability" standard for charging violations, where the mental state or intention of the defendant is irrelevant. Since mental state requirements only preclude criminal enforcement for a small subset of violations, the factor that ultimately determines which environmental violations result in

criminal prosecution is the judgment of prosecutors. The scope of prosecutorial discretion assumes a particularly critical role in environmental cases, because so much conduct potentially falls within the criminal provisions of the environmental laws.

12 See Lawrence Culleen & Thomas Glazer, "Let's Make A Deal: Twenty Years of EPA's Audit Policy" (Winter 2016) 30 Nat Resources & Env 3.

13 "Incentives for Self-Policing: Discovery, Disclosure, Correction and Prevention of Violations," 60 Federal Register 66706 (22 December 1995).

14 "Audit Policy Interpretive Guidance," 15 January 1997, online: <http://www.epa.gov/sites/production/files/documents/audpolintepgui-mem.pdf>.

15 See EPA revised final policy re "Incentives for Self-Policing: Discovery, Disclosure, Correction and Prevention of Violations," 65 Federal Register 19618–19627 (11 April 2000) [Audit Policy], online: <https://www.gpo.gov/fdsys/pkg/FR-2000-04-11/pdf/00-8954.pdf> and EPA's 2007 Memorandum, "Issuance of Audit Policy: Frequently Asked Questions," online: <https://www.epa.gov/compliance/incentives/auditing/auditpolicy.html>.

16 "Systematic discovery" is defined as "the detection of a potential violation through an environmental audit or a compliance management system that reflects the entity's due diligence in preventing, detecting, and correcting violations." The gravity-based penalty waiver for companies that detect violations by a system of "systematic discovery" reflects EPA's recognition that "environmental auditing and compliance management systems play a critical role in protecting human health and the environment by identifying, correcting and ultimately preventing violations." Audit Policy, *supra* note 15 at 19620.

17 *Ibid.* The EPA also notes that this incentive will not be available where "corporate officials are consciously involved in or willfully blind to violations or conceal or condone noncompliance." Also, even though the EPA may not recommend criminal prosecution for disclosing entities, it recognizes that "ultimate prosecutorial discretion resides with the U.S. Department of Justice."

18 Effective 1 August 2008, the EPA issued its "Interim Approach to Applying the Audit Policy to New Owners," which, among other things, encourages new owners of existing facilities to disclose otherwise threatening violations discovered during acquisition due diligence, by giving the acquiring company nine months from the closing date to disclose the violations and enter into an audit agreement with EPA. See online: <https://www.epa.gov/compliance/epas-interim-approach-applying-audit-policy-new-owners>.

19 Audit Policy, *supra* note 15 at 19623.

20 See online: <https://www.epa.gov/ems>. The most commonly used environmental management system (EMS) is the one developed by the International Organization for Standardization for its ISO 14001 standard, first established in 1996.

21 Culleen & Glazer, *supra* note 12 at 6.

22 Deputy US Attorney General Sally Yates, *Memorandum re Individual Accountability for Corporate Wrongdoing*, 9 September 2015 [Yates Memo], online: <https://www.justice.gov/dag/file/769036/download>. Its intended scope and application is comprehensive, because it is addressed to the assistant attorneys general of the Department of Justice's Antitrust, Civil, Criminal, Environment and Natural Resources, National Security, and Tax divisions, as well as to the directors of the Federal Bureau of Investigation and the Executive Office for United States Trustees.

23 Jonathan Segal & Daniel Walworth (Duane Morris LLP), *Individual Accountability and Investigations*, 20 November 2015 webinar.

24 See online: <https://www.justice.gov/usam/united-states-attorneys-manual>,

*United States Attorneys' Manual* (USAM), at Title 9, ch 9-28 (titled "Principles of Federal Prosecution of Business Organizations"), and within Title 4 (Civil) of the USAM, a new s 4-3.100 (titled "Pursuit of Claims Against Individuals").

25 *USAM* at 9-28.700. The requirement for "complete disclosure" as a condition to receipt of *any* cooperation credit is more relaxed in the civil enforcement than in the criminal enforcement context.

26 Yates Memo, *supra* note 22 at 3 (fn omitted; emphasis in original).

27 *USAM* at 9-28.720.

28 *Ibid* at 9-28.710.

29 Yates Memo, *supra* note 22 at 3. On a subsequent occasion, Yates elaborated: "As we all know, legal advice is privileged. Facts are not. If a law firm interviews a corporate employee during an investigation, the notes and memos generated from that interview may be protected, at least in part, by attorney-client privilege or as attorney work product. The corporation need not produce the protected material in order to receive cooperation credit and prosecutors will not request it. But to earn cooperation credit, the corporation does need to produce all relevant facts—including the facts learned through those interviews—unless identical information has already been provided. We will respect the privilege, but we will also expect companies to respect its boundaries and not to wrongly exploit its legitimate purpose by using it to shield non-privileged information from investigators." Remarks of Deputy Attorney General Sally Yates to American Bankers Association and American Bar Association Money Laundering Conference, Washington, DC, 16 November 2015, online: <http://www.justice.gov/opa/speech/deputy-attorney-general-sally-quillian-yates-delivers-remarks-american-banking-0>.

30 Only parts of these situations can be examined here. A discussion of when independent counsel should be provided to an employee at the expense of the company and when the company should indemnify the employee is beyond the scope of this chapter.

31 Jessica Ching-yi Kao, EPA Region IX Regional Counsel, "Knock, Knock, Knocking on Office Doors: A 'How-to Guide' to Responding to Environmental Enforcement Agency Investigations" (Remarks at State Bar of California Environmental Law Section Annual Yosemite Conference Webinar, October 2014) [Knock, Knock].

32 Not only do criminal investigations typically dispense with opening conferences, but investigators may appear, present credentials, enter the facility, and proceed with inspecting, sampling, seizing, and removing evidence, and interviewing employees. See Craig D Galli & Gregory E Goldberg (Holland & Hart LLP), "Methodology and Ethics of Internal Investigations of Environmental Crimes – Domestic and International Considerations" (2015) 61 Rocky Mtn Mineral Law Inst 24.

33 Knock, Knock, *supra* note 31. Under RCRA, EPA is required to provide split samples if requested and to promptly disclose all analytical results: RCRA s 3007(a), at 42 USC § 6927(a). Although neither the *Clean Air Act* nor the *Clean Water Act* requires EPA to provide split samples or analytical results, EPA guidance and general practice recognize these as duties. See EPA, *NPDES Compliance Inspection Manual* (2004) at 2-17; *EPA Multi-Media Investigation Manual* (1992) at App M-8.

34 In the author's experience, this is true for EPA Region IX and for California environmental regulatory agencies. However, individual agency practices can vary as can the practices of the same agency from region to region.

35 See, 18 USC § 1501 *et seq* (ch 73, "Obstruction of Justice").

36 "Knock, Knock," *supra*, note 31, remarks of Deborah Schmall, Partner, Paul Hastings LLP.

37 In these situations, facility personnel are strongly advised to immediately call outside counsel so counsel can try to get to the facility before the inspection begins. Until counsel arrives, the facility employee "in charge" should ask the inspectors if they will wait for the company's outside counsel; if they refuse, then counsel must consider whether to advise the inspectors that the facility refuses to consent to their entry and their interviewing of employees unless corporate counsel is present, or to allow the inspection and possible employee interviews to proceed in his or her absence. If the inspection proceeds without corporate counsel's presence, then facility employees need to be even more than normally vigilant in documenting exactly what the inspectors say, what parts of the facility they visit and photograph, and where they take samples.

38 Documents containing trade secrets or confidential business information (CBI) cannot be withheld from seizure pursuant to a warrant or from production during a warrantless inspection. Instead, every single page in any document that contains trade secret data or CBI must be prominently marked with the appropriate identification, or else the company will be held to have waived its right to assert that protection in later proceedings where the government seeks to introduce those documents for evidentiary purposes or to object to their release to the public pursuant to the federal *Freedom of Information Act* or the *California Public Records Act*. Even if the assertion of trade secret or CBI protection is properly asserted, the documents will be taken and the company will have to prove to a judge in a later proceeding that the documents at issue cannot be disclosed without causing real and significant damage to the company's protected commercial interests.

39 Galli & Goldberg, *supra* note 32 at 24–28. If the warrant execution proceeds in the absence of corporate counsel, then the lead facility employee(s) must be prepared to shadow the inspectors at their every step to verify that their inspection is constrained by the scope of the warrant and, if the employee(s) believe at any point that the inspection exceeds the scope of the warrant, the employee(s) must immediately and with specificity object to the inspectors, ensure the inspectors note their objection, and then permit the inspectors to continue without interference that might be construed as obstruction of justice.

40 The limited scope of this chapter allows only the most abbreviated discussion of a small portion of the relevant legal issues associated with the conduct of governmental agency inspections, internal corporate investigations (including employee interviews), and the application of the attorney-client privilege to those investigations. The discussion of those issues presented here is not and cannot (and, therefore, is not intended to) be comprehensive or dispositive for any given set of facts.

41 *Upjohn Co v United States*, 449 US 383 (1981). This decision affirmed the application of the attorney-client privilege to communications between a company's in-house counsel and the company's upper-echelon employees in an internal investigation context, and then expanded its applicability in such internal investigations to cover communications made to in-house counsel not only by upper-echelon employees responsible for directing the company's response to legal advice but also to middle- and lower-level employees "whose actions within the scope of their employment can embroil the corporation in serious legal difficulties." While *Upjohn* involved an investigation conducted jointly by in-house and outside counsel, the DC Circuit Court of Appeals recently held that the privilege is applicable to an internal investigation where an employee is interviewed by a non-attorney at the direction of in-house counsel. *In re Kellogg, Brown & Root, Inc*, 756 F 3d 754 (DC Cir 2014). Clearly,

therefore, the privilege will apply when in-house counsel alone directly conducts the employee interview.

42 See generally Galli & Goldberg, *supra*, note 32.

43 See *United States v Ruehle*, 583 F 3d 600 (9th Cir 2009).

44 Docket No 15-0603 (2d Cir, 16 June 2016)

45 Because the underlying investigation and prosecution were instigated by the New York State Attorney General's Office and because the Second Circuit determined that Delaware law governed the interpretation of Marsh's employment contracts with Gilman and McNenney, no US federal law enforcement statutes, regulations, or guidelines were involved in this particular case.

46 See, e.g.: the *Clean Air Act*, 42 USC § 7622(a); the *Comprehensive Environmental Response, Compensation, and Liability Act* (Superfund or CERCLA), 42 USC § 9610(a); the *Clean Water Act*, 33 USC § 1367(a)); the *Solid Waste Disposal Act* (RCRA), 42 USC § 6971(a); the *Surface Mining Control and Reclamation Act* (SMCRA), 30 USC § 1293(a); the *Toxic Substances Control Act* (TSCA), 15 USC § 2622(a); and the *Pipeline Safety Improvement Act*, 49 USC § 60129(a). These provisions are by no means identical, and some of them provide fewer whistleblower protections than others.

47 *USAM* at 9.28-710 (Attorney-Client and Work Product Protections), quoting *Upjohn Co v United States*, *supra* note 41 at 389.

48 See Segal & Walworth, *supra*, note 23; Galli & Goldberg, *supra*, note 32; and Craig Galli, "A Compliance Crisis Is a Terrible Things to Waste: Counsel's Role to Enhance Corporate Culture" (Winter 2015) 30 Nat Resources & Env 3.

# Contributors

PAUL ADAMS, Senior Counsel, Public Prosecution Service Canada, Halifax

NATASHA AFFOLDER, Associate Dean, Faculty of Law, University of British Columbia, Vancouver

ANDREA C. AKELAITIS, Letcher Akelaitis LLP, Vancouver

PETER BOXALL, Professor, Department of Resource Economics & Environmental Sociology, University of Alberta, Edmonton

JAMES BUNTING, Davies, Ward, Phillips & Vineberg LLP, Toronto

CINDY CHIASSON, Alberta Energy Regulator, Edmonton

JOHN S.G. CLARK, Department of Justice, Vancouver

JOHN D. CLIFFE, Q.C., Cliffe Tobias, Vancouver

LYNDA COLLINS, Professor, Faculty of Law, Common Law, University of Ottawa

JACK D. COOP, Fogler, Rubinoff LLP, Toronto

CHARLES-EMMANUEL CÔTÉ, Professor, Faculty of Law, Laval University

PETER J. CRAIG, Senior Crown Attorney, Nova Scotia Public Prosecution Service, Dartmouth

PIERRE-OLIVIER DESMARCHAIS, Policy Analyst, Policy Horizons Canada, Government of Canada

ADAM DRIEDZIC, Staff Counsel, Environmental Law Centre (Alberta) Society, Edmonton

ERIN EACOTT, Public Prosecution Service of Canada, Edmonton

JENNIFER FAIRFAX, Partner, Osler, Hoskin & Harcourt LLP, Toronto

JAMES FLAGAL, Counsel, Ontario Ministry of the Environment and Climate Change, Toronto

SHAUN FLUKER, Associate Professor, Faculty of Law, University of Calgary

HADLEY FRIEDLAND, Assistant Professor, Faculty of Law, University of Alberta, Edmonton

PAULE HALLEY, Professor, Faculty of Law, Laval University

CHARLES HATT, Staff Lawyer, Ecojustice, Toronto

BRENDA HEELAN POWELL, Staff Counsel, Environmental Law Centre, Edmonton

NICHOLAS R. HUGHES, McCarthy Tétrault, Vancouver

ALEX IKEJIANI, Department of Justice, Fisheries and Oceans Legal Services, Government of Canada, Ottawa

ALLAN E. INGELSON, Associate Professor, Faculty of Law, University of Calgary

ASHA JAMES, Managing Associate, Falconers LLP, Toronto

MEREDITH JAMES, Environmental Lawyer, City of Toronto

ALBERT KOEHL, Former Staff Lawyer, Ecojustice, Toronto

DAVID LAIDLAW, Research Fellow, Canadian Institute of Resources Law, Calgary

JONATHAN LEO, Former Attorney, State Bar of California

GARY A. LETCHER, Letcher Akelaitis LLP, Vancouver

ALASTAIR R. LUCAS, Q.C., Professor, Faculty of Law, University of Calgary

FRED MAEFS, Crown Counsel, Ontario Ministry of the Environment and Climate Change, Toronto

SHARON MASCHER, Professor, Faculty of Law, University of Calgary

MARC McAREE, Partner, Willms & Shier Environmental Lawyers LLP, Toronto

PAUL McCULLOCH, Crown Counsel, Ministry of the Environment and Climate Change, Ottawa

HEATHER McLEOD-KILMURRAY, Professor, Faculty of Law, Common Law, University of Ottawa

SUSAN McRORY, Former Environmental Prosecutor, Specialized Prosecutions Branch, Government of Alberta, Edmonton

DANIELLE MEULEMAN, Crown Counsel, Ontario Ministry of the Attorney General, Toronto

NICKIE NIKOLAOU, Associate Professor, Faculty of Law, University of Calgary

TERRI-LEE OLENIUK, Osler, Hoskin & Harcourt LLP, Calgary

MARTIN OLSZYNSKI, Associate Professor, Faculty of Law, University of Calgary

KATIA OPALKA, Senior Manager, Pratt & Whitney Canada Corp, Quebec

JEAN PIETTE, Norton Rose Fulbright, Québec

SARAH POWELL, Davies, Ward, Phillips & Vineberg, Toronto

PHILLIP SAUNDERS, Professor, Schulich School of Law, Dalhousie University, Halifax

MONIKA A. SAWICKA, McCarthy Tétrault, Vancouver

DR. DIANNE SAXE, Environmental Commissioner of Ontario, Government of Ontario, Toronto

CHERYL SHARVIT, Mandell Pinder LLP, Vancouver

ANAND SRIVASTAVA, Associate Lawyer, Willms & Shier Environmental Lawyers LLP, Toronto

BARRY STUART, Retired Judge, Vancouver

JOHN SWAIGEN, Staff Lawyer, Ecojustice, Toronto

CHRIS TOLLEFSON, Professor, Faculty of Law, University of Victoria

RONDA M. VANDERHOEK, Counsel, Public Prosecution Service of Canada, Halifax

JASMINE VAN SCHOUWEN, Faculty of Law, University of Ottawa

MICHAEL M. WENIG, Natural Resources Conservation Board, Calgary

ROBERT WOON, Associate Lawyer, Willms & Shier Environmental Lawyers LLP, Toronto

# Index

## D



## E

## F



## G



## H



## I

## S



## T



## U



## V



## W

www.ingramcontent.com/pod-product-compliance
Lightning Source LLC
LaVergne TN
LVHW052111210926
848482LV00025B/538